Adjustments to Net Income (Loss) Using the Indirect Method:

Net income (loss)	$ XXX	
Adjustments to reconcile net income to net cash flow from operating activities:		
Depreciation of fixed assets	XXX	
Amortization of intangible assets	XXX	
Losses on disposal of assets	XXX	
Gains on disposal of assets	(XXX)	
Changes in current operating assets and liabilities:		
Increases in noncash current operating assets	(XXX)	
Decreases in noncash current operating assets	XXX	
Increases in current operating liabilities	XXX	
Decreases in current operating liabilities	(XXX)	
Net cash flow from operating activities		$XXX

Subtract	Add
Increases in accounts receivable	Decreases in accounts receivable
Increases in inventory	Decreases in inventory
Increases in prepaid expenses	Decreases in prepaid expenses
Decreases in accounts payable	Increases in accounts payable
Decreases in accrued expenses payable	Increases in accrued expenses payable
Decreases in income taxes payable	Increases in income taxes payable

Summary of Metrics

Liquidity and Solvency Metrics

Working Capital	Current Assets − Current Liabilities
Current Ratio	Current Assets / Current Liabilities
Quick Ratio	Quick Assets / Current Liabilities
Accounts Receivable Turnover	Sales / Average Accounts Receivable
Days' Sales in Receivables	Average Accounts Receivable / Average Daily Sales
Inventory Turnover	Cost of Goods Sold / Average Inventory
Days' Sales in Inventory	Average Inventory / Average Daily Cost of Goods Sold
Net Assets	Total Assets − Total Liabilities
Debt Ratio	Total Liabilities / Total Assets
Ratio of Liabilities to Stockholders' Equity	Total Liabilities / Total Stockholders' Equity
Ratio of Fixed Assets to Long-Term Liabilities	Fixed Assets (net) / Long-Term Liabilities
Times Interest Earned	(Income Before Income Tax + Interest Expense) / Interest Expense

Profitability Metrics

Asset Turnover	Sales / Average Long-Term Operating Assets
Return on Total Assets	(Net Income + Interest Expense) / Average Total Assets
Return on Stockholders' Equity	Net Income / Average Total Stockholders' Equity
Return on Common Stockholders' Equity	(Net Income − Preferred Dividends) / Average Common Stockholders' Equity
Earnings per Share on Common Stock	(Net Income − Preferred Dividends) / Shares of Common Stock Outstanding
Price-Earnings Ratio	Market Price per Share of Common Stock / Earnings per Share on Common Stock
Dividends per Share	Common Stock Dividends / Shares of Common Stock Outstanding
Dividend Yield	Dividends per Share of Common Stock / Market Price per Share of Common Stock

USING FINANCIAL ACCOUNTING

Completing the puzzle of using accounting to understand business.

USING FINANCIAL ACCOUNTING

Completing the puzzle of using accounting to understand business.

Carl S. Warren
Professor Emeritus of Accounting
University of Georgia, Athens

Jefferson P. Jones
Associate Professor of Accounting
Auburn University

Amanda G. Farmer
Lecturer of Accounting
University of Georgia, Athens

Australia • Brazil • Canada • Mexico • Singapore • United Kingdom • United States

Using Financial Accounting
Carl S. Warren, Jefferson P. Jones, Amanda G. Farmer

Senior Vice President, Higher Education & Skills Product: Erin Joyner

Product Director: Joseph Sabatino

Product Manager: Melody Sorkhabi

Product Assistant: Matt Schiesl

Learning Designer: Kristen Meere

Senior Digital Delivery Lead: Sally Nieman

Senior Content Manager: Tim Bailey

Executive Marketing Manager: Nathan Anderson

Intellectual Property Analyst: Ashley Maynard

Manufacturing Planner: Ron Montgomery

Production Service: SPi Global

Text and Cover Designer: Christopher Doughman

Cover Image: iStockPhoto.com/RudyBalaskos

Library of Congress Control Number: 2021902394

Student Edition ISBN: 978-0-357-50785-8

Loose-leaf Edition ISBN: 978-0-357-50786-5

Cengage
20 Channel Center Street
Boston, MA 02210
USA

Cengage is a leading provider of customized learning solutions with employees residing in nearly 40 different countries and sales in more than 125 countries around the world. Find your local representative at **www.cengage.com.**

To learn more about Cengage platforms and services, register or access your online learning solution, or purchase materials for your course, visit **www.cengage.com**.

Throughout this text, real-world companies are used in the narrative, illustrations, and end-of-chapter assignments. These companies are identified in boldface color type, and any data presented was adapted from or based upon annual reports, Securities and Exchange Commission filings, or other publicly available sources. Any other individuals or companies used in illustrations and homework are fictional, and any resemblance to actual persons, living or dead, businesses or companies is entirely coincidental.

Printed in Mexico
Print Number: 01 Print Year: 2021

Preface

Using Financial Accounting is designed for a one-term introductory financial accounting course. Written for students who have no prior knowledge of accounting, this text emphasizes how managers, investors, and other business stakeholders use accounting. It provides an overview of the basic topics in financial accounting, without using debits and credits or extraneous topics that must be skipped or otherwise modified to fit into a one-term course.

A major objective of *Using Financial Accounting* is to create an inclusive learning experience for all students that recognizes the wide diversity in student demographics, abilities, and experiences. This edition has been revised with a learner-centric approach that understands and acknowledges that a student's learning experience may be influenced by a variety of mental, sensory, and physical factors. As a result, this edition and its ancillaries have been designed to create an accessible learning experience for all students.

Using Financial Accounting also recognizes students have unique backgrounds and perspectives. As a result, chapter content, illustrations, and homework are designed to be respectful and inclusive of differences in student race, ethnicity, sexual orientation, gender, religion, age, and culture. Finally, the authors welcome suggestions and comments on how to be even more inclusive in future editions.

Hallmark Features

Using Financial Accounting uses innovative features and design elements to help instructors and enhance the learning experience of students. These features include the following:

- **Integrated Financial Statement Framework** clearly illustrates the impact of transactions on the balance sheet, income statement, and the statement of cash flows and the corresponding relationships among these financial statements. The IFS framework moves the student from the simple to the complex and explains the how and why of financial statements.

  Chapter 1 introduces students to this integration in the form of actual company financials from **The Hershey Company (HSY)**, a well-known manufacturer of chocolates.

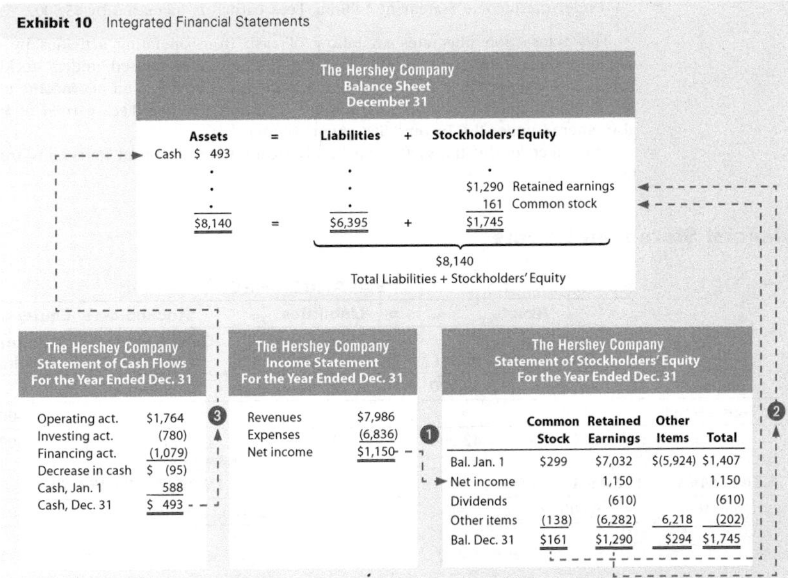

Chapter 2 begins with the format of the integrated framework that will be used throughout the financial chapters. Using this framework shown below, students will gain a greater understanding of how transactions impact a company's financial statements, which add valuable insight into the financial condition and operations of the business.

Exhibit 1 Integrated Financial Statement Framework

Integrated Financial Statement Framework

BALANCE SHEET

	Assets	=	Liabilities	+	Stockholders' Equity		
	Assets	=	Liabilities	+	Common Stock	+	Retained Earnings
Transaction	XXX		XXX		XXX		XXX
	XXX						
	XXX		XXX		XXX		XXX

STATEMENT OF CASH FLOWS

+/– Operating activities	XXX
+/– Investing activities	XXX
+/– Financing activities	XXX
Increase or decrease in cash	XXX
Beginning cash	XXX
Ending cash	XXX

INCOME STATEMENT

Revenues	XXX
Expenses	XXX
Net income or loss	XXX

To illustrate, Chapter 2 uses the integrated financial statement framework to illustrate the impact of transactions on Family Health Care as follows:

Transaction d

During the first month of operations, Family Health Care earned patient fees of $5,500, receiving the fees in cash.

The effects of this transaction on Family Health Care's financial statements are recorded as follows:

1. Under the Statement of Cash Flows column, Cash from Operating activities is increased by $5,500.
2. Under the Balance Sheet column, Cash under Assets is increased by $5,500. To balance the accounting equation, Retained Earnings under Stockholders' Equity is also increased by $5,500.
3. Under the Income Statement column, Fees earned is increased by $5,500.

This transaction illustrates an inflow of cash from operating activities by earning revenues (fees earned) of $5,500. Retained Earnings is increased under Stockholders' Equity by $5,500 because fees earned contribute to net income and net income increases stockholders' equity. Since fees earned are a type of revenue, Fees earned of $5,500 is also entered under the Income Statement column.

The effects of this transaction on Family Health Care's financial statements are shown below.

Financial Statement Effects

BALANCE SHEET

	Assets			=	Liabilities	+	Stockholders' Equity		
	Cash	+	Land	=	Notes Payable	+	Common Stock	+	Retained Earnings
Balances	4,000		12,000		10,000		6,000		
d. Fees earned	5,500								5,500
Balances	9,500		12,000		10,000		6,000		5,500

STATEMENT OF CASH FLOWS

d. Operating	5,500

INCOME STATEMENT

d. Fees earned	5,500

The preceding design illustrates sound pedagogy in its use of color, which engages students and clearly presents the material. The Solutions Manual also includes color screens matching this presentation. This facilitates covering homework assignments and reinforces the integration of the financial statements and effects of transactions.

- **Metric-Based Analyses** uses common business metrics to assess a company's financial condition and operations. Metrics are assessed at the Transaction Level and Financial Statement Level.

  At the transaction level, the effect of each transaction on the financial statements is shown using the Integrated Financial Statement spreadsheet. In addition, the **transaction metric effects** on common liquidity and profitability metrics are also shown. To illustrate, assume that on January 3, TechSource sells merchandise for $1,800 that cost $1,200 for cash. The effect of the cash sale is on the accounts and financial statements as follows:

Financial Statement Effects

BALANCE SHEET

	Assets		= Liabilities +	Stockholders' Equity
	Cash	**+ Inventory =**		**Retained Earnings**
Jan 3.	1,800	(1,200)		600

STATEMENT OF CASH FLOWS

Jan. 3. Operating	1,800

INCOME STATEMENT

Jan. 3. Sales	1,800
Cost of goods sold	(1,200)
Gross profit	600

Transaction Metric Effects

The effects of the cash sale on the liquidity and profitability metrics are as follows:

LIQUIDITY

Working Capital	$600

PROFITABILITY

Gross Profit Percent (33%)	Increases ability to achieve minimum of 20%

Since Cash increased by $1,800 and Inventory decreased by $1,200, working capital increased by $600 ($1,800 – $1,200). We assume that TechSource desires a minimum overall gross profit percent of 20%. Since the gross profit percent for this sale is 33% [($1,800 – $1,200) ÷ $1,800], this sale increases TechSource's ability to achieve its overall minimum gross profit percent of 20%.

The preceding transaction metric effects design illustrates sound pedagogy in its use of color, which engages students and clearly presents the material. The Solutions Manual also includes color screens matching the this presentation. This facilitates covering homework assignments.

At the **financial statement level** common metrics are used to analyze a company's overall financial statements. An example of the use of the accounts receivable turnover metric is as follows:

The **accounts receivable turnover** is computed as follows:

$$\textbf{Accounts Receivable Turnover} = \frac{\textbf{Sales}}{\textbf{Average Accounts Receivable}}$$

Although accounts receivable are just related to "credit" sales, total sales is normally used to compute accounts receivable turnover. This is because credit sales are normally not reported to external users. The average accounts receivable is computed as the beginning accounts receivable plus the ending accounts receivable for the period divided by two.

To illustrate, assume the following data for Downing Inc. for the year ending December 31, 20Y4:

Sales for 20Y4	$9,125,000
Accounts Receivable, Jan. 1, 20Y4	400,000
Accounts Receivable, Dec. 31, 20Y4	600,000

The accounts receivable turnover of 18.3 for Downing Inc. is computed as follows:

$$\text{Accounts Receivable Turnover} = \frac{\$9{,}125{,}000}{(\$400{,}000 + \$600{,}000) \div 2} = \frac{\$9{,}125{,}000}{\$500{,}000} = 18.3^{*}$$

* Rounded to one decimal place.

At the end of each chapter, the Metric Analyses are clearly identified wtih a separate screen of color. This allows for quick identification of the analyses through the chapters and text. This separate screen of color also identifies the end-of-chapter section for assigning homework.

- **Using Data Analytics** examples have been added to each chapter, which describe an application of data analytics to each chapter's content.

Using Data Analytics

Sales

Retail businesses, such as **Target Corporation (TGT)**, use data analytics to answer questions such as the following:

- What are our best-selling products?
- What products are generating returns?
- What percent of our customers are using self-checkouts?
- What time of the day do we have the most sales?
- What percent of our customers use credit cards?
- What percent of our customers use debit cards?

Target has used data (predictive) analytics to improve the retail experience of its customers as well as to increase its sales. For example, Target uses data analytics to decide which products should earn shelf space in its brick-and-mortar stores and which are best serviced with its online sales app.

See Case 4-6 for a homework assignment using data analytics.

Source: Dina Gerdeman, "On Target: Rethinking the Retail Website," *Forbes*, December 4, 2018, www.forbes.com/sites/hbsworkingknowledge/2018/12/04/on-target-rethinking-the-retail-website/#2690a20916fb.

- **Data Analytic Cases** have been added to several chapters. These cases use a dataset related to the chapter content that requires a student to analyze and develop reports using Excel and Tableau. The chapters with data analytic cases are as follows:

  Chapter 4: Accounting for Retail Businesses
  Case 4-6 "Sales analysis using data analytics" (Excel application)
  Chapter 5: Internal Control and Cash
  Case 5-6 "Evaluating internal controls for inventory shrinkage" (Tableau application)
  Chapter 6: Receivables
  Case 6-6 "Collectability of receivables by customer type" (Excel application)
  Chapter 7: Inventories
  Case 7-5 "Out-of-stock items" (Excel application)
  Chapter 8: Long-Term Operating Assets
  Case 8-5 "Equipment maintenance, downtime, and costs" (Excel and Tableau applications)
  Chapter 9: Liabilities
  Case 9-6 "Supplier (vendor) analyses" (Excel application)

  The following is the data analytic case for Chapter 4.

USING DATA ANALYTICS

Case 4-6 Sales analysis

Michelle Horowitz is the manager of AAAA Office Supplies, a locally owned office supply store for schools and businesses. Michelle is concerned about the large variety of products the store carries, which ties up storage space and working capital. Michelle has asked you to analyze the store's inventory and sales to determine if there are products that may be worth discontinuing.

Michelle has asked you for the following:

1. A list of the quantity of each product sold for a recent month.
2. Recommendations for any products that should be discontinued.

Go to CengageNOWv2 to complete this assignment.

Other Features

Using Financial Accounting uses other features and design elements to help instructors and enhance the learning experience of students. These include the following:

- **Infographic Art** examples help students visualize important accounting concepts within chapters. Some examples include the following:

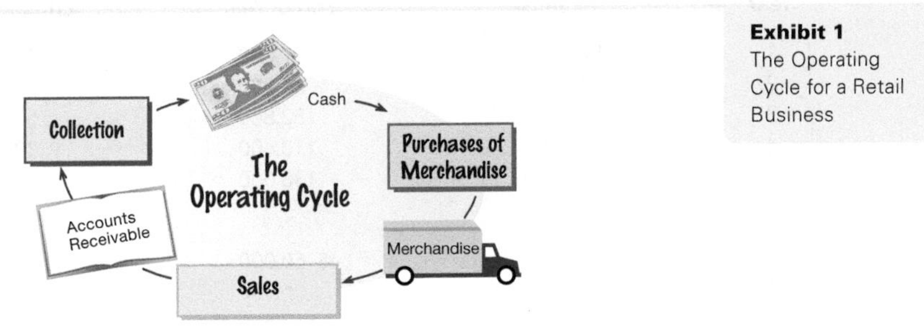

Exhibit 1 The Operating Cycle for a Retail Business

Exhibit 2 Inventory Cost Flows

	Cost Flow Assumption	
1. Cost flow is in the order in which the costs were incurred.	2. Cost flow is in the reverse order in which the costs were incurred.	3. Cost flow is an average of the costs.
	Inventory Costing Method	
First-In, First-Out (FIFO)	**Last-In, First-Out (LIFO)**	**Average Cost**

- **Illustrative Problems** help students apply what they learn by walking them through problems that cover the most important concepts addressed within the chapter. An example of an Illustrative Problem from Chapter 8, "Long-term Operating Assets," is as follows:

Illustrative Problem

McCollum Company, a furniture wholesaler, acquired new equipment at a cost of $150,000 at the beginning of the fiscal year. The equipment has an estimated life of five years and an estimated residual value of $12,000. Ellen McCollum, the president, has requested information regarding alternative depreciation methods.

Instructions

Determine the annual depreciation for each of the five years of estimated useful life of the equipment, the accumulated depreciation at the end of each year, and the book value of the equipment at the end of each year by (a) the straight-line method and (b) the double-declining-balance method.

Solution

	Year	Depreciation Expense	Accumulated Depreciation, End of Year	Book Value, End of Year
a.	1	$27,600*	$ 27,600	$122,400
	2	27,600	55,200	94,800
	3	27,600	82,800	67,200
	4	27,600	110,400	39,600
	5	27,600	138,000	12,000

*$27,600 = ($150,000 − $12,000) ÷ 5

	Year	Depreciation Expense	Accumulated Depreciation, End of Year	Book Value, End of Year
b.	1	$60,000**	$ 60,000	$ 90,000
	2	36,000	96,000	54,000
	3	21,600	117,600	32,400
	4	12,960	130,560	19,440
	5	7,440***	138,000	12,000

**$60,000 = $150,000 × 40%

***The asset is not depreciated below the estimated residual value of $12,000.

- **Integrity, Objectivity, and Ethics in Business** features describe real-world dilemmas, helping students apply accounting concepts within an ethical context, using integrity and objectivity.

Integrity, Objectivity, and Ethics in Business

Bank Error in Your Favor

At some point, you might experience a bank error in your favor, such as a misposted deposit. Such errors are not a case of "found money," as in the Monopoly® game. Bank control systems quickly discover most errors and make automatic adjustments. Even so, you have a legal responsibility to report the error and return the money to the bank.

stephenkirsh/Shutterstock.com

- **Business Insight** vignettes emphasize practical ways in which businesses apply accounting concepts when generating profit strategies.

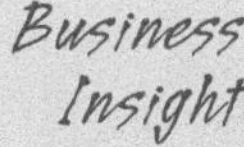

Business Insight

The retail environment has changed rapidly during the last 40 years with the emergence of (1) discount merchandising, (2) category killers, and (3) Internet retailing. Walmart (WMT) led the development of discount merchandising by providing consumers discounted prices over a wide array of grocery, household, and electronic products. Category killers include Best Buy (BBY) (electronics), Home Depot (HD) (home improvement), and Office Depot (ODP) (office supplies). Each of these companies provides a wide selection of competitively priced goods within their market segment. Internet retailers, such as Amazon.com (AMZN), allow consumers to shop quickly for a wide variety of products using online platforms. Retailing will continue to evolve as consumer tastes, lifestyles, and technology change.

- **Appendix A: Selected Topics** allows instructors the flexibility to cover a variety of topics that may be relevant to their students. The topics include the following:

  Topic 1: Investments
  Topic 2: Foreign Currency Transactions
  Topic 3: Corporate Taxes
  Topic 4: Reporting Unusual Items and Comprehensive Income
  Topic 5: Revenue Recognition
  Topic 6: International Accounting Standards

  Each topic is designed as a self-contained learning module with its own assignment materials. The modules have been written so that instructors have the flexibility of covering one or more of the modules at a variety of different places in their course depending upon their students' needs.

- **Appendix B: Nike Annual Report (10-K)** includes student assignments. A Nike annual report assignment with the related learning objective is included for each chapter. An instructor could use "all" the chapter assignments as an "annual report" project of the course. Alternatively, an instructor might use some assignments and not others.

  The assignments are included with the annual report in Appendix B so that students have the annual report and assignments in one place in the text. The annual report assignments are also reference at the end of each chapter following the Metric-Based Analysis section.

- **Appendix C: Double-Entry Accounting Systems** includes a brief overview of the double-entry accounting systems. This appendix can be used by instructors who want to introduce their students to double-entry accounting without having to cover it throughout the text.

Technology

What is CengageNOWv2?

CengageNOWv2 is a powerful course management and online homework tool that provides robust intructor control and customization to optimize the student learning experience and meet desired outcomes.

CengageNOWv2 includes the following:

- Integrated eBook
- End-of-Chapter homework with static and algorithmic versions
- Excel Online Algorithmic Activities
- Adaptive Study Plan with quizzing and multimedia study tools
- Test Bank
- Course management tools and flexible assignment options
- Reporting and grade book options
- Tell Me More eLectures with quizzes
- Show Me How demonstration videos
- Quick Lessons videos with quizzes

CengageNOWv2 for Warren's *Using Financial Accounting* is designed to help students learn more effectively by providing engaging resources at unique points in the learning process:

When to use it?	What to use?	How will it help?
Preparing for Class	Lecture Activities Quick Lessons	Recall Understand
Completing Homework	Show Me How Videos Enhanced Feedback	Apply

Cengage Mobile App

The Cengage Mobile App lets students study wherever and whenever the mood strikes. Now available with CengageNOWv2, it features a full interactive eBook—readable online or off—with 24/7 course access and study tools to power on-the-go learning. Plus, the app allows you to engage your students with instant in-class polling and take attendance with a tap. Details at www.cengage.com/mobile-app/

Excel Online

Cengage and Microsoft have partnered in CNOWv2 to provide students with a uniform, authentic Excel experience. It provides instant feedback, built-in video tips, and easily accessible spreadsheet work. These features allow you to spend more time teaching college accounting applications and less time troubleshooting Excel.

These new algorithmic activities offer pre-populated data directly in Microsoft Excel Online. Each student receives his or her own version of the problem to perform the necessary data calculations in Excel Online. Their work is constantly saved in Cengage cloud storage as a part of homework assignments in CNOWv2. It's easily retrievable so students can review their answers without cumbersome file management and numerous downloads/uploads.

Preparing for Class

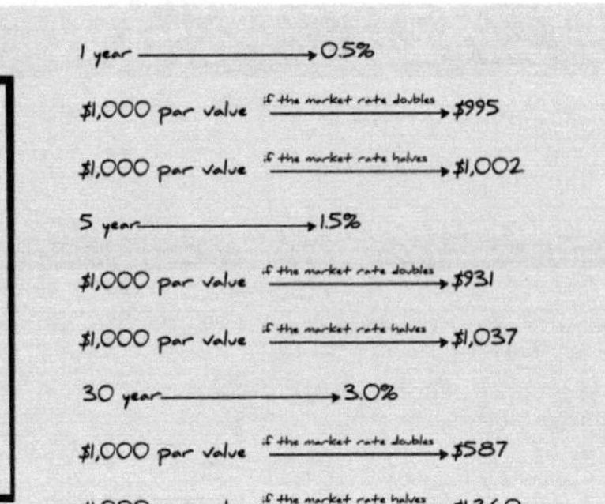

CengageNOWv2 helps you motivate students and prepare them for class with a host of resources. These resources were developed with visual learners and those that don't like to read textbooks in mind. Available in the Study Tools tab in CengageNOWv2, students may access these resources on demand. Each resource is fully assignable and gradable!

Tell Me More Lecture Activities are available and correlate to each Learning Objective (LO). These Lecture Assignments review the material covered in each LO, giving students a way to review what is covered in each objective in a digestible video activity format so they come to class more prepared and ready to participate.

Quick Lessons are available for selected chapters. Quick Lessons are assignable/gradable videos that visually explain and guide students through selected core topics. Each activity uses a realistic company example to illustrate how the concepts relate to the everyday activities of a business. After finishing the video, a student is expected to answer questions based on what they've seen. These activities offer excellent resources for students prior to coming to lecture and will especially appeal to visual learners.

By using these resources, you have a powerful suite of content to help you ensure students can familiarize themselves with content prior to coming to class, which is an excellent way to help you flip the classroom!

Completing Homework

Students sometimes struggle with accounting homework. By using CengageNOWv2's powerful instructor tools you can fine-tune the amount of help that your students receive as they work on their homework. Help your students succeed by making the right amount of assistance available at the right time!

Show Me How videos are available for the most commonly assigned end-of-chapter assignments. *Linked only to algorithms*, these videos provide students with both a detailed walk-through of a similar problem and problem-solving strategies without giving away the answer.

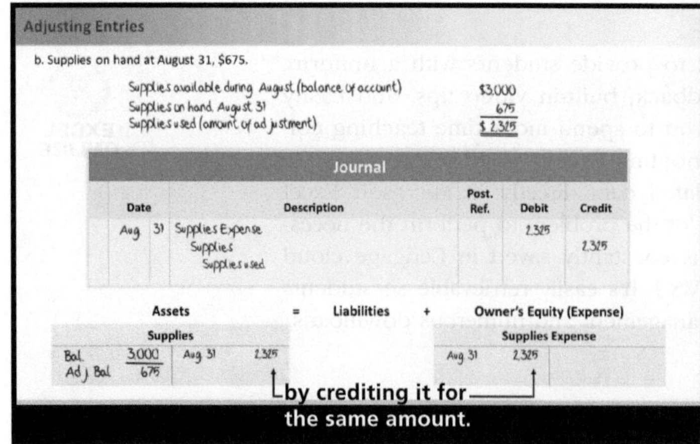

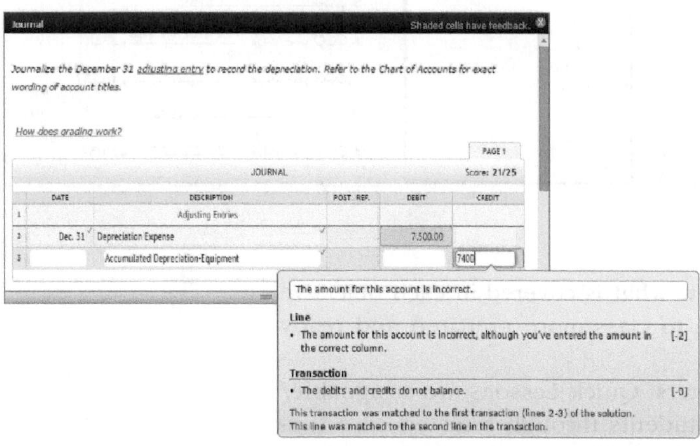

CengageNOWv2 provides multiple layers of guidance to keep students on track and progressing.

- Check My Work Feedback provides general guidance and hints as students work through homework assignments.
- Check My Work Feedback in CengageNOWv2 only reports on what students have attempted, which prevents them from "guessing" their way through assignments.
- Explanations are available after the assignment has been submitted and provide a detailed description of how the student should have arrived at the solution.

To view a demo of CengageNOWv2, please visit: https://www.cengage.com/cnowv2/

CENGAGE *UNLIMITED*

Cengage Unlimited is a first- of-its-kind digital subscription designed specifically to lower costs. Students get total access to everything Cengage has to offer on demand—in one place. That's over 20,000 eBooks, 2,300 digital learning products, and dozens of study tools across 70 disciplines and over 675 courses. Currently available in select markets. Details at www.cengage.com/unlimited.

Supplements for the Instructor

Additional instructor resources for this product are available online. Instructor assets include an Educator's Guide, Solutions Manual, PowerPoint® slides, and a test bank powered by Cognero®. Sign up or sign in at www.cengage.com to search for and access this product and its online resources.

- **Test Bank Available with Cengage Testing Powered by Cognero®** is a flexible, online system that allows you to:
  - author, edit, and manage test bank content from multiple Cengage solutions
  - create multiple test versions in an instant
  - deliver tests from your LMS, your classroom, or wherever you want.
- **PowerPoint® Presentation Slides** Included on the product companion site, each presentation enhances lectures and simplifies class preparation.
- **Solutions Manual** The Solutions Manual contains answers to all exercises, problems, and cases that appear in the text. As always, the solutions are author-written and verified multiple times for numerical accuracy and consistency with the core text.

Acknowledgments

Many people deserve thanks for their contributions to this text over the past several editions. Amanda Farmer, Mark Sears, LuAnn Bean Mangold, and Brenda Bindschatel provided a thorough technical review and verification of the end-of-chapter materials. Robin Browning and Tomeika Williams did a thorough review of the CNOWv2 content. The comments from the following reviewers also influenced recent edition of the text as well as the current edition:

Sharon Agee, *Rollins College*
Tim Alzheimer, *Montana State University, Bozeman*
Scott R. Berube, *University of New Hampshire, Whittemore School of Business & Economics*
Jekabs Bikis, *Dallas Baptist University*
Jerold Braun, *Daytona State College*
Suzanne Lyn Cercone, *Keystone College*
H. Edward Gallatin, *Indiana State University*
Robert E. Holtfreter, *Central Washington University*
José Luis Hortensi, *Miami Dade College*
Daniel Kerch, *Pennsylvania Highlands Community College*
William J. Lavelle, *Ave Maria University*
Ann E. Martel, *Marquette University*
Edna C. Mitchell, *Polk State College*
Tami Park, *University of Great Falls*
Craig Pence, *Highland Community College*
Patricia G. Roshto, *University of Louisiana at Monroe*
Geeta Shankar, *University of Dayton*
Alice Sineath, *Forsyth Technical Community College*
Hans Sprohge, *Wright State University*
Gary Volk, *Wayne State College*

Your comments and suggestions as you use this text are sincerely appreciated.

Carl S. Warren, Jefferson P. Jones, and Amanda G. Farmer

About the Authors

TERRY R. SPRAY/INHISIMAGE STUDIOS

Carl S. Warren

Dr. Carl S. Warren is Professor Emeritus of Accounting at the University of Georgia, Athens. For over 25 years, Professor Warren has taught all levels of accounting classes. In recent years, Professor Warren has focused his teaching efforts on principles of accounting and auditing courses. Professor Warren has taught classes at the University of Iowa, Michigan State University, and University of Chicago. Professor Warren received his doctorate degree (PhD) from Michigan State University and his undergraduate (BBA) and master's (MA) degrees from the University of Iowa. During his career, Professor Warren published numerous articles in professional journals, including *The Accounting Review*, *Journal of Accounting Research*, *Journal of Accountancy*, *The CPA Journal*, and *Auditing: A Journal of Practice & Theory*. Professor Warren's outside interests include handball, skiing, hiking, fly-fishing, and golf. Professor Warren also spends time backpacking U.S. national parks (Yellowstone and the Grand Canyon), playing with his grandchildren, and riding ATVs and motorcycles.

Jefferson P. Jones

Dr. Jefferson P. Jones is an Associate Professor of Accounting in the School of Accountancy at Auburn University where he teaches financial accounting and applied financial research courses. He received his Bachelor's in Accounting and Master of Accountancy degrees from Auburn University and his PhD from Florida State University. Dr. Jones has received numerous teaching awards, including the Auburn University Beta Alpha Psi Outstanding Teaching Award (eight times); the Auburn University Outstanding Master of Accountancy Professor Teaching Award (five times); the Auburn University Outstanding Distance Master of Accountancy Teaching Award (three times); and the Auburn University College of Business McCartney Teaching Award. In addition, he has made numerous presentations around the country on research and pedagogical issues. Dr. Jones has public accounting experience as an auditor with Deloitte and Touche, holds a CPA certificate in the state of Alabama (inactive), and is a member of the American Accounting Association, the American Institute of Certified Public Accountants (AICPA), and the Alabama Society of CPAs (ASCPA). His research interests focus on financial accounting, specifically investigating the quality of reported accounting information, and accounting education. He has published articles in numerous journals, including *Advances in Accounting*, *Review of Quantitative Finance and Accounting*, *Issues in Accounting Education*, *International Journal of Forecasting*, and *The CPA Journal*. When not at work, Dr. Jones enjoys playing golf and watching college football.

THE UNIVERSITY OF GEORGIA

Amanda G. Farmer

Amanda G. Farmer, CPA, has been a full-time lecturer in the JM Tull School of Accounting at the University of Georgia since 2006. Farmer is a University of Georgia alumna. She received her Bachelor of Business Administration (BBA) and Master of Accountancy (MAcc) from the University. After graduation, Farmer worked for Trinity Accounting Group in Athens, Georgia, and ran her own company, DolCor, Inc., which provided tax and accounting services to business and individual clients. Her primary area of teaching is managerial accounting. She has taught courses in principles of accounting, managerial accounting, survey of accounting, and professional accounting. Farmer's outside interests include working out, practicing yoga, cooking, and spending time with her daughters.

Brief Contents

Contents

7 Inventories 271

8 Long-Term Operating Assets 308

9 Liabilities 349

10 Stockholders' Equity 381

11 Statement of Cash Flows 418

12 Metric-Based Analysis of Financial Statements 459

Chapter 1 The Role of Accounting in Business

What's Covered:

Topics: The Role of Accounting in Business

Nature of Business
- Types of Business (Obj. 1)
- Forms of Business (Obj. 1)
- Business Strategies (Obj. 1)
- Business Stakeholders (Obj. 1)
- Business Activities (Obj. 2)

Role of Accounting
- Financial and Managerial Accounting (Obj. 3)
- Income Statement (Obj. 4)
- Statement of Stockholders' Equity (Obj. 4)
- Balance Sheet (Obj. 4)
- Statement of Cash Flows (Obj. 4)
- Accounting Concepts (Obj. 5)

Metric-Based Analysis
- Types of Analyses (Obj. 6)
- Return on Assets (Obj. 6)

Learning Objectives

Obj.1 Describe the types and forms of businesses, how businesses make money, and business stakeholders.

Obj.2 Describe the three business activities of financing, investing, and operating.

Obj.3 Define accounting and describe its role in business.

Obj.4 Describe and illustrate the basic financial statements and how they are integrated.

Obj.5 Describe eight accounting concepts underlying financial reporting.

Obj.6 Describe types of metrics and analyze a company's performance using return on assets.

Chapter Metrics

Use the following metrics to analyze transactions and financial statements

TRANSACTIONS*

Liquidity: N/A

Profitabililty: N/A

FINANCIAL STATEMENTS

Return on Assets

*There are no transactions in this chapter.

Snap Inc.

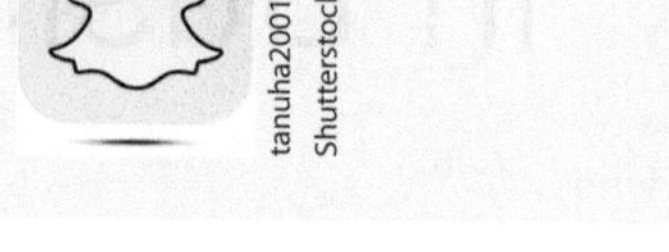

tanuha2001/Shutterstock.com

How much are you willing to pay for stock of a company that has never been traded on a public market? Investors must come up with an answer to this question for companies that offer stock to the public for the first time, which is called an *initial public offering*.

In the United States, before such companies can offer stock for sale, they must file a prospectus (Form S-1) with the Securities and Exchange Commission. The prospectus includes background information on the company, including its business strategy and the range of prices that the stock is expected to sell for in the market. Also included in the prospectus are the company's financial statements for the past three years.

Snap Inc. (SNAP) is a camera company with the objective of reinventing the camera by providing people an ability to communicate and express themselves with pictures. Snap's primary product is Snapchat, which is a camera application that allows people to send Snaps (images, emojis, and videos). On average, more than 180 million people use Snapchat daily creating more than three billion snaps.

In its prospectus filed with the Securities and Exchange Commission in 2017, Snap Inc. indicated that it anticipated a price for its Class A common stock of between $14.00 and $16.00 per share. At the end of its first day of trading, its stock closed at $24.48 per share and had traded as high at $26.05 per share. At $24 per share, Snap Inc.'s stock is worth more than $30 billion.

Was Snap Inc.'s stock really worth $24.48 at the end of its first day of trading on March 2, 2017?* To answer this question, investors analyze Snap Inc.'s financial condition and performance using public information, including its financial statements.

In this chapter, the nature, types, and activities of businesses, such as Snap Inc., are described and illustrated. In addition, the roles of accounting in business—including financial statements, basic accounting concepts, and how to use metrics to evaluate a business's performance—are also described and illustrated.

* As of the close of the market on October 2, 2020, Snap Inc. common stock was trading at $26.64 per share.

Objective 1
Describe the types and forms of businesses, how businesses make money, and business stakeholders.

Nature of Business and Accounting

A **business**[1] is an organization in which basic resources (inputs), such as materials and labor, are assembled and processed to provide goods or services (outputs) to customers. Businesses come in all sizes, from a local coffee house to **Starbucks (SBUX)**, which sells over $22 billion of coffee and related products each year.

The objective of most businesses is to earn a profit. **Profit** is the difference between the amounts received from customers for goods or services and the amounts paid for the inputs used to provide the goods or services. In this text, we focus on businesses operating to earn a profit. However, many of the same concepts and principles also apply to not-for-profit organizations such as hospitals, churches, and government agencies.

Types of Businesses

Three types of businesses operated for profit include service, merchandising, and manufacturing businesses. Each type of business and some examples are described below.

Service businesses provide services rather than products to customers.

Delta Air Lines (DAL) (transportation services)
The Walt Disney Company (DIS) (entertainment services)

Merchandising businesses sell products they purchase from other businesses to customers.

Walmart (WMT) (general merchandise)
Amazon.com (AMZN) (general merchandise)

1. A complete glossary of terms appears at the end of the text.

Manufacturing businesses change basic inputs into products that are sold to customers.

General Motors Corporation (GM) (cars, trucks, vans)
Intel Corporation (INTC) (computer microprocessors)

Snap Inc. is a service business that provides users an ability to communicate and express themselves to family and friends with short videos and images.

Snap Inc. Connection

Forms of Business

A business is normally organized in one of the following four forms:

- proprietorship
- partnership
- corporation
- limited liability company

A **proprietorship** is owned by one individual. More than 70% of the businesses in the United States are organized as proprietorships. The frequency of this form is due to the ease and low cost of organizing. The primary disadvantage of proprietorships is that the financial resources are limited to the individual owner's resources. In addition, the owner has unlimited liability to creditors for the debts of the company.

A **partnership** is owned by two or more individuals. About 10% of the businesses in the United States are organized as partnerships. Like a proprietorship, a partnership may outgrow the financial resources of its owners. Also, the partners have unlimited liability to creditors for the debts of the company.

A **corporation** is organized under state or federal statutes as a separate legal entity. The ownership of a corporation is divided into shares of stock. A corporation issues the stock to individuals or other companies, who then become owners or stockholders of the corporation. A primary advantage of the corporate form is the ability to obtain large amounts of resources by issuing shares of stock. In addition, the stockholders' liability to creditors for the debts of the company is limited to their investment in the corporation.

Snap Inc. is organized as a corporation in Delaware even though its offices are in Venice, California. Many companies incorporate in Delaware because of its favorable legal and business environment.

Snap Inc. Connection

A **limited liability company (LLC)** combines attributes of a partnership and a corporation. The primary advantage of the limited liability company form is that it operates similar to a partnership, but its owners' (or members') liability for the debts of the company is limited to their investment. Many professional practices such as lawyers, doctors, and accountants are organized as limited liability companies.

In addition to the ease of formation, ability to raise capital, and liability for the debts of the business, other factors such as taxes and legal life of the business should be considered when forming a business. For example, corporations are taxed as separate legal entities, while the income of sole proprietorships, partnerships, and limited liability companies is passed through to the owners and taxed on the owners' tax returns. As separate legal entities, corporations also continue on, regardless of the lives of the individual owners. In contrast, sole proprietorships, partnerships, and limited liability companies may terminate their existence with the death of an individual owner.

The characteristics of sole proprietorships, partnerships, corporations, and limited liability companies are summarized in the following table.

Organizational Form	Ease of Formation	Legal Liability	Taxation	Limitation on Life of Entity	Access to Capital
Proprietorship	Simple	No limitation	Nontaxable (pass-through) entity	Yes	Limited
Partnership	Simple	No limitation	Nontaxable (pass-through) entity	Yes	Average
Corporation	Complex	Limited liability	Taxable entity	No	Extensive
Limited liability company	Moderate	Limited liability	Nontaxable (pass-through) entity by election	Yes	Average

The three types of businesses we discussed earlier—manufacturing, merchandising, and service—may be proprietorships, partnerships, corporations, or limited liability companies. However, businesses that require a large amount of resources, such as many manufacturing businesses, are corporations. Likewise, most large retailers such as **Walmart (WMT)** and **Target (TGT)** are corporations.

Because most large businesses are corporations, they tend to dominate the economic activity in the United States. For this reason, this text focuses on the corporate form of organization. However, many of the concepts and principles discussed also apply to proprietorships, partnerships, and limited liability companies.

How Do Businesses Make Money?

The objective of a business is to earn a profit by providing goods or services to customers. How does a company decide which products or services to offer its customers? Many factors influence this decision. Ultimately, however, the decision is based on how the company plans to gain an advantage over its competitors and, in doing so, maximize its profits.

Companies try to maximize their profits by generating high revenues while maintaining low costs, which results in high profits. However, a company's competitors are also trying to do the same, and thus, a company can only maximize its profits by gaining an advantage over its competitors.

Generally, companies gain an advantage over their competitors by using one of the following strategies:

- A **low-cost strategy**, where a company designs and produces products or services at a lower cost than its competitors. Such companies often sell no-frills, standardized products and services.
- A **premium-price strategy**, where a company tries to design and produce products or services that serve unique market needs, allowing it to charge premium prices. Such companies often design and market their products so that customers perceive their products or services as having a unique quality, reliability, or image.

Walmart Inc. (WMT) and **Southwest Airlines Co. (LUV)** are examples of companies using a low-cost strategy. **Deere & Company (DE)** and **Tiffany & Co. (TIF)** are examples of companies using a premium-price strategy.

Since business is highly competitive, it is difficult for a company to sustain a competitive advantage over time. For example, a competitor of a company using a low-cost strategy may copy the company's low-cost methods or develop new methods that achieve even lower costs. Likewise, a competitor of a company using a premium-price strategy may develop products that are perceived as more desirable by customers.

Examples of companies utilizing low-cost and premium-price strategies include:

- Local pharmacies who develop personalized relationships with their customers. By doing so, they are able to charge premium (higher) prices. In contrast, Walmart's pharmacies use the low-cost emphasis and compete on cost.
- Grocery stores such as **Kroger (KR)** develop relationships with their customers by issuing preferred customer cards. These cards allow the stores to track consumer preferences and buying habits for use in purchasing and advertising campaigns.

- **Honda (HMC)** promotes the reliability and quality ratings of its automobiles and thus charges premium prices. In contrast, **Kia Motors (KRX)** uses a low-cost strategy.
- **Harley-Davidson (HOG)** emphasizes that its motorcycles are "Made in America" and promotes its "rebel" image as a means of charging higher prices.

Companies sometimes struggle to find a competitive advantage. For example, **JCPenney (JCP)** and **Macy's (M)** have difficulty competing on low costs against **Walmart (WMT)**, **Kohl's (KSS)**, **T.J. Maxx (TJX)**, and **Target (TGT)**. At the same time, JCPenney and Macy's have difficulty charging premium prices against competitors such as **The GAP (GPS)** and **Urban Outfitters (UOF)**. Likewise, **Delta Air Lines (DAL)** and **United Airlines (UA)** have difficulty competing against low-cost airlines such as **Southwest (LUV)**. At the same time, Delta and United don't offer any unique services for which their passengers are willing to pay a premium price.

Exhibit 1 summarizes low-cost and premium-price strategies with common examples of companies that employ each strategy.

Exhibit 1 Business Strategies and Industries

	Industry					
Business Strategy	**Airline**	**Freight**	**Automotive**	**Retail**	**Financial Services**	**Hotel**
Low cost	Southwest	Union Pacific	Hyundai	Sam's Club	Ameritrade	Super 8
Premium price	Virgin Atlantic	FedEx	BMW	Talbot's	Morgan Stanley	Ritz-Carlton

Snap Inc. Connection

Snap Inc.'s strategy is to provide an innovative, free platform for people to express themselves through images. Snap believes that images contain more context and richer information than text alone. Snap generates revenues (monetizes itself) primarily through advertising.

Business Stakeholders

A **business stakeholder** is a person or entity with an interest in the economic performance and well-being of a company. For example, owners, suppliers, customers, and employees are all stakeholders in a company.

Business stakeholders can be classified into one of the four categories illustrated in Exhibit 2.

Exhibit 2 Business Stakeholders

Business Stakeholder	Interest in the Business	Examples
Capital market stakeholders	Providers of major financing for the business	Banks, owners, stockholders
Product or service market stakeholders	Buyers of products or services and vendors to the business	Customers and suppliers
Government stakeholders	Collect taxes and fees from the business and its employees	Federal, state, and city governments
Internal stakeholders	Individuals employed by the business	Employees and managers

Capital market stakeholders provide the financing for a company to begin and continue its operations. Banks and other long-term creditors have an economic interest in receiving the amount loaned plus interest. Owners want to maximize the economic value of their investments.

Product or service market stakeholders purchase the company's products or services or sell their products or services to the company. Customers have an economic interest in the continued success of the company. For example, customers who purchase advance tickets on **Delta Air Lines (DAL)** are depending on Delta continuing in business. Likewise, suppliers depend on continued success of their customers. For example, if a customer fails or cuts back on purchases, the supplier's business will also decline.

Government stakeholders, such as federal, state, county, and city governments, collect taxes from companies. The better a company does, the more taxes the government collects. In addition, workers who are laid off by a company can file claims for unemployment compensation, which results in a financial burden for the state and federal governments.

Internal stakeholders, such as managers and employees, depend upon the continued success of the company for keeping their jobs. Managers of companies that perform poorly are often fired by the owners. Likewise, during economic downturns companies often lay off workers. Business stakeholders are illustrated in Exhibit 3.

Snap Inc. Connection

Snap Inc.'s stakeholders include common stockholders, bondholders, network members, employees, and U.S. and state governments who receive taxes.

Exhibit 3
Business Stakeholders

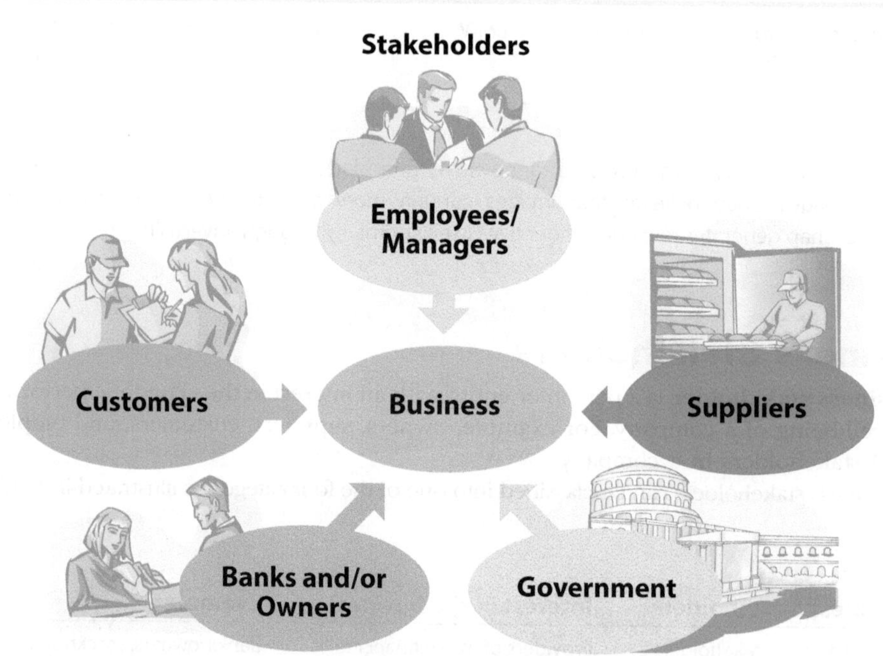

Business Insight

Inclusivity

Business stakeholders are increasingly concerned not only about whether a company is making money, but also about a company's impact on society. For example, a company that practices inclusivity has as an objective that every person should have equal rights, support, consideration, and opportunities to achieve their full potential. To achieve this objective, an inclusive company will enact policies and procedures that are accommodating and respectful of a person's race, ethnicity, sexual orientation, gender identity, physical abilities, religion, age, and culture.

Business Activities

Objective 2
Describe the three business activities of financing, investing, and operating.

All companies engage in the following three business activities:

- **Financing activities** to obtain the necessary funds (monies) to organize and operate the company
- **Investing activities** to obtain assets such as buildings and equipment to begin and operate the company
- **Operating activities** to earn revenues and profits

The preceding business activities are illustrated in Exhibit 4.

Exhibit 4
Business Activities

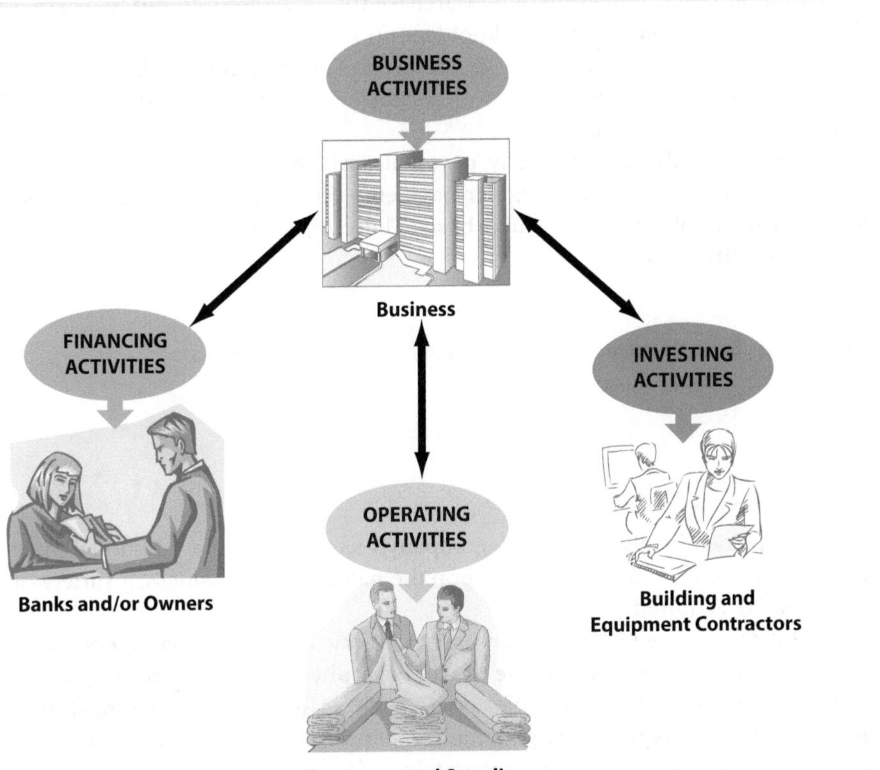

Financing Activities

Financing activities involve obtaining funds to begin and operate a business. Companies obtain financing through the use of capital markets by:

- borrowing
- issuing shares of ownership

When a company borrows money, it incurs a liability. A **liability** is a legal obligation to repay the amount borrowed according to the terms of the borrowing agreement. When a company borrows from a vendor or supplier, the liability is called an **account payable**. In such cases, the company promises to pay according to the terms set by the vendor or supplier. Most vendors and suppliers require payment within a relatively short time, such as 30 days.

On a recent balance sheet, **Snap Inc.** reported $46.9 million of accounts payable.

Snap Inc. Connection

A company may also borrow money by issuing bonds. *Bonds* are sold to investors and require repayment normally with interest. The amount of the bonds, called the *face value*, usually requires repayment several years in the future. Thus, bonds are a form of long-term financing. The interest on the bonds, however, is normally paid semiannually. Bond obligations are reported as **bonds payable**, and any interest that is due is reported as **interest payable**.

Many companies borrow by issuing notes payable. A **note payable** requires payment of the amount borrowed plus interest. Notes payable are similar to bonds except that they may be issued on either a short-term or a long-term basis.

A company may finance its operations by issuing shares of ownership. For a corporation, shares of ownership are issued in the form of shares of stock. Although corporations may issue a variety of different types of stock, the basic type of stock issued to owners is called **common stock**.[2] Investors who purchase the stock are referred to as **stockholders**.

The claims of creditors and stockholders on the assets of a corporation are different. **Assets** are the resources owned by a corporation (company). Creditors have first claim on the company's assets. Only after the creditors' claims are satisfied do the stockholders have a right to the corporate assets.

Creditors normally receive timely payments, which may include interest. In contrast, stockholders are not entitled to regular payments. However, many corporations distribute earnings to stockholders on a regular basis. These distributions of earnings to stockholders are called **dividends**.

Snap Inc. Connection

In a recent year, **Snap Inc.** engaged in the financing activity of issuing stock.

Investing Activities

Investing activities involve using the company's assets to obtain additional assets to start and operate the business. Depending upon the nature of the business, a variety of different assets must be acquired.

Most businesses need assets such as machinery, buildings, computers, office furnishings, trucks, and automobiles. These assets have physical characteristics and as such are **tangible assets**. Long-term tangible assets such as machinery, buildings, and land are reported separately as property, plant, and equipment. Short-term tangible assets such as cash and inventories are reported separately.

A business may also need **intangible assets**. For example, a business may obtain patent rights to use in manufacturing a product. Long-term assets such as patents, goodwill, and copyrights are reported separately as intangible assets.

A company may also prepay for items such as insurance or rent. Such items, which are assets until they are consumed, are reported as **prepaid expenses**. In addition, rights to payments from customers who purchase merchandise or services on credit are reported as **accounts receivable**.

Snap Inc. Connection

For a recent year, **Snap Inc.** engaged in investing activities such as the purchasing of property and equipment.

Operating Activities

Operating activities involve using assets to earn revenues and profits. The management of a company does this by implementing one of the business strategies discussed earlier.

2. Other types of stock are discussed in Chapter 10, "Stockholders' Equity."

Revenue is the increase in assets from selling products or services. Revenues are normally identified according to their source. For example, revenues received from selling products are called **sales**. Revenues received from providing services are called **fees earned**.

In a recent year, **Snap Inc.** reported $1,715 million of revenue.

Snap Inc. Connection

To earn revenue, a business incurs costs, such as wages of employees, salaries of managers, rent, insurance, advertising, freight, and utilities. Costs used to earn revenue are called **expenses** and are identified and reported in a variety of ways. For example, the cost of products sold is referred to as the **cost of goods sold**, **cost of merchandise sold**, or **cost of sales**. Other expenses are normally classified as either selling expenses or administrative expenses. **Selling expenses** include those costs directly related to the selling of a product or service. For example, selling expenses include such costs as sales salaries, sales commissions, freight, and advertising costs. **Administrative expenses** include other costs not directly related to the selling such as officer salaries and other costs of the corporate office.

By comparing the revenues for a period to the related expenses, it can be determined whether the company has earned net income or incurred a net loss. **Net income** results when revenues exceed expenses. A **net loss** results when expenses exceed revenues.

In a recent year, **Snap Inc.** reported loss from operations of $1.1 billion.

Snap Inc. Connection

As discussed next, the major role of accounting is to provide stakeholders with information on the financing, investing, and operating activities of businesses. Financial statements are one source of such information.

What Is Accounting and Its Role in Business?

Objective 3

Define accounting and describe its role in business.

The *role of accounting* is to provide information about the financing, investing, and operating activities of a company to its stakeholders. For example, accounting provides information for managers to use in operating the business. In addition, accounting provides information to other stakeholders, such as creditors, for assessing the economic performance and condition of the company.

Accounting is often called the "language of business." In a general sense, **accounting** is defined as an information system that provides reports to stakeholders about the economic activities and condition of a business. This text focuses on accounting and its role in business. However, many of the concepts discussed also apply to individuals, governments, and not-for-profit organizations. For example, individuals must account for their hours worked, checks written, and bills paid. Stakeholders for individuals include creditors, dependents, and the government.

A primary purpose of accounting is to summarize the financial performance of a business for external stakeholders, such as banks and governmental agencies. The branch of accounting that is associated with preparing reports for users external to the business is called **financial accounting**. Accounting also can be used to guide management in making financing, investing, and operations decisions for the company. This branch of accounting is called **managerial accounting**. Financial and managerial accounting may overlap. For example, financial reports for external stakeholders are often used by managers in assessing the potential impact of their decisions on the company. The head of the accounting department in a company is called **comptroller** or **chief financial officer** (CFO).

Snap Inc. Connection

The Chief Financial Officer of **Snap Inc.** is Derek Andersen, who has a BBA from Acadia University and an MBA from the University of California, Berkeley. During a recent year, Mr. Andersen's compensation, including stock awards, was over $9 million.

The two major objectives of financial accounting are:

- To report the financial condition of a business at a point in time
- To report changes in the financial condition of a business over a period of time

The relationship between these two financial accounting objectives is shown in Exhibit 5.

Exhibit 5
Objectives of Financial Accounting

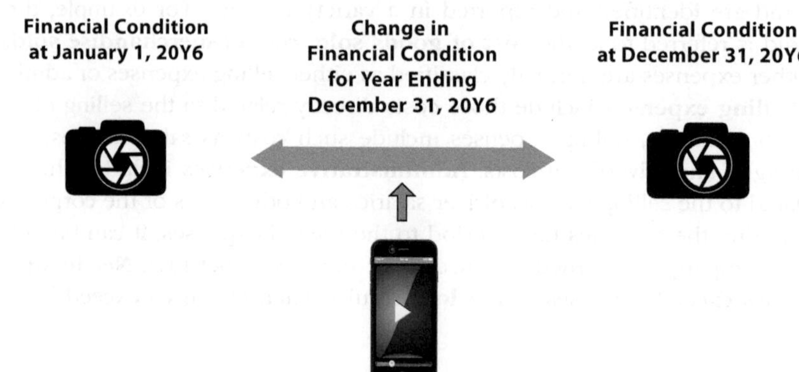

The first objective can be thought of as a still photograph (snapshot) of the company's financial (economic) condition as of a point in time. The second objective can be thought of as a moving picture (video) of the company's financial (economic) performance over time.

The objectives of accounting are achieved by (1) recording the economic events affecting a business and then (2) summarizing the impact of these events on the business in financial reports, called **financial statements**.

Using Data Analytics

What Is It?

A company's success will increasingly rely on the ability to collect, interpret, and gather insights from massive volumes of data. **Data analytics** is the science of analyzing raw data to discover patterns, identify anomalies, or gain other useful insights. The four basic types of data analytics are as follows:

Descriptive analytics Describes and summarizes outcomes.
Example: a sales report by product, region of country, and customer.

Diagnostic analytics Tries to explain results by identifying relationships among data.
Example: determining whether a YouTube video featuring a product increased sales within 48 hours after its first showing.

Predictive analytics Uses statistical methods to predict future outcomes.
Example: predicting the effects of methods for creating customer satisfaction on future sales.

Prescriptive analytics Recommends future actions for achieving company goals and objectives.
Example: analyzing the effects of energy saving alternatives on meeting the company's goal of reducing greenhouse gas emissions by 25%.

Data analytics is conducted using a variety of mathematical models, algorithms, and visualizations. Because of accounting's role in providing useful information, accountants are increasingly using data analytics to help businesses make better decisions. For this reason, we provide suggestions for the use of data analytics throughout the remainder of this text.

Financial Statements

Objective 4
Describe and illustrate the basic financial statements and how they are integrated.

Financial statements report the financial condition of a business at a point in time and changes in the financial condition over a period of time. The four basic financial statements and their relationship to the objectives of financial accounting are as follows.

Financial Statement	Financial Accounting Objective
Income statement	Reports changes in financial condition
Statement of stockholders' equity	Reports changes in financial condition
Balance sheet	Reports financial condition
Statement of cash flows	Reports changes in financial condition

The order in which each financial statement is prepared and the nature of each statement is as follows.

Order Prepared	Financial Statement	Description of Statement
1	Income statement	A summary of the revenue and expenses for a specific period of time, such as a month or a year.
2	Statement of stockholders' equity	A summary of the changes in the stockholders' equity in the corporation for a specific period of time, such as a month or a year.
3	Balance sheet	A list of the assets, liabilities, and stockholders' equity as of a specific date, usually at the close of the last day of a month or a year.
4	Statement of cash flows	A summary of the cash receipts and cash payments for a specific period of time, such as a month or a year.

The preceding four financial statements are described and illustrated in Exhibits 6 through 9 using **The Hershey Company (HSY)**. These illustrations will introduce you to the financial statements that you will be studying throughout this text. The data for the statements are adapted from a recent annual report of The Hershey Company.[3]

Income Statement

The **income statement** reports the change in financial condition due to the operations of the company. The time period covered by the income statement may vary depending upon the needs of stakeholders. Public corporations are required to file quarterly and annual income statements with the Securities and Exchange Commission (SEC). The income statement for a year ended December 31 for The Hershey Company is shown in Exhibit 6.

Since the objective of business operations is to generate revenues, the income statement begins by listing the revenues for the period. During the year, Hershey generated sales of $7,986 million. These sales are listed under "Revenues." The numbers shown in Exhibit 6 are expressed in millions of dollars. It is common for large companies to express their financial statements in thousands or millions of dollars.

3. The financial statements for Hershey shown in Exhibits 6–9 are for the year ended December 31, 2019. The most recent statements may be found at http://www.sec.gov/edgar/searchedgar/companysearch.html. Enter Hershey's stock market symbol "HSY" in the Fast Search box, enter "10-K" in the Filing Type box, and click on the latest 10-K.

Exhibit 6 Income Statement: The Hershey Company

The Hershey Company Income Statement For the Year Ended December 31 (in millions)		
Revenues:		
Sales		$7,986
Expenses:		
Cost of sales	$4,364	
Selling and administrative expenses	1,906	
Interest expense	144	
Income taxes expense	234	
Other expenses	188	(6,836)
Net income		$ 1,150

Following the revenues, the expenses used in generating the revenues are listed. For Hershey, these expenses include cost of sales, selling and administrative, interest, income taxes, and other expenses. By reporting the expenses and the related revenues for a period, the expenses are said to be matched against the revenues. This is known in accounting as the *matching concept*, which is discussed later in this chapter.

When revenues exceed expenses for a period, the company has *net income*. If expenses exceed revenues, the company has a *net loss*. Net income means that the business increased its net assets through its operations. That is, the assets created by the revenues exceeded the assets used in generating those revenues.

The objective of most companies is to maximize net income or profit. A net loss means that the business decreased its net assets through its operations. While a business might survive in the short run by reporting net losses, in the long run a business must earn net income to survive.

Exhibit 6 shows that Hershey earned net income of $1,150 million. Is this good or bad? Certainly, net income is better than a net loss. However, the stakeholders must assess net income according to their objectives. For example, a creditor might be satisfied that the net income is sufficient to ensure that it will be repaid. In contrast, a stockholder might assess the corporation's profitability as less than its competitors' profits and thus be disappointed. Throughout this text, various methods of assessing corporate performance will be described and illustrated.

Statement of Stockholders' Equity

The **statement of stockholders' equity** reports the changes in financial condition due to changes in stockholders' equity for a period. Changes to stockholders' equity normally involve common stock and retained earnings. **Retained earnings** are the portion of a corporation's net income retained in the business. A corporation may retain all of its net income for expanding operations, or it may pay a portion or all of its net income as dividends. For example, high-growth companies often do not distribute dividends but instead retain profits for future expansion. In contrast, more mature corporations normally pay a regular dividend.

Snap Inc. doesn't intend to pay cash dividends in the foreseeable future. Instead, it retains its cash to use in the expansion of its operations.

Since retained earnings depend upon net income, the period covered by the statement of stockholders' equity is the same period as the income statement. The statement of stockholders' equity for Hershey for the year ended December 31 is shown in Exhibit 7.

Exhibit 7 Statement of Stockholders' Equity

The Hershey Company
Statement of Stockholders' Equity
For the Year Ended December 31 (in millions)

	Common Stock	Retained Earnings	Other Items	Total
Balances, January 1	$299	$7,032	$(5,924)	$1,407
Net income		1,150		1,150
Dividends		(610)		(610)
Other items	(138)	(6,282)	6,218	(202)
Balances, December 31	$161	$1,290	$ 294	$1,745

During the year, common stock decreased by $138 million due to the purchase and retirement of a portion of its common stock. The purchase of a company's common stock (called treasury stock) is discussed in a later chapter.

During the year, Hershey's retained earnings was increased by its net income of $1,150 million and decreased by dividends of $610 million. Dividends are reported on the statement of stockholders' equity rather than the income statement. This is because dividends are not an expense but a distribution of net income to stockholders.

Hershey's retained earnings also decreased by an other item of $6,282 million, which was related to its purchase and retirement of common stock. The Other Items column of Exhibit 7 includes paid-in capital (amounts contributed in excess of the par value of stock) and losses from noncontrolling interests in subsidiaries.

Balance Sheet

The balance sheet reports the financial condition *as of a point in time*. This is in contrast to the income statement, statement of stockholders' equity, and statement of cash flows, which report changes in financial condition *for a period of time*. The financial condition of a business as of a point in time is measured by its total assets and claims or rights to those assets.

The claims on a company's assets consist of rights of creditors and stockholders. The rights of creditors are *liabilities*. The rights of stockholders are referred to as **stockholders' equity** or **owners' equity**. Thus, the financial condition of a business can be expressed in equation form as:

Assets = Liabilities + Stockholders' Equity

This equation is called the **accounting equation**. This equation is the foundation of accounting information systems, which are discussed in later chapters.

The **balance sheet**, sometimes called the **statement of financial condition**, is prepared using the accounting equation. The balance sheet is prepared by listing the accounting equation in vertical rather than horizontal form as follows:

Step 1. Each *asset* is listed and added to arrive at *total assets*.
Step 2. Each *liability* is listed and added to arrive at *total liabilities*.
Step 3. Each *stockholders' equity* item is listed and added to arrive at *total stockholders' equity*.
Step 4. Total liabilities and total stockholders' equity is added to arrive at *total liabilities and stockholders' equity*.
Step 5. Total assets must equal total liabilities and stockholders' equity.

The accounting equation must balance in Step 5; hence, the name balance sheet. The balance sheet for The Hershey Company as of December 31 is shown in Exhibit 8.

Exhibit 8 reports total assets of $8,140 million equal to its total liabilities of $6,395 million plus its total stockholders' equity of $1,745 million.

Exhibit 8 Balance Sheet: The Hershey Company

The Hershey Company Balance Sheet December 31 (in millions)	
Assets	
Cash	$ 493
Accounts receivable	569
Inventories	815
Prepaid expenses	240
Property, plant, and equipment	2,153
Intangibles	3,327
Other assets	543
Total assets	$8,140
Liabilities	
Accounts payable	$ 551
Accrued liabilities	722
Notes and other debt	4,922
Income taxes payable	200
Total liabilities	$6,395
Stockholders' Equity	
Common stock	$ 161
Retained earnings	1,290
Other equity items	294
Total stockholders' equity	$1,745
Total liabilities and stockholders' equity	$8,140

Statement of Cash Flows

The **statement of cash flows** reports the change in financial condition due to the changes in cash during a period. The statement of cash flows is organized around the three business activities of financing, investing, and operating. Any changes in cash must be related to one or more of these activities.

The *net cash flows from operating activities* is reported first. This is because cash flows from operating activities is a primary focus of the company's stakeholders. In the short term, creditors use cash flows from operating activities to assess whether the company's operating activities are generating enough cash to repay them. In the long term, a company cannot survive unless it generates positive cash flows from operating activities. Thus, cash flows from operating activities is also a focus of employees, managers, suppliers, customers, and other stakeholders who are interested in the long-term success of the company.

The *net cash flows from investing activities* is reported second. This is because investing activities directly impact the operations of the company. Cash receipts from selling property, plant, and equipment are reported in this section. Likewise, any purchases of property, plant, and equipment are reported as cash payments. Companies that are expanding rapidly, such as start-up companies, normally report negative net cash flows from investing activities. In contrast, companies that are downsizing or selling segments of the business may report positive net cash flows from investing activities.

The *net cash flows from financing activities* is reported third. Any cash receipts from issuing debt or stock are reported in this section as cash receipts. Likewise, cash payments of debt and dividends are reported in this section.

The statement of cash flows is completed by adding the net cash flows from operating, investing, and financing activities to determine the *net increase or decrease in cash* for the period. This net increase or decrease in cash is then added to the *cash at the beginning of the period* to arrive at the *cash at the end of the period.*

The statement of cash flows for The Hershey Company for the year ended December 31 is shown in Exhibit 9.

During the year, Hershey's *operating activities* generated a positive net cash flow of $1,764 million. Hershey's *investing activities* used $780 million of cash to purchase property, plant, equipment, and other long-term assets. Hershey's *financing activities* used $1,079 million of cash. This cash was used to pay dividends, pay debt, and purchase its own stock. A company may purchase its own common stock if the corporate management believes its stock is undervalued or for providing stock to employees or managers as part of an incentive (stock option) plan.[4] Hershey also received $990 million of cash by borrowing from creditors.

Exhibit 9 Statement of Cash Flows: The Hershey Company

The Hershey Company Statement of Cash Flows For the Year Ended December 31 (in millions)		
Cash flows from (used for) operating activities:		
Net cash flows from operating activities		$1,764
Cash flows from (used for) investing activities:		
Investments in property, plant, equipment, and other long-term assets		(780)
Cash flows from (used for) financing activities:		
Cash receipts from financing activities, including debt	$990	
Dividends paid to stockholders	(610)	
Repurchase of stock	(527)	
Other, including repayment of debt	(932)	
Net cash flows used for financing activities		(1,079)
Net decrease in cash during year		$ (95)
Cash as of January 1		588
Cash as of December 31		$ 493

During the year, Hershey decreased its cash by $95 million. This decrease is deducted from the cash at the beginning of the period of $588 million to arrive at net cash at the end of the period of $493 million.

Overall, Hershey's statement of cash flows indicates that Hershey generated $1,764 million in cash flows from its operations. It used this cash to expand its operations and pay dividends to stockholders. Thus, Hershey appears to be in a strong operating position.

Integrated Financial Statements

The financial statements are prepared in the following order:

1. income statement
2. statement of stockholders' equity
3. balance sheet
4. statement of cash flows

Preparing the financial statements in the preceding order is important because the financial statements are integrated as follows:

1. The income statement and statement of stockholders' equity are integrated. The net income or net loss reported on the income statement also appears on the statement of stockholders' equity as either an addition (net income) to or deduction (net loss) from the beginning retained earnings.[5]

4. The accounting for a company's purchase of its own stock, termed treasury stock, is discussed in a later chapter.

5. Depending upon the method of preparing cash flows from operating activities, net income may also appear on the statement of cash flows. This method of preparing the statement of cash flows is called the indirect method. This method is illustrated in a later chapter. In addition, Chapter 2 illustrates how cash flows from operating activities may equal net income.

2. The statement of stockholders' equity and the balance sheet are integrated. The common stock and retained earnings at the end of the period on the statement of stockholders' equity also appear on the balance sheet.
3. The balance sheet and statement of cash flows are integrated. The cash on the balance sheet also appears as the end-of-period cash on the statement of cash flows.

To illustrate, The Hershey Company's financial statements in Exhibits 6, 7, 8, and 9 are integrated as follows:

1. *Net income* of $1,150 million is also reported on the statement of stockholders' equity as an addition to the beginning retained earnings.
2. *Retained earnings* of $1,290 million and common stock of $161 as of December 31 are also reported on the balance sheet.
3. *Cash* of $493 million on the December 31 balance sheet is also reported as the end-of-period cash on the statement of cash flows.

The preceding integrations are shown in Exhibit 10. These integrations are important in analyzing (1) financial statements and (2) the impact of transactions on the financial statements. In addition, these integrations serve as a check on whether the financial statements have been prepared correctly. For example, if the ending cash on the statement of cash flows doesn't agree with the balance sheet cash, then an error has occurred.

Exhibit 10 Integrated Financial Statements

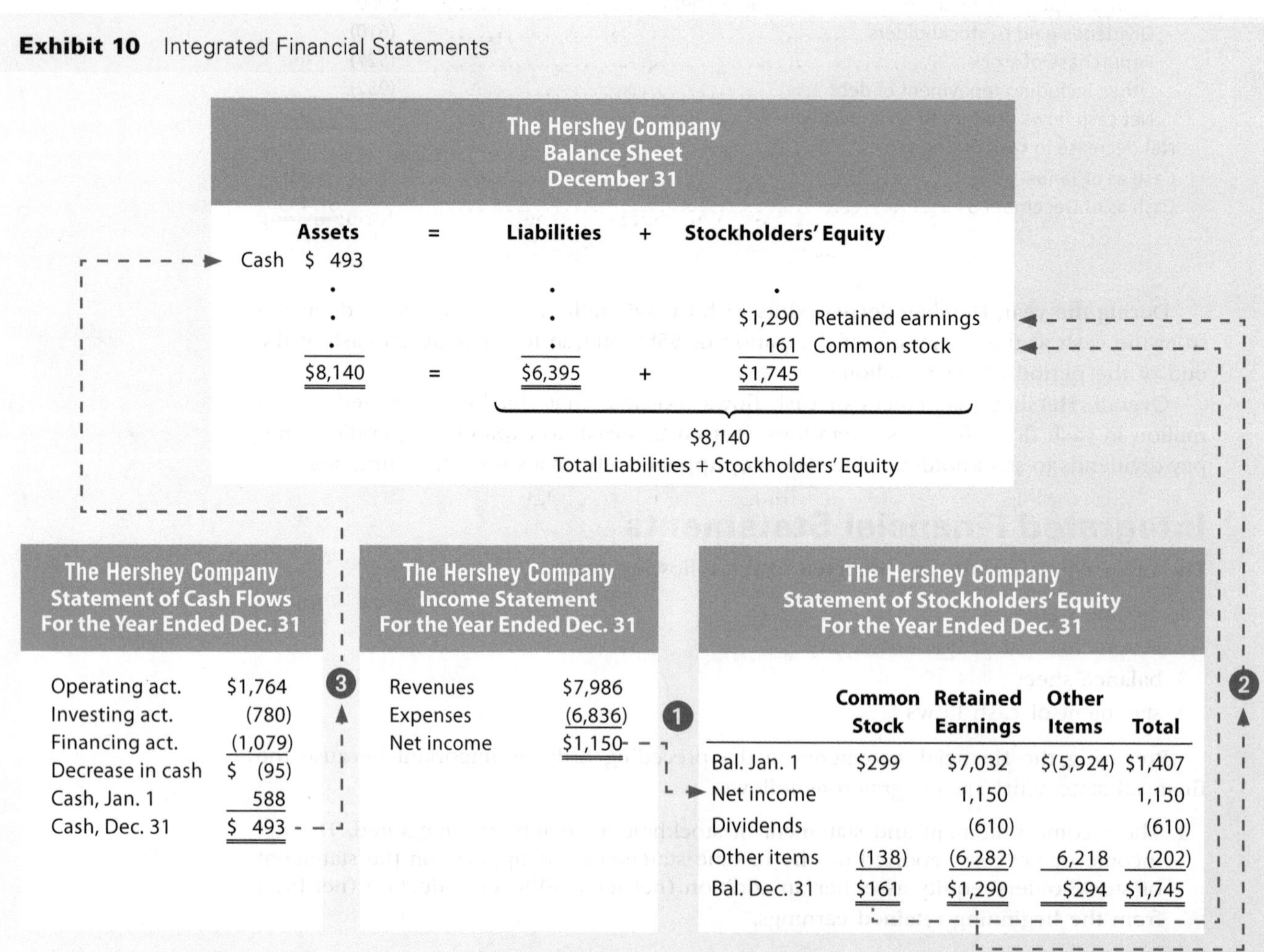

Accounting Concepts

Objective 5
Describe eight accounting concepts underlying financial reporting.

The four corporate financial statements described and illustrated in the preceding section were prepared using accounting "rules," called **generally accepted accounting principles (GAAP)**. Generally accepted accounting principles (GAAP) are necessary so that stakeholders can compare companies across time. If the management of a company could prepare financial statements as they saw fit, the comparability between companies and across time would be impossible.

Accounting principles and concepts are developed from research, accepted accounting practices, and pronouncements of regulators. Within the United States, the **Financial Accounting Standards Board (FASB)** has the primary responsibility for developing accounting principles. The FASB publishes *Statements of Financial Accounting Standards* as well as interpretations of these *Standards*.

The **Securities and Exchange Commission (SEC)**, an agency of the U.S. government, also has authority over the accounting and financial disclosures for corporations whose stock is traded and sold to the public. The SEC normally accepts the accounting principles set forth by the FASB. However, the SEC may issue *Staff Accounting Bulletins* on accounting matters that may not have been addressed by the FASB.

Many countries outside the United States use generally accepted accounting principles adopted by the **International Accounting Standards Board (IASB)**. The IASB issues *International Financial Reporting Standards (IFRS)*. Significant differences currently exist between FASB and IASB accounting principles. However, the FASB and IASB are working together to reduce and eliminate these differences toward the goal of developing a single set of accounting principles. Such a set of worldwide accounting principles would help facilitate investment and business in an increasingly global economy.

Generally accepted accounting principles (GAAP) rely upon eight supporting accounting concepts, as shown in Exhibit 11. Throughout this text, emphasis is on accounting principles and concepts. In this way, you will gain an understanding of "why" as well as "how" accounting is applied in business. Such an understanding is essential for analyzing and interpreting financial statements.

Business Entity Concept

The **business entity concept** limits the economic data recorded in an accounting system to data related to the activities of that company. In other words, the company is viewed as an entity separate from its owners, creditors, or other companies. For example, a company with one owner records the activities of only that company and does not record the personal activities, property, or debts of the owner. A business entity may take the form of a proprietorship, partnership, corporation, or limited liability company (LLC).

To illustrate, the accounting for The Hershey Company, a corporation, is separate from the accounting of its stakeholders. In other words, the accounting for transactions and events of individual stockholders, creditors, or other Hershey stakeholders is not included in The Hershey Company's financial statements. Only the transactions and events of the corporation are included.

Covid-19 Pandemic

Business Insight

The coronavirus (COVID-19) pandemic is causing significant disruptions to the companies and their business operations in the United States (U.S.) and throughout the world. As a result, the Financial Accounting Standards Board (FASB) has delayed the effective date of several accounting standards and is considering how to apply generally accepted accounting principles (GAAP) to a variety of issues generated by the pandemic. For example, companies with less than 500 employees may have received payroll loans under the Payroll Protection Program (PPP). Some or all of these PPP loans may be forgiven if certain conditions are met. Currently, GAAP does not have specific guidance on how to account for and disclose this type of government assistance.

Exhibit 11
Accounting Principles and Concepts

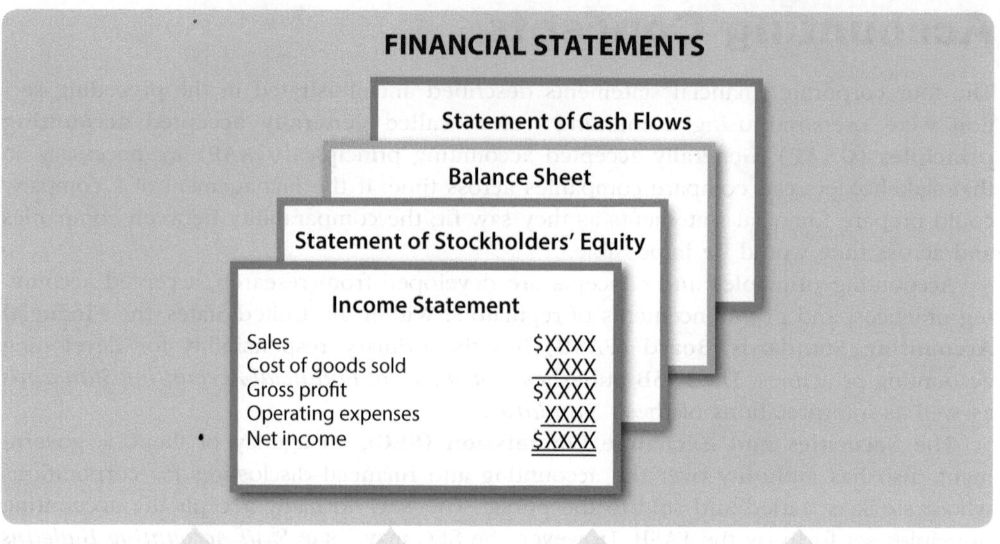

Generally Accepted Accounting Principles (GAAP)

ACCOUNTING CONCEPTS

- Business Entity Concept
- Cost Concept
- Going Concern Concept
- Matching Concept
- Objectivity Concept
- Unit of Measure Concept
- Adequate Disclosure Concept
- Accounting Period Concept

International Connection

Adoption or Convergence?

The largest public accounting firms, known as the Big Four, have pushed for the "adoption" of IFRS in the United States. Such a strategy of adoption would generate millions of dollars of consulting and accounting work within the United States for the Big Four: Deloitte Touche Tohmatsu, PwC (PriceWaterhouseCoopers), Ernst & Young, and KPMG.

In contrast, others have argued for a strategy of gradual "convergence" to IFRS over time. Currently, it appears that regulators within the United States and the FASB are favoring convergence rather than adoption. For example, the FASB and IASB have completed several projects to converge U.S. and IFRS standards.*

* FASB.org, "Progress Report on IASB-FASB Convergence Work," April 21, 2011.

Cost Concept

The **cost concept** initially records assets in the accounting records at their cost or purchase price. To illustrate, assume that Aaron Publishers purchased the following land on August 3, 20Y4, for $150,000:

Price listed by seller on March 1, 20Y4	$160,000
Aaron Publishers' initial offer to buy on January 31, 20Y4	140,000
Estimated selling price on December 31, 20Y8	220,000
Assessed value for property taxes, December 31, 20Y8	190,000

Under the cost concept, Aaron Publishers records the purchase of the land on August 3, 20Y4, at the purchase price of $150,000. The other amounts listed above have no effect on the accounting records.

The fact that the land has an estimated selling price of $220,000 on December 31, 20Y8, indicates that the land has increased in value. However, to use the $220,000 in the accounting records would be to record an illusory or unrealized profit. If Aaron Publishers sells the land on January 9, 20Y9, for $240,000, a profit of $90,000 ($240,000 − $150,000) is then realized and recorded. The new owner would record $240,000 as its cost of the land.

Going Concern Concept

The **going concern concept** assumes that a company will continue in business indefinitely. This assumption is made because the amount of time that a company will continue in business is not known.

The going concern concept justifies the use of the cost concept for recording purchases, such as land. For example, in the preceding illustration Aaron Publishers plans to build a plant on the land. Since Aaron Publishers does not plan to sell the land, reporting changes in the market value of the land is irrelevant. That is, the amount Aaron Publishers could sell the land for if it went out of business is not important. This is because Aaron Publishers plans to continue its operations.

If, however, there is strong evidence that a company is planning on discontinuing its operations, then the accounting records are revised. To illustrate, the assets and liabilities of businesses in receivership or bankruptcy are valued from a quitting concern or liquidation point of view, rather than from the going concern point of view.

Matching Concept

The **matching concept** reports the revenues earned by a company for a period with the expenses incurred in generating the revenues. That is, expenses are *matched* against the revenues they generated.

Revenues are normally recorded at the time a product is sold or a service is rendered, which is referred to as the **revenue recognition principle**. At the point of sale, the sale price has been agreed upon, the buyer acquires ownership of the product or acquires the service, and the seller has a legal claim against the buyer for payment.

The expenses incurred in generating revenue should be reported in the same period as the related revenue. This is called the **expense recognition principle**. By matching revenues and expenses, net income or loss for the period can properly be determined and reported.

Snap Inc. recognizes (records) revenue when the services have been provided or delivered, the fees are fixed or determinable, and collectability of the related receivable is reasonably assured.

Snap Inc. Connection

Objectivity Concept

The **objectivity concept** requires that entries in the accounting records and the data reported on financial statements be based on verifiable or objective evidence. For example, invoices, bank statements, and a physical count of supplies on hand are all objective and verifiable. Thus, they can be used for entering amounts in the accounting system. In some cases, judgments, estimates, and other subjective factors may have to be used in preparing financial statements. In such situations, the most objective evidence available is used.

Unit of Measure Concept

In the United States, the **unit of measure concept** requires that all economic data be recorded in dollars. Other relevant, nonfinancial information may also be recorded, such as terms of contracts. However, it is only through using dollar amounts that the various transactions and activities of a business can be measured, summarized, reported, and compared. Money is common to all business transactions and thus is the unit of measurement for financial reporting.

Adequate Disclosure Concept

The **adequate disclosure concept** requires that the financial statements, including related notes, contain all relevant data a stakeholder needs to understand the financial condition and performance of the company. Nonessential data are excluded to avoid clutter.

Accounting Period Concept

The **accounting period concept** requires that accounting data be recorded and summarized in financial statements for periods of time. For example, transactions are recorded for a period of time such as a month or a year. The accounting records are then summarized and updated before preparing the financial statements.

The financial history of a company may be shown by a series of balance sheets and income statements. If the life of a company is expressed by a line moving from left to right, the financial history of the company may be graphed as shown in Exhibit 12.

Exhibit 12 Financial History of a Company

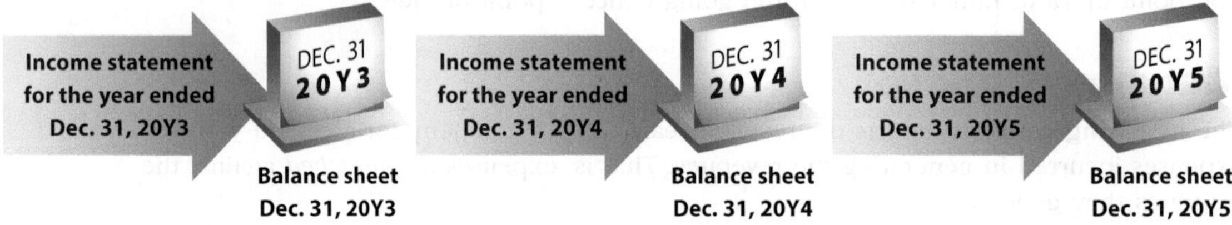

The annual accounting period adopted by a company is called its **fiscal year**. The fiscal year most commonly used is the calendar year beginning January 1 and ending December 31, as shown above. However, other periods are not unusual, especially for companies organized as corporations. For example, corporations often use a fiscal year that ends when its annual business operations have reached the lowest point. Such a fiscal year is called the **natural business year**. For example, Walmart Inc.'s fiscal year begins on February 1 and ends on January 31.

Responsible and Ethical Reporting

The reliability of the financial reporting system is important to the economy and for the ability of businesses to raise money from investors. That is, stockholders and creditors require accurate financial reporting before they will invest their money. Scandals and financial reporting frauds threaten the confidence of investors. Exhibit 13 is a list of some financial reporting frauds and abuses.

The companies listed in Exhibit 13 were caught in the midst of ethical lapses that led to fines, firings, and criminal or civil prosecution.

Integrity, Objectivity, and Ethics in Business

Doing the Right Thing

Time magazine named three women as "Persons of the Year 2002." Each of these not-so-ordinary women had the courage, determination, and integrity to do the right thing. Each risked their personal careers to expose shortcomings in their organizations. Sherron Watkins, an **Enron (ENRN)** vice president, wrote a letter to Enron's chairman, Kenneth Lay, warning him of improper accounting that eventually led to Enron's collapse. Cynthia Cooper, an internal accountant, informed **WorldCom**'s Board of Directors of phony accounting that allowed WorldCom to cover up over $3 billion in losses and forced WorldCom into bankruptcy. Coleen Rowley, an FBI staff attorney, wrote a memo to FBI Director Robert Mueller, exposing how the Bureau brushed off her pleas to investigate Zacarias Moussaoui, who was indicted as a co-conspirator in the September 11 terrorist attacks.

Exhibit 13
Accounting and Business Frauds

Company	Nature of Accounting or Business Fraud	Result
Countrywide	CEO misled investors.	CEO paid $22.5 million penalty and was permanently banned from serving as an officer or director of a public company.
Enron	Fraudulently inflated its financial results	Bankruptcy. Senior executives criminally convicted. More than $60 billion in stock market losses.
Goldman Sachs	Misstated and omitted key facts from investors.	Company agreed to pay $550 million fine and reformed business practices.
Wells Fargo	Improperly opened customer accounts without their permission.	CEO fined $17.5 million and banned from banking Industry for life.
Xerox Corporation	Recognized $3 billion in sales prior to when it should have been recorded.	Company fined $10 million. Six executives forced to pay $22 million.

What went wrong for the managers and companies listed in Exhibit 13? The answer normally involved one or both of the following factors:

- *Failure of Individual Character*. Ethical managers and accountants are honest and fair. However, managers and accountants often face pressures from supervisors to meet company and investor expectations. In many of the cases in Exhibit 13, managers and accountants justified small ethical violations to avoid such pressures. However, these small violations became big violations as the company's financial problems became worse.
- *Culture of Greed and Ethical Indifference*. By their behavior and attitude, senior managers set the company culture. In most of the companies listed in Exhibit 13, the senior managers created a culture of greed and indifference to the truth.

Ponzi Schemes

Business Insight

A Ponzi scheme is a scam or fraudulent operation where to attract investors an individual or entity promises high returns with little or no risk. To meet their claims, the perpetrators (fraudsters) pay early investors with monies obtained from attracting new investors. To succeed, a Ponzi scheme requires a constant stream of money from new investors. Eventually, Ponzi schemes become so large that they collapse. One of the most recent Ponzi schemes was perpetrated by Bernard Madoff, who admitted to defrauding clients of up to $50 billion over a number of years. He is serving a sentence of 150 years in prison.

As a result of accounting and business frauds, the United States Congress passed laws to monitor the behavior of accounting and business. For example, the Sarbanes-Oxley Act of 2002 (SOX) was enacted. SOX established a new oversight body for the accounting profession called the Public Company Accounting Oversight Board (PCAOB). In addition, SOX established standards for independence, corporate responsibility, and disclosure.

How does one behave ethically when faced with financial or other types of pressure? Guidelines for behaving ethically are shown in Exhibit 14.

Exhibit 14
Guidelines for Ethical Conduct

1. Identify an ethical decision by using your personal ethical standards of honesty and fairness.
2. Identify the consequences of the decision and its effect on others.
3. Consider your obligations and responsibilities to those that will be affected by your decision.
4. Make a decision that is ethical and fair to those affected by it.

Many companies have ethical standards of conduct for managers and employees.

Snap Inc. Connection

Snap Inc.'s code of conduct can be found at https://investor.snap.com/governance/governance-documents/default.aspx.

Objective 6
Describe types of metrics and analyze a company's performance using return on assets.

Metric-Based Analysis: Return on Assets

In analyzing and assessing a company's financial condition and performance, a variety of quantitative measures may be used. Quantitative measures are referred to as **metrics**. Throughout this text, we use a variety of metrics to assess a company's financial condition and performance. In addition, the effects of management's decisions on metrics are also described and illustrated. We call this use of metrics to assess financial condition, performance, and decisions **metric-based analysis**.

Types of Metrics

The two basic types of metrics used in this text are ratios and amounts. For example, the return on assets ratio is described and illustrated in this chapter. An example of a metric amount is passenger miles flown by an airline or grade point average of a student.

Snap Inc. Connection

Some metrics that **Snap Inc.** uses to assess its performance include average daily active users and average revenue per user.

Level of Application

We apply metric analysis at the following levels:

- Financial statement level
- Transaction level

Financial statement level. Metric-based analysis is commonly applied at the financial statement level. At this level, various financial ratios are computed and analyzed. In the next section, we apply metric-based analysis at the financial statement level using the ratio return on assets (net income divided by average total assets).

Transaction level. We also apply metric-based analysis at the transaction level. When a company enters into a transaction, it changes the company's assets, liabilities, and stockholders' equity. Since we assume companies operate to maximize their profits, we assess the effects of a transaction on one or more of a company's profitability metrics.

Companies also attempt to maintain a minimum degree of liquidity so they can pay their liabilities and respond quickly to new opportunities to expand or enhance their operations. **Liquidity** refers to the degree to which a company has cash or assets that can be readily converted to cash. For example, investments in marketable securities can readily be converted to cash. In contrast, property, plant, and equipment are less liquid and could take months or years to convert to cash.

Liquidity differs from solvency. **Solvency** refers to the ability of a company to pay its long-term debts. Companies that cannot pay their debts are said to be insolvent, which usually involves filing for bankruptcy. Liquidity affects a company's ability to pay its debts. However, a company may have a large portion of assets that cannot be readily converted to cash but still be profitable and solvent.

In addition to assessing the effects of a transaction on one or more of a company's profitability metrics, we also assess the effects on one or more of a company's liquidity metrics. In Chapter 2, we begin our metric-based analysis of transactions by assessing the effects of each transaction on cash and net income. In later chapters, we expand this analysis to include a variety of profitability and liquidity metrics.

Return on Assets

In the remainder of this chapter, we describe and illustrate metric-based analysis at the financial statement level using return on assets. The return on assets is a profitability metric often used to compare a company's performance over time and with competitors.

Return on assets is normally expressed as a percent such as 12%. However, it may also be expressed as an amount per dollar invested. For example, a 12% return on assets could also be expressed as $0.12 return per $1 invested. In other words, the company is earning 12 cents per dollar invested.

The **return on assets** percentage is computed as follows:

$$\textbf{Return on Assets} = \frac{\textbf{Net Income}}{\textbf{Average Total Assets}}$$

To illustrate, return on assets is computed for **Apple Inc. (AAPL)** and **HP Inc. (HPQ)** (formerly **Hewlett-Packard**). The computations use data (in millions) from recent financial statements.

	Apple Inc.	HP Inc.
Net income	$ 55,256	$ 3,152
Total assets at beginning of year	$365,725	$34,622
Total assets at end of year	$338,516	$33,467
Average total assets:*		
Apple Inc. [($365,725 + $338,516) ÷ 2]	$352,121	
HP Inc. [($34,622 + $33,467) ÷ 2]		$34,045
Return on assets:**		
Apple Inc. ($55,256 ÷ $352,121)	15.7%	
HP Inc. ($3,152 ÷ $34,045)		9.3%

*Rounded to nearest dollar.

**Rounded to one decimal place.

As shown, Apple is 1.7 (15.7% ÷ 9.3%) times more profitable, as measured by return on assets, than is HP Inc. Apple's profitability is largely due to its innovative technology, including its iPad, iPhone, iPod, and Mac computers.

Comparing rates of return among companies that use different tax strategies or different methods of financing their operations may be misleading. In the case of companies using different tax strategies, tax expense may be added to net income to reduce the impact of taxes. Likewise, some companies finance their operations primarily by debt, while other companies finance their operations primarily by equity. In this case, interest expense may be added to net income to reduce the impact of differences in financing.

Key Points

1. Describe the types and forms of businesses, how businesses make money, and business stakeholders.

The three types of businesses operated for profit include manufacturing, merchandising, and service businesses. Such businesses may be organized as proprietorships, partnerships, corporations, and limited liability companies. A business may make money (profits) by gaining an advantage over its competitors using a low-cost or a premium-price emphasis. Under a low-cost emphasis, a business designs and produces products or services at a lower cost than its competitors. Under a premium-price emphasis, a business tries to design products or services that possess unique attributes or characteristics for which customers are willing to pay more. A business' economic performance is of interest to its stakeholders. Business stakeholders include four categories: capital market stakeholders, product or service market stakeholders, government stakeholders, and internal stakeholders.

2. Describe the three business activities of financing, investing, and operating.

All businesses engage in financing, investing, and operating activities. Financing activities involve obtaining funds to begin and operate a business. Investing activities involve obtaining the necessary resources to start and operate the business. Operating activities involve using the business's resources according to its business emphasis.

3. Define accounting and describe its role in business.

Accounting is an information system that provides reports to stakeholders about the economic activities and condition of a business. Accounting is the "language of business."

4. Describe and illustrate the basic financial statements and how they are integrated.

The principal financial statements of a corporation are the income statement, the statement of stockholders' equity, the balance sheet, and the statement of cash flows. The income statement reports a period's net income or net loss, which also appears on the statement of stockholders' equity. The ending balances reported on the statement of stockholders' equity are also reported on the balance sheet. The ending cash balance is reported on the balance sheet and the statement of cash flows.

5. Describe eight accounting concepts underlying financial reporting.

The eight accounting concepts discussed in this chapter include the business entity, cost, going concern, matching, objectivity, unit of measure, adequate disclosure, and accounting period concepts.

6. Describe types of metrics and analyze a company's performance using return on assets.

A metric is any quantitative measure. Metric analysis may be performed at the financial statement, transaction, or managerial decision level. At the financial statement level, return on assets is computed by dividing net income by average total assets. Return on assets is useful in assessing the percentage (rate) that a company is earnings on its invested assets. Return on assets can also be expressed as dollars earned for each dollar invested.

Key Terms

Accounting (9)
Accounting equation (13)
Accounting period concept (20)
Accounts payable (7)
Accounts receivable (8)
Adequate disclosure concept (20)
Administrative expenses (9)
Assets (8)
Balance sheet (13)
Bonds payable (8)
Business (2)
Business entity concept (17)
Business stakeholder (5)
Chief financial officer (9)
Common stock (8)
Comptroller (9)
Corporation (3)
Cost concept (19)
Cost of goods sold (9)
Cost of merchandise sold (9)
Cost of sales (9)
Data analytics (10)
Dividends (8)
Expenses (9)
Expense recognition principle (19)
Fees earned (9)
Financial accounting (9)
Financial Accounting Standards Board (FASB) (17)
Financial statements (10)
Financing activities (7)
Fiscal year (20)
Generally accepted accounting principles (GAAP) (17)
Going concern concept (19)
Income statement (11)
Intangible assets (8)
Interest payable (8)
International Accounting Standards Board (IASB) (17)
Investing activities (7)
Liabilities (7)
Limited liability company (LLC) (3)
Liquidity (23)
Low-cost strategy (4)
Managerial accounting (9)
Manufacturing business (3)
Matching concept (19)
Merchandising business (2)
Metric (22)
Metric-based analysis (22)
Natural business year (20)
Net income (9)
Net loss (9)
Note payable (8)
Objectivity concept (20)
Operating activities (7)
Partnership (3)
Premium-price strategy (4)
Prepaid expenses (8)
Profit (2)
Proprietorship (3)
Retained earnings (12)
Return on assets (23)
Revenue (9)
Revenue recognition principle (19)
Sales (9)
Securities and Exchange Commission (SEC) (17)
Selling expenses (9)
Service business (2)
Solvency (23)
Statement of cash flows (14)
Statement of financial condition (13)
Statement of stockholders' equity (12)
Stockholders (8)
Stockholders' equity (13)
Tangible assets (8)
Unit of measure concept (20)

Illustrative Problem

The financial statements at the end of Spratlin Consulting's first month of operations follow.

SPRATLIN CONSULTING
Income Statement
For the Month Ended June 30, 20Y8

Fees earned		$ 36,000
Operating expenses:		
Wages expense	$12,000	
Rent expense	7,640	
Utilities expense	(a)	
Miscellaneous expense	1,320	
Total operating expenses		(23,120)
Net income		$ (b)

SPRATLIN CONSULTING
Statement of Stockholders' Equity
For the Month Ended June 30, 20Y8

	Common Stock	Retained Earnings
Balances, June 1, 20Y8	$ 0	$ 0
Issued common stock	48,000	
Net income		(c)
Dividends		(d)
Balances, June 30, 20Y8	$48,000	$(e)

SPRATLIN CONSULTING
Balance Sheet
June 30, 20Y8

Assets	
Cash	$ 5,600
Land	50,000
Total assets	$ (f)
Liabilities	
Accounts payable	$ 1,920
Stockholders' Equity	
Common stock	$ (g)
Retained earnings	(h)
Total stockholders' equity	$ (i)
Total liabilities and stockholders' equity	$ (j)

SPRATLIN CONSULTING
Statement of Cash Flows
For the Month Ended June 30, 20Y8

Cash flows from operating activities:		
Cash received from customers	$36,000	
Cash paid for operating expenses	(k)	
Net cash flows from operating activities		$14,800
Cash flows from investing activities:		
Cash paid for acquisition of land		(l)
Cash flows from financing activities:		
Cash received from issuing common stock	$48,000	
Dividends paid to stockholders	(7,200)	
Net cash flows from financing activities		(m)
Net increase in cash during month		$ (n)
Cash as of June 1		0
Cash as of June 30		$ (n)

Instructions

By analyzing how the four financial statements are integrated, determine the proper amounts for (a) through (n).

Solution

a. Utilities expense, $2,160 ($23,120 – $12,000 – $7,640 – $1,320)
b. Net income, $12,880 ($36,000 – $23,120)
c. Net income, $12,880 [same as (b)]
d. Dividends, $(7,200) (from statement of cash flows)
e. Retained earnings, $5,680 ($12,880 – $7,200)
f. Total assets, $55,600 ($5,600 + $50,000)
g. Common stock, $48,000 (from the statement of stockholders' equity or statement of cash flows)
h. Retained earnings, $5,680 [same as (e)]
i. Total stockholders' equity, $53,680 ($48,000 + $5,680)
j. Total liabilities and stockholders' equity, $55,600 ($1,920 + $53,680) [same as (f)]

k. Cash paid for operating expenses, $(21,200) ($36,000 – $14,800)
l. Cash paid for acquisition of land, $(50,000) (from balance sheet)
m. Net cash flows from financing activities, $40,800 ($48,000 – $7,200)
n. Net increase in cash and June 30, 20Y8, cash balance, $5,600 ($14,800 – $50,000 + $40,800)

Self-Examination Questions

(Answers appear at the end of chapter.)

1. A profit-making business operating as a separate legal entity and in which ownership is divided into shares of stock is known as a:
   A. proprietorship.
   B. service business.
   C. partnership.
   D. corporation.
2. The resources owned by a business are called:
   A. assets.
   B. liabilities.
   C. the accounting equation.
   D. stockholders' equity.
3. A listing of a business entity's assets, liabilities, and stockholders' equity as of a specific date is:
   A. a balance sheet.
   B. an income statement.
   C. a statement of stockholders' equity.
   D. a statement of cash flows.
4. If total assets are $20,000 and total liabilities are $12,000, the amount of stockholders' equity is:
   A. $32,000.
   B. $(32,000).
   C. $(8,000).
   D. $8,000.
5. If revenue was $45,000, expenses were $37,500, and dividends were $10,000, the amount of net income or net loss would be:
   A. $45,000 net income.
   B. $7,500 net income.
   C. $37,500 net loss.
   D. $2,500 net loss.

Class Discussion Questions

1. What is the objective of most businesses?
2. What is the difference between a manufacturing business and a merchandising business? Give an example of each type of business.
3. What is the difference between a manufacturing business and a service business? Is a restaurant a manufacturing business, a service business, or both?
4. Why are most large companies like Apple (AAPL), Pepsico (PEP), General Electric (GE), and Intel (INTC) organized as corporations?
5. Both Kia Motors (KRX) and BMW (BMW) produce and sell automobiles. Describe and contrast the business emphasis of KIA and BMW.
6. Assume that a friend of yours operates a family-owned pharmacy. A Walmart Supercenter, scheduled to open in the next several months, will also offer pharmacy services. What business emphasis would your friend use to compete with the Super Walmart pharmacy?
7. What services does eBay (EBAY) offer its customers?
8. A business's stakeholders can be classified into capital market, product or service market, government, and internal stakeholders. Will the interests of all the stakeholders within a classification be the same? Use bankers and stockholders of the capital market as an example in answering this question.

9. The three business activities are financing, investing, and operating. Using Southwest Airlines (LUV), give an example of each type of activity.
10. What is the role of accounting in business?
11. Briefly describe the nature of the information provided by each of the following financial statements: the income statement, the statement of stockholders' equity, the balance sheet, and the statement of cash flows. In your descriptions, indicate whether each of the financial statements covers a period of time or is for a specific date.
12. For a recent year ended January 31, Target Corporation (TGT) had revenues of $72,618 million and total expenses of $74,254 million. Did Target Corporation report a net loss or a net income?
13. What particular item of financial or operating data appears on both the income statement and the statement of stockholders' equity? What items appear on both the balance sheet and the statement of stockholders' equity? What item appears on both the balance sheet and statement of cash flows?
14. Billy Jessop is the owner of Valley Delivery Service. Recently, Billy paid interest of $6,000 on a personal loan of $75,000 that he used to begin the business. Should Valley Delivery Service record the interest payment? Explain.
15. On October 1, Wok Repair Service extended an offer of $100,000 for land that had been priced for sale at $150,000. On December 19, Wok Repair Service accepted the seller's counteroffer of $110,000. Describe how Wok Repair Service should record the land.
16. Land with an assessed value of $500,000 for property tax purposes is acquired by a business for $600,000. Four years later, the plot of land has an assessed value of $750,000 and the business receives an offer of $975,000 for it. Should the monetary amount assigned to the land in the business records now be increased?

Exercises

Obj. 1

E1-1 Types of businesses

Indicate whether each of the following companies is primarily a service, merchandise, or manufacturing business. If you are unfamiliar with the company, you may use the Internet to locate the company's home page or use the finance Web site of Yahoo.com.

1. AFLAC (AFL)
2. Best Buy (BBY)
3. Boeing (BA)
4. Caterpillar (CAT)
5. Citigroup (C)
6. CVS Health Corp. (CVS)
7. DowDuPont Inc. (DWDP)
8. Exxon Mobil (XOM)
9. Facebook (FB)
10. Ford Motor (F)
11. General Electric (GE)
12. Hilton Hotels
13. H&R Block Inc. (HRD)
14. Oracle (ORCL)
15. Target (TGT)

Obj. 1

E1-2 Business emphasis

Identify the primary business emphasis of each of the following companies as (a) a low-cost emphasis or (b) a premium-price emphasis. If you are unfamiliar with the company, you may use the Internet to locate the company's home page or use the finance Web site of Yahoo.com.

1. Allegiant Travel Services (ALGT)
2. Best Buy (BBY)
3. BMW
4. Dollar Tree (DLTR)
5. E*TRADE (ETFC)
6. Goldman Sachs Group (GS)
7. Lowe's (LOW)
8. Nike (NKE)
9. Starbucks
10. Walmart
11. Sub-Zero
12. Mercedes-Benz

E1-3 Accounting equation

Obj. 4

✔ Best Buy, $3,479

The total assets and total liabilities for a recent year of Best Buy (BBY) and Gamestop (GME) are shown below.

	Best Buy (in millions)	Gamestop (in millions)
Assets	$15,591	$2,820
Liabilities	12,112	2,208

Determine the stockholders' equity of each company.

E1-4 Accounting equation

Obj. 4

✔ Apple, $90,488

The total assets and total liabilities for a recent year of Apple (AAPL) and Microsoft (MSFT) are shown here.

	Apple (in millions)	Microsoft (in millions)
Assets	$338,516	$286,556
Liabilities	248,028	184,226

Determine the stockholders' equity of each company.

E1-5 Accounting equation

Obj. 4

SHOW ME HOW

✔ a. $712,500

Determine the missing amount for each of the following:

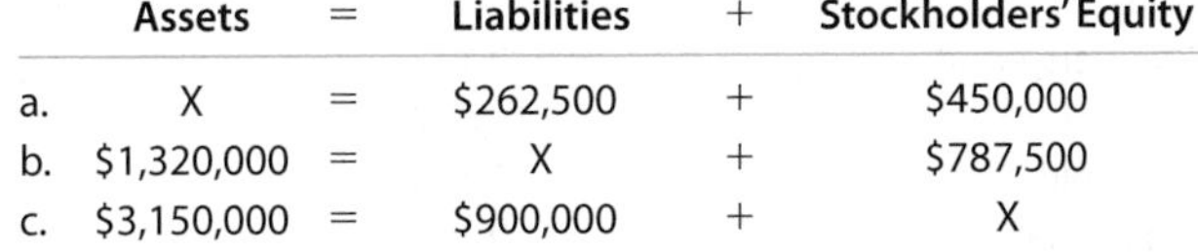

	Assets	=	Liabilities	+	Stockholders' Equity
a.	X	=	$262,500	+	$450,000
b.	$1,320,000	=	X	+	$787,500
c.	$3,150,000	=	$900,000	+	X

E1-6 Accounting equation

Obj. 4

✔ a. $15,584

Determine the missing amounts (in millions) for the condensed balance sheets shown below.

	Costco (COST)	Target (TGT)	Walmart (WMT)
Assets	$45,400	$42,779	$ (c)
Liabilities	29,816	(b)	161,826
Stockholders' equity	(a)	11,833	74,669

E1-7 Net income and dividends

Obj. 4

The income statement of a corporation for the month of November indicates a net income of $90,000. During the same period, $100,000 in cash dividends were paid. Would it be correct to say that the business incurred a net loss of $10,000 during the month? Discuss.

Obj. 4

✔ Company Chang: Net income, $225,000

E1-8 Net income and stockholders' equity for four businesses

Four different companies—Chang, Henry, Nagel, and Wilcox—show the same balance sheet data at the beginning and end of a year. These data, exclusive of the amount of stockholders' equity, are summarized as follows:

	Total Assets	Total Liabilities
Beginning of the year	$775,000	$400,000
End of the year	900,000	300,000

On the basis of the preceding data and the following additional information for the year, determine the net income (or loss) of each company for the year. (*Hint:* First determine the amount of increase or decrease in stockholders' equity during the year.)

Company Chang: No additional common stock was issued, and no dividends were paid.

Company Henry: No additional common stock was issued, but dividends of $90,000 were paid.

Company Nagel: Common stock of $125,000 was issued, but no dividends were paid.

Company Wilcox: Common stock of $125,000 was issued, and dividends of $90,000 were paid.

Obj. 4

✔ a. (1) $5,138

E1-9 Accounting equation and income statement

Office Depot, Inc. (ODP) is a leading provider of business services, supplies, products, and technology solutions to small, medium, and enterprise businesses. The following financial statement data were adapted from recent financial statements of Staples:

	Year 2 (in millions)	Year 1 (in millions)
Total assets	$ 7,311	$6,166
Total liabilities	(1)	4,040
Total stockholders' equity	2,173	(2)
Sales	10,647	
Cost of goods sold	8,183	
Operating expenses	2,101	
Other expense (net)	217	
Income tax expense	47	

a. Determine the missing data indicated for (1) and (2).

b. Using the income statement data for Year 2, determine the amount of net income or loss.

Obj. 4

E1-10 Balance sheet items

From the following list of selected items taken from the records of Mermaid Stories, Inc. as of a specific date, identify those that would appear on the balance sheet.

1. Accounts Receivable
2. Common Stock
3. Cash
4. Fees Earned
5. Rent Expense
6. Salaries Expense
7. Salaries Payable
8. Supplies
9. Supplies Expense
10. Utilities Expense

Obj. 4

E1-11 Income statement items

Based on the data presented in Exercise 1-10, identify those items that would appear on the income statement.

E1-12 Financial statement items

Obj. 4

Identify each of the following items as (a) an asset, (b) a liability, (c) revenue, (d) an expense, or (e) a dividend:

1. Amounts due from customers
2. Amounts owed to suppliers
3. Cash on hand
4. Cash paid to stockholders
5. Cash sales
6. Equipment
7. Note payable owed to the bank
8. Rent paid for the month
9. Sales commissions paid to salespersons
10. Wages paid to employees

E1-13 Statement of stockholders' equity

Obj. 4

✔ Retained earnings, June 30, 20Y7, $217,500

Financial information related to All Seasons Company for the month ended June 30, 20Y7, is as follows:

Common stock, June 1, 20Y7	$ 30,000
Stock issued in June	20,000
Net income for June	87,500
Dividends during June	15,000
Retained earnings, June 1, 20Y7	145,000

Prepare a statement of stockholders' equity for the month ended June 30, 20Y7.

E1-14 Income statement

Obj. 4

✔ Net income: $633,750

JLM Services was organized on August 1, 20Y5. A summary of the revenue and expense transactions for August follows:

Fees earned	$2,550,000
Wages expense	1,612,500
Miscellaneous expense	41,250
Rent expense	240,000
Supplies expense	22,500

Prepare an income statement for the month ended August 31.

E1-15 Missing amounts from balance sheet and income statement data

Obj. 4

✔ (a) $90,000

One item is omitted in each of the following summaries of balance sheet and income statement data for four different corporations, AL, CO, KS, and MT.

	AL	CO	KS	MT
Beginning of the year:				
Assets	$400,000	$300,000	$550,000	$ (d)
Liabilities	200,000	130,000	325,000	350,000
End of the year:				
Assets	800,000	460,000	660,000	1,200,000
Liabilities	450,000	110,000	360,000	700,000
During the year:				
Additional issue of common stock	(a)	50,000	100,000	100,000
Dividends	50,000	20,000	(c)	90,000
Revenue	175,000	(b)	115,000	420,000
Expenses	65,000	70,000	130,000	480,000

Determine the missing amounts, identifying them by letter. [*Hint:* First determine the amount of increase or decrease in stockholders' equity during the year.]

Obj. 4

✔ b. $53,000

E1-16 Balance sheets, net income

Financial information related to Montana Interiors for October and November 20Y8 is as follows:

	October 31, 20Y8	November 30, 20Y8
Accounts payable	$ 40,000	$ 65,000
Accounts receivable	75,000	118,000
Common stock	60,000	60,000
Retained earnings	?	?
Cash	110,000	140,000
Supplies	15,000	20,000

a. Prepare balance sheets for Montana Interiors as of October 31 and as of November 30, 20Y8.

b. Determine the amount of net income for November, assuming that no additional common stock was issued and no dividends were paid during the month.

c. Determine the amount of net income for November, assuming that no additional common stock was issued but dividends of $20,000 were paid during the month.

Obj. 4

E1-17 Financial statements

Each of the following items is shown in the financial statements of ExxonMobil Corporation. Identify the financial statement (balance sheet or income statement) in which each item would appear.

a. Accounts payable
b. Cash equivalents
c. Crude oil inventory
d. Equipment
e. Exploration expenses
f. Income taxes payable
g. Investments
h. Long-term debt
i. Marketable securities
j. Notes and loans payable
k. Operating expenses
l. Prepaid taxes
m. Retained earnings
n. Sales
o. Selling expenses

Obj. 4

E1-18 Statement of cash flows

Indicate whether each of the following cash activities would be reported on the statement of cash flows as (a) an operating activity, (b) an investing activity, or (c) a financing activity.

1. Issued common stock
2. Paid rent
3. Paid for office equipment
4. Sold services
5. Issued a note payable
6. Sold equipment
7. Paid officers' salaries
8. Paid for advertising
9. Paid insurance
10. Paid dividends

Obj. 4

E1-19 Statement of cash flows

Indicate whether each of the following activities would be reported on the statement of cash flows as (a) an operating activity, (b) an investing activity, or (c) a financing activity.

1. Cash received from investment by stockholders
2. Cash received from fees earned
3. Cash paid for expenses
4. Cash paid for land

E1-20 Statement of cash flows

Obj. 4

✔ **Net cash flows from operating activities, $220,000**

Looney Inc. was organized on July 1, Year 1. A summary of cash flows for July follows.

Cash receipts:	
Cash received from customers	$600,000
Cash received from issuing common stock	200,000
Cash received from note payable	75,000
Cash payments:	
Cash paid out for expenses	$380,000
Cash paid out for purchase of equipment	95,000
Cash paid as dividends	25,000

Prepare a statement of cash flows for the month ended July 31, Year 1.

E1-21 Using financial statements

Obj. 4

A company's stakeholders often differ in their financial statement focus. For example, some stakeholders focus primarily on the income statement, while others focus primarily on the statement of cash flows or the balance sheet. For each of the following situations, indicate which financial statement would be the likely focus for the stakeholder. Choose either the income statement, balance sheet, or statement of cash flows, and justify your choice.

Situation 1: Assume that you are considering purchasing a personal computer from Dell (DELL).

Situation 2: Assume that you are considering investing in LinkedIn (capital market stakeholder).

Situation 3: Assume that you are employed by Campbell Soup Co. (CPB) (product market stakeholder) and are considering whether to extend credit for a 60-day period to a new grocery store chain that has recently opened throughout the Midwest.

Situation 4: Assume that you are considering taking a job (internal stakeholder) with either Sears or JCPenney (JCP).

Situation 5: Assume that you are a banker for US Bank (capital market stakeholder), and you are considering whether to grant a major credit line (loan) to Target (TGT). The credit line will allow Target to borrow up to $400 million for a five-year period at the market rate of interest.

E1-22 Financial statement items

Obj. 4

Amazon.com, Inc. (AMZN) operates as an online retailer in North America and internationally. Both Amazon and third parties, via the Amazon.com Web site, sell products across various product categories.

The following items were adapted from a recent annual report of Amazon.com for the year ended December 31:

	In millions
1. Accounts payable	$ 47,183
2. Accounts receivable	20,816
3. Cash	36,092
4. Cost of sales	165,536
5. Income tax expense	2,374
6. Interest expense	1,600
7. Inventories	20,497
8. Net cash provided by operating activities	38,514
9. Net cash flows used for investing activities	(24,281)
10. Net sales	280,522
11. Other expense	14
12. Other income	1,035
13. Property and equipment, net	72,705
14. Operating expenses	100,445
15. Retained earnings (Dec. 31)	31,220

Using the following notations, indicate on which financial statement you would find each of the preceding items. (*Note:* An item may appear on more than one statement.)

IS	Income statement
SE	Statement of stockholders' equity
BS	Balance sheet
SCF	Statement of cash flows

Obj. 4

✔ Net income $11,588

E1-23 Income statement

Based on the Amazon.com, Inc. (AMZN) financial statement data shown in Exercise 1-22, prepare an income statement for the year ended December 31.

Obj. 4

E1-24 Financial statement items

Though the McDonald's (MCD) menu of hamburgers, cheeseburgers, the Big Mac®, Quarter Pounder®, Filet-O-Fish®, and Chicken McNuggets® is easily recognized, McDonald's financial statements may not be as familiar. The following items were adapted from a recent annual report of McDonald's Corporation:

1. Accounts payable
2. Accrued interest payable
3. Cash
4. Cash provided by operations
5. Common stock
6. Food and packaging costs used in operations
7. Income tax expense
8. Interest expense
9. Inventories
10. Long-term debt payable
11. Net income
12. Net increase in cash
13. Notes payable
14. Notes receivable
15. Occupancy and rent expense
16. Payroll expense
17. Prepaid expenses not yet used in operations
18. Property and equipment
19. Retained earnings
20. Sales

Identify the financial statement on which each of the preceding items would appear. An item may appear on more than one statement. Use the following notations:

IS	Income statement
SE	Statement of stockholders' equity
BS	Balance sheet
SCF	Statement of cash flows

Obj. 4

✔ Correct amount of total assets is $200,000

E1-25 Financial statements

Outlaw Realty, organized August 1, 20Y7, is owned and operated by Julie Baxter. How many errors can you find in the following financial statements for Outlaw Realty, prepared after its first month of operations? Assume that the cash balance on August 31, 20Y7, is $51,600 and that cash flows from operating activities is reported correctly.

OUTLAW REALTY
Income Statement
August 31, 20Y7

Sales commissions		$ 408,400
Operating expenses:		
Office salaries expense	$272,600	
Rent expense	31,200	
Miscellaneous expense	2,200	
Automobile expense	7,900	
Total operating expenses		(313,900)
Net income		$ 134,500

JULIE BAXTER
Statement of Stockholders' Equity
August 31, Year 1

	Common Stock	Retained Earnings	Total
Balances, August 1, 20Y7	$ 0	$ 7,800	$ 7,800
Issued common stock			100,000
Net income		134,500	134,500
Dividends		12,000	12,000
Balances, August 31, 20Y7	$100,000	$154,300	$254,300

Balance Sheet
For the Month Ended August 31, 20Y7

Assets		
Cash		$ 51,600
Accounts payable		17,500
Land		60,000
Total assets		$129,100
Liabilities		
Accounts receivable		$ 81,200
Prepaid expenses		7,200
Stockholders' Equity		
Common stock	$100,000	
Retained earnings	140,300	240,300
Total liabilities and stockholders' equity		$328,700

Statement of Cash Flows
August 31, 20Y7

Cash flows from (used for) operating activities:		
Cash received from customers	$327,200	
Cash paid for operating expenses	(303,600)	
Net cash flows from operating activities		$ 23,600
Cash flows from (used for) financing activities:		
Cash received from issuing common stock	$100,000	
Dividends paid to stockholders	(12,000)	
Net cash flows from financing activities		88,000
Net increase in cash and cash balance as of August 31, 20Y7		$111,600

E1-26 Accounting concepts

Obj. 5

Match each of the following statements with the appropriate accounting concept. Some concepts may be used more than once, while others may not be used at all. Use the notations shown to indicate the appropriate accounting concept.

Accounting Concept	Notation
Accounting period concept	P
Adequate disclosure concept	D
Business entity concept	B
Cost concept	C
Going concern concept	G
Matching concept	M
Objectivity concept	O
Unit of measure concept	U

Statements

1. Assume that a business will continue forever.
2. Material litigation involving the corporation is described in a note.
3. Monthly utilities costs are reported as expenses along with the monthly revenues.
4. Personal transactions of owners are kept separate from the business.
5. This concept supports relying on an independent actuary (statistician), rather than the chief operating officer of the corporation, to estimate a pension liability.
6. Changes in the use of accounting methods from one period to the next are described in the notes to the financial statements.
7. Land worth $800,000 is reported at its original purchase price of $220,000.
8. This concept justifies recording only transactions that are expressed in dollars.
9. If this concept was ignored, the confidence of users in the financial statements could not be maintained.
10. The changes in financial condition are reported at the end of the month.

Obj. 5

E1-27 Business entity concept

Crazy Mountain Sports sells hunting and fishing equipment and provides guided hunting and fishing trips. Crazy Mountain is owned and operated by Karl Young, a well-known sports enthusiast and hunter. Karl's wife, Mila, owns and operates Mila's Boutique, a women's clothing store. Karl and Mila have established a trust fund to finance their children's college education. The trust fund is maintained by First Bank in the names of their children, Steve and Isabelle.

For each of the following transactions, identify which of the entities listed should record the transaction in its records.

Entities	
C	Crazy Mountain Sports
B	First Bank Trust Fund
M	Mila's Boutique
X	None of the above

1. Karl paid a local doctor for a physical, which was required by the workmen's compensation insurance policy carried by Crazy Mountain Sports.
2. Karl received a cash advance from customers for a guided hunting trip.
3. Mila paid her dues to the YWCA.
4. Karl paid a breeder's fee for an English Springer spaniel to be used as a hunting guide dog.
5. Mila deposited a $10,000 personal check in the trust fund at First Bank.
6. Karl paid for an advertisement in a hunters' magazine.
7. Mila authorized the trust fund to purchase mutual fund shares.
8. Mila donated several dresses from the store's inventory to a local charity auction for the benefit of a women's abuse shelter.
9. Karl paid for dinner and a movie to celebrate the couple's fifteenth wedding anniversary.
10. Mila purchased two dozen spring dresses from a Boise designer for a special spring sale.

Problems

P1-1 Income statement, statement of stockholders' equity, and balance sheet

Obj. 4

✔ 1. Net income: $103,500

The amounts of the assets and liabilities of Viva Travel Service as of September 30, 20Y6, the end of the current year, and its revenue and expenses for the year are listed below. The retained earnings were $135,000 and the common stock was $45,000 as of October 1, 20Y5, the beginning of the current year. Dividends of $9,000 were paid during the year.

Accounts payable	$157,500
Accounts receivable	288,900
Cash	149,400
Common stock	63,000
Fees earned	810,000
Miscellaneous expense	33,300
Rent expense	162,000
Supplies	11,700
Supplies expense	34,200
Taxes expense	27,000
Utilities expense	67,500
Wages expense	382,500

Instructions

1. Prepare an income statement for the current year ended September 30, 20Y6.
2. Prepare a statement of stockholders' equity for the current year ended September 30, 20Y6.
3. Prepare a balance sheet as of September 30, 20Y6.

P1-2 Missing amounts from financial statements

Obj. 4

✔ j. $314,000

The financial statements at the end of Paradise Realty's first month of operations are shown below.

PARADISE REALTY
Income Statement
For the Month Ended November 30, 20Y3

Fees earned		$149,300
Operating expenses:		
Wages expense	$ (a)	
Rent expense	14,400	
Supplies expense	12,000	
Utilities expense	8,100	
Miscellaneous expense	4,950	
Total operating expenses		(69,300)
Net income		$ (b)

PARADISE REALTY
Statement of Stockholders' Equity
For the Month Ended November 30, 20Y3

	Common Stock	Retained Earnings	Total
Balances, Nov. 1, 20Y3	$ 0	$ 0	$ 0
Issued common stock	270,000		270,000
Net income		(c)	(c)
Dividends		(d)	(d)
Balances, Nov. 30, 20Y3	$270,000	$(e)	$314,000

PARADISE REALTY
Balance Sheet
November 30, 20Y3

Assets		
Cash		$ 99,200
Supplies		6,000
Land		(f)
Total assets		$ (g)
Liabilities		
Notes payable		$ 7,200
Stockholders' Equity		
Common stock	$ (h)	
Retained earnings	(i)	
Total stockholders' equity		(j)
Total liabilities and stockholders' equity		$ (k)

PARADISE REALTY
Statement of Cash Flows
For the Month Ended November 30, 20Y3

Cash flows from (used for) operating activities:		
Cash received from customers	$ (l)	
Cash paid for expenses and to creditors	(68,100)	
Net cash flows from operating activities		$ (m)
Cash flows used for investing activities:		
Cash paid for acquisition of land		(216,000)
Cash flows from (used for) financing activities:		
Cash received from issuing common stock	$270,000	
Deduct dividends	(36,000)	
Net cash flows from financing activities		(n)
Net increase in cash during month		$ (o)
Cash as of November 1		0
Cash as of November 30		$ (o)

Instructions

1. Would you classify a realty business such as Hamel Realty as a manufacturing, merchandising, or service business?
2. By analyzing the interrelationships among the financial statements, determine the proper amounts for (a) through (o).

Obj. 4

✔ 1. Net income $3,281

P1-3 Income statement, statement of stockholders' equity, and balance sheet

The following financial data were adapted from a recent annual report of Target Corporation (TGT) for the year ended January 31.

	In millions
Accounts payable	$ 9,920
Cash	2,577
Common stock	42
Cost of sales	54,864
Debt and other borrowings	11,499
Income tax expense	921
Interest expense	477
Inventory	8,992
Other assets	4,927
Other expenses	2,336
Other liabilities	9,527
Property and equipment, net	26,283
Sales	78,112
Selling, general, and administrative expenses	16,233

Instructions

1. Prepare Target's income statement for the year ended January 31.
2. Prepare Target's statement of stockholders' equity for the year ended January 31.

   Use the following additional information for the year:

Common stock, Feb. 1 of prior year	$ 43
Retained earnings Feb. 1 of prior year	6,017
Other stockholder equity items on Feb. 1 of prior year	5,237
Dividends	1,345
Other items affecting retained earnings	(1,520)
Other items affecting common stock	(1)
Other items affecting stockholders' equity	121

3. Prepare a balance sheet as of January 31.

P1-4 Statement of cash flows

Obj. 4

✔ Net increase in cash, $1,797

The following cash data for the year ended December 31 were adapted from a recent annual report of Alphabet (GOOG), formerly known as Google. The cash balance as of January 1 was $16,701 (in millions).

	In millions
Payments on debt	$ 585
Proceeds from disposals of property and equipment	589
Purchases of investments (marketable securities)	100,315
Net cash provided by operating activities*	54,497
Other net cash flows provided by investing activities	70,235
Other net cash flows used by financing activities	22,624

*Adjusted for effect of exchange rate changes on cash and cash equivalents

Instructions

Prepare Alphabet's statement of cash flows for the year ended December 31.

P1-5 Financial statements, including statement of cash flows

Obj. 4

✔ 1. Net income, $335,000

Pendray Systems Corporation began operations on January 1, 20Y5 as an online retailer of computer software and hardware. The following financial statement data were taken from Pendray's records at the end of its first year of operations, December 31, 20Y5.

Accounts payable	$ 40,000
Accounts receivable	88,000
Cash	?
Cash payments for operating activities	896,000
Cash receipts from operating activities	1,087,000
Common stock	120,000
Cost of sales	650,000
Dividends	90,000
Income tax expense	87,000
Income taxes payable	15,000
Interest expense	3,000
Inventories	111,000
Note payable (due in 10 years)	80,000
Property, plant, and equipment	265,000
Retained earnings	?
Sales	1,175,000
Selling and administrative expenses	100,000

Instructions

1. Prepare an income statement for the year ended December 31, 20Y5.
2. Prepare a statement of stockholders' equity for the year ended December 31, 20Y5.
3. Prepare a balance sheet as of December 31, 20Y5.
4. Prepare a statement of cash flows for the year ended December 31, 20Y5.

Metric-Based Analysis

Obj. 6

MBA 1-1 Quantitative metrics

Interpublic Group of Companies Inc. (IPG) is an advertising and marketing service company that operates throughout the world. In addition, the company provides event planning, public relations, and brand management services. Twitter Inc. (TWTR) operates as a worldwide platform for individuals to communicate with each other by sending Tweets using their mobile devices.

For each company, go to the Securities and Exchange Commission (SEC) Internet site *http://www.sec.gov/edgar/searchedgar/companysearch.html*. In the search box "Fast Search," enter the Central Index Key (stock market ticker symbol) shown next to the company name. Once the EDGAR Search screen appears, type in "10-K" for Filing Type. Open the most recent 10-K file and search the file for "metric" using the "Edit and Find" functions.

1. List the quantitative metrics that appear in each company's 10-K.
2. Comment on the differences in the metrics for each company listed in (1).

Obj. 6

MBA 1-2 Quantitative metrics

JetBlue Airways Corporation (JBLU) is a passenger airline with flights to destinations throughout the United States, the Caribbean, and Latin America. Costco (COST) operates membership retail warehouses offering a variety of products including foods, electronics, appliances, and clothing.

For each company, go to the Securities and Exchange Commission (SEC) Internet site *http://www.sec.gov/edgar/searchedgar/companysearch.html*. In the search box "Fast Search," enter the Central Index Key (stock market ticker symbol) shown next to the company name. Once the EDGAR Search screen appears, type in "10-K" for Filing Type. Open the most recent 10-K file and search the file for "metric" using the "Edit and Find" functions.

1. List the quantitative metrics that appear in each company's 10-K.
2. Comment on the differences in the metrics for each company listed in (1).

Obj. 6

MBA 1-3 Return on assets

The financial statements of The Hershey Company (HSY) are shown in Exhibits 6 through 9 of this chapter. Based upon these statements, answer the following questions.

1. What are Hershey's sales (in millions)?
2. What is Hershey's cost of sales (in millions)?
3. What is Hershey's net income (in millions)?
4. What is Hershey's percent of the cost of sales to sales? Round to one decimal place.
5. The percent that a company adds to its cost of sales to determine the selling price is called a markup. What is Hershey's markup percent? Round to one decimal place.
6. What is the percentage of net income to sales for Hershey? Round to one decimal place.
7. Hershey had total assets of $7,703 (million) at the beginning of the year. Compute the return on assets for Hershey for the year shown in Exhibits 6 through 9 of this chapter.

MBA 1-4 Return on assets

Obj. 6

The following data (in millions) were adapted from recent financial statements of Tootsie Roll Industries Inc. (TR):

Sales	$524
Cost of sales	329
Net income	64
Average total assets	963

1. What is Tootsie Roll's percent of the cost of sales to sales? Round to one decimal place.
2. The percent a company adds to its cost of sales to determine selling price is called a markup. What is Tootsie Roll's markup percent? Round to one decimal place.
3. What is the percentage of net income to sales for Tootsie Roll? Round to one decimal place.
4. Compute the return on assets for Tootsie Roll.
5. Using your answers to MBA 1-3, compare the markup percentages and return on assets for Hershey and Tootsie Roll.

MBA 1-5 Return on assets

Obj. 6

Pfizer Inc. (PFE) discovers, produces, and distributes medicines, including Celebrex and Lipitor. General Motors (GM) develops, markets, and produces automobiles and trucks. Microsoft Corporation (MSFT) develops, produces, and distributes a variety of computer software and hardware products including Windows, Office, Excel, and the Xbox.

1. Without computing the return on assets, list from highest to lowest how you would expect Pfizer, Ford, and Microsoft to rank in terms of their return on assets.
2. The following data (in millions) were taken from recent financial statements of each company:

	Pfizer	General Motors	Microsoft
Net income	$ 16,273	$ 6,581	$ 39,240
Total assets at the beginning of the year	159,422	227,339	258,848
Total assets at the end of the year	167,489	228,037	286,556

Compute the return on assets for each company using the preceding data, and rank the companies' return on assets from highest to lowest. Round the return on assets to one decimal place.

3. Analyze and explain the rankings in (2).

MBA 1-6 Return on assets

Obj. 6

ExxonMobil Corporation (XOM) explores, produces, and distributes oil and natural gas. The Coca-Cola Company (KO) produces and distributes soft drink beverages, including Coke. Walmart Stores, Inc. (WMT) operates retail stores and supermarkets.

1. Without computing the return on assets, list from highest to lowest how you would expect ExxonMobil, Coca-Cola, and Walmart to rank in terms of their return on assets.
2. The following data (in millions) were taken from recent financial statements of each company:

	ExxonMobil	Coca-Cola	Walmart
Net income	$ 14,340	$ 8,920	$ 14,881
Total assets at the beginning of the year	346,196	83,216	219,295
Total assets at the end of the year	362,597	86,381	236,495

Compute the return on assets for each company using the preceding data, and rank the companies' return on assets from highest to lowest. Round the return on assets to one decimal place.

3. Analyze and explain the rankings in (2).

Obj. 6

MBA 1-7 Return on assets

Tiffany & Co. (TIF) designs and sells jewelry including rings, watches, and necklaces throughout the world. The following data (in millions) were taken from recent financial statements of Tiffany:

Net income	$ 541
Total assets at the beginning of the year	5,333
Total assets at the end of the year	6,660

1. Compute the return on assets for Tiffany using the preceding data. Round to one decimal place.
2. Using your answers to MBA 1-6, compare the return on assets for Walmart to that of Tiffany.

Cases

Case 1-1 Integrity, objectivity, and ethics at The Hershey Company

ETHICS

The management of The Hershey Company (HSY) has asked union workers in two of its highest-cost Pennsylvania plants to accept higher health insurance premiums and take a wage cut. The workers' portion of the insurance cost would double from 6% of the premium to 12%. In addition, workers hired after January 2000 would have their hourly wages cut by $4, which would be partially offset by a 2% annual raise. Management says that the plants need to be more cost competitive. Management has indicated that if the workers accept the proposal, the company would invest $30 million to modernize the plants and move future projects to the plants. Management has refused, however, to guarantee more work at the plants even if the workers approve the proposal. If the workers reject the proposal, management implies that it would move future projects to other plants and that layoffs might be forthcoming. Do you consider management's actions ethical?

Source: Susan Govzdas, "Hershey to Cut Jobs or Wages," *Central Penn Business Journal*, September 24, 2004.

Case 1-2 Ethics and professional conduct in business

GROUP PROJECT

ETHICS

Loretta Smith, president and owner of Custom Enterprises, applied for a $250,000 loan from City National Bank. The bank requested financial statements from Custom Enterprises as a basis for granting the loan. Loretta has told her accountant to provide the bank with a balance sheet. Loretta has decided to omit the other financial statements because there was a net loss during the past year.

In groups of three or four, discuss the following questions:

1. Is Loretta behaving in a professional manner by omitting some of the financial statements?
2. a. What types of information about their businesses would owners be willing to provide bankers? What types of information would owners not be willing to provide?
   b. What types of information about a business would bankers want before extending a loan?
   c. What common interests are shared by bankers and business owners?

Case 1-3 How businesses make money

GROUP PROJECT

Assume that you are the chief executive officer for a national poultry producer. The company's operations include hatching chickens through the use of breeder stock and feeding, raising, and processing the mature chicks into finished products. The finished products include breaded chicken nuggets and patties and deboned, skinless, and marinated chicken. The company sells its products to schools, military services, fast-food chains, and grocery stores.

In groups of four or five, discuss the following business emphasis and risk issues:

1. In a commodity business like poultry production, what do you think is the dominant business emphasis? What are the implications in this dominant emphasis for how you would run the company?
2. Identify at least two major business risks for operating the company.
3. How could the company try to differentiate its products?

Case 1-4 Net income versus cash flow

On January 9, 20–, Dr. Susan Tempkin established DocMed, a medical practice organized as a professional corporation. The below conversation took place the following September between Dr. Tempkin and a former medical school classmate, Dr. Phil Anzar, at an American Medical Association convention in London.

Dr. Anzar: Susan, good to see you again. Why didn't you call when you were in Chicago? We could have had dinner together.

Dr. Tempkin: Actually, I never made it to Chicago this year. My husband and kids went to our Wisconsin Dells condo twice, but I got stuck in New York. I opened a new consulting practice this January and haven't had any time for myself since.

Dr. Anzar: I heard about it . . . Doc . . . something . . . right?

Dr. Tempkin: Yes, DocMed. My husband chose the name.

Dr. Anzar: I've thought about doing something like that. Are you making any money? I mean, is it worth your time?

Dr. Tempkin: You wouldn't believe it. I started by opening a bank account with $40,000, and my August bank statement shows a balance of $215,000. Not bad for eight months—all pure profit.

Dr. Anzar: Maybe I'll try it in Chicago. Let's have breakfast together tomorrow and you can fill me in on the details.

Comment on Dr. Tempkin's statement that the difference between the opening bank balance ($40,000) and the August statement balance ($215,000) is pure profit.

Case 1-5 The accounting equation

Review financial statements for three well-known companies, such as Ford Motor Co. (F), General Motors (GM), International Business Machines (IBM), Microsoft (MSFT), or Amazon (AMZN). The financial statements may be found at http://www.sec.gov/edgar/searchedgar/companysearch.html. Enter the company's stock market symbol in the Fast Search box, enter "10-K" in the Filing Type box, and click on the latest 10-K. If you wish, you can save the whole 10-K report to your computer.

Examine the balance sheet for each company and determine the total assets, liabilities, and stockholders' equity. Verify that total assets equal the total of the liabilities plus stockholders' equity.

Case 1-6 Financial analysis of Enron Corporation

Enron Corporation (ENRN), headquartered in Houston, Texas, provided products and services for natural gas, electricity, and communications to wholesale and retail customers. Enron's operations were conducted through a variety of subsidiaries and affiliates that involved transporting gas through pipelines, transmitting electricity, and managing energy commodities. The following data were taken from Enron's December 31, 2000, financial statements:

	In millions
Total revenues	$100,789
Total costs and expenses	98,836
Operating income	1,953
Net income	979
Total assets	65,503
Total liabilities	54,033
Total stockholders' equity	11,470
Net cash flows from operating activities	4,779
Net cash flows from investing activities	(4,264)
Net cash flows from financing activities	571
Net increase in cash	1,086

At the end of 2000, the market price of Enron's stock was approximately $83 per share. Eventually, however, Enron's stock was selling for $0.22 per share.

Review the preceding financial statement data and search the Internet for articles on Enron Corporation. Briefly explain why Enron's stock dropped so dramatically in such a short time.

The annual report (10-K) assignment for this chapter is in Appendix B: Nike Annual Report, Chapter 1.

Answers to Self-Examination Questions

1. **D** A corporation, organized in accordance with state or federal statutes, is a separate legal entity in which ownership is divided into shares of stock (answer D). A proprietorship (answer A) is an unincorporated business owned by one individual. A service business (answer B) provides services to its customers. It can be organized as a proprietorship, partnership, or corporation. A partnership (answer C) is an unincorporated business owned by two or more individuals.

2. **A** The resources owned by a business are called assets (answer A). The debts of the business are called liabilities (answer B), and the equity of the owners is called stockholders' equity (answer D). The relationship among assets, liabilities, and stockholders' equity is expressed as the accounting equation (answer C).

3. **A** The balance sheet is a listing of the assets, liabilities, and stockholders' equity of a business at a specific date (answer A). The income statement (answer B) is a summary of the revenue and expenses of a business for a specific period of time. The statement of stockholders' equity (answer C) summarizes the changes in stockholders' equity during a specific period of time. The statement of cash flows (answer D) summarizes the cash receipts and cash payments for a specific period of time.

4. **D** The accounting equation is:

   Assets = Liabilities + Stockholders' Equity

   Therefore, if assets are $20,000 and liabilities are $12,000, stockholders' equity is $8,000 (answer D), as indicated in the following computation:

Assets	= Liabilities + Stockholders' Equity
+$20,000	= $12,000 + Stockholders' Equity
+$20,000 − $12,000	= Stockholders' Equity
+$8,000	= Stockholders' Equity

5. **B** Net income is the excess of revenue over expenses, or $7,500 (answer B). If expenses exceed revenue, the difference is a net loss. Dividends are the opposite of the stockholders investing in the business and do not affect the amount of net income or net loss.

Chapter 2

Basic Accounting Systems: Cash Basis

What's Covered:

Topics: Basic Accounting Systems: Cash Basis

Systems Elements
- Rules (Obj. 1)
- Framework (Obj. 1)
- Controls (Obj. 1)

Recording Transactions
- First-Period Transactions (Obj. 2)
- First-Period Financial Statements (Obj. 3)
- Second-Period Transactions (Obj. 4)
- Second-Period Financial Statements (Obj. 5)

Metric-Based Analysis
- Transactions
  - Liquidity: Cash (Obj. 2, 4)
  - Profitability: Net Income (Obj. 2,4)
- Financial Statements
  - Common-Sized Statements (Obj. 6)

Learning Objectives

Obj.1 Describe the basic elements of a financial accounting system.

Obj.2 Analyze, record, and summarize transactions for a corporation's first period of operations.

Obj.3 Prepare financial statements for a corporation's first period of operations.

Obj.4 Analyze, record, and summarize transactions for a corporation's second period of operations.

Obj.5 Prepare financial statements for a corporation's second period of operations.

Obj.6 Describe and illustrate the use of common-sized income statements in assessing a company's performance.

Chapter Metrics

Use the following metrics to analyze transactions and financial statements.

TRANSACTIONS

Liquidity: Cash

Profitability: Net Income—Cash Basis

FINANCIAL STATEMENTS

Common-Sized Statements

Twitter Connection

tanuha2001/ Shutterstock.com

Every day it seems like you get an incredible amount of incoming e-mail messages; you get them from your friends, relatives, subscribed e-mail lists, and even spammers! But how do you organize all of these messages? You might create folders to sort messages by sender, topic, or project. Perhaps you use keyword search utilities. You might even use filters or rules to automatically delete spam or send messages from your best friend to a special folder. In any case, you are organizing information so that it is simple to retrieve and allows you to more easily understand, respond to, or refer to the messages.

In the same way that you organize your e-mail, companies develop an organized method for processing, recording, and summarizing financial transactions. For example, **Twitter (TWTR)** is an information network used by millions to share messages of up to 140 characters. Such messages, called Tweets, are available free to the public. Twitter earns revenue by selling advertisements on the Internet as "Promoted Tweets," "Promoted Trends," or "Promoted Accounts." In order to analyze revenue by these three sources, Twitter records and summarizes its revenues by each advertising category. In addition, Twitter records and summarizes various metrics for its customers such as Retweets, clicks, replies, mentions, and follows. In doing so, Twitter has an integrated information system that includes an accounting component.

This chapter describes the basic elements of financial accounting systems. Such systems process, record, and summarize financial transactions, allowing for the preparation of financial statements, as discussed in Chapter 1.

The simplest form of an accounting system records and summarizes only transactions involving the receipt and payment of cash. For this reason, this chapter describes and illustrates a cash basis accounting system. This serves as a foundation for later discussions of more complex accounting systems and financial reporting issues.

Objective 1
Describe the basic elements of a financial accounting system.

Elements of an Accounting System

A financial accounting system is designed to produce financial statements. The financial statements include the income statement, statement of stockholders' equity, balance sheet, and statement of cash flows.

The basic elements of a **financial accounting system** include:

- *Rules* for determining what, when, and the amount that should be recorded
- A *framework* for preparing financial statements
- *Controls* to determine whether errors may have arisen in the recording process

Rules

The rules for determining what, when, and the amount recorded are derived from the eight concepts discussed in Chapter 1. These concepts are the basis of generally accepted accounting principles (GAAP), which require the recording of transactions affecting elements of the financial statements.

A **transaction** is an economic event that under GAAP affects the financial statements. A transaction may affect one, two, or more items within the financial statements. For example, equipment purchased for cash affects only assets. That is, one asset (equipment) increases while another asset (cash) decreases. If, on the other hand, the equipment is purchased on credit, assets (equipment) and liabilities (accounts or notes payable) increase.

Twitter records transactions using generally accepted accounting principles (GAAP).

Framework

Transactions must be analyzed, recorded, and summarized using a framework. The accounting equation is the basis for all such frameworks. The accounting equation is expressed as follows:

Assets = Liabilities + Stockholders' Equity

Twitter Connection

Using the accounting equation as a framework, **Twitter** reported in recent financial statements (in millions) assets of \$12,703, liabilities of \$3,999, and stockholders equity of \$8,704, which can be expressed in the form of the accounting equation as: \$12,703 = \$3,999 + \$8,704.

By expanding the accounting equation, as shown in Exhibit 1, an integrated financial statement approach can be designed for analyzing, recording, and summarizing transactions. This is done by including columns for the statement of cash flows, balance sheet, and income statement.

The *left-hand* column in Exhibit 1 shows the effects of transactions on the statement of cash flows. Each cash transaction is recorded and classified as an operating, investing, or financing activity. This serves as a basis for preparing the statement of cash flows.

The cash at the beginning of the period plus or minus the cash flows from operating, investing, and financing activities equals the end-of-period cash. This end-of-period cash amount is reported as Cash on the balance sheet. Thus, the statement of cash flows is integrated with the balance sheet in Exhibit 1.

Twitter Connection

Twitter reported cash of \$1,799 million on its balance sheet and statement of cash flows.

Exhibit 1 Integrated Financial Statement Framework

Integrated Financial Statement Framework

BALANCE SHEET

	Assets	=	Liabilities	+	Stockholders' Equity		
	Assets	**=**	**Liabilities**	**+**	**Common Stock**	**+**	**Retained Earnings**
Transaction	XXX		XXX		XXX		XXX
	XXX						
	XXX		XXX		XXX		XXX

STATEMENT OF CASH FLOWS

+/– Operating activities	XXX
+/– Investing activities	XXX
+/– Financing activities	XXX
Increase or decrease in cash	XXX
Beginning cash	XXX
Ending cash	XXX

INCOME STATEMENT

Revenues	XXX
Expenses	XXX
Net income or loss	XXX

The *right-hand* column in Exhibit 1 shows the effects of transactions on the income statement. Each revenue and expense transaction is recorded and classified as a revenue or expense. This serves as a basis for preparing the income statement.

Net income for the period (revenues less expenses) is added to beginning retained earnings.[1] Thus, revenue and expense transactions are also recorded under the Retained Earnings column of the balance sheet. By doing so, the balance sheet is integrated with the income statement in Exhibit 1.

Exhibit 1 also illustrates the importance of the balance sheet as the connecting link between the statement of cash flows and the income statement.[2] This integrated financial statement approach for analyzing, recording, and summarizing transactions is illustrated later in this chapter.

The integrated financial statement approach shown in Exhibit 1 is an invaluable tool for analyzing transactions and their effects on the financial statements. It is also an aid for analyzing and interpreting a company's financial statements. This is because, without understanding how a company's financial statements are integrated, important trends or events may be missed or misinterpreted.

To illustrate, assume a company reports net income (profits) on its income statement. As a result, it might be mistakenly concluded that the company's operations are doing well and no major changes are necessary. In fact, the company might be experiencing a continuing negative net cash flow from operations and thus be headed toward bankruptcy. This is why it is essential to analyze all the financial statements and their integration.

Controls

The integrated financial statement approach shown in Exhibit 1 has built-in controls to ensure that all transactions are correctly analyzed, recorded, and summarized. These controls include the following:[3]

1. The accounting equation must balance.
2. The ending cash on the statement of cash flows must equal the cash on the balance sheet.
3. The net income on the income statement must equal the net effects of revenues and expenses on retained earnings.

These controls are illustrated throughout the remainder of this chapter as transactions are recorded and financial statements are prepared.

In **Twitter's** annual report, it includes a report on its controls and procedures for preparing accurate financial statements.

Recording a Corporation's First Period of Operations

Objective 2
Analyze, record, and summarize transactions for a corporation's first period of operations.

The integrated financial statement framework shown in Exhibit 1 is illustrated using the transactions for a corporation's first period of operations. Assume that on September 1, 20Y5, Lee Landry, M.D., organizes a professional corporation to practice general medicine. The business is to be known as Family Health Care, P.C., where P.C. refers to a *professional corporation*.

Each of Family Health Care's transactions during September is described and recorded in this section. The transactions begin with Dr. Landry's investment to establish the business.

1. A net loss for the period, which occurs when expenses exceed revenues, is subtracted from beginning retained earnings.
2. In Chapter 3, the use of the balance sheet to reconcile net cash flows from operating activities with net income is described and illustrated.
3. Additional accounting controls are discussed in Chapter 5.

Transaction a

Dr. Landry deposits $6,000 in a bank account in the name of Family Health Care, P.C., in return for shares of common stock in the corporation.

In recording this transaction, increases are recorded as positive numbers, while decreases are recorded as negative numbers. Negative amounts are shown in parentheses.

The effects of this transaction on Family Health Care's financial statements are recorded as follows:

1. Under the Statement of Cash Flows column, Cash from Financing activities is increased by $6,000.
2. Under the Balance Sheet columns, Cash under Assets is increased by $6,000. To balance the accounting equation, Common Stock under Stockholders' Equity is also increased by $6,000.

Since no revenues or expenses are affected, there are no entries under the Income Statement column. The recording of transaction (a) relates only to the business, Family Health Care, P.C. Dr. Landry's personal assets (such as a home or a personal bank account) and personal liabilities are excluded. This is because under the business entity concept, Family Health Care is treated as a separate entity, with cash of $6,000 and stockholders' equity of $6,000.

The effects of this transaction on Family Health Care's financial statements are as follows:

Financial Statement Effects

BALANCE SHEET

	Assets	=	Liabilities	+	Stockholders' Equity
Transaction	Cash	=			Common Stock
a. Investment by Dr. Landry	6,000				6,000

STATEMENT OF CASH FLOWS	
a. Financing	6,000

INCOME STATEMENT

Got the Flu? Why Not Chew Some Gum?

Business Insight

Facing a slumping market for sugared chewing gum—such as Juicy Fruit™ and Doublemint™—**Wm. Wrigley Jr. Company**, a subsidiary of **Mars Incorporated**, is reinventing itself by expanding its product lines and introducing new chewing gum applications. Wrigley's new products include sugarless breath mints and more powerful flavored mint chewing gum, like Extra Polar Ice™. In addition, Wrigley is experimenting with health-care applications of chewing gum. For example, the company founded the Wrigley Science Institute™ with the objective of promoting scientific research on the benefits of chewing gum. Specifically, the Institute sponsors research in such areas as weight reduction, management and stress relief, and cognitive focus. The Institute provides grants to leading researchers who investigate the role of chewing gum in health and wellness.

Sources: Wrigley.com and *USA Today*, "Wrigley Wants Science to Prove Gum-Chewing Benefits," by Dave Carpenter, The Associated Press, March 28, 2006.

Transaction Metric Effects

The effects of each transaction on liquidity and profitability metrics for Family Health Care are also illustrated. Cash is used as the liquidity metric and net income (revenues less expenses) as the profitability metric. Since this chapter illustrates only cash transactions, the profitability metric is termed Net Income – Cash Basis.

The effects of issuing $6,000 of common stock on Family Health Care's liquidity and profitability metrics are as follows:

LIQUIDITY	
Cash	$6,000

PROFITABILITY	
Net Income—Cash Basis	No Effect

Transaction b

Family Health Care borrows $10,000 from First National Bank to finance its operations.

To borrow the $10,000, Dr. Landry signs a note payable with First National Bank in the name of Family Health Care. The note payable is a liability that Family Health Care must pay in the future. The note payable also requires the payment of interest of $100 per month until the note of $10,000 is paid on September 30, 20Y9. The interest is to be paid at the end of each month.

The effects of this transaction on Family Health Care's financial statements are recorded as follows:

1. Under the Statement of Cash Flows column, Cash from Financing activities is increased by $10,000.
2. Under the Balance Sheet columns, Cash under Assets is increased by $10,000. To balance the accounting equation, Notes Payable under Liabilities is also increased by $10,000.

This transaction changes assets and liabilities on the balance sheet but does not change Family Health Care's stockholders' equity of $6,000. Since no revenues or expenses are affected, no entries are made under the Income Statement column.

The effects of this transaction on Family Health Care's financial statements are as follows:

Financial Statement Effects

BALANCE SHEET

	Assets	=	Liabilities	+	Stockholders' Equity
	Cash	=	Notes Payable	+	Common Stock
Balances	6,000				6,000
b. Issued note pay.	10,000		10,000		
Balances	16,000		10,000		6,000

STATEMENT OF CASH FLOWS	
b. Financing	10,000

INCOME STATEMENT

Transaction Metric Effects

The effects of borrowing $10,000 on Family Health Care's liquidity and profitability metrics are as follows:

LIQUIDITY	
Cash	$10,000

PROFITABILITY	
Net Income—Cash Basis	No Effect

Transaction c

Family Health Care buys land for $12,000 cash.

The land is located near a new suburban hospital that is under construction. Dr. Landry plans to rent office space and equipment for several months. When the hospital is completed, Family Health Care will build on the land.

The effects of this transaction on Family Health Care's financial statements are recorded as follows:

1. Under the Statement of Cash Flows column, Cash from Investing activities is decreased by $12,000.
2. Under the Balance Sheet columns, Cash under Assets is decreased by $12,000. To balance the accounting equation, Land under Assets is increased by $12,000.

This transaction illustrates the use of cash for an investing activity. As a result, $(12,000) was entered under the Statement of Cash Flows column. In addition, the mix of assets changes on the balance sheet. Since no revenues or expenses are affected, no entries are made under the Income Statement column.

The effects of this transaction on Family Health Care's financial statements are as follows:

Financial Statement Effects

	BALANCE SHEET						
	Assets			=	Liabilities	+	Stockholders' Equity
	Cash	+	Land	=	Notes Payable	+	Common Stock
Balances	16,000				10,000		6,000
c. Purchase of land	(12,000)		12,000				
Balances	4,000		12,000		10,000		6,000

STATEMENT OF CASH FLOWS	
c. Investing	(12,000)

INCOME STATEMENT

Transaction Metric Effects

The effects of the $12,000 purchase of the land on Family Health Care's liquidity and profitability metrics are as follows:

LIQUIDITY	
Cash	$(12,000)

PROFITABILITY	
Net Income—Cash Basis	No Effect

Transaction d

During the first month of operations, Family Health Care earned patient fees of $5,500, receiving the fees in cash.

The effects of this transaction on Family Health Care's financial statements are recorded as follows:

1. Under the Statement of Cash Flows column, Cash from Operating activities is increased by $5,500.
2. Under the Balance Sheet columns, Cash under Assets is increased by $5,500. To balance the accounting equation, Retained Earnings under Stockholders' Equity is also increased by $5,500.
3. Under the Income Statement column, Fees earned is increased by $5,500.

This transaction illustrates an inflow of cash from operating activities by earning revenues (fees earned) of $5,500. Retained Earnings is increased under Stockholders' Equity by $5,500 because fees earned contribute to net income and net income increases stockholders' equity. Since fees earned are a type of revenue, Fees earned of $5,500 is also entered under the Income Statement column.

The effects of this transaction on Family Health Care's financial statements are as follows:

Financial Statement Effects

BALANCE SHEET

	Assets			=	Liabilities	+	Stockholders' Equity		
					Notes		Common		Retained
	Cash	+	Land	=	Payable	+	Stock	+	Earnings
Balances	4,000		12,000		10,000		6,000		
d. Fees earned	5,500								5,500
Balances	9,500		12,000		10,000		6,000		5,500

STATEMENT OF CASH FLOWS	
d. Operating	5,500

INCOME STATEMENT	
d. Fees earned	5,500

Transaction Metric Effects

The effects of receiving $5,500 of patient fees on Family Health Care's liquidity and profitability metrics are as follows:

LIQUIDITY	
Cash	$5,500

PROFITABILITY	
Net Income—Cash Basis	$5,500

Transaction e

Family Health Care paid expenses during September as follows: wages, $1,125; rent, $950; utilities, $450; interest, $100; and miscellaneous, $275.

Miscellaneous expenses include small amounts paid for such items as postage, newspapers, and magazines. The effects of this transaction on Family Health Care's financial statements are recorded as follows:

1. Under the Statement of Cash Flows column, Cash from Operating activities is decreased by $2,900, which is the sum of the expenses ($1,125 + $950 + $450 + $100 + $275).

2. Under the Balance Sheet columns, Cash under Assets is decreased by $2,900. To balance the accounting equation, Retained Earnings under Stockholders' Equity is also decreased by $2,900.
3. Under the Income Statement column, each expense is listed as a negative amount.

This transaction illustrates an outflow of cash of $2,900 for operating activities (paying expenses). Thus, $(2,900) is entered in the Statement of Cash Flows column as an Operating activity. Expenses have the opposite effect from revenues on net income and retained earnings. As a result, $(2,900) is entered for Retained Earnings under Stockholders' Equity. In addition, each expense is listed under the Income Statement column as a negative amount.

The effects of this transaction on Family Health Care's financial statements are as follows:

Financial Statement Effects

BALANCE SHEET

	Assets			=	Liabilities	+	Stockholders' Equity		
	Cash	+	Land	=	Notes Payable	+	Common Stock	+	Retained Earnings
Balances	9,500		12,000		10,000		6,000		5,500
e. Paid expenses	(2,900)								(2,900)
Balances	6,600		12,000		10,000		6,000		2,600

STATEMENT OF CASH FLOWS

e. Operating	(2,900)

INCOME STATEMENT

e. Wages expense	(1,125)
Rent expense	(950)
Utilities expense	(450)
Interest expense	(100)
Misc. expense	(275)

Transaction Metric Effects

The effects of paying $2,900 in expenses on Family Health Care's liquidity and profitability metrics are as follows:

LIQUIDITY

Cash	$(2,900)

PROFITABILITY

Net Income—Cash Basis	$(2,900)

Transaction f

Family Health Care paid $1,500 to stockholders (Dr. Lee Landry) as dividends.

Dividends are distributions of a company's earnings to stockholders. Dividends should not be confused with expenses. Dividends do not represent assets consumed or services used in earning revenues. Instead, dividends are a distribution of earnings to the stockholders.

The effects of this transaction on Family Health Care's financial statements are recorded as follows:

1. Under the Statement of Cash Flows column, Cash from Financing activities is decreased by $1,500.
2. Under the Balance Sheet columns, Cash under Assets is decreased by $1,500. To balance the accounting equation, Retained Earnings under Stockholders' Equity is also decreased by $1,500.

This transaction illustrates an outflow of cash of $1,500 for financing activities (paying dividends). Thus, $(1,500) is entered in the Statement of Cash Flows column as a Financing activity. Dividends decrease retained earnings; thus, $(1,500) is entered for Retained Earnings under Stockholders' Equity. Since dividends are not an expense, no entry is made under the Income Statement column.

The effects of this transaction on Family Health Care's financial statements are as follows:

Financial Statement Effects

BALANCE SHEET

	Assets			=	Liabilities	+	Stockholders' Equity		
	Cash	+	**Land**	=	**Notes Payable**	+	**Common Stock**	+	**Retained Earnings**
Balances	6,600		12,000		10,000		6,000		2,600
f. Paid dividends	(1,500)								(1,500)
Balances	5,100		12,000		10,000		6,000		1,100

STATEMENT OF CASH FLOWS	
f. Financing	(1,500)

INCOME STATEMENT

Transaction Metric Effects

The effects of paying dividends of $1,500 on Family Health Care's liquidity and profitability metrics are as follows:

LIQUIDITY	
Cash	$(1,500)

PROFITABILITY	
Net Income—Cash Basis	No Effect

Family Heath Care's September transactions are summarized in Exhibit 2 using the integrated financial statement format. Each transaction is identified by letter.

Exhibit 2 illustrates the three controls that are built into the integrated financial statement approach. These controls are as follows:

1. The accounting equation under the Balance Sheet columns balances. That is, total assets of $17,100 ($5,100 + $12,000) equals total liabilities plus stockholders' equity of $17,000 ($10,000 + $6,000 + $1,100).
2. The ending cash under the Statement of Cash Flows column of $5,100 equals the cash balance under the Balance Sheet columns of $5,100.
3. The net income under the Income Statement column of $2,600 equals the net effects of revenues of $5,500 and expenses of $2,900 on retained earnings ($5,500 − $2,900).

Exhibit 2 Family Health Care's Summary of Transactions for September

Financial Statement Effects for September

BALANCE SHEET

	Assets			=	Liabilities	+	Stockholders' Equity		
	Cash	**+**	**Land**	**=**	**Notes Payable**	**+**	**Common Stock**	**+**	**Retained Earnings**
a. Investment by Dr. Landry	6,000						6,000		
b. Issued note pay.	10,000				10,000				
c. Purchase of land	(12,000)		12,000						
d. Fees earned	5,500								5,500
e. Paid expenses	(2,900)								(2,900)
f. Paid dividends	(1,500)								(1,500)
Balances, Sept. 30	5,100		12,000		10,000		6,000		1,100

STATEMENT OF CASH FLOWS

a. Financing	6,000
b. Financing	10,000
c. Investing	(12,000)
d. Operating	5,500
e. Operating	(2,900)
f. Financing	(1,500)
Increase in cash and Sept. 30 cash	5,100

INCOME STATEMENT

d. Fees earned	5,500
e. Wages expense	(1,125)
Rent expense	(950)
Utilities expense	(450)
Interest expense	(100)
Misc. expense	(275)
Net income	2,600

Integrity, Objectivity, and Ethics in Business

A History of Ethical Conduct

The **Wm. Wrigley Jr. Company**, which is now a subsidiary of **Mars Incorporated**, has a long history of integrity, objectivity, and ethical conduct. When pressured to become part of a cartel, known as the Chewing Gum Trust, the company founder, William Wrigley Jr., said, "We prefer to do business by fair and square methods or we prefer not to do business at all." In 1932, Phillip K. Wrigley, called "PK" by his friends, became president of the Wrigley Company after his father, William Wrigley Jr., died. PK also was president of the Chicago Cubs, which played in Wrigley Field. He was financially generous to his players and frequently gave them advice on and off the field. However, as a man of integrity and high ethical standards, PK docked (reduced) his salary as president of the Wrigley Company for the time he spent working on Cubs-related activities and business.

Richard B. Levine/Newscom

Source: *St. Louis Post-Dispatch*, "Sports—Backpages," January 26, 2003.

In reviewing Exhibit 2, you should note that the following apply to all companies:

- The Balance Sheet columns reflect the accounting equation (Assets = Liabilities + Stockholders' Equity).
- The two sides of the accounting equation are always equal.
- Every transaction affects (increases or decreases) one or more of the balance sheet elements—assets, liabilities, or stockholders' equity.
- A transaction may or may not affect (increase or decrease) an element of the statement of cash flows or the income statement. Some transactions affect elements of both statements, some transactions affect only one statement and not the other, and some transactions affect neither statement.
- Every cash transaction increases or decreases the asset (cash) on the balance sheet. Every cash transaction also increases or decreases an operating, investing, or financing activity on the statement of cash flows.
- The ending balance of Cash under the Statement of Cash Flows column ($5,100 in Exhibit 2) agrees with the ending cash balance shown on the balance sheet. Since September was Family Health Care's first period of operations, this ending cash balance equals the net increase in cash for the period. In future periods, the net increase (decrease) in cash is added to (or subtracted from) the beginning cash balance to equal the ending cash balance. This ending cash balance is reported in the statement of cash flows and balance sheet.
- The stockholders' equity is increased by amounts invested by stockholders (common stock).
- Revenues increase stockholders' equity (retained earnings) and expenses decrease stockholders' equity (retained earnings). The effects of revenue and expense transactions are also shown in the Income Statement column.
- Stockholders' equity (retained earnings) is decreased by dividends paid to stockholders.
- The change in retained earnings for the period is the net income minus dividends. For a net loss, the change in retained earnings is the net loss plus dividends.
- The statement of cash flows is linked to the balance sheet through cash.
- The income statement is linked to the balance sheet through revenues and expenses (net income or loss), which affects retained earnings.

Exhibit 3 summarizes the effects of the various transactions affecting stockholders' equity.

Exhibit 3 Effects of Transactions on Stockholders' Equity

Transaction Metric Effects

The effects of September's transactions on Family Health Care's liquidity and profitability metrics are as follows:

LIQUIDITY

Transaction	Cash
a. Issued stock	$ 6,000
b. Issued note pay.	10,000
c. Purchased land	(12,000)
d. Earned fees	5,500
e. Paid expenses	(2,900)
f. Paid dividends	(1,500)
Total	$ 5,100

PROFITABILITY

	Net Income—Cash Basis
a. Issued stock	—
b. Issued note pay.	—
c. Purchased land	—
d. Earned fees	$ 5,500
e. Paid expenses	(2,900)
f. Paid dividends	—
Total	$ 2,600

September's transactions had the effect of increasing Family Health Care's liquidity metric (Cash) by $5,100. Since this is Family Health Care's first period of operations, this is also the ending balance of cash. September's transactions increased Family Health Care's profitability metric, Net Income—Cash Basis, by $2,600, which is also the amount that will be reported as net income on the income statement for September.

Financial Statements for a Corporation's First Period of Operations

Objective 3

Prepare financial statements for a corporation's first period of operations.

Exhibit 2 lists Family Health Care's September transactions in the order they occurred. Exhibit 2, however, does not group and summarize like transactions together. The accounting reports that provide this summarized information are financial statements.

Family Health Care's September financial statements can be prepared from Exhibit 2. These financial statements are shown in Exhibit 4.

The financial statements shown in Exhibit 4 are prepared from Exhibit 2 as follows:

1. The income statement is prepared using the Income Statement column.
2. The statement of stockholders' equity is prepared next because the ending balance of common stock and retained earnings is needed to prepare the balance sheet. The retained earnings column is prepared using net income from the income statement and the amount recorded for dividends.
3. The balance sheet is prepared next using the balances shown under the Balance Sheet columns.
4. The statement of cash flows is prepared last using the Statement of Cash Flows column.

Each financial statement is identified by the name of the business, the title of the statement, and the date or period of time covered by the statement.

Income Statement

The income statement for Family Health Care shown in Exhibit 4 reports fees earned of $5,500, total operating expenses of $2,900, and net income of $2,600. The $5,500 of fees earned is taken from the Income Statement column of Exhibit 2. Likewise, the expenses are summarized from the Income Statement column of Exhibit 2. These expenses are reported under the heading "Operating expenses." Operating expenses are normally listed in order of size, beginning with the largest expense. Miscellaneous expense is usually shown as the last item, regardless of amount.

Statement of Stockholders' Equity

The statement of stockholders' equity shown in Exhibit 4 reports two columns for common stock and retained earnings. Since this is the first month of Family Health Care's operations, the beginning balances of common stock and retained earnings are zero. Common stock of $6,000 is taken from Exhibit 2. Ending retained earnings of $1,100 is created by net income of $2,600 less dividends of $1,500.

Exhibit 4 Family Health Care's Financial Statements for September

Family Health Care, P.C.
Income Statement
For the Month Ended September 30, 20Y5

Fees earned		$5,500
Operating expenses:		
Wages expense	$1,125	
Rent expense	950	
Utilities expense	450	
Interest expense	100	
Miscellaneous expense	275	
Total operating expenses		(2,900)
Net income		$2,600

Family Health Care, P.C.
Statement of Stockholders' Equity
For the Month Ended September 30, 20Y5

	Common Stock	Retained Earnings	Total
Balances, Sept. 1, 20Y5	$ 0	$ 0	$ 0
Issued common stock	6,000		6,000
Net income		2,600	2,600
Dividends		(1,500)	(1,500)
Balances, Sept. 30, 20Y5	$ 6,000	$ 1,100	$7,100

Family Health Care, P.C.
Balance Sheet
September 30, 20Y5

Assets		
Cash		$ 5,100
Land		12,000
Total assets		$17,100
Liabilities		
Notes payable		$10,000
Stockholders' Equity		
Common stock	$6,000	
Retained earnings	1,100	
Total stockholders' equity		7,100
Total liabilities and stockholders' equity		$17,100

(Continued)

Exhibit 4 Family Health Care's Financial Statements for September (Concluded)

Family Health Care, P.C.
Statement of Cash Flows
For the Month Ended September 30, 20Y5

Cash flows from (used for) operating activities:		
Cash received from customers	$ 5,500	
Cash paid for expenses	(2,900)	
Net cash flows from operating activities		$ 2,600
Cash flows from (used for) investing activities:		
Cash paid for acquisition of land		(12,000)
Cash flows from (used for) financing activities:		
Cash received from issuing common stock	$ 6,000	
Cash received from notes payable	10,000	
Cash paid as dividends to stockholder	(1,500)	
Net cash flows from financing activities		14,500
Net increase in cash during September		$ 5,100
Cash as of September 1, 20Y5		0
Cash as of September 30, 20Y5		$ 5,100

Balance Sheet

Family Health Care's assets, liabilities, and stockholders' equity as of September 30, 20Y5, are taken from the last line of the Balance Sheet columns of Exhibit 2. The September 30, 20Y5, balance sheet is shown in Exhibit 4.

In the Assets section of the balance sheet, assets are normally listed in order of liquidity, starting with cash. **Liquidity** refers to the ability to convert an asset to cash. Land is less liquid than cash and thus would be listed second in Family Health Care's balance sheet.

In the Liabilities section of Family Health Care's balance sheet, notes payable is the only liability. When there are two or more categories of liabilities, each should be listed and the total amount reported. Liabilities should be presented in the order that they will be paid in cash. Thus, the notes payable due in 20Y9 would be listed after the liabilities that are due earlier.

The stockholders' equity for Family Health Care as of September 30, 20Y5, consists of $6,000 of common stock and retained earnings of $1,100. The retained earnings is the ending retained earnings reported on the statement of stockholders' equity.

Statement of Cash Flows

Family Health Care's statement of cash flows for September is prepared from the Statement of Cash Flows column of Exhibit 2. Cash increased from a zero balance at the beginning of the month to $5,100 at the end of the month.

The $5,100 increase in cash during September was created by:

1. Operating activities that generated $2,600 of cash
2. Investing activities that used $12,000 of cash
3. Financing activities that generated $14,500 of cash

The details of how the operating, investing, and financing activities generated or used cash is reported on the statement of cash flows. For example, financing activities generated $6,000 from the sale of common stock and $10,000 from borrowing by issuing a note payable. Financing activities used $1,500 for paying dividends.

Integration of Financial Statements

Exhibit 5 shows how Family Health Care's financial statements for September are integrated. As shown in Exhibit 5, these statements are integrated as follows:

1. The ending cash balance of $5,100 on the balance sheet equals the ending cash balance reported on the statement of cash flows.

2. The net income of $2,600 is reported on the income statement and the statement of stockholders' equity.
3. The ending common stock of $6,000 and retained earnings of $1,100 are reported in the statement of stockholders' equity and balance sheet.
4. The cash flows from operating activities of $2,600 reported on the statement of cash flows equals the net income on the income statement. The relationship between cash flows from operating activities and net income is further described and illustrated in Chapter 3.

Exhibit 5 Family Health Care Integrated Financial Statements for September

Family Health Care, P.C.
Balance Sheet
September 30, 20Y5

Assets			=	Liabilities	+	Stockholders' Equity		
Cash	+	Land	=	Notes Payable	+	Common Stock	+	Retained Earnings
$5,100		$12,000		$10,000		$6,000		$1,100
$17,100 Total Assets			=	$17,100 Total Liabilities + Stockholders' Equity				

Family Health Care, P.C.
Statement of Cash Flows
For the Month Ended Sept. 30, 20Y5

Operating act.	$ 2,600
Investing act.	(12,000)
Financing act.	14,500
Increase in cash and Sept. 30 cash	$ 5,100

Family Health Care, P.C.
Income Statement
For the Month Ended Sept. 30, 20Y5

Revenues	$5,500
Expenses	(2,900)
Net income	$2,600

Family Health Care, P.C.
Statement of Stockholders' Equity
For the Month Ended Sept. 30, 20Y5

	Common Stock	Retained Earnings	Total
Bal. Sept. 1	$ 0	$ 0	$ 0
Issued stock	6,000		6,000
Net income		2,600	2,600
Dividends		(1,500)	(1,500)
Bal. Sept. 30	$ 6,000	$ 1,100	$7,100

Using Data Analytics

Extracting Data

When a company uses data analytics to solve a problem, it must first *extract* (gather) relevant data. In many cases, this requires the company to collect data from a variety of sources. For example, a service company analyzing the effectiveness of its marketing efforts might extract data from its customer data base as well as publicly available data bases, such as those reporting market share and competitor revenue growth.

The nature of the problem to be solved dictates the type of data extracted, which may be quantitative or categorical in nature. *Quantitative data* can be used to perform mathematical operations, such as computing the average revenue per customer for a service company. *Categorical data* are often based on occurrences or observations of qualitative data, which is often summarized as a proportion or percentage. For example, a qualitative metric used by airlines is the number of "on-time" arrivals, which is normally reported as a percentage.

The data analytic process of extracting data is in some ways similar to the process of analyzing and recording transactions that is described and illustrated in this chapter. For example, quantitative transaction data (expressed in dollars) are collected and summarized in categorical (asset, liability, stockholders' equity, revenue, and expense) accounts.

Recording a Corporation's Second Period of Operations

Objective 4
Analyze, record, and summarize transactions for a corporation's second period of operations.

During October, Family Health Care entered into the following transactions:

a. Received cash fees of $6,400
b. Paid expenses as follows: wages, $1,370; rent, $950; utilities, $540; interest, $100; and miscellaneous, $220
c. Paid cash dividends of $1,000

Family Heath Care's October transactions are summarized in Exhibit 6 using the integrated financial statement format. Each transaction is identified by letter.

The Balance Sheet columns of Exhibit 6 begin with the ending balances as of September 30, 20Y5, taken from Exhibit 2. This is because the balance sheet is the cumulative total of the entity's assets, liabilities, and stockholders' equity since the company's inception.

As of October 1, 20Y5, Family Health Care has cash of $5,100, land of $12,000, notes payable of $10,000, common stock of $6,000, and retained earnings of $1,100. In contrast, the statement of cash flows and the income statement report only transactions for a period and are not cumulative.

Exhibit 6 Family Health Care's Summary of Transactions for October

Financial Statement Effects for October

BALANCE SHEET

	Assets			=	Liabilities	+	Stockholders' Equity		
	Cash	+	**Land**	=	**Notes Payable**	+	**Common Stock**	+	**Retained Earnings**
Balances, Oct. 1	5,100		12,000		10,000		6,000		1,100
a. Fees earned	6,400								6,400
b. Paid expenses	(3,180)								(3,180)
c. Paid dividends	(1,000)								(1,000)
Balances, Oct. 31	7,320		12,000		10,000		6,000		3,320

STATEMENT OF CASH FLOWS

a. Operating	6,400
b. Operating	(3,180)
c. Financing	(1,000)
Increase in cash	2,220

INCOME STATEMENT

a. Fees earned	6,400
b. Wages expense	(1,370)
Rent expense	(950)
Utilities expense	(540)
Interest expense	(100)
Misc. expense	(220)
Net income	3,220

Transaction Metric Effects

The effects of October's transactions on Family Health Care's liquidity and profitability metrics are as follows:

LIQUIDITY

Transaction	Cash
a. Fees earned	$6,400
b. Paid expenses	(3,180)
c. Paid dividends	(1,000)
Total	$2,220

PROFITABILITY

Net Income—Cash Basis	
a. Fees earned	$6,400
b. Paid expenses	(3,180)
Total	$3,220

October's transactions had the effect of increasing Family Health Care's liquidity metric (Cash) by $2,220. Since the beginning cash balance on October 1 was $5,100, the increase of $2,220 yields an ending cash balance of $7,320, which will be reported on the October 31, 20Y5, balance sheet. October's transactions increased Family Health Care's profitability metric, Net Income—Cash Basis, by $3,220, which is also the amount that will be reported as net income on the October income statement.

Financial Statements for a Corporation's Second Period of Operations

Objective 5

Prepare financial statements for a corporation's second period of operations.

Family Health Care's financial statements for October are shown in Exhibit 7. These statements were prepared from Exhibit 6.

Exhibit 7 Family Health Care's Financial Statements for October

Family Health Care, P.C.
Income Statement
For the Month Ended October 31, 20Y5

Fees earned		$6,400
Operating expenses:		
Wages expense	$1,370	
Rent expense	950	
Utilities expense	540	
Interest expense	100	
Miscellaneous expense	220	
Total operating expenses		(3,180)
Net income		$3,220

Family Health Care, P.C.
Statement of Stockholders' Equity
For the Month Ended October 31, 20Y5

	Common Stock	Retained Earnings	Total
Balances, Oct. 1, 20Y5	$6,000	$1,100	$7,100
Net income		3,220	3,220
Dividends		(1,000)	(1,000)
Balances, Oct. 31, 20Y5	$6,000	$3,320	$9,320

(Continued)

Exhibit 7 Family Health Care's Financial Statements for October (Concluded)

Family Health Care, P.C. Balance Sheet October 31, 20Y5		
Assets		
Cash		$ 7,320
Land		12,000
Total assets		$19,320
Liabilities		
Notes payable		$10,000
Stockholders' Equity		
Common stock	$6,000	
Retained earnings	3,320	
Total stockholders' equity		9,320
Total liabilities and stockholders' equity		$19,320

Family Health Care, P.C. Statement of Cash Flows For the Month Ended October 31, 20Y5		
Cash flows from (used for) operating activities:		
Cash received from customers	$6,400	
Cash paid for expenses	(3,180)	
Net cash flows from operating activities		$ 3,220
Cash flows from (used for) investing activities		0
Cash flows from (used for) financing activities:		
Cash paid as dividends to stockholder		(1,000)
Net increase in cash during October		$ 2,220
Cash as of October 1, 20Y5		5,100
Cash as of October 31, 20Y5		$ 7,320

Income Statement

The income statement for October reports net income of $3,220. This is an increase of $620, or 23.8% ($620 ÷ $2,600), from September's net income of $2,600. The increase in net income was due to fees increasing from $5,500 to $6,400, a $900, or 16.4% ($900 ÷ $5,500), increase from September. At the same time, total operating expenses increased only $280 ($3,180 − $2,900), or 9.7% ($280 ÷ $2,900). This suggests that Family Health Care's operations are profitable and expanding.

Statement of Stockholders' Equity

The statement of stockholders' equity shown in Exhibit 7 starts with the balances of common stock and retained earnings as of October 1, 20Y5. These are the same balances as of September 30, 20Y5, shown in Exhibit 4. Since no common stock was issued during October, the common stock balance on October 31, 20Y5, is $6,000. October's net income of $3,220 is added and dividends of $1,000 are deducted from the beginning retained earnings of $1,100 to yield retained earnings of $3,320 as of October 31, 20Y5.

Balance Sheet

The total assets increased from $17,100 on September 30, 20Y5 (Exhibit 4), to $19,320 on October 31 (Exhibit 7). This increase of $2,220 ($19,320 − $17,100) was due to an increase in cash from $5,100 to $7,320. Total liabilities of $10,000 remained the same.

Since total assets increased by $2,220 and total liabilities remained the same, total stockholders' equity must also have increased by $2,220. This is because the accounting equation must always balance. Exhibit 7 shows that total stockholders' equity did increase by $2,220, which is the increase in retained earnings.

Statement of Cash Flows

Family Health Care's statement of cash flows for October indicates that cash increased by $2,220. This increase is cash generated from operating activities of $3,220 less cash used by financing activities to pay dividends of $1,000.

The net increase in cash of $2,220 is added to the beginning cash balance of $5,100 to yield the ending cash balance of $7,320. This ending cash balance of $7,320 also appears on the October 31, 20Y5, balance sheet.

Integration of Financial Statements

Exhibit 8 illustrates that Family Health Care's financial statements for October are integrated as follows:

1. The ending cash balance of $7,320 on the balance sheet equals the ending cash balance reported on the statement of cash flows.
2. The net income of $3,220 is reported on the income statement and the statement of stockholders' equity.
3. The ending common stock of $6,000 and retained earnings of $3,320 are reported on the statement of stockholders' equity and the balance sheet.
4. The cash flows from operating activities of $3,220 reported on the statement of cash flows equals the net income on the income statement. The relationship between cash flows from operating activities and net income is further described and illustrated in Chapter 3.

Exhibit 8 Family Health Care's Integrated Financial Statements for October

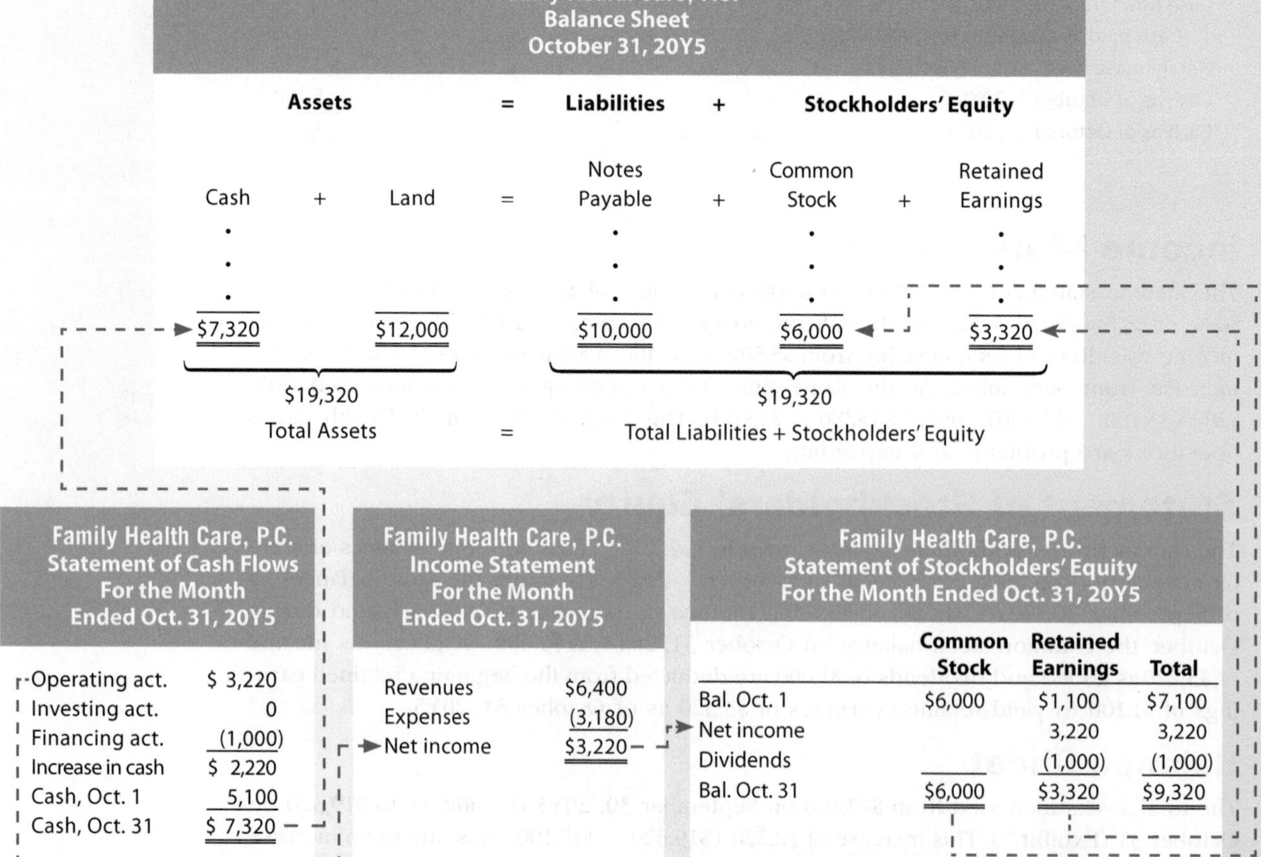

Metric-Based Analysis: Common-Sized Statements

Objective 6

Describe and illustrate the use of common-sized income statements in assessing a company's performance.

Common-sized financial statements are useful in assessing a company's financial condition and performance over time. Common-sized financial statements are also useful in comparing companies with one another.

Common-sized financial statements are prepared by expressing financial statement amounts as a percent of a base amount. A **common-sized income statement** is prepared by expressing income statement amounts as a percent of sales. A **common-sized balance sheet** is prepared by expressing each asset as a percent of total assets. Each liability and stockholders' equity item is expressed as a percent of total liabilities plus stockholders' equity.[4]

To illustrate common-sized income statements, we use data (in millions) adapted from recent financial statements of **The Kroger Co. (KR)**. Kroger operates over 2,700 supermarkets, 2,200 pharmacies, and 1,500 fueling centers. The following operating data were adapted from recent income statements of Kroger.

	Year 2	Year 1
Sales	$121,162	$122,662
Cost of sales	(94,894)	(95,662)
Gross profit	$ 26,268	$ 27,000
Operating expenses:		
Selling and administrative	$ (20,305)	$ (21,041)
Other expenses	(3,349)	(3,347)
Total operating expenses	$ (23,654)	$ (24,388)
Operating income	$ 2,614	$ 2,612

Kroger's common-sized income statements (rounded to one decimal place) for Year 1 and Year 2 are provided. Each item is expressed as a percent of sales. For example, the cost of sales for Year 2 of 78.3% is computed as $94,894 ÷ $121,162.

	Year 2	Year 1	Increase (Decrease)
Sales	100.0%	100.0%	n/a
Cost of sales	(78.3)	(78.0)	0.3%
Gross profit	21.7%	22.0%	(0.3)%
Operating expenses:			
Selling and administrative	(16.8)%	(17.2)%	(0.4)%
Other expenses	(2.7)	(2.7)	0.0
Total operating expenses	(19.5)%	(19.9)%	(0.4)%
Operating income	2.2%	2.1%	0.1%

The common-sized income statements for Kroger indicate that the cost of sales increased by 0.3% between Year 1 and Year 2. This increase in cost of goods sold in Year 2 was partially offset by a decrease in operating expenses of 0.4%. As a result, Kroger's operating income increased by only 0.1% between Year 1 and Year 2. These results imply that Kroger's operations did not change significantly between years.

When comparing operating performance across companies within the same industry, common-sized income statements are often prepared only through operating income rather than through net income. This is because other income and expenses are influenced by a variety of factors that are independent of operations and that can vary significantly across companies. For example, differences in the financing and tax strategies used by companies affect the comparability.

4. Since total assets equals total liabilities plus total stockholders' equity, common-sized balance sheets can be prepared simply by expressing each balance sheet item as a percent of total assets.

Key Points

1. Describe the basic elements of a financial accounting system.

The basic elements of a financial accounting system include (1) a set of rules for determining what, when, and the amount that should be recorded; (2) a framework for preparing financial statements; and (3) one or more controls to determine whether errors may have arisen in the recording process.

2. Analyze, record, and summarize transactions for a corporation's first period of operations.

Using the integrated financial statement framework, September transactions for Family Health Care are recorded and summarized in Exhibit 2.

3. Prepare financial statements for a corporation's first period of operations.

The financial statements for Family Health Care for September, its first period of operations, are shown in Exhibit 4.

4. Analyze, record, and summarize transactions for a corporation's second period of operations.

Using the accounting equation as a basic framework, October transactions for Family Health Care are recorded and summarized in Exhibit 6.

5. Prepare financial statements for a corporation's second period of operations.

The financial statements for Family Health Care for October, its second period of operations, are shown in Exhibit 7.

6. Describe and illustrate the use of common-sized income statements in assessing a company's performance.

A common-sized income statement is prepared by expressing each income statement amount as a percent of sales.

Key Terms

Common-sized balance sheet (65)
Common-sized financial statements (65)
Common-sized income statement (65)
Financial accounting system (46)
Liquidity (59)
Transaction (46)

Illustrative Problem

Beth Sumner established an insurance agency on April 1, 20Y4, and completed the following transactions during April:

a. Opened a business bank account in the name of Sumner Insurance Inc., with a deposit of $15,000 in exchange for common stock.
b. Borrowed $8,000 by issuing a note payable.
c. Received cash from fees earned, $11,500.
d. Paid rent on office and equipment for the month, $3,500.
e. Paid automobile expenses for the month, $650, and miscellaneous expenses, $300.
f. Paid office salaries, $1,400.
g. Paid interest on the note payable, $60.
h. Purchased land as a future building site, paying cash of $20,000.
i. Paid dividends, $1,000.

Instructions

1. Indicate the effect of each transaction and the balances after each transaction, using the integrated financial statement framework.
2. Indicate the effects of each transaction on liquidity metric Cash and profitability metric Net Income—Cash Basis.
3. Prepare an income statement and statement of stockholders' equity for April.
4. Prepare a balance sheet as of April 30, 20Y4.
5. Prepare a statement of cash flows for April.

Solution

1.

Financial Statement Effects

BALANCE SHEET

	Assets			=	Liabilities	+	Stockholders' Equity		
	Cash	+	Land	=	Notes Payable	+	Common Stock	+	Retained Earnings
a. Investment	15,000						15,000		
b. Issued note payable	8,000				8,000				
Balances	23,000				8,000		15,000		
c. Fees earned	11,500								11,500
Balances	34,500				8,000		15,000		11,500
d. Rent expense	(3,500)								(3,500)
Balances	31,000				8,000		15,000		8,000
e. Paid expenses	(950)								(950)
Balances	30,050				8,000		15,000		7,050
f. Paid salary expense	(1,400)								(1,400)
Balances	28,650				8,000		15,000		5,650
g. Paid interest expense	(60)								(60)
Balances	28,590				8,000		15,000		5,590
h. Purchased land	(20,000)		20,000						
Balances	8,590		20,000		8,000		15,000		5,590
i. Paid dividends	(1,000)								(1,000)
Balances, April 30	7,590		20,000		8,000		15,000		4,590

STATEMENT OF CASH FLOWS

a. Financing	$ 15,000
b. Financing	8,000
c. Operating	11,500
d. Operating	(3,500)
e. Operating	(950)
f. Operating	(1,400)
g. Operating	(60)
h. Investing	(20,000)
i. Financing	(1,000)
Increase in cash and April 30 cash	$ 7,590

INCOME STATEMENT

c. Fees earned	$11,500
d. Rent expense	(3,500)
e. Auto expense	(650)
e. Misc. expense	(300)
f. Salary expense	(1,400)
g. Interest expense	(60)
Net income	$ 5,590

2.

Transaction Metric Effects

LIQUIDITY

Transaction	Cash
a. Issued stock	$ 15,000
b. Issued note pay.	8,000
c. Earned fees	11,500
d. Paid rent exp.	(3,500)
e. Paid expenses	(950)
f. Paid salaries	(1,400)
g. Paid interest	(60)
h. Purchased land	(20,000)
i. Paid dividends	(1,000)
Total	$ 7,590

PROFITABILITY

	Net Income—Cash Basis
a. Issued stock	—
b. Issued note pay.	—
c. Earned fees	$11,500
d. Paid rent exp.	(3,500)
e. Paid expenses	(950)
f. Paid salaries	(1,400)
g. Paid interest	(60)
h. Purchased land	—
i. Paid dividends	—
Total	$ 5,590

3.

SUMNER INSURANCE, INC.
Income Statement
For the Month Ended April 30, 20Y4

Revenues:		
Fees earned		$11,500
Expenses:		
Rent expense	$3,500	
Salaries expense	1,400	
Automotive expense	650	
Interest expense	60	
Miscellaneous expense	300	
Total expenses		(5,910)
Net income		$ 5,590

SUMNER INSURANCE, INC.
Statement of Stockholders' Equity
For the Month Ended April 30, 20Y4

	Common Stock	Retained Earnings	Total
Balances, Apr. 1, 20Y4	$ 0	$ 0	$ 0
Issued common stock	15,000		15,000
Net income		5,590	5,590
Dividends		(1,000)	(1,000)
Balances, Apr. 30, 20Y4	$15,000	$ 4,590	$19,590

4.

SUMNER INSURANCE, INC.
Balance Sheet
April 30, 20Y4

Assets		
Cash		$ 7,590
Land		20,000
Total assets		$27,590
Liabilities		
Note payable		$ 8,000
Stockholders' Equity		
Common stock	$15,000	
Retained earnings	4,590	
Total stockholders' equity		19,590
Total liabilities and stockholders' equity		$27,590

5.

SUMNER INSURANCE, INC.
Statement of Cash Flows
For the Month Ended April 30, 20Y4

Cash flows from (used for) operating activities:		
Cash received from operating activities	$11,500	
Cash paid for operating activities	(5,910)	
Net cash flows from operating activities		$ 5,590
Cash flows from (used for) investing activities:		
Cash paid for land		(20,000)
Cash flows from (used for) financing activities:		
Cash received from issuing common stock	$15,000	
Cash received from issuing note payable	8,000	
Cash paid as dividends	(1,000)	
Net cash flows from financing activities		22,000
Net increase in cash during April		$ 7,590
Cash as of April 1, 20Y4		0
Cash as of April 30, 20Y4		$ 7,590

Self-Examination Questions

(Answers appear at the end of chapter)

1. The purchase of land for $50,000 cash was incorrectly recorded as an increase in land and an increase in notes payable. Which of the following statements is correct?
   A. The accounting equation will not balance because cash is overstated by $50,000.
   B. The accounting equation will not balance because notes payable are overstated by $50,000.
   C. The accounting equation will not balance because assets will exceed liabilities by $50,000.
   D. Even though a recording error has been made, the accounting equation will balance.

2. The receipt of $8,000 cash for fees earned was recorded by Langley Consulting as an increase in cash of $8,000 and a decrease in retained earnings (revenues) of $8,000. What is the effect of this error on the accounting equation?
   A. Total assets will exceed total liabilities and stockholders' equity by $8,000.
   B. Total assets will be less than total liabilities and stockholders' equity by $8,000.
   C. Total assets will exceed total liabilities and stockholders' equity by $16,000.
   D. The error will not affect the accounting equation.

3. If total assets increased $20,000 during a period and total liabilities increased $12,000 during the same period, the amount and direction (increase or decrease) of the change in stockholders' equity for that period is:
   A. a $32,000 increase.
   B. a $32,000 decrease.
   C. an $8,000 increase.
   D. an $8,000 decrease.

4. If revenue was $90,000, expenses were $75,000, and dividends were $20,000, the amount of net income or net loss would be:
   A. $90,000 net income.
   B. $15,000 net income.
   C. $75,000 net loss.
   D. $5,000 net loss.

5. Which of the following transactions changes only the mix of assets and does not affect liabilities or stockholders' equity?
   A. Borrowed $40,000 from First National Bank
   B. Purchased land for $50,000 cash
   C. Received $3,800 for fees earned
   D. Paid $4,000 for office salaries

Class Discussion Questions

1. What are the basic elements of a financial accounting system? Do these elements apply to all businesses, from a local restaurant to Alphabet (Google) Inc. (GOOGL)? Explain.
2. Provide an example of a transaction that affects (a) only one element of the accounting equation, (b) two elements of the accounting equation, (c) three elements of the accounting equation.
3. Indicate whether the following error would cause the accounting equation to be out of balance and, if so, indicate how it would be out of balance. The payment of utilities of $1,200 was recorded as a decrease in cash of $1,200 and a decrease in retained earnings (utilities expense) of $2,100.
4. For each of the following errors, indicate whether the error would cause the accounting equation to be out of balance and, if so, indicate how it would be out of balance. (a) The purchase of land for $85,000 cash was recorded as an increase in land of $85,000 and a decrease in cash of $58,000. (b) The receipt of $7,000 for fees earned was recorded as an increase in cash of $7,000 and an increase in liabilities of $7,000.
5. What is a primary control for determining the accuracy of a business's record keeping?
6. Capstone Consulting Services acquired land 5 years ago for $200,000. Capstone recently signed an agreement to sell the land for $375,000. In accordance with the sales agreement, the buyer transferred $375,000 to Capstone's bank account on February 20. How would elements of the accounting equation be affected by the sale?
7. (a) How does the payment of dividends of $15,000 affect the three elements of the accounting equation? (b) Is net income affected by the payment of dividends? Explain.
8. Assume that Esquire Consulting erroneously recorded the payment of $30,000 of dividends as salary expense. (a) How would this error affect the equality of the accounting equation? (b) How would this error affect the income statement, statement of stockholders' equity, balance sheet, and statement of cash flows?
9. Assume that Larsh Realty Inc. borrowed $75,000 from Country Bank and Trust. In recording the transaction, Larsh erroneously recorded the receipt as an increase in cash, $75,000, and an increase in fees earned, $75,000. (a) How would this error affect the equality of the accounting equation? (b) How would this error affect the income statement, statement of stockholders' equity, balance sheet, and statement of cash flows?
10. Assume that as of January 1, 20Y8, Sylvester Consulting has total assets of $500,000 and total liabilities of $150,000. As of December 31, 20Y8, Sylvester has total liabilities of $200,000 and total stockholders' equity of $400,000. (a) What was Sylvester's stockholders' equity as of January 1, 20Y8? (b) Assume that Sylvester did not pay any dividends during 20Y8. What was the amount of net income for 20Y8?
11. Using the January 1 and December 31, 20Y8, data given in Question 10, answer the following question: If Sylvester Consulting paid $18,000 of dividends during 20Y8, what was the amount of net income for 20Y8?

Exercises

Obj. 1

✔ a. $950,000

E2-1 Accounting equation

Determine the missing amount for each of the following:

	Assets	=	Liabilities	+	Stockholders' Equity
a.	X	=	$357,500	+	$592,500
b.	$300,000	=	X	+	$255,000
c.	$ 56,200	=	$11,875	+	X

E2-2 Accounting equation

Obj. 1

✔ a. $52,832

The Walt Disney Company (DIS) had the following assets and liabilities (in millions) at the end of Year 1.

Assets	$98,598
Liabilities	45,766

a. Determine the stockholders' equity of Walt Disney at the end of Year 1.

b. During Year 2, Disney purchased Twenty-First Century Fox, Inc. If assets increased by $95,386 million and stockholders' equity increased by $41,067 million, what was the increase or decrease in liabilities for Year 2?

c. What were the total assets, liabilities, and stockholders' equity at the end of Year 2?

d. Based upon your answer to (c), does the accounting equation balance?

E2-3 Accounting equation

Obj. 1

✔ a. $1,373

Campbell Soup Co. (CPB) had the following assets and liabilities (in millions) at the end of Year 1.

Assets	$14,529
Liabilities	13,156

a. Determine the stockholders' equity of Campbell Soup at the end of Year 1.

b. If assets decreased by $1,381 million and liabilities decreased by $1,120 million, what was the increase or decrease in stockholders' equity for Year 2?

c. What were the total assets, liabilities, and stockholders' equity at the end of Year 2?

d. Based upon your answer to (c), does the accounting equation balance?

E2-4 Accounting equation

Obj. 1

✔ (a) $258,578

The following are recent year summaries of balance sheet and income statement data (in millions) for Apple Inc. (AAPL) and Verizon Communications (VZ).

	Apple	Verizon
Year 1:		
Assets	$365,725	(e)
Liabilities	(a)	(f)
Stockholders' equity	(b)	$ 54,710
Increase (decrease) in assets, liabilities, and stockholders' equity during Year 2:		
Assets	$ (27,209)	(g)
Liabilities	(10,550)	$ 18,773
Stockholders' equity	(16,659)	(h)
Year 2:		
Assets	(c)	$291,727
Liabilities	$248,028	(i)
Stockholders' equity	(d)	62,835

Determine the amounts of the missing items (a) through (i).

E2-5 Accounting equation

Obj. 1

✔ b. $895,000

Alex Hayden is the sole stockholder and operator of Elevate and Succeed, a motivational consulting business. At the end of its accounting period, December 31, 20Y7, Elevate and Succeed has assets of $1,200,000 and liabilities of $375,000. Using the accounting equation and considering each case independently, determine the following amounts:

a. Stockholders' equity, as of December 31, 20Y7.
b. Stockholders' equity, as of December 31, 20Y8, assuming that assets increased by $150,000 and liabilities increased by $80,000 during 20Y8.
c. Stockholders' equity, as of December 31, 20Y8, assuming that assets decreased by $200,000 and liabilities increased by $100,000 during 20Y8.
d. Stockholders' equity, as of December 31, 20Y8, assuming that assets increased by $400,000 and liabilities decreased by $75,000 during 20Y8.
e. Net income (or net loss) during 20Y8, assuming that as of December 31, 20Y8, assets were $1,275,000, liabilities were $290,000, and there were no dividends and no additional common stock was issued.

Obj. 2, 4

SHOW ME HOW

E2-6 Effects of transactions on stockholders' equity

For Target Corporation (TGT), indicate whether the following transactions would (1) increase, (2) decrease, or (3) have no effect on stockholders' equity.

a. Borrowed money from the bank.
b. Paid creditors.
c. Made cash sales to customers.
d. Purchased store equipment.
e. Paid dividends.
f. Paid store rent.
g. Paid interest expense.
h. Sold store equipment at a gain.
i. Received interest revenue.
j. Paid taxes.

Obj. 1, 2, 4

E2-7 Effects of transactions on accounting equation

Describe how the following business transactions affect the three elements of the accounting equation.

a. Received cash for services performed.
b. Paid for utilities used in the business.
c. Borrowed cash at local bank.
d. Issued common stock for cash.
e. Purchased land for cash.

Obj. 1, 2, 4

EXCEL ONLINE

✔ (1) Assets decreased by $140,000

E2-8 Effects of transactions on accounting equation

A vacant lot acquired for $500,000, on which there is a balance owed of $300,000, is sold for $660,000 in cash. The seller pays the $300,000 owed. What is the effect of these transactions on the total amount of the seller's (1) assets, (2) liabilities, and (3) stockholders' equity?

Obj. 2, 4

E2-9 Effects of transactions on stockholders' equity

Indicate whether each of the following types of transactions will (a) increase stockholders' equity or (b) decrease stockholders' equity.

1. Issued common stock for cash.
2. Received cash for fees earned.
3. Paid cash for utilities expense.
4. Paid cash for rent expense.
5. Paid cash dividends.

E2-10 Effects of transactions on accounting equation

Obj. 1, 2, 4

JIT Delivery Service had the following selected transactions during November:

1. Received cash from issuance of common stock, $37,500.
2. Paid rent expense for November, $2,500.
3. Paid advertising expense, $1,500.
4. Received cash for providing delivery services, $17,250.
5. Borrowed $5,000 from Second National Bank to finance its operations.
6. Purchased a delivery van for cash, $12,500.
7. Paid interest on note from Second National Bank, $50.
8. Paid salaries and wages for November, $5,000.
9. Paid dividends, $1,000.

Indicate the effect of each transaction on the accounting equation by listing the numbers identifying the transactions, (1) through (9), in a vertical column, and inserting at the right of each number the appropriate letter from the following list:

a. Increase in an asset, decrease in another asset.
b. Increase in an asset, increase in a liability.
c. Increase in an asset, increase in stockholders' equity.
d. Decrease in an asset, decrease in a liability.
e. Decrease in an asset, decrease in stockholders' equity.

E2-11 Nature of transactions

Obj. 1, 2, 4

✔ b. $11,000 decrease

Cheryl Alder operates her own catering service. Summary financial data for March are presented in the following equation form. Each line, designated by a number, indicates the effect of a transaction on the balance sheet. Each increase and decrease in retained earnings, except transaction (4), affects net income.

	Cash	+	Land	=	Liabilities	+	Common Stock	+	Retained Earnings
Bal.	40,000		100,000		16,000		24,000		100,000
1.	28,000								28,000
2.	(20,000)		20,000						
3.	(18,000)								(18,000)
4.	(1,000)								(1,000)
Bal.	29,000		120,000		16,000		24,000		109,000

a. Describe each transaction.
b. What is the net decrease in cash during the month?
c. What is the net increase in retained earnings during the month?
d. What is the net income for the month?
e. How much of the net income for the month was retained in the business?
f. What is the net cash flows from (used for) operating activities?
g. What is the net cash flows from (used for) investing activities?
h. What is the net cash flows from (used for) financing activities?

E2-12 Net income and dividends

Obj. 3, 5

The income statement of a corporation for the month of February indicates a net income of $32,000. During the same period, $40,000 in cash dividends were paid.

Would it be correct to say that the business incurred a net loss of $8,000 during the month? Discuss.

Obj. 1, 3, 5

✔ Company Yankee: Net income, $86,000

E2-13 Net income and stockholders' equity for four businesses

Four different companies, Sierra, Tango, Yankee, and Zulu, show the same balance sheet data at the beginning and end of a year. These data, exclusive of the amount of stockholders' equity, are summarized as follows:

	Total Assets	Total Liabilities
Beginning of the year	$490,000	$175,000
End of the year	770,000	294,000

On the basis of the preceding data and the following additional information for the year, determine the net income (or loss) of each company for the year. (*Suggestion:* First determine the amount of increase or decrease in stockholders' equity during the year.)

Sierra:	No additional common stock was issued, and no dividends were paid.
Tango:	No additional common stock was issued, but dividends of $55,000 were paid.
Yankee:	Common stock of $75,000 was issued, but no dividends were paid.
Zulu:	Common stock of $75,000 was issued, and dividends of $55,000 were paid.

Obj. 1, 3, 5

✔ (a) 76,500

E2-14 Missing amounts from balance sheet and income statement data

One item is omitted from each of the following summaries of balance sheet and income statement data for four different corporations.

	Carbon	Krypton	Fluorine	Radium
Beginning of the year:				
Assets	$333,000	$250,000	$100,000	(d)
Liabilities	118,000	130,000	76,000	$120,000
End of the year:				
Assets	495,000	350,000	90,000	248,000
Liabilities	160,000	110,000	80,000	136,000
During the year:				
Additional issuance of common stock	(a)	50,000	10,000	40,000
Dividends	7,500	16,000	(c)	60,000
Revenue	90,000	(b)	115,000	112,000
Expenses	39,000	64,000	122,500	128,000

Determine the amounts of the missing items, identifying them by letter. (*Suggestion:* First determine the amount of increase or decrease in stockholders' equity during the year.)

Obj. 3, 5

EXCEL ONLINE

✔ a. $1,465.7

E2-15 Net income, retained earnings, and dividends

The following data (in millions) are provided for Twitter, Inc. (TWTR), for a recent year:

Retained earnings, beginning of year	$(1,454.1)
Retained earnings, end of year	11.6
Net cash flows from operating activities	1,303.4
Net decrease in cash	(94.2)
Net cash flows used for investing activities	(1,116.0)

a. Determine Twitter's net income for the year, assuming no dividends were paid during the year.

b. Determine the net cash flows from (used for) financing activities for the year.

E2-16 Balance sheet, net income, and cash flows

Obj. 3, 5

✔ b. $147,000

Financial information related to Abby's Interiors for October and November of 20Y6 is as follows:

	October 31, 20Y6	November 30, 20Y6
Notes payable	$200,000	$250,000
Land	500,000	575,000
Common stock	75,000	90,000
Retained earnings	?	?
Cash	50,000	175,000

a. Prepare balance sheets for Abby's Interiors as of October 31 and November 30, 20Y6.

b. Determine the amount of net income for November, assuming that dividends of $12,000 were paid.

c. Determine the net cash flows from (used for) operating activities for November.

d. Determine the net cash flows from (used for) investing activities for November.

e. Determine the net cash flows from (used for) financing activities for November.

f. Determine the net increase or decrease in cash for November.

E2-17 Income statement

Obj. 1, 3

✔ Net income, $40,000

After its first month of operations, the following amounts were taken from the accounting records of West Coast Dreams Realty Inc. as of June 30, 20Y9.

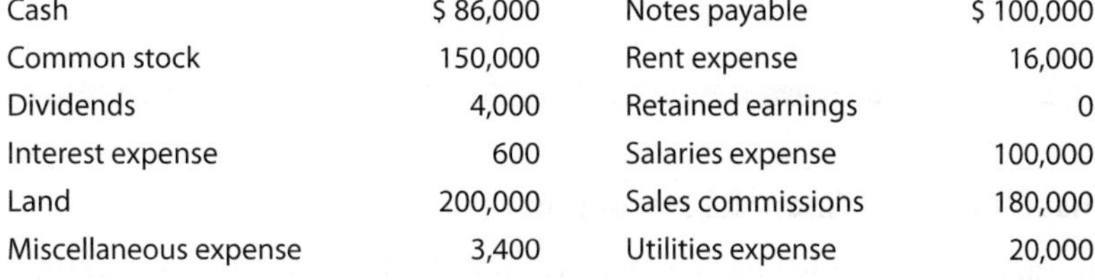

Cash	$ 86,000	Notes payable	$ 100,000
Common stock	150,000	Rent expense	16,000
Dividends	4,000	Retained earnings	0
Interest expense	600	Salaries expense	100,000
Land	200,000	Sales commissions	180,000
Miscellaneous expense	3,400	Utilities expense	20,000

Prepare an income statement for the month ended June 30, 20Y9.

E2-18 Statement of stockholders' equity

Obj. 3, 5

Using the financial data shown in Exercise 2-17 for West Coast Dreams Realty Inc., prepare a statement of stockholders' equity for the month ended June 30, 20Y9.

E2-19 Balance sheet

Obj. 3, 5

Using the financial data shown in Exercise 2-17 for West Coast Dreams Realty Inc., prepare a balance sheet as of June 30, 20Y9.

E2-20 Statement of cash flows

Obj. 3, 5

✔ Net cash flows from financing activities, $246,000

Using the financial data shown in Exercise 2-17 for West Coast Dreams Realty Inc., prepare a statement of cash flows for the month ended June 30, 20Y9.

Obj. 1, 2, 4

E2-21 Effects of transactions on accounting equation

Describe how the following transactions of McDonald's Corp. (MCD) would affect the three elements of the accounting equation.

a. Paid research and development expenses for the current year.
b. Purchased machinery and equipment for cash.
c. Received cash from issuing stock.
d. Received cash from the issuance of long-term debt.
e. Made cash sales.
f. Paid selling expenses.
g. Paid employee pension expenses for the current year.
h. Received cash from selling manufacturing equipment for a gain on the sale.
i. Paid officer salaries.
j. Paid taxes.
k. Paid off long-term debt.
l. Paid dividends.

Obj. 3, 5

E2-22 Statement of cash flows

For each transaction listed for McDonald's Corp. (MCD) in Exercise 2-21, indicate whether it would be reported as an operating, investing, or financing activity on the statement of cash flows.

Problems

Obj. 1, 2, 3

SHOW ME HOW

✔ 3. Net income, $7,250

P2-1 Transactions and financial statements

Roger Smith established an insurance agency on July 1, 20Y5, and completed the following transactions during July:

a. Opened a business bank account in the name of Smith Insurance Inc., with a deposit of $30,000 in exchange for common stock.
b. Borrowed $50,000 by issuing a note payable.
c. Received cash from fees earned, $15,000.
d. Paid rent on office and equipment for the month, $2,500.
e. Paid automobile expense for the month, $1,250, and miscellaneous expense, $500.
f. Paid office salaries, $3,250.
g. Paid interest on the note payable, $250.
h. Purchased land as a future building site, paying cash of $60,000.
i. Paid dividends, $1,500.

Instructions

1. Indicate the effect of each transaction and the balances after each transaction, using the integrated financial statement framework. After all transactions are recorded, enter Net income under the Income Statement column.
2. Briefly explain why the stockholders' investments and revenues increased stockholders' equity, while dividends and expenses decreased stockholders' equity.
3. Prepare an income statement and statement of stockholders' equity for July.
4. Prepare a balance sheet as of July 31, 20Y5.
5. Prepare a statement of cash flows for July.

P2-2 Transactions and financial statements

Obj. 1, 2, 3

✔ 4. Net cash flows from financing activities, $64,000

Aaron Lee established Restart Technology Services on August 1, 20Y4. The effect of each transaction and the balances after each transaction for August are shown in the integrated financial statement framework that follows.

Instructions

1. Prepare an income statement for the month ended August 31, 20Y4.
2. Prepare a statement of stockholders' equity for the month ended August 31, 20Y4.
3. Prepare a balance sheet as of August 31, 20Y4.
4. Prepare a statement of cash flows for the month ended August 31, 20Y4.

Financial Statement Effects

BALANCE SHEET

	Assets		= Liabilities +	Stockholders' Equity	
	Cash +	Land =	Notes Payable +	Common Stock +	Retained Earnings
a. Issued common stock	50,000			50,000	
b. Fees earned	54,000				54,000
Balances	104,000			50,000	54,000
c. Rent expense	(5,000)				(5,000)
Balances	99,000			50,000	49,000
d. Issued notes payable	20,000		20,000		
Balances	119,000		20,000	50,000	49,000
e. Purchased land	(80,000)	80,000			
Balances	39,000	80,000	20,000	50,000	49,000
f. Paid expenses	(3,800)				(3,800)
Balances	35,200	80,000	20,000	50,000	45,200
g. Paid salary expense	(9,200)				(9,200)
Balances	26,000	80,000	20,000	50,000	36,000
h. Paid dividends	(6,000)				(6,000)
Balances, Aug. 31	20,000	80,000	20,000	50,000	30,000

STATEMENT OF CASH FLOWS

a. Financing	$ 50,000
b. Operating	54,000
c. Operating	(5,000)
d. Financing	20,000
e. Investing	(80,000)
f. Operating	(3,800)
g. Operating	(9,200)
h. Financing	(6,000)
Increase in cash	$ 20,000

INCOME STATEMENT

b. Fees earned	$ 54,000
c. Rent expense	(5,000)
f. Auto expense	(2,400)
f. Misc. expense	(1,400)
g. Salary expense	(9,200)
Net income	$ 36,000

Obj. 3

✔ 1. Net income, $27,000

P2-3 Financial statements

The following amounts were taken from the accounting records of Dust, Sweep, Repeat Services, Inc., as of December 31, 20Y7. The company began its operations on January 1, 20Y7.

Cash	$ 12,000
Common stock	15,000
Dividends	3,000
Fees earned	124,000
Interest expense	960
Land	43,000
Miscellaneous expense	2,040
Notes payable	16,000
Rent expense	14,000
Salaries expense	54,400
Taxes expense	8,600
Utilities expense	17,000

Instructions

1. Prepare an income statement for the year ended December 31, 20Y7.
2. Prepare a statement of stockholders' equity for the year ended December 31, 20Y7.
3. Prepare a balance sheet as of December 31, 20Y7.
4. Prepare a statement of cash flows for the year ended December 31, 20Y7.

Obj. 5

✔ 1. Net income, $100,000

P2-4 Financial statements

Dust, Sweep, Repeat Services, Inc. began its operations on January 1, 20Y7 (see Problem 2-3). After its second year of operations, the following amounts were taken from the accounting records of Dust, Sweep, Repeat Services, Inc., as of December 31, 20Y8.

Cash	?
Common stock	$ 55,000
Dividends	25,000
Fees earned	443,000
Interest expense	3,600
Land	170,000
Miscellaneous expense	6,900
Notes payable	60,000
Rent expense	50,000
Salaries expense	190,000
Taxes expense	32,500
Utilities expense	60,000

Instructions

1. Prepare an income statement for the year ended December 31, 20Y8.
2. Prepare a statement of stockholders' equity for the year ended December 31, 20Y8. (*Note:* The retained earnings at January 1, 20Y8, was $24,000.)
3. Prepare a balance sheet as of December 31, 20Y8.
4. Prepare a statement of cash flows for the year ended December 31, 20Y8. (*Hint:* You should compare the asset and liability amounts of December 31, 20Y8, with those of December 31, 20Y7, to determine cash used in investing and financing activities. See your solution to Problem 2-3 for the December 31, 20Y7, balance sheet amounts.)

P2-5 Missing amounts from financial statements

Obj. 3, 5

✔ a. $125,000

The financial statements at the end of Network Realty, Inc.'s first month of operations are provided. By analyzing the interrelationships among the financial statements, fill in the proper amounts for (a) through (r).

NETWORK REALTY, INC.
Income Statement
For the Month Ended December 31, 20Y4

Fees earned		$ (a)
Operating expenses:		
Wages expense	$33,120	
Rent expense	18,000	
Utilities expense	(b)	
Interest expense	1,800	
Miscellaneous expense	3,960	
Total operating expenses		67,500
Net income		$ (c)

NETWORK REALTY, INC.
Statement of Stockholders' Equity
For the Month Ended December 31, 20Y4

	Common Stock	Retained Earnings	Total
Balances, Dec. 1, 20Y4	$ 0	$ (d)	$ 0
Issued common stock	75,000		75,000
Net income		57,500	57,500
Dividends		(e)	(e)
Balances, Dec. 31, 20Y4	$75,000	$ (f)	$ (g)

NETWORK REALTY, INC.
Balance Sheet
December 31, 20Y4

Assets		
Cash		$ (h)
Land		175,000
Total assets		$225,500
Liabilities		
Notes payable		$105,000
Stockholders' Equity		
Common stock	$(i)	
Retained earnings	(j)	
Total stockholders' equity		(k)
Total liabilities and stockholders' equity		$ (l)

NETWORK REALTY, INC.
Statement of Cash Flows
For the Month Ended December 31, 20Y4

Cash flows from (used for) operating activities:		
Cash received from customers	$125,000	
Cash paid for expenses	(67,500)	
Net cash flows from operating activities		$ (m)
Cash flows from (used for) investing activities:		
Cash paid for purchase of land		(175,000)
Cash flows from (used for) financing activities:		
Cash received from issuing common stock	$ 75,000	
Cash received from issuing notes payable	(n)	
Cash paid as dividends to stockholders	(12,000)	
Net cash flows from financing activities		(o)
Net increase in cash during December		$ (p)
Cash as of December 1, 20Y4		(q)
Cash as of December 31, 20Y4		$ (r)

Obj. 3, 5

P2-6 Financial statements

Alpine Realty, Inc., organized July 1, 20Y8, is operated by Angela Griffin. The following financial statements for Alpine Realty, Inc., were prepared after its first month of operations.

ALPINE REALTY, INC.
Income Statement
July 31, 20Y8

Sales commissions		$60,000
Operating expenses:		
Office salaries expense	$20,000	
Rent expense	6,000	
Automobile expense	3,500	
Dividends	2,000	
Miscellaneous expense	1,500	
Total operating expenses		(33,000)
Net income		$27,000

ANGELA GRIFFIN
Statement of Stockholders' Equity
July 31, 20Y7

Net income for the month	$27,000
Retained earnings, July 31, 20Y7	$27,000

Balance Sheet
For the Month Ended July 31, 20Y7

Assets		
Cash		$32,000
Notes payable		20,000
Total assets		$52,000
Liabilities		
Land		$30,000
Stockholders' Equity		
Common stock	$15,000	
Retained earnings	27,000	
Total stockholders' equity		42,000
Total liabilities and stockholders' equity		$72,000

ALPINE REALTY, INC.
Statement of Cash Flows
July 31, 20Y8

Cash flows from (used for) operating activities:	
Cash received from sales commissions	$ 60,000
Cash flows from (used for) investing activities:	
Cash paid for land	(30,000)
Cash flows from (used for) financing activities:	
Cash received from retained earnings	27,000
Net increase in cash during July	$ 57,000
Cash as of July 1, 20Y8	0
Cash as of July 31, 20Y8	$ 57,000

Instructions

1. Identify the errors in the preceding financial statements of Alpine Realty, Inc.
2. Prepare corrected financial statements for Alpine Realty, Inc.

Metric-Based Analysis

MBA 2-1 Metric analysis of transactions

Obj. 2, 4

Using transactions listed in P2-1 for Smith Insurance Inc. indicate the effects of each transaction on the liquidity metric Cash and profitability metric Net Income—Cash Basis.

MBA 2-2 Metric analysis of transactions

Obj. 2, 4

Using transactions listed in P2-2 for Restart Technology Services indicate the effects of each transaction on the liquidity metric Cash and profitability metric Net Income—Cash Basis.

MBA 2-3 Common-sized income statements

Obj. 6

Delta Air Lines, Inc. (DAL) provides cargo and passenger services throughout the world. The following operating data (in millions) were adapted from recent financial statements of Delta.

	Year 2	Year 1
Revenue	$ 47,007	$ 44,438
Operating expenses:		
Fuel	$ (8,519)	$ (9,020)
Aircraft related	(12,742)	(11,573)
Selling and general	(17,357)	(16,858)
Other expenses	(1,771)	(1,723)
Total operating expenses	$(40,389)	$(39,174)
Operating income	$ 6,618	$ 5,264

1. Prepare common-sized income statements for Years 1 and 2. Round to one decimal place.
2. Using your answer to (1), analyze and comment on the performance of Delta in Year 2.

MBA 2-4 Common-sized income statements

Obj. 6

Southwest Airlines Co. (LUV) provides passenger services throughout the United States, Mexico, Jamaica, the Bahamas, Aruba, and the Dominican Republic. The following operating data (in millions) were adapted from recent financial statements of Southwest.

	Year 2	Year 1
Revenue	$ 22,428	$ 21,965
Operating expenses:		
Fuel	$ (4,347)	$ (4,616)
Aircraft related	(3,805)	(3,642)
Selling and general	(8,293)	(7,649)
Other expenses	(3,026)	(2,852)
Total operating expenses	$(19,471)	$(18,759)
Operating income	$ 2,957	$ 3,206

1. Prepare common-sized income statements for Years 1 and 2. Round to one decimal place.
2. Using your answer to (1), analyze and comment on the performance of Southwest in Year 2.

MBA 2-5 Common-sized income statements

Obj. 6

Using your answers to MBA 2-3 and MBA 2-4, compare and comment on the operating results of Delta and Southwest.

Obj. 6

MBA 2-6 Common-sized income statements

Kellogg Company (K) produces, markets, and distributes cereal and food products including Cheez-It, Coco Pops, Rice Krispies, and Pringles. The following partial income statements (in millions) were adapted from recent financial statements.

	Year 2	Year 1
Sales	$13,578	$13,547
Cost of goods sold	(9,197)	(8,821)
Gross profit	$ 4,381	$ 4,726
Selling and administrative expenses	(2,980)	(3,020)
Operating income	$ 1,401	$ 1,706

1. Prepare common-sized income statements for Years 1 and 2. Round to one decimal place.
2. Using your answer to (1), analyze the performance of Kellogg in Year 2.

Obj. 6

MBA 2-7 Common-sized income statements

General Mills Inc. (GIS) produces, markets, and distributes cereal and food products including Cheerios, Wheaties, Cocoa Puffs, Yoplait, and Pillsbury branded products. The following partial income statements (in millions) were adapted from recent financial statements.

	Year 2	Year 1
Sales	$ 16,865	$ 15,740
Cost of goods sold	(11,108)	(10,305)
Gross profit	$ 5,757	$ 5,435
Selling and administrative expenses	(2,936)	(2,850)
Operating income	$ 2,821	$ 2,585

1. Prepare common-sized income statements for Years 1 and 2. Round to one decimal place.
2. Using your answer to (1), analyze the performance of General Mills in Year 2.

Obj. 6

MBA 2-8 Common-sized income statements

Using your answers to MBA 2-6 and MBA 2-7, compare and analyze Year 2 common-sized income statements of Kellogg (K) to those of General Mills (GIS).

Obj. 6

MBA 2-9 Common-sized balance sheets

The following end-of-year balance sheets (in millions) were adapted from recent financial statements of Apple (AAPL).

	Year 2	Year 1
Current assets:		
Cash	$ 48,844	$ 25,913
Marketable securities	51,713	40,388
Accounts receivable	22,926	23,186
Inventories	4,106	3,956
Other	35,230	37,896
Total current assets	$162,819	$131,339
Long-term assets:		
Long-term marketable securities	$105,341	$170,799
Property, plant, and equipment	37,378	41,304
Other long-term assets	32,978	22,283
Total long-term assets	$175,697	$234,386
Total assets	$338,516	$365,725

Current liabilities:		
Accounts payable	$ 46,236	$ 55,888
Current portion of long-term debt	10,260	8,784
Other	49,222	51,257
Total current liabilities	$105,718	$115,929
Long-term liabilities	142,310	142,649
Total liabilities	$248,028	$258,578
Stockholders' equity:		
Common stock	$ 45,174	$ 40,201
Retained earnings	45,898	70,400
Other items	(584)	(3,454)
Total stockholders' equity	$ 90,488	$107,147
Total liabilities and stockholders' equity	$338,516	$365,725

1. Prepare common-sized balance sheets for Apple for Years 1 and 2. Round to one decimal place.
2. Comment on your answer in (1).

Cases

Case 2-1 Business emphasis

Assume that you are considering developing a nationwide chain of women's clothing stores. You have contacted a Seattle-based firm that specializes in financing new business ventures and enterprises. Such firms, called venture capital firms, finance new businesses in exchange for a percentage of the ownership.

1. In groups of four or five, discuss the different business emphases that you might use in your venture.
2. For each emphasis you listed in (1), provide an example of a real-world business using the same emphasis.
3. What percentage of the ownership would you be willing to give the venture capital firm in exchange for its financing?

Case 2-2 Cash accounting

On August 1, 20Y7, Dr. Ruth Turner established SickCo, a medical practice organized as a professional corporation. The following conversation occurred the following February between Dr. Turner and a former medical school classmate, Dr. Shonna Rees, at an American Medical Association convention in New York City.

Dr. Rees: Ruth, good to see you again. Why didn't you call when you were in Denver? We could have had dinner together.

Dr. Turner: Actually, I never made it to Denver this year. My husband and kids went up to our Vail condo twice, but I got stuck in Fort Lauderdale. I opened a new consulting practice this August and haven't had any time for myself since.

Dr. Rees: I heard about it ... Sick... something ... right?

Dr. Turner: Yes, SickCo. My husband chose the name.

Dr. Rees: I've thought about doing something like that. Are you making any money? I mean, is it worth your time?

Dr. Turner: You wouldn't believe it. I started by opening a bank account with $45,000, and my January bank statement shows a balance of $100,000. Not bad for six months—all pure profit.

Dr. Rees: Maybe I'll try it in Denver! Let's have breakfast together tomorrow and you can fill me in on the details.

Comment on Dr. Turner's statement that the difference between the opening bank balance ($45,000) and the January statement balance ($100,000) is pure profit.

Case 2-3 Business emphasis

Amazon.com (AMZN), an Internet retailer, was incorporated in the early 1990s and opened its virtual doors on the Web shortly thereafter. On its statement of cash flows, would you expect Amazon.com's net cash flows from (used for) operating, investing, and financing activities to be positive or negative for its first three years of operations? Use the following format for your answers, and briefly explain your logic.

	Year 1	Year 2	Year 3
Net cash flows from (used for) operating activities	negative		
Net cash flows from (used for) investing activities			
Net cash flows from (used for) financing activities			

Case 2-4 Financial information

Yahoo.com's (YHOO) finance Internet site provides summary financial information about public companies, such as stock quotes, recent financial filings with the Securities and Exchange Commission, and recent news stories. Go to Yahoo.com's financial Web site (**http://finance.yahoo.com/**) and enter Apple, Inc.'s (AAPL). Answer the following questions concerning Apple, Inc. by clicking on the various tabs provided under Apple Inc. (AAPL) on the Web site.

1. At what price did Apple's stock last trade?
2. What is the 52-week range of Apple's stock?
3. When was Apple's stock's 52-week high?
4. Has there been any insider selling or buying of Apple's stock? If so, by whom?
5. Who is the chief executive officer and director of Apple Inc.?
6. What was the salary of the chief executive officer of Apple Inc.?
7. What is the annual dividend rate of Apple's stock?
8. How many current broker recommendations are strong buy, buy, hold, sell, or strong sell? What is the recommendation rating?
9. What is the net cash flows from (used for) operating activities for this year?
10. What is the operating margin for this year?

The annual report (10-K) assignment for this chapter is in Appendix B: Nike Annual Report, Chapter 2.

Answers to Self-Examination Questions

1. **D** Even though a recording error has been made, the accounting equation will balance (answer D). However, assets (cash) will be overstated by $50,000, and liabilities (notes payable) will be overstated by $50,000. Answer A is incorrect because although cash is overstated by $50,000, the accounting equation will balance. Answer B is incorrect because although notes payable are overstated by $50,000, the accounting equation will balance. Answer C is incorrect because the accounting equation will balance and assets will not exceed liabilities.
2. **C** Total assets will exceed total liabilities and stockholders' equity by $16,000. This is because stockholders' equity (retained earnings) was decreased instead of increased by $8,000. Thus, stockholders' equity will be understated by a total of $16,000.
3. **C** The accounting equation is:

   Assets = Liabilities + Stockholders' Equity

   Therefore, if assets increased by $20,000 and liabilities increased by $12,000, stockholders' equity must have increased by $8,000 (answer C), as indicated in the following computation:

Assets	**= Liabilities + Stockholders' Equity**
+$20,000	= $12,000 + Stockholders' Equity
+$20,000 − $12,000	= Stockholders' Equity
+$8,000	= Stockholders' Equity

4. **B** Net income is the excess of revenue over expenses, or $15,000 (answer B). If expenses exceed revenue, the difference is a net loss. Dividends are the opposite of the stockholders investing in the business and do not affect the amount of net income or net loss.
5. **B** The purchase of land for cash (answer B) changes the mix of assets and does not affect liabilities or stockholders' equity. Borrowing cash from a bank (answer A) increases assets and liabilities. Receiving cash for fees earned (answer C) increases cash and stockholders' equity (retained earnings). Paying office salaries (answer D) decreases cash and stockholders' equity (retained earnings).

Chapter 3

Basic Accounting Systems: Accrual Basis

What's Covered:

Topics: Basic Accounting Systems: Accrual Basis

Accrual Concepts
- Matching Concept (Obj. 1)
- Revenue Recognition (Obj. 1)
- Expense Recognition (Obj. 1)

Accrual Accounting
- Transactions (Obj. 2)
- Adjustment Process (Obj. 3)
- Financial Statements (Obj. 4)

Why Accrual Basis Is Used
- Cash vs. Accrual Basis (Obj. 5)
- Advantage of Accrual Basis (Obj. 5)
- Accounting Cycle (Obj. 5)

Metric-Based Analysis
- Transactions
  - Liquidity: Quick Assets (Obj. 2,3)
  - Profitability: Net Income (Obj. 2,3)
- Financial Statements
  - Quick Ratio (Obj. 6)

Learning Objectives

Obj.1 Describe accrual accounting concepts, including the matching concept, revenue recognition, and expense recognition principles.

Obj.2 Use the accrual basis of accounting to analyze, record, and summarize transactions.

Obj.3 Describe and illustrate the end-of-period adjustment process.

Obj.4 Prepare financial statements using the accrual basis of accounting, including a classified balance sheet.

Obj.5 Describe why generally accepted accounting principles (GAAP) require the accrual basis of accounting.

Obj.6 Describe and illustrate the use of the quick ratio in assessing a company's liquidity.

Chapter Metrics

Use the following metrics to analyze transactions and financial statements.

TRANSACTIONS

- **Liquidity: Quick Assets**
- **Profitability: Net Income—Accrual Basis**

FINANCIAL STATEMENTS

- **Quick Ratio**

Apple Inc.

DisobeyArt/Shutterstock.com

Have you ever purchased an iTunes gift card that can be redeemed online at the iTunes Store? If so, when do you think **Apple Inc. (AAPL)** should record the revenue from the sale of the gift card?

As we discussed and illustrated in Chapter 2, sometimes revenues are earned at the point cash is received. However, in some cases, a company renders a service or delivers a product before cash is received. In other cases, cash is received before a company renders a service or delivers a product. In these cases, companies normally record revenue when the service is rendered or the product is delivered to the customer.

One company that receives cash before the service is rendered or the product delivered is Apple Inc. In the case of iTunes gift cards, Apple receives cash before the customer downloads music, movies, or other content from its online iTunes Store. When cash is received for the gift card, Apple defers recording the revenue until the customer redeems the card. Likewise, revenue from AppleCare, which provides computer support and repair services, is recorded over the service period covered by the AppleCare contract. For example, Apple offers AppleCare on its iPads for up to a two-year period.

In this chapter, we continue our discussion of financial statements and financial reporting systems. In doing so, we focus on accrual concepts of accounting such as how Apple would record revenue. In addition, our discussions will include how to record transactions under accrual accounting concepts, update accounting records, and prepare accrual financial statements. Because all large companies, and many small ones, use accrual concepts of accounting, a thorough understanding of this topic is important for your business studies and future career.

Accrual Accounting Concepts

Objective 1
Describe accrual accounting concepts, including the matching concept, revenue recognition, and expense recognition principles.

Family Health Care's transactions and financial statements for September and October were illustrated in Chapter 2. These illustrations used many of the eight accounting concepts described in Chapter 1. For example, the business entity concept was used to account for Family Health Care as a separate entity, independent of the owner-manager, Dr. Lee Landry. The cost, unit of measure, going concern, accounting period, full disclosure, and objectivity concepts were also used.

The one accounting concept not used in Chapter 2 was the matching concept. This is because all the transactions in Chapter 2 were structured so that cash was either received or paid. This was done to simplify the recording of transactions and preparing of the financial statements. For example, all revenues were received in cash at the time the services were rendered and all expenses were paid in cash at the time they were incurred. In doing so, this allowed us to illustrate the cash basis of accounting in its simplest form.

In the real world, cash may be received or paid at a different time from when revenues are earned or expenses are incurred. In fact, companies often earn revenue before or after cash is received and incur expenses before or after cash is paid.

To illustrate, a real estate company might spend months or years developing land for a business complex or subdivision. During this period, the company earns no revenues but makes payments for materials, wages, insurance, and other construction items. Thus, if revenues were recorded only when cash is received and expenses recorded only when cash is paid, the company would report a series of losses on its income statement while the land is being developed. In such cases, the income statements would not provide a realistic picture of the company's operations. In fact, the development might become highly successful and the early losses misleading.

Accrual basis accounting is designed to avoid misleading information arising from the timing of cash receipts and payments. Under accrual accounting, transactions are recorded as they occur and thus affect the accounting equation (assets, liabilities, and stockholders' equity). Specifically, the **accrual basis of accounting** records revenue as it is earned and matches expenses against the revenue they generate. Since the receipt or payment of cash affects assets (cash), all cash receipts and payments are recorded in the accounts under accrual accounting. Additionally, under accrual accounting, transactions are recorded even though cash is not received or paid until a later point.

To illustrate, Family Health Care may provide services to patients who are covered by health insurance. Periodically, Family Health Care files claims with the insurance companies requesting payment. In this case, revenue is recorded, referred to as *recognized*, when the services are provided even though the cash is to be received later. When services are provided with the cash to be received at a later time, the services are said to be provided *on account*. In such cases, an *account receivable* for the amount of the services is recorded as an asset.

Likewise, a company may purchase supplies from a supplier (vendor), with terms that allow the company to pay for the purchase at a later time. In this case, the supplies are said to be purchased *on account* and an *account payable* for the amount to be paid is recorded as a liability.

In accounting, the term *recognized* is used to refer to when a transaction is recorded. Under the **revenue recognition principle**, revenue is recorded when services have been provided or when a product has been delivered to a customer. For Family Health Care, revenue is recorded when services have been provided to the patient. At this point, the revenue-earning process is complete and the patient is legally obligated to pay for the services.

Under the **expense recognition principle**, expenses are recorded in the same period that they generate revenue. This is required by the **matching concept** so net income or net loss for the period is properly determined.

Accrual accounting also recognizes liabilities at the time the business incurs the obligation to pay for the services or goods purchased. For example, the purchase of supplies on account is recorded when the supplies are received and the business has incurred the obligation to pay for the supplies.

Apple uses the accrual basis of accounting in recording transactions and reporting its financial statements.

Family Health Care's November Transactions

Objective 2
Use the accrual concepts of accounting to analyze, record, and summarize transactions.

To illustrate accrual accounting, the following November 20Y5 Family Health Care transactions are used:

a. On November 1, received $1,800 from ILS Company as rent for the use of Family Health Care's land as a temporary parking lot from November 20Y5 through March 20Y6.

Business Insight

Not Cutting Corners

Have you ever ordered a hamburger from **Wendy's (WEN)** and noticed that the meat patty is square? The square meat patty reflects a business emphasis instilled in Wendy's by its founder, Dave Thomas. Mr. Thomas emphasized offering high-quality products at a fair price in a friendly atmosphere, without "cutting corners"; hence, the square meat patty. In the highly competitive fast-food industry, Dave Thomas's approach has enabled Wendy's to become one of the largest fast-food restaurant chains in the world.

Source: Douglas Martin, "Dave Thomas, 69, Wendy's Founder, Dies," *New York Times*, January 9, 2002.

b. On November 1, paid a premium of $2,400 for a two-year general business insurance policy that covers risks from fire and theft.
c. On November 1, paid $6,000 for an insurance premium on a six-month medical malpractice policy.
d. Dr. Landry invested an additional $5,000 in the business in exchange for common stock.
e. Purchased supplies for $240 on account.
f. Purchased $8,500 of office equipment. Paid $1,700 cash as a down payment, with the remaining $6,800 ($8,500 − $1,700) due in five monthly installments of $1,360 ($6,800 ÷ 5) beginning January 1, 20Y6.
g. Provided services of $6,100 to patients on account.
h. Received $5,500 for services provided to patients who paid cash.
i. Received $4,200 from insurance companies on patients' accounts for services that were provided in transaction g.
j. Paid $100 on account for supplies that were purchased in transaction e.
k. Expenses paid during November were as follows: wages, $2,790; rent, $800; utilities, $580; interest, $100; and miscellaneous, $420.
l. Paid dividends of $1,200 to stockholder (Dr. Landry).

In analyzing and recording the November transactions for Family Health Care, the integrated financial statement framework is used. Transactions that increase or decrease a financial statement element are recorded. These financial statement elements are referred to as **accounts**.

In addition, the effects of each transaction on liquidity and profitability metrics for Family Health Care are illustrated. In this chapter, we use quick assets as our liquidity metric. **Quick assets** include cash and other assets that can be readily converted to cash such as receivables and marketable securities. Inventory is normally not included as a quick asset since inventory must be sold and any related receivable collected before it is converted to cash. Since Family Health Care has no marketable securities, quick assets consist of cash and accounts receivable.

In this chapter, we use net income (revenue − expenses) as our profitability metric. Since this chapter illustrates accrual transactions, the profitability metric is termed **Net Income—Accrual Basis**.

Transaction a

On November 1, received $1,800 from ILS Company as rent for the use of Family Health Care's land as a temporary parking lot from November 20Y5 through March 20Y6.

In this transaction, Family Health Care entered into a rental agreement for the use of its land for five months. The agreement requires a payment of a rental fee of $1,800 in advance. The rental agreement also gives ILS Company the option of renewing the agreement for an additional four months.

By entering into this rental agreement and accepting the $1,800, Family Health Care has incurred a liability to make the land available for ILS's use. If Family Health Care canceled the agreement on November 1, after accepting the $1,800, it would have to repay the $1,800.

Family Health Care records this transaction as an increase in Cash and an increase in a liability for $1,800. Because the liability relates to rent that has not yet been earned, it is recorded as Unearned Revenue.

The effects of this transaction on Family Health Care's financial statements are recorded as follows.

Financial Statement Effects

BALANCE SHEET

	Assets		=	Liabilities		+	Stockholders' Equity	
	Cash	+ Land	=	Notes Payable	+ Unearned Revenue	+	Common Stock	+ Retained Earnings
Balances, Nov. 1	7,320	12,000		10,000			6,000	3,320
a. Received rent in advance	1,800				1,800			
Balances	9,120	12,000		10,000	1,800		6,000	3,320

STATEMENT OF CASH FLOWS	
a. Operating	1,800

INCOME STATEMENT

The November 1 balances shown in the preceding integrated financial statement spreadsheet are the ending balances from October 31. That is, the cash balance of $7,320 is the ending cash balance as of October 31, 20Y5. Likewise, the other balances are carried forward from the preceding month. In this sense, the Balance Sheet columns are a cumulative financial history of Family Health Care.

The receipt of the $1,800 of cash from ILS Company increases cash flows from Operating activities under the Statement of Cash Flows column. Since no rental revenue has yet been earned, there are no entries under the Income Statement column.

As time passes, Family Health Care will earn the rental revenue. For example, at the end of November, $360 ($1,800 ÷ 5 months) will be earned. Recording the $360 of earned rent revenue at the end of November is described and illustrated later in this chapter.

Transaction Metric Effects

The effects of each transaction on liquidity and profitability metrics for Family Health Care are illustrated throughout the chapter. Quick assets is used as the liquidity metric. Quick assets include cash and other assets that can be readily converted to cash such as receivables and marketable securities. Inventory is normally not included in quick assets. Since Family Health Care has no marketable securities, quick assets consist of cash and accounts receivable.

Net income (revenue – expenses) is used as the profitability metric. Since this chapter illustrates accrual transactions, the profitability metric is **Net Income—Accrual Basis**. The transaction did not affect revenues or expenses and thus, there is no effect on the profitability metric.

The effects of the receipt of the rent of $1,800 on the liquidity and profitability metrics are as follows:

LIQUIDITY	
Quick Assets	$1,800

PROFITABILITY	
Net Income—Accrual Basis	No Effect

Transaction b

On November 1, paid a premium of $2,400 for a two-year general business insurance policy that covers risks from fire and theft.

By paying the premium, Family Health Care has purchased an asset, insurance coverage, in exchange for cash. The effects of this transaction on Family Health Care's financial statements are recorded as follows.

Financial Statement Effects

BALANCE SHEET

	Assets			=	Liabilities		+ Stockholders' Equity	
	Cash	+ Prepaid Insurance	+ Land	=	Notes Payable	+ Unearned Revenue	+ Common Stock	+ Retained Earnings
Balances	9,120		12,000		10,000	1,800	6,000	3,320
b. Paid insurance for two years	(2,400)	2,400						
Balances	6,720	2,400	12,000		10,000	1,800	6,000	3,320

STATEMENT OF CASH FLOWS	
b. Operating	(2,400)

INCOME STATEMENT

In the Balance Sheet columns the mix of assets has changed, with Cash decreasing by $2,400 and Prepaid Insurance increasing by $2,400. The payment of cash also decreases cash flows from Operating activities under the Statement of Cash Flows column. Since no revenue or expenses are affected, there are no entries under the Income Statement column.

Prepaid insurance is unique in that it expires with the passage of time. For example, $100 ($2,400 ÷ 24 months) of Family Health Care's insurance will expire each month. Such assets are called **prepaid expenses** or **deferred expenses**.

Transaction Metric Effects

The effects of paying the insurance premium of $2,400 on the liquidity and profitability metrics are as follows:

LIQUIDITY	
Quick Assets	$(2,400)

PROFITABILITY	
Net Income—Accrual Basis	No Effect

Transaction c

On November 1, paid $6,000 for an insurance premium on a six-month medical malpractice policy.

This transaction is similar to the preceding transaction, except that Family Health Care has purchased medical malpractice insurance that is renewable every six months. The effects of this transaction on Family Health Care's financial statements are recorded as follows.

Financial Statement Effects

BALANCE SHEET

	Assets			=	Liabilities		+ Stockholders' Equity	
	Cash	+ Prepaid Insurance	+ Land	=	Notes Payable	+ Unearned Revenue	+ Common Stock	+ Retained Earnings
Balances	6,720	2,400	12,000		10,000	1,800	6,000	3,320
c. Paid insurance for two years	(6,000)	6,000						
Balances	720	8,400	12,000		10,000	1,800	6,000	3,320

STATEMENT OF CASH FLOWS	
c. Operating	(6,000)

INCOME STATEMENT

Transaction Metric Effects

The effects of paying the insurance premium of $6,000 on the liquidity and profitability metrics are as follows:

LIQUIDITY	
Quick Assets	$(6,000)

PROFITABILITY	
Net Income—Accrual Basis	No Effect

Apple maintains insurance coverage for cyber risks.

Transaction d

Dr. Landry invested an additional $5,000 in the business in exchange for common stock.

This transaction is similar to the initial transaction in which Dr. Landry established Family Health Care. The effects of these transactions are recorded as follows.

Financial Statement Effects

BALANCE SHEET

	Assets			=	Liabilities		+ Stockholders' Equity	
	Cash	+ Prepaid Insurance	+ Land	=	Notes Payable	+ Unearned Revenue	+ Common Stock	+ Retained Earnings
Balances	720	8,400	12,000		10,000	1,800	6,000	3,320
d. Issued common stock	5,000						5,000	
Balances	5,720	8,400	12,000		10,000	1,800	11,000	3,320

STATEMENT OF CASH FLOWS	
d. Financing	5,000

INCOME STATEMENT

Transaction Metric Effects

The effects of issuing $5,000 of common stock on the liquidity and profitability metrics are as follows:

LIQUIDITY	
Quick Assets	$5,000

PROFITABILITY	
Net Income—Accrual Basis	No Effect

In a recent year, **Apple** reported receiving $781 million from issuing common stock and had 4,754,986 shares of common stock outstanding.

Transaction e

Purchased supplies for $240 on account.

This transaction is similar to transactions b and c, in that purchased supplies are assets until they are used in the generation of revenue. Family Health Care has purchased and received the supplies, with a promise to pay in the near future. Such liabilities that are incurred in the normal operations are called **accounts payable**. The effects of this transaction on Family Health Care's financial statements are recorded as follows.

Financial Statement Effects

BALANCE SHEET

	Assets				=	Liabilities			+ Stockholders' Equity	
	Cash +	Prepaid Insurance +	Supplies +	Land	=	Accounts Payable	+ Notes Payable	+ Unearned Revenue	+ Common Stock	+ Retained Earnings
Balances	5,720	8,400		12,000			10,000	1,800	11,000	3,320
e. Purchased supplies			240			240				
Balances	5,720	8,400	240	12,000		240	10,000	1,800	11,000	3,320

STATEMENT OF CASH FLOWS

INCOME STATEMENT

Under the Balance Sheet columns, the asset Supplies increases by $240 and the liability Accounts Payable increases by $240. Since no cash is paid or received, there are no entries under the Statement of Cash Flows column. Likewise, since no revenue or expenses are affected, there are no entries under the Income Statement column.

Transaction Metric Effects

The effects of purchasing $240 of supplies on credit on the liquidity and profitability metrics are as follows:

LIQUIDITY	
Quick Assets	No Effect

PROFITABILITY	
Net Income—Accrual Basis	No Effect

On a recent balance sheet, **Apple** reported $49,049 million of accounts payable.

Transaction f

Purchased $8,500 of office equipment. Paid $1,700 cash as a down payment, with the remaining $6,800 ($8,500 − $1,700) due in five monthly installments of $1,360 ($6,800 ÷ 5) beginning January 1, 20Y6.

In this transaction, the asset Office Equipment increases by $8,500, Cash decreases by $1,700, and Notes Payable increases by $6,800. Since cash was paid, cash flows from Investing activities is decreased by $1,700 under the Statement of Cash Flows column. No revenues or expenses are affected, so no entries under the Income Statement column are necessary.

The effects of transaction on Family Health Care's financial statements are recorded as follows.

Financial Statement Effects

BALANCE SHEET

	Assets					=	Liabilities			+ Stockholders' Equity	
	Cash +	Prepaid Insur. +	Supp. +	Office Equip. +	Land	=	Accts. Pay. +	Notes Pay. +	Unearned Revenue +	Common Stock +	Retained Earnings
Balances	5,720	8,400	240		12,000		240	10,000	1,800	11,000	3,320
f. Purchased office equipment	(1,700)			8,500				6,800			
Balances	4,020	8,400	240	8,500	12,000		240	16,800	1,800	11,000	3,320

STATEMENT OF CASH FLOWS

f. Investing	(1,700)

INCOME STATEMENT

Transaction Metric Effects

The effects of purchasing $8,500 of office equipment by paying cash of $1,700 and issuing $6,800 in notes payable on the liquidity and profitability metrics are as follows:

LIQUIDITY	
Quick Assets	$(1,700)

PROFITABILITY	
Net Income—Accrual Basis	No Effect

Transaction g

Provided services of $6,100 to patients on account.

This transaction is similar to the revenue transactions recorded for Family Health Care in September and October. This transaction is different in that instead of receiving cash, the services were provided *on account.*

Family Health Care will collect cash from the patients' insurance companies in the future. Such amounts that are to be collected in the future and that arise from the normal operations are called **accounts receivable**. Since a valid claim exists for future collection, accounts receivable are assets. Thus, the asset Accounts Receivable is increased by $6,100 under the Balance Sheet columns. In addition, Retained Earnings are increased under the Balance Sheet columns and Fees earned is increased under the Income Statement column.

The effects of transaction on Family Health Care's financial statements are recorded as follows.

Financial Statement Effects

BALANCE SHEET

	Assets						=	Liabilities			+ Stockholders' Equity	
	Cash +	Accts. Rec. +	Prepaid Insur.	+ Supp.	+ Office Equip.	+ Land	= Accts. Pay.	+ Notes Pay.	+ Unearned Revenue	+ Common Stock	+ Retained Earnings
Balances	4,020		8,400	240	8,500	12,000	240	16,800	1,800	11,000	3,320
g. Fees earned on acct.		6,100									6,100
Balances	4,020	6,100	8,400	240	8,500	12,000	240	16,800	1,800	11,000	9,420

STATEMENT OF CASH FLOWS

INCOME STATEMENT

g. Fees earned	6,100

Transaction Metric Effects

The effects of earning $6,100 of patient fees on account on the liquidity and profitability metrics are as follows:

LIQUIDITY	
Quick Assets	$6,100

PROFITABILITY	
Net Income—Accrual Basis	$6,100

On a recent balance sheet, **Apple** reported $22,926 million of accounts receivable. *Apple Connection*

Transaction h

Received $5,500 for services provided to patients who paid cash.

This transaction is similar to the revenue transactions that Family Health Care recorded in September and October. The effects of this transaction on Family Health Care's financial statements are recorded as follows.

Financial Statement Effects

BALANCE SHEET

	Assets						=	Liabilities			+ Stockholders' Equity	
	Cash +	Accts. Rec. +	Prepaid Insur.	+ Supp.	+ Office Equip.	+ Land	=	Accts. Pay. +	Notes Pay.	+ Unearned Revenue +	Common Stock	+ Retained Earnings
Balances	4,020	6,100	8,400	240	8,500	12,000		240	16,800	1,800	11,000	9,420
h. Fees earned for cash	5,500											5,500
Balances	9,520	6,100	8,400	240	8,500	12,000		240	16,800	1,800	11,000	14,920

STATEMENT OF CASH FLOWS

h. Operating	5,500

INCOME STATEMENT

h. Fees earned	5,500

Transaction Metric Effects

The effects of earning cash patient fees of $5,500 on the liquidity and profitability metrics are as follows:

LIQUIDITY

Quick Assets	$5,500

PROFITABILITY

Net Income—Accrual Basis	$5,500

Transaction i

Received $4,200 from insurance companies on patients' accounts for services that were provided in transaction g.

This transaction is similar to transaction in that only the mix of assets changes. Cash is increased and Accounts Receivable is decreased by $4,200 under the Balance Sheet columns. The effects of this transaction on Family Health Care's financial statements are recorded as follows.

Financial Statement Effects

BALANCE SHEET

	Assets						=	Liabilities			+ Stockholders' Equity	
	Cash +	Accts. Rec. +	Prepaid Insur.	+ Supp.	+ Office Equip.	+ Land	=	Accts. Pay. +	Notes Pay.	+ Unearned Revenue +	Common Stock	+ Retained Earnings
Balances	9,520	6,100	8,400	240	8,500	12,000		240	16,800	1,800	11,000	14,920
i. Collected receivables	4,200	(4,200)										
Balances	13,720	1,900	8,400	240	8,500	12,000		240	16,800	1,800	11,000	14,920

STATEMENT OF CASH FLOWS

i. Operating	4,200

INCOME STATEMENT

Transaction Metric Effects

The effects of receiving $4,200 from insurance companies for payments on account on the liquidity and profitability metrics are as follows:

LIQUIDITY	
Quick Assets	No Effect

PROFITABILITY	
Net Income—Accrual Basis	No Effect

Since cash and accounts receivable are quick assets, the increase in cash and decrease in accounts receivable offset each other, with the result that there is no effect on quick assets.

Transaction j

Paid $100 on account for supplies that were purchased in transaction e.

The cash was paid for supplies purchased on account. Thus, this transaction decreases Cash and Accounts Payable by $100 under the Balance Sheet columns. Since the supplies are used in the normal operations of Family Health Care, cash flows from Operating activities is also decreased under the Statement of Cash Flows column.

The effects of transaction on Family Health Care's financial statements are recorded as follows.

Financial Statement Effects

BALANCE SHEET

	Assets						=	Liabilities			+ Stockholders' Equity	
	Cash +	Accts. Rec. +	Prepaid Insur.	+ Supp.	+ Office Equip.	+ Land	= Accts. Pay.	+ Notes Pay.	+ Unearned Revenue	+ Common Stock	+ Retained Earnings	
Balances	13,720	1,900	8,400	240	8,500	12,000	240	16,800	1,800	11,000	14,920	
j. Paid on acct.	(100)						(100)					
Balances	13,620	1,900	8,400	240	8,500	12,000	140	16,800	1,800	11,000	14,920	

STATEMENT OF CASH FLOWS	
j. Operating	(100)

INCOME STATEMENT

Transaction Metric Effects

The effects of paying $100 on accounts payable on the liquidity and profitability metrics are as follows:

LIQUIDITY	
Quick Assets	$(100)

PROFITABILITY	
Net Income—Accrual Basis	No Effect

Transaction k

Expenses paid during November were as follows: wages, $2,790; rent, $800; utilities, $580; interest, $100; and miscellaneous, $420.

This transaction is similar to the September and October expense transactions for Family Health Care. The effects of this transaction on Family Health Care's financial statements are recorded as follows.

Financial Statement Effects

BALANCE SHEET

	Cash	+ Accts. Rec.	+ Prepaid Insur.	+ Supp.	+ Office Equip.	+ Land	= Accts. Pay.	+ Notes Pay.	+ Unearned Revenue	+ Common Stock	+ Retained Earnings
	Assets						**= Liabilities**			**+ Stockholders' Equity**	
Balances	13,620	1,900	8,400	240	8,500	12,000	140	16,800	1,800	11,000	14,920
k. Paid expenses	(4,690)										(4,690)
Balances	8,930	1,900	8,400	240	8,500	12,000	140	16,800	1,800	11,000	10,230

STATEMENT OF CASH FLOWS

k. Operating	(4,690)

INCOME STATEMENT

k. Wages expense	(2,790)
Rent expense	(800)
Utilities expense	(580)
Interest expense	(100)
Misc. expense	(420)

Transaction Metric Effects

The effects of paying expenses of $4,690 on the liquidity and profitability metrics are as follows:

LIQUIDITY

Quick Assets	$(4,690)

PROFITABILITY

Net Income—Accrual Basis	$(4,690)

Transaction l

Paid dividends of $1,200 to stockholder (Dr. Landry).

This transaction is similar to Family Health Care's dividend transactions in September and October. The effects of this transaction on Family Health Care's financial statements are recorded as follows.

Financial Statement Effects

BALANCE SHEET

	Cash	+ Accts. Rec.	+ Prepaid Insur.	+ Supp.	+ Office Equip.	+ Land	= Accts. Pay.	+ Notes Pay.	+ Unearned Revenue	+ Common Stock	+ Retained Earnings
	Assets						**= Liabilities**			**+ Stockholders' Equity**	
Balances	8,930	1,900	8,400	240	8,500	12,000	140	16,800	1,800	11,000	10,230
l. Paid dividends	(1,200)										(1,200)
Balances	7,730	1,900	8,400	240	8,500	12,000	140	16,800	1,800	11,000	9,030

STATEMENT OF CASH FLOWS

l. Financing	(1,200)

INCOME STATEMENT

Transaction Metric Effects

The effects of paying $1,200 in dividends on liquidity and profitability metrics are as follows:

LIQUIDITY	
Quick Assets	$(1,200)

PROFITABILITY	
Net Income—Accrual Basis	No Effect

For a recent year, **Apple** paid dividends of $14,119 million.

Apple Connection

The Adjustment Process

Objective 3

Describe and illustrate the end-of-period adjustment process.

Accrual accounting requires the updating of the accounting records prior to preparing financial statements. This updating is called the **adjustment process**. The adjustment process is needed to match revenues and expenses, which is an application of the matching concept and the revenue and expense recognition principles.

Adjustments are necessary because, at any point in time, some accounts (elements) of the accounting equation are not up to date. For example, as time passes, prepaid insurance expires and supplies are used. However, it is not efficient to record the daily expiration of prepaid insurance or the daily use of supplies. Instead, the accounting records are normally updated just prior to preparing financial statements.

Family Health Care's September and October financial statements were prepared in Chapter 2 without recording any adjustments. This is because Family Health Care only entered into cash transactions in September and October. When all of a company's transactions are cash transactions, no adjustments are necessary.

During November, however, Family Health Care entered into several accrual transactions. As a result, Family Health must adjust its accounts before preparing financial statements.

Deferrals and Accruals

Two types of accounts require adjustments as follows:

- **Deferrals**, which are created by recording a transaction in a way that delays or defers the recognition of an expense or revenue.
- **Accruals**, which are created when a revenue or expense has been earned or incurred but has not been recorded.

Common deferrals include prepaid expenses and unearned revenues.

Prepaid expenses or **deferred expenses** are initially recorded as assets but become expenses over time or through normal operations of the business. For Family Health Care, prepaid insurance is an example of a deferral that requires adjustment. Other examples include supplies, prepaid advertising, and prepaid interest.

Unearned revenues or **deferred revenues** are initially recorded as liabilities but become revenues over time or through normal operations of the business. For Family Health Care, unearned rent is an example of a deferral that requires adjustment. Other examples include tuition received in advance, an attorney's annual retainer fee, insurance premiums received in advance, and magazine subscriptions received in advance.

On a recent balance sheet, **Apple** reported unearned revenue of over $8.1 billion as a liability, which includes cash received for Apple gift cards.

Common accruals include accrued expenses and accrued revenues. **Accrued expenses** or **accrued liabilities** are expenses that have been incurred but are not recorded in the accounts. For Family Health Care, unpaid wages at the end of November are an example of an accrued expense. Other examples include accrued interest, utility expenses, and taxes.

Accrued revenues or **accrued assets** are revenues that have been earned but are not recorded in the accounts. For Family Health Care, revenue for patient services that have been earned but not billed at the end of November is an example of accrued revenue. Other examples include accrued interest on notes receivable and accrued rent on property rented to others.

Deferrals are normally the result of cash being received or paid *before* the revenue is earned or the expense is incurred. In contrast, accruals are normally the result of cash being received or paid *after* revenue has been earned or an expense has been incurred. Exhibit 1 summarizes the nature of deferrals and accruals.

Exhibit 1
Deferrals and Accruals

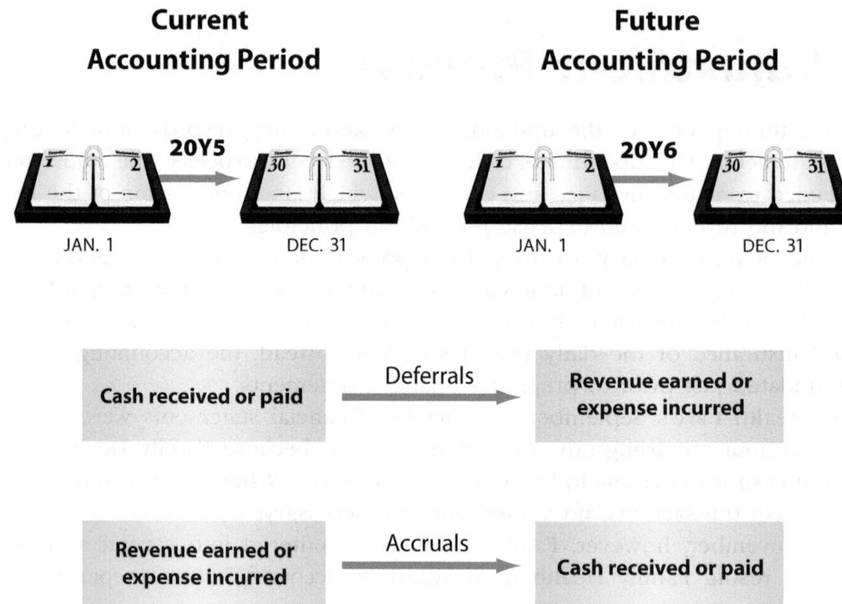

Integrity, Objectivity, and Ethics in Business

Dave's Legacy

When Dave Thomas, founder of **Wendy's (WEN)**, died in 2002, he left behind a corporate culture of integrity and high ethical conduct. When asked to comment on Dave's death, Jack Schuessler, chairman and chief executive officer of Wendy's, stated:

"People (could) relate to Dave, that he was honest and has integrity and he really cares about people.... There is no replacing Dave Thomas.... So you are left with ... the values that he gave us ... and you take care of the customer every day like Dave would want us to and good things will happen.

He's [Dave Thomas] taught us so much that when we get stuck, we can always look back and ask ourselves, how would Dave handle it?"

In a recent discussion of corporate earnings with analysts, Kerrii Anderson, then chief financial officer of Wendy's, stated: "We're confident about the future because of our unwavering commitment to our core values, such as quality food, superior restaurant operations, continuous improvement, and *integrity to doing the right thing* [emphasis added]."

Sources: Neil Cavuto, "Wendy's CEO—Interview," *Fox News: Your World*, February 11, 2002; "Q1 2003 Wendy's International Earnings Conference Call—Final," *Financial Disclosure Wire*, April 24, 2003.

Adjustments for Family Health Care

On November 30, 20Y5, the following adjustment data have been gathered for Family Health Care.

DEFERRALS

Deferred expenses:

a1. Prepaid insurance expired, $1,100.

a2. Supplies used, $150.

a3. Depreciation on office equipment, $160.

Deferred revenue:

a4. Unearned revenue earned, $360.

ACCRUALS

Accrued expense:

a5. Wages owed but not paid to employees, $220.

Accrued revenue:

a6. Services provided to patients but not billed to insurance companies, $750.

Adjustment a1

Prepaid insurance expired, $1,100.

During November, a portion of the prepaid insurance purchased on November 1 has expired. On November 1, Family Health Care paid for the following two policies:

1. General business policy for $2,400 (transaction b)
2. Malpractice policy for $6,000 (transaction c)

The general business policy is a two-year policy expiring at a rate of $100 ($2,400 ÷ 24) per month. The malpractice policy is a six-month policy that expires at a rate of $1,000 ($6,000 ÷ 6) per month. Thus, a total of $1,100 ($100 + $1,000) of prepaid insurance has expired by the end of November.

Adjustment a1 is recorded by decreasing the asset Prepaid Insurance and decreasing Retained Earnings under the Balance Sheet columns. In addition, Insurance expense under the Income Statement column is recorded as $(1,100). Since no cash was received or paid, no entries are necessary in the Statement of Cash Flows column.

The effects of Adjustment a1 on Family Health Care's financial statements are recorded as follows.

Financial Statement Effects

BALANCE SHEET

	Assets						=	Liabilities		+ Stockholders' Equity	
	Cash +	Accts. Rec. +	Prepaid Insur.	+ Supp. +	Office Equip. +	Land =	Accts. Pay. +	Notes Pay.	+ Unearned Revenue +	Common Stock +	Retained Earnings
Balances	7,730	1,900	8,400	240	8,500	12,000	140	16,800	1,800	11,000	9,030
a1. Insurance expense			(1,100)								(1,100)
Balances	7,730	1,900	7,300	240	8,500	12,000	140	16,800	1,800	11,000	7,930

STATEMENT OF CASH FLOWS

INCOME STATEMENT

a1. Insurance exp.	(1,100)

All adjustments affect the balance sheet and income statement, and thus, adjusting entries are recorded in the Balance Sheet and Income Statement columns. In contrast, *no adjustment* affects cash or the statement of cash flows, and thus, no adjusting entries are recorded in the Statement of Cash Flows column.

Adjustment Metric Effects

The effects of Adjustment a1 for $1,100 of expiring prepaid insurance on the liquidity and profitability metrics are as follows:

LIQUIDITY	
Quick Assets	No Effect

PROFITABILITY	
Net Income—Accrual Basis	$(1,100)

Prepaid insurance is not classified as a quick asset (cash or receivable).Thus, Adjustment a1 has no effect on quick assets. All adjustments will affect net income, and since insurance expense is increased by $1,100, net income decreases by $(1,100).

Adjustment a2

Supplies used, $150.

For November, supplies of $150 were used. This leaves $90 ($240 − $150) of supplies on hand as of November 30.

Adjustment a2 is recorded by decreasing the asset Supplies and decreasing Retained Earnings under the Balance Sheet columns. In addition, Supplies expense under the Income Statement column is recorded as $(150).

The effects of Adjustment a2 on Family Health Care's financial statements are recorded as follows:

Financial Statement Effects

BALANCE SHEET

	Assets						=	Liabilities		+ Stockholders' Equity		
	Cash +	Accts. Rec. +	Prepaid Insur.	+ Supp.	+ Office Equip.	+ Land	= Accts. Pay.	+ Notes Pay.	+ Unearned Revenue	+ Common Stock	+ Retained Earnings
Balances	7,730	1,900	7,300	240	8,500	12,000	140	16,800	1,800	11,000	7,930
a2. Supplies expense				(150)							(150)
Balances	7,730	1,900	7,300	90	8,500	12,000	140	16,800	1,800	11,000	7,780

STATEMENT OF CASH FLOWS

INCOME STATEMENT

a2. Supplies exp.	(150)

Adjustment Metric Effects

The effects of Adjustment a2 for $150 of supplies used on the liquidity and profitability metrics are as follows:

LIQUIDITY	
Quick Assets	No Effect

PROFITABILITY	
Net Income—Accrual Basis	$(150)

Supplies are not a quick asset and thus, there is no effect on the liquidity metric. Since supplies expense increases, the profitability metric Net Income—Accrual Basis decreases.

Adjustment a3

Depreciation on office equipment, $160.

Fixed assets such as office equipment lose their ability to provide service over time. This reduction in the ability of a fixed asset to provide service is called **depreciation**. However, it is difficult to objectively determine the physical decline in a fixed asset's ability to provide service. For this reason, depreciation is estimated based on the asset's useful life. Methods of estimating depreciation are covered in Chapter 7. In this chapter, the November depreciation for the office equipment is assumed to be $160.

A record of the initial cost of a fixed asset must be maintained for tax and other purposes. For this reason, the fixed asset account is not reduced directly for depreciation. Instead, an offsetting or *contra asset account*, called **accumulated depreciation**, is added to the Balance Sheet columns. On the balance sheet, the accumulated depreciation is subtracted from the cost of the fixed asset.

Adjustment a3 is recorded in the Accumulated Depreciation (Acc. Dep.) column under Assets in the Balance Sheet columns as $(160). Retained Earnings is also decreased under the Balance Sheet columns by $(160). In addition, Depreciation expense under the Income Statement column is recorded as $(160).

The effects of Adjustment a3 on Family Health Care's financial statements are recorded as follows.

Financial Statement Effects

BALANCE SHEET

	Assets							=	Liabilities			+ Stockholders' Equity	
	Cash +	Accts. Rec. +	Prepaid Insur. +	Supp. +	Office Equip. –	Acc. Depr. +	Land	=	Accts. Pay. +	Notes Pay. +	Unearned Revenue +	Common Stock +	Retained Earnings
Balances	7,730	1,900	7,300	90	8,500		12,000		140	16,800	1,800	11,000	7,780
a3. Depr. exp.						(160)							(160)
Balances	7,730	1,900	7,300	90	8,500	(160)	12,000		140	16,800	1,800	11,000	7,620

STATEMENT OF CASH FLOWS

INCOME STATEMENT

a3. Depreciation exp.	(160)

Three other points related to depreciation are:

1. Land is not depreciated, because it usually does not lose its ability to provide service.
2. The cost of the equipment is a type of deferred expense that is recognized as an expense over the fixed asset's useful life.
3. The cost of the fixed asset less the balance of its accumulated depreciation is called the asset's **book value**, or *carrying value*. For example, the book value of Family Health Care's office equipment, after the preceding adjustment, is $8,340 ($8,500 – $160).

Apple Connection

On a recent balance sheet, **Apple** reported property, plant, and equipment of $95,957 million and accumulated depreciation of $58,579 million for a book value of $37,378 million.

Adjustment Metric Effects

The effects of Adjustment a3 for depreciation of $160 on the liquidity and profitability metrics are as follows:

LIQUIDITY	
Quick Assets	No Effect

PROFITABILITY	
Net Income—Accrual Basis	$(160)

Adjustment a4

Unearned revenue earned, $360.

This adjustment recognizes that a portion of the unearned revenue is earned by the end of November. That is, of the $1,800 received for rental of the land for five months (November through March), one-fifth, or $360, would have been earned as of November 30.

Adjustment a4 is recorded by decreasing the liability Unearned Revenue by $360 and increasing Retained Earnings by $360 under the Balance Sheet columns. In addition, Rent revenue is increased by $360 under the Income Statement column.

The effects of Adjustment a4 on Family Health Care's financial statements are recorded as follows.

Financial Statement Effects

BALANCE SHEET

	Assets							=	Liabilities			+ Stockholders' Equity	
	Cash +	Accts. Rec. +	Prepaid Insur.	+ Supp. +	Office Equip. −	Acc. Depr. +	Land	=	Accts. Pay. +	Notes Pay.	+ Unearned Revenue +	Common Stock	+ Retained Earnings
Balances	7,730	1,900	7,300	90	8,500	(160)	12,000		140	16,800	1,800	11,000	7,620
a4. Rent rev.											(360)		360
Balances	7,730	1,900	7,300	90	8,500	(160)	12,000		140	16,800	1,440	11,000	7,980

STATEMENT OF CASH FLOWS

INCOME STATEMENT

a4. Rent revenue	360

Adjustment Metric Effects

The effects of Adjustment a4 for rent earned of $360 on the liquidity and profitability metrics are as follows:

LIQUIDITY	
Quick Assets	No Effect

PROFITABILITY	
Net Income—Accrual Basis	$360

Adjustment a5

Wages owed but not paid to employees, $220.

It is rare that employees are paid the same day that the accounting period ends. Thus, at the end of an accounting period, it is normal for businesses to owe wages to their employees.

Adjustment a5 recognizes that as of November 30, employees of Family Health Care have not been paid $220 for work they have performed. This adjustment is recorded by increasing the liability Wages Payable by $220 and decreasing Retained Earnings by $220 under the Balance Sheet columns. In addition, Wages expense under the Income Statement column is recorded as $(220).

Financial Statement Effects

BALANCE SHEET

	Assets							=	Liabilities				+ Stockholders' Equity	
	Cash +	Accts. Rec. +	Prepaid Insur. +	Supp. +	Office Equip. −	Acc. Depr. +	Land	=	Accts. Pay. +	Wages Pay. +	Notes Pay. +	Unearned Revenue +	Common Stock +	Retained Earnings
Balances	7,730	1,900	7,300	90	8,500	(160)	12,000		140		16,800	1,440	11,000	7,980
a5. Wages exp.										220				(220)
Balances	7,730	1,900	7,300	90	8,500	(160)	12,000		140	220	16,800	1,440	11,000	7,760

STATEMENT OF CASH FLOWS

INCOME STATEMENT

a5. Wages expense	(220)

Adjustment Metric Effects

The effects of Adjustment a5 for accrued wages of $220 on the liquidity and profitability metrics are as follows:

LIQUIDITY

Quick Assets	No Effect

PROFITABILITY

Net Income—Accrual Basis	$(220)

Apple has more than 137,000 full-time equivalent employees. *Apple Connection*

Adjustment a6

Services provided but not billed to insurance companies, $750.

This adjustment recognizes that Family Health Care has provided services of $750 to patients who have not yet been billed. Such services are usually provided near the end of the month.

This adjustment is recorded by increasing the asset Accounts Receivable (Accts. Rec.) and increasing Retained Earnings by $750 under the Balance Sheet columns. In addition, Fees earned under the Income Statement column is recorded as $750.

The effects of Adjustment a6 on Family Health Care's financial statements are as follows.

Financial Statement Effects

BALANCE SHEET

	Assets							=	Liabilities				+ Stockholders' Equity	
	Cash +	Accts. Rec. +	Prepaid Insur.	+ Supp.	+ Office Equip.	– Acc. Depr.	+ Land	= Accts. Pay.	+ Wages Pay.	+ Notes Pay.	+ Unearned Revenue	+ Common Stock	+ Retained Earnings	
Balances	7,730	1,900	7,300	90	8,500	(160)	12,000	140	220	16,800	1,440	11,000	7,760	
a6. Fees earned		750											750	
Balances	7,730	2,650	7,300	90	8,500	(160)	12,000	140	220	16,800	1,440	11,000	8,510	

STATEMENT OF CASH FLOWS

INCOME STATEMENT

a6. Fees earned	750

Adjustment Metric Effects

The effects of Adjustment a6 for fees earned but unbilled of $750 on the liquidity and profitability metrics are as follows:

LIQUIDITY	
Quick Assets	$750

PROFITABILITY	
Net Income—Accrual Basis	$750

Since Adjustment 6a increases accounts receivable by $750, the liquidity metric Quick Assets increases by $750. The profitability metric Net Income—Accrual Basis also increases for the fees earned of $750.

The November transactions and adjustments for Family Health Care are summarized in Exhibit 2. The net effects of November's transactions and adjustments on the Family Health Care's liquidity and profitability metrics are also shown in Exhibit 3.

Objective 4

Prepare financial statements using accrual concepts of accounting, including a classified balance sheet.

Financial Statements

Based on the summary of transactions and adjustments shown in Exhibit 2, Family Health Care's financial statements for November are described and illustrated in this section. These financial statements are shown in Exhibits 4, 5, 6, and 7.

Exhibit 2 Family Health Care's Summary of Transactions and Adjustments for November

Financial Statement Effects

BALANCE SHEET

	Assets							=	Liabilities			+ Stockholders' Equity	
	Cash	+ Accts. Rec.	+ Prepaid Insur.	+ Supp.	+ Office Equip.	– Acc. Depr.	+ Land	= Notes Pay.	+ Accts. Pay.	+ Wages Pay.	+ Unearned Revenue	+ Common Stock	+ Retained Earnings
Balances, Nov. 1	7,320						12,000	10,000				6,000	3,320
a. Received rent	1,800										1,800		
b. Paid insurancec	(2,400)		2,400										
c. Paid insurance	(6,000)		6,000										
d. Issued stock	5,000											5,000	
e. Pur. supplies				240					240				
f. Pur. off. equip.	(1,700)				8,500			6,800					
g. Fees earned		6,100											6,100
h. Fees earned	5,500												5,500
i. Collected rec.	4,200	(4,200)											
j. Paid on acct.	(100)								(100)				
k. Paid expenses	(4,690)												(4,690)
l. Dividends	(1,200)												(1,200)
a1. Insurance exp.			(1,100)										(1,100)
a2. Supplies exp.				(150)									(150)
a3. Depr. exp.						(160)							(160)
a4. Rent revenue											(360)		360
a5. Wages exp.										220			(220)
a6. Fees earned		750											750
Balances Nov. 30	7,730	2,650	7,300	90	8,500	(160)	12,000	16,800	140	220	1,440	11,000	8,510

STATEMENT OF CASH FLOWS

a. Operating	1,800
b. Operating	(2,400)
c. Operating	(6,000)
d. Financing	5,000
f. Investing	(1,700)
h. Operating	5,500
i. Operating	4,200
j. Operating	(100)
k. Operating	(4,690)
l. Financing	(1,200)
Increase in cash	410
Nov. 1 cash bal.	7,320
Nov. 30 cash bal.	7,730

INCOME STATEMENT

g. Fees earned	6,100
h. Fees earned	5,500
k. Wages expense	(2,790)
Rent expense	(800)
Utilities expense	(580)
Interest expense	(100)
Misc. expense	(420)
a1. Insurance expense	(1,100)
a2. Supplies expense	(150)
a3. Depreciation expense	(160)
a4. Rent revenue	360
a5. Wages expense	(220)
a6. Fees earned	750
Net income	6,390

Exhibit 3 Family Health Care's Summary of Metric Effects for November

LIQUIDITY	
Transaction and Adjustments	**Quick Assets**
a. Received rent	$1,800
b. Paid insurance	(2,400)
c. Paid insurance	(6,000)
d. Issued stock	5,000
e. Purchased supplies	–
f. Purchased office equipment	(1,700)
g. Fees earned	6,100
h. Fees earned	5,500
i. Collected receivable	–
j. Paid on account	(100)
k. Paid expenses	(4,690)
l. Paid dividends	(1,200)
Adjustments	
Adj. a1. Insurance expense	–
Adj. a2. Supplies expense	–
Adj. a3. Depr. expense	–
Adj. a4. Rent revenue	–
Adj. a5. Wages expense	–
Adj. a6. Fees earned	750
Total	$3,060

PROFITABILITY	
	Net Income—Accrual Basis
a. Received rent	–
b. Paid insurance	–
c. Paid insurance	–
d. Issued stock	–
e. Purchased supplies	–
f. Purchased office equipment	–
g. Fees earned	$6,100
h. Fees earned	5,500
i. Collected receivable	–
j. Paid on account	–
k. Paid expenses	(4,690)
l. Paid dividends	–
Adjustments	
Adj. a1. Insurance expense	(1,100)
Adj. a2. Supplies expense	(150)
Adj. a3. Depr. expense	(160)
Adj. a4. Rent revenue	360
Adj. a5. Wages expense	(220)
Adj. a6. Fees earned	750
Total	$6,390

Quick Assets increased by $3,060 and Net Income—Accrual Basis was $6,390 for November. The net income of $6,390 will be reported on Family Health Care's November income statement.

Income Statement

The income statement is shown in Exhibit 4. It is prepared by summarizing the revenue and expense transactions listed under the Income Statement column of Exhibit 2.

Revenues are a result of providing services or selling products to customers. Examples of revenues include fees earned, fares earned, commissions revenue, interest revenue, and rent revenue.

Revenues from the primary operations of the business are reported separately from other revenue. For example, Family Health Care has two types of revenues for November fees earned and rent revenue. Since the primary operation of the business is providing services to patients, rent revenue is reported under the heading of "Other revenue."

Expenses are assets used up or services consumed in the process of generating revenues. Expenses are matched against their related revenues to determine the net income or net loss for a period. Examples of typical expenses include wages expense, rent expense,

Exhibit 4 Family Health Care's Income Statement for November

Family Health Care, P.C. Income Statement For the Month Ended November 30, 20Y5		
Fees earned		$12,350
Operating expenses:		
Wages expense	$3,010	
Insurance expense	1,100	
Rent expense	800	
Utilities expense	580	
Depreciation expense	160	
Supplies expense	150	
Interest expense	100	
Miscellaneous expense	420	
Total operating expenses		(6,320)
Operating income		$ 6,030
Other revenue:		
Rent revenue		360
Net income		$ 6,390

utilities expense, supplies expense, and miscellaneous expense. Expenses are normally listed on the income statement from largest to smallest except for miscellaneous expense, which is always listed last. Expenses not related to the primary operations of the business are reported as "Other expenses."

Operating income is determined by deducting the operating expenses from the fees earned. Family Health Care has operating income of $6,030 in November. Other income consisting of $360 in rental revenue is then added to determine the net income for November of $6,390.

On a recent income statement, **Apple** reported operating income of $63,930 million and net income of $55,256 million.

Apple Connection

Statement of Stockholders' Equity

The statement of stockholders' equity shown in Exhibit 5 is prepared by adding the common stock issued in transaction d of $5,000 to the November 1 balance of common stock of $6,000. This yields the November 30 balance of common stock of $11,000. The November net income of $6,390 (from the income statement), less dividends of $1,200, added to the November 1 balance of retained earnings of $3,320 results in the November 30 retained earnings of $8,510. The November 30 balances of common stock and retained earnings are also reported on Family Health Care's November 30, 20Y5, balance sheet.

On a recent statement of stockholders' equity, **Apple** reported common stock of $45,174 million, retained earnings of $45,898 million, other equity items of $(584) million, and total stockholders' equity of $90.488 million.

Apple Connection

Exhibit 5 Family Health Care's Statement of Stockholders' Equity for November

Family Health Care, P.C.
Statement of Stockholders' Equity
For the Month Ended November 30, 20Y5

	Common Stock	Retained Earnings	Total
Balances, Nov. 1, 20Y5	$ 6,000	$3,320	$ 9,320
Issued common stock	5,000		5,000
Net income		6,390	6,390
Dividends		(1,200)	(1,200)
Balances, Nov. 30, 20Y5	$11,000	$8,510	$19,510

Balance Sheet

The balance sheet shown in Exhibit 6 is prepared from the ending balances shown in the Balance Sheet columns of Exhibit 2. The balance sheet shown in Exhibit 6 is a **classified balance sheet**. As the term implies, a classified balance sheet is prepared with various sections, subsections, and captions.

Exhibit 6 Family Health Care's Balance Sheet for November

Family Health Care, P.C.
Balance Sheet
November 30, 20Y5

Assets			
Current assets:			
Cash		$ 7,730	
Accounts receivable		2,650	
Prepaid insurance		7,300	
Supplies		90	
Total current assets			$17,770
Fixed assets:			
Office equipment	$8,500		
Less accumulated depreciation	(160)	$ 8,340	
Land		12,000	
Total fixed assets			20,340
Total assets			$38,110
Liabilities			
Current liabilities:			
Accounts payable		$ 140	
Wages payable		220	
Notes payable		6,800	
Unearned revenue		1,440	
Total current liabilities			$ 8,600
Long-term liabilities:			
Notes payable			10,000
Total liabilities			$18,600
Stockholders' Equity			
Common stock		$11,000	
Retained earnings		8,510	
Total stockholders' equity			19,510
Total liabilities and stockholders' equity			$38,110

A classified balance sheet normally reports assets as the following:

- Current assets
- Fixed assets
- Intangible assets

Current assets are cash and other assets that are expected to be converted to cash or sold or used up within one year or less, through normal operations. In addition to cash, the current assets normally include accounts receivable, notes receivable, supplies, and prepaid expenses.

Accounts receivable and notes receivable are current assets because they are normally converted to cash within one year or less. **Notes receivable** are written claims against debtors who promise to pay the amount of the note plus interest. From the creditor's point of view, a note receivable is a note payable.

Exhibit 6 indicates that Family Health Care has current assets of cash, accounts receivable, prepaid insurance, and supplies as of November 30, 20Y5. These current assets total $17,770.

Fixed assets are physical assets of a long-term nature. The fixed assets may also be reported on the balance sheet as *property, plant, and equipment* or *plant assets.* Fixed assets include equipment, machinery, buildings, and land. Except for land, fixed assets depreciate over a period of time. The cost less accumulated depreciation for each major type of fixed asset is normally reported on the classified balance sheet.

Exhibit 6 indicates that Family Health Care has fixed assets of office equipment and land. The book value, cost less accumulated depreciation, of the office equipment is $8,340. The land is reported at its cost of $12,000, which when added to the book value of the office equipment yields total fixed assets of $20,340.

Intangible assets represent rights of a long-term nature, such as patent rights, copyrights, and goodwill. Goodwill arises from such factors as name recognition, location, product quality, reputation, and managerial skill. Goodwill is recorded and reported on the balance sheet when a company purchases another company at a price above the normal market value of the purchased company's assets. Family Health Care has no intangible assets.

On a recent balance sheet, **Apple** reported current assets of $162,819 million and property, plant, and equipment of $37,378 million.

Apple Connection

A classified balance sheet normally reports liabilities as:

1. Current liabilities
2. Long-term liabilities

Current liabilities are due within a short time (usually one year or less) and are to be paid out of current assets. Common current liabilities include accounts payable and notes payable. Other current liabilities include wages payable, interest payable, taxes payable, and unearned revenue.

Exhibit 6 indicates that Family Health Care has total current liabilities of $8,600 that include accounts payable, wages payable, and notes payable. Unearned revenue (rent) is also reported as a current liability, since the revenue has not yet been earned.

Long-term liabilities are not due for a long time (usually more than one year). Long-term liabilities are reported following the current liabilities.

As long-term liabilities come due and are to be paid within one year, they are reported as current liabilities. If they are to be renewed rather than paid, they would continue to be classified as long term. When an asset is pledged as security for a long-term liability, the obligation may be called a *mortgage note payable* or a *mortgage payable.*

On a recent balance sheet, **Apple** reported current liabilities of $105,718 million and long-term debt of $91,807 million.

Apple Connection

Exhibit 2 indicates that Family Health Care has total notes payable of $16,800. Of these notes, $10,000 is not due until 20Y9 and is thus reported as a long-term liability in Exhibit 6. The note payable of $6,800 is due within the next year and is reported as a current liability in Exhibit 6.

A classified balance sheet normally reports stockholders' equity as:

1. Common stock, which has been invested in the company by the stockholders
2. Retained earnings, which is net income that has been retained in the corporation

Exhibit 6 reports common stock of $11,000 and the retained earnings of $8,510. These amounts are the November 30 balances for common stock and retained earnings reported on the statement of stockholders' equity in Exhibit 6.

Statement of Cash Flows

The statement of cash flows shown in Exhibit 7 is prepared by summarizing the November cash transactions. These cash transactions are shown in the Statement of Cash Flows column of Exhibit 2.

The *Cash flows from operating activities* section is prepared from the Statement of Cash Flows column of Exhibit 2 by summarizing the *Operating* activity transactions. The cash receipts from revenue transactions are added, and the cash payments for operating transactions are subtracted to determine the cash flows from operating activities.

Exhibit 7 indicates that the cash received from revenue transactions consists of $9,700 ($5,500 + $4,200) received from patients and $1,800 received from rental of the land. The cash payments for operating transactions of $13,190 ($2,400 + $6,000 + $100 + $4,690) is determined by adding the negative cash payments for operating activities shown in Exhibit 2.

The *Cash flows from investing activities* is prepared from the Statement of Cash Flows column of Exhibit 2 by summarizing the *Investing* activity transactions. During November, Family Health Care has only one investing transaction of $1,700 for the purchase of office equipment.

The *Cash flows from financing activities* section is prepared from the Statement of Cash Flows column of Exhibit 2 by summarizing the *Financing* activity transactions. During November, Family Health Care received an additional investment from Dr. Landry of $5,000 and paid dividends of $1,200.

Exhibit 7 Family Health Care's Statement of Cash Flows for November

Family Health Care, P.C.
Statement of Cash Flows
For the Month Ended November 30, 20Y5

Cash flows from (used for) operating activities:		
Cash received from patients	$ 9,700	
Cash received from rental of land	1,800	
Cash paid for expenses	(13,190)	
Net cash flows used for operating activities		$ (1,690)
Cash flows from (used for) investing activities:		
Cash paid for office equipment		(1,700)
Cash flows from (used for) financing activities:		
Cash received from issuing common stock	$ 5,000	
Cash paid as dividends	(1,200)	
Net cash flows from financing activities		3,800
Net increase in cash during November		$ 410
Cash as of November 1, 20Y5		7,320
Cash as of November 30, 20Y5		$ 7,730

On a recent statement of cash flows, **Apple** reported net cash flows from operating activities of $69,391 million, net cash flows from investing activities of $45,896 million, and net cash flows used in financing activities of $(90,976) million for a net increase in cash of $24,311 million.

Integration of Financial Statements

Exhibit 8 shows the integration of Family Health Care's financial statements for November. The reconciliation of net income and net cash flows from operations is shown in the appendix at the end of this chapter.

Exhibit 8 Family Health Care's Integrated Financial Statements for November

Family Health Care, P.C.
Balance Sheet
November 30, 20Y5

Assets			=	Liabilities	+	Stockholders' Equity		
Cash	+	Noncash Assets	=			Common Stock	+	Retained Earnings
$7,730		$30,380		$18,600		$11,000		$8,510
$38,110 Total Assets			=	$38,110 Total Liabilities + Stockholders' Equity				

Family Health Care, P.C.
Statement of Cash Flows
For the Month Ended Nov. 30, 20Y5

Operating act.	$(1,690)
Investing act.	(1,700)
Financing act.	3,800
Increase in cash	$ 410
Cash, Nov. 1	7,320
Cash, Nov. 30	$ 7,730

Family Health Care, P.C.
Income Statement
For the Month Ended Nov. 30, 20Y5

Revenues	$12,350
Expenses	(6,320)
Operating income	$ 6,030
Other revenue	360
Net income	$ 6,390

Family Health Care, P.C.
Statement of Stockholders' Equity
For the Month Ended Nov. 30, 20Y5

	Common Stock	Retained Earnings	Total
Bal. Nov. 1	$ 6,000	$3,320	$ 9,320
Issued common stock	5,000		5,000
Net income		6,390	6,390
Dividends		(1,200)	(1,200)
Bal. Nov. 30	$11,000	$8,510	$19,510

Objective 5
Describe why generally accepted accounting principles (GAAP) require the accrual basis of accounting.

Accrual and Cash Bases of Accounting

The accrual basis of accounting was used in this chapter to record Family Health Care's November transactions. The accrual basis of accounting is required by generally accepted accounting principles (GAAP) and is used by large corporations whose stock is publicly traded, such as **Alphabet (GOOG)**. Understanding why the accrual basis of accounting is required by generally accepted accounting principles (GAAP)is essential for your ability to analyze and evaluate financial statements.

To understand why the accrual basis of accounting is required, it is first necessary to consider the alternative. The primary alternative to GAAP is the **cash basis of accounting**, which records transactions only when cash is received or paid.[1] For example, revenue is recorded when cash is received from a customer regardless of when the services or goods have been provided or delivered. Likewise, expenses are recorded when the cash is paid regardless of when the related revenues are recorded. In other words, revenues and expenses are reported on the income statement in the period in which cash is received or paid.

All of Family Health Care's September and October transactions involved the receipt or payment of cash. As a result, the financial statements shown in Exhibit 4 and Exhibit 7 in Chapter 2 are the same under the cash and accrual bases of accounting.

In November, however, Family Health Care entered into accrual accounting transactions. For example, in November Family Health Care purchased supplies on account (transaction e) and provided services to patients on account (transaction g). Additional accruals and deferrals were created by Family Health Care's November transactions that required updating using the adjustment process (adjustments a1 through a6).[2] As a result, Family Health Care's November financial statements differ significantly under the cash and accrual bases.

To illustrate, the November and October income statements for Family Health Care under the accrual and cash bases of accounting are shown in summary form in Exhibit 9. Exhibit 9 shows that the October income statements for the accrual and cash bases are the same and report net income of $3,220.[3] The November income statements, however, differ significantly.

Using Data Analytics

Transforming Data

When a company uses data analytics to solve a problem, it must not only extract relevant data but also transform the raw data. *Transforming* raw data involves the process of cleansing and assembling the extracted data into a data set. Extracted data may include erroneous or missing data, including values that are not meaningful, such as outliers. The process of transforming the data evaluates, resolves, and "cleans" the data of erroneous and missing values. Once the extracted data are cleansed, they are combined into a data set for analysis.

The data analytic process of transforming data is similar to the adjusting process that is described and illustrated in this chapter. For example, the unadjusted accounts must be transformed (updated) into adjusted accounts. In addition, the accounts must be evaluated (cleansed) for any erroneous or missing accounts. For example, a credit balance in Supplies indicates an error.

1. Some companies use a *modified cash basis of accounting*, which includes "some" accrual accounting. The modified cash basis of accounting is discussed in advanced accounting courses.
2. Because the cash basis does not record accruals or deferrals, there is no adjustment process under the cash basis of accounting.
3. Net income (loss) under the cash basis is the same as the amount reported for net cash flows from (used for) operating activities on the statement of cash flows, as shown in Exhibit 7 for November.

Exhibit 9 Accrual- and Cash-Basis Income Statements for November and October

Family Health Care, P.C.
Income Statements

Accrual Basis of Accounting

	November	October	Increase (Decrease)
Revenue	$12,710	$6,400	$6,310
Operating expenses	(6,320)	(3,180)	3,140
Net income (loss)	$ 6,390	$3,220	3,170

Cash Basis of Accounting

	November	October	Increase (Decrease)
Revenue	$11,500	$6,400	$5,100
Operating expenses	(13,190)	(3,180)	10,010
Net income (loss)	$(1,690)	$3,220	(4,910)

Why the Accrual Basis Is Required by GAAP

Exhibit 9 illustrates why the accrual basis of accounting is required by GAAP. Under the accrual basis, Family Health Care's income statements indicate favorable changes from October. Specifically, revenue almost doubled from $6,400 in October to $12,710 in November, a change of $6,310. While revenue increased by $6,310, operating expenses increased by only $3,140. As a result, Family Health Care's net income almost doubled from $3,220 in October to $6,390 in November. These results suggest that Family Health Care is a profitable, rapidly expanding business.

In contrast, under the cash basis, Family Health Care's income statements indicate several unfavorable changes and raise concerns about Family Health Care's future. Specifically, while revenue increased by $5,100, from $6,400 in October to $11,500 in November, operating expenses increased almost twice as fast from $3,180 to $13,190, a change of $10,010. As a result, Family Health Care reported a net loss of $(1,690) in November, a decline in profitability of $4,910 or over 150% ($4,910 ÷ $3,220) from October. These results suggest that Family Health Care is in trouble and may not be able to continue without major changes to its operations.

Exhibit 9 shows that the accrual basis better reports the underlying operating performance of Family Health Care's November operations. It does this by better matching revenues and expenses using the revenue and expense recognition principles. This is why accrual accounting is required by generally accepted accounting principles (GAAP).

The Accounting Cycle

The **accounting cycle** is the process that begins with analyzing transactions and ends with preparing financial statements. Using the integrated financial statement framwork, the accounting cycle for the cash basis of accounting consists of the following two steps:

1. Identify, analyze, and record the effects each *cash transaction* on the balances sheet, statement of cash flows, and income statement elements (accounts).
2. Prepare financial statements.

The preceding steps for Family Health Care's September and October transactions were illustrated in Chapter 2.

Using the integrated financial statement framework, the accounting cycle for the accrual basis of accounting consists of the following three steps:

1. Using the matching concept, including the revenue and expense recognition principles, identify, analyze, and record the effects each transaction on the balances sheet, statement of cash flows, and income statement elements (accounts).
2. Assemble adjustment data and record end-of-the period adjustments.
3. Prepare financial statements.

The preceding steps for Family Health Care's November transactions were illustrated in this chapter. The Illustrative Problem at the end of this chapter illustrates these steps for Family Health Care's December transactions.

When using the integrated financial statement framework for recording transactions, the balances of the Balance Sheet columns carry forward from period to period. In contrast, the Statement of Cash Flows and Income Statement columns begin each period with no amounts or balances. This is because the statement of cash flows and income statement report the company's performance for each period independent of other periods. The balance sheet, however, reports the cumulative results of the company's performance on its financial condition.

Advanced accounting systems use a double-entry accounting system where transactions are recorded separate accounts using rules of debit and credit. The accounting cycle for a double-entry accounting system is more complex and involves more steps than the integrated financial statement framework.[4]

The double-entry accounting system is taught in accounting courses where the focus is on the mechanics of recording transactions and preparing financial statements. This focus is especially relevant for accounting majors. In contrast, we use the integrated financial statement framework to focus more on the effects of transactions on financial statements and metrics used to assess a company's performance and condition.

Objective 6
Describe and illustrate the use of the quick ratio in assessing a company's liquidity.

Metric-Based Analysis: Quick Ratio

An important aspect of a company's financial condition is its ability to pay its short-term liabilities as they become due. The liquidity metric Quick Assets measures the "amount" of cash and other assets that a company has on hand to pay its current liabilities. The quick ratio is a related metric used to assess a company's ability to pay its current liabilities.

The **quick ratio** is computed as quick assets divided by current liabilities. The quick ratio is a better metric than quick assets for comparing companies because, as a ratio, it eliminates the effect of size differences among companies.

To illustrate, the following data for Fly Creek Company and Huron Inc. are used.

	Fly Creek Company	Huron Inc.
Current assets:		
Cash	$ 60,000	$ 120,000
Accounts receivable	120,000	600,000
Inventories	202,000	300,000
Prepaid assets	18,000	60,000
Total current assets	$400,000	$1,080,000
Current liabilities	$150,000	$ 800,000

4. A double-entry accounting system is described and illustrated in Appendix C at the end of this text.

Fly Creek Company has $180,000 ($60,000 + $120,00) of quick assets compared to Huron Inc.'s quick assets of $720,000 ($120,000 + $600,000). Since Huron has four times ($720,000 ÷ $180,000) the amount of quick assets as Fly Creek, it would appear that Huron is in a stronger liquidity position.

However, the quick ratios for each company differ significantly, as shown below.

Fly Creek Company:

$$\text{Quick Ratio} = \frac{\text{Quick Assets}}{\text{Current Liabilities}} = \frac{(\$60{,}000 + \$120{,}000)}{\$150{,}000} = \frac{\$180{,}000}{\$150{,}000} = 1.2$$

Huron Inc.:

$$\text{Quick Ratio} = \frac{\text{Quick Assets}}{\text{Current Liabilities}} = \frac{(\$120{,}000 + \$600{,}000)}{\$800{,}000} = \frac{\$720{,}000}{\$800{,}000} = 0.9$$

The quick ratios indicate that Fly Creek is in a stronger liquidity position than Huron Inc. Huron's quick ratio of less than 1.0 raises concerns as to whether it will be able to pay its current liabilities on time.

Although quick ratios vary by industry, a quick ratio of at least 1.0 is normal. A quick ratio of less than 1.0, such as Huron Inc.'s ratio of 0.9, raises liquidity concerns for creditors.

Appendix

Reconciliation: Net Cash Flows from (Used for) Operating Activities and Net Income[5]

As shown in Exhibit 9, long-run profitability is best analyzed using accrual accounting and net income. The ability of the company to pay debts as they become due is best analyzed using net cash flows from operating activities. For example, in the long run, a business cannot survive if it continually reports negative cash flows from operating activities. This is true even though the company may report net income. In other words, a business *must* generate positive cash flows from operating activities in the long term in order to survive. For this reason, generally accepted accounting principles (GAAP) require reporting net cash flows from (used for) operating activities as well as net income. This illustrates why financial statements must be analyzed and interpreted together rather than individually. This is the primary reason the integrated financial statement approach is used throughout this text.

Because both net income and net cash flows from operations are important for analyzing and interpreting financial statements, this appendix examines the relationship between the two. We do this using the financial statements of Family Health Care.

Chapter 2 illustrates the financial statements for Family Health Care for September and October 20Y5. Because all the September and October transactions were cash transactions, the net cash flows from operating activities shown on the statement of cash flows equals the net income shown on the income statements as follows:

	Net Cash Flows from Operating Activities	Net Income
September (cash basis)	$2,600	$2,600
October (cash basis)	3,220	3,220

When all of a company's transactions are cash transactions or when a company uses the cash basis of accounting, net cash flows from operating activities always equals net income. This is not true, however, under the accrual basis of accounting.

During November and December, Family Health Care used the accrual basis of accounting. The November financial statements are illustrated in Exhibits 4 through 7 of this

5. This reconciliation is referred to as the indirect method of reporting cash flows from (used for) operating activities.

chapter. The December financial statements for Family Health Care are illustrated in the Illustrative Problem at the end of this chapter. The net cash flows from (used for) operating activities and net income for November and December are as follows.

	Net Cash Flows from (Used for) Operating Activities	Net Income
November (Accrual basis)	$(1,690)	$ 6,390
December (Accrual basis)	8,760	10,825

As shown, net cash flows from (used for) operating activities will normally not be the same as net income under accrual accounting. Any difference can be reconciled by considering the effects of deferrals and accruals on the income statement.

Exhibit 10 illustrates the November reconciliation of Family Health Care's net income with net cash flows used for operating activities.

Exhibit 10 November's Reconciliation of Net Income and Net Cash Flows Used for Operating Activities

Net income		$ 6,390
Depreciation expense	$ 160	
Changes in noncash current operating assets and liabilities:		
Increase in accounts receivable	(2,650)	
Increase in prepaid insurance	(7,300)	
Increase in supplies	(90)	
Increase in accounts payable	140	
Increase in wages payable	220	
Increase in unearned revenue	1,440	(8,080)
Net cash flows used for operating activities		$(1,690)

Exhibit 10 begins with net income and then adds or deducts the effects of accruals or deferrals that affect net income but do not result in the receipt or payment of cash. By doing so, Exhibit 10 ends with net cash flows used for operating activities.

The effect of an accrual or deferral on net income is a net increase or decrease during the period. For example, during November, depreciation expense of $160 was recorded (a deferred expense) and thus deducted in arriving at net income. Yet no cash was paid. Thus, to arrive at net cash flows used for operating activities, depreciation expense is added back to net income.

Accounts receivable increased by $2,650 during November and thus was recorded as part of revenue in arriving at net income. However, no cash was received. Thus, this increase in accounts receivable is deducted in arriving at net cash flows used for operating activities.

Prepaid insurance increased by $7,300 during November. This represents an $8,400 payment of cash for insurance premiums less $1,100 of premiums deducted in arriving at net income. Thus, the remaining $7,300 (the increase in prepaid insurance) is deducted in arriving at net cash flows used for operating activities. Similarly, the increase in supplies of $90 is deducted.

Accounts payable also increased during November by $140, and a related expense was recorded. But, no cash was paid. Similarly, wages payable increased during November by $220, and the related wages expense was deducted in arriving at net income. However, the $220 was not paid until the next month. Thus, for November, the increases of $140 in accounts payable and $220 in wages payable are added back to net income.

Unearned revenue increased by $1,440 during November, which represents land rented to ILS Company. ILS Company initially paid Family Health Care $1,800 in advance. Of the $1,800, one-fifth ($360) was recorded as revenue for November. However, under the cash basis, the entire $1,800 would have been recorded as revenue. Thus, $1,440 (the increase in the unearned revenue) is added back to net income to arrive at net cash flows used for operating activities.

During November, all the current assets are related to Family Health Care's operations. In addition, current liabilities for accounts payable and wages payable are also related to Family Health Care's operations. However, the increase in the current liability for notes payable, which increased by $6,800, is not included in the reconciliation shown in Exhibit 10. This is because the note payable is related to the purchase of office equipment, which is an investing activity rather than an operating activity.

During November, Family Health Care did not have any decreases in current assets or current liabilities. Thus, the effects of these items are not shown in Exhibit 10. Normally, however, both increases and decreases in current assets and liabilities are included in reconciling net income and net cash flows from (used for) operating activities. For example, Family Health Care's December reconciliation, shown in the Illustrative Problem, includes increases and decreases in current assets and current liabilities.

The reconciliation of net income to net cash flows from (used for) operating activities is normally prepared as shown in Exhibit 11.

Exhibit 11 Reconciling Items

Net income		$XXX
Depreciation expense	$XXX	
Changes in noncash current operating assets and liabilities:		
Decreases in current assets	XXX	
Increases in current liabilities	XXX	
Increases in current assets	(XXX)	
Decreases in current liabilities	(XXX)	XXX
Net cash flows from (used for) operating activities		$XXX

Key Points

1. Describe basic accrual accounting concepts, including the matching concept.

Under accrual concepts of accounting, revenue is recognized when it is earned. When revenues are earned and recorded, all expenses incurred in generating the revenues are recorded so that revenues and expenses are properly matched in determining the net income or loss for the period. Liabilities are recorded at the time a business incurs the obligation to pay for the services or goods purchased.

2. Use the accrual concepts of accounting to analyze, record, and summarize transactions.

Using the integrated financial statement framework, November transactions for Family Health Care were recorded. Family Health Care's November transactions involved accrual accounting transactions.

3. Describe and illustrate the end-of-period adjustment process.

The accrual concepts of accounting require the accounting records to be updated prior to preparing financial statements. This updating process, called the adjustment process, is necessary to match revenues and expenses. The adjustment process involves two types of adjustments—deferrals and accruals. Adjustments for deferrals may involve deferred expenses or deferred revenues. Adjustments for accruals may involve accrued expenses or accrued revenues.

4. Prepare financial statements using accrual concepts of accounting, including a classified balance sheet.

A classified balance sheet includes sections for current assets; property, plant, and equipment (fixed assets); and intangible assets. Liabilities are classified as current liabilities or long-term liabilities. The income statement normally reports sections for revenues, operating expenses, other income and expense, and net income.

5. Describe why generally accepted accounting principles (GAAP) require the accrual basis of accounting.

Under the accrual basis, net income is a better indicator of the long-term profitability of a business. For this reason, the accrual basis of accounting is required by generally accepted accounting principles (GAAP), except for very small businesses.

The accounting cycle is the process that begins with analyzing transactions and ends with preparing the accounting records for the next accounting period. The basic steps in the accrual basis accounting cycle are (1) identifying, analyzing, and recording the effects of transactions on the accounting equation; (2) identifying, analyzing, and recording adjustment data; and (3) preparing financial statements.

6. Metric-Based Analysis: Describe and illustrate the use of the quick ratio in assessing a company's liquidity.

A company's liquidity is its ability to convert assets to cash. The quick ratio is quick assets divided by current liabilities. Quick assets are normally cash, receivables, and short-term investments. The higher the quick ratio, the more liquid the company and the better its ability to pay current liabilities as they become due.

Key Terms

Account (89)
Accounting cycle (115)
Accounts payable (93)
Accounts receivable (94)
Accrual basis of accounting (87)
Accruals (99)
Accrued assets (100)
Accrued expenses (100)
Accrued liabilities (100)
Accrued revenues (100)
Accumulated depreciation (103)
Adjustment process (99)
Book value (103)
Cash basis of accounting (114)
Classified balance sheet (110)
Current assets (111)
Current liabilities (111)
Deferrals (99)
Deferred expenses (91, 99)
Deferred revenues (99)
Depreciation (103)
Expense recognition principle (88)
Fixed assets (111)
Intangible assets (111)
Long-term liabilities (111)
Matching concept (88)
Net income—accrual basis (89)
Notes receivable (111)
Prepaid expenses (91, 99)
Quick assets (89)
Quick ratio (116)
Revenue recognition principle (88)
Unearned revenues (99)

Illustrative Problem

Assume that the December transactions for Family Health Care are as follows:

a. Received cash of $1,900 from patients for services provided on account during November.
b. Provided services of $10,800 on account.
c. Received $6,500 for services provided for patients who paid cash.
d. Purchased supplies on account, $400.
e. Received $6,900 from insurance companies that paid on patients' accounts for services that had been previously billed.
f. Paid $310 on account for supplies that had been purchased.
g. Expenses paid during December were as follows: wages, $4,200, including $220 accrued at the end of November; rent, $800; utilities, $610; interest, $100; and miscellaneous, $520.
h. Paid dividends of $1,200 to stockholder (Dr. Landry).

Instructions

1. Record the December transactions, using the integrated financial statement framework as shown below. The beginning balances of December 1 have already been entered. After each transaction, you should enter a balance for each item. The transactions are recorded similarly to those for November. You should note that in transactions, the $4,200 of wages paid includes wages of $220 that were accrued at the end of November. Thus, only $3,980 ($4,200 − $220) should be recorded as wages expense for December. The remaining $220 reduces the wages payable.

Financial Statement Effects

BALANCE SHEET

	Assets							=	Liabilities				+ Stockholders' Equity	
	Cash +	Accts. Rec. +	Prepaid Insur. +	Supp. +	Office Equip. −	Acc. Depr. +	Land	=	Accts. Pay. +	Wages Pay. +	Notes Pay. +	Unearned Revenue +	Common Stock +	Retained Earnings
Balances, Dec. 1	7,730	2,650	7,300	90	8,500	(160)	12,000		140	220	16,800	1,440	11,000	8,510

STATEMENT OF CASH FLOWS

INCOME STATEMENT

2. The adjustment data for December are as follows:

Deferred expenses:

a1. Prepaid insurance expired, $1,100.

a2. Supplies used, $275.

a3. Depreciation on office equipment, $160.

Deferred revenue:

a4. Unearned revenue earned, $360.

Accrued expense:

a5. Wages owed employees but not paid, $340.

Accrued revenue:

a6. Services provided but not billed to insurance companies, $1,050.

Enter the adjustments in the integrated financial statement framework. Identify each adjustment by "a" and the number of the related adjustment item. For example, the adjustment for prepaid insurance should be identified as (a1).

3. Prepare the December financial statements, including the income statement, statement of stockholders' equity, balance sheet, and statement of cash flows. Note that the current portion of notes payable is $6,800.
4. Indicate the effects of each transaction on liquidity metric Quick Assets and profitability metric Net Income—Accrual Basis.
5. (Appendix) Reconcile the December net income with the net cash flows from (used for) operating activities. (*Note:* In computing increases and decreases in amounts, use adjusted balances.)

Solution

1. and 2. Family Health Care summary of transactions and adjustments for December:

Financial Statement Effects

BALANCE SHEET

	Assets							= Liabilities				+ Stockholders' Equity	
	Cash +	Accts. Rec. +	Prepaid Insur.	+ Supp.	+ Office Equip. –	Acc. Depr. +	Land =	Accts. Pay.	Wages Pay. +	Notes Pay.	Unearned Revenue +	Common Stock +	Retained Earnings
Balances, Dec. 1	7,730	2,650	7,300	90	8,500	(160)	12,000	140	220	16,800	1,440	11,000	8,510
a. Collected rec.	1,900	(1,900)											
Balances	9,630	750	7,300	90	8,500	(160)	12,000	140	220	16,800	1,440	11,000	8,510
b. Fees earned		10,800											10,800
Balances	9,630	11,550	7,300	90	8,500	(160)	12,000	140	220	16,800	1,440	11,000	19,310
c. Fees earned	6,500												6,500
Balances	16,130	11,550	7,300	90	8,500	(160)	12,000	140	220	16,800	1,440	11,000	25,810
d. Pur. supplies				400				400					
Balances	16,130	11,550	7,300	490	8,500	(160)	12,000	540	220	16,800	1,440	11,000	25,810
e. Collected rec.	6,900	(6,900)											
Balances	23,030	4,650	7,300	490	8,500	(160)	12,000	540	220	16,800	1,440	11,000	25,810
f. Paid on acct.	(310)							(310)					
Balances	22,720	4,650	7,300	490	8,500	(160)	12,000	230	220	16,800	1,440	11,000	25,810
g. Paid expenses	(6,230)								(220)				(6,010)
Balances	16,490	4,650	7,300	490	8,500	(160)	12,000	230	0	16,800	1,440	11,000	19,800
h. Paid dividends	(1,200)												(1,200)
Balances	15,290	4,650	7,300	490	8,500	(160)	12,000	230	0	16,800	1,440	11,000	18,600
a1. Insurance exp.			(1,100)										(1,100)
Balances	15,290	4,650	6,200	490	8,500	(160)	12,000	230	0	16,800	1,440	11,000	17,500
a2. Supplies exp.				(275)									(275)
Balances	15,290	4,650	6,200	215	8,500	(160)	12,000	230	0	16,800	1,440	11,000	17,225
a3. Depr. exp.						(160)							(160)
Balances	15,290	4,650	6,200	215	8,500	(320)	12,000	230	0	16,800	1,440	11,000	17,065
a4. Rent revenue											(360)		360
Balances	15,290	4,650	6,200	215	8,500	(320)	12,000	230	0	16,800	1,080	11,000	17,425
a5. Wages exp.									340				(340)
Balances	15,290	4,650	6,200	215	8,500	(320)	12,000	230	340	16,800	1,080	11,000	17,085
a6. Fees earned		1,050											1,050
Balances, Dec. 31	15,290	5,700	6,200	215	8,500	(320)	12,000	230	340	16,800	1,080	11,000	18,135

STATEMENT OF CASH FLOWS

a. Operating	1,900
c. Operating	6,500
e. Operating	6,900
f. Operating	(310)
g. Operating	(6,230)
h. Financing	(1,200)
Increase in cash	7,560
Dec. 1 cash bal.	7,730
Dec. 31 cash bal.	15,290

INCOME STATEMENT

b. Fees earned	10,800
c. Fees earned	6,500
g. Wages expense	(3,980)
Rent expense	(800)
Utilities expense	(610)
Interest expense	(100)
Misc. expense	(520)
a1. Insurance expense	(1,100)
a2. Supplies expense	(275)
a3. Depreciation expense	(160)
a4. Rent revenue	360
a5. Wages expense	(340)
a6. Fees earned	1,050
Net income	10,825

3.

FAMILY HEALTH CARE, P.C.
Income Statement
For the Month Ended December 31, 20Y5

Fees earned		$18,350
Operating expenses:		
Wages expense	$4,320	
Insurance expense	1,100	
Rent expense	800	
Utilities expense	610	
Supplies expense	275	
Depreciation expense	160	
Interest expense	100	
Miscellaneous expense	520	
Total operating expenses		(7,885)
Operating income		$10,465
Other revenue:		
Rent revenue		360
Net income		$10,825

FAMILY HEALTH CARE, P.C.
Statement of Stockholders' Equity
For the Month Ended December 31, 20Y5

	Common Stock	Retained Earnings	Total
Balances, Dec. 1, 20Y5	$11,000	$ 8,510	$19,510
Net income		10,825	10,825
Dividends		(1,200)	(1,200)
Balances, Dec. 31, 20Y5	$11,000	$18,135	$29,135

FAMILY HEALTH CARE, P.C.
Balance Sheet
December 31, 20Y5

Assets			
Current assets:			
Cash		$15,290	
Accounts receivable		5,700	
Prepaid insurance		6,200	
Supplies		215	
Total current assets			$27,405
Fixed assets:			
Office equipment	$8,500		
Less accumulated depreciation	(320)	$ 8,180	
Land		12,000	
Total fixed assets			20,180
Total assets			$47,585
Liabilities			
Current liabilities:			
Accounts payable		$ 230	
Wages payable		340	
Notes payable		6,800	
Unearned revenue		1,080	
Total current liabilities			$ 8,450
Long-term liabilities:			
Notes payable			10,000
Total liabilities			$18,450
Stockholders' Equity			
Common stock		$11,000	
Retained earnings		18,135	
Total stockholders' equity			29,135
Total liabilities and stockholders' equity			$47,585

FAMILY HEALTH CARE, P.C.
Statement of Cash Flows
For the Month Ended December 31, 20Y5

Cash flows from (used for) operating activities:		
Cash received from patients	$15,300	
Cash paid for expenses	(6,540)	
Net cash flows from operating activities		$ 8,760
Cash flows from (used for) investing activities		0
Cash flows from (used for) financing activities:		
Cash paid as dividends		(1,200)
Net increase in cash		$ 7,560
Cash as of December 1, 20Y5		7,730
Cash as of December 31, 20Y5		$15,290

4.

Metric Effects

LIQUIDITY

Transaction and Adjustments	Quick Assets
a. Collected receivables	–
b. Fees earned	$10,800
c. Fees earned	6,500
d. Purchased supplies	–
e. Collected receivables	–
f. Paid on account	(310)
g. Paid expenses	(6,230)
h. Paid dividends	(1,200)
Adjustments	
Adj. a1. Insurance expense	–
Adj. a2. Supplies expense	–
Adj. a3. Depr. expense	–
Adj. a4. Rent revenue	–
Adj. a5. Wages expense	–
Adj. a6. Fees earned	1,050
Total	$10,610

PROFITABILITY

	Net Income—Accrual Basis
a. Collected receivables	–
b. Fees earned	$10,800
c. Fees earned	6,500
d. Purchased supplies	–
e. Collected receivables	–
f. Paid on account	–
g. Paid expenses	(6,010)
h. Paid dividends	–
Adjustments	
Adj. a1. Insurance expense	(1,100)
Adj. a2. Supplies expense	(275)
Adj. a3. Depr. expense	(160)
Adj. a4. Rent revenue	360
Adj. a5. Wages expense	(340)
Adj. a6. Fees earned	1,050
Total	$10,825

Note: The December 31 balance sheet indicates quick assets of $20,990 ($15,290 + $5,700), which equals the December 1 quick assets of $10,380 plus the December increase in quick assets of $10,610.

Appendix

5. December's reconciliation of net income with net cash flows from (used for) operating activities:

Net income		$10,825
Depreciation expense	$ 160	
Changes in noncash current operating assets and liabilities:		
Increase in accounts receivable	(3,050)	
Decrease in prepaid insurance	1,100	
Increase in supplies	(125)	
Increase in accounts payable	90	
Increase in wages payable	120	
Decrease in unearned revenue	(360)	(2,065)
Net cash flows from operating activities		$ 8,760

Self-Examination Questions

(Answers appear at the end of the chapter.)

1. Assume that a lawyer bills her clients $15,000 on June 30, for services rendered during June. The lawyer collects $8,500 of the billings during July and the remainder in August. Under the accrual basis of accounting, when would the lawyer record the revenue for the fees?
   A. June, $15,000; July, $0; and August, $0
   B. June, $0; July, $6,500; and August, $8,500
   C. June, $8,500; July, $6,500; and August, $0
   D. June, $0; July, $8,500; and August, $6,500
2. On January 24, 20Y8, Niche Consulting collected $5,700 it had billed its clients for services rendered on December 31, 20Y7. How would you record the January 24 transaction, using the accrual basis?
   A. Increase Cash, $5,700; decrease Fees Earned, $5,700
   B. Increase Accounts Receivable, $5,700; increase Fees Earned, $5,700
   C. Increase Cash, $5,700; decrease Accounts Receivable, $5,700
   D. Increase Cash, $5,700; increase Fees Earned, $5,700
3. Which of the following items represents a deferral?
   A. Prepaid insurance
   B. Wages payable
   C. Fees earned
   D. Accumulated depreciation
4. If the supplies account indicated a balance of $2,250 before adjustment on May 31 and supplies on hand at May 31 totaled $950, the adjustment would be:
   A. Increase Supplies, $950; decrease Supplies Expense, $950.
   B. Increase Supplies, $1,300; decrease Supplies Expense, $1,300.
   C. Increase Supplies Expense, $950; decrease Supplies, $950.
   D. Increase Supplies Expense, $1,300; decrease Supplies, $1,300.
5. The balance in the unearned rent account for Jones Co. as of December 31 is $1,200. If Jones Co. failed to record the adjusting entry for $600 of rent earned during December, the effect on the balance sheet and income statement for December would be:
   A. Assets understated by $600; net income overstated by $600.
   B. Liabilities understated by $600; net income understated by $600.
   C. Liabilities overstated by $600; net income understated by $600.
   D. Liabilities overstated by $600; net income overstated by $600.

Class Discussion Questions

1. Would AT&T (T) and Microsoft (MFST) use the cash basis or the accrual basis of accounting? Explain.
2. How are revenues and expenses reported on the income statement under (a) the cash basis of accounting and (b) the accrual basis of accounting?
3. Fees for services provided are billed to a customer during 20Y6. The customer remits the amount owed in 20Y7. During which year would the revenues be reported on the income statement under (a) the cash basis? (b) the accrual basis?
4. Employees performed services in 20Y8, but the wages were not paid until 20Y9. During which year would the wages expense be reported on the income statement under (a) the cash basis? (b) the accrual basis?
5. Which of the following accounts would appear only in an accrual basis accounting system, and which could appear in either a cash basis or an accrual basis accounting system? (a) Common Stock, (b) Fees Earned, (c) Accounts Receivable, (d) Land, (e) Utilities Expense, and (f) Wages Payable.
6. Is the Land balance before the accounts have been adjusted the amount that should normally be reported on the balance sheet? Explain.
7. Is the Supplies balance before the accounts have been adjusted the amount that should normally be reported on the balance sheet? Explain.
8. Why are adjustments needed at the end of an accounting period?

9. Identify the four different categories of adjustments frequently required at the end of an accounting period.
10. If the effect of an adjustment is to increase the balance of a liability account, which of the following statements describes the effect of the adjustment on the other account?
    a. Increases the balance of a revenue account
    b. Increases the balance of an expense account
    c. Increases the balance of an asset account
11. If the effect of an adjustment is to increase the balance of an asset account, which of the following statements describes the effect of the adjustment on the other account?
    a. Increases the balance of a revenue account
    b. Increases the balance of a liability account
    c. Increases the balance of an expense account
12. Does every adjustment have an effect on determining the amount of net income for a period? Explain.
13. (a) Explain the purpose of the accounts Depreciation Expense and Accumulated Depreciation. (b) Is it customary for the balances of the two accounts to be equal? (c) In what financial statements, if any, will each account appear?
14. Describe the nature of the assets that compose the following sections of a balance sheet: (a) current assets, (b) property, plant, and equipment.

Exercises

Obj. 2

E3-1 Transactions using accrual accounting

Alex Vera organized Succulent Express at the beginning of February 20Y4. During February, Succulent Express entered into the following transactions:

a. Terry Mason invested $30,000 in Succulent Express in exchange for common stock.
b. Paid $5,400 on February 1 for an insurance premium on a one-year policy.
c. Purchased supplies on account, $1,800.
d. Received fees of $57,000 during February.
e. Paid expenses as follows: wages, $21,600; rent, $6,400; utilities, $2,800; and miscellaneous, $3,200.
f. Paid dividends of $8,000.

Record the preceding transactions using the integrated financial statement framework. After each transaction, you should enter a balance for each item.

Obj. 3

E3-2 Adjustment process

Using the data from Exercise 3-1, record the adjustments at the end of February to record the insurance expense and supplies expense. There was $300 of supplies on hand as of February 28. Identify the adjustment for insurance as (a1) and supplies as (a2). Enter the Net income under the Income Statement column after recording both adjustments.

Obj. 4

✔ Net income, $21,050

E3-3 Financial statements

Using the data from Exercises 3-1 and 3-2, prepare financial statements for February, including income statement, statement of stockholders' equity, balance sheet, and statement of cash flows.

E3-4 Appendix Reconcile net income and net cash flows from operating activities

Using the income statement and statement of cash flows you prepared in Exercise 3-3, reconcile net income with the net cash flows from operating activities.

E3-5 Accrual basis of accounting

Obj. 2

Margie Van Epps established Health Services, P.C., a professional corporation, in March of the current year. Health Services offers healthy living advice to its clients. The effect of each transaction on the balance sheet and the balances after each transaction for March are as follows. Each increase or decrease in Retained Earnings, except transaction h, affects net income.

Financial Statement Effects

BALANCE SHEET

	Assets			= Liabilities +	Stockholders' Equity	
	Cash	+ Accounts Receivable	+ Supplies =	Accounts Payable +	Common Stock +	Retained Earnings
a.	35,000				35,000	
b.			1,800	1,800		
Bal.	35,000		1,800	1,800	35,000	
c.	(800)			(800)		
Bal.	34,200		1,800	1,000	35,000	
d.	31,300					31,300
Bal.	65,500		1,800	1,000	35,000	31,300
e.	(25,000)					(25,000)
Bal.	40,500		1,800	1,000	35,000	6,300
f.			(1,250)			(1,250)
Bal.	40,500		550	1,000	35,000	5,050
g.		8,900				8,900
Bal.	40,500	8,900	550	1,000	35,000	13,950
h.	(6,000)					(6,000)
Bal.	34,500	8,900	550	1,000	35,000	7,950

STATEMENT OF CASH FLOWS

a. Financing	35,000
c. Operating	(800)
d. Operating	31,300
e. Operating	(25,000)
h. Financing	(6,000)
	34,500

INCOME STATEMENT

d. Fees earned	31,300
e. Expenses	(25,000)
f. Expenses	(1,250)
g. Fees earned	8,900
	13,950

a. Describe each transaction.

b. What is the amount of the net income for March?

Obj. 3

E3-6 Classify accruals and deferrals

Classify the following items as (a) deferred expense (prepaid expense), (b) deferred revenue (unearned revenue), (c) accrued expense (accrued liability), or (d) accrued revenue (accrued asset).

1. Subscriptions received in advance by a magazine publisher.
2. A three-year premium paid on a fire insurance policy.
3. Fees received but not yet earned.
4. Fees earned but not yet received.
5. Utilities owed but not yet paid.
6. Supplies on hand.
7. Salary owed but not yet paid.
8. Taxes owed but payable in the following period.

Obj. 3

E3-7 Classify adjustments

The following accounts were taken from the unadjusted trial balance of Inter Circle Co., a congressional lobbying firm. Indicate whether or not each account would normally require an adjusting entry. If the account normally requires an adjusting entry, use the following notations to indicate the type of adjustment:

AE—Accrued Expense

AR—Accrued Revenue

DR—Deferred Revenue

DE—Deferred Expense

To illustrate, the answer for the first account is as follows.

Account	Answer
a. Accounts Receivable	Normally requires adjustment (AR)
b. Accumulated Depreciation	
c. Common Stock	
d. Dividends	
e. Interest Payable	
f. Interest Receivable	
g. Land	
h. Office Equipment	
i. Prepaid Rent	
j. Supplies	
k. Unearned Fees	
l. Wages Expense	

Obj. 3

SHOW ME HOW

EXCEL ONLINE

✔ a. $4,800

E3-8 Adjustment for supplies

Answer each of the following independent questions concerning supplies and the adjustment for supplies.

a. The balance in the supplies account, before adjustment at the end of the year, is $7,000. What is the amount of the adjustment if the amount of supplies on hand at the end of the year is $2,200?

b. The supplies account has a balance of $1,300, and the supplies expense account has a balance of $3,900 at the end of the first year of operations. What was the amount of supplies purchased during the year?

E3-9 Adjustment for prepaid insurance

Obj. 3

The prepaid insurance account had a balance of $19,200 at the beginning of the year. The account was increased for $57,600 for premiums on policies purchased during the year. What is the adjustment required at the end of the year for each of the following independent situations? Indicate each account affected, whether the account is increased or decreased, and the amount of the increase or decrease.

a. The amount of unexpired insurance applicable to future periods is $24,000.

b. The amount of insurance expired during the year is $62,400.

E3-10 Adjustment for unearned fees

Obj. 3

The balance in the unearned fees account, before adjustment at the end of the year, is $1,375,000. What is the adjustment if the amount of unearned fees at the end of the year is $1,100,000? Indicate each account affected, whether the account is increased or decreased, and the amount of the increase or decrease.

E3-11 Adjustment for unearned revenue

Obj. 3

For a recent year, Microsoft Corporation (MSFT) reported short-term unearned revenue of $32,676 million. For the same year, Microsoft also reported total revenues of $125,843 million.

a. Assuming that Microsoft recognized $3,000 million of unearned revenue as revenue during the year, what entry for unearned revenue did Microsoft make during the year? Indicate each account affected, whether the account is increased or decreased, and the amount of the increase or decrease.

b. What percentage of total revenues is the short-term unearned revenue? Round to one decimal place.

E3-12 Effect of omitting adjustment

Obj. 3

At the end of August, the first month of the business year, the usual adjustment transferring rent earned of $36,750 to a revenue account from the unearned rent account was omitted. Indicate which items will be incorrectly stated because of the error on (a) the income statement for August and (b) the balance sheet as of August 31. Also indicate whether the items in error will be overstated or understated.

E3-13 Adjustment for accrued salaries

Obj. 3

Laguna Realty Co. pays weekly salaries of $8,000 on Friday for a five-day week ending on that day. What is the adjustment at the end of the accounting period, assuming that the period ends (a) on Monday or (b) on Wednesday? Indicate each account affected, whether the account is increased or decreased, and the amount of the increase or decrease.

E3-14 Determine wages paid

Obj. 3

The balances of the two accounts related to wages at October 31, after adjustments at the end of the first year of operations, are Wages Payable, $11,900, and Wages Expense, $825,000. Determine the amount of wages paid during the year.

E3-15 Effect of omitting adjustment

Obj. 3

Accrued salaries of $6,750 owed to employees for December 30 and 31 were not considered when preparing the financial statements for the year ended December 31, 20Y6. Indicate which items will be erroneously stated because of the error on (a) the income statement for December 20Y6 and (b) the balance sheet as of December 31, 20Y6. Also indicate whether the items in error will be overstated or understated.

Obj. 3

E3-16 Effect of omitting adjustment

Assume that the error in Exercise 3-15 was not corrected and that the $6,750 of accrued salaries was included in the first salary payment in January 20Y7. Indicate which items will be erroneously stated because of failure to correct the initial error on (a) the income statement for January 20Y7 and (b) the balance sheet as of January 31, 20Y7.

Obj. 3

E3-17 Effects of errors on financial statements

For a recent year, the balance sheet for The Campbell Soup Company (CPB) includes accrued liabilities of $367 million. The income before taxes for the year was $625 million.

a. Assume the accruals apply to the current year and were not recorded at the end of the year. By how much would income before taxes have been misstated?

b. What is the percentage of the misstatement in (a) to the reported income of $625 million? Round to one decimal place.

Obj. 3

✔ 1. (a) Revenue understated, $175,000

E3-18 Effects of errors on financial statements

The accountant for Healthy Medical Co., a medical services consulting firm, mistakenly omitted adjusting entries for (a) unearned revenue earned during the year ($175,000) and (b) accrued wages ($12,300). Indicate the effect of each error, considered individually, on the income statement for the current year ended August 31. Also indicate the effect of each error on the August 31 balance sheet. Set up a table similar to the following, and record your answers by inserting the dollar amount in the appropriate spaces. Insert a zero if the error does not affect the item.

	Error (a)		Error (b)	
	Over-stated	Under-stated	Over-stated	Under-stated
1. Revenue for the year would be	$____	$____	$____	$____
2. Expenses for the year would be	$____	$____	$____	$____
3. Net income for the year would be	$____	$____	$____	$____
4. Assets at August 31 would be	$____	$____	$____	$____
5. Liabilities at August 31 would be	$____	$____	$____	$____
6. Stockholders' equity at August 31 would be	$____	$____	$____	$____

Obj. 3

EXCEL ONLINE

E3-19 Effects of errors on financial statements

If the net income for the current year had been $2,224,600 in Exercise 3-18, what would have been the correct net income if the proper adjustments had been made?

Obj. 3

E3-20 Adjustment for accrued fees

At the end of the current year, $47,700 of fees have been earned but not billed to clients.

a. What is the adjustment to record the accrued fees? Indicate each account affected, whether the account is increased or decreased, and the amount of the increase or decrease.

b. If the cash basis rather than the accrual basis had been used, would an adjustment have been necessary? Explain.

Obj. 3

E3-21 Adjustments for unearned and accrued fees

The balance in the unearned fees account, before adjustment at the end of the year, is $900,000. Of these fees, $775,000 have been earned. In addition, $289,500 of fees have been earned but not billed to clients. What are the adjustments (a) to adjust the unearned fees account and (b) to record the accrued fees? Indicate each account affected, whether the account is increased or decreased, and the amount of the increase or decrease.

E3-22 Effect on financial statements of omitting adjustment

Obj. 3

The adjustment for accrued fees of $13,400 was omitted at July 31, the end of the current year. Indicate which items will be in error because of the omission on (a) the income statement for the current year and (b) the balance sheet as of July 31. Also indicate whether the items in error will be overstated or understated.

E3-23 Adjustment for depreciation

Obj. 3

SHOW ME HOW

The estimated amount of depreciation on equipment for the current year is $133,000.

a. How is the adjustment recorded? Indicate each account affected, whether the account is increased or decreased, and the amount of the increase or decrease.

b. If the adjustment in (a) was omitted, which items would be erroneously stated on (1) the income statement for the year and (2) the balance sheet as of December 31?

E3-24 Adjustments

Obj. 3

Clean Air Company is a consulting firm specializing in pollution control. The following adjustments were made for Clean Air Company:

Account	Adjustments Increase (Decrease)
Accounts Receivable	$11,250
Supplies	(1,350)
Prepaid Insurance	(1,800)
Accumulated Depreciation—Equipment	7,500
Wages Payable	4,500
Unearned Rent	(9,000)
Fees Earned	11,250
Wages Expense	4,500
Supplies Expense	1,350
Rent Revenue	9,000
Insurance Expense	1,800
Depreciation Expense—Equipment	7,500

Identify each of the six pairs of adjustments. For each adjustment, indicate the account, whether the account is increased or decreased, and the amount of the adjustment. No account is affected by more than one adjustment. Use the following format. The first adjustment is shown as an example.

Adjustment	Account	Increase or Decrease	Amount
1.	Accounts Receivable	Increase	$11,250
	Fees Earned	Increase	11,250

E3-25 Book value of fixed assets

Obj. 4

For a recent year, Barnes & Noble Inc. (BKS) reported (in thousands) *Property and Equipment* of $2,651,932 and *Accumulated Depreciation* of $2,395,142.

a. What was the book value of the fixed assets?

b. Would the book values of Barnes & Noble's fixed assets normally approximate their fair market values?

E3-26 Classify assets

Obj. 4

Identify each of the following as (a) a current asset or (b) property, plant, and equipment:

1. Accounts Receivable
2. Building
3. Cash
4. Office Equipment
5. Prepaid Insurance
6. Supplies

Obj. 4

E3-27 Balance sheet classification

At the balance sheet date, a business owes a five-year mortgage note payable of $480,000, the terms of which provide for monthly payments of $8,000. Explain how the liability should be classified on the balance sheet.

Obj. 4

✔ Total assets, $592,500

E3-28 Classified balance sheet

Eleven-Eleven, Inc. creates guided meditation programs for individuals. On November 30, 20Y9, the balances of selected accounts of Eleven-Eleven, Inc. are as follows:

Accounts Payable	$67,800	Prepaid Insurance	$ 14,400
Accounts Receivable	64,500	Prepaid Rent	10,800
Accum. Depreciation—Equipment	60,000	Retained Earnings	427,500
Cash	?	Salaries Payable	13,200
Common Stock	75,000	Supplies	24,000
Equipment	495,000	Unearned Fees	9,000

Prepare a classified balance sheet that includes the correct balance for Cash.

Obj. 4

✔ Total assets, $1,059,790

E3-29 Classified balance sheet

La-Z-Boy Inc. (LZB) is one of the world's largest manufacturer of furniture and is best known for its reclining chairs. The following data (in thousands) were adapted from recent financial statements:

Accounts payable	$ 65,365
Accounts receivable	143,288
Accrued expenses	173,091
Accumulated depreciation	347,065
Common stock	46,955
Cash	129,819
Intangible assets	215,774
Inventories	196,899
Debt due within one year	180
Long-term debt	19
Other current assets	71,112
Other long-term assets	102,375
Other long-term liabilities	124,159
Other stockholders' equity items	324,174
Property, plant, and equipment	547,588
Retained earnings	325,847

Prepare a classified balance sheet as of April 30. List intangible assets as its own separate item after fixed assets.

Obj. 4

E3-30 Balance sheet

The following balance sheet was prepared for Atlas Services Co.

ATLAS SERVICES CO.
Balance Sheet
For the Year Ended May 31, 20Y5

Assets		
Current assets:		
Cash	$ 12,000	
Accounts payable	47,900	
Supplies	4,800	
Prepaid insurance	17,400	
Land	400,000	
Total current assets		$482,100
Fixed assets:		
Building	$225,000	
Equipment	90,000	
Total fixed assets		315,000
Total assets		$797,100

Continued

Liabilities		
Current liabilities:		
Accounts receivable	$ 40,800	
Accumulated depreciation—building	54,600	
Accumulated depreciation—equipment	32,400	
Net loss	44,200	
Total liabilities		$172,000
Stockholders' Equity		
Wages payable	$ 8,100	
Common stock	200,000	
Retained earnings	447,000	
Total stockholders' equity		655,100
Total liabilities and stockholders' equity		$797,100

a. List any errors in the preceding balance sheet.

b. Prepare a corrected balance sheet.

Problems

P3-1 Accrual basis of accounting

Obj. 2

SLO Health Care Inc. is owned and operated by Morgan Denby, the sole stockholder. During January 20Y6, SLO Health Care entered into the following transactions:

Jan.	1	Received $13,500 from Glenn Company as rent for the use of a vacant office in SLO Health Care's building. Glenn paid the rent nine months in advance.
	1	Paid $3,000 for a one-year general insurance business policy.
	6	Purchased supplies of $900 on account.
	9	Collected $16,000 for services provided to customers on account.
	11	Paid creditors $2,500 on account.
	18	Invested an additional $5,000 in the business in exchange for common stock.
	20	Billed patients $26,000 for services provided on account.
	25	Received $7,500 for services provided to customers who paid cash.
	30	Paid expenses as follows: wages, $15,500 utilities, $4,250 rent on medical equipment, $2,650 interest, $100 and miscellaneous, $1,500.
	30	Paid dividends of $4,000 to stockholder (Dr. Denby).

Instructions

Analyze and record the January transactions for SLO Health Care Inc., using the integrated financial statement framework. Record each transaction by date, and show the balance for each item after each transaction. Do not enter net income under the Income Statement column. The January 1, 20Y6, balances for the balance sheet are as follows:

	Assets							=	**Liabilities**				+ **Stockholders' Equity**	
	Cash +	Accts. Rec. +	Pre. Ins. +	Supp. +	Building −	Acc. Depr. +	Land	=	Accts. Pay. +	Un. Rev. +	Wages Pay. +	Notes Pay. +	Common Stock +	Retained Earnings
Bal., Jan.1	10,000	22,250	350	600	75,000	(5,600)	60,000		3,850	0	0	15,000	25,000	118,750

Obj. 3

P3-2 Adjustment process

Adjustment data for SLO Health Care Inc. for January are as follows:

1. Insurance expired, $450.
2. Supplies on hand on January 31, $600.
3. Depreciation on building, $1,150.
4. Unearned rent revenue earned, $1,500.
5. Wages owed employees but not paid, $1,450.
6. Services provided but not billed to patients, $2,500.

Instructions

Based on the transactions recorded in January for Problem 3-1, record the adjustments for January using the integrated financial statement framework. Enter the net income under Income Statement column after recording all the adjustments.

Obj. 4

✔ Net income, $9,550

P3-3 Financial statements

Data for SLO Health Care for January are provided in Problems 3-1 and 3-2.

Instructions

Prepare an income statement, statement of stockholders' equity, and a classified balance sheet for January. The note payable is due in ten years.

Obj. 4

✔ Net cash flows from operating activities, $7,500

P3-4 Statement of cash flows

Data for SLO Health Care for January are provided in Problems 3-1, 3-2, and 3-3.

Instructions

1. Prepare a statement of cash flows for January.
2. (Appendix) Reconcile the net cash flows from operating activities with the net income for January. (*Hint:* See the appendix to this chapter and use adjusted balances in computing increases and decreases in accounts.)

Obj. 3

✔ Corrected net income, $127,075

P3-5 Adjustments and errors

At the end of May, the first month of operations, the following selected data were taken from the financial statements of Julie Mortenson, Attorney at Law, P.C.:

Net income for May	$127,500
Total assets at May 31	480,000
Total liabilities at May 31	150,000
Total stockholders' equity at May 31	330,000

In preparing the financial statements, adjustments for the following data were overlooked:

a1. Unbilled fees earned at May 31, $9,700

a2. Depreciation of equipment for May, $8,000

a3. Accrued wages at May 31, $1,150

a4. Supplies used during May, $975

Instructions

Determine the correct amount of net income for May and the total assets, liabilities, and stockholders' equity at May 31. In addition to indicating the corrected amounts, indicate the effect of each omitted adjustment by setting up and completing a columnar table similar to the following. Adjustment a1 is presented as an example.

	Net Income	Total Assets	=	Total Liabilities	+	Total Stockholders' Equity
Reported amounts	$127,500	$480,000		$150,000		$330,000
Corrections:						
Adjustment a1	9,700	9,700		0		9,700
Adjustment a2	______	______		______		______
Adjustment a3	______	______		______		______
Adjustment a4	______	______		______		______
Corrected amounts	______	______		______		______

P3-6 Adjustment process and financial statements

Obj. 3, 4

✔ 2. Net income, $82,750

Adjustment data for Ms. Ellen's Laundry Inc. for the year ended December 31, 20Y8, are as follows:

a1. Wages accrued but not paid at December 31, $2,150

a2. Depreciation of equipment during the year, $12,500

a3. Laundry supplies on hand at December 31, $1,500

a4. Insurance premiums expired, $4,600

Instructions

1. Using the following integrated financial statement framework, record each adjustment to the appropriate accounts, identifying each adjustment by its letter. After all adjustments are recorded, determine the balances.

Financial Statement Effects

BALANCE SHEET

	Assets					= Liabilities		+ Stockholders' Equity	
	Cash	+ Laundry Supplies	+ Prepaid Insurance	+ Laundry Equip.	– Acc. Depr.	= Accts. Payable	+ Wages Payable	+ Common Stock	+ Retained Earnings
Unadjusted Balances Dec. 31, 20Y8	53,000	9,000	6,000	250,000	(65,000)	7,000	0	50,000	196,000

STATEMENT OF CASH FLOWS

Operating (Revenues)	275,000
Financing (Common Stock)	25,000
Operating (Expenses)	(200,000)
Investing (Equipment)	(50,000)
Financing (Dividends)	(15,000)
Net increase in cash	35,000
Jan. 1 cash balance	18,000
Dec. 31 cash balance	53,000

INCOME STATEMENT

Laundry revenue	275,000
Wages expense	(110,000)
Rent expense	(30,000)
Utilities expense	(18,000)
Misc. expense	(7,500)

2. Prepare an income statement and statement of stockholders' equity for the year ended December 31, 20Y8. The common stock balance as of January 1, 20Y8, was $25,000. The retained earnings balance as of January 1, 20Y8, was $101,500.
3. Prepare a classified balance sheet as of December 31, 20Y8.
4. Prepare a statement of cash flows for the year ended December 31, 20Y8.

Metric-Based Analysis

Obj. 2

MBA 3-1 Metric analysis of transactions

Using the transactions listed in E3-5 for Health Services, P.C., indicate the effects of each transaction on the liquidity metric Quick Assets and the profitability metric Net Income—Accrual Basis.

Obj. 2

MBA 3-2 Metric analysis of transactions

Using the transactions listed in P3-1 for SLO Health Care, indicate the effects of each transaction on the liquidity metric Quick Assets and the profitability metric Net Income—Accrual Basis.

Obj. 3

MBA 3-3 Metric analysis of transactions

Using the adjustment data listed in P3-2 for SLO Health Care, indicate the effects of each adjustment on the liquidity metric Quick Assets and the profitability metric Net Income—Accrual Basis.

Obj. 3

MBA 3-4 Metric analysis of transactions

Using the adjustment data listed in P3-6 for Ms. Ellen's Laundry, indicate the effects of each adjustment on the liquidity metric Quick Assets and the profitability metric Net Income—Accrual Basis.

Obj. 6

MBA 3-5 Quick ratio

GameStop Corporation (GME) has over 7,000 retail stores worldwide and sells new and used video games. The following asset and liability data (in millions) were adapted from recent financial statements.

	Year 2	Year 1
Current assets:		
Cash	$ 499	$1,624
Accounts receivable	35	45
Inventory	860	1,251
Prepaid and other current assets	240	208
Total current assets	$1,634	$3,128
Total current liabilities	$1,238	$2,181

1. Compute quick assets for Years 2 and 1.
2. Compute the quick ratio for Years 2 and 1. Round to two decimal places.
3. Analyze and assess any changes in liquidity for Years 2 and 1.
4. Comment on any competitive pressures that you think GameStop may be experiencing.

MBA 3-6 Quick ratio

Obj. 6

The Gap Inc. (GPS) operates specialty retail stores under such brand names as GAP, Old Navy, and Banana Republic. The following asset and liability data (in millions) were adapted from recent financial statements.

	Year 2	Year 1
Current assets:		
Cash	$1,654	$1,369
Accounts receivable	316	359
Inventory	2,156	2,131
Prepaid and other current assets	390	392
Total current assets	$4,516	$4,251
Total current liabilities	$3,209	$2,174

1. Compute quick assets for Years 2 and 1.
2. Compute the quick ratio for Years 2 and 1. Round to two decimal places.
3. Analyze and assess any changes in liquidity for Years 2 and 1.

MBA 3-7 Quick ratio

Obj. 6

American Eagle Outfitters Inc. (AEO) operates specialty retail stores, selling clothing such as denim, sweaters, t-shirts, and fleece outerwear that targets 15-to-25-year-old men and women. The following asset and liability data (in millions) were adapted from recent financial statements.

	Year 2	Year 1
Current assets:		
Cash	$ 417	$ 425
Accounts receivable	62	48
Inventory	446	424
Prepaid and other current assets	123	149
Total current assets	$1,048	$ 1,046
Total current liabilities	$ 752	$ 543

1. Compute quick assets for Years 2 and 1.
2. Compute the quick ratio for Years 2 and 1. Round to two decimal places.
3. Analyze and assess any changes in liquidity for Years 2 and 1.

MBA 3-8 Quick ratios

Obj. 6

Compare The Gap Inc. (MBA 3-6) and American Eagle Outfitters Inc. (MBA 3-7) liquidity positions for Year 2. Comment on the differences.

MBA 3-9 Quick ratios

Obj. 6

Walmart Stores Inc. (WMT) operates over retail stores throughout the world. In contrast, Alphabet Inc. (GOOG) is a technology company, formerly known as Google, that provides a variety of online services.

1. Do you think Walmart or Alphabet has a higher quick ratio?
2. Using the following data (in millions) adapted from financial statements of a recent year, compute the quick ratios for Walmart and Alphabet. Round to two decimal places.

	Alphabet (Google)	Walmart
Current assets	$152,578	$61,806
Quick assets	145,001	15,749
Total current liabilities	45,221	77,790

3. Explain the results in (2).

Cases

Case 3-1 Accrued revenue

The following is an excerpt from a conversation between Monte Trask and Jamie Palk just before they boarded a flight to Berlin on **American Airlines (AAL)**. They are going to Berlin to attend their company's annual sales conference.

Monte: Jamie, aren't you taking an introductory accounting course at college?

Jamie: Yes, I decided it's about time I learned something about accounting. You know, our annual bonuses are based on the sales figures that come from the accounting department.

Monte: I guess I never really thought about it.

Jamie: You should think about it! Last year, I placed a $900,000 order on December 27. But when I got my bonus, the $900,000 sale wasn't included. They said it didn't ship until January 5, so it would have to count in next year's bonus.

Monte: A real bummer!

Jamie: Right! I was counting on that bonus including the $900,000 sale.

Monte: Did you complain?

Jamie: Yes, but it didn't do any good. Sophia, the head accountant, said something about matching revenues and expenses. Also, something about not recording revenues until the sale is final. I figured I'd take the accounting course and find out whether she's just jerking me around.

Monte: I never really thought about it. When do you think American Airlines will record its revenues from this flight?

Jamie: Hmmm, I guess it could record the revenue when it sells the ticket . . . or when the boarding passes are taken at the door . . . or when we get off the plane . . . or when our company pays for the tickets . . . or I don't know. I'll ask my accounting instructor.

Discuss when American Airlines should recognize the revenue from ticket sales to properly match revenues and expenses.

Case 3-2 Adjustments for financial statements

Several years ago, your brother opened Ready Appliance Repairs. He made a small initial investment and added money from his personal bank account as needed. He withdrew money for living expenses at irregular intervals. As the business grew, he hired an assistant. He is now considering adding more employees, purchasing additional service trucks, and purchasing the building he now rents. To secure funds for the expansion, your brother submitted a loan application to the bank and included the most recent financial statements prepared from accounts maintained by a part-time bookkeeper, as follows:

READY APPLIANCE REPAIRS
Income Statement
For the Year Ended March 31, 20Y6

Service revenue		$182,500
Less: Rent paid	$41,200	
Wages paid	34,750	
Supplies paid	7,000	
Utilities paid	6,500	
Insurance paid	3,600	
Miscellaneous payments	9,100	(102,150)
Net income		$ 80,350

READY APPLIANCE REPAIRS Balance Sheet March 31, 20Y6	
Assets	
Cash	$ 25,900
Amounts due from customers	18,750
Truck	55,350
Total assets	$100,000
Equities	
Owner's equity	$100,000

After reviewing the financial statements, the loan officer at the bank asked your brother if he used the accrual basis of accounting for revenues and expenses. Your brother responded that he did and that is why he included an account for "Amounts Due from Customers." The loan officer then asked whether or not the accounts were adjusted prior to the preparation of the statements. Your brother answered that they had not been adjusted.

a. Why do you think the loan officer suspected that the accounts had not been adjusted prior to the preparation of the statements?

b. Indicate possible accounts that might need to be adjusted before an accurate set of financial statements could be prepared.

Case 3-3 Business emphasis

GROUP PROJECT

Assume that you and two friends are debating whether to open an automotive and service retail chain that will be called Auto-Mart. Initially, Auto-Mart will open three stores locally, but the business plan anticipates going nationwide within five years.Currently, you and your future business partners are debating whether to focus Auto-Mart on a "do-it-yourself" or "do-it-for-me" business. A do-it-yourself business emphasizes the sale of retail auto parts that customers will use themselves to repair and service their cars. A do-it-for-me business emphasizes the offering of maintenance and service for customers.

1. In groups of three or four, discuss whether to implement a do-it-yourself or do-it-for-me business emphasis. List the advantages of each emphasis, and arrive at a conclusion as to which emphasis to implement.
2. Provide examples of real-world businesses that use do-it-yourself or do-it-for-me business emphases.

Case 3-4 Accrual versus cash net income

Cigna Corp. (CI) provides insurance services, and Deere & Company (DE) manufactures and sells farm and construction equipment. The following data (in millions) were adapted from recent financial statements of each company.

	Cigna	Deere
Net income (accrual basis)	$2,232	$2,159
Cash flows from operating activities	4,086	2,200
Depreciation	566	1,716

1. Compute the difference between cash flows from operating activities and net income for Cigna and Deere.
2. Express the difference in (1) as a percent of accrual net income. Round to two decimal places.
3. Which company's accrual based net income is closer to what would be reported if the company used the cash basis? Why?

Case 3-5 Analysis of income and cash flows

The following data (in millions) were taken from http://finance.yahoo.com.

	Year 3	Year 2	Year 1
Company A			
Revenues	$ 70,697	$ 55,838	$ 40,653
Operating income	23,986	24,913	20,203
Net income	18,485	22,112	15,934
Net cash flows from operating activities	36,314	29,274	24,216
Net cash flows used for investing activities	(19,864)	(11,603)	(20,038)
Net cash flows used for financing activities	(7,299)	(15,572)	(5,235)
Total assets	97,334	84,524	64,961
Company B			
Revenues	$ 77,147	$ 79,590	$ 79,139
Operating income	10,631	13,285	11,855
Net income	9,431	8,728	5,753
Net cash flows from operating activities	14,770	15,247	16,724
Net cash flows used for investing activities	(26,936)	(4,913)	(7,096)
Net cash flows from (used for) financing activities	9,043	(10,470)	(6,417)
Total assets	123,382	125,356	117,470
Company C			
Revenues	$260,174	$265,595	$229,234
Operating income	63,930	70,898	61,344
Net income	55,256	59,531	48,351
Net cash flows from operating activities	69,391	77,434	63,598
Net cash flows from (used for) investing activities	45,896	16,066	(46,446)
Net cash flows used for financing activities	(90,976)	(87,876)	(17,347)
Total assets	365,725	375,319	321,686
Company D			
Revenues	$122,286	$121,162	$122,662
Operating income	2,251	2,614	2,085
Net income	1,659	3,110	1,907
Net cash flows from operating activities	4,664	4,164	3,413
Net cash flows used for investing activities	(2,611)	(1,186)	(2,707)
Net cash flows used for financing activities	(2,083)	(2,896)	(681)
Total assets	38,118	37,197	36,505

1. Match each of the following companies with the data for Company A, B, C, or D:

   Apple Inc. (AAPL)

   Facebook, Inc. (FB)

   International Business Machines Corporation (IBM)

   Kroger (KR)

2. Explain the logic underlying your matches.

The annual report (10-K) assignment for this chapter is in Appendix B: Nike Annual Report, Chapter 3.

Answers to Self-Examination Questions

1. **A** Under the accrual basis of accounting, revenues are recorded when the services are rendered. Since the services were rendered during June, all the fees should be recorded in June (answer A). This is an example of accrued revenue. Under the cash basis of accounting, revenues are recorded when the cash is collected, not necessarily when the fees are earned. Thus, no revenue would be recorded in June, $8,500 of revenue would be recorded in July, and $6,500 of revenue would be recorded in August (answer D). Answers B and C are incorrect and are not used under either the accrual or cash basis.

2. **C** The collection of a $5,700 accounts receivable is recorded as an increase in Cash, $5,700, and a decrease in Accounts Receivable, $5,700 (answer C). The initial recording of the fees earned on account is recorded as an increase in Accounts Receivable and an increase in Fees Earned (answer B). Services rendered for cash are recorded as an increase in Cash and an increase in Fees Earned (answer D). Answer A is incorrect and would result in the accounting equation being out of balance because total assets would exceed total liabilities and stockholders' equity by $11,400.

3. **A** A deferral is the delay in recording an expense already paid, such as prepaid insurance (answer A). Wages payable (answer B) is considered an accrued expense or accrued liability. Fees earned (answer C) is a revenue item. Accumulated depreciation (answer D) is a contra account to a fixed asset.

4. **D** The balance in the supplies account, before adjustment, represents the amount of supplies available during the period. From this amount, $2,250, is subtracted the amount of supplies on hand, $950, to determine the supplies used, $1,300. The used supplies is recorded as an increase in Supplies Expense, $1,300, and a decrease in Supplies, $1,300 (answer D).

5. **C** The failure to record the adjusting entry increasing Rent Revenue, $600, and decreasing Unearned Rent, $600, would have the effect of overstating liabilities by $600 and understating net income by $600 (answer C).

Chapter **4**

Accounting for Retail Businesses

What's Covered:

Topics: Accounting for Retail Businesses

Nature of Retail Businesses
- Operating cycle (Obj. 1)
- Financial statements (Obj. 1)

Retail Transactions
- Purchase of merchandise (Obj. 2)
- Sale of merchandise (Obj. 3)
- Freight (Obj. 4)
- Seller and buyer (Obj. 5)

Financial Statements
- Adjustments (Obj. 6)
- Income statement (Obj. 7)
- Statement of stockholders' equity (Obj. 7)
- Balance sheet (Obj. 7)
- Statement of cash flows (Obj. 7

Metric-Based Analysis
- Transactions:
  Liquidity: Working capital (Obj. 2, 3, 6)
  Profitability: Gross profit percent (Obj. 2, 3, 6)
- Financial statements:
  Markup percent (Obj. 8)

Learning Objectives

Obj.1 Distinguish the operations and financial statements of a service business from those of a retail business.

Obj.2 Describe the accounting for the purchase of merchandise.

Obj.3 Describe the accounting for the sale of merchandise.

Obj.4 Describe the accounting for freight.

Obj.5 Illustrate the dual nature of merchandising transactions.

Obj.6 Describe and illustrate adjustments for retail operations.

Obj.7 Describe and illustrate the financial statements of a retail company.

Obj.8 Describe and illustrate the markup percent.

Chapter Metrics

Use the following metrics to analyze transactions and financial statements.

TRANSACTIONS

Liquidity: Working Capital

Profitabililty: Gross Profit Percent

FINANCIAL STATEMENTS

Markup Percent

Amazon.com

rvlsoft/Shutterstock.com

Jeff Bezos, the founder of **Amazon.com (AMZN)**, started Amazon's operations from the garage of his two-bedroom home in Seattle where he set up 3 workstations and designed a computer code that would work across various computer platforms. Amazon.com began its operations in July, 1995, by selling books over the Internet. By September, Amazon was growing rapidly and was selling $20,000 books per week. To expand, Jeff solicited monies from friends and family with a 70% chance that investors would lose everything.

When Amazon started its retail operations, its primary competitor was **Barnes & Noble (BKS)**, which had yet to develop its Internet operations. To continue its growth, Amazon.com offered its common stock for sale to the public on May 15, 1997, at $16 per share. Assuming you purchased one share at $16, you would now have 12 shares worth over $40,000.

Amazon is guided by four principles: customer obsession rather than competitor focus, passion for invention, commitment to operational excellence, and long-term thinking. Amazon, which was named after the South American river that has numerous branches, has expanded its products beyond books to various products, including electronics, movies, clothing, Kindle e-readers, and Fire tablets. In addition, Amazon allows sellers to offer their products on its website as well as offering digital services, such as cloud storage.

This chapter focuses on accounting issues unique to retailers. This discussion includes the recording of purchase and sales transactions as well as how retail financial statements differ from those of a service business.

Nature of Retail Operations

Objective 1
Distinguish the operations and financial statements of a service business from those of a retail business.

Retail businesses sell merchandise that they have purchased from other companies to consumers. Companies selling the merchandise to retailers are called suppliers or vendors. The transactions between suppliers and retailers are called **business-to-business (B2B)** transactions. Transactions between retailers and consumers are called **business-to-consumer (B2C)** transactions. For example, the selling of a variety of health and beauty products by **Procter & Gamble (PG)** to **Target (TGT)** is a B2B transaction. In contrast, the selling of Procter & Gamble's products such as *Tide* and *Charmin* to customers by Target is a B2C transaction.

The activities of a service business differ from those of a retail business. These differences are reflected in the operating cycles of a service and retail business as well as in their financial statements.

Operating Cycle

The **operating cycle** of a business is the process it takes for the business to spend cash to generate revenue, earn revenues, and receive cash from customers. The operating cycle for a retail business differs from a service business in that it must purchase merchandise for sale to customers. The operating cycle for a retail business, which purchases and sells merchandise on account, is shown in Exhibit 1.

Exhibit 1
The Operating Cycle for a Retail Business

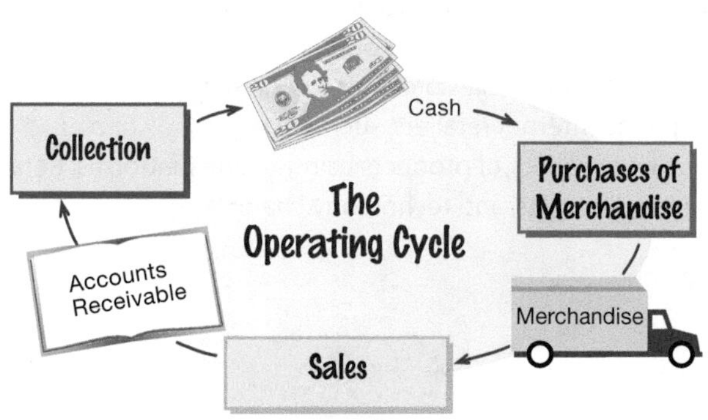

The length of time to complete an operating cycle differs among retail businesses. Grocery stores normally have short operating cycles because much of their merchandise is perishable with fixed selling dates. For example, milk has an expiration date of a week or two by which it must be sold. In contrast, jewelry stores carry expensive items often displayed months before being sold to customers.

Amazon.com Connection

Because Amazon.com sells its inventory quickly, it has a short operating cycle.

Financial Statements

The differences between retail and service businesses are also reflected in their financial statements. These differences are illustrated in the following income statements:

Retail Business		Service Business	
Sales	$XXX	Fees earned	$XXX
Cost of goods sold	(XXX)	Operating expenses	(XXX)
Gross profit	$XXX	Operating income	$XXX
Operating expenses	(XXX)		
Operating income	$XXX		

The revenue activities of a retail business involve the buying and selling of merchandise. A retail business first purchases merchandise to sell to its customers. When this merchandise is sold, the revenue is reported as **sales**. The cost of the merchandise sold is reported as **cost of goods sold** or *cost of merchandise sold*. The cost of goods sold is subtracted from sales to arrive at **gross profit** or *gross margin*. This amount is called gross profit because it is the profit *before* deducting operating expenses. The operating expenses are subtracted from gross profit to arrive at *operating income*.

Amazon.com Connection

In a recent income statement, Amazon.com reported net sales of $280,522 million and cost of goods sold of $165,536 million, resulting in a gross profit of $114,986 million.

In contrast, the revenue activities of a service business involve providing services to customers. These revenues from services are reported on the income statement as *fees earned*. The operating expenses incurred in providing the services are subtracted from the fees earned to arrive at *operating income*.

The balance sheet of a retail business differs from a service business in that there is normally merchandise on hand (not sold) at the end of a period. This merchandise is reported as **inventory** or *merchandise inventory* in the current asset section of the balance sheet.

Business Insight

The retail environment has changed rapidly during the last 40 years with the emergence of (1) discount merchandising, (2) category killers, and (3) Internet retailing. Walmart (WMT) led the development of discount merchandising by providing consumers discounted prices over a wide array of grocery, household, and electronic products. Category killers include Best Buy (BBY) (electronics), Home Depot (HD) (home improvement), and Office Depot (ODP) (office supplies). Each of these companies provides a wide selection of competitively priced goods within their market segment. Internet retailers, such as Amazon.com (AMZN), allow consumers to shop quickly for a wide variety of products using online platforms. Retailing will continue to evolve as consumer tastes, lifestyles, and technology change.

Purchase Transactions

Objective 2
Describe the accounting for the purchase of merchandise.

To illustrate merchandise transactions, we use TechSource, a retailer of computer hardware and software. TechSource's business strategy is to offer personalized service to individuals and small businesses who are upgrading or purchasing new computer systems. TechSource's personal service includes a no-obligation, on-site assessment of the customer's computer needs. By providing personalized service and follow-up, TechSource hopes to compete effectively against retailers, such as **Best Buy (BBY)**.

The effects of each merchandise transaction on TechSource's financial statements are illustrated using the integrated financial statement framework. In addition, the effects of each transaction on liquidity and profitability metrics are illustrated. In this chapter, we use **working capital** as our liquidity metric. Working capital is defined as current assets minus current liabilities. We use **gross profit percent** as our profitability metric. The gross profit percent is computed as follows:

$$\text{Gross Profit Percent} = \frac{\text{Sales} - \text{Cost of Goods Sold}}{\text{Sales}} = \frac{\text{Gross Profit}}{\text{Sales}}$$

To illustrate, assume TechSource has sales of $708,255 and cost of goods sold of $520,305. TechSource's gross profit percent is 26.5%, computed as follows:

$$\text{Gross Profit Percent} = \frac{\text{Sales} - \text{Cost of Goods Sold}}{\text{Sales}} = \frac{\$708{,}255 - \$520{,}305}{\$708{,}255} = \frac{\$187{,}950}{\$708{,}255} = 26.5\%$$

In analyzing the effects of transactions, we assume that TechSource desires a *minimum* gross profit percent of 20%.

Inventory Systems

Two systems for recording and accounting for merchandise transactions exist: perpetual and periodic. In a **perpetual inventory system**, each purchase and sale of merchandise is recorded. In this way, the amount of merchandise available for sale (on hand), and the amount sold are continuously (perpetually) updated in the inventory records. Perpetual inventory records consist of the Inventory account, called the **controlling account**, and a subsidiary record of each item of inventory, called a **subsidiary ledger**. The sum of the balances of the inventory items in the subsidiary ledger equals the balance of the Inventory (controlling) account. The Inventory account and related items in the subsidiary ledger are updated for each purchase and sale.

In a **periodic inventory system**, the inventory does not show the amount of merchandise available for sale (on hand) and the amount sold. Instead, a listing of inventory on hand, called a **physical inventory**, is prepared at the end of the accounting period. This physical inventory is used to determine the cost of inventory on hand at the end of the period, which is the amount reported as Inventory on the balance sheet.

The cost of goods sold for the period is determined as follows:

Beginning inventory	$XXX
Purchases	XXX
Merchandise available for sale	$XXX
Ending inventory (from physical count)	(XXX)
Cost of goods sold	$XXX

To illustrate, assume that on January 1, 20Y5, Jones Inc. had $250,000 of inventory on hand and purchased $3,140,000 of merchandise during 20Y5. On December 31, 20Y5,

Jones Inc. conducted its physical inventory and determined that $315,000 of inventory was on hand. Jones Inc.'s cost of goods sold for 20Y5 is $3,075,000, computed as follows:

Inventory, Jan. 1, 20Y5	$ 250,000
Purchases	3,140,000
Merchandise available for sale	$3,390,000
Inventory (from physical count) Dec. 31, 20Y5	(315,000)
Cost of goods sold	$3,075,000

Most retail companies use computerized perpetual inventory systems. Such systems use bar codes or radio frequency identification codes embedded in a product. An optical scanner or radio frequency identification device is then used to read the product codes and track inventory on hand and sold. Because computerized perpetual inventory systems are widely used, this chapter illustrates merchandise transactions using a perpetual inventory system.

Purchase of Merchandise for Cash

Assume that TechSource purchases $5,000 of merchandise for cash on September 3. The effects of the purchase on the TechSource's financial statements are recorded as follows:

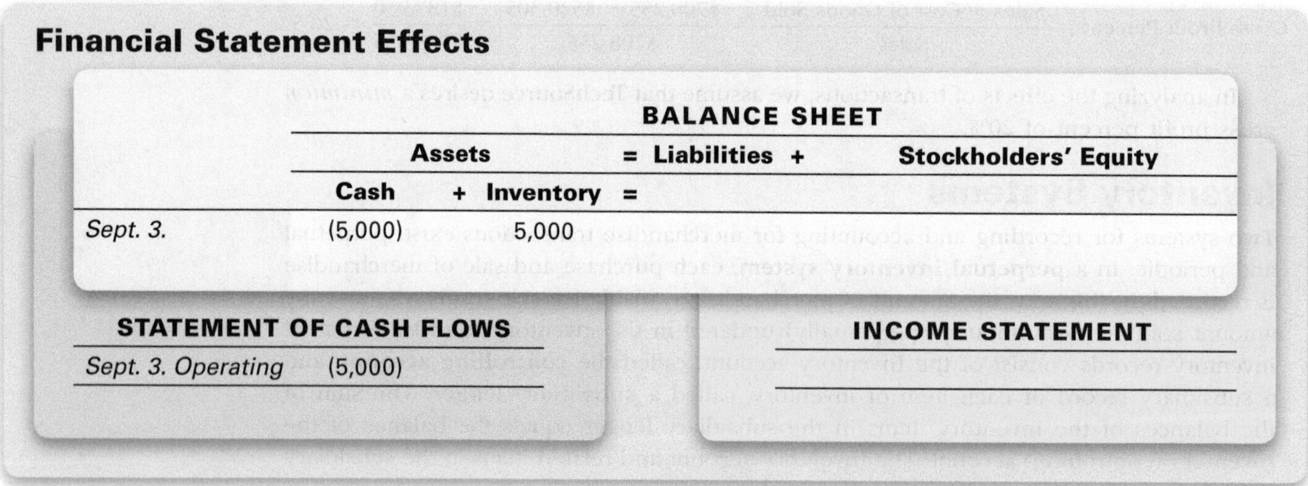

Financial Statement Effects

BALANCE SHEET

	Assets		= Liabilities +	Stockholders' Equity
	Cash	+ Inventory =		
Sept. 3.	(5,000)	5,000		

STATEMENT OF CASH FLOWS

Sept. 3. Operating	(5,000)

INCOME STATEMENT

Transaction Metric Effects

The effects of purchasing $5,000 of merchandise for cash on the liquidity and profitability metrics are as follows:

LIQUIDITY	
Working Capital	No Effect

PROFITABILITY	
Gross Profit Percent	No Effect

Since cash and inventory are both current assets, there was no effect on working capital. Likewise, since no sale of merchandise occurred, there was no effect on the gross profit percent.

Purchase of Merchandise on Account

When merchandise is purchased on account, the terms of the purchase are normally indicated on the **invoice** or bill that the seller sends the buyer. An example of an invoice from ABC Printers for a purchase by TechSource of printers on May 29, 20Y7 is shown in Exhibit 2.

Exhibit 2 Invoice

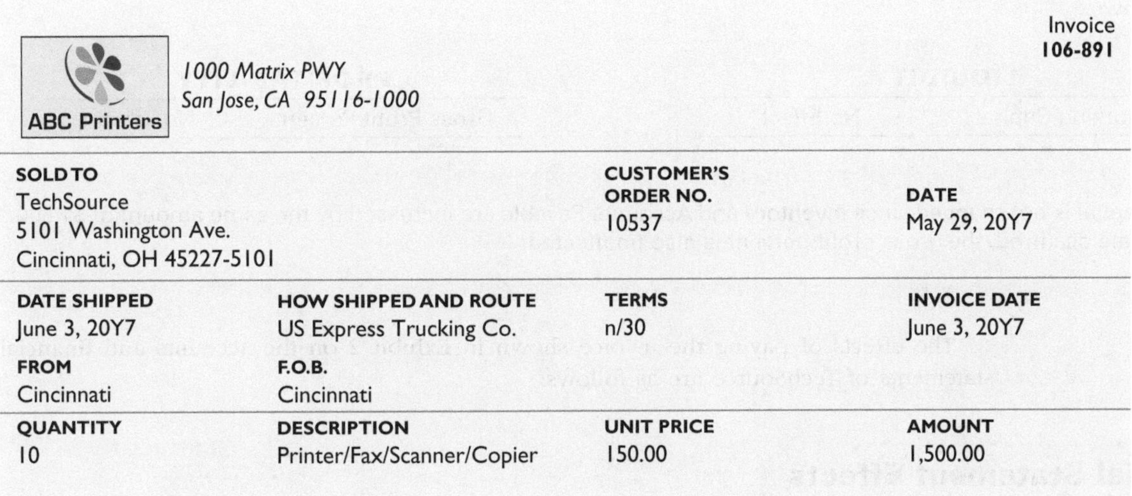

Invoice
106-891

ABC Printers
1000 Matrix PWY
San Jose, CA 95116-1000

SOLD TO		CUSTOMER'S ORDER NO.	DATE
TechSource 5101 Washington Ave. Cincinnati, OH 45227-5101		10537	May 29, 20Y7
DATE SHIPPED	**HOW SHIPPED AND ROUTE**	**TERMS**	**INVOICE DATE**
June 3, 20Y7	US Express Trucking Co.	n/30	June 3, 20Y7
FROM	**F.O.B.**		
Cincinnati	Cincinnati		
QUANTITY	**DESCRIPTION**	**UNIT PRICE**	**AMOUNT**
10	Printer/Fax/Scanner/Copier	150.00	1,500.00

The terms for when payments for merchandise are to be made, agreed on by the buyer and the seller, are called the **credit terms**. If payment is required on delivery, the terms are *cash* or *net cash*. Otherwise, the buyer is allowed an amount of time in which to pay, known as the **credit period**.

Payment may be due within a stated number of days after the invoice date, such as 15 days or 30 days. In these cases, the terms are net 15 days or net 30 days and are normally expressed as n/15 or n/30. If payment is due by the end of the month in which the sale was made, the terms are written as *n/eom*.

To illustrate, the due date for TechSource to pay the invoice shown in Exhibit 2 is July 3, 20Y7, computed as follows:

Credit terms, n/30	30 days
Less days in June (30 – 3)	(27) days
Days in July	3 days

The effects of the purchase shown in Exhibit 2 on the accounts and financial statements of TechSource are as follows:

Financial Statement Effects

	BALANCE SHEET				
	Assets	=	**Liabilities**	+	**Stockholders' Equity**
	Inventory	=	**Accounts Payable**		
June 3.	1,500		1,500		

STATEMENT OF CASH FLOWS

INCOME STATEMENT

Transaction Metric Effects

The effects of purchasing merchandise on account with credit terms n/30 on the liquidity and profitability metrics are as follows:

LIQUIDITY	
Working Capital	No Effect

PROFITABILITY	
Gross Profit Percent	No Effect

Working capital is not changed since Inventory and Accounts Payable are increased by the same amount of $1,500. Since no sale occurred, the gross profit percent is also unaffected.

The effects of paying the invoice shown in Exhibit 2 on the accounts and financial statements of TechSource are as follows:

Financial Statement Effects

BALANCE SHEET

	Assets	**=**	**Liabilities**	**+**	**Stockholders' Equity**
	Cash	**=**	**Accounts Payable**		
July 3.	(1,500)		(1,500)		

STATEMENT OF CASH FLOWS	
July 3. Operating	(1,500)

INCOME STATEMENT

Transaction Metric Effects

The effects of paying the invoice within the credit period on the liquidity and profitability metrics are as follows:

LIQUIDITY	
Working Capital	No Effect

PROFITABILITY	
Gross Profit Percent	No Effect

Working capital is not changed since Cash and Accounts Payable are decreased by the same amount of $1,500. Since no sale occurred, the gross profit percent is also unaffected.

Purchase Returns and Allowances

Purchase returns and allowances result when merchandise received by a buyer is defective, damaged in shipment, or not what was ordered. In these cases, the buyer may request a price adjustment or return the merchandise for full credit. The buyer normally notifies the seller of his or her intent by issuing a **debit memorandum**. The debit memorandum, sometimes called a *debit memo*, informs the seller of the amount the buyer proposes to decrease the account payable due the seller and why.

To illustrate, assume that TechSource issued the debit memo shown in Exhibit 3.

Exhibit 3 Debit Memorandum

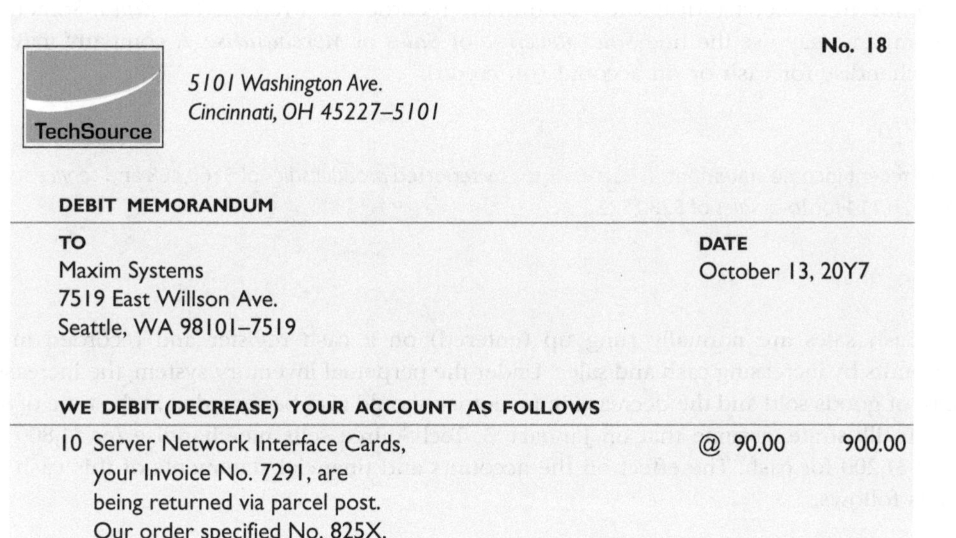

No. 18

TechSource
5101 Washington Ave.
Cincinnati, OH 45227–5101

DEBIT MEMORANDUM

TO
Maxim Systems
7519 East Willson Ave.
Seattle, WA 98101–7519

DATE
October 13, 20Y7

WE DEBIT (DECREASE) YOUR ACCOUNT AS FOLLOWS

10 Server Network Interface Cards, your Invoice No. 7291, are being returned via parcel post. Our order specified No. 825X. @ 90.00 900.00

The effects of the purchase return shown in Exhibit 3 on the accounts and financial statements of TechSource are as follows:

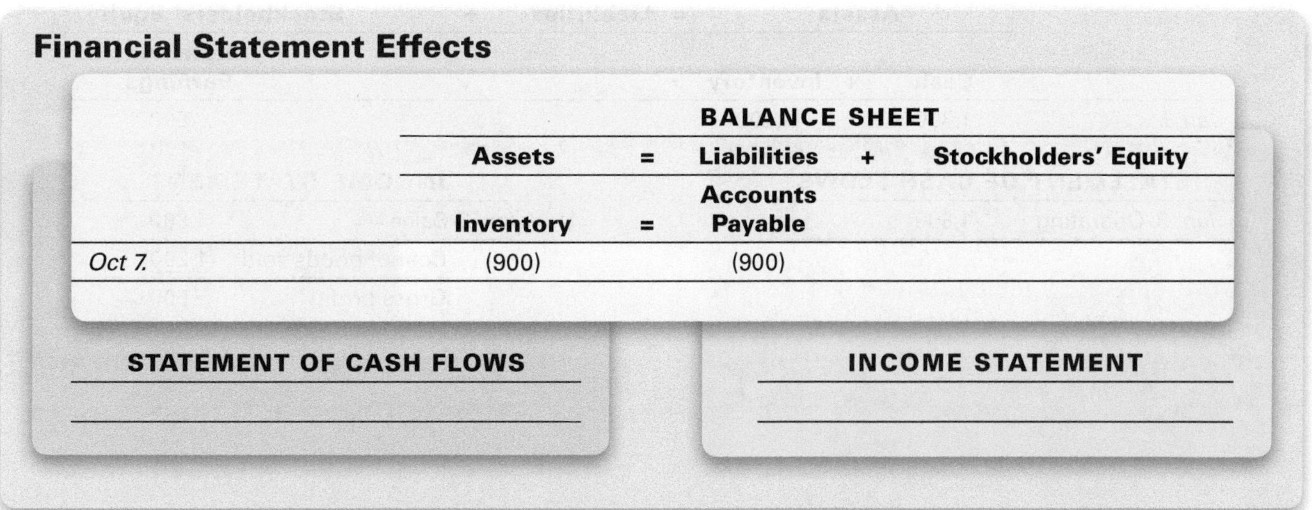

Financial Statement Effects

	BALANCE SHEET				
	Assets	**=**	**Liabilities**	**+**	**Stockholders' Equity**
	Inventory	**=**	**Accounts Payable**		
Oct 7.	(900)		(900)		

STATEMENT OF CASH FLOWS

INCOME STATEMENT

Transaction Metric Effects

The effects of the return of merchandise on the liquidity and profitability metrics are as follows:

LIQUIDITY	
Working Capital	No Effect

PROFITABILITY	
Gross Profit Percent	No Effect

Working capital is not changed since Inventory and Accounts Payable are decreased by the same amount of $900. Since no sale occurred, the gross profit percent is also unaffected.

Sales Transactions

Objective 3
Describe the accounting for the sale of merchandise.

Revenue from merchandise sales is normally recorded and reported as *Sales*. Sometimes a company may use the title *Sales Revenue* or *Sales* of *Merchandise*. A company may sell merchandise for cash or on account (on credit).

Amazon.com Connection

On a recent income statement, **Amazon.com** reported *product sales* of $160,408 and *service sales* of $120,114 for *Total sales* of $280,522.

Cash sales are normally rung up (entered) on a cash register and recorded in the accounts by increasing cash and sales. Under the perpetual inventory system, the increase in cost of goods sold and the decrease in inventory should also be recorded at the time of sale.

To illustrate, assume that on January 3, TechSource sells merchandise for $1,800 that cost $1,200 for cash. The effect on the accounts and financial statements of this cash sale is as follows:

Financial Statement Effects

BALANCE SHEET

	Assets		= Liabilities	+ Stockholders' Equity
	Cash	+ Inventory	=	Retained Earnings
Jan 3.	1,800	(1,200)		600

STATEMENT OF CASH FLOWS

Jan. 3. Operating	1,800

INCOME STATEMENT

Jan. 3. Sales	1,800
Cost of goods sold	(1,200)
Gross profit	600

Integrity, Objectivity, and Ethics in Business

The Case of the Fraudulent Price Tags

One of the challenges for a retailer is policing its sales return policy. There are many ways in which customers can unethically or illegally abuse such policies. In one case, a couple was accused of attaching Marshall's store price tags to cheaper merchandise bought or obtained elsewhere. The couple then returned the cheaper goods and received the substantially higher refund amount. Company security officials discovered the fraud and had the couple arrested after they had allegedly bilked the company for over $1 million.

Transaction Metric Effects

The effects of the cash sale on the liquidity and profitability metrics are as follows:

LIQUIDITY	
Working Capital	$600

PROFITABILITY	
Gross Profit Percent (33%)	Increases ability to achieve minimum of 20%

Since Cash increased by $1,800 and Inventory decreased by $1,200, working capital increased by $600 ($1,800 – $1,200). We assume that TechSource desires a minimum overall gross profit percent of 20%. Since the gross profit percent for this sale is 33% [($1,800 – $1,200) ÷ $1,800], this sale increases TechSource's ability to achieve its overall minimum gross profit percent of 20%.

Sales may be made to customers using **debit cards**, sometimes called **bank cards**. When a customer uses a debit card, the money required by the purchase is deducted from the customer's bank account and deposited in the retailer's account. For this reason, debit card sales are recorded as cash sales.

Sales may also be made to customers using credit cards such as MasterCard or VISA. Credit card sales are normally processed by a clearinghouse that contacts the bank that issued the card. The issuing bank then electronically transfers the cash directly to the retailer's bank account. Since the retailer receives the cash within a few days of making the sale, credit card sales are recorded as cash sales.[1]

When a retailer allows customers to use debit or credit cards, the retailer is normally charged a processing fee by the clearinghouse or issuing bank. Such fees are recorded as an expense.

A retailer may sell merchandise on credit (on account). The effects of sales on account are similar to those for cash sales except that Accounts Receivable is increased instead of Cash. When the customer pays the amount, Accounts Receivable is decreased and Cash is increased.

Sales Coupons and Rebates

Retailers frequently offer sales promotions to increase sales. Sales promotions are often distributed by retailers through newspapers, magazines, the Internet, and direct mailings. Such incentives and promotions often take the form of coupons and rebates. A **coupon** provides the customer a discount when purchasing a product(s). A **rebate** provides the customer a refund after the product is purchased. The accounting for a coupon or rebate depends upon its terms and how it can be redeemed by the customer.

A coupon has no value and the retailer has no obligation until a customer purchases merchandise and presents the coupon. As a result, no liability is recorded by the retailer when the coupon is issued. Instead, the retailer reduces Sales (revenue) by the amount of the coupon at the time of sale. These types of coupons are commonly issued by companies such as **Bed Bath & Beyond (BBBY)** and **Michaels (MIK)** and are referred to as *point-of-sale coupons.*

To illustrate, assume Welborn Stores offers a coupon on its website for $3 off the customer's next purchase of $15 or more. Assume that Becky Lewis purchases $45 of merchandise, submits the $3 coupon, and pays cash. The $3 coupon reduces the revenue

1. CyberSource is one of the major credit card clearinghouses. A description of its services can be found on its website at www.cybersource.com.

from the sale from $45 to $42 ($45 − $3 coupon). Assuming the merchandise cost Welborn Stores $27, the effects of the sale on the accounts and financial statements are as follows:

Financial Statement Effects

BALANCE SHEET

Assets		= Liabilities	+ Stockholders' Equity
Cash	**+ Inventory**	=	**Retained Earnings**
42	(27)		15

STATEMENT OF CASH FLOWS

Operating	42

INCOME STATEMENT

Sales	42
Cost of goods sold	(27)
Gross profit	15

Transaction Metric Effects

Assuming that Welborn Stores desires a minimum gross profit percent of 20%, the effects of the sale on the liquidity and profitability metrics are as follows:

LIQUIDITY

Working Capital	$15

PROFITABILITY

Gross Profit Percent (35.7%)	Increases ability to achieve minimum of 20%

Since Cash increased by $42 and Inventory decreased by $27, working capital increases by $15 ($42 – $27). Since the gross profit percent for this sale is 35.7% [($42 – $27) ÷ $42], the sale has the effect of increasing Welborn's ability to achieve an overall gross profit percent of at least 20%.

If instead of $3 off, the coupon had been for 10% off, Welborn Stores would have recorded a sale of $40.50 [($45 − ($45 × 10%)]. In both cases, the coupon reduces revenue at the time of sale.

In contrast, assume that a coupon is issued when customers purchase merchandise. The coupon appears on the bottom of the customer's sales receipt and may be redeemed for *future* purchases. In this case, when the retailer sold the merchandise, it incurred a future obligation (liability) to the customer. As a result, the retailer must estimate the dollar value of coupons that will be redeemed, reduce sales, and record a related liability.[2]

To illustrate, assume that to stimulate summer sales Grande Stores prints a coupon on the bottom of its May 20Y6 sales receipts for $3 off the customer's next purchase of over $20. The coupons may be redeemed June 1–August 31, 20Y6. During May, Grande Stores

2. *Revenue from Contracts with Customers, Topic 606, FASB Accounting Standards Update*, Financial Accounting Standards Board, Norwalk, CT, May 2014, para. 606-10-32-25b.

sold merchandise for $40,000,000, which generated 6,000,000 sales receipts. The cost of the merchandise sold was $21,500,000. Grande Stores estimates that 20% of the coupons will be redeemed before they expire on August 31. Assuming Grande Stores accepts only cash, VISA, or MasterCard, the effects on the accounts and financial statements of the May sales and issuance of the coupons are as follows:

Financial Statement Effects

BALANCE SHEET

	Assets		=	Liabilities	+	Stockholders' Equity
	Cash	**+ Inventory**	**=**	**Estimated Coupons Payable**	**+**	**Retained Earnings**
May 31.	40,000,000	(21,500,000)		3,600,000		14,900,000

STATEMENT OF CASH FLOWS

Operating	40,000,000

INCOME STATEMENT

Sales	36,400,000
Cost of goods sold	(21,500,000)
Gross profit	14,900,000

As of May 31, 20Y6, Grande Stores has incurred a current liability, called **Estimated Coupons Payable**, to its May customers who may redeem its $3 coupons. Since it is estimated that only 20% of its May customers will redeem a coupon, 1,200,000 coupons (6,000,000 sales receipts × 20%) are estimated to be redeemed. Because each coupon is for $3, the estimated coupon liability is $3,600,000 (1,200,000 coupons × $3). This estimated liability reduces the sales of $40,000,000 to $36,400,000 ($40,000,000 – $3,600,000).[3]

Transaction Metric Effects

Assuming that Grande Stores desires a minimum gross profit percent of 20%, the effects of the May sales and issuance of coupons on the liquidity and profitability metrics are as follows:

LIQUIDITY

Working Capital	$14,900,000

PROFITABILITY

Gross Profit Percent (40.9%)	Increases ability to achieve minimum of 20%

Working capital increases by $14,900,000 ($40,000,000 – $21,500,000 – $3,600,000). Since the gross profit percent for this sale is 40.9% [($36,400,000 – $21,500,000) ÷ $36,400,000], the sale has the effect of increasing Grande's ability to achieve an overall gross profit percent of at least 20%.

When customers redeem the coupons, the Estimated Coupons Payable is decreased. To illustrate, assume that during June, Grande Stores sold $52,500,000 of merchandise that

3. Ibid.

cost $28,100,000 and that 800,000 of the May coupons were redeemed. The effects of the June sales and redeemed coupons on the accounts and financial statements are as follows:

Financial Statement Effects

BALANCE SHEET

	Assets		=	Liabilities	+	Stockholders' Equity
	Cash	**+ Inventory**	**=**	**Estimated Coupons Payable**		**Retained Earnings**
June 30.	50,100,000	(28,100,000)		2,400,000		24,400,000

STATEMENT OF CASH FLOWS

Operating	50,100,000

INCOME STATEMENT

Sales	52,500,000
Cost of goods sold	(28,100,000)
Gross profit	24,400,000

Transaction Metric Effects

The effects of the June sales and redeemed coupons on the liquidity and profitability metrics are as follows:

LIQUIDITY

Working Capital	$24,400,000

PROFITABILITY

Gross Profit Percent (46.5%)	Increases ability to achieve minimum of 20%

Working capital increases by $24,400,000 ($50,100,000 − $28,100,000 + $2,400,000). Since the gross profit percent for this sale is 46.5% [($52,500,000 − $28,100,000) ÷ $52,500,000], the sale has the effect of increasing Grande Stores' ability to achieve an overall gross profit percent of at least 20%.

Grande Stores would record its July and August sales in a similar manner.

Since the May coupon liability is based on an estimate, Estimated Coupons Payable may have a balance on August 31, 20Y6. To illustrate, assume that on August 31, 20Y6, Estimated Coupons Payable has a balance of $175,000. Since the coupon period has expired, Grande Stores does not have any further coupon liability to its customers. As a result, the Estimated Coupons Payable balance of $175,000 should be added back to Sales. The effects on the accounts and financial statements of recording the expired coupons are as follows.

Financial Statement Effects

BALANCE SHEET

	Assets	=	Liabilities	+	Stockholders' Equity
		=	**Estimated Coupons Payable**		**Retained Earnings**
Aug. 31.			(175,000)		175,000

STATEMENT OF CASH FLOWS

INCOME STATEMENT

Sales	175,000

Transaction Metric Effects

The effects of the expired coupons on the liquidity and profitability metrics are as follows:

LIQUIDITY	
Working Capital	$175,000

PROFITABILITY	
Gross Profit Percent	Increases ability to achieve minimum of 20%

Since current liabilities decrease by $175,000 with no change in current assets, working capital increases by $175,000. Since sales and gross profit increase by $175,000 eliminating the expired coupons has the effect of increasing Grande Stores' ability to achieve an overall gross profit percent of at least 20%.

If on August 31, 20Y6, Estimated Coupons Payable had a balance of $(50,000), Grande Stores would have underestimated the percent of coupons that were redeemed. As a result, Grande Stores would decrease Sales and increase the Estimated Coupons Payable. The effects on the accounts and financial statements of recording the underestimation of the redeemed coupons are as follows:

Financial Statement Effects

BALANCE SHEET

	Assets	=	Liabilities	+	Stockholders' Equity
			Estimated Coupons Payable		**Retained Earnings**
Aug. 31.			50,000		(50,000)

STATEMENT OF CASH FLOWS

INCOME STATEMENT	
Sales	(50,000)

Transaction Metric Effects

The effects of the underestimation of redeemed coupons on the liquidity and profitability metrics are as follows:

LIQUIDITY	
Working Capital	($50,000)

PROFITABILITY	
Gross Profit Percent	Increases ability to achieve minimum of 20%

Since current liabilities increase by $50,000 with no change in current assets, working capital decreases by $50,000. Since sales and gross profit decrease by $50,000, underestimating redeemed coupons has the effect of decreasing Grande Stores' ability to achieve an overall gross profit percent of at least 20%.

After the coupon period has expired, Estimated Coupons Payable should have a zero balance.

Rebates normally entitle customers to receive cash if they mail in a coupon, receipt of purchase, and barcode from the item purchased. Mail-in rebates are normally distributed to customers in the form of a check or preloaded VISA or MasterCard. Retailers often advertise merchandise net of the rebate. For example, Mike's Appliances might advertise a Whirlpool side-by-side refrigerator with a retail list price of $1,799 for $1,499 with a $300 mail-in rebate.

The accounting for rebates is similar to that for coupons. Instant rebates, which are redeemed at the time of purchase, reduce the revenue at the time of sale. Mail-in rebates require the retailer to estimate the dollar value of rebates that will be redeemed, reduce sales, and record a related liability.

Amazon.com Connection

In notes to recent financial statements, **Amazon.com** reports that promotional discounts and rebates are accounted for as a reduction of revenues.

Customer Returns, Refunds, and Allowances

A buyer may return merchandise that is defective, damaged during shipment, or does not meet the buyer's expectations. If the buyer has already paid for the merchandise, the seller may pay the buyer a cash refund. If the buyer has an outstanding accounts receivable with the seller, the buyer may request an offset against the accounts receivable. A buyer could also keep the merchandise and request a partial refund or price allowance.

Amazon.com Connection

In a recent annual report, **Amazon** reported an allowance for customer returns of $712 million.

At the end of the accounting period, a seller must estimate the amount of returns, refunds, and allowances that may have to be issued to customers in the future. Based upon these estimates, sellers record two adjustments:

1. The first adjustment decreases Sales and increases Customer Refunds Payable for the estimated refunds and allowances that will be granted to customers in the future. **Customer Refunds Payable** is a current liability for refunds and allowances that will be granted to customers.
2. The second adjustment increases Estimated Returns Inventory for merchandise that is expected to be returned and decreases Cost of Goods Sold. **Estimated Returns Inventory** is a current asset for merchandise that is expected to be returned by customers.[4]

To illustrate, assume that on December 31, 20Y6, TechSource estimates that from 20Y6 sales it will have to refund or grant customers allowances of $7,000 during 20Y7. In addition, TechSource estimates that $5,500 of merchandise will be returned. Based upon these estimates, TechSource would record two adjustments on December 31, 20Y6. The effects of these adjustments on the accounts and financial statements are as follows.

4. This accounting is consistent with *Revenue from Contracts with Customers, Topic 606, FASB Accounting Standards Update*, Financial Accounting Standards Board, Norwalk, CT, May 2014, para. 606-10-32b.

Financial Statement Effects
Adjustment 1: Estimated Refunds and Allowances

	BALANCE SHEET				
	Assets	=	Liabilities	+	Stockholders' Equity
			Customer Refunds Payable		Retained Earnings
20Y6					
Dec. 31.			7,000		(7,000)

STATEMENT OF CASH FLOWS

INCOME STATEMENT	
Sales	(7,000)

Financial Statement Effects
Adjustment 2: Estimated Mechandise Returns

	BALANCE SHEET				
	Assets	=	Liabilities	+	Stockholders' Equity
	Estimated Returns Inventory				Retained Earnings
20Y6					
Dec. 31.	5,500				5,500

STATEMENT OF CASH FLOWS

INCOME STATEMENT	
Cost of goods sold	(5,500)

The first entry decreases 20Y6 sales to an amount that is expected to be received from customers and establishes a related liability for customer refunds and allowances. The second entry recognizes the inventory that is expected to be returned and decreases the related cost of goods sold.[5]

Transaction Metric Effects

The effects of the adjustments on the liquidity and profitability metrics are as follows:

LIQUIDITY		
Adjustment 1	Working Capital	$ (7,000)
Adjustment 2	Working Capital	5,500
		$(1,500)

PROFITABILITY	
Gross Profit Percent	Increases ability to achieve minimum of 20%

The combined effects of the adjustments reduce working capital by $(1,500). The effects of the adjustments are to reduce Sales by $7,000 and Cost of Goods Sold by $5,500. These adjustments reduce gross profit by $1,500 and, thus, decrease TechSource's ability to achieve an overall gross profit of at least 20%.

5. This accounting is consistent with *Revenue from Contracts with Customers, Topic 606, FASB Accounting Standards Update*, Financial Accounting Standards Board, Norwalk, CT, May 2014, para. 606-10-32b.

Assume that on March 4, 20Y7, Blake & Sons returned merchandise to TechSource with a selling price of $1,800 for a full **cash refund**. The merchandise originally cost TechSource $875. The effects of the cash refund and the return on the accounts and financial statements are as follows:

Cash Refund

Financial Statement Effects

BALANCE SHEET

	Assets	=	Liabilities	+	Stockholders' Equity
	Cash	=	Customer Refunds Payable		
20Y7 Mar. 4.	(1,800)		(1,800)		

STATEMENT OF CASH FLOWS

Operating	(1,800)

INCOME STATEMENT

Return of Merchandise

Financial Statement Effects

BALANCE SHEET

	Assets			=	Liabilities	+	Stockholders' Equity
	Inventory*	+	Estimated Returns Inventory	=			
20Y7 Mar. 4.	875		(875)				

STATEMENT OF CASH FLOWS

INCOME STATEMENT

* Because of wear, tear, and damage, companies may segregate returned items from normal inventory by using a separate returns inventory account.

Transaction Metric Effects

The effects of the refund and return on the liquidity and profitability metrics are as follows:

LIQUIDITY	
Working Capital	No effect

PROFITABILITY	
Gross Profit Percent	No effect on ability to achieve minimum of 20%

Since current assets decrease by $1,800 (−$1,800 + $875 − $875) and current liabilities decrease by $1,800, there is no effect on working capital. Since Sales and Cost of Goods Sold were not changed, there is no effect on the ability to achieve a minimum gross profit percent of 20%.

A buyer who has already paid for merchandise may decide to keep the merchandise and accept a partial refund from the seller. To illustrate, assume that in the prior example Blake & Sons agrees to keep the merchandise in return for a partial refund of $900 from TechSource. The effects of the partial refund on the accounts and financial statements are as follows:

Financial Statement Effects

BALANCE SHEET

	Assets		=	Liabilities	+	Stockholders' Equity
	Cash	+	=	Customer Refunds Payable		
20Y7 *Mar. 4.*	(900)			(900)		

STATEMENT OF CASH FLOWS	
Operating	(900)

INCOME STATEMENT

Transaction Metric Effects

The effects of the partial refund on the liquidity and profitability metrics are as follows:

LIQUIDITY	
Working Capital	No Effect

PROFITABILITY	
Gross Profit Percent	No Effect

Since current assets and liabilities both decrease by the same amount, there is no effect on working capital. Since Sales and Cost of Goods Sold were not changed, there is no effect on the ability to achieve a minimum gross profit percent of 20%.

A buyer who receives defective or damaged merchandise may not have paid for the merchandise. In other words, the seller has an outstanding account receivable balance due from the buyer. In this case, the seller may grant a sales allowance against the customer's account receivable. When this is done, the seller sends the buyer a **credit memorandum**, or *credit memo*, indicating its intent to decrease the customer's account receivable.

To illustrate, assume that instead of returning the merchandise, Blake & Sons agrees to accept a sales allowance of $900. TechSource notifies Blake & Sons its granting of the allowance by issuing the credit memo shown in Exhibit 4.

Exhibit 4
Credit Memorandum

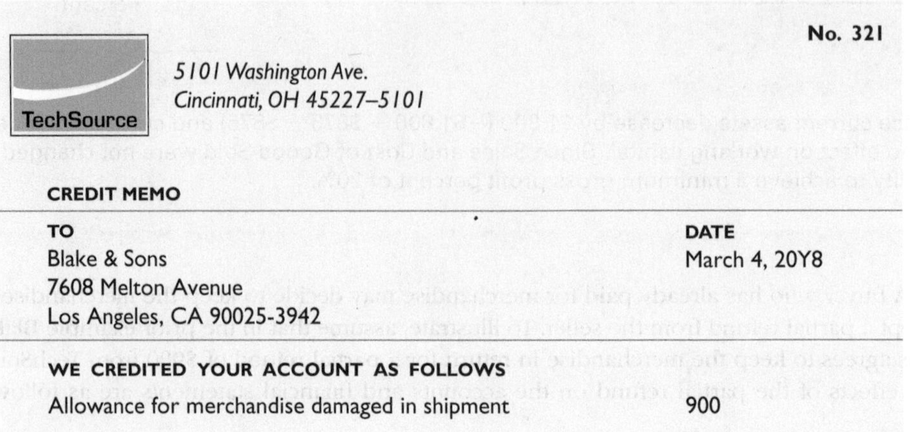

No. 321

TechSource

5101 Washington Ave.
Cincinnati, OH 45227–5101

CREDIT MEMO

TO	**DATE**
Blake & Sons 7608 Melton Avenue Los Angeles, CA 90025-3942	March 4, 20Y8

WE CREDITED YOUR ACCOUNT AS FOLLOWS

Allowance for merchandise damaged in shipment	900

The credit memo indicates that TechSource intends to decrease Blake & Sons' account receivable by $900. The effects of granting the customer allowance on the accounts and financial statements are as follows:

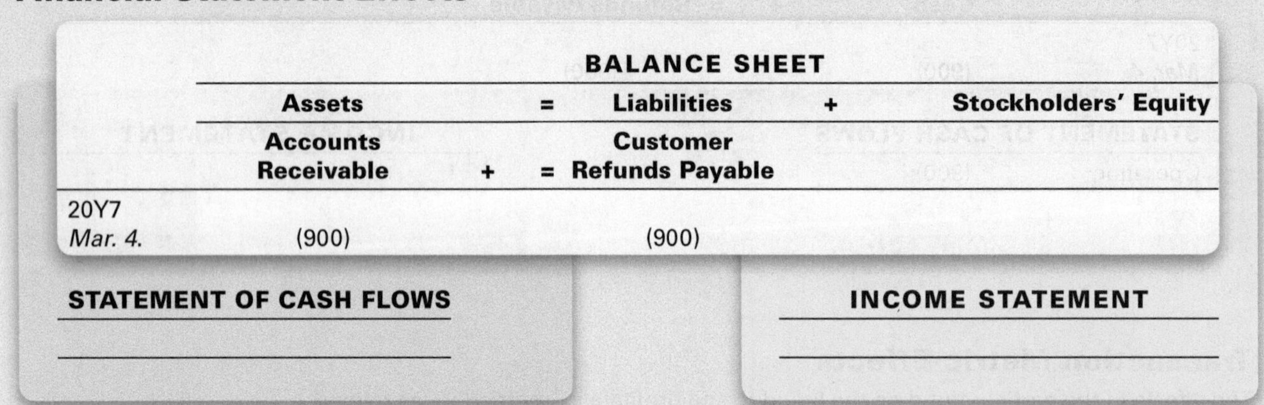

Financial Statement Effects

BALANCE SHEET

	Assets		=	Liabilities	+	Stockholders' Equity
	Accounts Receivable	+	=	Customer Refunds Payable		
20Y7 Mar. 4.	(900)			(900)		

STATEMENT OF CASH FLOWS

INCOME STATEMENT

Transaction Metric Effects

The effects of granting the customer allowance on the liquidity and profitability metrics are as follows:

LIQUIDITY	
Working Capital	No Effect

PROFITABILITY	
Gross Profit Percent	No Effect

Since current assets and liabilities both decrease by the same amount, there is no effect on working capital. Since Sales and Cost of Goods Sold were not changed, there is no effect on the ability to achieve a minimum gross profit percent of 20%.

Using Data Analytics

Sales

Retail businesses, such as Target Corporation (TGT), use data analytics to answer questions such as the following:

- What are our best-selling products?
- What products are generating returns?
- What percent of our customers are using self-checkouts?
- What time of the day do we have the most sales?
- What percent of our customers use credit cards?
- What percent of our customers use debit cards?

Target has used data (predictive) analytics to improve the retail experience of its customers as well as to increase its sales. For example, Target uses data analytics to decide which products should earn shelf space in its brick-and-mortar stores and which are best serviced with its online sales app.

See Case 4-6 for a homework assignment using data analytics.

Source: Dina Gerdeman, "On Target: Rethinking the Retail Website," *Forbes*, December 4, 2018, www.forbes.com/sites/hbsworkingknowledge/2018/12/04/on-target-rethinking-the-retail-website/#2690a20916fb.

Trade Discounts

Wholesale businesses are companies that sell merchandise to other businesses (B2B transactions) rather than to the public (B2C transactions). Wholesalers may offer their business customers special discounts off their normal list prices. Such discounts are called **trade discounts**.

To illustrate, assume Korf Inc. offers its wholesalers a 15% trade discount off normal list prices for orders placed before March 1. On February 14, Yang Stores ordered merchandise with a list price of $500,000. Korf Inc. would record the sale as $425,000 [$500,000 − ($500,000 × 15%)]. Likewise, Yang Stores would record the purchase as $425,000.

Regardless of the type of trade discount, sellers and buyers record sales and purchases *net* of any discount. That is, sales are recorded at the amount expected to be received by the seller and purchases are recorded at the net cost to the buyer.

Amounts received by Amazon.com from its vendors (suppliers) for volume purchases and other incentives are recorded as a reduction of the cost of its inventory. *Amazon.com Connection*

Sales Taxes

Almost all states and many other taxing units levy a tax on sales of merchandise.[6] The liability for the sales tax is incurred at the time the sale is made. For a cash sale, the seller collects the sales tax and increases Cash for the total amount collected from the customer, Sales are increased for the amount of the sale, and Sales Tax Payable is increased for the amount of the tax collected that must be remitted to the taxing authority.

Amazon collects sales tax from states that have a statewide sales tax. *Amazon.com Connection*

6. Merchandise purchased by a business for later resale to others (B2B transactions) are normally exempt from sales taxes. Only final buyers of merchandise (B2C transactions) normally pay sales taxes.

To illustrate, assume that on June 9 Dempski Products Inc. sold $4,750 of merchandise to customers using MasterCard subject to a 6% state sales tax. Assuming the merchandise cost, Dempski Products Inc. $2,000, the effects of the sales on the accounts and financial statements are as follows:

Financial Statement Effects

BALANCE SHEET

	Assets		=	Liabilities	+	Stockholders' Equity
	Cash	+ Inventory	=	Sales Tax Payable*		Retained Earnings
June 9.	5,035	(2,000)		285*		2,750

STATEMENT OF CASH FLOWS

Operating	5,035

INCOME STATEMENT

Sales	4,750
Cost of goods sold	(2,000)
Gross profit	2,750

* $4,750 × 6% = $285

At regular intervals, the seller pays to the taxing authority the amount of the sales tax collected. To illustrate, assume that Dempski Products Inc. pays the state $9,300 of sales taxes on June 30. The effects on the accounts and financial statements of remitting the sales taxes are as follows:

Financial Statement Effects

BALANCE SHEET

	Assets	=	Liabilities	+	Stockholders' Equity
	Cash	=	Sales Tax Payable		
June 30.	(9,300)		(9,300)		

STATEMENT OF CASH FLOWS

Operating	(9,300)

INCOME STATEMENT

Transaction Metric Effects

Assuming that Dempski Products Inc. desires a minimum gross profit percent of 20%, the effects of the sales and remittance of sales taxes on the liquidity and profitability metrics are as follows:

LIQUIDITY	
Sales of merchandise:	
Working Capital	$2,750
Remittance of sales taxes:	
Working Capital	No Effect

PROFITABILITY	
Sales of merchandise:	
Gross Profit Percent	Increases ability to achieve minimum of 20%
Remittance of sales:	
Gross Profit Percent	No Effect

The effects of the sales increase current assets by $3,035 ($5,035 – $2,000) and increase current liabilities by $285, thus working capital increases by $2,750 ($3,035 – $285). The gross profit on the sale is 57.9% ($2,750 ÷ $4,750) and thus, increases Dempski's ability to achieve an overall gross profit percent of at least 20%. The remittance of the sales taxes decreases current assets and liabilities by the same amount and thus, has no effect on working capital. Since the remittance of the sales taxes does not effect revenues or expenses, there is no effect on the profitability metric.

Freight

Objective 4
Describe the accounting for freight.

Retail businesses incur **freight** in selling and purchasing merchandise. The terms of a sale should indicate when the ownership (title) of the merchandise passes to the buyer. This point determines which party, the buyer or the seller, must pay the freight costs.[7]

The ownership of the merchandise may pass to the buyer when the seller delivers the merchandise to the freight carrier or transportation company. In this case, the terms are said to be **FOB (free on board) shipping point**. This term means that the buyer pays the freight costs from the shipping point (factory) to the final destination. Such costs are part of the buyer's total cost of purchasing inventory and should be added to the cost of the inventory by increasing Inventory.

To illustrate, assume that on December 10, TechSource buys merchandise from Magna Data on account, $900, terms FOB shipping point, and pays the freight cost of $50. The effects on the accounts and financial statements of these transactions are as follows:

Financial Statement Effects

	BALANCE SHEET			
	Assets		**= Liabilities +**	**Stockholders' Equity**
	Cash	**+ Inventory =**	**Accounts Payable**	
Dec. 10.	(50)	950	900	

STATEMENT OF CASH FLOWS	
Dec. 10. Operating	(50)

INCOME STATEMENT

7. The passage of title also determines whether the buyer or seller must pay other costs, such as the cost of insurance, while the merchandise is in transit.

Transaction Metric Effects

The effects on the liquidity and profitability metrics are as follows:

LIQUIDITY	
Working Capital	No Effect

PROFITABILITY	
Gross Profit Percent	No Effect

Working capital is not changed since the net increase of $900 ($950 – $50) in current assets equals the increase in Accounts Payable. Since no sale occurred, the gross profit percent is also unaffected.

The ownership of the merchandise may pass to the buyer when the buyer receives the merchandise. In this case, the terms are said to be **FOB (free on board) destination**. This term means that the seller delivers the merchandise to the buyer's final destination, free of freight charges to the buyer. The seller thus pays the freight costs to the final destination. The seller increases Delivery Expense, or Freight Out, which is reported on the seller's income statement as an expense.

Shipping terms, the passage of title, and whether the buyer or seller is to pay the transportation costs are summarized in Exhibit 5.

Exhibit 5
Freight Terms

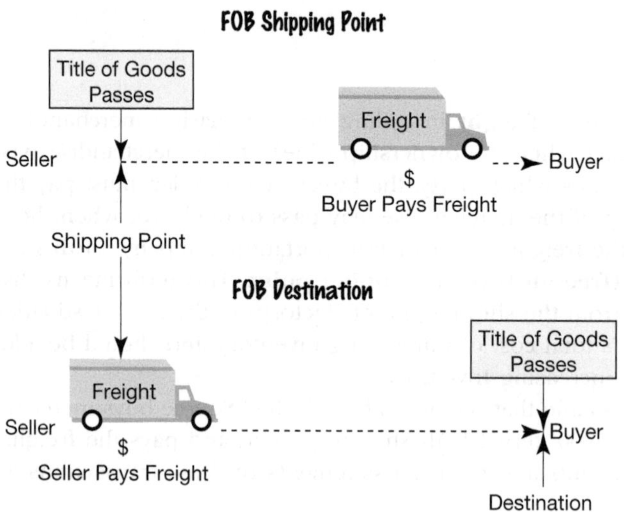

Amazon.com Connection

In a recent annual report, **Amazon.com** reported having incurred shipping costs of $37.9 billion. Shipping costs incurred to purchase merchandise were included in inventory. Shipping costs incurred from selling merchandise to customers were included in cost of goods sold.

Objective 5
Illustrate the dual nature of merchandising transactions.

Dual Nature of Merchandise Transactions

Each merchandising transaction affects a buyer and a seller. The following illustration shows how the same transactions would be recorded by both the seller and the buyer. In this example, the seller is Scully Company and the buyer is Burton Co.[8]

On July 1, Scully Company sold merchandise on account to Burton Co., $7,500, terms FOB destination; n/30. The cost of the merchandise sold was $4,500.

8. The metric effects of the transactions are not shown.

Scully Company (Seller)

Financial Statement Effects

BALANCE SHEET

	Assets		= Liabilities +	Stockholders' Equity
	Accounts Receivable	+ Inventory	=	Retained Earnings
July 1.	7,500	(4,500)		3,000

STATEMENT OF CASH FLOWS

INCOME STATEMENT

July 1.	Sales	7,500
	Cost of goods sold	(4,500)
	Gross profit	3,000

Burton Co. (Buyer)

Financial Statement Effects

BALANCE SHEET

	Assets	=	Liabilities	+	Stockholders' Equity
	Inventory	=	Accounts Payable		
July 1.	7,500		7,500		

STATEMENT OF CASH FLOWS

INCOME STATEMENT

On July 5, Scully Company pays transportation charges of $300 for delivery of the merchandise sold on July 1 to Burton Co.

Scully Company (Seller)

Financial Statement Effects

BALANCE SHEET

	Assets	=	Liabilities	+	Stockholders' Equity
	Cash	=			Retained Earnings
July 5.	(300)				(300)

STATEMENT OF CASH FLOWS

July 5. Operating	(300)

INCOME STATEMENT

July 5. Delivery exp.	(300)

Burton Co. (Buyer) No effect on the accounts and financial statements.

On July 6, Scully Company issues a credit memorandum for $400 for damaged merchandise. The merchandise was not returned.

Scully Company (Seller)

Financial Statement Effects

BALANCE SHEET

	Assets	=	Liabilities	+	Stockholders' Equity
	Accounts Receivable	=	Customer Refunds Payable		
July 6.	(400)		(400)		

STATEMENT OF CASH FLOWS

INCOME STATEMENT

Burton Co. (Buyer)

Financial Statement Effects

BALANCE SHEET

	Assets	=	Liabilities	+	Stockholders' Equity
	Inventory	=	Accounts Payable		
July 6.	(400)		(400)		

STATEMENT OF CASH FLOWS

INCOME STATEMENT

On August 1, Scully Company received payment from Burton Co.

Scully Company (Seller)

Financial Statement Effects

BALANCE SHEET

	Assets			=	Liabilities	+	Stockholders' Equity
	Cash	+	Accounts Receivable				
Aug. 1.	7,100*		(7,100)				

STATEMENT OF CASH FLOWS

Aug. 1. Operating	7,100

INCOME STATEMENT

* $7,500 – $400 = $7,100

Burton Co. (Buyer)

Financial Statement Effects

	BALANCE SHEET				
	Assets	**=**	**Liabilities**	**+**	**Stockholders' Equity**
	Cash	**=**	**Accounts Payable**		
Aug. 1.	(7,100)		(7,100)		

STATEMENT OF CASH FLOWS	
Aug. 1. Operating	(7,100)

INCOME STATEMENT

Adjustments for Retail Operations

Objective 6
Describe and illustrate adjustments for retail operations.

The adjusting process for a retail operation is similar to what we illustrated for Family Health Care in Chapter 3. For example, retail companies using the accrual basis of accounting need to record adjustments for deferrals, accruals, and depreciation. However, because of the nature of retail operations, several additional adjustments are necessary. These adjustments include the following:

- Inventory shrinkage
- Estimated customer refunds and allowances
- Estimated customer merchandise returns

These adjustments are described and illustrated in this section.

Inventory Shrinkage

Under the perpetual inventory system, the inventory account is continually updated for purchase and sales transactions. As a result, the balance of the inventory account is the amount of merchandise available for sale at that point in time. However, retailers normally experience some loss of inventory due to shoplifting, employee theft, or errors. Thus, the physical inventory on hand at the end of the accounting period is usually less than the balance of Inventory. This difference is called **inventory shrinkage** or **inventory shortage**.

To illustrate, TechSource's inventory records indicate the following on December 31, 20Y7:

	Dec. 31, 20Y7
Account balance of Inventory	$ 63,950
Physical merchandise inventory on hand	(62,150)
Inventory shrinkage	$ 1,800

The effect of the shrinkage on the accounts and financial statements is as follows:

Financial Statement Effects

	BALANCE SHEET				
	Assets	**=**	**Liabilities**	**+**	**Stockholders' Equity**
	Inventory	**=**			**Retained Earnings**
Dec. 31. Adjustments	(1,800)				(1,800)

STATEMENT OF CASH FLOWS

INCOME STATEMENT	
Dec. 31. Cost of goods sold	(1,800)

After the shrinkage is recorded, the balance of Inventory agrees with the physical inventory on hand at the end of the period. Since inventory shrinkage cannot be totally eliminated, it is considered a normal cost of operations and is included in the cost of goods sold.

Transaction Metric Effects

The effects of the shrinkage adjustment on the liquidity and profitability metrics are as follows:

LIQUIDITY	
Working Capital	$(1,800)

PROFITABILITY	
Gross Profit Percent	Decreases ability to achieve minimum of 20%

Since Inventory decreased by $1,800, working capital will decrease by $1,800. Since cost of goods sold increased by $1,800, gross profit will decrease by $1,800, which will have the effect of decreasing TechSource's ability to achieve an overall gross profit percent of at least 20%.

Customer Refunds, Allowances, and Returns

Retailers can normally estimate, based upon past operations, the percent of sales resulting in customer refunds and allowances. Using this percent, the Customer Refund Payable account is adjusted to reflect future refunds and allowances. An adjustment is also made to reflect estimated customer merchandise returns occurring in the future.

To illustrate, assume the following data for TechSource for the year ending December 31, 20Y7.

Unadjusted Balances
December 31, 20Y7

Account	**Balances***
Estimated Returns Inventory	$ 300
Customer Refunds Payable	800
Sales	715,409
Cost of Goods Sold	513,505
Adjustment Data	
Estimated percent of sales that is expected to be refunded or issued an allowance in 20Y8	1%
Estimated cost of inventory that is expected to be returned in 20Y8	$ 5,000

* Assume all normal balances

Based upon the preceding data, TechSource expects that customers of 20Y7 sales will be issued refunds or allowances of $7,154 ($715,409 × 1%) in 20Y8. As a result, an adjustment increasing Customer Refunds Payable by $7,154 and decreasing Sales by $7,154 is necessary. In addition, inventory costing $5,000 is expected to be returned in 20Y8. As a result, an adjustment increasing Estimated Returns Inventory by $5,000 and decreasing Cost of Goods Sold by $5,000 is necessary.[9]

The effects of these adjustments on the accounts and financial statements are as follows:

Financial Statement Effects

BALANCE SHEET

	Assets	=	Liabilities	+	Stockholders' Equity
	Estimated Returns Inventory	=	Customer Refunds Payable	+	Retained Earnings
Dec. 31.	5,000		7,154		(2,154)

STATEMENT OF CASH FLOWS

INCOME STATEMENT

Dec. 31.	Sales	(7,154)
	Cost of goods sold	5,000
	Gross profit	(2,154)

After the preceding adjustments, Estimated Returns Inventory will have a balance of $5,300 ($300 + $5,000) and Customer Refunds Payable will have a balance of $7,954 ($800 + $7,154). Estimated Returns Inventory is reported on the balance sheet as a current asset following Inventory. Customer Refunds Payable is reported on the balance sheet as a current liability following Accounts Payable.

Transaction Metric Effects

The effects of the preceding adjustments on liquidity and profitability metrics are as follows:

LIQUIDITY

Working Capital	$(2,154)

PROFITABILITY

Gross Profit Percent (30.1%)	Decrease ability to achieve minimum of 20%

Current assets (Estimated Returns Inventory) increased by $5,000 and current liabilities (Customer Refunds Payable) increased by $7,154. As a result, working capital decreased by $2,154. The gross profit percent on Sales of $7,154 and Cost of Goods Sold of $5,000 is 30.1% [($7,154 – $5,000) ÷ $7,154]. As a result, the adjustments decrease TechSource's ability to achieve an overall gross profit percent of at least 20%.

9. Because the specific items of inventory that will be returned in 20Y8 is unknown, Estimated Returns Inventory is increased rather than Inventory. In this way, the controlling account Inventory will still equal the sum of the Inventory subsidiary ledger accounts.

Objective 7
Describe and illustrate the financial statements of a retail company.

Financial Statements for a Retail Business

The financial statements for a retail company are illustrated in this section. As a basis for illustration, we use the financial statements of TechSource. We begin by illustrating multiple-step and single-step income statements.

Multiple-Step Income Statement

The 20Y7 income statement for TechSource is shown in Exhibit 6. This form of income statement, called a **multiple-step income statement**, contains several sections, subsections, and subtotals.

Exhibit 6 Multiple-Step Income Statement for Retail Company

TechSource Income Statement For the Year Ended December 31, 20Y7			
Sales			$ 708,255
Cost of goods sold			(520,305)
Gross profit			$ 187,950
Operating expenses:			
Selling expenses:			
Sales salaries expense	$53,430		
Advertising expense	10,860		
Depreciation expense—store equipment	3,100		
Delivery expense	2,800		
Miscellaneous selling expense	630		
Total selling expenses		$70,820	
Administrative expenses:			
Office salaries expense	$21,020		
Rent expense	8,100		
Depreciation expense—office equipment	2,490		
Insurance expense	1,910		
Office supplies expense	610		
Miscellaneous administrative expense	760		
Total administrative expenses		34,890	
Total operating expenses			(105,710)
Operating income			$ 82,240
Other revenue and expense:			
Rent revenue		$ 600	
Interest expense		(2,440)	(1,840)
Net income			$ 80,400

Sales

Sales is the total amount charged customers for merchandise sold, including cash sales and sales on account. During 20Y7, TechSource sold merchandise of $708,255.

Cost of Goods Sold

The cost of goods sold, sometimes called *cost of merchandise sold*, is the cost of the goods sold to customers. TechSource reported cost of goods sold of $520,305 during 20Y7.

Gross Profit

Gross profit is computed by subtracting the cost of goods sold from sales.

Sales	$708,255
Cost of goods sold	(520,305)
Gross profit	$187,950

Operating Income

Operating income, sometimes called *income from operations*, is determined by subtracting operating expenses from gross profit. Operating expenses are normally classified as either selling expenses or administrative expenses.

Selling expenses are incurred directly in the selling of merchandise. Examples of selling expenses include sales salaries, store supplies used, depreciation of store equipment, delivery expense, and advertising.

Administrative expenses, sometimes called **general expenses**, are incurred in the administration or general operations of the business. Examples of administrative expenses include office salaries, depreciation of office equipment, and office supplies used.

Each selling and administrative expense may be reported separately, as shown in Exhibit 6. However, many companies report selling, administrative, and operating expenses as single line items, as follows for TechSource.

Gross profit		$ 187,950
Operating expenses:		
Selling expenses	$70,820	
Administrative expenses	34,890	
Total operating expenses		(105,710)
Operating income		$ 82,240

Other Revenue and Expense

Other revenue and expense items are not related to the primary operations of the business. **Other revenue** is revenue from sources other than the primary operating activity of a business. Examples of other revenue include income from interest, rent, and gains resulting from the sale of fixed assets. **Other expense** is an expense that cannot be traced directly to the normal operations of the business. Examples of other expenses include interest expense and losses from disposing of fixed assets.

Other revenue and other expense are offset against each other on the income statement. If the total of other revenue exceeds the total of other expense, the difference is added to operating income to determine net income. If the reverse is true, the difference is subtracted from operating income. The other revenue and expense items of TechSource are reported as follows:

Operating income		$82,240
Other revenue and expense:		
Rent revenue	$ 600	
Interest expense	(2,440)	(1,840)
Net income		$80,400

Amazon's income statement uses the multiple-step form.

Amazon.com Connection

Single-Step Income Statement

An alternate form of income statement is the **single-step income statement**. As shown in Exhibit 7, the income statement for TechSource deducts the total of all expenses *in one step* from the total of all revenues.

The single-step form emphasizes total revenues and total expenses in determining net income. A criticism of the single-step form is that gross profit and operating income are not reported.

Exhibit 7 Single-Step Income Statement for Retail Company

TechSource
Income Statement
For the Year Ended December 31, 20Y7

Revenues:		
Sales		$708,255
Rent revenue		600
Total revenues		$708,855
Expenses:		
Cost of goods sold	$520,305	
Selling expenses	70,820	
Administrative expenses	34,890	
Interest expense	2,440	
Total expenses		(628,455)
Net income		$ 80,400

Statement of Stockholders' Equity

The statement of stockholders' equity for TechSource is shown in Exhibit 8. This statement is prepared in the same manner as for a service business.

Exhibit 8 Statement of Stockholders' Equity for Retail Company

	Common Stock	Retained Earnings	Total
Balances, Jan. 1, 20Y7	$25,000	$128,800	$153,800
Net income		80,400	80,400
Dividends		(18,000)	(18,000)
Balances, Dec. 31, 20Y7	$25,000	$191,200	$216,200

Amazon reported total stockholders' equity of $62,060 million on a recent statement of stockholders' equity.

Balance Sheet

As discussed and illustrated in Chapters 1–3, the balance sheet is presented in a downward sequence in three sections. The balance sheet for TechSource is shown in Exhibit 9. Inventory and estimated returns inventory are reported as current assets. Customer refunds payable and the current portion of the note payable of $5,000 are reported as current liabilities.

Amazon.com Connection

On a recent balance sheet, **Amazon** reported Inventories of $20,497 million and total current assets of $96,334 million.

Exhibit 9 Balance Sheet for Retail Company

TechSource Balance Sheet December 31, 20Y7			
Assets			
Current assets:			
Cash			$ 52,650
Accounts receivable			91,080
Inventory			62,150
Estimated returns inventory			5,300
Office supplies			480
Prepaid insurance			2,650
Total current assets			$214,310
Property, plant, and equipment:			
Land		$ 20,000	
Store equipment	$27,100		
Less accumulated depreciation	(5,700)	21,400	
Office equipment	$15,570		
Less accumulated depreciation	(4,720)	10,850	
Total property, plant, and equipment			52,250
Total assets			$266,560
Liabilities			
Current liabilities:			
Accounts payable		$ 12,466	
Customer refunds payable		7,954	
Estimated coupons payable		2,000	
Note payable (current portion)		5,000	
Salaries payable		1,140	
Unearned rent		1,800	
Total current liabilities			$ 30,360
Long-term liabilities:			
Note payable (final payment due in ten years)			20,000
Total liabilities			$ 50,360
Stockholders' Equity			
Common stock		$ 25,000	
Retained earnings		191,200	
Total stockholders' equity			216,200
Total liabilities and stockholders' equity			$266,560

Statement of Cash Flows

The statement of cash flows for TechSource is shown in Exhibit 10. It indicates that cash increased during 20Y7 by $16,450. This increase is generated from a positive cash flow from operating activities of $52,120 which is partially offset by negative cash flows from investing and financing activities of $(12,670) and $(23,000).

Amazon.com Connection On a recent statement of cash flows, **Amazon** reported cash from operating activities of $38,514 million, cash used for investing activities of $(24,281) million, cash used for financing activities of $(9,996) million, and a net increase in cash of $4,237 million.

The net cash flows from operating activities is shown in Exhibit 10 using a method known as the **indirect method**. This method, which reconciles net income with net cash flows from operating activities, is widely used among publicly held corporations.[10] Note that the December 31, 20Y7, cash balance reported on the statement of cash flows agrees with the amount reported for cash on the December 31, 20Y7, balance sheet shown in Exhibit 9.

Exhibit 10 Statement of Cash Flows for Retail Company

TechSource Statement of Cash Flows For the Year Ended December 31, 20Y7		
Cash flows from (used for) operating activities:		
Net income		$80,400
Depreciation expense—store equipment	$ 3,100	
Depreciation expense—office equipment	2,490	
Changes in noncash current operating assets and liabilities:		
Increase in accounts receivable	(38,080)	
Increase in inventory	(2,450)	
Increase in estimated returns inventory	(1,000)	
Decrease in office supplies	120	
Decrease in prepaid insurance	350	
Increase in accounts payable	7,250	
Increase in estimated coupons payable	400	
Increase in customer refunds payable	500	
Decrease in salaries payable	(360)	
Decrease in unearned rent	(600)	(28,280)
Net cash flows from operating activities		$52,120
Cash flows from (used for) investing activities:		
Cash paid for store equipment	$ (7,100)	
Cash paid for office equipment	(5,570)	
Net cash flows from investing activities		(12,670)
Cash flows from (used for) financing activities:		
Cash paid on note payable	$ (5,000)	
Cash paid as dividends	(18,000)	
Net cash flows from financing activities		(23,000)
Net increase in cash		$ 16,450
Cash as of January 1, 20Y7		36,200
Cash as of December 31, 20Y7		$ 52,650

10. The indirect method is briefly described and illustrated in the Appendix to Chapter 3, "Reconciliation: Net Cash Flows from (Used for) Operating Activities and Net Income." An alternative method of preparing the "Cash flows from (used for) operating activities" section is called the direct method. The direct method was used in preparing the statement of cash flows in Chapters 2 and 3. The direct and indirect methods are further discussed in Chapter 11.

Amazon uses the indirect method for preparing its statement of cash flows.

Amazon.com Connection

The integration of TechSource's financial statements is shown in Exhibit 11.

Exhibit 11 Integrated Financial Statements for TechSource

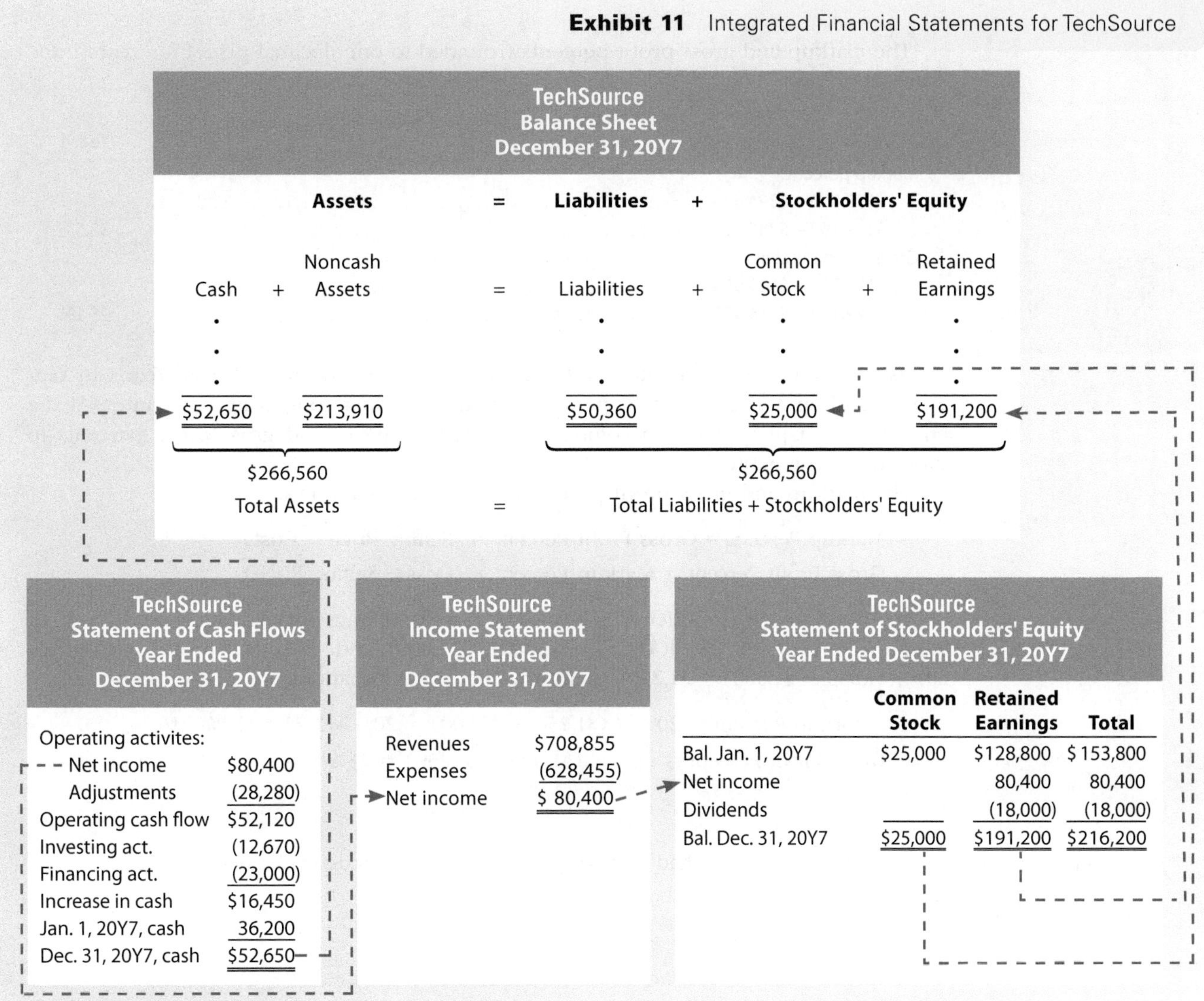

Metric-Based Analysis: Markup Percent

Objective 8

Describe and illustrate the markup percent.

A related metric to the gross profit percent is the markup percent. The **markup percent** is multiplied by a product's cost to determine the product's selling price. For example, assuming a product costs $1,000 and the desired markup percent is 25%, the selling price would be $1,250 [$1,000 + ($1,000 × 25%)].

The markup percent is computed as follows:

$$\text{Markup Percent} = \frac{\text{Gross Profit}}{\text{Cost of Goods Sold}}$$

To illustrate, data (in millions) for **Walmart Inc. (WMT)** are used. The following data were taken from two recent years' financial statements of Walmart.

	Year 2	Year 1
Sales	$523,964	$514,405
Cost of goods sold	(394,605)	(385,301)
Gross profit	$129,359	$129,104

The markup and gross profit percents (rounded to one decimal place) for Years 1 and 2 are as follows:

	Year 2	Year 1
Markup percent:		
$129,359 ÷ $394,605	32.8%	
$129,104 ÷ $385,301		33.5%
Gross profit percent:		
$129,359 ÷ $523,964	24.7%	
$129,104 ÷ $514,405		25.1%

As shown above, the markup and gross profit percents decreased from Year 1 to Year 2. The markup and gross profit percents are useful when comparing companies. At the end of this chapter, MBA 4-6 compares Walmart's markup and gross profit percents to those of its competitor, **Target Corporation (TGT)**.

The markup and gross profit percents are related as follows:

$$\text{Markup Percent} = \text{Gross Profit Percent} \times (\text{Selling Price} \div \text{Cost})$$

$$\text{Gross Profit Percent} = \text{Markup Percent} \times (\text{Cost} \div \text{Selling Price})$$

To illustrate, a product costing $1,000 and selling for $1,250 would have a markup percent of 25% [($1,250 − $1,000) ÷ $1,000] and a gross profit percent of 20% [($1,250 − $1,000) ÷ $1,250]. Using the preceding equations yields the following:

$$\text{Markup Percent} = 20\% \times (\$1{,}250 \div \$1{,}000) = 20\% \times 1.25 = 25\%$$

$$\text{Gross Profit Percent} = 25\% \times (\$1{,}000 \div \$1{,}250) = 25\% \times 0.8 = 20\%$$

Amazon.com Connection

For a recent year, **Amazon** had a gross profit percent of 41.0% and a markup percent of 69.5%.

Key Points

1. Distinguish the operations and financial statements of a service business from those of a retail business.

The operating cycle of a business is the process it takes for the business to spend cash to generate revenue, earn revenues, and receive cash from customers. The operating cycle for a retail business differs from a service business in that it must purchase merchandise for sale to customers. The differences between retail and service businesses are also reflected in their financial statements. A retail business reports sales, cost of goods sold, and gross profit on its income statement and inventory on its balance sheet.

2. Describe the accounting for the purchase of merchandise.

Purchases of merchandise for cash or on account are recorded in a perpetual inventory system by increasing Inventory. For purchases of merchandise on account, the credit terms allow payment at a later date. When merchandise is returned or a price adjustment is granted, the buyer decreases Inventory.

3. Describe the accounting for the sale of merchandise.

Sales of merchandise for cash or on account are recorded in a perpetual inventory system by increasing Sales. The cost of goods sold and the reduction in inventory are also recorded for the sale. A seller may offer customers a variety of sales incentives, promotions, and discounts in the form of coupons and rebates. A point-of-sale coupon is recorded as a decrease in Sales (revenue) at the time of the customer's purchase. If a coupon or rebate is issued at the time of the customer's purchase, the seller incurs a future liability. In this case, the seller estimates the dollar value of the coupons that will be redeemed, decreases Sales (revenue) by that amount, and increases Estimated Coupons Payable. When customers redeem the coupons, Estimated Coupons Payable is decreased. When the coupon period has expired, any remaining balance of Estimated Coupons Payable is transferred to Sales (revenue) as an increase or decrease. Rebates are accounted for in a similar manner as coupons.

A seller may pay a customer a refund or grant a price allowance for defective, returned, or damaged merchandise. At the end of the accounting period, a seller must estimate future returns, refunds, and allowances. Based upon this estimate, sellers record two adjustments. The first adjustment decreases Sales and increases Customer Refunds Payable. The second adjusting entry increases Estimated Returns Inventory and decreases Cost of Goods Sold.

When a customer is issued a refund or allowance, Customer Refunds Payable is decreased and either Cash, if the customer has already paid for the merchandise, or Accounts Receivable is decreased. If merchandise is returned, Inventory is increased for the cost of the returned merchandise and Estimated Returns Inventory is decreased.

On the balance sheet, Estimated Returns Inventory is reported as a current asset and Estimated Coupons Payable and Customer Refunds Payable are reported as a current liabilities.

Sales subject to sales or trade discounts are recorded net of the discounts. The liability for sales tax is incurred when the sale is made and is recorded by the seller as an increase in Sales Tax Payable. When the amount of the sales tax is paid to the taxing authority, Sales Tax Payable and Cash are decreased.

4. Describe the accounting for freight.

When merchandise is shipped FOB shipping point, the buyer pays the freight and increases Inventory. When merchandise is shipped FOB destination, the seller pays the freight and increases Delivery Expense or Freight Out.

5. Illustrate the dual nature of merchandising transactions.

Each merchandising transaction affects a buyer and a seller. The illustration in this chapter shows how the same transactions would be recorded by both.

6. Describe and illustrate adjustments for retail operations.

Because of the nature of retail operations, adjustments are necessary for inventory shrinkage, estimated customer refunds and allowances, and estimated customer merchandise returns.

The physical inventory taken at the end of the accounting period could differ from the amount of inventory shown in the inventory records. The difference, called *inventory shrinkage*, requires an adjusting entry increasing Cost of Goods Sold and decreasing Inventory. After this entry has been recorded, the adjusted Inventory (book inventory) in the accounting records agrees with the actual physical inventory at the end of the period.

The adjustment for estimated customer refunds or allowances decreases Sales and increases Customer Refunds Payable. The adjustment for estimated customer returns increases Estimated Returns Inventory and decreases Cost of Goods Sold.

7. Describe and illustrate the financial statements of a retail company.

The multiple-step income statement of a retail company reports sales, cost of goods sold, and gross profit. Operating income is determined by subtracting operating expenses from gross profit. Operating expenses are normally classified as selling or administrative expenses. Net income is determined by subtracting income taxes and other expense and adding other revenue. The income statement may also be reported in a single-step form. The statement of stockholders' equity and the statement of cash flows are similar to those for a service business. The balance sheet reports inventory and estimated returns inventory at the end of the period as current assets. In addition, customer returns payable is reported as a current liability.

8. Describe and illustrate the markup percent.

The markup percent is computed by dividing gross profit by cost of goods sold. It is useful for analyzing a company's performance and is related to the gross profit percent.

Key Terms

Administrative expenses (171)
Business-to-business (B2B) (143)
Business-to-consumer (B2C) (143)
Cash refund (158)
Controlling account (145)
Cost of goods sold (144)
Coupon (151)
Credit memorandum (160)
Credit period (147)
Credit terms (147)
Customer Refunds Payable (156)
Debit (bank) cards (151)
Debit memorandum (148)
Estimated Coupons Payable (153)
Estimated Returns Inventory (156)
FOB (free on board) destination (164)
FOB (free on board) shipping point (163)
Freight (163)
General expenses (171)
Gross profit (144)
Gross profit percent (145)
Indirect method (174)
Inventory (144)
Inventory shortage (167)
Inventory shrinkage (167)
Invoice (146)
Markup percent (175)
Multiple-step income statement (170)
Operating cycle (143)
Operating income (171)
Other expense (171)
Other revenue (171)
Periodic inventory system (145)
Perpetual inventory system (145)
Physical inventory (145)
Purchase returns and allowances (148)
Rebate (151)
Sales (144)
Selling expenses (171)
Single-step income statement (172)
Trade discounts (161)
Subsidiary ledger (145)
Working capital (145)

Illustrative Problem

Selected Accounts and their current balances of Sciatic Co. for the fiscal year ended July 31, 20Y5 are as follows:

Cash	$123,000	Retained earnings	$301,600
Accounts receivable	96,800	Dividends	28,000
Inventory	125,000	Sales	992,000
Estimated returns inventory	15,000	Cost of goods sold	620,000
Office supplies	4,480	Sales salaries expense	138,560
Prepaid insurance	2,720	Advertising expense	35,040
Office equipment	68,000	Depreciation expense—store equipment	5,120
Accumulated depreciation—office equipment	10,240	Miscellaneous selling expense	1,280
Store equipment	122,400	Office salaries expense	67,320
Accumulated depreciation—store equipment	27,360	Rent expense	25,080
Accounts payable	26,480	Depreciation expense—office equipment	10,160
Customer refunds payable	12,000	Insurance expense	3,120
Estimated coupons payable	6,000	Office supplies expense	1,040
Salaries payable	1,920	Miscellaneous administrative expense	1,280
Note payable (final payment due in seven years)	44,800	Interest expense	4,000
Common stock	75,000		

Instructions

1. Prepare a single-step income statement.
2. Prepare a multiple-step income statement.
3. Prepare a statement of stockholders' equity. Common stock of $15,000 was issued during the year. The retained earnings balance on August 1, 20Y4 was $301,600.
4. Prepare a balance sheet, assuming that the current portion of the note payable is $6,400

Solution

1.

SCIATIC CO.
Income Statement
For the Year Ended July 31, 20Y5

Sales		$ 992,000
Expenses:		
Cost of goods sold	$620,000	
Selling expenses	180,000	
Administrative expenses	108,000	
Interest expense	4,000	
Total expenses		(912,000)
Net income		$ 80,000

2.

SCIATIC CO.
Income Statement
For the Year Ended July 31, 20Y5

Sales			$ 992,000
Cost of goods sold			(620,000)
Gross profit			$ 372,000
Operating expenses:			
Selling expenses:			
Sales salaries expense	$138,560		
Advertising expense	35,040		
Depreciation expense—store equipment	5,120		
Miscellaneous selling expense	1,280		
Total selling expenses		$180,000	
Administrative expenses:			
Office salaries expense	$ 67,320		
Rent expense	25,080		
Depreciation expense—office equipment	10,160		
Insurance expense	3,120		
Office supplies expense	1,040		
Miscellaneous administrative expense	1,280		
Total administrative expenses		108,000	
Total operating expenses			(288,000)
Operating income			$ 84,000
Other expense:			
Interest expense			4,000
Net income			$ 80,000

3.

SCIATIC CO.
Statement of Stockholders' Equity
For the Year Ended July 31, 20Y5

	Common Stock	Retained Earnings	Total
Balances, Aug. 1, 20Y4	$60,000	$301,600	$361,600
Issued common stock	15,000		15,000
Net income		80,000	80,000
Dividends		(28,000)	(28,000)
Balances, July 31, 20Y5	$75,000	$353,600	$428,600

4.

SCIATIC CO.
Balance Sheet
July 31, 20Y5

Assets			
Current assets:			
Cash		$123,000	
Accounts receivable		96,800	
Inventory		125,000	
Estimated returns inventory		15,000	
Office supplies		4,480	
Prepaid insurance		2,720	
Total current assets			$367,000
Property, plant, and equipment:			
Office equipment	$ 68,000		
Less accumulated depreciation	(10,240)	$ 57,760	
Store equipment	$122,400		
Less accumulated depreciation	(27,360)	95,040	
Total property, plant, and equipment			152,800
Total assets			$519,800
Liabilities			
Current liabilities:			
Accounts payable		$ 26,480	
Customer refunds payable		12,000	
Estimated coupons payable		6,000	
Note payable (current portion)		6,400	
Salaries payable		1,920	
Total current liabilities			$ 52,800
Long-term liabilities:			
Note payable (final payment due in seven years)			38,400
Total liabilities			$ 91,200
Stockholders' Equity			
Common stock		$ 75,000	
Retained earnings		353,600	
Total stockholders' equity			428,600
Total liabilities and stockholders' equity			$519,800

Self-Examination Questions

(Answers appear at the end of the chapter.)

1. If merchandise purchased on account is returned, the buyer can inform the seller of the details by issuing:
   A. A debit memorandum
   B. A credit memorandum
   C. An invoice
   D. A bill

2. During January Tri-City Foods printed a $2 coupon at the bottom of its sales receipts. The coupon can be redeemed in February for purchases of $20 or more. In January, Tri-City Foods sold groceries and other merchandise for $30,000,000, which generated 400,000 printed receipts. Tri-City Foods estimates that 25% of the coupons will be redeemed in February. What is Tri-City Foods coupon liability (if any) as of January 31?
   A. $0
   B. $200,000
   C. $600,000
   D. $800,000

3. The income statement in which the total of all expenses is deducted from the total of all revenues is termed:
   A. Multiple-step form
   B. Single-step form
   C. Account form
   D. Report form

4. On a multiple-step income statement, the excess of sales over the cost of goods sold is called:
   A. Operating income
   B. Income from operations
   C. Gross profit
   D. Net income

5. As of December 31, 20Y4, Ames Corporation's physical inventory was $275,000, and its book inventory was $290,000. The effect of the inventory shrinkage on the accounts is:
   A. To increase Cost of Goods Sold and Inventory by $15,000
   B. To increase Cost of Goods Sold and decrease Inventory by $15,000
   C. To decrease Cost of Goods Sold and increase Inventory by $15,000
   D. To decrease Cost of Goods Sold and Inventory by $15,000

Class Discussion Questions

1. What distinguishes a retail business from a service business?
2. Describe how the periodic method differs from the perpetual method of accounting for merchandise inventory.
3. What is the difference between a sales coupon and a sales rebate?
4. What is the nature of (a) a credit memorandum issued by the seller of merchandise and (b) a debit memorandum issued by the buyer of merchandise?
5. Who bears the freight when the terms of sale are (a) FOB shipping point or (b) FOB destination?
6. When you purchase a new car, the "sticker price" includes a "destination" charge. Are you purchasing the car FOB shipping point or FOB destination? Explain.
7. How are sales to customers using MasterCard and VISA recorded?
8. Differentiate between the multiple and single-step forms of the income statement.
9. What are the major advantages and disadvantages of the single-step form of the income statement compared to the multiple-step form?
10. Can a business earn a gross profit but incur a net loss? Explain.
11. What type of revenue is reported in the "Other revenue" section of the multiple-step income statement?
12. Office Outfitters Inc., which uses a perpetual inventory system, experienced a inventory shrinkage of $3,750. What accounts would be increased and decreased to record the adjustment for the inventory shrinkage at the end of the accounting period?

Exercises

Obj. 1

SHOW ME HOW

EXCEL ONLINE

E4-1 Determining gross profit

During the current year, merchandise is sold for $3,200,000. The cost of the goods sold is $2,688,000.

a. What is the amount of the gross profit?

b. Compute the gross profit percent.

c. Will the income statement necessarily report a net income? Explain.

Obj. 1

E4-2 Determining cost of goods sold

For a recent year, Target Corporation (TGT) reported revenue of $78,112 million. Its gross profit was $23,248 million. What was the amount of Target's cost of goods sold?

Obj. 2

SHOW ME HOW

E4-3 Purchase-related transactions

Shepherd Company purchased merchandise on account from a supplier for $9,000, terms FOB shipping point, n/30. The seller paid freight of $75 as an accommodation to Shepherd Company. Shepherd Company returned $1,500 of the merchandise before payment was made and received full credit.

a. What is the amount of cash required for the payment by Shepherd Company?

b. Which accounts are decreased by Shepherd Company to record the return?

Obj. 2

SHOW ME HOW

✔ c. Cash, decreased $104,000

E4-4 Purchase-related transactions

Milan Co., a women's clothing store, purchased $120,000 of merchandise from a supplier on account, terms FOB destination, n/30. Milan Co. returned $16,000 of the merchandise, receiving a credit memorandum, and then paid the amount due. Illustrate the effects on the accounts and financial statements of Milan Co. to record (a) the purchase, (b) the merchandise return, and (c) the payment.

Obj. 2

✔ e. Cash, increased $12,500

E4-5 Purchase-related transactions

Illustrate the effects on the accounts and financial statements of the following related transactions of Bigsur Inc.

a. Purchased $200,000 of merchandise from Central Coast Co. on account, terms n/30.

b. Paid the amount owed on the invoice within the credit period.

c. Discovered that $30,000 of the merchandise was defective and returned items, receiving credit.

d. Purchased $17,500 of merchandise from Central Coast Co. on account, terms n/30.

e. Received a check from Central Coast Co. for the balance owed from the return in (c), after deducting for the purchase in (d).

Obj. 2, 4

✔ a. $11,800

E4-6 Determining amounts to be paid on invoices

Determine the amount to be paid in full settlement of each of the following invoices, assuming that credit for returns and allowances was received prior to payment and that all invoices were paid within the credit period.

	Merchandise	Freight Paid by Seller	Terms	Returns and Allowances
a.	$ 12,800	—	FOB shipping point, n/30	$ 1,000
b.	6,000	$ 175	FOB shipping point, n/30	500
c.	30,000	2,500	FOB destination, n/30	5,000
d.	28,500	1,100	FOB shipping point, n/eom	2,500
e.	7,700	250	FOB destination, n/30	—

E4-7 Sales-related transactions, including the use of credit cards

Obj. 3

Illustrate the effects on the accounts and financial statements of recording the following transactions:

a. Sold merchandise for cash, $62,500. The cost of the goods sold was $30,000.

b. Sold merchandise on account, $27,800, terms n/30. The cost of the goods sold was $16,000.

c. Sold merchandise to customers who used MasterCard and VISA, $287,500. The cost of the merchandise sold was $170,000.

E4-8 Sales-related transactions

Obj. 3

After the amount due on a sale of $16,000, terms n/eom, is received from a customer within the credit period, the seller consents to the return of the entire shipment. The cost of the merchandise returned was $10,000. (a) What is the amount of the refund owed to the customer? (b) Illustrate the effects on the accounts and financial statements of the seller of the return and the refund.

E4-9 Sales promotions

Obj. 3

Assume that Stacey Bauer clipped from a newspaper advertisement a coupon for $2 off any 20″ pizza from Rosa & Gene's Pizzeria. Stacey ordered a 20″ pizza with three toppings for $18.75. When the pizza arrived, Stacey gave the delivery person $20.

a. How much change should Stacey receive from the delivery person?

b. How much would Rosa & Gene's Pizzeria record for the sale of the pizza to Stacey?

c. Did Rosa & Gene's Pizzeria incur a liability when it placed the $2-off coupon advertisement in the newspaper?

E4-10 Sales promotions

Obj. 3

At the bottom of all its February sales receipts, Seifert Stores Inc. printed $2-off coupons. The coupons may be redeemed March 1–April 30. The liability for the $2-off coupons is recorded at the end of February in part (c). Seifert Stores Inc. accepts only cash, MasterCard, or VISA. During February, Seifert Stores completed the following selected transactions:

Feb. 6. Sold merchandise to Marci Andrews with a list price of $175 that cost Seifert Stores Inc. $80. Marci presented a $5-off coupon, which she clipped out of the local newspaper. Marci used her VISA card for the purchase.

18. Sold merchandise to Chris Johnson with a list price of $50 that cost Seifert Stores $24. The bottom of Chris Johnson's cash receipt includes the $2-off coupon. Chris paid cash for his purchase.

a. Illustrate the effects of the February 6 sale to Marci Andrews on the accounts and financial statements of Seifert Stores Inc.

b. Illustrate the effects of the February 18 sale to Chris Johnson on the accounts and financial statements of Seifert Stores Inc.

c. Illustrate the effects of the coupons Seifert Stores Inc. printed at the bottom of its February sales receipts on the accounts and financial statements. Assume that Seifert Stores sold $25,000,000 of merchandise in February, which generated 12,500,000 printed sales receipts. The merchandise sold cost $16,500,000. Siefert Stores estimates that 15% of the $2-off coupons printed in February will be redeemed before they expire April 30.

Obj. 3

SHOW ME HOW

E4-11 Sales promotions

Using the data in E4-10, assume that Seifert Stores Inc. sold $40,000,000 of merchandise in March and that 1,400,000 of the $2-off coupons were redeemed. The cost of the merchandise sold was $23,600,000.

a. Illustrate the effects of the March sales on the accounts and financial statements of Seifert Stores Inc.

b. Assume that Seifert Stores Inc. sold $33,500,000 of merchandise in April and that 440,000 of the $2-off coupons were redeemed. The cost of the merchandise sold was $19,100,000. Illustrate the effects of the April sales on the accounts and financial statements of Seifert Stores Inc.

c. What is the balance of Estimated Coupons Payable on April 30?

d. Illustrate the effects of the remaining unredeemed (expired) coupons as of April 30 on the accounts and financial statements of Seifert Stores Inc.

Obj. 3

E4-12 Sales promotions

On January 1, 20Y5, Seagrave Appliances offered a $150 mail-in rebate to any customer who purchases a TV or appliance with a list price of $1,000 or more. The rebate offer expires January 31 and checks will be mailed to customers starting February 1. During January, Seagrave Appliances issued 800 rebates to its customers.

a. Illustrate the effects of the liability for the mail-in rebates on the accounts and financial statements as of January 31. Assume all rebates will be redeemed.

b. Illustrate the effects of the payment of $115,000 of mail-in rebates on February 5 on the accounts and financial statements.

Obj. 3

E4-13 Sales incentives

Delta Air Lines, Inc. (DAL) operates its SkyMiles loyalty program to give its members (passengers) an incentive to fly Delta. Passengers earn mileage credit (SkyMiles) by flying on Delta, which can be redeemed for airline flights, car rentals, hotel stays, as well as other benefits.

How should Delta Air Lines record the sale of a $500 round-trip ticket that earns 1,500 Sky-Miles? Assume an average value of $0.012 per SkyMile.

Obj. 3

E4-14 Sales rebate

Goodyear Tire & Rubber Company (GT) published the following promotion on its Web site for the purchase of Wrangler TrailRunner AT tires: *$25 back with purchase of 4 tires by rebate via MasterCard prepaid card.*

Assume that Jeanne Blanchard purchases four Wrangler TrailRunner AT tires for her jeep at a list price of $120 per tire with free installation plus 5% sales tax.

a. When Goodyear posts the rebate on its Web site, should it record an estimated rebate liability?

b. Assuming Jeanne pays with her VISA, how much would be charged to her credit card?

c. How much would Goodyear record as sales (revenue) from the sale to Jeanne? Assume that Jeanne redeems the $25 rebate.

Obj. 3

E4-15 Customer refund

Senger Company sold merchandise of $15,500, terms n/30, to Burris Inc. on April 12. Burris paid Senger for the merchandise on May 12. On June 1, Senger paid Burris $650 for costs incurred by Burris to repair defective merchandise.

a. Illustrate the effects of the June 1 customer refund to Burris Inc. on the accounts and financial statements.

b. Assume that instead of paying Burris cash, Senger issued a credit memo on June 1 to Burris to be used against Burris's outstanding account receivable balance. Illustrate the effects of the credit memo on the accounts and financial statements.

E4-16 Customer return and refund

Obj. 3

On December 28, 20Y3, Silverman Enterprises sold $18,500 of merchandise to Beasley Co. with terms n/30. The cost of the goods sold was $11,200. On December 31, 20Y3, Silverman prepared its adjusting entries and yearly financial statements. On January 3, 20Y4, Silverman Enterprises issued Beasley Co. a credit memo for returned merchandise. The invoice amount of the returned merchandise was $4,000 and the merchandise originally cost Silverman Enterprises $2,350.

Illustrate the effects of the following on the accounts and financial statements of Silverman Enterprises of (a) the December 28, 20Y3, sale to Beasley Co., (b) the merchandise returned by Beasley Co. on January 3, 20Y4, and (c) the receipt of the amount due from Beasley Co. on January 7, 20Y4.

E4-17 Sales tax

Obj. 3

✔ c.$5,400

A sale of merchandise on account for $5,000, terms n/30, is subject to an 8% sales tax. (a) Should the sales tax be recorded at the time of sale or when payment is received? (b) What is the amount of the sale? (c) What is the amount of the increase to Accounts Receivable? (d) What is the title of the account in which the $400 ($5,000 × 8%) is recorded?

E4-18 Sales tax transactions

Obj. 3

Illustrate the effects on the accounts and financial statements of recording the following selected transactions:

a. Sold $22,500 of merchandise on account, terms n/30, subject to a sales tax of 6%. The cost of the merchandise sold was $13,500.

b. Paid sales tax to the state sales tax department for taxes collected on the preceding sale.

E4-19 Sales-related transactions

Obj. 3, 5

Steritech Co., a furniture wholesaler, sells merchandise to Butler Co. on account, $86,000, terms n/30. The cost of the merchandise sold is $51,600. Steritech Co. issues a credit memorandum for $5,000 for merchandise that was damaged in shipment. Butler Co. agreed to keep the damaged merchandise. Illustrate the effects on the accounts and financial statements of Steritech Co. for (a) the sale, including the cost of the merchandise sold, (b) the credit memorandum and (c) the receipt of the check for the amount due from Butler Co.

E4-20 Purchase-related transactions

Obj. 2, 5

Based on the data presented in Exercise 4-19, illustrate the effects on the accounts and financial statements of Butler Co. for (a) the purchase, (b) the credit for damaged merchandise, and (c) the payment of the invoice.

E4-21 Adjustment for merchandise inventory shrinkage

Obj. 6

Intrax Inc.'s perpetual inventory records indicate that $815,400 of merchandise should be on hand on December 31, 20Y4. The physical inventory indicates that $798,300 of merchandise is actually on hand. Illustrate the effects on the accounts and financial statements of the inventory shrinkage for Intrax Inc. for the year ended December 31, 20Y4.

Obj. 6

E4-22 Adjustment for customer refunds and returns

Assume the following data for Alpine Technologies for the year ending July 31, 20Y2.

Sales	$900,000
Estimated percent of sales expected to be refunded or issued an allowance in 20Y3	1.5%
Estimated cost of inventory expected to be returned in 20Y3	$6,000

Illustrate the effects of the adjustments for customer refunds and returns on the accounts and financial statements of Alpine Technologies for the year ended July 31, 20Y2.

Obj. 7

E4-23 Income statement for merchandiser

The following expenses were incurred by a retail business during the year. In which expense section of the income statement should each be reported: (a) selling, (b) administrative, or (c) other?

1. Advertising expense
2. Depreciation expense on store equipment
3. Insurance expense on office equipment
4. Interest expense on notes payable
5. Rent expense on office building
6. Salaries of office personnel
7. Salary of sales manager
8. Sales supplies used

Obj. 7

SHOW ME HOW

✔ a. Net income: $2,427,500

E4-24 Multiple-step income statement

On March 31, 20Y5, the balances of the accounts appearing in the ledger of Vibe Tribe Inc. are as follows:

Administrative Expenses	$ 475,000	Inventory	$ 400,000
Accumulated Dep.—Building	2,000,000	Notes Payable	450,000
Building	9,500,000	Office Supplies	25,000
Common Stock	500,000	Retained Earnings	6,182,500
Cash	1,485,000	Sales	8,925,000
Cost of Goods Sold	5,175,000	Selling Expenses	825,000
Dividends	100,000	Store Supplies	75,000
Interest Expense	22,500		

a. Prepare a multiple-step income statement for the year ended March 31, 20Y5.

b. Compare the major advantages and disadvantages of the multiple-step and single-step forms of income statements.

Obj. 7

✔ Net income: $4,100,000

E4-25 Single-step income statement

Summary operating data for Loma Company during the current year ended April 30, 20Y6, are as follows: cost of goods sold, $7,500,000; administrative expenses, $750,000; interest expense, $100,000; rent revenue, $120,000; sales, $13,580,000 and selling expenses, $1,250,000. Prepare a single-step income statement.

E4-26 Multiple-step income statement

Obj. 7

The following multiple-step income statement was prepared for Carlsbad Company:

CARLSBAD COMPANY Income Statement For the Year Ended February 28, 20Y8		
Sales		$4,220,000
Cost of goods sold		(2,650,000)
Operating income		$1,930,000
Expenses:		
Selling expenses	$ 800,000	
Administrative expenses	600,000	
Delivery expense	50,000	
Total expenses		(1,450,000)
Gross profit		$ 480,000
Other expense:		
Interest revenue		40,000
Net income		$ 440,000

a. Identify the errors in the preceding income statement.

b. Prepare a corrected income statement.

Problems

P4-1 Purchase-related transactions

Obj. 2, 4

The following selected transactions were completed by SUP Co. during August of the current year:

Aug. 3. Purchased merchandise on account for $16,700, terms FOB destination, n/30.

9. Issued debit memorandum for $1,250 for merchandise from the August 3 purchase that was kept, but was damaged in shipment.

10. Purchased merchandise on account, $12,500, terms FOB shipping point, n/eom. Paid $300 cash to the freight company for delivery of the merchandise.

13. Paid for invoice of August 3, less debit memorandum of August 9.

31. Paid for invoice of August 10.

Instructions

Illustrate the effects of each of the preceding transactions on the accounts and financial statements of SUP Co. Identify each transaction by date.

Obj. 3, 4

P4-2 Sales-related transactions

The following selected transactions were completed by Affordable Supplies Co., which sells supplies primarily to wholesalers and occasionally to retail customers.

Jan. 6. Sold merchandise on account, $14,000, terms FOB shipping point, n/eom. The cost of merchandise sold was $8,400.

7. Sold merchandise for $30,000 to retail customers who used MasterCard. The cost of the goods sold was $19,400. The printed receipts for retail customers included a coupon for $2 off the customer's next purchase. It is estimated that 2,000 of the coupons will be redeemed.

8. Sold merchandise on account, $20,000, terms FOB destination, n/15. The cost of merchandise sold was $14,000.

16. Sold merchandise on account, $19,500, terms FOB shipping point, n/15. The cost of merchandise sold was $11,700.

19. Issued credit memorandum for $4,500 for merchandise returned from sale on January 16. The cost of the merchandise returned was $2,700.

23. Received check for amount due for sale on January 8.

25. Sold $18,000 of merchandise to retail customers who used MasterCard and who redeemed 850 of the $2 coupons issued on January 7. The cost of the goods sold was $10,500.

31. Received check for amount due for sale on January 16 less credit memorandum of January 19.

31. Paid Cashell Delivery Service $3,000 for merchandise delivered during January to customers under shipping terms of FOB destination.

31. Received check for amount due for sale of January 6.

31. Paid local magazine $1,200 for advertising that included point-of-sale coupons for $15 off February purchases of $75 or more. It is estimated that 500 of the coupons will be redeemed.

Instructions

Illustrate the effects of each of the preceding transactions on the accounts and financial statements of Affordable Supplies Co. Identify each transaction by date.

Obj. 3, 4, 5

P4-3 Sales and purchase-related transactions for seller and buyer

The following selected transactions were completed during June between Snipes Company and Beejoy Company:

June 8. Snipes Company sold merchandise on account to Beejoy Company, $18,250, terms FOB destination, n/15. The cost of the merchandise sold was $10,000. Snipes Company paid transportation costs of $400 for delivery of the merchandise.

12. Beejoy Company returned merchandise with a selling price of $5,000 purchased on June 8 from Snipes Company. The cost of the merchandise returned was $3,000.

23. Beejoy Company paid Snipes Company for purchase of June 8, less refund on return of June 12.

24. Snipes Company sold merchandise on account to Beejoy Company, $15,000, terms FOB shipping point, n/eom. The cost of the merchandise sold was $9,000.

26. Beejoy Company paid transportation charges of $375 on June 24 purchase from Snipes Company.

30. Beejoy Company paid Snipes Company on account for purchase of June 24.

Instructions

Illustrate the effects of each of the preceding transactions on the accounts and financial statements of (1) Snipes Company and (2) Beejoy Company. Identify each transaction by date.

P4-4 Multiple-step income statement and report form of balance sheet

Obj. 7

✔ 1. Net income, $1,550,000

The following selected accounts and their current balances appear in the ledger of Prescott Inc. for the fiscal year ended September 30, 20Y8:

Cash	$ 167,000	Retained Earnings	$ 507,600
Accounts Receivable	300,000	Dividends	250,000
Inventory	735,000	Sales	7,134,000
Estimated Returns Inventory	25,000	Cost of Goods Sold	4,350,000
Office Supplies	30,000	Sales Salaries Expense	777,600
Prepaid Insurance	24,000	Advertising Expense	91,800
Office Equipment	230,400	Depreciation Expense—Store Equipment	16,600
Accumulated Depreciation—Office Equipment	99,000	Miscellaneous Selling Expense	4,000
Store Equipment	1,023,000	Office Salaries Expense	154,800
Accumulated Depreciation—Store Equipment	373,400	Rent Expense	79,800
Accounts Payable	47,000	Insurance Expense	45,900
Customer Refunds Payable	30,200	Depreciation Expense—Office Equipment	32,400
Estimated Coupons Payable	20,000	Office Supplies Expense	3,300
Salaries Payable	19,200	Miscellaneous Administrative Expense	3,800
Note Payable (final payment due in five years)	108,000	Interest Expense	24,000
Common Stock	30,000		

Instructions

1. Prepare a multiple-step income statement.
2. Prepare a statement of stockholders' equity. No common stock was issued during the year.
3. Prepare a balance sheet, assuming that the current portion of the note payable is $16,000.
4. Briefly explain how multiple-step and single-step income statements differ.

P4-5 Single-step income statement

Obj. 7

Selected accounts and related amounts for Prescott Inc. for the fiscal year ended September 30, 20Y8, are presented in Problem 4-4.

Instructions

1. Prepare a single-step income statement in the format shown in Exhibit 8.
2. Prepare a statement of stockholders' equity. No common stock was issued during the year.

Metric-Based Analysis

Obj. 2, 4, 8

MBA 4-1 Purchase transactions

Using transactions listed in P4-1, indicate the effects of each transaction on the liquidity metric working capital and profitability metric gross profit percent.

Obj. 3, 4, 8

MBA 4-2 Sales transactions

Using transactions listed in P4-2, indicate the effects of each transaction on the liquidity metric working capital and profitability metric gross profit percent. Indicate the gross profit percent for each sale (rounding to one decimal place) in parentheses next to the effect of the sale on the company's ability to attain an overall gross profit percent of 30%.

Obj. 6, 8

MBA 4-3 Inventory shrinkage

Using adjustment data listed in E4-21, indicate the effects the inventory shrinkage adjustment on the liquidity metric working capital and profitability metric gross profit percent.

Obj. 6, 8

MBA 4-4 Customer refunds and returns

Using adjustment data listed in E4-22, indicate the effects the adjustment for estimated customer refunds and returns on the liquidity metric working capital and profitability metric gross profit percent. Indicate in parentheses the effect of the adjustment for sales and cost of goods sold on the company's ability to attain an overall gross profit percent of 30%.

Obj. 8

MBA 4-5 Gross margin percent and markup percent

Target Corp. (TGT) operates retail stores throughout the United States and is a major competitor of Walmart (WMT). The following data (in millions) were adapted from recent financial statements of Target.

	Year 2	Year 1
Sales	$78,112	$75,356
Cost of goods sold	(54,864)	(53,299)
Gross profit	$23,248	$22,057

1. Compute the gross profit percent for Years 1 and 2. Round to one decimal place.
2. Compute the average markup percent for Years 1 and 2. Round to one decimal place.
3. Compare the results in parts (1) and (2) for Years 1 and 2. Comment on your comparison.

Obj. 8

MBA 4-6 Gross profit percent and markup percent

Compare the Target (TGT) results in MBA 4-5 with those of Walmart (WMT) shown in the chapter illustration on page 176. Comment on the differences.

MBA 4-7 Gross profit percent and markup percent

Obj. 8

Deere & Company (DE) produces and sells tractors, loaders, combines, lawnmowers, and a variety of other equipment. The following data (in millions) were adapted from recent financial statements of Deere.

	Year 2	Year 1
Sales	$39,281	$37,355
Cost of goods sold	(28,449)	(27,115)
Gross profit	$10,832	$10,240

1. Compute the gross profit percent for Years 1 and 2. Round to one decimal place.
2. Compute the average markup percent for Years 1 and 2. Round to one decimal place.
3. Compare the results in parts (1) and (2) for Years 1 and 2. Comment on your comparison.

MBA 4-8 Gross profit percent and markup percent

Obj. 8

Caterpillar Inc. (CAT) produces and sells various types of equipment, including tractors, loaders, and mining equipment. The following data (in millions) were adapted from recent financial statements of Caterpillar.

	Year 2	Year 1
Sales	$53,800	$54,722
Cost of goods sold	(36,508)	(36,815)
Gross profit	$17,292	$17,907

1. Compute the gross profit percent for Years 1 and 2. Round to one decimal place.
2. Compute the average markup percent for Years 1 and 2. Round to one decimal place.
3. Compare the results in parts (1) and (2) for Years 1 and 2. Comment on your comparison.

MBA 4-9 Gross profit percent, markup percent, and ratio of sales to assets

Obj. 8

Compare the gross profit percent, average markup percent, and ratio of sales to assets for Deere & Company (DE) and Caterpillar Inc. (CAT) using the results of MBA 4-7 and MBA 4-8. Comment on any differences.

MBA 4-10 Gross profit percent and markup percent

Obj. 8

Companies with low gross profit and markup percents often have higher volumes of sales than companies with high gross profit and markup percents.

1. Comment on the preceding statement.
2. The following data (in millions) were adapted from recent financial statements of The Kroger Co. (KR) and Tiffany & Co. (TIF) Kroger operates supermarkets, while Tiffany designs and sells jewelry, china, watches, and other expensive merchandise.

	Kroger	Tiffany
Sales	$122,286	$4,424
Cost of goods sold	(95,294)	(1,662)
Gross profit	$ 26,992	$2,762

Compute the gross profit percent and average markup percent for Kroger and Tiffany. Round to one decimal place.

3. Comment on the results in part (2).

Cases

Case 4-1 Determining cost of purchase

The following is an excerpt from a conversation between Eric Jackson and Carlie Miller. Eric is debating whether to buy a stereo system from First Audio, a locally owned electronics store, or Dynamic Sound Systems, an online electronics company.

Eric: Carlie, I don't know what to do about buying my new stereo.

Carlie: What's the problem?

Eric: Well, I can buy it locally at First Audio for $890.00. But Dynamic Sound Systems has the same system listed for $899.99.

Carlie: So what's the big deal? Buy it from First Audio.

Eric: It's not quite that simple. Dynamic Sound Systems said something about not having to pay sales tax, since I was out of state.

Carlie: Yes, that's a good point. If you buy it at First Audio, they'll charge you 6% sales tax.

Eric: But Dynamic Sound Systems charges $13.99 for shipping and handling. If I have them send it next-day air, it'll cost $44.99 for shipping and handling.

Carlie: I guess it is a little confusing.

Eric: That's not all. First Audio will give an additional 1% discount if I pay cash. Otherwise, they will let me use my VISA, or I can pay it off in three monthly installments.

Carlie: Anything else???

Eric: Well ... Dynamic Sound Systems says I have to charge it on my VISA. They don't accept checks.

Carlie: I am not surprised. Many online stores don't accept checks.

Eric: I give up. What would you do?

1. Assuming that Dynamic Sound Systems doesn't charge sales tax on the sale to Eric, which company is offering the best buy?
2. What might be some considerations other than price that might influence Eric's decision on where to buy the stereo system?

Case 4-2 Inventory shrinkage adjustment

ETHICS

Margie Johnson is a staff accountant at ToolEx Company, a manufacturer of tools and equipment. The company is under pressure from investors to increase earnings, and the president of the company expects the Accounting Department to "make this happen." Margie's boss, who has been a mentor to her, is concerned that if earnings do not increase, he will be terminated.

Shortly after the end of the fiscal year, the company performs a physical count of the inventory. When Margie compares the physical count to the balance in the inventory account, she finds a significant amount of inventory shrinkage. The amount is so large that it will result in a significant drop in earnings this period. Margie's boss asks her not to make the adjusting entry for shrinkage this period. He assures her that they will get "caught up" on shrinkage in the next period, after the pressure is off to reach this period's earnings goal. Margie's boss asks her to do this as a personal favor to him.

What should Margie do in this situation? Why?

Case 4-3 Real word annual report

GROUP PROJECT

In teams, obtain **Dollar Tree, Inc.**'s **(DLTR)** most recent annual report on Form 10-K. The Form 10-K is a company's annually required filing with the Securities and Exchange Commission (SEC). It includes the company's financial statements and accompanying notes. The

Form 10-K can be obtained either (a) from the investor relations section of the company's Web site or (b) by using the company search feature of the SEC's EDGAR database service found at www.sec.gov/edgar/searchedgar/companysearch.html.

1. Based on the information in the company's most recent annual report, determine each of the following:
   a. Gross profit for each year reported.
   b. Gross profit percentage (gross profit ÷ sales) for each year reported. Round to one decimal place.
   c. Operating income for each year reported.
   d. Percentage change in operating income for the most recent year. Round to one decimal place.
   e. Net income for each year reported.
2. Based solely on your responses to item 1, has the company's performance improved, remained constant, or deteriorated over the periods presented? Briefly explain your answer.

Case 4-4 Effects of sales promotion

Your sister operates Harbor Ready Parts Company, an online boat parts distributorship that is in its third year of operation. The following income statement was recently prepared for the year ended October 31, 20Y6:

HARBOR READY PARTS COMPANY
Income Statement
For the Year Ended October 31, 20Y6

Revenues:		
Sales		$1,200,000
Interest revenue		15,000
Total revenues		$1,215,000
Expenses:		
Cost of goods sold	$800,000	
Selling expenses	135,000	
Administrative expenses	75,000	
Interest expense	21,650	
Total expenses		(1,031,650)
Net income		$ 183,350

Your sister is considering a proposal to increase net income by offering sales promotions, including coupons and rebates and by shipping all merchandise FOB shipping point. It is estimated that the sales promotion will increase sales by 15%, but will also increase the ratio of cost of goods sold to sales to 68%. The cost of the sales promotions will increase selling expenses from $135,000 to $150,000. All merchandise is currently shipped FOB destination. All other expenses are expected to remain unchanged, except for store supplies, miscellaneous selling, office supplies, and miscellaneous administrative expenses, which are expected to increase proportionately with increased sales. The amounts of these preceding items for the year ended October 31, 20Y6, were as follows:

Store supplies expense	$18,000	Office supplies expense	$4,000
Miscellaneous selling expense	5,000	Miscellaneous administrative expense	2,000

The other revenue and other expense items will remain unchanged. The shipment of all merchandise FOB shipping point will eliminate all delivery expenses, which for the year ended October 31, 20Y6, were $28,000.

1. Prepare a projected single-step income statement for the year ending October 31, 20Y7, based on the proposal. Assume all sales are collected within the credit period.
2. Based on the projected income statement in part (1), would you recommend implementation of the proposed changes?
3. Describe any possible concerns you may have related to the proposed changes described in part (1).

GROUP PROJECT

Case 4-5 Shopping for a television

Assume that you are planning to purchase a Samsung LED-LCD, 55-inch television. In groups of three or four, determine the lowest cost for the television, considering the available alternatives and the advantages and disadvantages of each alternative. For example, you could purchase locally, through mail order, or through an Internet shopping service. Consider such factors as delivery charges, interest-free financing, discounts, coupons, and availability of warranty services. Prepare a report for presentation to the class.

USING DATA ANALYTICS

Case 4-6 Sales analysis

Michelle Horowitz is the manager of AAAA Office Supplies, a locally owned office supply store for schools and businesses. Michelle is concerned about the large variety of products the store carries, which ties up storage space and working capital. Michelle has asked you to analyze the store's inventory and sales to determine if there are products that may be worth discontinuing.

Michelle has asked you for the following:

1. A list of the quantity of each product sold for a recent month.
2. Recommendations for any products that should be discontinued.

Go to CengageNOWv2 to complete this assignment.

ANNUAL REPORT

The annual report (10-K) assignment for this chapter is in Appendix B: Nike Annual Report, Chapter 4.

Answers to Self-Examination Questions

1. **A** A debit memorandum (answer A), issued by the buyer, indicates the amount the buyer proposes to decrease the accounts payable account. A credit memorandum (answer B), issued by the seller, indicates the amount the seller proposes to decrease the accounts receivable account. An invoice (answer C) or a bill (answer D), issued by the seller, indicates the amount and terms of the sale.
2. **B** The estimated coupon liability on January 31 is based on the estimated coupons that will be redeemed in February. Since 25% of the coupons are estimated to be redeemed, the estimated coupon liability on January 31 is $200,000 (answer B), which is computed as 400,000 coupons × 25% × $2 per coupon.
3. **B** The single-step form of income statement (answer B) is so named because the total of all expenses is deducted in one step from the total of all revenues. The multiple-step form (answer A) includes numerous sections and subsections with several subtotals. The account form (answer C) and the report form (answer D) are two forms of the balance sheet.
4. **C** Gross profit (answer C) is the excess of sales over the cost of goods sold. Operating income (answer A) or income from operations (answer B) is the excess of gross profit over operating expenses. Net income (answer D) is the final figure on the income statement after all revenues and expenses have been reported.
5. **B** The inventory shrinkage, $15,000, is the difference between the book inventory, $290,000, and the physical inventory, $275,000. The effect of the inventory shrinkage on the accounts is to increase Cost of Goods Sold and decrease Inventory by $15,000.

Chapter 5

Internal Control and Cash

What's Covered:

Topics: Internal Control and Cash

Internal Control
- Sarbanes-Oxley Act (Obj. 1)
- Control objectives (Obj. 2)
- Control elements (Obj. 2)
- Controls for cash receipts (Obj. 3)
- Controls for cash payments (Obj. 3)

Bank Accounts
- Bank statement (Obj. 4)
- Bank reconciliation (Obj. 5)
- Special-purpose funds (Obj. 6)

Financial Reporting
- Cash (Obj. 7)
- Cash equivalents (Obj. 7)

Metric-Based Analysis
- Financial statements: Cash to monthly cash expenses (Obj. 8)

Learning Objectives

Obj.1 Describe the Sarbanes-Oxley Act and its impact on internal controls and financial reporting.

Obj.2 Describe and illustrate the objectives and elements of internal control.

Obj.3 Describe and illustrate the application of internal controls to cash.

Obj.4 Describe the nature of a bank account and its use in controlling cash.

Obj.5 Describe and illustrate the use of a bank reconciliation in controlling cash.

Obj.6 Describe the accounting for special-purpose cash funds.

Obj.7 Describe and illustrate the reporting of cash and cash equivalents in the financial statements.

Obj.8 Describe and illustrate the ratio of cash to monthly cash expenses in assessing the ability of a company to continue operating.

Chapter Metrics

Use the following metrics to analyze transactions and financial statements:

TRANSACTIONS*

Liquidity: N/A

Profitability: N/A

FINANCIAL STATEMENTS

Ratio of Cash to Monthly Cash Expenses

* Because of the few number of transactions in this chapter, liquidity and profitablity metrics are not illustrated.

eBay Inc.

rvlsoft/Shutterstock.com

Controls are a part of your everyday life. At one extreme, laws are used to limit your behavior. For example, the speed limit is a control on your driving, designed for traffic safety. In addition, you are also affected by many nonlegal controls. For example, recording checks in your checkbook is a control that you can use at the end of the month to verify the accuracy of your bank statement. In addition, banks give you a personal identification number (PIN) as a control against unauthorized access to your cash if you lose your automated teller machine (ATM) card. As you can see, you use and encounter controls every day.

Just as there are many examples of controls throughout society, businesses must also implement controls to help guide the behavior of their managers, employees, and customers. For example, **eBay Inc. (EBAY)** maintains an Internet-based marketplace for the sale of goods and services. Using eBay's online platform, buyers and sellers can browse, buy, and sell a wide variety of items including antiques and used cars. However, in order to maintain the integrity and trust of its buyers and sellers, eBay must have controls to ensure that buyers pay for their items and sellers don't misrepresent their items or fail to deliver sales. One such control eBay uses is a feedback forum that estabilishes buyer and seller reputations. A prospective buyer or seller can view the member's reputation and feedback comments before completing a transaction. Dishonest or unfair trading can lead to a negative reputation and even suspension or cancellation.

This chapter discusses controls that can be included in accounting systems to provide reasonable assurance that the financial statements are reliable. Controls over cash that you can use to determine whether your bank has made any errors in your account are also discussed. This chapter begins by discussing the Sarbanes-Oxley Act and its impact on controls and financial reporting.

Sarbanes-Oxley Act

Objective 1
Describe the Sarbanes-Oxley Act and its impact on internal controls and financial reporting.

When companies commit financial fraud, stockholders, creditors, and other investors often lose billions of dollars.[1] To reduce the likelihood and mitigate the impact of financial fraud, the U.S. Congress passed the **Sarbanes-Oxley Act**. This act, often referred to as *Sarbanes-Oxley*, is one of the most important laws affecting U.S. companies. The purpose of Sarbanes-Oxley is to restore public confidence and trust in the financial reporting of companies.

Sarbanes-Oxley applies only to companies whose stock is traded on public exchanges, referred to as *publicly held companies*. However, Sarbanes-Oxley highlights the importance of assessing the financial controls and reporting of all companies. As a result, companies of all sizes have been influenced by Sarbanes-Oxley.

eBay Connection

eBay designs and maintains its internal controls in conformity with Sarbanes-Oxley.

Sarbanes-Oxley emphasizes the importance of effective internal control.[2] **Internal control** is defined as the procedures and processes used by a company to:

1. Safeguard its assets.
2. Process information accurately.
3. Ensure compliance with laws and regulations.

Sarbanes-Oxley requires companies to maintain effective internal controls over the recording of transactions and the preparing of financial statements. Such controls are important because they deter fraud and prevent misleading financial statements as shown in Exhibit 1.

1. Exhibit 13 in Chapter 1 briefly summarizes these scandals.
2. Sarbanes-Oxley also has important implications for corporate governance and the regulation of the public accounting profession. This chapter, however, focuses on the internal control implications of Sarbanes-Oxley.

Exhibit 1
Effect of Sarbanes-Oxley

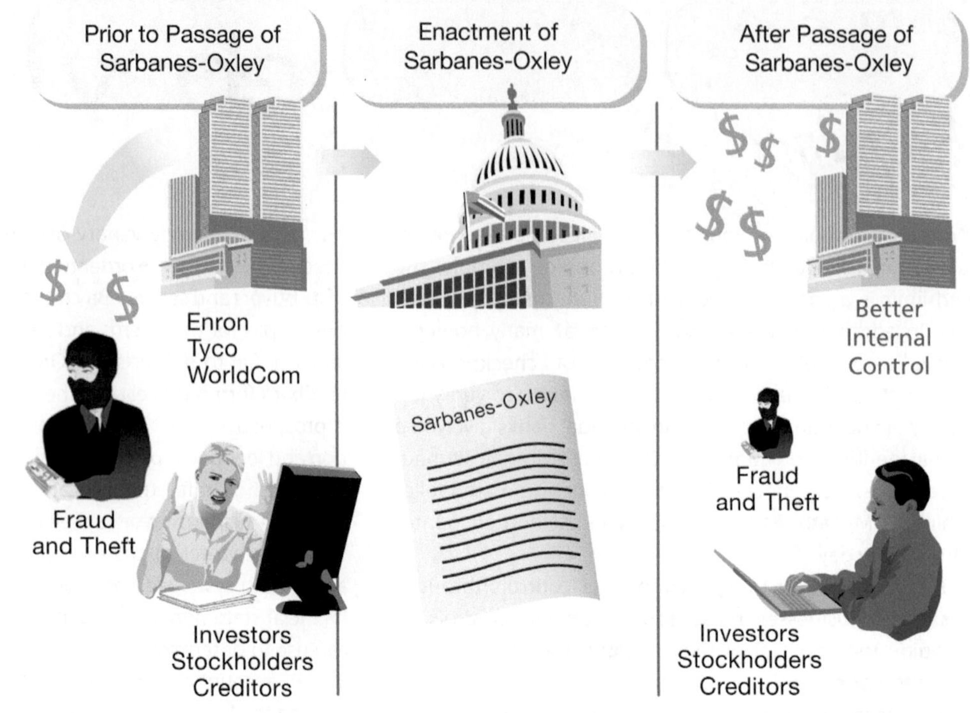

Sarbanes-Oxley also requires companies and their independent accountants to report on the effectiveness of the company's internal controls.[3] These reports are required to be filed with the company's annual 10-K report with the Securities and Exchange Commission. Companies are also encouraged to include these reports in their annual reports to stockholders. An example of such a report by the management of **eBay (EBAY)** is shown in Exhibit 2.

Exhibit 2 Sarbanes-Oxley Report of eBay

eBay Connection

Management's Report on Internal Control over Financial Reporting

Our management is responsible for establishing and maintaining adequate internal control over financial reporting. Our management, including our principal executive officer and principal financial officer, conducted an evaluation of the effectiveness of our internal control over financial reporting based on the framework in Internal Control—Integrated Framework (2013) issued by the Committee of Sponsoring Organizations of the Treadway Commission.

Based on its evaluation under the framework in Internal Control—Integrated Framework, our management concluded that our internal control over financial reporting was effective.

Source: eBay Inc., *Form 10-K*.

Exhibit 2 indicates that **eBay (EBAY)** based its evaluation of internal controls on *Internal Control—Integrated Framework*, which was issued by the Committee of Sponsoring Organizations (COSO) of the Treadway Commission. This framework is the standard by which companies design, analyze, and evaluate internal controls.

3. These reporting requirements are required under Section 404 of the act. As a result, these requirements and reports are often referred to as 404 requirements and 404 reports.

Internal Control

Objective 2
Describe and illustrate the objectives and elements of internal control.

Internal Control—Integrated Framework is used as the basis for discussing internal controls.[4] In this section, the objectives of internal control are described, followed by a discussion of how these objectives can be achieved through the *Integrated Framework*'s five elements of internal control.

Objectives of Internal Control

The objectives of internal control are to provide reasonable assurance that:

1. Assets are safeguarded and used for business purposes.
2. Business information is accurate.
3. Employees and managers comply with laws and regulations.

These objectives are illustrated in Exhibit 3.

Exhibit 3
Objectives of Internal Control

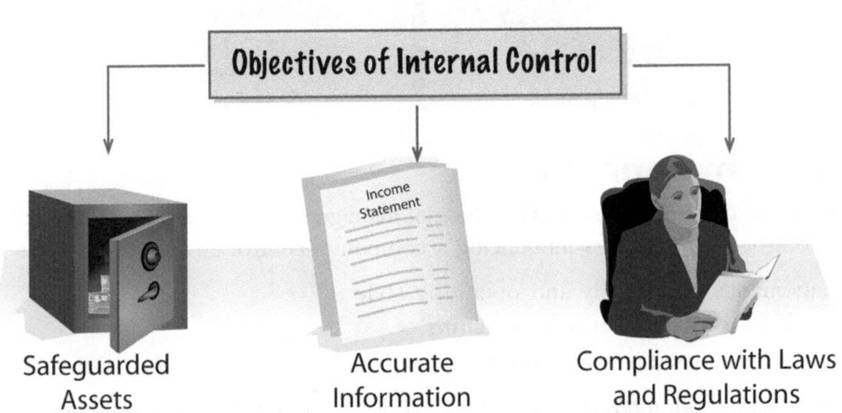

Internal control can safeguard assets by preventing theft, fraud, misuse, or misplacement. A serious concern of internal control is preventing employee fraud. **Employee fraud** is the intentional act of deceiving an employer for personal gain. Such fraud may range from minor overstating of a travel expense report to stealing millions of dollars. Employees stealing from a business often adjust the accounting records in order to hide their fraud. Thus, employee fraud usually affects the accuracy of business information.

Accurate information is necessary to successfully operate a business. Businesses must also comply with laws, regulations, and financial reporting standards. Examples of such standards include environmental regulations, safety regulations, and generally accepted accounting principles (GAAP).

Elements of Internal Control

The three internal control objectives can be achieved by applying the five **elements of internal control** set forth by the *Integrated Framework*.[5] These elements are as follows:

1. Control environment
2. Risk assessment
3. Control procedures
4. Monitoring
5. Information and communication

The elements of internal control are illustrated in Exhibit 4. In this exhibit, the elements of internal control form an umbrella over the business to protect it from control threats.

4. Internal Control—Integrated Framework by the Committee of Sponsoring Organizations of the Treadway Commission, 1992.
5. Ibid., pp. 12–14.

The control environment is the size of the umbrella. Risk assessment, control procedures, and monitoring are the fabric of the umbrella, which keep it from leaking. Information and communication connect the umbrella to management.

Exhibit 4
Elements of Internal Control

Control Environment

The control environment is the overall attitude of management and employees about the importance of controls. Three factors influencing a company's control environment are as follows:

1. Management's philosophy and operating style
2. The company's organizational structure
3. The company's personnel policies

Management's philosophy and operating style relates to whether management emphasizes the importance of internal controls. An emphasis on controls and adherence to control policies creates an effective control environment. In contrast, overemphasizing operating goals and tolerating deviations from control policies creates an ineffective control environment.

eBay Connection

eBay has a *Code of Business Conduct and Ethics* that applies to all employees.

A business's *organizational structure* is the framework for planning and controlling operations. For example, a retail store chain might organize each of its stores as separate business units. Each store manager has full authority over pricing and other operating activities. In such a structure, each store manager has the responsibility for establishing an effective control environment.

A business's *personnel policies* involve the hiring, training, evaluation, compensation, and promotion of employees. In addition, job descriptions, employee codes of ethics, and conflict-of-interest policies are part of the personnel policies. Such policies can enhance the internal control environment if they provide reasonable assurance that only competent, honest employees are hired and retained.

Risk Assessment

All businesses face risks such as changes in customer requirements, competitive threats, regulatory changes, and changes in economic factors. Management should identify such risks, analyze their significance, assess their likelihood of occurring, and take any necessary actions to minimize them.

eBay faces competitive risks from various online companies including **Amazon.com** and **Home Shopping Network**.

Control Procedures

Control procedures provide reasonable assurance that business goals will be achieved, including the prevention of fraud. Control procedures, which constitute one of the most important elements of internal control, include the following:

1. Competent personnel, rotating duties, and mandatory vacations
2. Separating responsibilities for related operations
3. Separating operations, custody of assets, and accounting
4. Proofs and security measures

Competent Personnel, Rotating Duties, and Mandatory Vacations A successful company needs competent employees who are able to perform the duties that they are assigned. Procedures should be established for properly training and supervising employees. It is also advisable to rotate duties of accounting personnel and mandate vacations for all employees. In this way, employees are encouraged to adhere to procedures. Cases of employee fraud are often discovered when a long-term employee, who never took vacations, missed work because of an illness or another unavoidable reason.

Separating Responsibilities for Related Operations The responsibility for related operations should be divided among two or more persons. This decreases the possibility of errors and fraud. For example, if the same person orders supplies, verifies the receipt of the supplies, and pays the supplier, the following abuses may occur:

1. Orders may be placed on the basis of friendship with a supplier, rather than on price, quality, and other objective factors.
2. The quantity and quality of supplies received may not be verified; thus, the company may pay for supplies not received or that are of poor quality.
3. Supplies may be stolen by the employee.
4. The validity and accuracy of invoices may not be verified; hence, the company may pay false or inaccurate invoices.

Separating Operations, Custody of Assets, and Accounting The responsibilities for operations, custody of assets, and accounting should be separated. In this way, the accounting records serve as an independent check on the operating managers and the employees who have custody of assets.

To illustrate, employees who handle cash receipts should not record cash receipts in the accounting records. To do so would allow employees to borrow or steal cash and hide the theft in the accounting records. Likewise, operating managers should not also record the results of operations. To do so would allow the managers to distort the accounting reports to show favorable results, which might allow them to receive larger bonuses.

Proofs and Security Measures Proofs and security measures are used to safeguard assets and ensure reliable accounting data. Proofs involve procedures such as authorization, approval, and reconciliation. For example, an employee planning to travel on company business may be required to complete a "travel request" form for a manager's authorization and approval.

Documents used for authorization and approval should be prenumbered, accounted for, and safeguarded. Prenumbering of documents helps prevent transactions from being recorded more than once or not at all. In addition, accounting for and safeguarding prenumbered documents helps prevent fraudulent transactions from being recorded. For example, blank checks are prenumbered and safeguarded. Once a payment has been properly authorized and approved, the checks are filled out and issued.

Reconciliations are also an important control. Later in this chapter, the use of bank reconciliations as an aid in controlling cash is described and illustrated.

Security measures involve measures to safeguard assets. For example, cash on hand should be kept in a cash register or safe. Inventory not on display should be stored in a locked storeroom or warehouse. Accounting records such as the accounts receivable subsidiary ledger should also be safeguarded to prevent their loss. For example, electronically maintained accounting records should be safeguarded with access codes and backed up so that any lost or damaged files could be recovered if necessary.

Monitoring

Monitoring the internal control system is used to locate weaknesses and improve controls. Monitoring often includes observing employees' behavior and the accounting system for indicators of control problems. Some such indicators are shown in Exhibit 5.[6]

Exhibit 5
Warning Signs of Internal Control Problems

Warning signs with regard to people

1. Abrupt change in lifestyle (without winning the lottery).
2. Close social relationships with suppliers.
3. Refusing to take a vacation.
4. Frequent borrowing from other employees.
5. Excessive use of alcohol or drugs.

Warning signs from the accounting system

1. Missing documents or gaps in transaction numbers (could mean documents are being used for fraudulent transactions).
2. An unusual increase in customer refunds (refunds may be phony).
3. Differences between daily cash receipts and bank deposits (could mean receipts are being pocketed before being deposited).
4. Sudden increase in slow payments (employee may be pocketing the payments).
5. Backlog in recording transactions (possibly an attempt to delay detection of fraud).

Evaluations of controls are often performed when there are major changes in strategy, senior management, business structure, or operations. Internal auditors, who are independent of operations, usually perform such evaluations. Internal auditors are also responsible for day-to-day monitoring of controls. External auditors evaluate and report on internal control as part of their annual financial statement audit.

Information and Communication

Information and communication is an essential element of internal control. Information about the control environment, risk assessment, control procedures, and monitoring is used by management for guiding operations and ensuring compliance with reporting, legal, and regulatory requirements. Management also uses external information to assess events and conditions that impact decision making and external reporting. For example, management uses pronouncements of the Financial Accounting Standards Board (FASB) to assess the impact of changes in reporting standards on the financial statements.

6. Edwin C. Bliss, "Employee Theft," *Boardroom Reports,* July 15, 1994, pp. 5–6.

In its annual 10-K filing with the Securities and Exchange Commission, eBay reports on its business strategies, risk factors affecting its business, legal matters, and analysis of its current operating results and condition. Its financial statements are also included in the filing.

Limitations of Internal Control

Internal control systems can provide only reasonable assurance for safeguarding assets, processing accurate information, and complying with laws and regulations. In other words, internal controls are not a guarantee. This is due to the following factors:

1. The human element of controls
2. Cost-benefit considerations

The *human element* recognizes that controls are applied and used by humans. As a result, human errors can occur because of fatigue, carelessness, confusion, or misjudgment. For example, an employee may unintentionally shortchange a customer or miscount the amount of inventory received from a supplier. In addition, two or more employees may collude together to defeat or circumvent internal controls. This latter case often involves fraud and the theft of assets. For example, the cashier and the accounts receivable clerk might collude to steal customer payments on account.

Cost-benefit considerations recognize that the costs of internal controls should not exceed their benefits. For example, retail stores could eliminate shoplifting by searching all customers before they leave the store. However, such a control procedure would upset customers and result in lost sales. Instead, retailers use cameras or signs saying they prosecute all shoplifters.

Using Data Analytics

Evaluating Internal Controls

Loss of inventory from shoplifting is a major concern for large retail chains such as **Walmart Inc. (WMT)** and **Target Corporation (TGT)**. The National Association for Shoplifting Prevention (NASP) estimates that stores lose more than $45 million a day to shoplifting.

Retailers can implement a variety of controls to prevent and detect shoplifting, including the following:

1. Place rounded mirrors throughout stores to better enable employees to detect shoplifters.
2. Install electronic tags on high-value items that must be removed before exiting the store.
3. Put up signs indicating the store's willingness to prosecute shoplifters.
4. Hire a person to check bags and receipts of all customers exiting the store.
5. Hire a greeter to monitor customers bringing bags or other items that can be used to hide shoplifted items.
6. Install security cameras throughout stores.
7. Place high-value items in locked cases.
8. Monitor dressing rooms closely.

Before implementing a control, retailers should carefully consider the cost of the control and whether the cost exceeds its potential benefit. For example, the cost of putting up signs and mirrors is low compared to the cost of installing security cameras, using electronic tags, or hiring greeters. Data analytics can be used by large retail chains such as Walmart and Target to monitor shoplifting and to assess the cost-benefit of various shoplifting controls across their stores.

See Case 5-6 for a homework assignment using data analytics.

Source: www.shopliftingprevention.org/the-shoplifting-problem/

Cash Controls Over Receipts and Payments

Objective 3
Describe and illustrate the application of internal controls to cash.

Cash includes coins, currency (paper money), checks, and money orders. Money on deposit with a bank or other financial institution that is available for withdrawal is also considered cash. Normally, you can think of cash as anything that a bank would accept for deposit in your account. For example, a check made payable to you could normally be deposited in a bank and thus is considered cash.

Businesses usually have several bank accounts. For example, a business might have one bank account for general cash payments and another for payroll. For example, a general bank account at City Bank could be identified as *Cash in Bank—City Bank*. To simplify, we will assume that a company has only one bank account, which is identified as *Cash*.

Cash is the asset most likely to be stolen or used improperly in a business. For this reason, businesses must carefully control cash and cash transactions.

Control of Cash Receipts

To protect cash from theft and misuse, a business must control cash from the time it is received until it is deposited in a bank. Businesses normally receive cash from two main sources as shown in Exhibit 6.

1. Customers purchasing products or services
2. Customers making payments on account

Exhibit 6 Cash Received from Customers

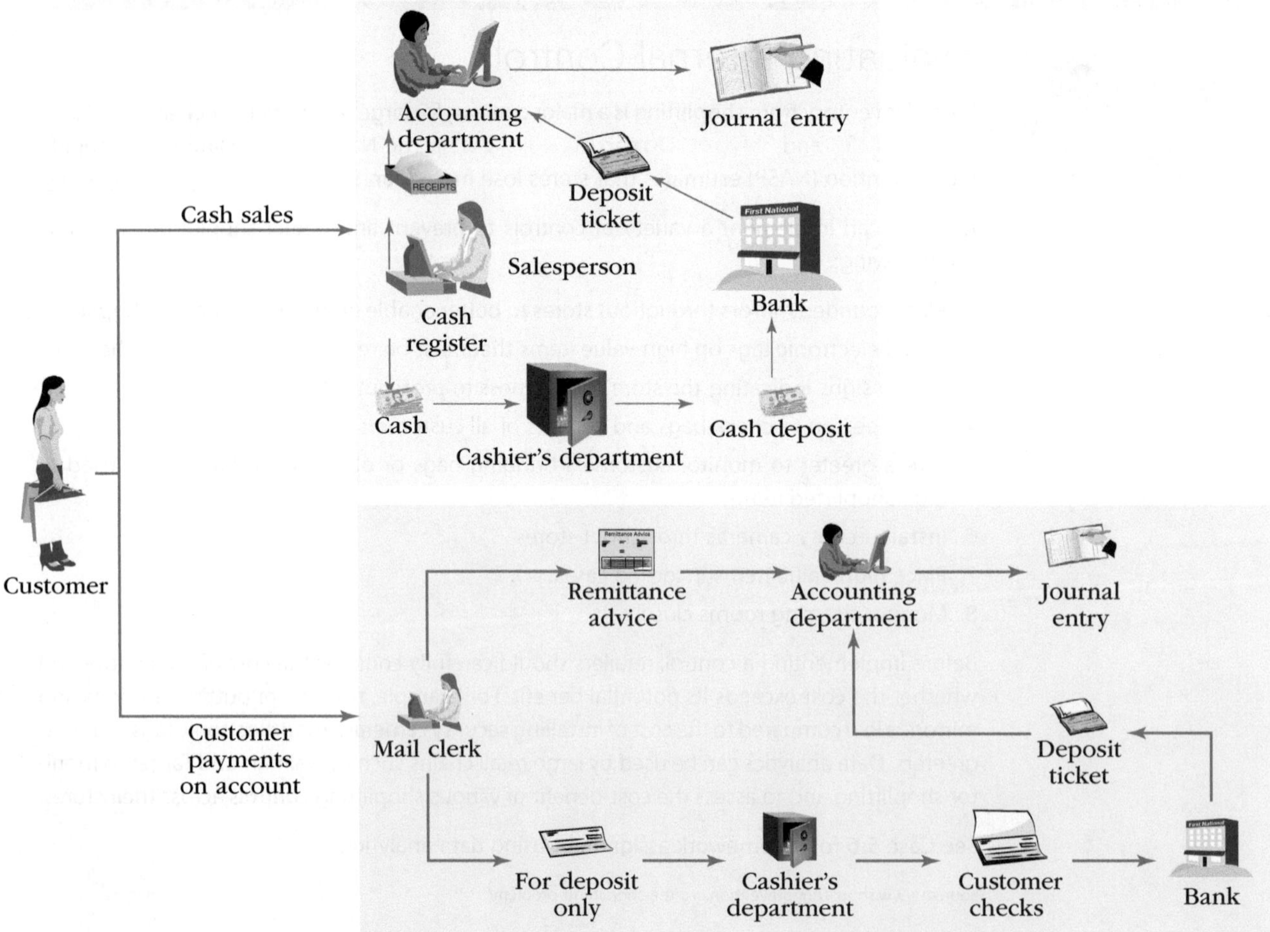

Cash Received from Cash Sales An important control to protect cash received in over-the-counter sales is a cash register. The use of a cash register to control cash is shown in Exhibit 6.

A cash register controls cash as follows:

1. Each cash register clerk is given a cash drawer containing a predetermined amount of cash. This amount is used for making change for customers and is sometimes called a *change fund*.
2. When the clerk enters the amount of a sale, the cash register displays the amount to the customer. This allows the customer to verify that the clerk has charged the correct amount. The customer also receives a cash receipt.
3. The clerk and a supervisor count the cash in the clerk's cash drawer each time a new clerk takes control of the cash register. The amount of cash in the clerk's drawer should equal the beginning amount of cash plus the cash sales.
4. The supervisor takes the cash to the Cashier's Department where it is placed in a safe.
5. The supervisor forwards the clerk's cash register receipts to the Accounting Department.
6. The cashier prepares a bank deposit ticket.
7. The cashier deposits the cash in the bank, or the cash is picked up by an armored car service, such as **Wells Fargo (WFC)**.
8. The Accounting Department summarizes the cash receipts and records the day's cash sales.
9. When cash is deposited in the bank, the bank normally stamps a duplicate copy of the deposit ticket or sends an electronic receipt of the amount received. The bank receipt is returned to the Accounting Department, where it is compared to the total amount that should have been deposited. This control helps ensure that all the cash is deposited and that no cash is lost or stolen on the way to the bank. Any shortages are thus promptly detected.

Cash register clerks may make errors in making change for customers or in ringing up cash sales. As a result, the amount of cash on hand may differ from the amount of cash sales. Such differences are recorded as **cash short and over**.

To illustrate, assume the following cash register data for May 3:

Cash register total for cash sales	$35,690
Cash receipts from cash sales	35,668

The cash sales are recorded in the normal manner. The cash shortage of $22 ($35,690 − $35,668) is recorded as a normal operating expense. This is done by recording a negative $22 under the account titled Cash Short and Over.

A cash overage is recorded as a positive amount in Cash Short and Over. At the end of the period, a negative balance in Cash Short and Over is reported as an Other operating expense. A positive balance in Cash Short and Over is reported as Other revenue.

Cash Received in the Mail Cash is received in the mail when customers pay their bills. This cash is usually in the form of checks and money orders. Most companies design their invoices so that customers return a portion of the invoice, called a *remittance advice*, with their payment. Remittance advices may be used to control cash received in the mail as shown in Exhibit 6.

1. An employee opens the incoming mail and compares the amount of cash received with the amount shown on the remittance advice. If a customer does not return a remittance advice, the employee prepares one. The remittance advice serves as a record of the cash initially received. It also helps ensure that the posting to the customer's account is for the amount of cash received.
2. The employee opening the mail stamps checks and money orders "For Deposit Only" in the bank account of the business.
3. The remittance advices and their summary totals are delivered to the Accounting Department.
4. All cash, money orders, and customer checks are delivered to the Cashier's Department.
5. The cashier prepares a bank deposit ticket.
6. The cashier deposits the cash in the bank, or the cash is picked up by an armored car service, such as **Wells Fargo (WFC)**.

7. An accounting clerk records the cash received and posts the amounts to the customer accounts.
8. When cash is deposited in the bank, the bank normally stamps a duplicate copy of the deposit ticket with the amount received. This bank receipt is returned to the Accounting Department, where it is compared to the total amount that should have been deposited. This control helps ensure that all cash is deposited and that no cash is lost or stolen on the way to the bank. Any shortages are thus promptly detected.

Separating the duties of the Cashier's Department, which handles cash, and the Accounting Department, which records cash, is a control. If Accounting Department employees both handle and record cash, an employee could steal cash and change the accounting records to hide the theft.

Cash Received by EFT Cash also may be received from customers through **electronic funds transfer (EFT)**. For example, customers may authorize automatic electronic transfers from their checking accounts to pay monthly bills for such items as cell phone, Internet services, and utilities. In such cases, the company sends the customer's bank a signed form from the customer authorizing the monthly electronic transfers. Each month, the company notifies the customer's bank of the amount of the transfer and the date the transfer should take place. On the due date, the company records the electronic transfer as a receipt of cash to its bank account and posts the amount paid to the customer's account.

Companies encourage customers to use EFT for the following reasons:

1. EFTs cost less than receiving cash payments through the mail.
2. EFTs enhance internal controls over cash since the cash is received directly by the bank without any employees handling cash.
3. EFTs reduce late payments from customers and speed up the processing of cash receipts.

In a recent year, **eBay** generated over $3 billion of cash from its operations.

Control of Cash Payments

The control of cash payments should provide reasonable assurance that:

1. Payments are made for only authorized transactions.
2. Cash is used effectively and efficiently. For example, controls should ensure that all available purchase discounts are taken.

In a small business, an owner/manager may authorize payments based on personal knowledge. In a large business, however, purchasing goods, inspecting the goods received, and verifying the invoices are usually performed by different employees. These duties must be coordinated to ensure that proper payments are made to creditors. One system used for this purpose is the voucher system.

Voucher System A **voucher system** is a set of procedures for authorizing and recording liabilities and cash payments. A **voucher** is any document that serves as proof of authority to pay cash or issue an electronic funds transfer. An invoice that has been approved for payment could be considered a voucher. In many businesses, however, a voucher is a special form used to record data about a liability and the details of its payment.

In a manual system, a voucher is normally prepared after all necessary supporting documents have been received. For the purchase of goods, a voucher is supported by the supplier's invoice, a purchase order, and a receiving report. After a voucher is prepared, it is submitted for approval. Once approved, the voucher is recorded in the accounts and filed by due date. Upon payment, the voucher is recorded in the same manner as the payment of an account payable.

In a computerized system, data from the supporting documents (such as purchase orders, receiving reports, and suppliers' invoices) are entered directly into computer files. At the due date, the checks are automatically generated and mailed to creditors. At that time, the voucher is electronically transferred to a paid voucher file.

Cash Paid by EFT Cash can also be paid by electronic funds transfer systems. For example, many companies pay their employees by EFT. Under such a system, employees authorize the deposit of their payroll checks directly into their checking accounts. Each pay period, the company transfers the employees' net pay to their checking accounts through the use of EFT. Many companies also use EFT systems to pay their suppliers and other vendors.

eBay Connection

PayPal provides **eBay** customers a convenient way for eBay users to receive and pay cash. In 2015, PayPal was spun off by eBay into a separate company.

Bank Accounts

Objective 4
Describe the nature of a bank account and its use in controlling cash.

A major reason that companies use bank accounts is for internal control. Some of the control advantages of using bank accounts are as follows:

1. Bank accounts reduce the amount of cash on hand.
2. Bank accounts provide an independent recording of cash transactions. Reconciling the balance of the cash account in the company's records with the cash balance according to the bank is an important control.
3. Use of bank accounts facilitates the transfer of funds using EFT systems.

Bank Statement

Banks usually maintain a record of all checking account transactions. A summary of all transactions, called a **bank statement**, is mailed, usually each month, to the company (depositor) or made available online. The bank statement shows the beginning balance, additions, deductions, and the ending balance. A typical bank statement is shown in Exhibit 7.

Exhibit 7
Bank Statement

MEMBER FDIC — PAGE 1

Mariner National Bank
5000 NE 75th Street
Bellevue, WA 98005

ACCOUNT NUMBER 1627042
FROM 6/30/20Y7 TO 7/31/20Y7
BALANCE 4,218.60
22 DEPOSITS 13,749.75
52 WITHDRAWALS 14,698.57
3 OTHER DEBITS AND CREDITS 90.00CR
NEW BALANCE 3,359.78

Colter Inc.
200 West Main Street
Bozeman, MT 59715

CHECKS AND OTHER DEBITS						DEPOSITS	DATE	BALANCE
No. 850	819.40	No. 852	122.54			585.75	07/01	3,862.41
No. 854	369.50	No. 853	20.15			421.53	07/02	3,894.29
No. 851	600.00	No. 856	190.70	No. 857	52.50	781.30	07/03	3,832.39
No. 855	25.93	No. 858	160.00			662.50	07/05	4,308.96
No. 860	921.20	NSF	300.00			503.18	07/07	3,590.94
No. 880	32.26	No. 877	535.09			ACH 932.00	07/29	4,136.66
No. 881	21.10	No. 879	732.26	No. 882	126.20	705.21	07/30	3,962.31
		SC	18.00			MS 408.00	07/30	4,352.31
No. 874	26.12	ACH	1,615.13			648.72	07/31	3,359.78

EC — ERROR CORRECTION
ACH — AUTOMATED CLEARING HOUSE
MS — MISCELLANEOUS
SC — SERVICE CHARGE
NSF — NOT SUFFICIENT FUNDS

* * * * * * * * *

THE RECONCILEMENT OF THIS STATEMENT WITH YOUR RECORDS IS ESSENTIAL.
ANY ERROR OR EXCEPTION SHOULD BE REPORTED IMMEDIATELY.

Checks or copies of the checks listed in the order that they were paid by the bank may accompany the bank statement. If paid checks are returned, they are stamped "Paid," together with the date of payment. Many banks no longer return checks or check copies. Instead, the check payment information is available online.

The depositor's checking account balance in the bank records is a liability. A credit memo entry on the bank statement indicates an increase in the depositor's account. Likewise, a debit memo entry on the bank statement indicates a decrease in the depositor's account.

A bank issues credit memos for the following:

1. Deposits made by electronic funds transfer (EFT)
2. Collections of note receivable for the company
3. Proceeds for a loan made to the company by the bank
4. Interest earned on the company's account
5. Correction of bank errors

A bank issues debit memos for the following:

1. Payments made by electronic funds transfer (EFT)
2. Service charges
3. Customer checks returned for not sufficient funds
4. Correction of bank errors

Customers' checks returned for not sufficient funds, called *NSF checks*, are customer checks that were initially deposited but not paid by the customer's bank. Since the company's bank increased the company's account when the customer's check was deposited, the bank decreases the company's account (issues a debit memo) when the check is returned without payment.

The reason for a credit or debit memo entry is indicated on the bank statement. Exhibit 7 identifies the following types of credit and debit memo entries:

EC: Error correction to correct bank error
NSF: Not sufficient funds check
SC: Service charge
ACH: Automated clearing house entry for electronic funds transfer
MS: Miscellaneous item such as collection of a note receivable on behalf of the company or receipt of a loan by the company from the bank

The above list includes the notation "ACH" for electronic funds transfers. ACH is a network for clearing electronic funds transfers among individuals, companies, and banks.[7] Because electronic funds transfers may be either deposits or payments, ACH entries may indicate either a positive or negative entry to the company's account. Likewise, entries to correct bank errors and miscellaneous items may indicate a positive or negative entry to the company's account.

The relationship between the company's cash in bank asset account and the bank's liability account is shown in Exhibit 8.

7. For further information on ACH, go to www.nacha.org/. Click on "ACH" and then click on "What is ACH?"

Business Insight

Check Fraud

Check fraud involves counterfeiting, altering, or otherwise manipulating the information on a check in order to fraudulently obtain cash. According to Feature Space's *U.S. Consumer Fraud Sentiment Survey*, 38% of consumers experience at least one instance of fraud on an existing bank account. Check fraud can take a variety of forms including the following:

- Forging signatures on blank checks
- Forging endorsements on stolen checks
- Using counterfeit checks generated by color printers or copying machines
- Altering items on a legitimate check, such as changing the amount of the check

Consumers can prevent check fraud by carefully-storing blank checks, placing outgoing mail in postal mailboxes, and shredding canceled checks. Consumers can detect check fraud by closely monitoring their bank activity and statements.

Source: www.featurespace.com/us-consumer-fraud-survey-report

Exhibit 8 Relationship Between Bank and Company

Company			Bank	
Asset **Cash in Bank**			**Liability** **Company's Account**	
Beginning balance	**$XXX**	=	**Beginning balance**	**$XXX**
Increases in asset	XXX ←	Cash deposits EFT deposits Notes receivable collections Loan proceeds Interest earned Company or bank errors	→ Increases in liability (Credit memorandum)	XXX
Decreases in asset	(XXX) ←	Checks EFT payments Service charges NSF checks Company or Bank errors	→ Decrease in liability (Debit memorandum)	(XXX)
Ending balance	**$XXX**	=	**Ending balance**	**$XXX**

Using the Bank Statement as a Control Over Cash

The bank statement is a primary control that a company uses over cash. A company uses the bank's statement as a control by comparing the company's recording of cash transactions to those recorded by the bank.

The cash balance shown by a bank statement is usually different from the company's cash balance, as shown in Exhibit 9.

Exhibit 9 Colter Inc.'s Records and Bank Statement

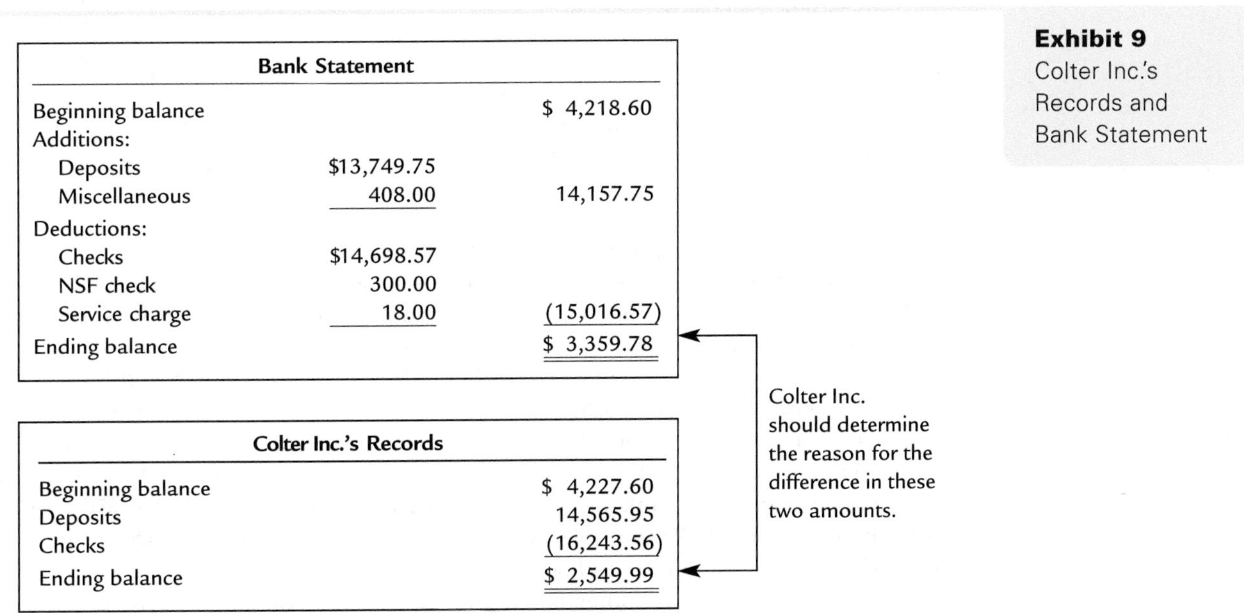

Bank Statement		
Beginning balance		$ 4,218.60
Additions:		
Deposits	$13,749.75	
Miscellaneous	408.00	14,157.75
Deductions:		
Checks	$14,698.57	
NSF check	300.00	
Service charge	18.00	(15,016.57)
Ending balance		$ 3,359.78

Colter Inc.'s Records	
Beginning balance	$ 4,227.60
Deposits	14,565.95
Checks	(16,243.56)
Ending balance	$ 2,549.99

Differences between the company and bank balances may arise because of a delay by either the company or bank in recording transactions. For example, there is normally a time lag of one or more days between the date a check is written and the date that it is paid by the bank. Likewise, there is normally a time lag between when the company mails a deposit to the bank (or uses the night depository) and when the bank receives and records the deposit.

Differences may also arise because the bank has increased or decreased the company's account for transactions that the company will not know about until the bank statement is received. Finally, differences may arise from errors made by either the company or the bank. For example, the company may incorrectly post to Cash a check written for $4,500 as $450. Further, a bank may incorrectly record the amount of a check.

Objective 5
Describe and illustrate the use of a bank reconciliation in controlling cash.

Bank Reconciliation

A **bank reconciliation** is an analysis of the items and amounts that result in the cash balance reported in the bank statement differing from the balance of the cash account in the ledger. The adjusted cash balance determined in the bank reconciliation is reported on the balance sheet.

A bank reconciliation is usually divided into two sections as follows:

1. The *bank section* begins with the cash balance according to the bank statement and ends with the *adjusted balance.*
2. The *company section* begins with the cash balance according to the company's records and ends with the *adjusted balance.*

The *adjusted balance* from bank and company sections must be equal. The format of the bank reconciliation is shown in Exhibit 10.

Exhibit 10
Bank Reconciliation Format

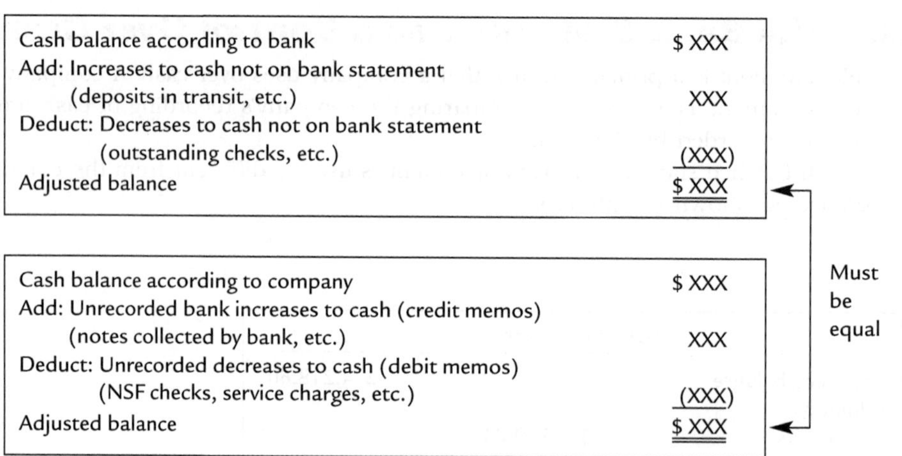

Cash balance according to bank	$ XXX
Add: Increases to cash not on bank statement (deposits in transit, etc.)	XXX
Deduct: Decreases to cash not on bank statement (outstanding checks, etc.)	(XXX)
Adjusted balance	$ XXX

Cash balance according to company	$ XXX
Add: Unrecorded bank increases to cash (credit memos) (notes collected by bank, etc.)	XXX
Deduct: Unrecorded decreases to cash (debit memos) (NSF checks, service charges, etc.)	(XXX)
Adjusted balance	$ XXX

A bank reconciliation is prepared using the steps shown in Exhibit 11.

The adjusted balances in the bank and company sections of the reconciliation must be equal. If the balances are not equal, an item has been overlooked and must be found.

Sometimes the adjusted balances are not equal because either the company or the bank has made an error. In such cases, the error is often discovered by comparing the amount of each item (deposit and check) on the bank statement with that in the company's records.

Any bank or company errors discovered should be added to or deducted from the bank or company section of the reconciliation depending on the nature of the error. For example, assume that the bank incorrectly recorded a company check for $50 as $500. This bank error of $450 ($500 − $50) would be added to the bank balance in the bank section of the reconciliation. In addition, the bank would be notified of the error so that it could be corrected. On the other hand, assume that the company recorded a deposit

Exhibit 11
Bank Reconciliation Steps

Bank Section of Reconciliation

Step 1. Enter the *Cash balance according to bank* from the ending cash balance according to the bank statement.

Step 2. *Add deposits not recorded by the bank.* Identify deposits not recorded by the bank by comparing each deposit listed on the bank statement with unrecorded deposits appearing in the preceding period's reconciliation and with the current period's deposits. Example: Deposits in transit at the end of the period.

Step 3. *Deduct outstanding checks that have not been paid by the bank.* Identify outstanding checks by comparing paid checks with outstanding checks appearing on the preceding period's reconciliation and with recorded checks. Example: Outstanding checks at the end of the period.

Step 4. Determine the *Adjusted balance* by adding Step 2 and deducting Step 3.

Company Section of Reconciliation

Step 5. Enter the *Cash balance according to company* from the ending cash balance in the ledger.

Step 6. *Add increases to cash (credit memos) that have not been recorded.* Identify the bank credit memos that have not been recorded by comparing the bank statement credit memos to entries in the journal. Examples: A note receivable and interest collected by the bank for the company.

Step 7. *Deduct decreases to cash (debit memos) that have not been recorded.* Identify the bank debit memos that have not been recorded by comparing the bank statement debit memos to entries in the journal. Examples: Customers' not sufficient funds (NSF) checks and bank service charges.

Step 8. Determine the *Adjusted balance* by adding Step 6 and deducting Step 7.

Verify that Adjusted Balances Are Equal

Step 9. Verify that the Adjusted balances determined in Steps 4 and 8 are equal.

of $1,200 as $2,100. This company error of $900 ($2,100 − $1,200) would be deducted from the cash balance in the company section of the bank reconciliation. The company would later correct the error in its records.

To illustrate, we will use the bank statement for Colter Inc. in Exhibit 7. This bank statement shows a balance of $3,359.78 as of July 31. The cash balance in Colter Inc.'s ledger on the same date is $2,549.99. Using the preceding steps, the following reconciling items were identified:

Step 2. Deposit of July 31, not recorded on bank statement: $816.20
Step 3. Outstanding checks:

Check No. 812	$1,061.00
Check No. 878	435.39
Check No. 883	48.60
Total	$1,544.99

Step 6. Note receivable of $400 plus interest of $8 collected by bank but not recorded by the company as indicated by a credit memo of $408.

Step 7. Check from customer (Thomas Ivey) for $300 returned by bank because of not sufficient funds (NSF) as indicated by a debit memo of $300.00. Bank service charges of $18 not recorded by the company as indicated by a debit memo of $18.00.

In addition, an error of $9 was discovered. This error occurred when Check No. 879 for $732.26 to Taylor Co., on account, was recorded by the company as $723.26.

The bank reconciliation, based on the Exhibit 7 bank statement and the preceding reconciling items, is shown in Exhibit 12.

Exhibit 12 Bank Reconciliation for Colter Inc.

Colter Inc.
Bank Reconciliation
July 31, 20Y7

Step			
Step 1 →	Cash balance according to bank statement		$3,359.78
Step 2 →	Add deposit of July 31, not recorded by bank		816.20
Step 3 →	Deduct outstanding checks:		
	No. 812	$1,061.00	
	No. 878	435.39	
	No. 883	48.60	(1,544.99)
Step 4 →	Adjusted balance		$2,630.99
Step 5 →	Cash balance according to Colter Inc.		$2,549.99
Step 6 →	Add note and interest collected by bank		408.00
Step 7 →	Deduct: Check returned because of insufficient funds	$ 300.00	
	Bank service charge	18.00	
	Error in recording Check No. 879	9.00	(327.00)
Step 8 →	Adjusted balance		$2,630.99

Step 9 (compare adjusted balances)

The company's records do not need to be updated for any items in the *bank section* of the reconciliation. This section begins with the cash balance according to the bank statement. However, the bank should be notified of any errors that need to be corrected.

The company's records do need to be updated for any items in the *company section* of the bank reconciliation. For example, entries should be made for any unrecorded bank memos and any company errors.

The effects on the accounts and financial statements of Colter Inc. of the bank reconciliation in Exhibit 12 are as follows:

Increases to Cash

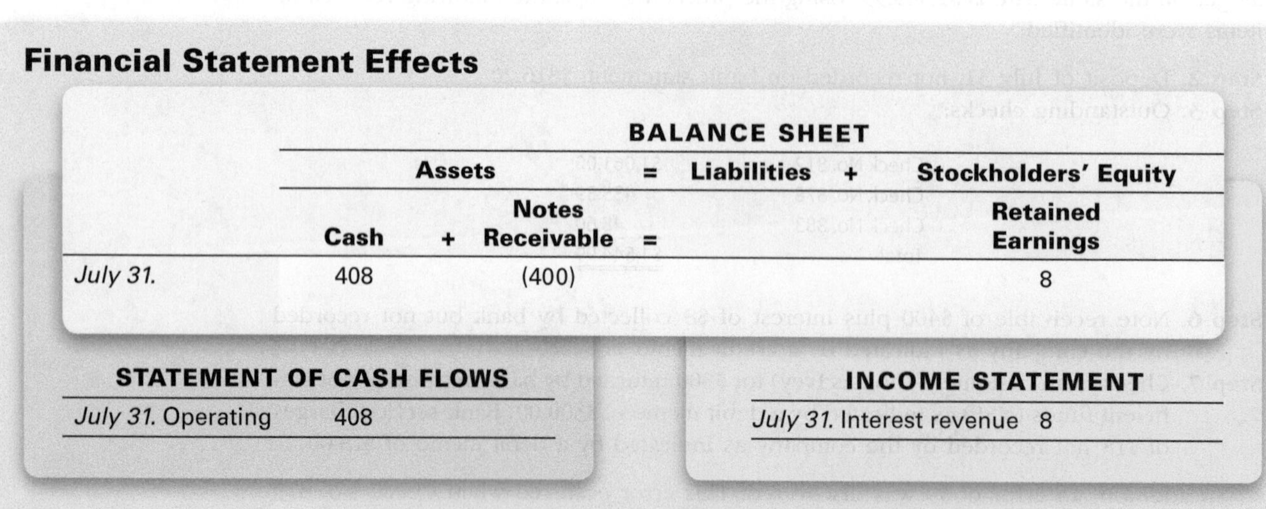

Financial Statement Effects

BALANCE SHEET

	Assets		= Liabilities +	Stockholders' Equity
	Cash	+ Notes Receivable	=	Retained Earnings
July 31.	408	(400)		8

STATEMENT OF CASH FLOWS	
July 31. Operating	408

INCOME STATEMENT	
July 31. Interest revenue	8

Decreases to Cash

Financial Statement Effects

BALANCE SHEET								
	Assets			=	Liabilities	+	Stockholders' Equity
	Cash	+	Accounts Receivable	=	Accounts Payable	+	Retained Earnings
July 31.	(327)		300		(9)		(18)

STATEMENT OF CASH FLOWS	
July 31. Operating	(327)

INCOME STATEMENT	
July 31. Misc. expense	(18)

After the preceding entries are recorded, the cash account will have a balance of $2,630.99. This cash balance agrees with the adjusted balance shown on the bank reconciliation. This is the amount of cash on July 31 and is the amount that is reported on Colter Inc.'s July 31 balance sheet.

Businesses may reconcile their bank accounts in a slightly different format from that shown in Exhibit 12. Regardless, the objective is to control cash by reconciling the company's records with the bank statement. In doing so, any errors or misuse of cash may be detected.

To enhance internal control, the bank reconciliation should be prepared by an employee who does not take part in or record cash transactions. Otherwise, mistakes may occur, and it is more likely that cash will be stolen or misapplied. For example, an employee who handles cash and also reconciles the bank statement could steal a cash deposit, omit the deposit from the accounts, and omit it from the reconciliation.

Bank reconciliations are also important in computerized systems where deposits and checks are stored in electronic files and records. Some systems use computer software to determine the difference between the bank statement and company cash balances. The software then adjusts for deposits in transit and outstanding checks. Any remaining differences are reported for further analysis.

Special-Purpose Cash Funds

Objective 6
Describe the accounting for special-purpose cash funds.

A company often has to pay small amounts for such items as postage, office supplies, or minor repairs. Although small, such payments may occur often enough to total a significant amount. Thus, it is desirable to control such payments. However, writing a check for each small payment is not practical. Instead, a special-purpose cash fund, called a **petty cash fund**, is used.

Integrity, Objectivity, and Ethics in Business

Bank Error in Your Favor

At some point, you might experience a bank error in your favor, such as a misposted deposit. Such errors are not a case of "found money," as in the Monopoly® game. Bank control systems quickly discover most errors and make automatic adjustments. Even so, you have a legal responsibility to report the error and return the money to the bank.

stephenkirsh/Shutterstock.com

A petty cash fund is established by estimating the amount of payments needed from the fund during a period, such as a week or a month. A check is then written and cashed for this amount. The money obtained from cashing the check is then given to an employee, called the *petty cash custodian*. The petty cash custodian disburses monies from the fund as needed. For control purposes, the company may place restrictions on the maximum amount and the types of payments that can be made from the fund. Each time money is paid from petty cash, the custodian records the details on a petty cash receipts form.

The petty cash fund is normally replenished at periodic intervals, when it is depleted, or reaches a minimum amount. When a petty cash fund is replenished, the accounts are updated by summarizing the petty cash receipts. A check is then written for this amount, payable to Petty Cash.

To illustrate normal petty cash fund entries, assume that a petty cash fund of $500 is established on August 1. The effect on the accounts and financial statements of recording this transaction is as follows:

Financial Statement Effects

BALANCE SHEET

	Assets		=	Liabilities	+	Stockholders' Equity
	Cash	**+ Petty Cash**	**=**			
Aug. 1.	(500)	500				

STATEMENT OF CASH FLOWS

INCOME STATEMENT

At the end of August, the petty cash receipts indicate expenditures for the following items:

Office supplies	$380
Postage (record as Office Supplies)	22
Store supplies	35
Miscellaneous administrative expense	30
Total	$467

The effect on the accounts and financial statements of replenishing the petty cash fund on August 31 is as follows:

Financial Statement Effects

BALANCE SHEET

	Assets			=	Liabilities	+	Stockholders' Equity
	Cash	**+ Office Supplies**	**+ Store Supplies**	**=**			**Retained Earnings**
Aug. 31.	(467)	402	35				(30)

STATEMENT OF CASH FLOWS

Aug. 31. Operating (467)

INCOME STATEMENT

Aug. 31. Misc. admin. expense (30)

Replenishing the petty cash fund restores the fund to its original amount of $500. There is no adjustment to Petty Cash when the fund is replenished. Petty Cash is adjusted only if the amount of the fund is later increased or decreased.

Companies often use **special-purpose cash funds** for other needs, such as payroll or travel expenses. For example, each salesperson might be given $1,000 for travel-related expenses. Periodically, each salesperson submits an expense report, and the fund is replenished. Special-purpose funds are established and controlled in a manner similar to that of the petty cash fund.

Financial Statement Reporting of Cash

Objective 7
Describe and illustrate the reporting of cash and cash equivalents in the financial statements.

Cash is normally listed as the first asset in the Current Assets section of the balance sheet. Most companies present only a single cash amount on the balance sheet by combining all their bank and cash fund accounts.

A company may temporarily have excess cash. In such cases, the company normally invests in highly liquid investments in order to earn interest. These investments are called **cash equivalents**.[8] Examples of cash equivalents include U.S. Treasury bills, notes issued by major corporations (referred to as commercial paper), and money market funds. In such cases, companies usually report *Cash and cash equivalents* as one amount on the balance sheet.

In a recent balance sheet, eBay reported cash and cash equivalents of $975 million.

eBay Connection

Banks may require that companies maintain minimum cash balances in their bank accounts. Such a balance is called a **compensating balance**. This is often required by the bank as part of a loan agreement or line of credit. A *line of credit* is a preapproved amount the bank is willing to lend to a customer upon request. Compensating balance requirements are normally disclosed in notes to the financial statements.

8. To be classified as a cash equivalent, according to *FASB Accounting Standards Codification*, Section 305.10, the investment is expected to be converted to cash within three months.

Metric-Based Analysis: Ratio of Cash to Monthly Cash Expenses

Objective 8
Describe and illustrate the ratio of cash to monthly cash expenses in assessing the ability of a company to continue operating.

The statement of cash flows reports "Net cash flows from operating activities." It is generally expected that a company will generate positive cash flows from operations. While a company may occasionally experience economic downturns that generate negative cash flows from operations, a company must generate positive cash flows from operations over the long term to remain in business.

When a company reports *negative* net cash flows from operations, one measure that is useful in assessing the ability of the company to continue to operate is the ratio of cash to monthly cash expenses. The **ratio of cash to monthly cash expenses** is computed as follows:

$$\text{Ratio of Cash to Monthly Cash Expenses} = \frac{\text{Cash and Cash Equivalents}}{\text{Monthly Cash Expenses}}$$

Cash and cash equivalents is the amount reported on the end-of-period balance sheet for the period that the net cash flows from operations is reported.

The **monthly cash expenses**, sometimes called **monthly cash burn**, are computed as follows:

$$\text{Monthly Cash Expenses} = \frac{\text{Net Cash Flows Used in Operating Activities}}{12}$$

The ratio of cash to monthly cash expenses is especially useful when assessing the ability of new companies to continue operating. A primary cause of failure of new companies is that they are undercapitalized. That is, the companies don't have sufficient funding (cash) from debt or equity financing to operate long enough to generate positive cash flows from operations.

To illustrate, assume the following data for Ztech Inc., a biotechnology startup company.

	Year 2	Year 1
Net cash flows used in operating activities..........	$(3,420,000)	$(3,600,000)
Cash and cash equivalents at end of year	1,824,000	2,550,000

The monthly cash expenses and ratio of cash to monthly cash expenses for Year 2 and Year 1 are as follows:

	Year 2	Year 1
Monthly cash expenses:		
$3,420,000 ÷ 12	$285,000	
$3,600,000 ÷ 12		$300,000
Ratio of cash to monthly cash expenses:		
$1,824,000 ÷ $285,000	6.4 months	
$2,550,000 ÷ $300,000		8.5 months

At the end of Year 1, Ztech had enough cash to continue operating for 8.5 months. To continue beyond 8.5 months, Ztech needed to do one or more of the following:

- Generate positive net cash flows from operations
- Obtain additional financing from issuing stock or debt

Assume that during Year 2 Ztech continued to operate by issuing additional common stock and debt. As a result, at the end of Year 2, the company had cash and cash equivalents of $1,824,000. Based on this amount and its monthly cash expenses, the company can continue to operate 6.4 months into Year 3. Ultimately, Ztech's ability to survive depends upon its ability to generate positive cash flows from its operations.

Startup companies, like Ztech, often experience negative cash flows from operations as they establish a customer base, generate revenue, and earn profits. As a result, startup companies must raise enough funds or have commitments from investors for additional funding to survive until they can generate positive cash flows from their operations.

Key Points

1. Describe the Sarbanes-Oxley Act and its impact on internal controls and financial reporting.

Sarbanes-Oxley requires companies to maintain strong and effective internal controls over the recording of transactions and the preparing of financial statements. Sarbanes-Oxley also requires companies and their independent accountants to report on the effectiveness of a company's internal controls.

2. Describe and illustrate the objectives and elements of internal control.

The objectives of internal control are to provide reasonable assurance that (1) assets are safeguarded and used for business purposes, (2) business information is accurate, and (3) compliance with laws and regulations is met. The elements of internal control are the control environment, risk assessment, control procedures, monitoring, and information and communication.

3. Describe and illustrate the application of internal controls to cash.

One of the most important controls to protect cash received in over-the-counter sales is a cash register. A remittance advice is a control for cash received through the mail. Separating the duties of handling cash and recording cash is also a control. A voucher system is a control system for cash payments that uses a set of procedures for authorizing and recording liabilities and cash payments. Many companies use electronic funds transfers to enhance their control over cash receipts and cash payments.

4. Describe the nature of a bank account and its use in controlling cash.

Businesses use bank accounts as a means of controlling cash. Bank accounts reduce the amount of cash on hand and facilitate the transfer of cash between businesses and locations. In addition, banks send monthly statements to their customers, summarizing all of the transactions for the month. The bank statement allows a business to reconcile the cash transactions recorded in the accounting records to those recorded by the bank.

5. Describe and illustrate the use of a bank reconciliation in controlling cash.

The first section of the bank reconciliation begins with the cash balance according to the bank statement. This balance is adjusted for the company's changes in cash that do not appear on the bank statement and for any bank errors. The second section begins with the cash balance according to the company's records. This balance is adjusted for the bank's changes in cash that do not appear on the company's records and for any company errors. The adjusted balances for the two sections must be equal. No adjustments are necessary on the company's records as a result of the information included in the bank section of the bank reconciliation. However, the items in the company section require adjustments on the company's records.

6. Describe the accounting for special-purpose cash funds.

Businesses often use special-purpose cash funds, such as a petty cash fund or travel funds, to meet specific needs. Each fund is initially established by cashing a check for the amount of cash needed. The cash is then given to a custodian who is authorized to disburse monies from the fund. At periodic intervals or when it is depleted or reaches a minimum amount, the fund is replenished and the disbursements recorded.

7. Describe and illustrate the reporting of cash and cash equivalents in the financial statements.

Cash is listed as the first asset in the Current Assets section of the balance sheet. Companies that have invested excess cash in highly liquid investments usually report *Cash and cash equivalents* on the balance sheet.

8. Metric-Based Analysis: Describe and illustrate the ratio of cash to monthly cash expenses in assessing the ability of a company to continue operating.

The ratio of cash to monthly cash expenses can be used to assess how long a company with negative cash flows from operations can continue to operate. It is computed as cash and cash equivalents divided by monthly cash expenses. Monthly cash expenses are computed as net cash flows used in operating activities divided by 12.

Key Terms

Bank reconciliation (210)
Bank statement (207)
Cash (204)
Cash equivalents (215)
Cash short and over (205)
Compensating balance (215)
Electronic funds transfer (EFT) (206)
Elements of internal control (199)
Employee fraud (199)
Internal control (197)
Monthly cash burn (216)
Monthly cash expenses (216)
Petty cash fund (213)
Ratio of cash to monthly cash expenses (215)
Sarbanes-Oxley Act (197)
Special-purpose cash funds (215)
Voucher (206)
Voucher system (206)

Illustrative Problem

The bank statement for Urethane Company for June 30, 20Y5, indicates a balance of $9,143.11. All cash receipts are deposited each evening in a night depository, after banking hours.

The accounting records indicate the following summary data for cash receipts and payments for June:

Cash balance as of June 1	$ 3,943.50
Total cash receipts for June	28,971.60
Total amount of checks issued in June	28,388.85

Comparing the bank statement and the accompanying canceled checks and memorandums with the records reveals the following reconciling items:

a. The bank had collected for Urethane Company $1,030 on a customer's note left for collection. The face of the note was $1,000.

b. A deposit of $1,852.21, representing receipts of June 30, had been made too late to appear on the bank statement.

c. Checks outstanding totaled $5,265.27.

d. A check drawn for $157 had been incorrectly charged by the bank as $175.

e. A check for $30 returned with the statement had been recorded in the company's records as $300. The check was for the payment of an obligation to Avery Equipment Company for the purchase of office supplies on account.

f. Bank service charges for June amounted to $78.20.

Instructions

1. Prepare a bank reconciliation for June.
2. Record the effects on the accounts and financial statements that should be made by Urethane Company based upon the bank reconciliation.

Solution

1.

URETHANE COMPANY
Bank Reconciliation
June 30, 20Y5

Cash balance according to bank statement		$ 9,143.11
Add: Deposit of June 30, not recorded by bank	$1,852.21	
Bank error in charging check as $175 instead of $157	18.00	1,870.21
Deduct: Outstanding checks		(5,265.27)
Adjusted balance		$ 5,748.05
Cash balance according to company's records		$ 4,526.25*
Add: Proceeds of note collected by bank, including $30 interest	$1,030.00	
Error in recording check	270.00	1,300.00
Deduct: Bank service charges		(78.20)
Adjusted balance		$ 5,748.05

*$3,943.50 + $28,971.60 − $28,388.85

2.

Increases to Cash

Financial Statement Effects

BALANCE SHEET

	Assets		=	Liabilities	+	Stockholders' Equity
	Cash	+ Notes Receivable	=	Accounts Payable	+	Retained Earnings
June 30.	1,300.00	(1,000.00)		270.00		30.00

STATEMENT OF CASH FLOWS

June 30. Operating 1,300.00

INCOME STATEMENT

June 30. Interest revenue 30.00

Decreases to Cash

Financial Statement Effects

BALANCE SHEET

	Assets	=	Liabilities	+	Stockholders' Equity
	Cash	=			Retained Earnings
June 30.	(78.20)				(78.20)

STATEMENT OF CASH FLOWS

June 30. Operating (78.20)

INCOME STATEMENT

June 30. Misc. admin. exp. (78.20)

Self-Examination Questions

(Answers appear at the end of the chapter.)

1. Which of the following is not an element of internal control?
   A. Control environment
   B. Monitoring
   C. Compliance with laws and regulations
   D. Control procedures
2. The bank erroneously charged Tropical Services' account for $450.50 for a check that was correctly written and recorded by Tropical Services as $540.50. To reconcile the bank account of Tropical Services at the end of the month, you would:
   A. add $90 to the cash balance according to the bank statement.
   B. add $90 to the cash balance according to Tropical Services' records.
   C. deduct $90 from the cash balance according to the bank statement.
   D. deduct $90 from the cash balance according to Tropical Services' records.
3. In preparing a bank reconciliation, the amount of checks outstanding would be:
   A. added to the cash balance according to the bank statement.
   B. deducted from the cash balance according to the bank statement.
   C. added to the cash balance according to the company's records.
   D. deducted from the cash balance according to the company's records.
4. Adjustments to the company's records based on the bank reconciliation are required for:
   A. additions to the cash balance according to the company's records.
   B. deductions from the cash balance according to the company's records.
   C. both A and B.
   D. neither A nor B.
5. A petty cash fund is:
   A. used to pay relatively small amounts.
   B. established by estimating the amount of cash needed for disbursements of relatively small amounts during a specified period.
   C. reimbursed when the amount of money in the fund is reduced to a predetermined minimum amount.
   D. all of the above.

Class Discussion Questions

1. (a) Why did Congress pass the Sarbanes-Oxley Act? (b) What was the purpose of the Sarbanes-Oxley Act?
2. Define internal control.
3. (a) Name and describe the five elements of internal control. (b) Is any one element of internal control more important than another?
4. How does a policy of rotating clerical employees from job to job aid in strengthening the control procedures within the control environment? Explain.
5. Why should the responsibility for a sequence of related operations be divided among different persons? Explain.
6. Why should the employee who handles cash receipts not have the responsibility for maintaining the accounts receivable records? Explain.
7. In an attempt to improve operating efficiency, one employee was made responsible for all purchasing, receiving, and storing of supplies. Is this organizational change wise from an internal control standpoint? Explain.
8. The ticket seller at a movie theater doubles as a ticket taker for a few minutes each day while the ticket taker is on a break. Which control procedure of a business's system of internal control is violated in this situation?

9. Why should the responsibility for maintaining the accounting records be separated from the responsibility for operations?

10. Assume that Leslie Hunter, accounts payable clerk for Campland Inc., stole $185,000 by paying fictitious invoices for goods that were never received. The clerk set up accounts in the names of fictitious companies and cashed the checks at a local bank. Describe a control procedure that would have prevented or detected the fraud.

11. Before a voucher for the purchase of merchandise is approved for payment, supporting documents should be compared to verify the accuracy of the liability. Give an example of a supporting document for the purchase of merchandise.

12. The accounting clerk pays all obligations by prenumbered checks. What are the strengths and weaknesses in the internal control over cash payments in this situation?

13. The balance of Cash is likely to differ from the bank statement balance. What two factors are likely to be responsible for the difference?

14. What is the purpose of preparing a bank reconciliation?

15. Do items reported as a credit memorandum on the bank statement represent (a) additions made by the bank to the company's balance or (b) deductions made by the bank from the company's balance? Explain.

16. Seatow Inc. has a petty cash fund of $2,500. (a) Since the petty cash fund is only $2,500, should Seatow Inc. implement controls over petty cash? (b) What controls, if any, could be used for the petty cash fund?

17. (a) How are cash equivalents reported on the financial statements? (b) What are some examples of cash equivalents?

Exercises

E5-1 Sarbanes-Oxley internal control report

Obj. 1

Using Wikipedia (www.wikipedia.org.), look up the entry for the Sarbanes-Oxley Act. Look over the table of contents and find the section that describes Section 404. What does Section 404 require of management's internal control report?

E5-2 Internal controls

Obj. 2, 3

Jittery Joe has recently been hired as the manager of Loyola's Coffee, a national chain of franchised coffee shops. During his first month as store manager, Jittery encountered the following internal control situations:

a. Loyola's Coffee has one cash register. Prior to Jittery joining the coffee shop, each employee working on a shift would take a customer order, accept payment, and then prepare the order. Jittery made one employee on each shift responsible for taking orders and accepting the customer's payment. Other employees prepare the orders.

b. Since only one employee uses the cash register, that employee is responsible for counting the cash at the end of the shift and verifying that the cash in the drawer matches the amount of cash sales recorded by the cash register. Jittery expects each cashier to balance the drawer to the penny *every* time—no exceptions.

c. Jittery caught an employee putting a case of single-serving tea bags in her car. Not wanting to create a scene, Jittery smiled and said, "I don't think you're putting those tea bags on the right shelf. Don't they belong inside the coffee shop?" The employee returned the tea bags to the stockroom.

State whether you agree or disagree with Jittery's method of handling each situation and explain your answer.

E5-3 Internal controls

Obj. 2, 3

Honeybee Hippie is a retail store specializing in women's clothing. The store has established a liberal return policy for the holiday season in order to encourage gift purchases.

Any item purchased during November and December may be returned through January 31, with a receipt, for cash or exchange. If the customer does not have a receipt, cash will still be refunded for any item less than $200. If the item is more than $200, a check is mailed to the customer.

Whenever an item is returned, a store clerk completes a return slip, which the customer signs. The return slip is placed in a special box. The store manager visits the return counter approximately once every two hours to authorize the return slips. Clerks are instructed to place the returned merchandise on the proper rack on the selling floor as soon as possible.

This year, returns at Honeybee Hippie reached an all-time high. There are a large number of returns of less than $200 without receipts.

a. How can sales clerks employed at Honeybee Hippie use the store's return policy to steal money from the cash register?

b. What internal control weaknesses do you see in the return policy that make cash thefts easier?

c. Would issuing a store credit in place of a cash refund for all merchandise returned without a receipt reduce the possibility of theft? List some advantages and disadvantages of issuing a store credit in place of a cash refund.

d. Assume that Honeybee Hippie is committed to the current policy of issuing cash refunds without a receipt. What changes could be made in the store's procedures regarding customer refunds in order to improve internal control?

Obj. 2, 3

E5-4 Internal controls

Republic City Bank provides loans to businesses in the community through its Commercial Lending Department. Small loans (less than $250,000) may be approved by an individual loan officer, while larger loans (greater than $250,000) must be approved by a board of loan officers. Once a loan is approved, the funds are made available to the loan applicant under agreed-upon terms. The president of Republic City Bank has instituted a policy whereby he has the individual authority to approve loans up to $4,000,000. The president believes that this policy will allow flexibility to approve loans to valued clients much quicker than under the previous policy.

As an internal auditor of Republic City Bank, how would you respond to this change in policy?

Obj. 2, 3

E5-5 Internal controls

One of the largest losses in history from unauthorized securities trading involved a securities trader for a French bank. The trader was able to circumvent internal controls and create over a billion in trading losses. The trader apparently escaped detection by using knowledge of the bank's internal control systems learned from a previous back-office monitoring job. Much of this monitoring involved the use of software to monitor trades. The traders were usually kept to tight spending limits. However, these controls failed in this case.

What general weaknesses in internal controls contributed to the occurrence and size of the losses?

Obj. 2, 3

E5-6 Internal controls

An employee of a trucking company was responsible for resolving roadway accident claims under $25,000. The employee created fake accident claims and wrote settlement checks of between $5,000 and $25,000 to friends or acquaintances acting as phony "victims." One friend recruited subordinates at his place of work to cash some of the checks. Beyond this, the employee also recruited lawyers, who he paid to represent both the trucking company and the fake victims in the bogus accident settlements. When the lawyers cashed the checks, they allegedly split the money with the corrupt employee. This fraud went undetected for two years.

Why would it take so long to discover such a fraud?

E5-7 Internal controls

Obj. 2, 3

Awesome Sound Inc. discovered a fraud wherein one of its front office administrative employees used company funds to purchase goods, such as computers, digital cameras, DVD players, and other electronic items, for her own use. The fraud was discovered when employees noticed an increase in delivery frequency from vendors and the use of unusual vendors. After some investigation, it was discovered that the employee would alter the description or change the quantity on an invoice in order to explain the cost on the bill.

Comment on control strengths and weaknesses related to this fraud.

E5-8 Financial statement fraud

Obj. 2, 3

A former chairman, chief financial officer, and controller of an apparel company pleaded guilty to financial statement fraud. These managers used false journal entries to record fictitious sales, hid inventory in public warehouses so that it could be recorded as "sold," and required sales orders to be backdated so that the sale could be moved back to an earlier period. The combined effect of these actions caused millions in phony quarterly sales.

a. Why might control procedures listed in this chapter be insufficient in stopping this type of fraud?

b. How could this type of fraud be stopped?

E5-9 Internal control of cash receipts

Obj. 2, 3

At the close of each day's business, the sales clerks count the cash in their respective cash drawers and compare the total cash to the cash register tapes. They then prepare a cash memo noting any discrepancies between the actual cash and the cash tapes. An employee from the cashier's office then recounts the cash, compares the total with the memo, and takes the cash to the cashier's office.

a. Indicate the weak link in internal control.

b. How can the weakness be corrected?

E5-10 Internal control of cash receipts

Obj. 2, 3

Jodi Rostad works at the drive-through window of Mamma's Burgers. Occasionally, when a drive-through customer orders, Jodi fills the order and pockets the customer's money. She does not ring up the order on the cash register.

Identify the internal control weaknesses that exist at Mamma's Burgers, and discuss what can be done to prevent this theft.

E5-11 Internal control of cash receipts

Obj. 2, 3

The mailroom employees send all remittances and remittance advices to the cashier. The cashier deposits the cash in the bank and forwards the remittance advices and duplicate deposit slips to the Accounting Department.

a. Indicate the weak link in internal control in the handling of cash receipts.

b. How can the weakness be corrected?

E5-12 Entry for cash sales; cash short

Obj. 2, 3

EXCEL ONLINE

The actual cash received from the day's cash sales was $3,625, and the amount indicated by the cash register total was $3,640.

a. What is the amount deposited in the bank for the day's sales?

b. What is the amount recorded for the day's sales?

c. How should the difference be recorded?

d. If a cashier is consistently over or short, what action should be taken?

Obj. 2, 3

EXCEL ONLINE

E5-13 Recording cash sales; cash over

The actual cash received from the day's cash sales was $9,380 and the amount indicated by the cash register total was $9,300.

a. What is the amount deposited in the bank for the day's sales?
b. What is the amount recorded for the day's sales?
c. How should the difference be recorded?
d. If a cashier is consistently over or short, what action should be taken?

Obj. 2, 3

E5-14 Internal control of cash payments

Greenleaf Co. is a small merchandising company with a manual accounting system. An investigation revealed that in spite of a sufficient bank balance, a significant amount of available cash discounts had been lost because of failure to make timely payments. In addition, it was discovered that the invoices for several purchases had been paid twice.

Outline procedures for the payment of vendors' invoices, so that the possibilities of losing available cash discounts and of paying an invoice a second time will be minimized.

Obj. 2, 3

E5-15 Internal control of cash payments

Torpedo Digital Company, a communications equipment manufacturer, recently fell victim to a fraud scheme developed by one of its employees. To understand the scheme, it is necessary to review Torpedo's procedures for the purchase of services.

The purchasing agent is responsible for ordering services (such as repairs to a photocopy machine or office cleaning) after receiving a service requisition from an authorized manager. However, since no tangible goods are delivered, a receiving report is not prepared. When the Accounting Department receives an invoice billing Torpedo for a service call, the accounts payable clerk calls the manager who requested the service in order to verify that it was performed.

The fraud scheme involves Ross Dunbar, the manager of plant and facilities. Ross arranged for his uncle's company, Capo Industrial Supplies and Service, to be placed on Torpedo's approved vendor list. Ross did not disclose the family relationship.

On several occasions, Ross would submit a requisition for services to be provided by Capo Industrial Supplies and Service. However, the service requested was really not needed, and it was never performed. Capo Industrial Supplies and Service would bill Torpedo for the service and then split the cash payment with Ross.

Explain what changes should be made to Torpedo's procedures for ordering and paying for services in order to prevent such occurrences in the future.

Obj. 5

E5-16 Bank reconciliation

Identify each of the following reconciling items as: (a) an addition to the cash balance according to the bank statement, (b) a deduction from the cash balance according to the bank statement, (c) an addition to the cash balance according to the company's records, or (d) a deduction from the cash balance according to the company's records. (None of the transactions reported by bank debit and credit memos have been recorded by the company.)

1. Bank service charges, $20.
2. Check drawn by company for $174 but incorrectly recorded by company as $147.
3. Check for $10 incorrectly charged by bank as $100.
4. Check of a customer returned by bank to company because of insufficient funds, $240.
5. Deposit in transit, $2,475.
6. Outstanding checks, $7,385.
7. Note collected by bank, $5,300.

E5-17 Entries based on bank reconciliation

Obj. 5

Which of the reconciling items listed in Exercise 5-16 are required to be recorded in the company's accounts?

E5-18 Bank reconciliation

Obj. 5

✔ Adjusted balance: $7,385

The following data were accumulated for use in reconciling the bank account of Wolfpack Bread Inc. for August 20Y9:

a. Cash balance according to the company's records at August 31, $6,865.
b. Cash balance according to the bank statement at August 31, $9,165.
c. Checks outstanding, $2,855.
d. Deposit in transit, not recorded by bank, $1,075.
e. A check for $280 issued in payment of an account to a supplier was erroneously recorded by Wolfpack Bread Inc. as $820.
f. Bank debit memo for service charges, $20.

Prepare a bank reconciliation, using the format shown in Exhibit 10.

E5-19 Effects of bank reconciliation updates

Obj. 5

Using the data presented in Exercise 5-18, record the effects on the accounts and financial statements of the company based upon the bank reconciliation.

E5-20 Effects of bank reconciliation updates

Obj. 5

Accompanying a bank statement for Nite Lighting Company is a credit memo for $26,500, representing the principal ($25,000) and interest ($1,500) on a note that had been collected by the bank. The company had been notified by the bank at the time of the collection but had made no recording. Record the financial statement effect for the adjustment that should be made by the company to bring the accounting records up to date.

E5-21 Bank reconciliation

Obj. 5

✔ Adjusted balance: $15,310

An accounting clerk for Westwind Co. prepared the following bank reconciliation:

WESTWIND CO.
Bank Reconciliation
August 31, 20Y6

Cash balance according to company's records		$ 6,800
Add: Outstanding checks	$4,190	
Error by Westwind Co. in recording Check No. 1115 as $830 instead of $380	450	
Note for $7,500 collected by bank, including interest	8,100	12,740
		$19,540
Deduct: Deposit in transit on August 31	$2,175	
Bank service charges	40	(2,215)
Cash balance according to bank statement		$17,325

a. From the bank reconciliation data, prepare a new bank reconciliation for Westwind Co., using the format shown in Exhibit 10.

b. If a balance sheet were prepared for Westwind Co. on August 31, 20Y6, what amount should be reported for cash?

Obj. 5

✔ Corrected adjusted balance: $24,110

E5-22 Bank reconciliation

The following bank reconciliation was prepared for Dakota Co.

DAKOTA CO.
Bank Reconciliation
For the Month Ended June 30, 20Y3

Cash balance according to bank statement			$22,900
Add outstanding checks:			
No. 7715		$1,450	
7760		915	
7764		1,850	
7765		775	4,990
			$27,890
Deduct deposit of June 30, not recorded by bank			(6,200)
Adjusted balance			$21,690
Cash balance according to company's records			$15,625
Add: Proceeds of note collected by bank:			
Principal	$6,000		
Interest	360	$6,360	
Service charges		30	6,390
			$22,015
Deduct: Check returned because of insufficient funds		$ 545	
Error in recording June 20 deposit of $5,200 as $2,500		2,700	(3,245)
Adjusted balance			$18,770

a. Identify the errors in the preceding bank reconciliation.

b. Prepare a corrected bank reconciliation.

Obj. 2, 3, 5

E5-23 Using bank reconciliation to determine cash receipts stolen

Pala Co. records all cash receipts on the basis of its cash register tapes. Pala Co. discovered during April 20Y1 that one of its sales clerks had stolen an undetermined amount of cash receipts when she took the daily deposits to the bank. The following data have been gathered for April:

Cash in bank according to the company records	$19,565
Cash according to the April 30, 20Y1, bank statement	28,175
Outstanding checks as of April 30, 20Y1	12,100
Bank service charges for April	75
Note receivable, including interest collected by bank in April	3,710

No deposits were in transit on April 30.

a. Determine the amount of cash receipts stolen by the sales clerk.

b. What accounting controls would have prevented or detected this theft?

Obj. 6

SHOW ME HOW

E5-24 Effects of petty cash transactions

Illustrate the effect on the accounts and financial statements of the following transactions:

a. Established a petty cash fund of $750.

b. The amount of cash in the petty cash fund is now $140. Replenished the fund, based on the following summary of petty cash receipts: office supplies, $325; miscellaneous selling expense, $200; miscellaneous administrative expense, $85.

Obj. 6

E5-25 Effects of petty cash transactions

Illustrate the effect on the accounts and financial statements of the following transactions:

a. Established a petty cash fund of $500.

b. The amount of cash in the petty cash fund is now $45. Replenished the fund, based on the following summary of petty cash receipts: office supplies purchased, $175; miscellaneous selling expense, $190; miscellaneous administrative expense, $90.

Problems

P5-1 Evaluate internal control of cash

Obj. 2,3

The following procedures were recently implemented by SUP Yoga Co.:

a. Each cashier is assigned a separate cash register drawer to which no other cashier has access.

b. All sales are rung up on the cash register, and a receipt is given to the customer. All sales are recorded on a record locked inside the cash register.

c. At the end of a shift, each cashier counts the cash in his or her cash register, unlocks the cash register record, and compares the amount of cash with the amount on the record to determine cash shortages and overages.

d. Checks received through the mail are given daily to the accounts receivable clerk for recording collections on account and for depositing in the bank.

e. Vouchers and all supporting documents are stamped PAID after being paid by the treasurer.

f. Disbursements are made from the petty cash fund only after a petty cash receipt has been completed and signed by the payee.

g. The bank reconciliation is prepared by the accountant.

Instructions

Indicate whether each of the procedures of internal control over cash represents (1) a strength or (2) a weakness. For each weakness, indicate why it exists.

P5-2 Bank reconciliation and entries

Obj. 5

✔ 1. Adjusted balance: $25,000

The cash account for Deaver Consulting at October 31, 20Y6, indicated a balance of $15,750. The bank statement indicated a balance of $31,095 on October 31, 20Y6. Comparing the bank statement and the accompanying canceled checks and memos with the records revealed the following reconciling items:

a. Checks outstanding totaled $10,125.

b. A deposit of $4,120, representing receipts from October 31, had been made too late to appear on the bank statement.

c. The bank had collected $10,400 on a note left for collection. The face of the note was $10,000.

d. A check for $1,200 returned with the statement had been incorrectly recorded by Deaver Consulting as $120. The check was for the payment of an obligation to Oxford Office Supplies Co. for the purchase of office supplies on account.

e. A check drawn for $320 had been incorrectly charged by the bank as $230.

f. Bank service charges for October amounted to $70.

Instructions

1. Prepare a bank reconciliation.
2. Illustrate the effects on the accounts and financial statements of the bank reconciliation.

Obj. 5

✔ 1. Adjusted balance: $52,850

P5-3 Bank reconciliation and entries

The cash account for Highlander Diamond Co. on April 1, 20Y5, indicated a balance of $35,400. During April, the total cash deposited was $120,255, and checks written totaled $109,200. The bank statement indicated a balance of $60,927 on April 30, 20Y5. Comparing the bank statement, the canceled checks, and the accompanying memos with the records revealed the following reconciling items:

a. Checks outstanding totaled $21,450.

b. A deposit of $13,913, representing receipts of April 30, had been made too late to appear on the bank statement.

c. A check for $710 had been incorrectly charged by the bank as $170.

d. A check for $220 returned with the statement had been recorded by Highlander Diamond Co. as $2,200. The check was for the payment of an obligation to Dirt Dog Inc. on account.

e. The bank had collected for Highlander Diamond $6,480 on a note left for collection. The face of the note was $6,000.

f. Bank service charges for April amounted to $115.

g. A check for $1,950 from Fly Ball Co. was returned by the bank because of insufficient funds.

Instructions

1. Prepare a bank reconciliation as of April 30.
2. Illustrate the effects on the accounts and financial statements of the bank reconciliation.

Obj. 5

✔ 1. Adjusted balance: $10,798.88

P5-4 Bank reconciliation and entries

Rancho Foods deposits all cash receipts each Wednesday and Friday in a night depository, after banking hours. The data required to reconcile the bank statement as of May 31 have been taken from various documents and records and are reproduced as follows. The sources of the data are printed in capital letters.

CASH ACCOUNT:

Balance as of May 1 $9,578.00

CASH RECEIPTS FOR MONTH OF MAY $5,255.89

DUPLICATE DEPOSIT TICKETS:

Date and amount of each deposit in May:

Date	Amount	Date	Amount	Date	Amount
May 2	$569.50	May 12	$580.70	May 23	$ 731.45
5	701.80	16	600.10	26	601.50
9	189.24	19	701.26	31	580.34

CHECKS WRITTEN:

Number and amount of each check issued in May:

Check No.	Amount	Check No.	Amount	Check No.	Amount
614	$243.50	621	$309.50	628	$ 837.70
615	350.10	622	Void	629	329.90
616	279.90	623	Void	630	882.80
617	395.50	624	707.01	631	1,081.56
618	435.40	625	185.63	632	62.40
619	320.10	626	550.03	633	310.08
620	238.87	627	318.73	634	503.30

Total amount of checks issued in May $8,342.01

MEMBER FDIC		PAGE 1
AMERICAN NATIONAL BANK OF DETROIT	ACCOUNT NUMBER	
	FROM 5/01/20Y8 TO 5/31/20Y8	
DETROIT, MI 48201-2500 (313)933-8547	BALANCE	9,422.80
	9 DEPOSITS	6,086.35
	20 WITHDRAWALS	7,462.11
Rancho Foods	4 OTHER DEBITS AND CREDITS	3,650.00CR
	NEW BALANCE	11,697.04

CHECKS AND OTHER DEBITS					DEPOSITS	DATE	BALANCE
No.580	310.10	No.612	92.50		780.80	05/01	9,801.00
No.602	85.50	No.614	243.50		569.50	05/03	10,041.50
No.615	350.10	No.616	279.90		701.80	05/06	10,113.30
No.617	395.50	No.618	435.40		819.24	05/11	10,101.64
No.619	320.10	No.620	238.87		580.70	05/13	10,123.37
No.621	309.50	No.624	707.01		MS 4,000.00	05/14	13,106.86
No.625	158.63	No.626	550.03		MS 160.00	05/14	12,558.20
No.627	318.73	No.629	329.90		600.10	05/17	12,509.67
No.630	882.80	No.631	1,081.56	NSF 450.00		05/20	10,095.31
No.632	62.40	No.633	310.08		701.26	05/21	10,424.09
					731.45	05/24	11,155.54
					601.50	05/28	11,757.04
		SC	60.00			05/31	11,697.04

EC — ERROR CORRECTION   OD — OVERDRAFT
MS — MISCELLANEOUS   PS — PAYMENT STOPPED
NSF — NOT SUFFICIENT FUNDS   SC — SERVICE CHARGE

* * *   * * *   * * *

THE RECONCILEMENT OF THIS STATEMENT WITH YOUR RECORDS IS ESSENTIAL.
ANY ERROR OR EXCEPTION SHOULD BE REPORTED IMMEDIATELY.

BANK RECONCILIATION FOR PRECEDING MONTH (DATED APRIL 30):		
Cash balance according to bank statement		$ 9,422.80
Add deposit of April 30, not recorded by bank		780.80
Deduct outstanding checks:		
No. 580	$310.10	
No. 602	85.50	
No. 612	92.50	
No. 613	137.50	(625.60)
Adjusted balance		$ 9,578.00
Cash balance according to company's records		$ 9,605.70
Deduct service charges		(27.70)
Adjusted balance		$ 9,578.00

Instructions

1. Prepare a bank reconciliation as of May 31. If errors in recording deposits or checks are discovered, assume that the errors were made by the company. Assume that all deposits are from cash sales except for the note receivable of $4,000 and interest of $160 collected on May 14. All checks were written to satisfy accounts payable.
2. Illustrate the effects on the accounts and financial statements of the bank reconciliation.
3. What is the amount of Cash that should appear on the balance sheet as of May 31?
4. Assume that a canceled check for $50 has been incorrectly recorded by the bank as $500. Briefly explain how the error would be included in a bank reconciliation and how it should be corrected.

Metric-Based Analysis

MBA 5-1 Ratio of cash to monthly cash expenses

AcelRx Pharmaceuticals, Inc. (ACRX), develops therapies for pain relief for a variety of patients, including cancer and trauma patients. The following data (in thousands) were adapted from financial statements of a recent year.

Net cash flows used in operating activities	$(51,180)
End of the year cash and cash equivalents	87,975
Short-term investments*	17,740

*Includes U.S. short-term government securities that are readily convertible to cash.

1. Compute the monthly cash expenses. Round to nearest thousand.
2. Compute the ratio of cash to monthly cash expenses, excluding short-term investments. Round to one decimal place.
3. Including short-term investments as part of cash and cash equivalents, compute the ratio of cash to monthly cash expenses. Round to one decimal place.
4. Comment on the results from parts (2) and (3).
5. AceIRx had negative cash flows from operations for at least the past three years, yet cash and cash equivalents and short-term investments are $105,715 ($87,975 + $17,740). How could this have happened?

MBA 5-2 Ratio of cash to monthly cash expenses

Intercept Pharmaceuticals (ICPT) is a specialty pharmaceutical company focused on the development of treatments for chronic liver diseases.

The following data (in thousands) were adapted from recent financial statements.

	Year 2	Year 1
Operations:		
Net income (loss)	$(344,681)	$(309,242)
Net cash flows used in operating activities	(236,613)	(240,714)
Balance sheet:		
End of the year cash and cash equivalents excluding short-term investments	70,055	43,248
Short-term investments*	582,567	392,912
Financing activities:		
Issued common stock	227,260	261,362

*Includes various short-term securities that are readily convertible to cash.

1. Compute the monthly cash expenses for Years 1 and 2. Round to nearest thousand.
2. Compute the ratio of cash to monthly cash expenses for Years 1 and 2. Round to one decimal place.
3. Including short-term investments as part of cash and cash equivalents, compute the ratio of cash to monthly cash expenses for Years 1 and 2. Round to one decimal place.
4. Comment on the results from parts (2) and (3).

MBA 5-3 Ratio of cash to monthly cash expenses

Achaogen, Inc. (AKAOQ) is a biopharmaceutical company, which engages in the research, development, and commercialization of antibacterial treatments for drug resistant infections. The following data (in thousands) were adapted from recent financial statements.

	Year 3	Year 2	Year 1
Operations:			
Net income (loss)	$(186,512)	$(125,618)	$(71,227)
Net cash flows used in operating activities	(165,000)	(95,255)	(46,903)
Balance sheet:			
End of the year cash and cash equivalents excluding short-term investments	30,956	145,219	118,964
Short-term investments*	—	19,572	26,912
Financing activities:			
Issued common stock	31,416	134,160	124,311

*Includes various short-term securities that are readily convertible to cash.

1. Compute the monthly cash expenses for Years 1–3. Round to nearest thousand.
2. Compute the ratio of cash to monthly cash expenses for Years 1–3. Round to one decimal place.
3. Including short-term investments as part of cash and cash equivalents, compute the ratio of cash to monthly cash expenses for Years 1–3. Round to one decimal place.
4. Comment on the results from parts (2) and (3).
5. Achaogen continued to issue common stock in all three years analyzed. Based upon (2) and (3), would you purchase stock from Achaogen?

MBA 5-4 Ratio of cash to monthly cash expenses

Boston Scientific Corporation (BSX) is a competitor of **Achaogen, Inc.** (MBA 5-3). It was organized in 1979 and develops, produces, and sells medical devices. The following data (in millions) were adapted from Boston Scientific's recent financial statements.

	Year 2	Year 1
Net cash flows from operating activities	$310	$1,426
End of the year cash and cash equivalents	146	188

1. Compare the preceding data for Boston Scientific with Achaogen's data shown in MBA 5-3.
2. Would the computation of the ratio of cash to monthly cash expenses be meaningful for Boston Scientific?

Cases

Case 5-1 Ethics and professional conduct in business

ETHICS

During the preparation of the bank reconciliation for Apache Grading Co., Sarah Ferrari, the assistant controller, discovered that Rocky Spring Bank incorrectly recorded a $610 check written by Apache Grading Co. as $160. Sarah has decided not to notify the bank but wait for the bank to detect the error. Sarah plans to record the $450 error as Other Income if the bank fails to detect the error within the next three months.

Discuss whether Sarah is behaving in a professional manner.

Case 5-2 Internal controls

The following is an excerpt from a conversation between two sales clerks, Tracy Rawlin and Jeff Weimer. Both Tracy and Jeff are employed by Magnum Electronics, a locally owned and operated electronics retail store.

Tracy: Did you hear the news?

Jeff: What news?

Tracy: Bridget and Ken were both arrested this morning.

Jeff: What? Arrested? You're putting me on!

Tracy: No, really! The police arrested them first thing this morning. Put them in handcuffs, read them their rights—the whole works. It was unreal!

Jeff: What did they do?

Tracy: Well, apparently they were filling out merchandise refund forms for fictitious customers and then taking the cash.

Jeff: I guess I never thought of that. How did they catch them?

Tracy: The store manager noticed that returns were twice that of last year and seemed to be increasing. When he confronted Bridget, she became flustered and admitted to taking the cash, apparently over $15,000 in just three months. They're going over the last six months' transactions to try to determine how much Ken stole. He apparently started stealing first.

Suggest appropriate control procedures that would have prevented or detected the theft of cash.

Case 5-3 Internal controls

The following is an excerpt from a conversation between the store manager of La Food Grocery Stores, Amy Locke, and Steve Meyer, president of La Food Grocery Stores.

Steve: Amy, I'm concerned about this new scanning system.

Amy: What's the problem?

Steve: Well, how do we know the clerks are ringing up all the merchandise?

Amy: That's one of the strong points about the system. The scanner automatically rings up each item, based on its bar code. We update the prices daily, so we're sure that the sale is rung up for the right price.

Steve: That's not my concern. What keeps a clerk from pretending to scan items and then simply not charging his friends? If his friends were buying 10–15 items, it would be easy for the clerk to pass through several items with his finger over the bar code or just pass the merchandise through the scanner with the wrong side showing. It would look normal for anyone observing. In the old days, we at least could hear the cash register ringing up each sale.

Amy: I see your point.

Suggest ways that La Food Grocery Stores could prevent or detect the theft of merchandise as described.

Case 5-4 Ethics and professional conduct in business

Javier Meza and Sue Quan are both cash register clerks for Healthy Markets. Ingrid Perez is the store manager for Healthy Markets. The following is an excerpt of a conversation between Javier and Sue:

Javier: Sue, how long have you been working for Healthy Markets?

Sue: Almost five years this June. You just started two weeks ago, right?

Javier: Yes. Do you mind if I ask you a question?

Sue: No, go ahead.

Javier: What I want to know is, have they always had this rule that if your cash register is short at the end of the day, you have to make up the shortage out of your own pocket?

Sue: Yes, as long as I've been working here.

Javier: Well, it's the pits. Last week I had to pay in almost $30.

Sue: It's not that big a deal. I just make sure that I'm not short at the end of the day.

Javier: How do you do that?

Sue: I just shortchange a few customers early in the day. There are a few jerks that deserve it anyway. Most of the time, their attention is elsewhere and they don't think to check their change.

Javier: What happens if you're over at the end of the day?

Sue: Ingrid lets me keep it as long as it doesn't get to be too large. I've not been short in over a year. I usually clear about $10 to $40 extra per day.

Discuss this case from the viewpoint of proper controls and professional behavior.

Case 5-5 Observe internal controls over cash

Select a business in your community and observe its internal controls over cash receipts and cash payments. The business could be a bank or a bookstore, restaurant, department store, or other retailer. In groups of three or four, identify and discuss the similarities and differences in each business's cash internal controls.

Case 5-6 Evaluating internal controls for inventory shrinkage

Johnson Mercantile owns 20 retail stores throughout Utah. The Chief Executive Officer (CEO) and company Loss Prevention Officer (LPO) decided to evaluate the cost effectiveness of two types of controls for reducing shoplifting and the related inventory shrinkage. The first control is to hire store greeters during busy hours to monitor customers coming and leaving the store. The second control is to install monitoring cameras throughout the store.

Starting on January 1 of the past year, the stores were divided into four groups of five stores each. The groups were as follows:

Group 1: No change in controls
Group 2: Hired greeters
Group 3: Installed cameras
Group 4: Hired greeters and installed cameras

Using the data provided in the Excel spreadsheet for the past year, prepare the following:

1. A report that compares estimated inventory losses across control type (camera, greeters, combination, or none).
2. A report of stores that are experiencing high dollar volume of inventory losses.

Go to CengageNOWv2 to complete this assignment.

The annual report (10-K) assignment for this chapter is in Appendix B: Nike Annual Report, Chapter 5.

Answers to Self-Examination Questions

1. **C** Compliance with laws and regulations (answer C) is an objective, not an element, of internal control. The control environment (answer A), monitoring (answer B), control procedures (answer D), risk assessment, and information and communication are the five elements of internal control.

2. **C** The error was made by the bank, so the cash balance according to the bank statement needs to be adjusted. Since the bank deducted $90 ($540.50 − $450.50) too little, the error of $90 should be deducted from the cash balance according to the bank statement (answer C).

3. **B** On any specific date, the cash account in a company's records may not agree with the account in the bank's records because of delays and/or errors by either party in recording transactions. The purpose of a bank reconciliation, therefore, is to determine the reasons for any differences between the two account balances. All errors should then be corrected by the company or the bank, as appropriate. In arriving at the adjusted cash balance according to the bank statement, outstanding checks must be deducted (answer B) to adjust for checks that have been written by the company but that have not yet been presented to the bank for payment.

4. **C** All reconciling items that are added to and deducted from the cash balance according to the company's records on the bank reconciliation (answer C) require that adjustments be recorded by the company to correct errors made in recording transactions or to bring the cash account up to date for delays in recording transactions.

5. **D** To avoid the delay, annoyance, and expense that is associated with paying all obligations by check, relatively small amounts (answer A) are paid from a petty cash fund. The fund is established by estimating the amount of cash needed to pay these small amounts during a specified period (answer B), and it is then reimbursed when the amount of money in the fund is reduced to a predetermined minimum amount (answer C).

Chapter 6 Receivables

What's Covered:

Topics: Receivables

Classifications
- Accounts receivable (Obj. 1)
- Notes receivable (Obj. 1)
- Other receivables (Obj. 1)

Uncollectible Receivables
- Bad debts (Obj.2)
- Direct write-off method (Obj. 3)
- Allowance method (Obj. 4)

Notes Receivable
- Characteristics (Obj. 5)
- Recording (Obj. 5)

Financial Reporting
- Balance sheet (Obj. 6):

Metric-Based Analysis
- Transactions:
  - Liquidity: Days' sales in receivables (Obj. 3, 4)
  - Profitability: Return on sales (Obj. 3, 4)
- Financial Statements:
  - Accounts receivable turnover (Obj. 7)

Learning Objectives

Obj.1 Describe the common classifications of receivables.

Obj.2 Describe the nature of and the accounting for uncollectible receivables.

Obj.3 Describe the direct write-off method of accounting for uncollectible receivables.

Obj.4 Describe the allowance method of accounting for uncollectible receivables.

Obj.5 Describe the accounting for notes receivable.

Obj.6 Describe the reporting of receivables on the balance sheet.

Obj.7 Describe and illustrate the accounts receivable turnover for assessing a company's liquidity and operations.

Chapter Metrics

Use the following metrics to analyze transactions and financial statements.

TRANSACTIONS

Liquidity: Days' Sales in Receivables

Profitability: Return on Sales

FINANCIAL STATEMENTS

Accounts Receivable Turnover

Under Armour, Inc.

@RaymondAsia Photography/ Alamy Stock Photo

A company generates revenues by providing goods or services to customers. For example, **Under Armour, Inc. (UAA)** sells performance apparel, footwear, and other accessories to national, regional, and specialty retailers. Under Armour also sells directly to consumers through its brand and factory house stores and Web site.

If you were to purchase an athletic shirt from the Under Armour Web site, you would use a credit card to complete the purchase. In this case, Under Armour would record the transaction as a cash sale. However, Under Armour allows its business customers to purchase its products "on account." Sales on account create accounts receivable with terms requiring payment within the credit period.

Unlike cash sales, not all credit sales will generate cash. That is, some customers will not pay their account receivable and the company will have to record a bad debt expense. Companies like Under Armour try to reduce uncollectible accounts by reviewing the customer's credit rating and payment history prior to a sale. Even with such procedures, however, companies will experience bad debts.

This chapter describes common classifications of receivables, including notes receivable. In addition, methods of accounting for and estimating uncollectible accounts are described and illustrated.

Finally, the reporting of receivables, the allowance for uncollectible accounts, and bad debt expense in the financial statements is described and illustrated.

Objective 1
Describe the common classifications of receivables.

Classification of Receivables

The receivables that result from sales on account are normally accounts receivable or notes receivable. The term **receivables** includes all money claims against other entities, including people, companies, and other organizations. Receivables are usually a significant portion of the total current assets.

Accounts Receivable

The most common transaction creating a receivable is selling merchandise or services on account (on credit). The receivable is recorded as an increase to Accounts Receivable. Such **accounts receivable** are normally collected within a short period, such as 30 or 60 days. They are classified on the balance sheet as a current asset.

Under Armour Connection

In a recent annual report, **Under Armour** reported accounts receivable of $708.7 million, a majority was due from large retailers such as **Dick's Sporting Goods (DKS)**.

Notes Receivable

Notes receivable are amounts that customers owe for which a formal, written instrument of credit has been issued. If notes receivable are expected to be collected within a year, they are classified on the balance sheet as a current asset.

Notes are often used for credit periods of more than 60 days. For example, an automobile dealer may require a down payment at the time of sale and accept a note or a series of notes for the remainder. Such notes usually provide for monthly payments.

Notes may also be used to settle a customer's account receivable. Notes and accounts receivables that result from sales transactions are sometimes called *trade receivables*. In this chapter, all notes and accounts receivables are from sales transactions.

Other Receivables

Other receivables include interest receivable, taxes receivable, and receivables from officers or employees. Other receivables are normally reported separately on the balance sheet.

If they are expected to be collected within one year, they are classified as current assets. If collection is expected beyond one year, they are classified as noncurrent assets and reported under the caption *Investments*.

Uncollectible Receivables

Objective 2
Describe the nature of and the accounting for uncollectible receivables.

In prior chapters, the accounting for sales of merchandise or services on account (on credit) was described and illustrated. A major issue that has not yet been discussed is that some customers will not pay their accounts. That is, some accounts receivable will be uncollectible.

Companies may shift the risk of uncollectible receivables to other companies. For example, some retailers do not accept sales on account but will only accept cash or credit cards. Such policies shift the risk to the credit card companies.

Companies may also sell their receivables. This is often the case when a company issues its own credit card. For example, **Macy's (M)** and **JCPenney (JCP)** issue their own credit cards. Selling receivables is called *factoring* the receivables. The buyer of the receivables is called a *factor*. An advantage of factoring is that the company selling its receivables immediately receives cash for operating and other needs. Also, depending on the factoring agreement, some of the risk of uncollectible accounts is shifted to the factor.

Regardless of how careful a company is in granting credit, some credit sales will be uncollectible. The operating expense recorded from uncollectible receivables is called **bad debt expense**, *uncollectible accounts expense*, or *doubtful accounts expense*.

There is no general rule for when an account becomes uncollectible. Some indications that an account may be uncollectible include the following:

- The receivable is past due.
- The customer does not respond to the company's attempts to collect.
- The customer files for bankruptcy.
- The customer closes its business.
- The company cannot locate the customer.

If a customer doesn't pay, a company may turn the account over to a collection agency. After the collection agency attempts to collect payment, any remaining balance in the account is considered worthless.

The two methods of accounting for uncollectible receivables are as follows:

1. The **direct write-off method** records bad debt expense only when an account is determined to be worthless.
2. The **allowance method** records bad debt expense by estimating uncollectible accounts at the end of the accounting period.

Warning Signs

One way a company can manage the risk of extending credit is by monitoring customer sales and collections. Early warning signs that a customer may have difficulty paying its account receivable include the following:

- You're only receiving partial payments.
- The customer's ordering pattern has declined dramatically, or the customer is seeking merchandise elsewhere.
- The customer requests frequent changes in the payment schedule.
- The customer is exceeding its credit limits.
- You are repeatedly told that late payments are in the mail.
- The customer is frequently making late payments.
- You can't reach your customer, or the customer refuses to acknowledge you.

Source: BARR Credit Services, "Six Early Warning Signs of Bad Debt," https://barrcredit.com/signs-of-bad-debt/

The direct write-off method is often used by small companies and companies with few receivables.[1] Generally accepted accounting principles (GAAP), however, require companies with a large amount of receivables to use the allowance method. As a result, most well-known companies such as **General Electric Company (GE)**, **Pepsi Co. Inc. (PEP)**, **Intel Corporation (INTC)**, and **FedEx Corporation (FDX)** use the allowance method.

Under Armour Connection

Under Armour uses the allowance method and estimates uncollectible accounts based upon historical experience, significant economic developments, and specific customer risk, such as a customer who is experiencing financial difficulties.

Direct Write-Off Method for Uncollectible Accounts

Objective 3
Describe the direct write-off method of accounting for uncollectible receivables.

Under the direct write-off method, bad debt expense is not recorded until the customer's account is determined to be worthless. At that time, the customer's account receivable is written off.

To illustrate, assume that on May 10 a $4,200 account receivable from Markieff Carson has been determined to be uncollectible. The effects on the accounts and financial statements of writing off the account are as follows:

Financial Statement Effects

BALANCE SHEET

	Assets	=	Liabilities	+	Stockholders' Equity
	Accounts Receivable	=			Retained Earnings
May 10.	(4,200)				(4,200)

STATEMENT OF CASH FLOWS

INCOME STATEMENT

May 10. Bad debt expense (4,200)

The liquidity metric related to accounts receivable transactions used throughout the chapter is days' sales in receivables. **Days' sales in receivables** estimates the average number of days it takes to collect accounts receivable. For example, a company with credit terms of n/30 would expect to collect receivables every 30 days and have 30 days of accounts receivable outstanding.

Days' sales in accounts receivable is computed as follows[2]:

$$\textbf{Days' Sales in Receivables} = \frac{\textbf{Average Accounts Receivables}}{\textbf{Average Daily Sales}}$$

Average daily sales is computed by dividing annual sales by 365 days. To illustrate, assume the following data for Downing Inc. for the year ending December 31, 20Y4.

Sales for year ending Dec. 31, 20Y4	$9,125,000
Accounts Receivable, Jan. 1, 20Y4	400,000
Accounts Receivable, Dec. 31, 20Y4	600,000

1. The direct write-off method is also required for federal income tax purposes.
2. Although accounts receivable are just related to "credit" sales, total sales is normally used to compute days' sales in receivables. This is because credit sales are normally not reported to external users.

The days' sales in receivables of 20 days is computed as follows:

$$\text{Days' Sales in Receivables} = \frac{\text{Average Accounts Receivables}}{\text{Average Daily Sales}} = \frac{(\$400{,}000 + \$600{,}000) \div 2}{\$9{,}125{,}000 \div 365 \text{ days}}$$

$$= \frac{\$500{,}000}{\$25{,}000} = 20 \text{ days}$$

The profitability metric related to accounts receivable transactions used throughout the chapter is **return on sales**. Return on sales is computed as follows:

$$\textbf{Return on Sales} = \frac{\textbf{Operating Income}}{\textbf{Sales}}$$

To illustrate, assume that Downing Inc. reported operating income of $1,460,000 for the year ending December 31, 20Y4. The return on sales of 16% is computed as follows:

$$\text{Return on Sales} = \frac{\text{Operating Income}}{\text{Sales}} = \frac{\$1{,}460{,}000}{\$9{,}125{,}000} = 16\%$$

Transaction Metric Effects

The effects of writing off an uncollectible account of $4,200 using the direct write-off method on the liquidity and profitability metrics are as follows:

LIQUIDITY	
Days' Sales in Receivables	Decrease

PROFITABILITY	
Return on Sales	Decrease

Writing off accounts receivable under the direct method decreases accounts receivable and increases bad debt expense. Because sales do not change and accounts receivable decrease, days' sales in receivables decrease. Because of the increase in bad debt expense and no change in sales, operating income decreases and the return on sales also decreases.

An account receivable that has been written off may be later collected. In such cases, the account is reinstated by reversing the write-off. The cash received in payment is then recorded as a receipt on account.

To illustrate, assume that the Markieff Carson account of $4,200 written off on May 10 is later collected on November 21. The effects on the accounts and financial statements of the reinstatement and the receipt of cash are as follows:

Reinstate Account

Financial Statement Effects

	BALANCE SHEET				
	Assets	=	Liabilities	+	Stockholders' Equity
	Accounts Receivable	=			Retained Earnings
Nov. 21.	4,200				4,200

STATEMENT OF CASH FLOWS

INCOME STATEMENT
Nov. 21. Bad debt expense 4,200

Collected Cash

Financial Statement Effects

	BALANCE SHEET				
	Assets		= Liabilities	+	Stockholders' Equity
	Cash	+ Accounts Receivable			
Nov. 21.	4,200	(4,200)			

STATEMENT OF CASH FLOWS	
Nov. 21. Operating	4,200

INCOME STATEMENT

Transaction Metric Effects

The effects of the reinstatement and collection of the $4,200 account on the liquidity and profitability metrics are as follows:

Date	Description	Liquidity Days' Sales in Receivables	Profitability Return on Sales
Nov. 21	Reinstate Account	Increase	Increase
21	Collected Cash	Decrease	No Effect

Days' sales in receivables is increased by the reinstatement of the account and decreased by its collection. Since bad debt expense is reduced by the reinstatement of the account, operating income and return on sales increase. Operating income and return on sales are not affected by collection of the account.

The direct write-off method is used by businesses that sell most of their goods or services for cash and accept only credit cards such as **MasterCard (MA)** or **VISA (V)**, which are recorded as cash sales. In such cases, receivables are a small part of the current assets and any bad debt expense would be small. Examples of such businesses are a local restaurant or convenience store.

Business Insight

Collecting Past Due Accounts

When customers fail to pay their accounts, a business has the option of seeking payment through a variety of means. The easiest recourse is to simply inquire about the cause of nonpayment and adjust terms to maximize the potential for collection. For large amounts, the cost and time of legal remedies may be appropriate. However, for smaller amounts, most businesses wish to minimize the time, effort, and cost of collecting amounts past due. Thus, after exhausting their internal efforts to collect, it is typical to use the services of a collection agency to collect overdue accounts. Such services must abide by a number of consumer protection laws in collecting overdue accounts. The final amount collected will often be less than the full amount due, of which the collection agency will often keep 25–45% as a fee. Thus, the collection agency is often the last resort before a final write-off.

Allowance Method for Uncollectible Accounts

Objective 4
Describe the allowance method of accounting for uncollectible receivables.

The allowance method estimates the uncollectible accounts receivable at the end of the accounting period. Based on this estimate, Bad Debt Expense is recorded by an adjustment.

To illustrate, assume that DPS Company began operations August 1, 20Y6. As of the end of its accounting period on December 31, 20Y6, DPS has an accounts receivable balance of $200,000. This balance includes some past due accounts. Based on industry averages, DPS estimates that $30,000 of the December 31 accounts receivable will be uncollectible. However, on December 31, DPS doesn't know which customer accounts will be uncollectible. Thus, specific customer accounts cannot be decreased. Instead, a contra asset account, **Allowance for Doubtful Accounts**, is used.

Using the $30,000 estimate, the effects on the accounts and financial statements of recording the adjustment on December 31 are as follows:

Financial Statement Effects

	BALANCE SHEET					
	Assets		=	Liabilities	+	Stockholders' Equity
	Accounts Receivable	– Allowance for Doubtful Accts.	=			Retained Earnings
Dec. 31.		(30,000)				(30,000)

STATEMENT OF CASH FLOWS

INCOME STATEMENT
Dec. 31. Bad debt expense (30,000)

The preceding adjustment affects the income statement and balance sheet. On the income statement, the $30,000 of Bad Debt Expense will be matched against the related revenues of the period. On the balance sheet, the value of the receivables is reported as the amount that is expected to be collected or realized. This amount, $170,000 ($200,000 − $30,000), is called the **net realizable value of accounts receivable**, sometimes referred to as net realizable value of receivables or net receivables.

After the preceding adjustment is recorded, Accounts Receivable still has a balance of $200,000. This balance is the total amount owed by customers on account at December 31 and is supported by the individual customer accounts.[3] The accounts receivable contra account, Allowance for Doubtful Accounts, has a negative balance of $(30,000).

3. The individual customer accounts are often maintained in a separate file or record called a subsidiary ledger. The sum of the individual customer accounts equals the balance of the accounts receivable, called the control account, reported on the balance sheet.

Adjustment Metric Effects

The effects of the adjustment of $30,000 on the liquidity and profitability metrics are as follows:

LIQUIDITY	
Days' Sales in Receivables	Decrease

PROFITABILITY	
Return on Sales	Decrease

Days' sales in receivables is normally computed using net realizable value of receivables (accounts receivable less the allowance for doubtful accounts). Since allowance for doubtful accounts increases, the net realizable value of receivables decreases and the days' sales in receivables decreases. Since bad debt expense increases, operating income decreases, which results in a decrease in the return on sales.

Write-Offs to the Allowance Account

When a customer's account is identified as uncollectible, it is written off against the allowance account. This requires the company to remove the specific accounts receivable and an equal amount from the allowance account. For example, the effect on the accounts and financial statements on January 21, 20Y7, of writing off Chandler Somers's account of $6,000 with DPS Company is as follows:

Financial Statement Effects

BALANCE SHEET

	Assets		=	Liabilities	+	Stockholders' Equity
	Accounts Receivable	– Allowance for Doubtful Accts.	=			
Jan. 21.	(6,000)	6,000				

STATEMENT OF CASH FLOWS

INCOME STATEMENT

Transaction Metric Effects

The effects of the write-off of the $6,000 account receivable on the liquidity and profitability metrics are as follows:

LIQUIDITY	
Days' Sales in Receivables	No Effect

PROFITABILITY	
Return on Sales	No Effect

Since the net realizable value of receivables does not change, the write-off has no effect on the days' sales in receivables. Since the write-off does not affect operating income, there is no effect on the profitability metric return on sales.

At the end of a period, the Allowance for Doubtful Accounts will normally have a balance. This is because the Allowance for Doubtful Accounts is based upon an estimate. As a result, the total write-offs to the allowance account during the period will rarely equal the balance of the account at the beginning of the period. The allowance account will have a negative balance at the end of the period if the write-offs during the period are less than the beginning balance. It will have a positive balance if the write-offs exceed the beginning balance. However, after the end-of-period adjustment is recorded, Allowance for Doubtful Accounts should always have a negative balance.

Exhibit 1 illustrates the allowance method, where the end-of-period adjustment increases the Allowance for Doubtful Accounts (fills the bucket), while writing off accounts decreases the Allowance for Doubtful Accounts (empties the bucket).

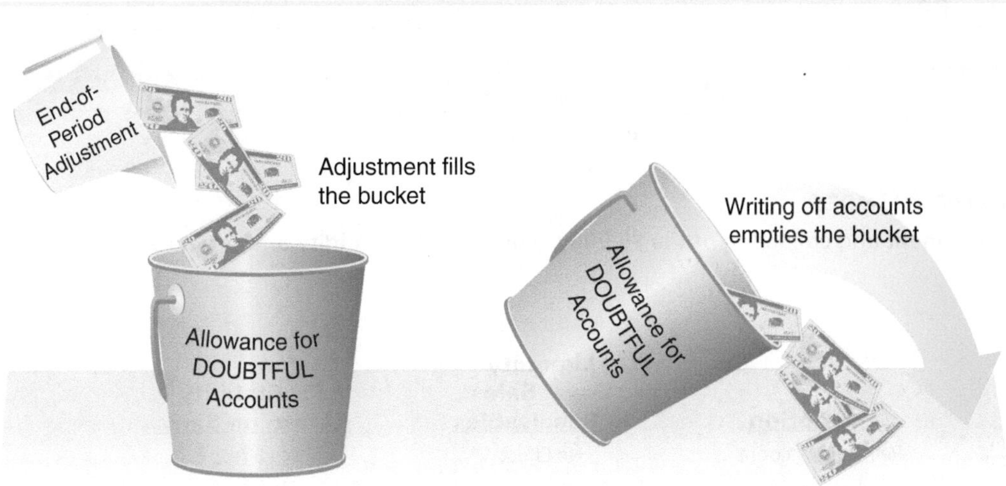

Exhibit 1 The Allowance Method

An account receivable that has been written off against the allowance account may be collected later. Like the direct write-off method, the account is reinstated by reversing the write-off. The cash received in payment is then recorded as a receipt on account.

To illustrate, assume that Nancy Smith's account of $5,000, which was written off on April 2, is later collected on June 10. DPS Company records the reinstatement and the collection as follows:

Reinstate Account

Financial Statement Effects

BALANCE SHEET

	Assets			=	Liabilities	+	Stockholders' Equity
	Accounts Receivable	–	Allowance for Doubtful Accts.	=			
June 10.	5,000		(5,000)				

STATEMENT OF CASH FLOWS

INCOME STATEMENT

Collected Cash

Financial Statement Effects

	BALANCE SHEET			
	Assets		= Liabilities +	Stockholders' Equity
	Cash +	Accounts Receivable =		
June 10.	5,000	(5,000)		

STATEMENT OF CASH FLOWS	
June 10. Operating	5,000

INCOME STATEMENT

Transaction Metric Effects

The effects of the reinstatement and collection of the $5,000 account on the liquidity and profitability metrics are as follows:

Date	Description	Liquidity Days' Sales in Receivables	Profitability Return on Sales
June 10	Reinstate Account	No Effect	No Effect
10	Collected Cash	Decrease	No Effect

The reinstatement of the account increases accounts receivable and the allowance for doubtful accounts. Since days' sales in receivables is normally computed using net accounts receivable, there is no effect on the liquidity metric as a result of the reinstatement. However, the collection of cash for the accounts receivable reduces accounts receivable and thus, decrease days' sales in receivables. Since revenues and expenses are not affected, there is no effect on the return on sales.

Estimating Uncollectibles

The allowance method requires an estimate of uncollectible accounts at the end of the period. This estimate of current credit losses is normally based on past experience, industry averages, current economic conditions, and forecasts of the future.

Integrity, Objectivity, and Ethics in Business

Collecting Past Due Accounts

Companies should make reasonable attempts (steps) to collect past due accounts, as we discussed in the previous Business Insight. Many companies first send a collection reminder as a first step. As a second step, a company may send a collection letter that offers options such as a willingness to negotiate a schedule for future payments. The next step is normally to turn the past due amount over to a collection agency or to file action in court. However, in no case should a company employee harass or misrepresent themselves as an attorney, collection agent, or agent of the court to the customer.

The two methods used to estimate uncollectible accounts are as follows:

1. Percent of sales method
2. Analysis of receivables method

Percent of Sales Method Since accounts receivable are created by credit sales, uncollectible accounts can be estimated as a percentage of credit sales. If the portion of credit sales to sales is relatively constant, the percent may be applied to total sales.

To illustrate, assume the following data for DPS Company on December 31, 20Y7, before any adjustments:

Balance of Accounts Receivable	\$240,000
Balance of Allowance for Doubtful Accounts	\$(3,250)
Total credit sales	\$3,000,000
Bad debt as a percent of credit sales	¾%

Bad Debt Expense is estimated as follows:

Bad Debt Expense = Credit Sales × Bad Debts as a Percent of Credit Sales

$$\text{Bad Debt Expense} = \$3,000,000 \times \tfrac{3}{4}\% = \$22,500$$

Under the percent of sales method, the amount of the adjustment is always the amount estimated for Bad Debt Expense, which in this case is \$22,500.

The effects of the adjustment on the accounts and financial statements on December 31 are as follows:

Financial Statement Effects

BALANCE SHEET

	Assets			=	Liabilities	+	Stockholders' Equity
	Accounts Receivable	–	Allowance for Doubtful Accts.	=			Retained Earnings
Dec. 31.			(22,500)				(22,500)

STATEMENT OF CASH FLOWS

INCOME STATEMENT

Dec. 31. Bad debt expense	(22,500)

After the adjustment, Bad Debt Expense will have an adjusted balance of \$22,500. Allowance for Doubtful Accounts will have a negative adjusted balance of \$(25,750) (\$3,250 + \$22,500).

Adjustment Metric Effects

The effects of the adjustment for uncollectible accounts using the allowance method on the liquidity and profitability metrics are as follows:

LIQUIDITY

Days' Sales in Receivables	Decrease

PROFITABILITY

Return on Sales	Decrease

The increase in the allowance for doubtful accounts decreases the net realizable value of the receivables and thus, the liquidity metric decreases. Since the increase in bad debt expense decreases operating income, return on sales also decreases.

Analysis of Receivables Method The analysis of receivables method is based on the assumption that the longer an account receivable is outstanding, the less likely that it will be collected. The analysis of receivables method is applied as follows:

Step 1. The due date of each account receivable is determined.
Step 2. The number of days each account is past due is determined. This is the number of days between the due date of the account and the date of the analysis.
Step 3. Each account is placed in an aged class according to its days past due. Typical aged classes include the following:

Not past due
1–30 days past due
31–60 days past due
61–90 days past due
91–180 days past due
181–365 days past due
Over 365 days past due

Step 4. The totals for each aged class are determined.
Step 5. The total for each aged class is multiplied by an estimated percentage of uncollectible accounts for that class.
Step 6. The estimated total of uncollectible accounts is determined as the sum of the uncollectible accounts for each aged class.

The preceding steps are summarized in an aging schedule, and this overall process is called **aging the receivables.**

To illustrate, assume that DPS Company uses the analysis of receivables method instead of the percent of sales method. DPS prepared an aging schedule for its accounts receivable of $240,000 as of December 31, 20Y7, as shown in Exhibit 2.

Exhibit 2 Aging-of-Receivables Schedule, December 31, 20Y7

		A	B	C	D	E	F	G	H	I
	1			Not	Days Past Due					
	2			Past						Over
Steps 1–3	3	Customer	Balance	Due	1–30	31–60	61–90	91–180	181–365	365
	4	Ashby & Co.	1,500			1,500				
	5	B. T. Barr	6,100					3,500	2,600	
	6	Brock Co.	4,700	4,700						
	21									
	22	Saxon Woods Co.	600					600		
Step 4 →	23	Total	240,000	125,000	64,000	13,100	8,900	5,000	10,000	14,000
Step 5 →	24	Percent uncollectible		2%	5%	10%	20%	30%	50%	80%
Step 6 →	25	Estimate of uncollectible accounts	26,490	2,500	3,200	1,310	1,780	1,500	5,000	11,200

Assume that DPS Company sold merchandise to Saxon Woods Co. on August 29, 20Y7, with terms n/30. Thus, the due date (Step 1) of Saxon Woods' account is September 28, as shown below.

Credit terms, net	30 days
Less two days in August (31 – 29)	(2)
Days in September	28 days

As of December 31, Saxon Woods' account is 94 days past due (Step 2), as follows:

Number of days past due in September (30 – 28)	2 days
Number of days past due in October	31
Number of days past due in November	30
Number of days past due in December	31
Total number of days past due	94 days

Exhibit 2 shows that the $600 account receivable for Saxon Woods Co. was placed in the 91–180 days past due class (Step 3).

The total for each of the aged classes is determined (Step 4). Exhibit 2 shows that $125,000 of the accounts receivable are not past due, while $64,000 are 1–30 days past due. DPS Company applies a different estimated percentage of uncollectible accounts to the totals of each of the aged classes (Step 5). As shown in Exhibit 2, the percent is 2% for accounts not past due, while the percent is 80% for accounts over 365 days past due.

The sum of the estimated uncollectible accounts for each aged class (Step 6) is the estimated uncollectible accounts on December 31, 20Y7. This is the desired adjusted balance for Allowance for Doubtful Accounts. For DPS Company, this amount is $26,490, as shown in Exhibit 2.

The amount of the adjustment for Bad Debt Expense is the amount that will yield an adjusted balance for Allowance for Doubtful Accounts equal to that estimated by the aging schedule. For DPS, the unadjusted balance of the allowance account is a negative balance of $(3,250). The amount to be added to this balance is therefore $(23,240) ($26,490 – $3,250).

The effects of the adjustment of $23,240 on the accounts and financial statements of DPS Company are as follows:

Financial Statement Effects

BALANCE SHEET

	Assets			=	Liabilities	+	Stockholders' Equity
	Accounts Receivable	–	**Allowance for Doubtful Accts.**	=			**Retained Earnings**
Dec. 31.			(23,240)				(23,240)

STATEMENT OF CASH FLOWS

INCOME STATEMENT

Dec. 31. Bad debt expense	(23,240)

After the preceding adjustment, Bad Debt Expense will have an adjusted balance of $23,240. Allowance for Doubtful Accounts will have an adjusted balance of $26,490, and the net realizable value of the receivables is $213,510 ($240,000 – $26,490).

Adjustment Metric Effects

The effects of the adjustment of $23,240 for uncollectible accounts on the liquidity and profitability metrics are as follows:

LIQUIDITY	
Days' Sales in Receivables	Decrease

PROFITABILITY	
Return on Sales	Decrease

The increase in the allowance for doubtful accounts decreases the net realizable value of the receivables, and thus, the liquidity metric decreases. Since the increase in bad debt expense decreases operating income, return on sales also decreases.

Under Armour Connection

For a recent year, **Under Armour** reported accounts receivable of $723.8 million, allowance for doubtful accounts of $15.1 million, and a net accounts receivable of $708.7 million.

Comparing Estimation Methods Both the percent of sales and analysis of receivables methods estimate uncollectible accounts. However, each method has a slightly different focus and financial statement emphasis.

Under the percent of sales method, Bad Debt Expense is the focus of the estimation process. The percent of sales method places more emphasis on matching revenues and expenses and thus emphasizes the income statement. That is, the amount of the adjustment is based on the estimate of Bad Debt Expense for the period. Allowance for Doubtful Accounts is then adjusted by this amount.

Under the analysis of receivables method, Allowance for Doubtful Accounts is the focus of the estimation process. The analysis of receivables method places more emphasis on the net realizable value of the receivables and thus emphasizes the balance sheet. That is, the amount of the adjustment is the amount that will yield an adjusted balance for Allowance for Doubtful Accounts equal to that estimated by the aging schedule. Bad Debt Expense is then adjusted by this amount.

Exhibit 3 summarizes these differences between the percent of sales and the analysis of receivables methods. Exhibit 3 also shows the results of the DPS Company illustration for the percent of sales and analysis of receivables methods. The amounts shown in

Exhibit 3 Differences Between Estimation Methods

			DPS Company Example	
Estimation Method	**Focus of Method**	**Financial Statement Emphasis**	**Bad Debt Expense (Adjustment Amount)**	**Allowance for Doubtful Accounts (After Adjustment)**
Percent of Sales Method	Bad Debt Expense Estimate	Income Statement	$22,500	$(25,750)* ($22,500 + $3,250)
Analysis of Receivables Method	Allowance for Doubtful Accounts Estimate	Balance Sheet	$23,240* ($26,490 − $3,250)	$(26,490)

*Indicates that the estimate was derived (sometimes called "plugged") from the estimate on which this method focuses.

Exhibit 3 assumes an unadjusted negative balance of $(3,250) for Allowance for Doubtful Accounts. While the methods normally yield different amounts for any one period, over several periods the amounts should be similar.

Comparing Direct Write-Off and Allowance Methods The primary differences between the direct write-off and allowance methods are summarized in Exhibit 4.

Exhibit 4
Direct Write-Off and Allowance Methods

	Direct Write-Off Method	Allowance Method
Bad debt expense is recorded	When the specific customer accounts are determined to be uncollectible.	Using an estimate based on: (1) a percent of sales or (2) an analysis of receivables.
Allowance account	No allowance account is used.	The allowance account is used.
Primary users	Small companies and companies with few receivables.	Large companies and those with a large amount of receivables.

Using Data Analytics

Collectability of Credit Sales

Most retail businesses accept only cash or credit card payments from customers. As a result, these companies do not have to assess the creditworthiness of their customers or the collectability of their credit sales (accounts receivable). For these businesses, "cash and carry" is an efficient way of doing business.

Other types of businesses, such as suppliers of merchandise to retail businesses, frequently ship merchandise on credit. For example, suppliers such as **The Procter & Gamble Company (PG)** sell merchandise to a variety of different types of retail stores, from local convenience stores to large retail chains such as **Costco (COST)**, **Target (TGT)**, and **Walmart (WMT)**.

Companies like Procter & Gamble can use data analytics to assess the collectability and timeliness of payments from different classes of customers. For example, large retail chains such as Costco would normally pay their receivables but might take longer to pay. In contrast, credit sales to small, locally owned stores might be more likely to be uncollectible. By using data analytics, a retail supplier might implement different credit procedures and credit terms for each class of customer.

See Case 6-6 for a homework assignment using data analytics.

Notes Receivable

Objective 5
Describe the accounting for notes receivable.

A note has some advantages over an account receivable. By signing a note, the debtor recognizes the debt and agrees to pay it according to its terms. Thus, a note is a stronger legal claim.

Characteristics of Notes Receivable

A promissory note receivable is a written promise to pay the face amount, usually with interest, on demand or at a date in the future.[4] Characteristics of a promissory note are as follows:

1. The *maker* is the party making the promise to pay.
2. The *payee* is the party to whom the note is payable.
3. The *face amount* is the amount the note is written for on its face.
4. The *issuance date* is the date a note is issued.
5. The *due date* or *maturity date* is the date the note is to be paid.
6. The *term* of a note is the amount of time between the issuance and due dates.
7. The *interest rate* is that rate of interest that must be paid on the face amount for the term of the note.

Exhibit 5 illustrates a promissory note.

Exhibit 5
Promissory Note

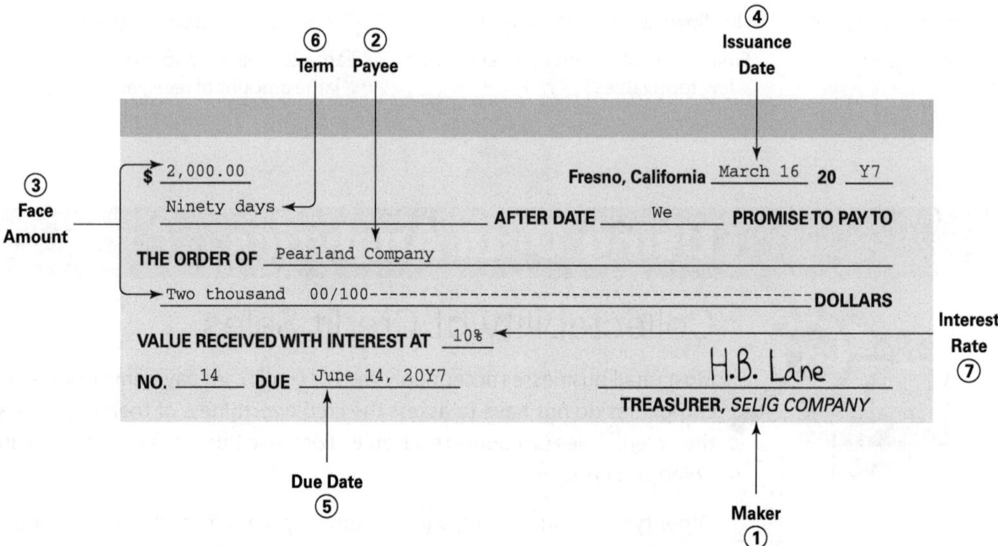

The maker of the note is Selig Company, and the payee is Pearland Company. The face value of the note is $2,000, and the issuance date is March 16, 20Y7. The term of the note is 90 days, which results in a due date of June 14, 20Y7, as follows:

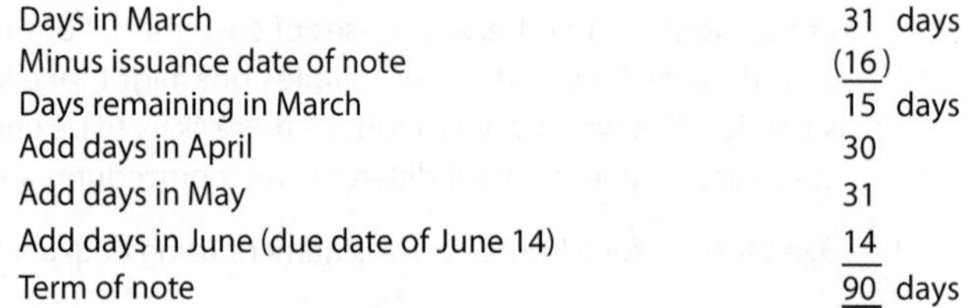

Days in March	31 days
Minus issuance date of note	(16)
Days remaining in March	15 days
Add days in April	30
Add days in May	31
Add days in June (due date of June 14)	14
Term of note	90 days

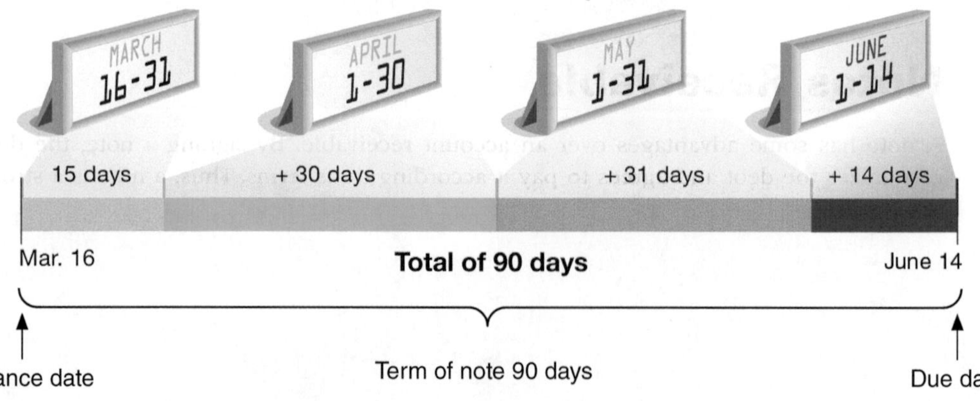

4. You may see references to non-interest-bearing notes. Such notes are not widely used and carry an assumed or implicit interest rate.

In Exhibit 5, the term of the note is 90 days and it has an interest rate of 10%. The interest on a note is computed as follows:

Interest = Face Amount × Interest Rate × Term/360 days

The interest rate is stated on an annual (yearly) basis, while the term is expressed in days. Thus, the interest on the note in Exhibit 1 is computed as follows:

Interest = $2,000 × 10% × 90/360 = $50

To simplify, 360 days per year are used in this chapter. In practice, companies such as banks and mortgage lenders use the exact number of days in a year, 365.

The **maturity value** is the amount that must be paid at the due date of the note, which is the sum of the face amount and the interest. The maturity value of the note in Exhibit 5 is $2,050 ($2,000 + $50).

Accounting for Notes Receivable

A promissory note may be received by a company from a customer to replace an account receivable. In such cases, the promissory note is recorded as a note receivable.

To illustrate, assume that Pearland Company accepted the 90-day, 10% note dated March 16 shown in Exhibit 5 in settlement of the account receivable of Selig Company, which is past due and has a balance of $2,000. The effect on the accounts and financial statements of Pearland Company of the receipt of the note is as follows:

BALANCE SHEET

	Assets		=	Liabilities	+	Stockholders' Equity
	Accounts Receivable	Notes Receivable				
Mar. 16.	(2,000)	2,000				

STATEMENT OF CASH FLOWS

INCOME STATEMENT

Transaction Metric Effects

The effects of accepting a note receivable to replace an account receivable on the liquidity and profitability metrics are as follows:

LIQUIDITY	
Days' Sales in Receivables	No Effect

PROFITABILITY	
Return on Sales	No Effect

When a company accepts notes receivable from customers, days' sales in receivables normally is computed using both notes and accounts receivable. Since the total trade receivables has not changed, there is no effect on the liquidity metric. Likewise, since revenues and expenses were not changed, there is no effect on the profitability metric.

On the due date of June 14, Pearland Company receive $2,050, which is the $2,000 face amount of the note plus interest of $50. The effects on the accounts and financial statements of the receipt of the amount due on the note are as follows:

Financial Statement Effects

BALANCE SHEET

	Assets		=	**Liabilities**	+	**Stockholders' Equity**
	Cash	+ **Notes Receivable**				**Retained Earnings**
June 14.	2,050	(2,000)				50

STATEMENT OF CASH FLOWS

June 14.	Operating	2,050

INCOME STATEMENT

June 14.	Interest revenue	50

Transaction Metric Effects

The effects on the liquidity and profitability metrics of receiving the amount due on the note receivable are as follows:

LIQUIDITY

Days' Sales in Receivables	Decrease

PROFITABILITY

Return on Sales	Increase

Since receivables decrease, the liquidity metric days' sales in receivables decreases. Since operating income increases, the profitability metric return on sales increases.

A company receiving a note should record an adjustment for any accrued interest at the end of the period. For example, assume that Crawford Company receives a $4,000, 90-day, 12% note dated December 1, 20Y3, to settle an account receivable. If Crawford Company's accounting period ends on December 31, 20Y3, it should record an adjustment for accrued interest of $40 ($4,000 × 12% × 30/360). The adjustment would increase both Interest Receivable and Interest Revenue by $40.

Objective 6
Describe the reporting of receivables on the balance sheet.

Reporting Receivables on the Balance Sheet

All receivables expected to be realized in cash within a year are presented in the "Current assets" section of the balance sheet as shown in Exhibit 6. Current assets are normally listed in the order of their liquidity, that is, the order in which they are expected to be converted to cash during normal operations.

Exhibit 6 Receivables on the Balance Sheet

Crabtree Co. Balance Sheet December 31, 20Y3		
Assets		
Current assets:		
Cash and cash equivalents		$119,500
Accounts receivable	$445,000	
Less allowance for doubtful accounts	(15,000)	430,000
Notes receivable		250,000
Interest receivable		14,500

The receivables (in thousands) reported on a recent **Under Armour, Inc. (UAA)** balance sheet are as follows:[5]

Assets (in millions)	Year 2	Year 1
Current assets:		
Cash and cash equivalents	$788,072	$557,403
Accounts receivable, net	708,714	652,546
Inventories	892,258	1,019,496
Prepaid expenses and other current assets	313,165	364,183
Total current assets	2,702,209	2,593,628

Under Armour Connection

Under Armour reports net accounts receivable of $708,714 and $652,546 for Years 2 and 1, respectively. The allowances for doubtful accounts of $15,100 and $22,200 are reported in a note to the financial statements. These allowances are subtracted from the gross accounts receivable to arrive at the net receivables.

Other disclosures related to receivables are presented either on the face of the financial statements or in the accompanying notes. Such disclosures include the market (fair) value of the receivables if significantly different from the reported value. In addition, if unusual credit risks exist within the receivables, the nature of the risks should be disclosed. For example, if the majority of the receivables are due from one customer or are due from customers located in one area of the country or one industry, these facts should be disclosed.

To illustrate, **Under Armour (UAA)** reported the following related to credit risks in its recent financial statements:

Concentration of Credit Risk

Financial instruments that subject the Company to significant concentration of credit risk consist primarily of accounts receivable. The majority of the Company's accounts receivable is due from large retailers. Credit is extended based on an evaluation of the customer's financial condition and collateral is not required. None of the Company's customers accounted for more than 10% of accounts receivable ...

Under Armour Connection

5. Adapted from Under Armour, Inc., *Form 10-K*.

Objective 7
Describe and illustrate the accounts receivable turnover for assessing a company's liquidity and operations.

Metric-Based Analysis: Accounts Receivable Turnover

Accounts receivable are large current assets for many companies. One of the primary objectives in managing receivables is to convert them to cash through collections. The accounts receivable turnover is a useful measure of liquidity and how efficiently a company is managing its operations.

The **accounts receivable turnover** is computed as follows:

$$\textbf{Accounts Receivable Turnover} = \frac{\textbf{Sales}}{\textbf{Average Accounts Receivable}}$$

Although accounts receivable are just related to "credit" sales, total sales is normally used to compute accounts receivable turnover. This is because credit sales are normally not reported to external users. The average accounts receivable is computed as the beginning accounts receivable plus the ending accounts receivable for the period divided by two.

To illustrate, assume the following data for Downing Inc. for the year ending December 31, 20Y4:

Sales for 20Y4	$9,125,000
Accounts Receivable, Jan. 1, 20Y4	400,000
Accounts Receivable, Dec. 31, 20Y4	600,000

The accounts receivable turnover of 18.3 for Downing Inc. is computed as follows:

$$\text{Accounts Receivable Turnover} = \frac{\$9{,}125{,}000}{(\$400{,}000 + \$600{,}000) \div 2} = \frac{\$9{,}125{,}000}{\$500{,}000} = 18.25$$

Under Armour Connection

For a recent year, **Under Armour** had an accounts receivable turnover of 7.7.

Accounts receivable turnover is related to the liquidity metric days' sales in receivables described earlier in this chapter. Specifically, these two metrics are related as follows:

$$\textbf{Days' Sales in Receivables} = \frac{\textbf{365 Days}}{\textbf{Accounts Receivable Turnover}}$$

To illustrate, the days' sales in receivables of 20 days for Downing Inc. can be computed as follows:

$$\text{Days' Sales in Receivables} = \frac{\text{365 Days}}{\text{Accounts Receivable Turnover}} = \frac{\text{365 Days}}{18.25} = 20 \text{ days}$$

or

$$\text{Days' Sales in Receivables} = \frac{\text{Average Accounts Receivable}}{\text{Average Daily Sales}} = \frac{(\$400{,}000 + \$600{,}000) \div 2}{\$9{,}125{,}000 \div 365}$$

$$= \frac{\$500{,}000}{\$25{,}000} = 20 \text{ days}$$

Downing Inc. is converting its accounts receivable to cash 18.25 times per year and on average collecting sales on account within 20 days. Assuming that Downing Inc.'s credit terms are net 30 days, these metrics are favorable. In other words, customers are paying within the credit period. When customers are paying faster and within the credit period, a company's liquidity is increased (improved).

Under Armour Connection

For a recent year, **Under Armour** had an average days' sales in receivables of 47 days.

Key Points

1. Describe the common classifications of receivables.

The term *receivables* includes all money claims against other entities, including people, business firms, and other organizations. Receivables are normally classified as accounts receivable, notes receivable, or other receivables.

2. Describe the nature of and the accounting for uncollectible receivables.

The two methods of accounting for uncollectible receivables are the direct write-off method and the allowance method. The direct write-off method recognizes the expense only when the account is judged to be uncollectible. The allowance method provides in advance for uncollectible receivables.

3. Describe the direct write-off method of accounting for uncollectible receivables.

Under the direct write-off method, writing off an account increases Bad Debt Expense and decreases Accounts Receivable. Neither an allowance account nor an adjustment is needed at the end of the period.

4. Describe the allowance method of accounting for uncollectible receivables.

A year-end adjustment provides for (1) the reduction of the value of the receivables to the amount of cash expected to be realized from them in the future and (2) the allocation to the current period of the expected expense resulting from such reduction. The adjustment affects Bad Debt Expense and the Allowance for Doubtful Accounts. When an account is believed to be uncollectible, it is written off against the allowance account.

When the estimate of uncollectibles is based on the amount of sales for the period, the adjustment is made without regard to the balance of the allowance account. When the estimate of uncollectibles is based on the amount and the age of the receivable accounts at the end of the period, the adjustment is recorded so that the balance of the allowance account will equal the estimated uncollectibles at the end of the period.

The allowance account, which will have a negative balance after the adjustment has been posted, is a contra asset account. The bad debt expense is generally reported on the income statement as an operating expense.

5. Describe the accounting for notes receivable.

A note received to settle an account receivable is recorded as an increase to Notes Receivable and a decrease to Accounts Receivable. When a note is paid at maturity, Cash is increased, Notes Receivable is decreased, and Interest Revenue is increased. An adjustment is necessary for any accrued interest at the end of the accounting period.

6. Describe the reporting of receivables on the balance sheet.

All receivables that are expected to be realized in cash within a year are presented in the Current Assets section of the balance sheet. It is normal to list the assets in the order of their liquidity, which is the order in which they can be converted to cash in normal operations. In addition to the allowance for doubtful accounts, additional receivable disclosures include the market value and unusual credit risks.

7. Metric-Based Analysis: Describe and illustrate the accounts receivable turnover for assessing a company's liquidity and operations.

The accounts receivable turnover is useful in assessing a company's liquidity and operations. The accounts receivable turnover is computed as sales divided by average accounts receivable. A high accounts receivable turnover implies that a company is efficient in managing its receivables.

Key Terms

Accounts receivable (236)
Accounts receivable turnover (254)
Aging the receivables (246)
Allowance for Doubtful Accounts (241)
Allowance method (237)
Bad debt expense (237)
Days' sales in receivables (238)
Direct write-off method (237)
Maturity value (251)
Net realizable value of accounts receivable (241)
Notes receivable (236)
Receivables (236)
Return on sales (239)

Illustrative Problem

Stewart Co. is a construction supply company that uses the allowance method of accounting for uncollectible accounts receivable. It is estimated that 3% of the credit sales of $1,375,000 for the year ended December 31 will be uncollectible.

Instructions

1. Determine the amount of the adjustment for uncollectible accounts as of December 31, 20Y5.
2. Illustrate the effects of the adjustment for uncollectible accounts on the accounts and financial statements of Stewart Co.
3. If the balance of Allowance for Doubtful Accounts was a negative $7,500, would the amount of adjustment determined in (1) change?

Solution

1. $41,250 ($1,375,000 × 3%)
2.

Financial Statement Effects

BALANCE SHEET

	Assets	=	Liabilities	+	Stockholders' Equity
	– Allowance for Doubtful Accts.	=			Retained Earnings
Dec. 31.	(41,250)				(41,250)

STATEMENT OF CASH FLOWS

INCOME STATEMENT

Dec. 31. Bad debt expense (41,250)

3. No. Under the percent of sales method, the amount of the adjustment is determined without considering the balance of Allowance for Doubtful Accounts. Under the analysis of receivables method, however, the balance of Allowance for Doubtful Accounts does affect the amount of the adjustment.

Self-Examination Questions

(Answers appear at the end of the chapter.)

1. At the end of the fiscal year, before the accounts are adjusted, Accounts Receivable has a balance of $200,000 and Allowance for Doubtful Accounts has a negative balance of $(2,500). Sales during the year were $1,250,000, and it is estimated that 1.2% of sales will be uncollectible. If the estimate of uncollectible accounts is determined by a percent of sales, the amount of bad debt expense is:
   A. $12,500
   B. $15,000
   C. $17,500
   D. $20,000

2. At the end of the fiscal year, before the accounts are adjusted, Accounts Receivable has a balance of $200,000 and Allowance for Doubtful Accounts has a negative balance of $(2,500). If the estimate of uncollectible accounts determined by aging the receivables is $8,500, the amount of bad debt expense is:
   A. $2,500
   B. $6,000
   C. $8,500
   D. $11,000

3. At the end of the fiscal year, Accounts Receivable has a balance of $100,000 and Allowance for Doubtful Accounts has a negative balance of $(7,000). The expected net realizable value of the accounts receivable is:
   A. $7,000
   B. $93,000
   C. $100,000
   D. $107,000

4. What is the maturity value of a 90-day, 12% note for $10,000?
   A. $8,800
   B. $10,000
   C. $10,300
   D. $11,200

5. What is the due date of a $12,000, 90-day, 8% note receivable dated August 5?
   A. October 31
   B. November 2
   C. November 3
   D. November 4

Class Discussion Questions

1. What are the three classifications of receivables?
2. What types of transactions give rise to accounts receivable?
3. In what section of the balance sheet should a note receivable be listed if its term is (a) 90 days, (b) 12 years?
4. Give two examples of other receivables.
5. Carter's Hardware is a small hardware store in the rural township of Oglethorpe that rarely extends credit to its customers in the form of an account receivable. The few customers that are allowed to carry accounts receivable are long-time residents of Oglethorpe and have a history of doing business at Carter's. What method of accounting for uncollectible receivables should Carter's Hardware use? Why?
6. Which of the two methods of accounting for uncollectible accounts provides for the recognition of the expense at the earlier date?
7. What kind of an account (asset, liability, etc.) is Allowance for Doubtful Accounts?
8. After the accounts are adjusted at the end of the fiscal year, Accounts Receivable has a balance of $475,000 and Allowance for Doubtful Accounts has a negative balance of $(46,800). Describe how Accounts Receivable and Allowance for Doubtful Accounts are reported on the balance sheet.
9. A firm has consistently adjusted its allowance account at the end of the fiscal year by adding a fixed percent of the period's sales on account. After 10 years, the balance in Allowance for Doubtful Accounts has become very large in relationship to the balance in Accounts Receivable. Give two possible explanations.
10. Which of the two methods of estimating uncollectible accounts receivable places more emphasis on the net realizable value of the receivables and the balance sheet?
11. Which of the two methods of estimating uncollectible accounts receivable places more emphasis on the matching of revenues and expenses and the income statement?
12. Neptune Company issued a note receivable to Sailfish Company. (a) Who is the payee? (b) What is the title of the account used by Sailfish Company in recording the note?
13. If a note provides for payment of principal of $85,000 and interest at the rate of 6%, will the interest amount to $5,100? Explain.
14. The maker of a $240,000, 6%, 90-day note receivable paid the note on the due date of November 30. What accounts should be increased and decreased by the payee to record the payment?
15. Under what section should accounts receivable be reported on the balance sheet.

Exercises

Obj. 1

E6-1 Classifications of receivables

Boeing (BA) is one of the world's major aerospace firms, with operations involving commercial aircraft, military aircraft, missiles, satellite systems, and information and battle management systems. Recently, Boeing reported $1,121 million of receivables involving U.S. government contracts and $2,218 million of receivables involving commercial aircraft customers, such as Delta Air Lines (DAL) and United Airlines (UAL).

Should Boeing report these receivables separately in the financial statements, or combine them into one overall accounts receivable amount? Explain.

Obj. 2

✔ a. 13.4%

E6-2 Nature of uncollectible accounts

MGM Resorts International (MGM) owns and operates casinos including the MGM Grand and the Bellagio in Las Vegas, Nevada. For a recent year, the MGM Resorts International reported accounts and notes receivable of $707,278,000 and allowance for doubtful accounts of $94,561,000.

International Business Machines (IBM) provides information technology services, including software, worldwide. For a recent year, IBM reported notes and accounts receivable of $8,169,000,000 and allowance for doubtful accounts of $299,000,000.

a. Compute the percentage of the allowance for doubtful accounts to the accounts and notes receivable for MGM. Round to one decimal place.

b. Compute the percentage of the allowance for doubtful accounts to the accounts receivable for IBM. Round to one decimal place.

c. Discuss possible reasons for the difference in the two ratios computed in (a) and (b).

Obj. 3

E6-3 Uncollectible accounts, using direct write-off method

Illustrate the effects on the accounts and financial statements of the following transactions in the accounts of Valley Care & Supplies Co., a local hospital supply company that uses the direct write-off method of accounting for uncollectible receivables:

March 18 Received $5,000 on an account and wrote off the remainder owed of $10,000 as uncollectible.

Aug. 29 Reinstated the account that had been written off on March 18 and received $10,000 cash in full payment.

Obj. 4

E6-4 Uncollectible receivables, using allowance method

Illustrate the effects on the accounts and financial statements of the following transactions in the accounts of Kitchen Depot Company, a restaurant supply company that uses the allowance method of accounting for uncollectible receivables:

July 3 Received $2,500 on an account and wrote off the remainder owed of $11,000 as uncollectible.

Oct. 8 Reinstated the account that had been written off on July 3 and received $11,000 cash in full payment.

Obj. 3, 4

E6-5 Writing off accounts receivable

Quantum Technologies, a computer consulting firm, has decided to write off the $13,000 balance of an account owed by a customer. Illustrate the effects on the accounts and financial statements to record the write-off (a) assuming that the direct write-off method is used, and (b) assuming that the allowance method is used.

E6-6 Estimating doubtful accounts

Obj. 4

Sun Valley Rides is a wholesaler of motorcycle supplies. An aging of the company's accounts receivable on December 31, 20Y3, and a historical analysis of the percentage of uncollectible accounts in each age category are as follows:

Age Interval	Balance	Percent Uncollectible
Not past due	$ 925,000	1%
1–30 days past due	375,000	2
31–60 days past due	50,000	6
61–90 days past due	30,000	14
91–180 days past due	22,500	60
Over 180 days past due	12,500	90
	$1,415,000	

Estimate what the balance of Allowance for Doubtful Accounts should be as of December 31, 20Y3.

E6-7 Adjustment for uncollectible accounts

Obj. 4

Using the data in Exercise 6-6, assume that the allowance for doubtful accounts for Sun Valley Rides had a negative balance of $(6,650) as of December 31, 20Y3.

Illustrate the effects of the adjustment for uncollectible accounts as of December 31, 20Y3, on the accounts and financial statements.

E6-8 Aging accounts receivable

Obj. 4

✔ c. $(106,974)

The accounts receivable clerk for Evers Industries prepared the following partially completed aging of receivables schedule as of the end of business on July 31:

	A	B	C	D	E	F	G
1			Not		Days Past Due		
2			Past				Over
3	Customer	Balance	Due	1–30	31–60	61–90	90
4	Acme Industries Inc.	3,000	3,000				
5	Alliance Company	4,500		4,500			
21	Zollinger Company	5,000			5,000		
22	Subtotals	1,050,000	600,000	220,000	115,000	85,000	30,000

The following accounts were unintentionally omitted from the aging schedule and not included in the preceding subtotals:

Customer	Balance	Due Date
Boyd Industries	$36,000	April 7
Hodges Company	11,500	May 29
Kent Creek Inc.	6,600	June 8
Lockwood Company	7,400	August 10
Van Epps Company	13,000	July 2

a. Determine the number of days past due for each of the preceding accounts as of July 31.

b. Complete the aging of receivables schedule by adding the omitted accounts to the bottom of the schedule and updating the totals.

c. Estimate what the balance of Allowance for Doubtful Accounts should be as of July 31. Assume Evers Industries has the following historical average of the percent of uncollectible accounts in each aged category:

Age Interval	Percent Uncollectible
Not past due	1%
1–30 days past due	3%
31–60 days past due	10%
61–90 days past due	30%
Over 90 days past due	80%

Obj. 4

E6-9 Adjustment for uncollectible accounts

Using your answer to part (c) of Exercise 6-8, assume that the "unadjusted" balance of Allowance for Doubtful Accounts is a positive $2,226 on July 31. Illustrate the effects of the adjustment for uncollectible accounts on the accounts and financial statements of Evers Industries.

Obj. 4

SHOW ME HOW

EXCEL ONLINE

✔ a. $172,500

✔ b. $181,500

E6-10 Providing for doubtful accounts

At the end of the current year, the accounts receivable account has a balance of $2,875,000 and sales for the year total $34,500,000. Determine the amount of the adjustment to provide for doubtful accounts under each of the following independent assumptions:

a. The allowance account before adjustment has a negative balance of $(18,500). Bad debt expense is estimated at ½ of 1% of sales.

b. The allowance account before adjustment has a negative balance of $(18,500). An aging of the accounts in the customer ledger indicates estimated doubtful accounts of $200,000.

c. The allowance account before adjustment has a positive balance of $9,000. Bad debt expense is estimated at ¾ of 1% of sales.

d. The allowance account before adjustment has a positive balance of $9,000. An aging of the accounts in the customer ledger indicates estimated doubtful accounts of $255,000.

Obj. 3, 4

E6-11 Effect of doubtful accounts on net income

During its first year of operations, Fisher Plumbing Supply Co. had sales of $2,780,000, wrote off $16,000 of accounts as uncollectible using the direct write-off method, and reported net income of $120,000. Determine what the net income would have been if the allowance method had been used, and the company estimated that 1% of sales would be uncollectible.

Obj. 3, 4

E6-12 Effect of doubtful accounts on net income

Using the data in Exercise 6-11, assume that during the second year of operations Fisher Plumbing Supply Co. had sales of $3,000,000, wrote off $20,000 of accounts as uncollectible using the direct write-off method, and reported net income of $140,000.

a. Determine what net income would have been in the second year if the allowance method (using 1% of sales) had been used in both the first and second years.

b. Determine what the balance of Allowance for Doubtful Accounts would have been at the end of the second year if the allowance method had been used in both the first and second years.

E6-13 Direct write-off and allowance methods

Obj. 3, 4

Casebolt Company wrote off $30,000 of accounts receivable as uncollectible for the first year of its operations ending December 31.

a. Assume that Casebolt Company uses the direct write-off method. Illustrate the effects of the $30,000 of write-offs of accounts receivable on the accounts and financial statements.

b. Assume that Casebolt Company uses the allowance method. Illustrate the effects of the $30,000 of write-offs of accounts receivable on the accounts and financial statements.

c. Assume that Casebolt Company uses the allowance method based on a percent of sales estimate. The company had $5,250,000 of credit sales during the year. Based on industry averages, ¾% of credit sales are expected to be uncollectible. Illustrate the effects of the adjustment for uncollectible accounts on the accounts and financial statements.

d. Assuming the Casebolt Company uses the allowance method in parts (b) and (c), what is the balance of Allowance for Doubtful Accounts on December 31?

e. How much higher (lower) would Casebolt Company's net income have been under the direct write-off method than under the allowance method?

E6-14 Direct write-off and allowance methods

Obj. 3, 4

Seaforth International wrote off $103,100 of accounts receivable as uncollectible for the year ended December 31. The company prepared the following aging schedule for its accounts receivable on December 31:

Aging Class (Number of Days Past Due)	Receivables Balance on December 31	Estimated Percent of Uncollectible Accounts
0–30 days	$ 735,000	1%
31–60 days	290,000	2
61–90 days	111,000	15
91–120 days	70,000	30
More than 120 days	94,000	60
Total receivables	$1,300,000	

a. Assume that Seaforth International uses the direct write-off method. Illustrate the effects of the $103,100 of write-offs of accounts receivable on the accounts and financial statements.

b. Assume that Seaforth International uses the allowance method. Illustrate the effects of the $103,100 of write-offs of accounts receivable on the accounts and financial statements.

c. Assume that Seaforth International uses the allowance method based on an aging of accounts receivable. The Allowance for Doubtful Accounts had a balance of $(89,000) at the beginning of the year. Illustrate the effects of the adjustment for uncollectible accounts on the accounts and financial statements.

d. Assuming the Seaforth International uses the allowance method in parts (b) and (c), what is the balance of Allowance for Doubtful Accounts on December 31?

e. How much higher (lower) would Seaforth International's net income have been under the direct write-off method than under the allowance method?

E6-15 Determine due date and interest on notes

Obj. 5

SHOW ME HOW

✔ a. Feb. 14, $125

Determine the due date and the amount of interest due at maturity on the following notes:

	Date of Note	Face Amount	Interest Rate	Term of Note
a.	January 15	$25,000	6%	30 days
b.	April 1	13,500	4	90 days
c.	June 22	20,000	6	45 days
d.	August 30	45,000	8	120 days
e.	October 16	36,000	5	50 days

To simplify, use 360 days per year to compute interest.

Obj. 5

E6-16 Determine due date and interest on notes

Determine the due date and the amount of interest due at maturity on the following notes:

	Date of Note	Face Amount	Interest Rate	Term of Note
a.	January 5*	$90,000	6%	120 days
b.	February15*	21,000	4	30 days
c.	May 19	68,000	8	45 days
d.	August 20	34,400	5	90 days
e.	October 19	50,000	7	90 days

* Assume a leap year in which February has 29 days.

To simplify, use 360 days per year to compute interest.

Obj. 5

E6-17 Notes receivable

Bork Furniture Company received a 120-day, 6% note for $80,000 dated April 20 from Valley Designs to replace an account receivable.

a. Illustrate the effects of accepting the note from Valley Designs on the accounts and financial statements of Bork Furniture Company.

b. Determine the due date of the note.

c. Determine the maturity value of the note. To simplify, use 360 days per year to compute interest.

d. Illustrate the effects of receiving payment of the note from Valley Designs at its maturity on the accounts and financial statements of Bork Furniture Company.

Obj. 6

E6-18 Receivables in the balance sheet

The following is a partial balance sheet for Zabel Company:

ZABEL COMPANY
Balance Sheet
December 31, 20Y4

Assets

Current assets:		
Cash		$ 75,000
Account receivable	$475,000	
Plus allowance for doubtful accounts	11,150	486,150
Notes receivable	$115,000	
Less interest receivable	9,000	106,000

Instructions

1. List any errors in the preceding balance sheet.
2. Prepare a corrected balance sheet.

Problems

PR 6-1 Allowance method

Obj. 4

The following transactions were completed by Irvine Company during the current fiscal year ended December 31:

Feb. 8. Received 40% of the $18,000 balance owed by DeCoy Co., a bankrupt business, and wrote off the remainder as uncollectible.

May 27. Reinstated the account of Seth Nelsen, which had been written off in the preceding year as uncollectible. Received $7,350 in full payment of Seth's account.

Aug. 13. Wrote off the $6,400 balance owed by Kat Tracks Co., which has no assets.

Oct. 31. Reinstated the account of Crawford Co., which had been written off in the preceding year as uncollectible. Received $3,880 in full payment of the account.

Dec. 31. Wrote off $23,200 of accounts as uncollectible.

31. Based on an analysis of the $1,785,000 of accounts receivable, it was estimated that $35,700 will be uncollectible. The beginning of the year balance on January 1 of Allowance for Doubtful Accounts was $(26,000).

Instructions

1. Assuming that Irvine Company uses the allowance method, illustrate the effects of the preceding transactions on the accounts and financial statements of Irvine Company.
2. What is the net realizable value of Irvine Company's accounts receivable after the adjustment for uncollectible accounts on December 31?
3. Assuming that instead of basing the provision for uncollectible accounts on an analysis of receivables, the adjustment on December 31 had been based on an estimated expense of ¼ of 1% of the sales of $18,200,000 for the year, determine the following:
   a. Bad debt expense for the year.
   b. Balance in the allowance account after the adjustment on December 31.
   c. Expected net realizable value of the accounts receivable as of December 31.

P6-2 Allowance method for doubtful accounts

Obj. 4

✔ 1. Estimate of uncollectible accounts, $59,350

Averys All-Natural Company supplies wigs and hair care products to beauty salons throughout Texas and the Southwest. The accounts receivable clerk for Averys All-Natural prepared the following aging-of-receivables schedule as of the end of business on December 31, 20Y7:

	A	B	C	D	E	F	G	H
1			Not	Days Past Due				
2			Past					
3	Customer	Balance	Due	1–30	31–60	61–90	91–120	Over 120
4	AAA Beauty	27,500	27,500					
5	Amelia's Wigs	3,750			3,750			
30	Zim's Beauty	1,650		1,650				
31	Totals	1,100,000	750,000	180,000	75,000	45,000	22,000	28,000

Averys All-Natural Company has a past history of uncollectible accounts by age category, as follows:

Age Class	Percent Uncollectible
Not past due	1%
1–30 days past due	3
31–60 days past due	7
61–90 days past due	16
91–120 days past due	40
Over 120 days past due	90

Instructions

1. Estimate the allowance for doubtful accounts, based on the aging-of-receivables schedule.
2. Assume that the allowance for doubtful accounts for Averys All-Natural Company has a negative balance of $(2,250) before adjustment on December 31, 20Y7. Illustrate the effect on the accounts and financial statements of the adjustment for uncollectible accounts.
3. Averys All-Natural Company reported credit sales of $2,400,000 during 20Y7. Assume that instead of using the analysis of receivables method of estimating uncollectible accounts, Averys All-Natural uses the percent of sales method and estimates that 2.5% of sales will be uncollectible. Illustrate the effect on the accounts and financial statements of the adjustment for uncollectible accounts using the percent of sales method.
4. Assume that on March 4, 20Y8, Averys All-Natural wrote off the $2,950 account of Superior Images as uncollectible. Illustrate the effect on the accounts and financial statements of the write-off of the Superior Images account.
5. Assume that on August 17, 20Y8, Superior Images paid $2,950 on its account. Illustrate the effect on the accounts and financial statements of reinstating and collecting the Superior Images account.
6. Assume that instead of using the allowance method, Averys All-Natural uses the direct write-off method. Illustrate the effect on the accounts and financial statements of the following:
   a. The write-off of the Superior Images account on March 4, 20Y8.
   b. The reinstatement and collection of the Superior Images account on August 17, 20Y8.

Obj. 4

P6-3 Estimate uncollectible accounts

✔ 1. a. 20Y2, $31,250

For several years, EquiPrime Co.'s sales have been on a "cash only" basis. On January 1, 20Y2, however, EquiPrime Co. began offering credit on terms of n/30. The amount of the adjustment to record the estimated uncollectible receivables at the end of each year has been ¼ of 1% of credit sales, which is the rate reported as the average for the industry. Credit sales and the year-end credit balances in Allowance for Doubtful Accounts for the past four years are as follows:

Year	Credit Sales	Allowance for Doubtful Accounts
20Y2	$12,500,000	$12,800
20Y3	12,600,000	23,000
20Y4	12,800,000	34,000
20Y5	13,000,000	49,000

Mandy Pulaski, president of EquiPrime Co., is concerned that the method used to account for and write off uncollectible receivables is unsatisfactory. She has asked for your advice in the analysis of past operations in this area and for recommendations for change.

1. Determine the amount of (a) the addition to Allowance for Doubtful Accounts and (b) the accounts written off for each of the four years.

2. a. Advise Mandy Pulaski as to whether the estimate of ¼ of 1% of credit sales appears reasonable.

   b. Assume that after discussing (a) with Mandy Pulaski, she asked you what action might be taken to determine what the balance of Allowance for Doubtful Accounts should be at December 31, 20Y5, and what possible changes, if any, you might recommend in accounting for uncollectible receivables. How would you respond?

P6-4 Compare two methods of accounting for uncollectible receivables

Obj. 3, 4

✔ 1. Year 4: Balance of allowance account, end of year, $53,750

Cyber Space Company, which operates a chain of 65 electronics supply stores, has just completed its fourth year of operations. The direct write-off method of recording bad debt expense has been used during the entire period. Because of substantial increases in sales volume and the amount of uncollectible accounts, the firm is considering changing to the allowance method. Information is requested as to the effect that an annual provision of ½% of sales would have had on the amount of bad debt expense reported for each of the past four years. It is also considered desirable to know what the balance of Allowance for Doubtful Accounts would have been at the end of each year. The following data have been obtained from the accounts:

			Year of Origin of Accounts Receivable Written Off as Uncollectible			
Year	Sales	Uncollectible Accounts Written Off	1	2	3	4
1	$2,300,000	$ 5,000	$5,000			
2	4,750,000	9,000	4,000	$ 5,000		
3	9,000,000	23,000	2,000	12,000	$ 9,000	
4	9,600,000	37,500		5,500	14,500	$17,500

Instructions

1. Assemble the desired data, using the following column headings:

	Bad Debt Expense			
Year	Expense Actually Reported	Expense Based on Estimate	Increase (Decrease) in Amount of Expense	Balance of Allowance Account, End of Year

2. Experience during the first four years of operations indicated that the receivables were either collected within two years or had to be written off as uncollectible. Does the estimate of ½% of sales appear to be reasonably close to the actual experience with uncollectible accounts originating during the first two years? Explain.

P6-5 Notes receivable

Obj. 5

Water Closet Co. wholesales bathroom fixtures. During the current year ending December 31, Water Closet received the following notes:

	Date of Note	Face Amount	Interest Rate	Term
1.	March 6	$75,000	4%	60 days
2.	April 7	40,000	6	45 days
3.	August 12	36,000	5	120 days
4.	October 22	27,000	8	30 days
5.	November 19	48,000	3	90 days
6.	December 15	72,000	5	45 days

Instructions

1. Determine for each note (a) the due date and (b) the amount of interest due at maturity, identifying each note by number. To simplify, use 360 days per year to compute interest.
2. Illustrate the effects on the accounts and financial statements of the receipt of the amount due on Note 3 at its maturity.
3. Compute the accrued interest on December 31 for Notes 5 and 6.
4. Illustrate the effects on the accounts and financial statements of the adjustment for accrued interest on December 31 for Notes 5 and 6.

Metric-Based Analysis

Obj. 3

MBA 6-1 Direct write-off method

Using transactions listed in E6-3, indicate the effects of each transaction on the liquidity metric days' sales in receivables and profitability metric return on sales.

Obj. 4

MBA 6-2 Allowance method

Using transactions listed in E6-4, indicate the effects of each transaction on the liquidity metric days' sales in receivables and profitability metric return on sales.

Obj. 4

MBA 6-3 Allowance method: adjustment

Referring to the adjustment for uncollectible accounts in E6-7, indicate the effects of the adjustment on the liquidity metric days' sales in receivables and profitability metric return on sales.

Obj. 7

MBA 6-4 Accounts receivable turnover

The following data (in millions) were adapted from recent financial statements of **Apple Inc.** (AAPL).

	Year 2	Year 1
Sales	$260,174	$265,595
Operating income	63,930	70,898
Average net accounts receivable	23,056	20,530

1. Compute the accounts receivable turnover for Years 1 and 2. Round to one decimal place.
2. Compute days' sales in receivables for Years 1 and 2. Round to the nearest day.
3. Compute the return on sales for Years 1 and 2. Round to one decimal place.
4. Comment on Apple's operations based upon the results in parts (1), (2), and (3).

Obj. 7

MBA 6-5 Accounts receivable turnover

The following data (in millions) were adapted from recent financial statements of **HP Inc.** (HPQ) formerly Hewlett-Packard Company.

	Year 2	Year 1
Sales	$58,756	$58,472
Operating income	3,877	3,705
Average accounts receivable	8,471	7,583

1. Compute the accounts receivable turnover for Years 1 and 2. Round to one decimal place.
2. Compute days' sales in receivables for Years 1 and 2. Round to nearest day.
3. Compute the return on sales for Years 1 and 2. Round to one decimal place.
4. Comment on HP's operations based upon the results in parts (1), (2), and (3).

MBA 6-6 Accounts receivable turnover

Obj. 7

Compare and comment on Apple and HP using the results of MBA 6-4 and MBA 6-5.

MBA 6-7 Accounts receivable turnover

Obj. 7

The following data (in millions) were adapted from recent financial statements of CVS Health Corporation (CVS):

	Year 2	Year 1
Sales	$256,776	$194,579
Operating income	12,467	10,170
Average accounts receivable	18,624	15,406

1. Compute the accounts receivable turnover for Years 1 and 2. Round to one decimal place.
2. Compute the days' sales in receivables for Years 1 and 2. Round to the nearest day.
3. Compute the return on sales for Years 1 and 2. Round to one decimal place.
4. Comment on CVS' operations based upon the results in parts (1), (2), and (3).

MBA 6-8 Accounts receivable turnover

Obj. 7

The following data (in millions) were adapted from recent financial statements of International Paper Company (IP) and Walmart Inc. (WMT):

	International Paper	Walmart
Sales	$22,376	$523,964
Operating income	2,130	20,568
Accounts receivable:		
Beginning of year	3,916	6,283
End of year	3,673	6,284

1. Compute the accounts receivable turnover for International Paper and Walmart. Round to one decimal place.
2. Compute the days' sales in receivables for International Paper and Walmart. Round to nearest day.
3. Compute the return on sales for International Paper and Walmart. Round to one decimal place.
4. Comment on and explain any differences in International Paper's and Walmart's management of receivables based upon the results in parts (1), (2), and (3).

Cases

Case 6-1 Ethics and professional conduct in business

ETHICS

Sybil Crumpton, vice president of operations for Bob Marshall Wilderness Bank, has instructed the bank's computer programmer to use a 365-day year to compute interest on depository accounts (payables). Sybil also instructed the programmer to use a 360-day year to compute interest on loans (receivables).

Discuss whether Sybil is behaving in a professional manner.

Case 6-2 Collecting accounts receivable

The following is an excerpt from a conversation between the office manager, Terry Holland, and the president of Northern Construction Supplies Co., Janet Austel. Northern Construction Supplies sells building supplies to local contractors.

Terry: Janet, we're going to have to do something about these overdue accounts receivable. One-third of our accounts are over 60 days past due, and I've had accounts that have stayed open for almost a year!

Janet: I didn't realize it was that bad. Any ideas?

Terry: Well, we could stop giving credit. Make everyone pay with cash or a credit card. We accept MasterCard and Visa already, but only the walk-in customers use them. Almost all of the contractors put purchases on their bills.

Janet: Yes, but we've been allowing credit for years. As far as I know, all of our competitors allow contractors credit. If we stopped giving credit, we'd lose many of our contractors. They'd just go elsewhere. You know, some of these guys run up bills as high as $50,000 or $75,000. There's no way they could put that kind of money on a credit card.

Terry: That's a good point. But we've got to do something.

Janet: How many of the contractor accounts do you actually end up writing off as uncollectible?

Terry: Not many. Almost all eventually pay. It's just that they take so long!

Suggest one or more solutions to Northern Construction Supplies Co.'s problem concerning the collection of accounts receivable.

Case 6-3 Ethics and professional conduct in business

ETHICS

Bud Lighting Co. is a retailer of commercial and residential lighting products. Gowen Geter, the company's chief accountant, is in the process of making year-end adjusting entries for uncollectible accounts receivable. In recent years, the company has experienced an increase in accounts that have become uncollectible. As a result, Gowen believes that the company should increase the percentage used for estimating doubtful accounts from 2% to 4% of credit sales. This change will significantly increase bad debt expense, resulting in a drop in earnings for the first time in company history. The company president, Tim Burr, is under considerable pressure to meet earnings goals. He suggests that this is "not the right time" to change the estimate. He instructs Gowen to keep the estimate at 2%. Gowen is confident that 2% is too low, but he follows Tim's instructions.

Evaluate the decision to use the lower percentage to improve earnings. Are Tim and Gowen acting in an ethical manner?

Case 6-4 Uncollectible accounts receivable

On January 1, Xtreme Co. began offering credit with terms of n/30. Uncollectible accounts are estimated to be 1% of credit sales, which is the average for the industry.

The CEO, Todd Hurley, has no background in accounting and is struggling to understand the allowance method.

Write a brief memo to Todd explaining the allowance method and how this information is reported in the financial statements.

Case 6-5 Allowance for doubtful accounts

For several years, Xtreme Co.'s sales have been on a "cash only" basis. On January 1, 20Y4, however, Xtreme Co. began offering credit on terms of n/30. The amount of the adjustment to record the estimated uncollectible receivables at the end of each year has been ½ of 1% of credit sales, which is the rate reported as the average for the industry. Credit sales and the year-end credit balances in Allowance for Doubtful Accounts for the past four years are as follows:

Year	Credit Sales	Allowance for Doubtful Accounts
20Y4	$4,000,000	$ 5,000
20Y5	4,400,000	8,250
20Y6	4,800,000	10,200
20Y7	5,100,000	14,400

Laurie Jones, president of Xtreme Co., is concerned that the method used to account for and write off uncollectible receivables is unsatisfactory. She has asked for your advice in the analysis of past operations in this area and for recommendations for change.

1. Determine the amount of (a) the addition to Allowance for Doubtful Accounts and (b) the accounts written off for each of the four years.
2. a. Advise Laurie Jones as to whether the estimate of ½ of 1% of credit sales appears reasonable.
   b. Assume that after discussing (a) with Laurie Jones, she asked you what action might be taken to determine what the balance of Allowance for Doubtful Accounts should be at December 31, 20Y7, and what possible changes, if any, you might recommend in accounting for uncollectible receivables. How would you respond?

Case 6-6 Data Analytics: Collectability of receivables by customer type

USING DATA ANALYTICS

Landry Marine is a national distributor of boat parts and supplies. Landry Marine's customers include the following categories of stores: locally owned, small regional chains, large regional chains, and national chains. Landry Marine's chief executive officer (CEO), Gene O'Neil, has requested your assistance in helping him further understand the company's credit sales, including collectability of accounts receivable and returns by customer type. Specifically, Gene O'Neil has asked you to answer the following questions based on the dataset provided:

1. What are the average days' sales in receivables by customer type? Assume that Landry Marine's credit terms are n/30 for all customers.
2. What are write-offs by customer type, in dollars and as a percent of credit sales?
3. What are returns as a percent of credit sales by customer type?
4. How could the CEO, Gene O'Neil, use the preceding analyses in managing Landry Marine?

Go to CengageNOWv2 to complete this assignment.

The annual report (10-K) assignment for this chapter is in Appendix B: Nike Annual Report, Chapter 6.

Answers to Self-Examination Questions

1. **B** The estimate of the uncollectible accounts is $15,000 ($1,250,000 × 1.2%). This is the amount that bad debt expense increased in the year-end adjustment for uncollectible accounts. It is also the amount reported on the income statement as bad debt expense for the year. After the adjustment, the allowance for doubtful accounts will have a negative balance of $(17,500) (answer C).

2. **B** The estimate of uncollectible accounts, $8,500 (answer C), is the amount of the desired balance of Allowance for Doubtful Accounts after adjustment. The amount of the current provision to be made for bad debt expense is thus $6,000 (answer B), which is the amount that must be added to the Allowance for Doubtful Accounts negative balance of $2,500 (answer A), so that the account will have the desired balance of $8,500.

3. **B** The amount expected to be realized from accounts receivable is the balance of Accounts Receivable, $100,000, less the balance of Allowance for Doubtful Accounts, $7,000, or $93,000 (answer B).

4. **C** Maturity value is the amount that is due at the maturity or due date. The maturity value of $10,300 (answer C) is determined as follows:

Face amount of note	$10,000
Plus interest ($10,000 × 12% × 90/360)	300
Maturity value of note	$10,300

5. **C** November 3 is the due date of a $12,000, 90-day, 8% note receivable dated August 5 [26 days in August (31 days − 5 days) + 30 days in September + 31 days in October + 3 days in November].

Chapter **7**

Inventories

What's Covered:

Topics: Inventories

Types
- Retail inventory (Obj. 1)
- Manufacturing inventories (Obj. 1)

Inventory Cost Flow Assumptions
- First-in, first-out cost flow (Obj.2)
- Last-in, first-out cost flow (Obj. 2)
- Weighted average cost flow (Obj. 2)

Inventory Costing Methods
- First-in, first-out method (Obj. 3)
- Last-in, first-out method (Obj. 3)
- Weighted average cost method (Obj. 3)

Comparing Costing Methods
- Income statement (Obj. 4)
- Balance sheet (Obj. 4)

Financial Reporting
- Lower of cost or market (Obj. 5)
- Balance sheet (Obj. 5)
- Effects of errors (Obj. 5)

Metric-Based Analysis
- Transactions:
  - Liquidity: Days' sales in inventory (Obj. 4, 5)
  - Profitability: Return on sales (Obj. 4, 5)
- Financial statements:
  - Inventory turnover (Obj. 6)

Learning Objectives

Obj.1 Describe the types of inventory for retail and manufacturing businesses.

Obj.2 Describe three inventory cost flow assumptions.

Obj.3 Determine the cost of inventory using the FIFO, LIFO, and weighted average cost methods.

Obj.4 Compare and contrast the effects of inventory costing methods on the income statement and balance sheet.

Obj.5 Describe and illustrate the financial reporting of inventories.

Obj.6 Metric-Based Analysis: Describe and illustrate the use of the inventory turnover for assessing a company's operations.

Chapter Metrics

Use the following metrics to analyze transactions and financial statements.

TRANSACTIONS

Liquidity: Days' Sales in Inventory

Profitability: Return on Sales

FINANCIAL STATEMENTS

Inventory Turnover

CVS

Susan Montgomery/ Shutterstock.com

CVS Health Care Corporation (CVS) operates more than 9,000 retail pharmacies and 1,000 walk-in medical clinics. In addition, CVS provides a mail-order pharmacy where customers can fill prescriptions using the mail, telephone, fax, or the Internet. Finally, CVS serves as a pharmacy benefits plan manager for employers, insurance companies, and health plans offered by private insurance exchanges. In this role, CVS serves more than 65 million customers.

CVS faces many operational challenges and risks. For example, in its pharmacy operations, CVS must comply with laws regulating the purchase, distribution, tracking, and dispensing of prescription drugs and other controlled substances. It must comply with privacy laws on the collection, disclosure, and transmission of customers' personal information. It must monitor patent expirations of brand drugs and the availability of generic substitutes. Finally, CVS must protect against the possibility of product tampering and incorrectly dispensing drugs to customers. In its retail operations, CVS also faces various competitive pressures from companies like **Walgreens (WBA)** and **Walmart (WMT)** as well as changing customer lifestyles and preferences.

As a retail business, CVS maintains inventories of prescription drugs as well as general merchandise, including cosmetics, snack foods, greeting cards, and soft drinks.

In this chapter, accounting and reporting issues related to inventories are described and illustrated. In doing so, the effects on the financial statements of inventory cost flow assumptions are emphasized.

Objective 1
Describe the types of inventory for retail and manufacturing businesses.

Types of Inventory

Inventories vary depending upon the type of business. For example, a retail business purchases products for resale, while a manufacturing business converts raw materials into finished products.

Retail Inventory

A retail business purchases products in a condition ready for resale, such as apparel, consumer electronics, hardware, or food items. Merchandise on hand (not sold) at the end of the period, called **inventory** or **merchandise inventory**, is reported on the balance sheet as a current asset. Inventory sold is reported as cost of goods sold or cost of merchandise sold on the income statement.

For a retail company, the cost of inventory includes its purchase price less any purchase discounts. The cost of merchandise inventory also includes other costs such as freight, insurance costs while in transit, and import duties. Inventory is a large asset for most retail companies, as illustrated for some well-known retailers in Exhibit 1.

Exhibit 1
Inventory Size for Retail Companies

	Inventory as a Percentage of	
	Current Assets	**Total Assets**
Best Buy (BBY)	58%	33%
CostCo (COST)	49	25
Kohl's (KSS)	76	24
Target (TGT)	70	21
Walmart (WMT)	72	19

CVS reported $17,516 million in inventories on a recent balance sheet, which was 35% of its current assets.

Manufacturing Inventories

Manufacturing businesses convert raw materials into finished products, which are often sold to retail companies. For example, The Hershey Foods Company (HSY) produces a variety of chocolate candies from cocoa and other raw materials, which it sells to retailers such as Walmart (WMT) and Target (TGT).

A manufacturing company has the following types of inventories:

- **Materials inventory** consisting of the cost of raw materials used in the manufacturing process.
- **Work in process inventory** consisting of the costs of partially completed products.
- **Finished goods inventory** consisting of the costs of completed products.

The following costs are included in the work in process and finished goods inventories of a manufactured product:

- **Direct materials** consists of the costs of acquiring a product's component materials. Direct materials enter production in the same stage as they are when purchased from vendors (suppliers).
- **Direct labor** consists of wages of factory workers directly involved in manufacturing the product.
- **Factory overhead** consists of all factory costs other than direct materials and direct labor, such as equipment depreciation, supervisory salaries, and utility costs.

Like retail inventory, manufacturing inventories are reported as current assets on the balance sheet. Manufacturers often report an aggregate amount for inventory with a detailed breakdown provided in the notes to the financial statements. For example, Hershey Company reported inventories (in thousands) of $984,665 with the following details in a note:

Raw materials	$271,125
Goods (work) in process	98,842
Finished goods	614,698
Total inventories	$984,665

When finished goods inventory is sold, it is reported as cost of goods sold on the income statement.

To simplify, the remainder of this chapter describes and illustrates the accounting for merchandise (retail) inventory. However, this discussion applies equally well to manufacturing inventories.[1]

1. The accounting for manufacturing inventories is discussed in more detail in managerial accounting courses and textbooks.

The Consumer Electronic Wars: Best Buy versus Amazon.com

Business Insight

How does Best Buy (BBY) compete against online retailers such as Amazon.com (AMZN) in the intensely competitive consumer electronic market? Best Buy believes that by offering high-quality customer service in its retail stores that it can compete effectively with online retailers like Amazon.com. An important part of this strategy is hiring, training, and retaining high-quality store employees and managers. In addition, Best Buy recently announced a "Perfect Match Promise" that provides customers (1) 30 days of free telephone support for any products purchased, (2) 30-day return policy with no restocking fees, and (3) 30 days of competitor price matching. Finally, Best Buy plans to enhance its customer loyalty program with free shipping, access to new products and technologies, free access to the Geek Squad, and extended return and price-matching options.

ZUMA Press/ZUMA Press Inc/Alamy Stock Photo

Source: Adapted from Best Buy Co., Inc.'s 10-K report.

Objective 2
Describe three inventory cost flow assumptions.

Inventory Cost Flow Assumptions

An accounting issue arises when identical units of inventory are acquired at different unit costs during a period. In such cases, when an item is sold, it is necessary to determine its cost using a cost flow assumption and related inventory cost flow method. Three common cost flow assumptions and related inventory cost flow methods are shown in Exhibit 2.

Exhibit 2 Inventory Cost Flows

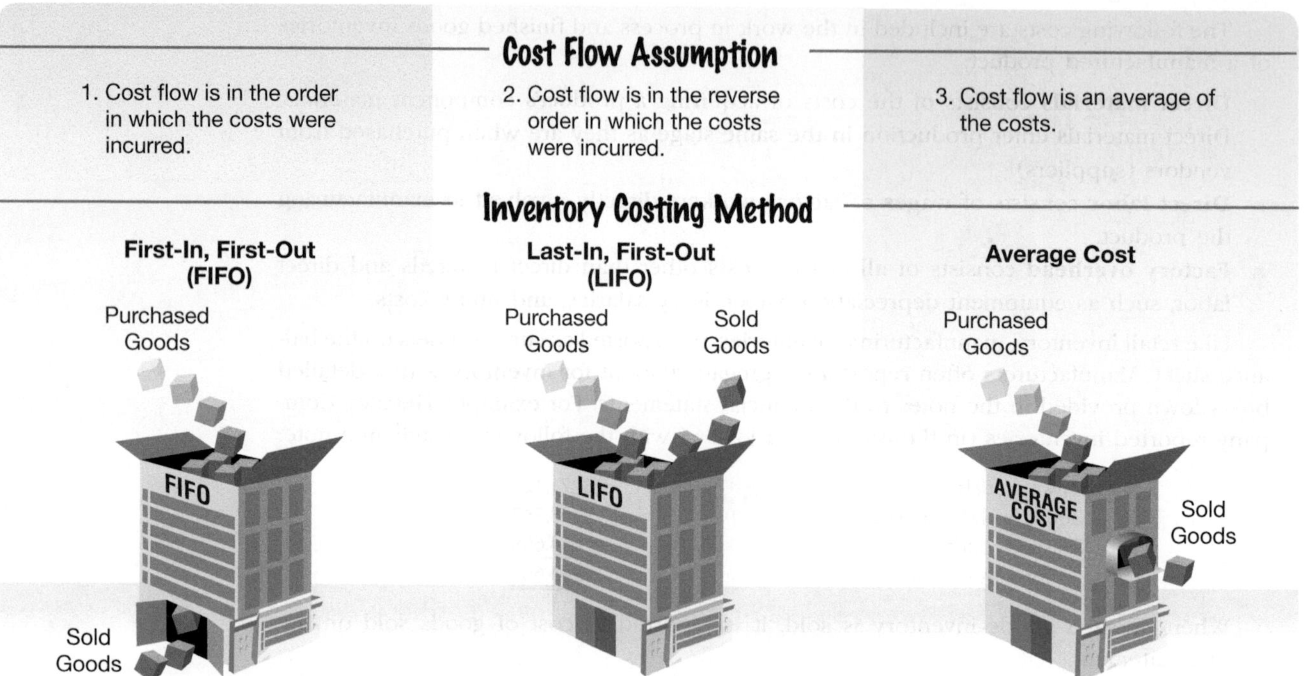

To illustrate, assume that three identical units of merchandise are purchased during May, as follows:

			Units	Cost
May	10	Purchase	1	$ 9
	18	Purchase	1	13
	24	Purchase	1	14
Total			3	$36

Average cost per unit: $12 ($36 ÷ 3 units)

Assume that one unit is sold on May 30 for $20. Depending upon which unit was sold, the gross profit varies from $11 to $6, as shown below.

	May 10 Unit Sold	May 18 Unit Sold	May 24 Unit Sold
Sales	$20	$20	$20
Cost of goods sold	(9)	(13)	(14)
Gross profit	$11	$ 7	$ 6
Ending inventory*	$27	$23	$22
	*($13 + $14)	*($9 + $14)	*($9 + $13)

Under the **specific identification inventory cost flow method**, the unit sold is identified with a specific purchase. The ending inventory is made up of the remaining units on hand. Thus, the gross profit, cost of goods sold, and ending inventory can vary as shown above. For example, if the May 18 unit was sold, the cost of goods sold is $13, the gross profit is $7, and the ending inventory is $23.

The specific identification method is not practical unless each inventory unit can be separately identified. For example, an automobile dealer may use the specific identification method since each automobile has a unique serial number. However, most businesses cannot identify each inventory unit separately. In such cases, one of the following three inventory cost flow methods is used.

Under the **first-in, first-out (FIFO) inventory cost flow method**, the first units purchased are assumed to be sold and the ending inventory is made up of the most recent purchases. In the preceding example, the May 10 unit would be assumed to have been sold. Thus, the gross profit would be $11, and the ending inventory would be $27 ($13 + $14).

Under the **last-in, first-out (LIFO) inventory cost flow method**, the last units purchased are assumed to be sold and the ending inventory is made up of the first purchases. In the preceding example, the May 24 unit would be assumed to have been sold. Thus, the gross profit would be $6, and the ending inventory would be $22 ($9 + $13).

Under the **weighted average cost inventory cost flow method**, the cost of the units sold and in ending inventory is an average of the purchase costs. In the preceding example, the cost of the unit sold would be $12 ($36 ÷ 3 units), the gross profit would be $8 ($20 − $12), and the ending inventory would be $24 ($12 × 2 units).

The three inventory cost flow methods—FIFO, LIFO, and average cost—are shown in Exhibit 3.

Exhibit 3 Inventory Costing Methods

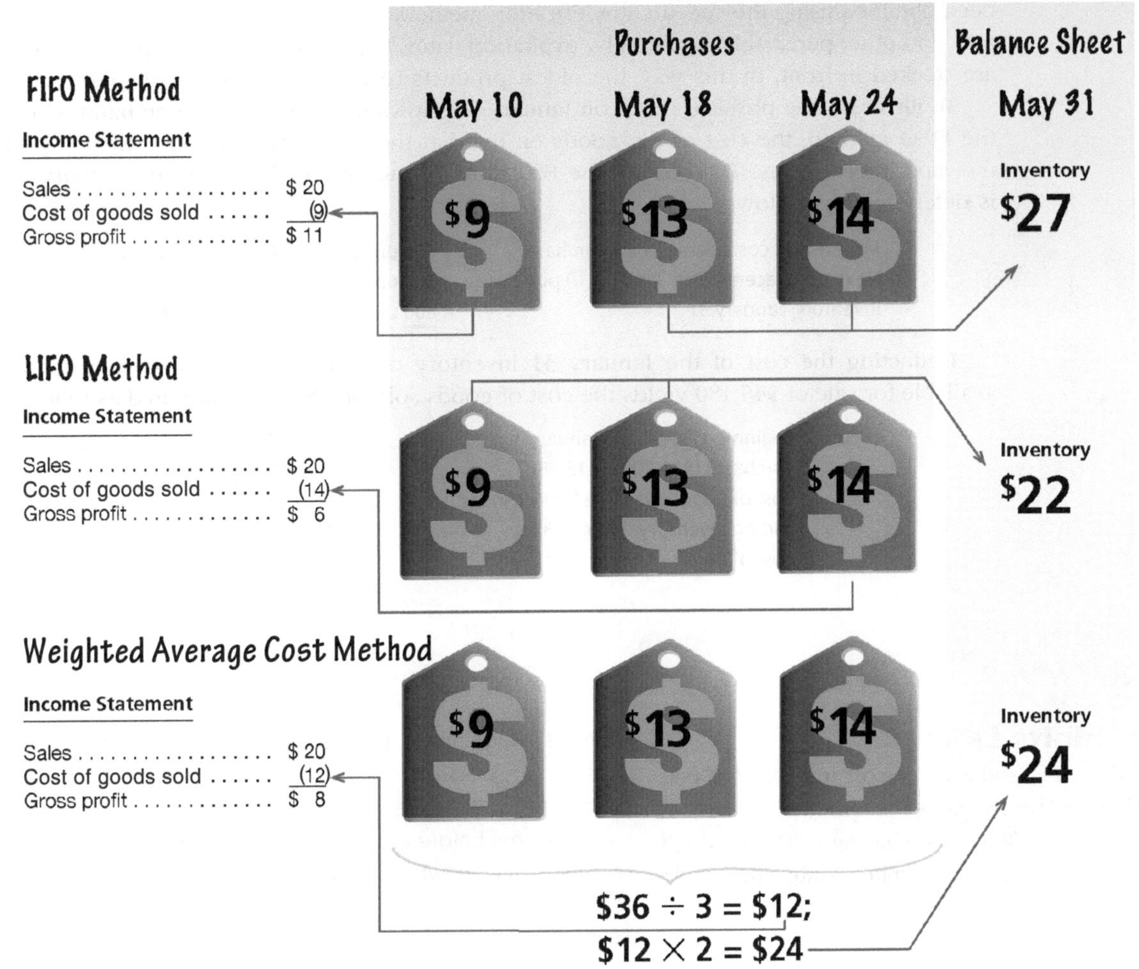

Purchases: May 10, May 18, May 24 — Balance Sheet: May 31

FIFO Method

Income Statement

Sales	$ 20
Cost of goods sold	(9)
Gross profit	$ 11

$9 $13 $14 — Inventory $27

LIFO Method

Income Statement

Sales	$ 20
Cost of goods sold	(14)
Gross profit	$ 6

$9 $13 $14 — Inventory $22

Weighted Average Cost Method

Income Statement

Sales	$ 20
Cost of goods sold	(12)
Gross profit	$ 8

$9 $13 $14 — Inventory $24

$36 ÷ 3 = $12;
$12 × 2 = $24

Objective 3

Determine the cost of inventory using the FIFO, LIFO, and weighted-average cost methods.

Inventory Costing Methods

As illustrated in the prior section, a cost flow assumption must be made when identical units are acquired at different unit costs during a period. In addition, a **physical inventory** or *count of inventory* should be taken at the end of an accounting period to verify that the quantity of inventory reported in the financial statements is accurate. After the quantity of inventory on hand is determined, the cost of the inventory is assigned for reporting in the financial statements. In assigning costs, the FIFO, LIFO, or weighted average cost method is normally used.

In this section, the FIFO, LIFO, and weighted average cost methods are illustrated using the following data for **Item 127B**:

Jan. 1	Inventory	1,000 units at	$20.00	$20,000
10	Purchase	500 units at	22.40	11,200
30	Purchase	600 units at	23.30	13,980
Available for sale during month		2,100		$45,180

Inventory cost flows are simpler to illustrate under the periodic inventory system. For this reason, the periodic inventory system is used to illustrate the FIFO, LIFO, and weighted average cost methods.The same illustrations for **Item 127B** using the perpetual inventory system are shown in the appendix to this chapter.

First-In, First-Out Method

When the FIFO method is used, costs are included in the cost of goods sold in the order in which they were purchased. This is often the same as the physical flow of the goods. Thus, the FIFO method often provides results that are about the same as those that would have been obtained using the specific identification method. For example, grocery stores shelve milk and other perishable products by expiration dates. Products with early expiration dates are stocked in front. In this way, the oldest products (earliest purchases) are sold first.

To illustrate, the physical count on January 31 shows that 800 units are on hand. Using the FIFO method, the cost of the goods on hand at the end of the period is made up of the most recent costs. The cost of the 800 units in the ending inventory on January 31 is determined as follows:

Most recent costs, January 30 purchase	600 units at	$23.30	$13,980
Next most recent costs, January 10 purchase	200 units at	22.40	4,480
Inventory, January 31	800 units		$18,460

Deducting the cost of the January 31 inventory of $18,460 from the cost of goods available for sale of $45,180 yields the cost of goods sold of $26,720, computed as follows:

Beginning inventory, January 1	$ 20,000
Purchases ($11,200 + $13,980)	25,180
Cost of goods available for sale in January	$ 45,180
Ending inventory, January 31	(18,460)
Cost of goods sold	$ 26,720

International Connection

IFRS Prohibits LIFO

While the FIFO, LIFO, and average cost methods are permitted within the United States, International Financial Reporting Standards (IFRS) prohibit the LIFO method. If IFRS were adopted within the United States, this could have a significant impact on a company's income. For example, **Deere & Company (DE)** reports its inventories using LIFO. If Deere & Company were to switch to FIFO, its income before taxes would decrease by approximately $1,398 million, which is over a 40% decrease.

The $18,460 cost of the ending inventory on January 31 is made up of the most recent costs. The $26,720 cost of goods sold is made up of the beginning inventory and the earliest costs. Exhibit 4 shows the relationship of the cost of goods sold for January and the ending inventory on January 31.

Exhibit 4 First-In, First-Out Flow of Costs

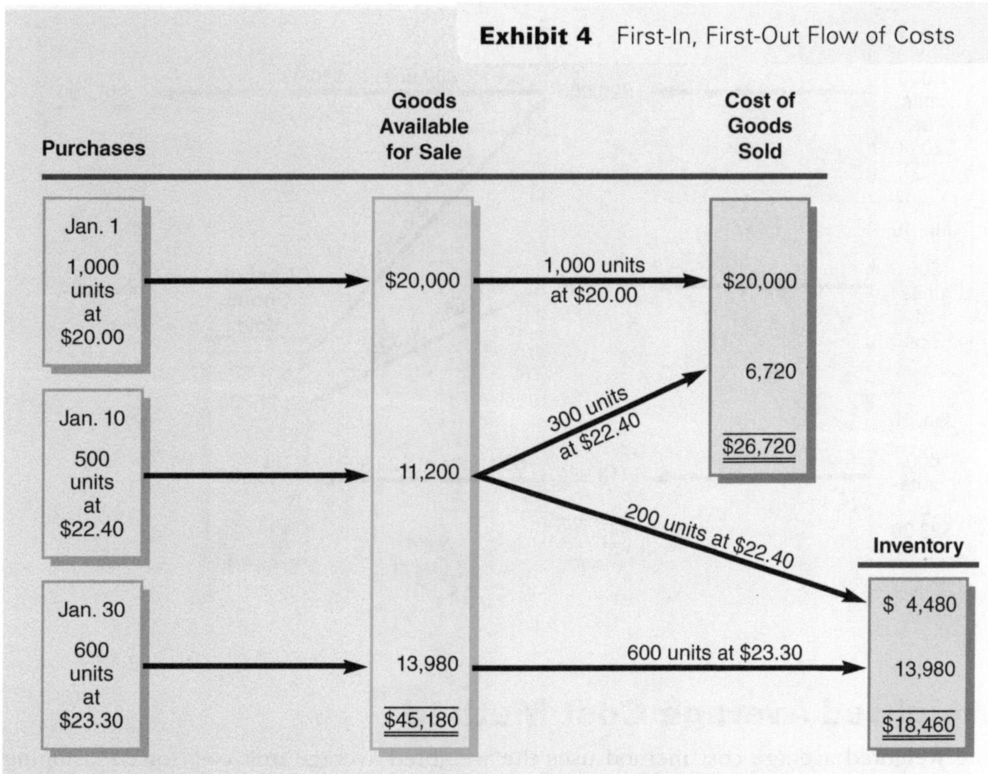

Last-In, First-Out Method

When the LIFO method is used, the cost of goods on hand at the end of the period is made up of the earliest costs. Based on the same data for **Item 127B** as in the FIFO example, the cost of the 800 units in ending inventory on January 31 is $16,000, which consists of 800 units from the beginning inventory at a cost of $20.00 per unit.

Deducting the cost of the January 31 inventory of $16,000 from the cost of goods available for sale of $45,180 yields the cost of goods sold of $29,180, computed as follows:

Beginning inventory, January 1	$ 20,000
Purchases ($11,200 + $13,980)	25,180
Cost of goods available for sale in January	$ 45,180
Ending inventory, January 31	(16,000)
Cost of goods sold	$ 29,180

The $16,000 cost of the ending inventory on January 31 is made up of the earliest costs. The $29,180 cost of goods sold is made up of the most recent costs. Exhibit 5 shows the relationship of the cost of goods sold for January and the ending inventory on January 31.

Exhibit 5 Last-In, First-Out Flow of Costs

Purchases | Goods Available for Sale | Inventory

Jan. 1 — 1,000 units at $20.00 → $20,000 → 800 units at $20.00 → $16,000

$20,000 → 200 units at $20.00 → Cost of Goods Sold

Jan. 10 — 500 units at $22.40 → 11,200 → 500 units at $22.40 → Cost of Goods Sold

Jan. 30 — 600 units at $23.30 → 13,980 → 600 units at $23.30 → Cost of Goods Sold

Goods Available for Sale: $20,000; 11,200; 13,980; $45,180

Cost of Goods Sold: $ 4,000; 11,200; 13,980; $29,180

Weighted Average Cost Method

The weighted average cost method uses the weighted average unit cost for determining the cost of goods sold and the ending inventory. If purchases are relatively uniform during a period, the weighted average cost method provides results that are similar to the physical flow of goods.

The weighted average unit cost is determined as follows:

$$\text{Weighted Average Unit Cost} = \frac{\text{Total Cost of Units Available for Sale}}{\text{Units Available for Sale}}$$

To illustrate, the data for **Item 127B** are used as follows:

$$\text{Weighted Average Unit Cost} = \frac{\text{Total Cost of Units Available for Sale}}{\text{Units Available for Sale}} = \frac{\$45{,}180}{2{,}100 \text{ units}}$$

$$= \$21.51 \text{ per unit (rounded)}$$

The cost of the January 31 ending inventory is as follows:

Inventory, January 31: $17,208 (800 units × $21.51)

Deducting the cost of the January 31 inventory of $17,208 from the cost of goods available for sale of $45,180 yields the cost of goods sold of $27,972, computed as follows:

Beginning inventory, January 1	$ 20,000
Purchases ($11,200 + $13,980)	25,180
Cost of goods available for sale in January	$ 45,180
Ending inventory, January 31	(17,208)
Cost of goods sold	$ 27,972

Exhibit 6 shows the relationship of the cost of goods sold for January and the ending inventory on January 31.

Exhibit 6 Weighted Average Flow of Costs

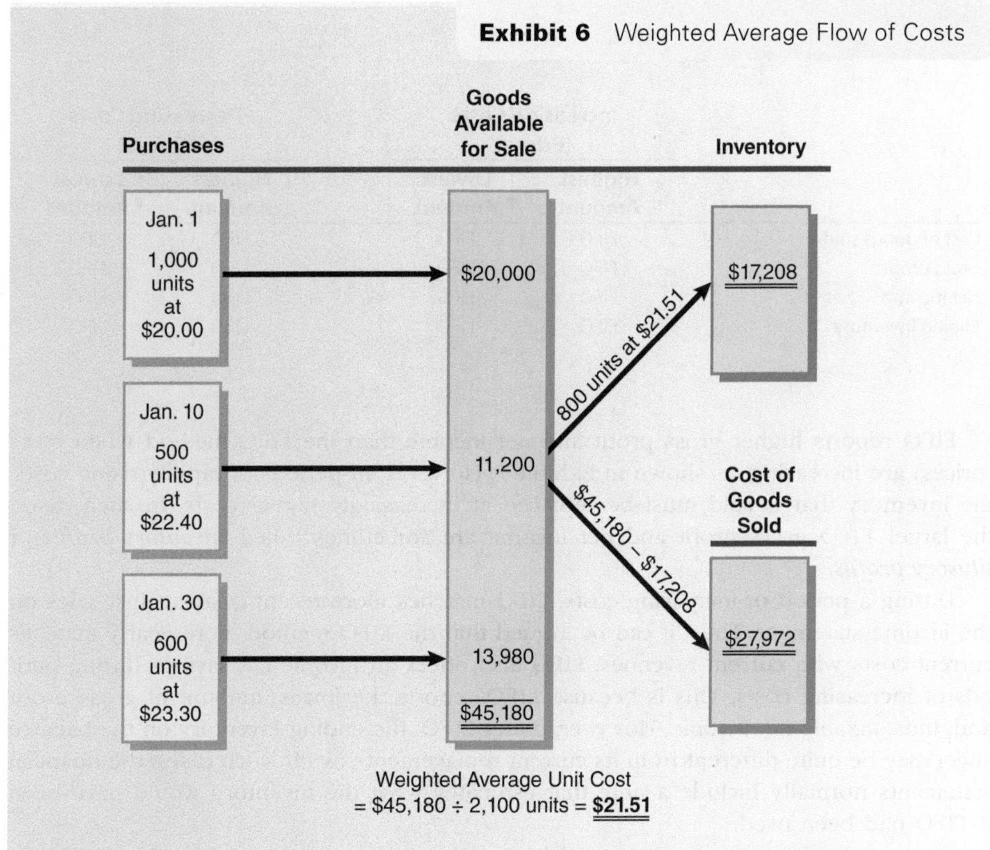

Comparing Inventory Costing Methods

Objective 4
Compare and contrast the effects of inventory costing methods on the income statement and balance sheet.

A different cost flow is assumed for the FIFO, LIFO, and weighted average inventory cost flow methods. As a result, the three methods normally yield different amounts for the following:

- Cost of goods sold
- Gross profit
- Ending inventory

Using the prior illustration for **Item 127B** with sales of $39,000 (1,300 units × $30), the following differences result:

Partial Income Statements

	First-In, First-Out	Weighted Average Cost	Last-In, First-Out
Sales	$ 39,000	$ 39,000	$ 39,000
Cost of goods sold	(26,720)	(27,972)	(29,180)
Gross profit	$ 12,280	$ 11,028	$ 9,820
Inventory, Jan. 31	$ 18,460	$ 17,208	$ 16,000

During January the cost of **Item 127B** increased from the $20 per unit on January1 to $23.30 for the purchase on January 30. Thus, the preceding differences show the effect of increasing costs (prices). If costs (prices) had remained the same, all three methods would have yielded the same results.

The financial statement effects of changing costs (prices) on the FIFO and LIFO methods are summarized in Exhibit 7. The weighted average cost method will always yield results between those of FIFO and LIFO.

Exhibit 7
Effects of Changing Costs (Prices): FIFO and LIFO Cost Method

	Increasing Costs (Prices)		Decreasing Costs (Prices)	
	↑ Highest Amount	↓ Lowest Amount	↑ Highest Amount	↓ Lowest Amount
Cost of goods sold	LIFO	FIFO	FIFO	LIFO
Gross profit	FIFO	LIFO	LIFO	FIFO
Net income	FIFO	LIFO	LIFO	FIFO
Ending inventory	FIFO	LIFO	LIFO	FIFO

FIFO reports higher gross profit and net income than the LIFO method when costs (prices) are increasing, as shown in Exhibit 7. However, in periods of rapidly rising costs, the inventory that is sold must be replaced at increasingly higher costs. In such cases, the larger FIFO gross profit and net income are sometimes called *inventory profits* or *illusory profits.*

During a period of increasing costs, LIFO matches more recent costs against sales on the income statement. Thus, it can be argued that the LIFO method more nearly matches current costs with current revenues. LIFO also offers an income tax savings during periods of increasing costs. This is because LIFO reports the lowest amount of gross profit and, thus, taxable net income. However, under LIFO, the ending inventory on the balance sheet may be quite different from its current replacement cost. In such cases, the financial statements normally include a note that estimates what the inventory would have been if FIFO had been used.

The weighted average cost method is, in a sense, a compromise between FIFO and LIFO. The effect of cost (price) trends is averaged in determining the cost of goods sold and the ending inventory. For a series of purchases, the weighted average cost will be the same, regardless of the direction of price trends. For example, reversing the sequence of unit costs presented in Exhibit 6 would not affect the reported cost of goods sold, gross profit, or ending inventory.

Exhibit 7 and the preceding paragraphs illustrate the effects of FIFO, LIFO, and weighted average cost flow methods on the financial statements with changing prices. The effects can also be illustrated using the integrated financial statement framework. For example, the effects on the accounts and financial statements of using FIFO rather than LIFO with *rising prices* are as follows:

Integrity, Objectivity, and Ethics in Business

Where's the Bonus?

Managers are often given bonuses based on reported earnings numbers. This can create a conflict. LIFO can improve the value of the company through lower taxes. However, in periods of rising costs (prices), LIFO also produces a lower earnings number and therefore lower management bonuses. Ethically, managers should select accounting procedures that will maximize the value of the firm, rather than their own compensation. Compensation specialists can help avoid this ethical dilemma by adjusting the bonus plan for the accounting procedure differences.

Financial Statement Effects

BALANCE SHEET

Assets	=	Liabilities	+	Stockholders' Equity
Inventory* (FIFO)	=			**Retained Earnings**
Higher				Higher

STATEMENT OF CASH FLOWS

INCOME STATEMENT

Sales	No Effect
Cost of goods sold	Lower
Net income	Higher

*Assuming rising prices.

The preceding effects of using FIFO rather than LIFO would be the opposite with *decreasing prices*. The effects of using the weighted average cost method would be between the effects of the FIFO and LIFO methods.

The selection of an inventory cost flow method also affects a company's liquidity and profitability metrics. For inventory, the liquidity metric **days' sales in inventory** is used. Days' sales in inventory estimates the average number of days it takes to sell inventory. For example, if a company's days' sales in inventory is 30, the company would expect to sell its inventory every 30 days. In other words, it expects to turnover its entire inventory 12 times a year.

Days' sales in inventory is computed as follows:

$$\textbf{Days' Sales in Inventory} = \frac{\textbf{Average Inventory}}{\textbf{Average Daily Cost of Goods Sold}}$$

Average daily cost of goods sold is computed as yearly cost of goods sold divided by 365 days. To illustrate, assume the following data for Downing Inc. for the year ending December 31, 20Y4.

Cost of goods sold for 20Y4	$4,745,000
Inventory, Jan. 1, 20Y4	285,000
Inventory, Dec. 31, 20Y4	339,000

Days' sales in inventory of 24 days is computed as follows:

$$\text{Days' Sales in Inventory} = \frac{\text{Average Inventory}}{\text{Average Cost of Goods Sold}} = \frac{(\$285,000 + \$339,000) \div 2}{\$4,745,000 \div 365 \text{ days}}$$

$$= \frac{\$312,000}{\$13,000} = 24 \text{ days}$$

The profitability metric is **return on sales**. Return on sales is computed as follows:

$$\text{Return on Sales} = \frac{\text{Operating Income}}{\text{Sales}}$$

Assuming that Downing Inc. has sales of $9,125,000 and operating income of $1,460,000, its return on sales is 16%, computed as follows:

$$\text{Return on Sales} = \frac{\text{Operating Income}}{\text{Sales}} = \frac{\$1,460,000}{\$9,125,000} = 16\%$$

Transaction Metric Effects

Assuming rising prices, the effects of selecting FIFO rather than LIFO on the liquidity and profitability metrics are as follows:

LIQUIDITY	
Days' Sales in Inventory	Increase

PROFITABILITY	
Return on Sales	Increase

Since ending inventory using FIFO will be higher than ending inventory using LIFO during periods of rising prices, days' sales in inventory will increase. Since cost of goods sold will be lower using FIFO rather than LIFO, operating income will be higher under FIFO and therefore, return on sales will increase.

Days' sales in inventory is higher using FIFO rather than LIFO. This implies that since the dollar amount of inventory is higher, the company's overall liquidity, which is the ability to convert assets to cash, will be higher. The inventory items being valued, however, are the same regardless of whether FIFO or LIFO is used. Since the inventory items are the same, the ability to sell the items and convert them to cash is the same regardless of whether FIFO or LIFO is used. For this reason, managers must distinguish between the "metric" used to assess liquidity and the "actual" liquidity, which is the ability to convert assets to cash.

CVS Connection

CVS uses the weighted average cost method for valuing the inventories.

Financial Statement Reporting of Inventories

Objective 5

Describe and illustrate the financial reporting of inventories.

Cost is the primary basis for valuing and reporting inventories in the financial statements. However, inventory may be valued at other than cost in the following cases:

- The cost of replacing items in inventory is below the recorded cost.
- The inventory cannot be sold at normal prices due to imperfections, style changes, spoilage, damage, obsolescence, or other causes.

Valuing at Lower of Cost or Market

If the market is lower than the purchase cost, the **lower-of-cost-or-market (LCM) method** is used to value the inventory. *Market*, as used in *lower of cost or market*, is the **net realizable value of the inventory**.[2] Net realizable value is determined as follows:

Net Realizable Value = Estimated Selling Price − Direct Costs of Disposal

2. Accounting Standards Update, *Inventory (Topic 330): Simplifying the Measurement of Inventory*, July 2015, FASB.

Direct costs of disposal include selling expenses such as special advertising or sales commissions on the sale. To illustrate, assume the following data about an item of damaged merchandise:

Original cost	$1,000
Estimated selling price	800
Selling expenses	150

The merchandise should be valued at its net realizable value of $650 as follows:

Net Realizable Value = $800 − $150 = $650

The lower-of-cost-or-market method can be applied in one of three ways by determining the cost, market price, and any declines for one of the following:

- each item in the inventory
- each major class or category of inventory
- total inventory as a whole

The amount of any price decline is included in the cost of goods sold. This in turn reduces gross profit and net income in the period in which the price declines occur. This matching of price declines to the period in which they occur is the primary advantage of using the lower-of-cost-or-market method.

To illustrate, assume the following data for 400 identical units of Item A in inventory on December 31, 20Y4:

Unit purchased cost	$10.25
Replacement cost on December 31, 20Y4	9.50

Since Item A could be replaced at $9.50 a unit, $9.50 is used under the lower-of-cost-or-market method.

Exhibit 8 illustrates applying the lower-of-cost-or-market method to each inventory item (A, B, C, and D). As applied on an item-by-item basis, the total lower of cost or market is $15,070, which is a market decline of $450 ($15,520 − $15,070). This market decline of $450 is included in the cost of goods sold.

In Exhibit 8, Items A, B, C, and D could be viewed as a class of inventory items. If the lower-of-cost-or-market method is applied to the class, the inventory would be valued at $15,472, which is a market decline of $48 ($15,520 − $15,472). Likewise, if Items A, B, C, and D make up the total inventory, the lower-of-cost-or-market method as applied to the total inventory would be the same amount, $15,472.

Exhibit 8
Determining Inventory at Lower of Cost or Market

	A	B	C	D	E	F	G
1			Cost	Market Value		Total	
2		Inventory	per	per Unit			
3	Item	Quantity	Unit	(Net Realizable Value)	Cost	Market	LCM
4	A	400	$10.25	$ 9.50	$ 4,100	$ 3,800	$ 3,800
5	B	120	22.50	24.10	2,700	2,892	2,700
6	C	600	8.00	7.75	4,800	4,650	4,650
7	D	280	14.00	14.75	3,920	4,130	3,920
8	Total				$15,520	$15,472	$15,070
9							

The effects of lower of cost or market on the financial statements are as follows:

Financial Statement Effects

BALANCE SHEET

Assets	=	Liabilities	+	Stockholders' Equity
Inventory	=			**Retained Earnings**
Lower				Lower

STATEMENT OF CASH FLOWS

INCOME STATEMENT

Sales	No Effect
Cost of goods sold	Higher
Net income	Lower

Transaction Metric Effects

The effects of lower of cost or market on liquidity and profitability metrics are as follows:

LIQUIDITY

Days' Sales in Inventory	Decrease

PROFITABILITY

Return on Sales	Decrease

Since lower of cost or market reduces the dollar amount of inventory, lower of cost or market decrease the days' sales in inventory. Since cost of goods sold is increased, return on sales is decreased.

CVS Connection

CVS values all its inventories using lower of cost or market.

Inventory on the Balance Sheet

Inventory is usually reported in the "Current assets" section of the balance sheet. In addition to this amount, the following are reported on the balance sheet or in the accompanying notes:

- The method of determining the cost of the inventory (FIFO, LIFO, or weighted average)
- The method of valuing the inventory (cost or the lower of cost or market)

The presentation for inventory for CVS within the "Current assets" section of the balance sheet and accompanying notes is as follows:

CVS Connection

CVS Health Corporation
Balance Sheet
December 31
(in millions)

Assets:	
Cash and cash equivalents	$ 5,683
Investments	2,373
Accounts receivable, net	19,617
Inventories	17,516
Other current assets	5,113
Total current assets	50,302

Note to the Financial Statements:

Inventories

Inventories are valued at the lower of cost or net realizable value using the weighted average cost method. Physical inventory counts are taken on a regular basis in each retail store and . . . pharmacy . . . to ensure that the amounts reflected in the . . . financial statements are properly stated.

It is not unusual for a large business to use different costing methods for segments of its inventories. Also, a business may change its inventory costing method. In such cases, the effect of the change and the reason for the change are disclosed in the notes to the financial statements.

Effects of Inventory Errors on the Financial Statements

Any errors in inventory will affect the balance sheet and income statement. Some reasons that inventory errors may occur include the following:

- Physical inventory on hand was miscounted.
- Costs were incorrectly assigned to inventory using an inventory costing method, such as FIFO, LIFO, or weighted average, that was incorrectly applied.
- Inventory in transit was incorrectly included or excluded from inventory.
- Consigned inventory was incorrectly included or excluded from inventory.

Inventory errors often arise when conducting end-of-year "physical" inventory. For example, merchandise that was ordered *FOB shipping point* may be in transit at the end of the year and thus, not counted as part of the physical inventory. Even though the inventory has not been received, the title to the merchandise passed to the buyer at the time of shipment and should be included in the buyer's physical inventory.

Likewise, manufacturers sometimes ship merchandise to retailers who act as the manufacturer's selling agent. The manufacturer, called the **consignor**, retains title until the goods are sold. Such merchandise, called **consigned inventory**, is said to be shipped *on consignment* to the retailer, called the **consignee**. Any unsold merchandise at year-end is a part of the manufacturer's (consignor's) inventory, even though the merchandise is in the hands of the retailer (consignee). At year-end, the retailer (consignee) may incorrectly include the consigned merchandise in its physical inventory or the manufacturer may incorrectly exclude it from its physical inventory.

Errors in the ending inventory affect not only the balance sheet, but also the income statement. In a perpetual inventory system, the end-of-year physical inventory is the basis for the inventory shrinkage adjustment illustrated in Chapter 4, *Accounting for Retail Operations*. This adjustment for inventory shrinkage increases Cost of Goods Sold and decreases Inventory. In a periodic inventory system, ending inventory is subtracted from goods available for sale in computing cost of goods sold. In addition, since the ending inventory becomes the beginning inventory of the next period, the income statement of the next period is also misstated.

Exhibit 9 illustrates the effects of inventory errors on the income statement and balance sheet.[3]

Exhibit 9 Effects of Inventory Errors

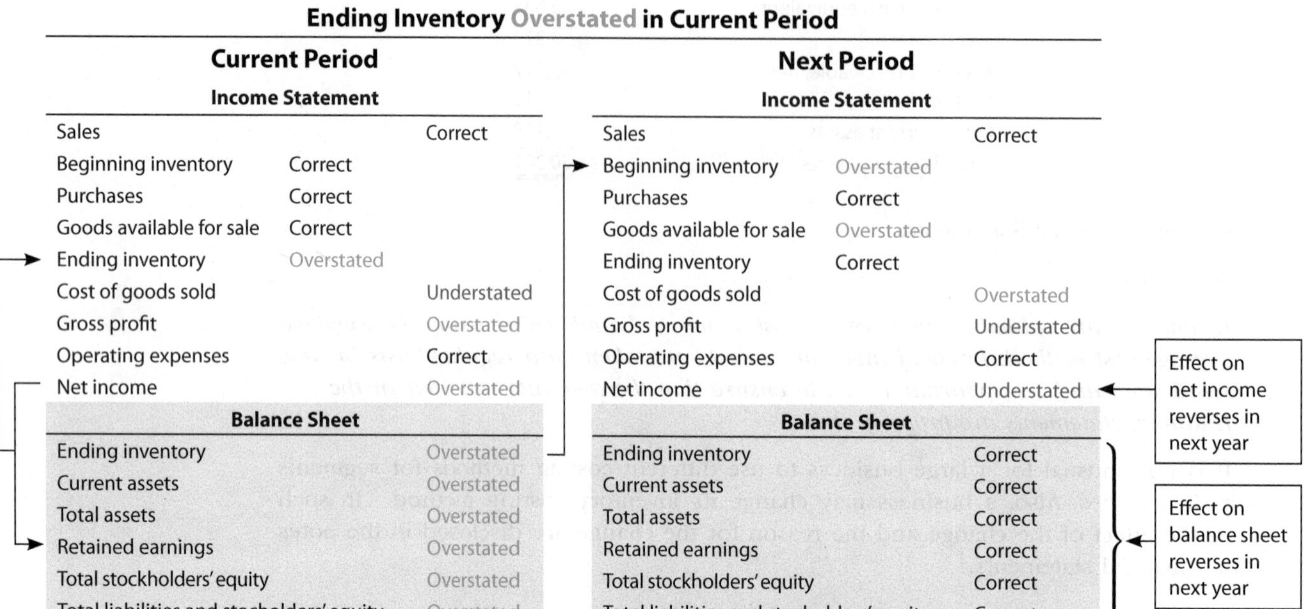

Ending Inventory Overstated in Current Period

Current Period — Income Statement			Next Period — Income Statement		
Sales		Correct	Sales		Correct
Beginning inventory	Correct		Beginning inventory	Overstated	
Purchases	Correct		Purchases	Correct	
Goods available for sale	Correct		Goods available for sale	Overstated	
Ending inventory	Overstated		Ending inventory	Correct	
Cost of goods sold		Understated	Cost of goods sold		Overstated
Gross profit		Overstated	Gross profit		Understated
Operating expenses		Correct	Operating expenses		Correct
Net income		Overstated	Net income		Understated
Balance Sheet			**Balance Sheet**		
Ending inventory		Overstated	Ending inventory		Correct
Current assets		Overstated	Current assets		Correct
Total assets		Overstated	Total assets		Correct
Retained earnings		Overstated	Retained earnings		Correct
Total stockholders' equity		Overstated	Total stockholders' equity		Correct
Total liabilities and stocholders' equity		Overstated	Total liabilities and stocholders' equity		Correct

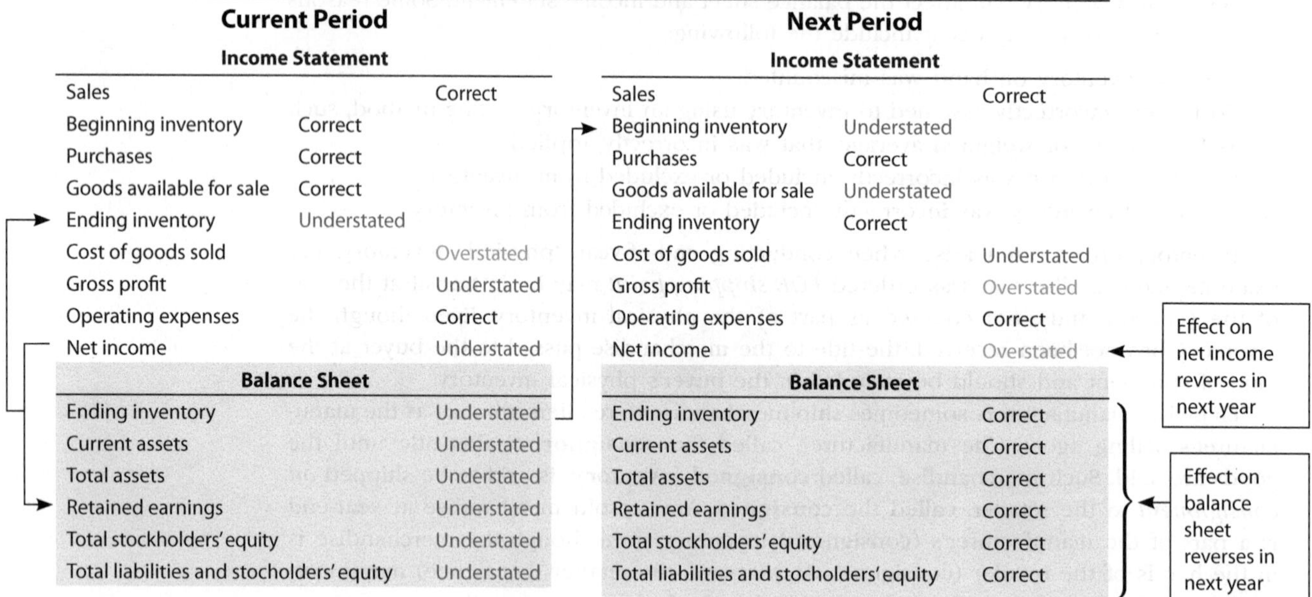

Ending Inventory Understated in Current Period

Current Period — Income Statement			Next Period — Income Statement		
Sales		Correct	Sales		Correct
Beginning inventory	Correct		Beginning inventory	Understated	
Purchases	Correct		Purchases	Correct	
Goods available for sale	Correct		Goods available for sale	Understated	
Ending inventory	Understated		Ending inventory	Correct	
Cost of goods sold		Overstated	Cost of goods sold		Understated
Gross profit		Understated	Gross profit		Overstated
Operating expenses		Correct	Operating expenses		Correct
Net income		Understated	Net income		Overstated
Balance Sheet			**Balance Sheet**		
Ending inventory		Understated	Ending inventory		Correct
Current assets		Understated	Current assets		Correct
Total assets		Understated	Total assets		Correct
Retained earnings		Understated	Retained earnings		Correct
Total stockholders' equity		Understated	Total stockholders' equity		Correct
Total liabilities and stocholders' equity		Understated	Total liabilities and stocholders' equity		Correct

To illustrate, assume that Zula Industries incorrectly counted its December 31, 20Y1, inventory at $250,000 instead of the correct amount of $220,000. The effect of the misstatement on Zula's income statement and balance sheet for 20Y1 (current year) and 20Y2 (following year) is shown in Exhibit 10.

3. To simplify, the periodic inventory system is used.

Exhibit 10 Effects of Inventory Errors—Zula Industries

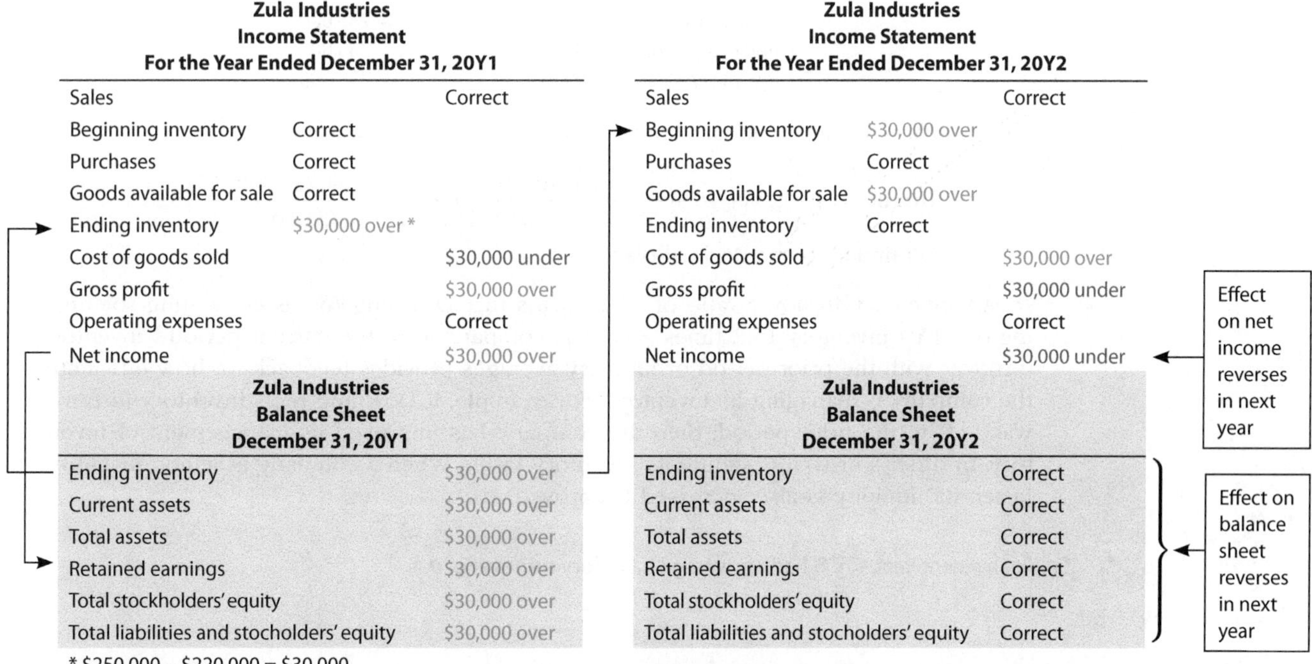

Zula Industries
Income Statement
For the Year Ended December 31, 20Y1

Sales		Correct
Beginning inventory	Correct	
Purchases	Correct	
Goods available for sale	Correct	
Ending inventory	$30,000 over *	
Cost of goods sold		$30,000 under
Gross profit		$30,000 over
Operating expenses		Correct
Net income		$30,000 over

Zula Industries
Balance Sheet
December 31, 20Y1

Ending inventory	$30,000 over
Current assets	$30,000 over
Total assets	$30,000 over
Retained earnings	$30,000 over
Total stockholders' equity	$30,000 over
Total liabilities and stocholders' equity	$30,000 over

* $250,000 – $220,000 = $30,000

Zula Industries
Income Statement
For the Year Ended December 31, 20Y2

Sales		Correct
Beginning inventory	$30,000 over	
Purchases	Correct	
Goods available for sale	$30,000 over	
Ending inventory	Correct	
Cost of goods sold		$30,000 over
Gross profit		$30,000 under
Operating expenses		Correct
Net income		$30,000 under

Effect on net income reverses in next year

Zula Industries
Balance Sheet
December 31, 20Y2

Ending inventory	Correct
Current assets	Correct
Total assets	Correct
Retained earnings	Correct
Total stockholders' equity	Correct
Total liabilities and stocholders' equity	Correct

Effect on balance sheet reverses in next year

Using Data Analytics

Inventories

A retailer can use data analytics to manage its inventory efficiently and, in doing so, increase its customer satisfaction and profitability. For example, **AutoZone, Inc. (AZO)** operates over 5,000 stores throughout the United States. Each store carries products for a variety of cars, sports utility vehicles, vans, and light trucks. However, stores cannot carry "all" parts for "all" vehicles. Therefore, each store manager must continually update and manage its inventory to best meet the demands (needs) of its customers.

Data analytics can be used by companies like AutoZone to track inventory and anticipate the needs of their customers. Doing so reduces lost sales due to out-of-stock items and enhances customer satisfaction and a company's reputation for meeting customer needs.

See Case 7-5 for a homework assignment using data analytics.

Metric-Based Analysis: Inventory Turnover

Objective 6
Describe and illustrate the use of the inventory turnover for assessing a company's operations.

Inventories are large current assets for many companies. One of the primary objectives in managing inventory is to maintain enough inventory to satisfy customer demands without carrying excess inventory. **Inventory turnover** is a useful measure of liquidity and how efficiently a company is managing its operations.

The inventory turnover is computed as follows:

$$\textbf{Inventory Turnover} = \frac{\textbf{Cost of Goods Sold}}{\textbf{Average Inventory}}$$

The average inventory is computed as the beginning inventory plus the ending inventory for the period divided by two.

To illustrate, assume the following data for Downing Inc. for the year ending December 31, 20Y4:

Cost of goods sold for 20Y4	$4,745,000
Inventory, Jan. 1, 20Y4	285,000
Inventory, Dec. 31, 20Y4	339,000

The inventory turnover of 15.2 times for Downing Inc. is computed as follows:

$$\text{Inventory Turnover} = \frac{\$4{,}745{,}000}{(\$285{,}000 + \$339{,}000) \div 2} = \frac{\$4{,}745{,}000}{\$312{,}000} = 15.2^*$$

*Rounded to one decimal place.

An inventory turnover ratio of 15.2 means that Downing Inc. is converting (or turning over) its inventory 15.2 times a year. A comparison of the current period's inventory turnover with the prior period or industry averages provides feedback on how efficiently the company is managing its inventory. For example, if Downing Inc.'s inventory turnover was 14.0 in the prior period, then the company has improved its management of inventory. In other words, it is selling its inventory faster. When a company is selling inventory faster, its liquidity is also increased (improved).

CVS Connection

For a recent year, **CVS** had an average inventory turnover of 9.4.

Inventory turnover is related to the liquidity metric days' sales in inventory described earlier in this chapter. Specifically, these two metrics are related as follows:

$$\textbf{Days' Sales in Inventory} = \frac{\textbf{365 Days}}{\textbf{Inventory Turnover}}$$

To illustrate, the days' sales in inventory of 24 days for Downing Inc. can be computed as follows:

$$\text{Days' Sales in Inventory} = \frac{\text{365 Days}}{\text{Inventory Turnover}} = \frac{\text{365 Days}}{15.2} = \text{24 days}^*$$

*Rounded to nearest day.

For a recent year, **CVS** had an average days' sales in inventory of 39 days (365 days ÷ 9.4).

Objective 7

Determine the cost of inventory using the FIFO, LIFO, and weighted average cost methods using the perpetual inventory system.

Appendix

Inventory Costing Methods: Perpetual Inventory System

This appendix illustrates the FIFO, LIFO, and weighted average cost methods using a perpetual inventory system. The following data for **Item 127B** are used:[4]

	Item 127B	Units	Cost
Jan. 1	Inventory	1,000	$20.00
4	Sale at $30 per unit	700	
10	Purchase	500	22.40
22	Sale at $30 per unit	360	
28	Sale at $30 per unit	240	
30	Purchase	600	23.30

4. This is the same data that was used in the chapter illustration except that the unit selling price, units sold, and date sold are also provided.

First-In, First-Out Method

When the FIFO method is used, costs are included in the cost of goods sold in the order in which they were purchased. This is often the same as the physical flow of the goods. Thus, the FIFO method often provides results that are about the same as those that would have been obtained using the specific identification method. For example, grocery stores shelve milk and other perishable products by expiration dates. Products with early expiration dates are stocked in front. In this way, the oldest products (earliest purchases) are sold first.

To illustrate, Exhibit 11 shows the use of FIFO under a perpetual inventory system for **Item 127B**.

Exhibit 11
Perpetual Inventory FIFO: Subsidiary Ledger Account

Item 127B

	Purchases			Cost of Goods Sold			Inventory		
Date	**Quantity**	**Unit Cost**	**Total Cost**	**Quantity**	**Unit Cost**	**Total Cost**	**Quantity**	**Unit Cost**	**Total Cost**
Jan. 1							1,000	20.00	20,000
4				700	20.00	14,000	300	20.00	6,000
10	500	22.40	11,200				300	20.00	6,000
							500	22.40	11,200
22				300	20.00	6,000			
				60	22.40	1,344	440	22.40	9,856
28				240	22.40	5,376	200	22.40	4,480
30	600	23.30	13,980				200	22.40	4,480
							600	23.30	13,980
31	Balances					26,720			18,460

Cost of goods sold

January 31 inventory

The entries in the subsidiary inventory ledger for Item 127B in Exhibit 11 are as follows:

1. The beginning balance on January 1 is $20,000 (1,000 units at a unit cost of $20.00).
2. On January 4, 700 units were sold at a price of $30 each for sales of $21,000 (700 units at a selling price of $30 per unit). The cost of goods sold is $14,000 (700 units at a unit cost of $20). After the sale, there remains $6,000 of inventory (300 units at a unit cost of $20).
3. On January 10, $11,200 is purchased (500 units at a unit cost of $22.40). After the purchase, the inventory is reported on two lines, $6,000 (300 units at a unit cost of $20.00) from the beginning inventory and $11,200 (500 units at a unit cost of $22.40) from the January 10 purchase.
4. On January 22, 360 units are sold at a price of $30 each for sales of $10,800 (360 units at a selling price of $30 per unit). Using FIFO, the cost of goods sold of $7,344 consists of $6,000 (300 units at a unit cost of $20.00) from the beginning inventory plus $1,344 (60 units at a unit cost of $22.40) from the January 10 purchase. After the sale, there remains $9,856 of inventory (440 units at a unit cost of $22.40) from the January 10 purchase.
5. The January 28 sale and January 30 purchase are recorded in a similar manner.
6. The ending balance on January 31 is $18,460. This balance is made up of two layers of inventory as follows:

	Date of Purchase	Quantity	Unit Cost	Total Cost
Layer 1:	Jan. 10	200	$22.40	$ 4,480
Layer 2:	Jan. 30	600	23.30	13,980
Total		800		$18,460

Last-In, First-Out Method

When the LIFO method is used, the cost of the units sold is the cost of the most recent purchases. The LIFO method was originally used in those rare cases where the units sold were taken from the most recently purchased units. LIFO is now widely used even when it does not represent the physical flow of units

To illustrate, Exhibit 12 shows the use of LIFO under a perpetual inventory system for **Item 127B**.

Exhibit 12
Perpetual Inventory LIFO: Subsidiary Ledger Account

Item 127B

	Purchases			Cost of Goods Sold			Inventory		
Date	**Quantity**	**Unit Cost**	**Total Cost**	**Quantity**	**Unit Cost**	**Total Cost**	**Quantity**	**Unit Cost**	**Total Cost**
Jan. 1							1,000	20.00	20,000
4				700	20.00	14,000	300	20.00	6,000
10	500	22.40	11,200				300	20.00	6,000
							500	22.40	11,200
22				360	22.40	8,064	300	20.00	6,000
							140	22.40	3,136
28				140	22.40	3,136	200	20.00	4,000
				100	20.00	2,000			
30	600	23.30	13,980				200	20.00	4,000
							600	23.30	13,980
31	Balances					27,200			17,980

Cost of goods sold ↑ (27,200) January 31 inventory ↑ (17,980)

The entries in the subsidiary inventory ledger for Item 127B in Exhibit 12 are as follows:

1. The beginning balance on January 1 is $20,000 (1,000 units at a unit of cost of $20.00).
2. On January 4, 700 units were sold at a price of $30 each for sales of $21,000 (700 units at a selling price of $30 per unit). The cost of goods sold is $14,000 (700 units at a unit cost of $20). After the sale, there remains $6,000 of inventory (300 units at a unit cost of $20).
3. On January 10, $11,200 is purchased (500 units at a unit cost of $22.40). After the purchase, the inventory is reported on two lines, $6,000 (300 units at a unit cost of $20.00) from the beginning inventory and $11,200 (500 units at a unit cost of $22.40) from the January 10 purchase.
4. On January 22, 360 units are sold at a price of $30 each for sales of $10,800 (360 units at a selling price of $30 per unit). Using LIFO, the cost of goods sold is $8,064 (360 units at unit cost of $22.40) from the January 10 purchase. After the sale, there remains $9,136 of inventory consisting of $6,000 (300 units at a unit cost of $20.00) from the beginning inventory and $3,136 (140 units at a unit cost of $22.40) from the January 10 purchase.
5. The January 28 sale and January 30 purchase are recorded in a similar manner.
6. The ending balance on January 31 is $17,980. This balance is made up of two layers of inventory as follows:

	Date of Purchase	Quantity	Unit Cost	Total Cost
Layer 1:	Beg. inv. (Jan. 1)	200	$20.00	$ 4,000
Layer 2:	Jan. 30	600	23.30	13,980
Total		800		$17,980

When the LIFO method is used, the subsidiary inventory ledger is sometimes maintained in units only. The units are converted to dollars when the financial statements are prepared at the end of the period.

Weighted Average Cost Method

When the weighted average cost method is used in a perpetual inventory system, a weighted average unit cost for each item is computed each time a purchase is made. This unit cost is used to determine the cost of each sale until another purchase is made and a new average is computed. This technique is called a *moving average.*

To illustrate, Exhibit 13 shows the use of weighted average under a perpetual inventory system for **Item 127B**.

Exhibit 13
Perpetual Inventory Weighted Average Cost: Subsidiary Ledger Account

Item 127B

	Purchases			Cost of Goods Sold			Inventory		
Date	**Quantity**	**Unit Cost**	**Total Cost**	**Quantity**	**Unit Cost**	**Total Cost**	**Quantity**	**Unit Cost**	**Total Cost**
Jan. 1							1,000	20.00	20,000
4				700	20.00	14,000	300	20.00	6,000
10	500	22.40	11,200				800	21.50	17,200
22				360	21.50	7,740	440	21.50	9,460
28				240	21.50	5,160	200	21.50	4,300
30	600	23.30	13,980				800	22.85	18,280
31	Balances					26,900	800	22.85	18,280

Cost of goods sold (26,900) — January 31 inventory (18,280)

The entries in the subsidiary inventory ledger for Item 127B in Exhibit 13 are as follows:

1. The beginning balance on January 1 is $20,000 (1,000 units at a unit cost of $20.00).
2. On January 4, 700 units were sold at a price of $30 each for sales of $21,000 (700 units at a selling price of $30 per unit). The cost of goods sold is $14,000 (700 units at a unit cost of $20). After the sale, there remains $6,000 of inventory (300 units at a unit cost of $20).
3. On January 10, $11,200 is purchased (500 units at a unit cost of $22.40). After the purchase, the weighted average unit cost of $21.50 is determined by dividing the total cost of the inventory on hand of $17,200 ($6,000 + $11,200) by the total quantity of inventory on hand of 800 (300 + 500) units. Thus, after the purchase, the inventory consists of 800 units at $21.50 per unit for a total cost of $17,200.
4. On January 22, 360 units are sold at a price of $30 each for sales of $10,800 (360 units at a selling price of $30 per unit). Using weighted average, the cost of goods sold is $7,740 (360 units × $21.50 per unit). After the sale, there remains $9,460 of inventory (440 units × $21.50 per unit).
5. The January 28 sale and January 30 purchase are recorded in a similar manner.
6. The ending balance on January 31 is $18,280 (800 units × $22.85 per unit).

Key Points

1. Describe types of inventory for retail and manufacturing businesses.

The goods held for sale by a retail business is a current asset called inventory or merchandise inventory. When inventory is sold, the cost is reported on the income statement as cost of goods sold.

A manufacturing business has three types of inventories: materials inventory, work in process inventory, and finished goods inventory. Work in process and finished goods inventories are made up of direct materials, direct labor, and factory overhead costs. Manufacturing inventories are a current asset on the balance sheet. When finished goods inventory is sold, the cost is reported on the income statement as cost of goods sold.

2. Describe three inventory cost flow assumptions.

When identical units of merchandise are acquired at different unit costs during a period, a cost flow assumption must be made as to which items are sold. Three common cost flow assumptions are first-in, first-out; last-in, first-out; and weighted average cost.

3. Determine the cost of inventory using the FIFO, LIFO, and weighted average cost methods.

The three inventory costing methods of FIFO, LIFO, and weighted average will normally yield different amounts for (1) the ending inventory, (2) the cost of goods sold for the period, and (3) the gross profit (and net income) for the period.

4. Compare and contrast the effects of inventory costing methods on the income statement and balance sheet.

During periods of inflation, the FIFO method yields the lowest amount for the cost of goods sold, the highest amount for gross profit (and net income), and the highest amount for the ending inventory. The LIFO method yields the opposite results. During periods of deflation, the effects are reversed. The weighted average cost method yields results that are between those of FIFO and LIFO.

5. Describe and illustrate the financial reporting of inventories.

Inventory is normally presented in the "Current assets" section of the balance sheet following receivables. If the market price of an item of inventory is lower than its cost, the lower market price is used to compute the value of the item. Market price is the net realizable value of the inventory. The lower of cost or market can be applied to each item in the inventory, to major classes or categories, or to the inventory as a whole.

Any errors in inventory will affect the balance sheet and income statement of the current period. Since the ending inventory of the current period becomes the beginning inventory of the next period, the income statement of the next period is also misstated. In the next (second) year, the income statement effects reverse. The result is that the balance sheet at the end of the second year will be correct.

6. Metric-Based Analysis: Describe and illustrate the use of the inventory turnover for assessing a company's operations.

Inventory turnover is useful in assessing a company's liquidity and operations. The inventory turnover is computed as cost of goods sold divided by average inventory. A high inventory turnover normally implies that a company is efficient in managing its operations.

Key Terms

Consigned inventory (285)
Consignee (285)
Consignor (285)
Days' sales in inventory (281)
Direct labor (273)
Direct materials (273)
Factory overhead (273)
First-in, first-out (FIFO) inventory cost flow method (275)
Finished goods inventory (273)
Inventory (272)
Inventory turnover (287)
Last-in, first-out (LIFO) inventory cost flow method (275)
Lower-of-cost-or-market (LCM) method (282)
Materials inventory (273)
Merchandise inventory (272)
Net realizable value of inventory (282)
Physical inventory (276)
Return on sales (281)
Specific identification inventory cost flow method (274)
Weighted average cost inventory cost flow method (275)
Work in process inventory (273)

Illustrative Problem

Stewart Co.'s beginning inventory and purchases during the year ended December 31, 20Y5, were as follows:

		Units	Unit Cost	Total Cost
January 1	Inventory	1,000	$50.00	$ 50,000
March 10	Purchase	1,200	52.50	63,000
August 30	Purchase	800	55.00	44,000
November 26	Purchase	2,000	56.00	112,000
Total		5,000		$269,000

Instructions

1. Assuming that 3,300 units were sold during the year, determine the cost of inventory on December 31, 20Y5, using each of the following inventory costing methods:
   a. First-in, first-out
   b. Last-in, first-out
   c. Weighted average cost
2. Which inventory costing method would yield the highest gross profit and net income?

Solution

1. a. First-in, first-out method: 1,700 units at $56 = $95,200
   b. Last-in, first-out method:

1,000	units at $50.00	$50,000
700	units at $52.50	36,750
1,700		$86,750

   c. Weighted average cost method:
   Weighted average cost per unit: $269,000 ÷ 5,000 units = $53.80
   Inventory, December 31, 20Y5: 1,700 units at $53.80 = $91,460
2. First-in, first-out. The per-unit cost of the purchases increased from $50 to $56 during the year. Thus, the first-in, first-out method will yield the highest gross profit and net income.

Self-Examination Questions

(Answers appear at the end of the chapter.)

1. When a retailer sells inventory, how is the related cost reported?
   A. As a current asset on the balance sheet
   B. As cost of goods sold on the income statement
   C. As revenue on the income statement
   D. As a long-term liability on the balance sheet
2. The inventory costing method that is based on the assumption that costs should be charged against revenue in the order in which they are incurred is:
   A. FIFO
   B. LIFO
   C. Weighted average cost
   D. Perpetual inventory

3. The following units of a particular item were available for sale during the period:

Beginning inventory	40 units at $20
First purchase	50 units at $21
Second purchase	50 units at $22
Third purchase	50 units at $23

What is the unit cost of the 35 units on hand at the end of the period as determined under the FIFO costing method?

A. $20
B. $21
C. $22
D. $23

4. If inventory is being valued at cost and the price level is steadily rising, the method of costing that will yield the highest net income is:

A. LIFO
B. FIFO
C. Weighted average
D. Periodic

5. If the inventory at the end of the year is understated by $7,500, the error will cause an:

A. Understatement of cost of goods sold for the year by $7,500
B. Overstatement of gross profit for the year by $7,500
C. Overstatement of beginning inventory for the following year by $7,500
D. Understatement of net income for the year by $7,500

Class Discussion Questions

1. Do the terms *FIFO* and *LIFO* refer to techniques used in determining quantities of the various classes of merchandise on hand? Explain.

2. Does the term *last-in* in the LIFO method mean that the items in the inventory are assumed to be the most recent (last) acquisitions? Explain.

3. If inventory is being valued at cost and the price level is steadily rising, which of the three methods of costing—FIFO, LIFO, or weighted average cost—will yield (a) the highest inventory cost, (b) the lowest inventory cost, (c) the highest gross profit, and (d) the lowest gross profit?

4. Which of the three methods of inventory costing—FIFO, LIFO, or weighted average cost—will in general yield an inventory cost most nearly approximating current replacement cost?

5. If inventory is being valued at cost and the price level is steadily rising, which of the three methods of costing—FIFO, LIFO, or weighted average cost—will yield the lowest annual income tax expense? Explain.

6. Using the following data, how should the inventory be valued under lower of cost or market?

Original cost	$1,350
Estimated selling price	1,475
Selling expenses	180

7. How is the method of determining the cost of inventory and the method of valuing it disclosed in the financial statements?

8. The inventory at the end of the year was understated by $14,750. (a) Did the error cause an overstatement or an understatement of the gross profit for the year? (b) Which items on the balance sheet at the end of the year were overstated or understated as a result of the error?

9. Hutch Co. sold merchandise to Bibbins Company on May 31, FOB shipping point. If the merchandise is in transit on May 31, the end of the fiscal year, which company would report it in its financial statements? Explain.

10. A manufacturer shipped merchandise to a retailer on a consignment basis. If the merchandise is unsold at the end of the period, in whose inventory should the merchandise be included?

Exercises

E7-1 Cost flow assumptions and methods

Obj. 2, 3

The following three identical units of Item P401C are purchased during April:

		Item P401C	Units	Cost	
Apr.	2	Purchase	1	$100	
	15	Purchase	1	120	
	20	Purchase	1	140	
	Total		3	$360	
	Average cost per unit			$120	($360 ÷ 3 units)

Assume that one unit is sold on April 27 for $300.

Determine the gross profit for April and ending inventory on April 30 using the (a) first-in, first-out (FIFO); (b) last-in, first-out (LIFO); and (c) weighted average cost methods.

E7-2 Inventory by three methods

Obj. 3

SHOW ME HOW

✔ b. $19,080

The units of an item available for sale during the year were as follows:

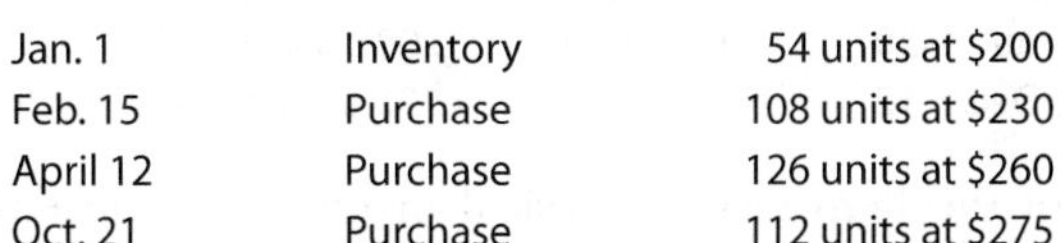

Jan. 1	Inventory	54 units at $200
Feb. 15	Purchase	108 units at $230
April 12	Purchase	126 units at $260
Oct. 21	Purchase	112 units at $275

There are 90 units of the item in the physical inventory at December 31. Determine the cost of ending inventory using (a) the first-in, first-out method, (b) the last-in, first-out method, and (c) the weighted average cost method.

E7-3 Inventory by three methods

Obj. 3

The units of an item available for sale during the year were as follows:

Jan.	1	Inventory	40 units at $165	$ 6,600
Aug.	13	Purchase	200 units at $180	36,000
Nov.	30	Purchase	60 units at $200	12,000
		Available for sale	300 units	$54,600

There are 75 units of the item in the physical inventory at December 31. The periodic inventory system is used. Determine the inventory cost using the (a) first-in, first-out (FIFO) method; (b) last-in, first-out (LIFO) method; and (c) weighted average cost method.

E7-4 Inventory by three methods

Obj. 3

EXCEL ONLINE

The units of an item available for sale during the year were as follows:

Jan.	1	Inventory	2,500 units at $5
Feb.	17	Purchase	3,300 units at $6
July	21	Purchase	3,000 units at $7
Nov.	23	Purchase	1,200 units at $8

There are 1,500 units of the item in the physical inventory at December 31. The periodic inventory system is used. Determine the inventory cost by the (a) first-in, first-out method, (b) last-in, first-out method, and (c) weighted average cost method.

Obj. 3

✔ a. Inventory, $22,700

E7-5 Inventory by three methods; cost of goods sold

The units of an item available for sale during the year were as follows:

Jan. 1	Inventory	10 units at $970 each
June 9	Purchase	45 units at $960 each
July 28	Purchase	30 units at $890 each
Nov. 1	Purchase	15 units at $920 each

There are 25 units of the item in the physical inventory at December 31. Determine the cost of ending inventory and the cost of goods sold by three methods, presenting your answers in the following form:

Inventory Method	Ending Inventory	Cost of Goods Sold
a. First-in, first-out	$	$
b. Last-in, first-out		
c. Weighted average		

Obj. 3

E7-6 Inventory by three methods; cost of goods sold

The units of an item available for sale during the year were as follows:

Jan. 1	Inventory	180 units at $108
Mar. 10	Purchase	224 units at $110
Aug. 30	Purchase	200 units at $116
Dec. 12	Purchase	196 units at $120

There are 208 units of the item in the physical inventory at December 31. The periodic inventory system is used. Determine the ending inventory cost and the cost of goods sold by three methods, presenting your answers in the following form:

Inventory Method	Ending Inventory	Cost of Goods Sold
a. First-in, first-out	$	$
b. Last-in, first-out		
c. Weighted average cost		

Obj. 4

E7-7 Comparing inventory methods

Assume that a firm separately determined inventory under FIFO and LIFO and then compared the results.

1. In each space below, place the correct sign [less than (<), greater than (>), or equal (=)] for each comparison, assuming periods of rising prices.
   a. FIFO ending inventory _____ LIFO ending inventory
   b. FIFO cost of goods sold _____ LIFO cost of goods sold
   c. FIFO net income _____ LIFO net income
   d. FIFO income tax _____ LIFO income tax
2. In periods of rising prices, why would management prefer to use LIFO over FIFO for preparing the company's income tax return?

Obj. 5

EXCEL ONLINE

E7-8 Lower-of-cost-or-market inventory

On the basis of the following data, determine the value of the inventory at the lower of cost or market. Apply lower of cost or market to each inventory item, as shown in Exhibit 8.

Item	Inventory Quantity	Cost per Unit	Market Value per Unit (Net Realizable Value)
JFW1	6,330	$10	$11
SAW9	1,140	36	34

E7-9 Lower-of-cost-or-market inventory

Obj. 5

SHOW ME HOW

EXCEL ONLINE

✔ LCM column total: $250,370

On the basis of the following data, determine the value of the inventory at the lower of cost or market. Apply lower of cost or market to each inventory item, as shown in Exhibit 8.

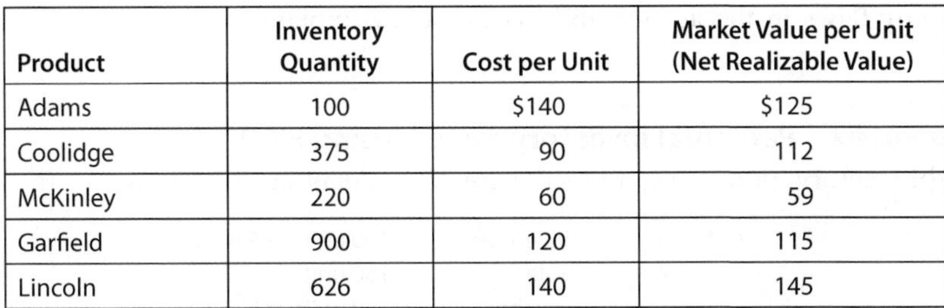

Product	Inventory Quantity	Cost per Unit	Market Value per Unit (Net Realizable Value)
Adams	100	$140	$125
Coolidge	375	90	112
McKinley	220	60	59
Garfield	900	120	115
Lincoln	626	140	145

E7-10 Inventory on the balance sheet

Obj. 5

Based on the data in Exercise 7-9 and assuming that cost was determined by the FIFO method, show how the inventory would appear on the balance sheet.

E7-11 Effects of inventory error

Obj. 5

During the taking of its physical inventory on December 31, 20Y3, Waterjet Bath Company incorrectly counted its inventory as $728,660 instead of the correct amount of $719,880. Indicate the effect of the misstatement on Waterjet Bath's December 31, 20Y3, balance sheet and income statement for the year ended December 31, 20Y3.

E7-12 Effects of inventory errors

Obj. 5

Madison River Supply Co. sells canoes, kayaks, whitewater rafts, and other boating supplies. During the taking of its physical inventory on December 31, 20Y8, Madison incorrectly counted its inventory as $545,000 instead of the correct amount of $555,400.

a. State the effects of the error on the December 31, 20Y8, balance sheet of Madison River Supply.

b. State the effects of the error on the income statement of Madison River Supply for the year ended December 31, 20Y8.

c. If uncorrected, what would be the effects of the error on the 20Y9 income statement?

d. If uncorrected, what would be the effects of the error on the December 31, 20Y9, balance sheet?

E7-13 Effects of inventory errors

Obj. 5

Fonda Motorcycle Shop sells motorcycles, ATVs, and other related supplies and accessories. During the taking of its physical inventory on December 31, 20Y1, Fonda incorrectly counted its inventory as $452,500 instead of the correct amount of $425,500.

a. State the effects of the error on the December 31, 20Y1, balance sheet of Fonda Motorcycle Shop.

b. State the effects of the error on the income statement of Fonda Motorcycle Shop for the year ended December 31, 20Y1.

c. If uncorrected, what would be the effects of the error on the 20Y2 income statement?

d. If uncorrected, what would be the effects of the error on the December 31, 20Y2, balance sheet?

Obj. 5

E7-14 Effects of inventory error

During 20Y5, the accountant discovered that the physical inventory at the end of 20Y4 had been understated by $42,750. Instead of correcting the error, however, the accountant assumed that the error would balance out (correct itself) in 20Y5.

Are there any flaws in the accountant's assumption? Explain.

Obj. 7

E7-15 Appendix Perpetual inventory system using FIFO

Beginning inventory, purchases, and sales for Item Zeta9 are as follows:

Oct.	1	Inventory	200 units at $30
	7	Sale	160 units
	15	Purchase	180 units at $33
	24	Sale	150 units

Assuming a perpetual inventory system and using the first-in, first-out (FIFO) method, determine (a) the cost of goods sold on October 24 and (b) the inventory on October 31.

Obj. 7

E7-16 Appendix Perpetual inventory system using LIFO

Beginning inventory, purchases, and sales for Item 88-HX are as follows:

July	1	Inventory	90 units at $52
	8	Sale	75 units
	15	Purchase	125 units at $58
	27	Sale	100 units

Assuming a perpetual inventory system and using the last-in, first-out (LIFO) method, determine (a) the cost of goods sold on July 27 and (b) the inventory on July 31.

Obj. 7

E7-17 Appendix Perpetual inventory system using weighted average

Beginning inventory, purchases, and sales for WCS12 are as follows:

Oct.	1	Inventory	320 units at $10
	13	Sale	180 units
	22	Purchase	360 units at $12
	29	Sale	300 units

Assuming a perpetual inventory system and using the weighted average method, determine (a) the weighted average unit cost after the October 22 purchase, (b) the cost of goods sold on October 29, and (c) the inventory on October 31.

Obj. 7

✔ Dec. 31 Inventory, $136,000

EXCEL ONLINE

E7-18 Appendix Perpetual inventory system using FIFO

A company purchased and sold the following items for the year ended December 31:

Jan.	1	Inventory	4,000 units at $40
Apr.	19	Sale	2,500 units
June	30	Purchase	4,500 units at $44
Sept.	2	Sale	5,000 units
Nov.	15	Purchase	2,000 units at $46

Determine the cost of goods sold for each sale and the inventory balance after each sale, using a perpetual inventory system and the first-in, first-out method. Present the data in the form illustrated in Exhibit 11.

E7-19 Appendix Perpetual inventory system using LIFO

Obj. 7

A company purchased and sold the following items for the year ended December 31.

Jan. 1	Inventory	4,000 units at $40
Apr. 19	Sale	2,500 units
June 30	Purchase	4,500 units at $44
Sept. 2	Sale	5,000 units
Nov. 15	Purchase	2,000 units at $46

Determine the cost of goods sold for each sale and the inventory balance after each sale, using a perpetual inventory system and the last-in, first-out method. Present the data in the form illustrated in Exhibit 12.

E7-20 Appendix Perpetual inventory system using weighted average

Obj. 7

A company purchased and sold the following items for the year ended December 31:

Jan. 1	Inventory	4,000 units at $40
Apr. 19	Sale	2,500 units
June 30	Purchase	4,500 units at $44
Sept. 2	Sale	5,000 units
Nov. 15	Purchase	2,000 units at $46

Determine the cost of goods sold for each sale and the inventory balance after each sale, using a perpetual inventory system and the weighted average cost method. Present the data in the form illustrated in Exhibit 13.

Problems

P7-1 FIFO cost method

Obj. 3, 4

✔ 1. Mar. 31 Inventory, $1,010,625

The beginning inventory at Midnight Supplies and data on purchases and sales for a three-month period ending March 31 are as follows:

Date	Transaction	Number of Units	Per Unit	Total
Jan. 1	Inventory	7,500	$ 75.00	$ 562,500
10	Purchase	22,500	85.00	1,912,500
28	Sale	11,250	150.00	1,687,500
30	Sale	3,750	150.00	562,500
Feb. 5	Sale	1,500	150.00	225,000
10	Purchase	54,000	87.50	4,725,000
16	Sale	27,000	160.00	4,320,000
28	Sale	25,500	160.00	4,080,000
Mar. 5	Purchase	45,000	89.50	4,027,500
14	Sale	30,000	160.00	4,800,000
25	Purchase	7,500	90.00	675,000
30	Sale	26,250	160.00	4,200,000

Instructions

1. Determine the cost of the 11,250 units of inventory on March 31 using the first-in, first-out (FIFO) cost method.
2. Determine the sales, cost of goods sold, and gross profit for the three-month period.

3. Based upon the preceding data and using the following table, indicate with a check mark (√) whether the item would be the same, higher, or lower if the last-in, first-out (LIFO) method had been used. The answer for sales is shown as an example.

	Using LIFO Rather Than FIFO		
	Same	Higher	Lower
Sales	√		
Cost of goods sold			
Gross profit			
Operating expenses			
Net income			
Ending inventory			

Obj. 3, 4

✔ 1. Mar. 31 Inventory, $881,250

P7-2 LIFO cost method

The beginning inventory at Midnight Supplies and data on purchases and sales for a three-month period are shown in P7-1.

Instructions

1. Determine the cost of the 11,250 units of inventory on March 31 using the last-in, first-out (LIFO) cost method.
2. Determine the sales, cost of goods sold, and gross profit for the three-month period.
3. Based upon the data in P7-1 and using the following table, indicate with a check mark (√) whether the item would be the same, higher, or lower if the first-in, first-out (FIFO) method had been used. The answer for sales is shown as an example.

	Using FIFO Rather Than LIFO		
	Same	Higher	Lower
Sales	√		
Cost of goods sold			
Gross profit			
Operating expenses			
Net income			
Ending inventory			

Obj. 3, 4

✔ 1. Mar. 31, inventory, $981,000

P7-3 Weighted average cost method

The beginning inventory at Midnight Supplies and data on purchases and sales for a three-month period are shown in P7-1.

Instructions

1. Determine the cost of the 11,250 units of inventory on March 31 using the weighted average cost method.
2. Determine the sales, cost of goods sold, and gross profit for the three-month period.
3. Using the weighted average cost method, will ending inventory always be valued between that of the first-in, first-out (FIFO) and last-in, first-out (LIFO) methods?

P7-4 Inventory by three cost flow methods

Obj. 3, 4

✔ 1. $10,700

Details regarding the inventory of appliances on January 1, 20Y7, purchases invoices during the year, and the inventory count on December 31, 20Y7, of Amsterdam Appliances are summarized as follows:

Model	Inventory, January 1	Purchases Invoices 1st	2nd	3rd	Inventory Count, December 31
A10	—	4 at $ 64	4 at $ 70	4 at $ 76	6
B15	8 at $176	4 at 158	3 at 170	6 at 184	8
E60	3 at 75	3 at 65	15 at 68	9 at 70	5
G83	7 at 242	6 at 250	5 at 260	10 at 259	9
J34	12 at 240	10 at 246	16 at 267	16 at 270	15
M90	2 at 108	2 at 110	3 at 128	3 at 130	5
Q70	5 at 160	4 at 170	4 at 175	7 at 180	8

Instructions

1. Determine the cost of the inventory on December 31, 20Y7, by the first-in, first-out method. Present data in columnar form, using the following headings:

Model	Quantity	Unit Cost	Total Cost

   If the inventory of a particular model comprises one entire purchase plus a portion of another purchase acquired at a different unit cost, use a separate line for each purchase.
2. Determine the cost of the inventory on December 31, 20Y7, by the last-in, first-out method, following the procedures indicated in (1).
3. Determine the cost of the inventory on December 31, 20Y7, by the average cost method, using the columnar headings indicated in (1).
4. Discuss which method (FIFO or LIFO) would be preferred for income tax purposes in periods of (a) rising prices and (b) declining prices.

P7-5 Lower-of-cost-or-market inventory

Obj. 5

✔ Total LCM, $41,855

Data on the physical inventory of Moyer Company as of December 31, 20Y9, are as follows:

Description	Inventory Quantity	Unit Market Price
112Aa	38	$ 83
B300t	33	115
C39f	41	64
Echo9	125	26
F900w	18	550
H687	60	15
J023	5	390
L33y	375	6
R66b	90	18
S77x	6	235
T882m	130	18
Z55p	12	746

Quantity and cost data from the last purchases invoice of the year and the next-to-the-last purchases invoice are summarized as follows:

	Last Purchases Invoice		Next-to-Last Purchases Invoice	
Description	Quantity Purchased	Unit Cost	Quantity Purchased	Unit Cost
112Aa	25	$ 80	30	$ 78
B300t	35	118	20	117
C39f	20	66	25	70
Echo9	150	25	100	24
F900w	10	565	10	560
H687	100	15	100	14
J023	10	385	5	384
L33y	500	6	500	6
R66b	80	22	50	21
S77x	5	250	4	260
T882m	100	20	75	19
Z55p	9	750	9	749

Instructions

Determine the inventory at cost and also at the lower of cost or market, using the first-in, first-out method. Record the appropriate unit costs on an inventory sheet and complete the pricing of the inventory. When there are two different unit costs applicable to an item, proceed as follows:

1. Draw a line through the quantity, and insert the quantity and unit cost of the last purchase.
2. On the following line, insert the quantity and unit cost of the next-to-the-last purchase.
3. Total the cost and market columns and insert the lower of the two totals in the LCM column. The first item on the inventory sheet has been completed below as an example.

Inventory Sheet
December 31, 20Y9

				Total		
Description	Inventory Quantity	Unit Cost Price	Unit Market Price	Cost	Market	LCM
112Aa	~~38~~ 25	$80	$83	$2,000	$2,075	
	13	78		1,014	1,079	
				$3,014	$3,154	$3,014

Obj. 7

✔ 2. Mar. 31 Inventory, $881,250

P7-6 Appendix Perpetual inventory using three cost methods

The beginning inventory at Midnight Supplies and data on purchases and sales for a three-month period ending March 31 are as follows:

Date		Transaction	Number of Units	Per Unit	Total
Jan.	1	Inventory	7,500	$ 75.00	$ 562,500
	10	Purchase	22,500	85.00	1,912,500
	28	Sale	11,250	150.00	1,687,500
	30	Sale	3,750	150.00	562,500
Feb.	5	Sale	1,500	150.00	225,000
	10	Purchase	54,000	87.50	4,725,000
	16	Sale	27,000	160.00	4,320,000
	28	Sale	25,500	160.00	4,080,000
Mar.	5	Purchase	45,000	89.50	4,027,500
	14	Sale	30,000	160.00	4,800,000
	25	Purchase	7,500	90.00	675,000
	30	Sale	26,250	160.00	4,200,000

Instructions

1. Record the inventory, purchases, and cost of goods sold data in a perpetual inventory record similar to the one illustrated in Exhibit 11, using the first-in, first-out (FIFO) method.
2. Record the inventory, purchases, and cost of goods sold data in a perpetual inventory record similar to the one illustrated in Exhibit 12, using the last-in, first-out (LIFO) method.
3. Record the inventory, purchases, and cost of goods sold data in a perpetual inventory record similar to the one illustrated in Exhibit 13, using the weighted average cost method.
4. Summarize the results of (1)–(3) in the following table:

	Cost Methods		
	FIFO	Weighted Average	LIFO
Sales			
Cost of goods sold			
Gross profit			
inventory, Mar. 31			

5. Will the first-in, first-out (FIFO) method always yield the highest inventory, lowest cost of goods sold, and highest gross profit?

Metric-Based Analysis

MBA 7-1 FIFO and LIFO

Obj. 3

Assuming periods of rising prices, indicate the effects of selecting FIFO and LIFO on the liquidity metric days' sales in inventory and profitability metric return on sales.

MBA 7-2 Lower of cost or market

Obj. 3

Using data in E7-9, indicate the effects of valuing inventory using lower of cost or market on the liquidity metric days' sales in inventory and profitability metric return on sales.

MBA 7-3 Inventory turnover

Obj. 6

The following data (in millions) were adapted from recent financial statements of **Apple Inc. (AAPL)**.

	Year 2	Year 1
Sales	$260,174	$265,595
Cost of goods sold	161,782	163,756
Operating income	63,930	70,898
Average inventory	4,031	4,406

1. Compute the inventory turnover for Years 1 and 2. Round to two decimal places.
2. Compute days' sales in inventory for Years 1 and 2. Round to nearest day.
3. Compute the return on sales for Years 1 and 2. Round to one decimal place.
4. Comment on Apple's operations based upon the results in parts (1), (2), and (3).

Obj. 6

MBA 7-4 Inventory turnover

The following data (in millions) were adapted from recent financial statements of HP Inc. (HPQ), formerly Hewlett-Packard Company.

	Year 2	Year 1
Sales	$58,756	$58,472
Cost of goods sold	47,586	47,803
Operating income	3,877	3,705
Average inventory	5,898	5,924

1. Compute the inventory turnover for Years 1 and 2. Round to two decimal places.
2. Compute days' sales in inventory for Years 1 and 2. Round to nearest day.
3. Compute the return on sales for Years 1 and 2. Round to one decimal place.
4. Comment on HP's operations based upon the results in parts (1), (2), and (3).

Obj. 6

MBA 7-5 Inventory turnover

Compare and comment on Apple and HP using the results of MBA 7-3 and MBA 7-4.

Obj. 6

MBA 7-6 Inventory Turnover

The following data (in millions) were adapted from recent financial statements of CVS Health Corporation (CVS):

	Year 2	Year 1
Sales	$256,766	$194,579
Cost of goods sold	158,719	156,447
Operating income	12,467	10,170
Average inventory	16,983	15,873

1. Compute the inventory turnover for Years 1 and 2. Round to two decimal places.
2. Compute the days' sales in inventory for Years 1 and 2. Round to the nearest day.
3. Compute the return on sales for Years 1 and 2. Round to one decimal place.
4. Comment on CVS's operations based upon the results in parts (1), (2), and (3).

Obj. 6

MBA 7-7 Inventory turnover

The following data (in millions) were adapted from recent financial statements of The Kroger Co. (KR) and Walmart Inc. (WMT):

	Kroger	Walmart
Sales	$122,286	$523,964
Cost of goods sold	95,294	394,605
Operating income	2,427	20,568
Inventory:		
Beginning of year	7,084	44,435
End of year	6,846	44,269

1. Compute the inventory turnover for Kroger and Walmart. Round to two decimal places.
2. Compute the days' sales in inventory for Kroger and Walmart. Round to nearest day.
3. Compute the return on sales for Kroger and Walmart. Round to one decimal place.
4. Comment on and explain any differences in Kroger's and Walmart's management of inventories based upon the results in parts (1), (2), and (3).

Cases

Case 7-1 Ethics and professional conduct in business

ETHICS

Mitchell Co. is experiencing a decrease in sales and operating income for the fiscal year ending December 31, 20Y1. Gene Lumpkin, controller of Mitchell Co., has suggested that all orders received before the end of the fiscal year be shipped by midnight, December 31, 20Y1, even if the shipping department must work overtime. Since Mitchell Co. ships all merchandise FOB shipping point, it would record all such shipments as sales for the year ending December 31, 20Y1, thereby offsetting some of the decreases in sales and operating income.

Discuss whether Gene Lumpkin is behaving in a professional manner.

Case 7-2 Ethics and professional conduct in business

Sizemo Elektroniks sells semiconductors that are used in games and small toys. The company has been extremely successful in recent years, recording an increase in earnings each of the past six quarters. At the end of the current quarter, Jay Shulz, the company's staff accountant, calculated the ending inventory for the semiconductors and was surprised to find that the quantity of the Hayden 537X model had not changed during the quarter. Jay confirmed his calculation with the inventory control manager, who indicated that sales of the Hayden 537X had stopped when the Hayden 637X semiconductor was released early in the quarter. Jay researched the issue further and found that the Hayden 637X semiconductor has the same applications as the Hayden 537X, but has more computing power and a lower cost than the 537X. Jay emailed this information to Tina Vereen, the chief financial officer, and recommended that the company apply the lower-of-cost-or-market method to the Hayden 537X semiconductors in inventory. Later that day, Tina emailed Jay back instructing him not to apply the lower-of-cost-or-market method to the 537X inventory because "the company is under considerable pressure to maintain its track record of earnings growth, and a lower-of-cost-or-market adjustment would result in a significant decline in earnings this quarter." Reluctantly, Jay followed Tina's instructions.

Evaluate the decision not to apply the lower-of-cost-or-market method in the current quarter.

1. Who benefits from this decision?
2. Who is harmed by this decision?
3. Are Jay and Tina acting in an ethical manner? Explain.

Case 7-3 LIFO and inventory flow

The following is an excerpt from a conversation between Evan Eberhard, the warehouse manager for Greenbriar Wholesale Co., and its accountant, Marty Hayes. Greenbriar operates a large regional warehouse that supplies produce and other grocery products to grocery stores in smaller communities.

Evan: Marty, can you explain what's going on here with these monthly statements?

Marty: Sure, Evan. How can I help you?

Evan: I don't understand this last-in, first-out inventory procedure. It just doesn't make sense.

Marty: Well, what it means is that we assume that the last goods we receive are the first ones sold. So the inventory is made up of the items we purchased first.

Evan: Yes, but that's my problem. It doesn't work that way! We always distribute the oldest produce first. Some of that produce is perishable! We can't keep any of it very long or it'll spoil.

Marty: Evan, you don't understand. We only assume that the products we distribute are the last ones received. We don't actually have to distribute the goods in this way.

Evan: I always thought that accounting was supposed to show what really happened. It all sounds like "make believe" to me! Why not report what really happens?

Respond to Evan's concerns.

Case 7-4 Inventory cost flow methods

Golden Eagle Company began operations on April 1 by selling a single product. Data on purchases and sales for the year are as follows:

Purchases:

Date	Units Purchased	Unit Cost	Total Cost
April 6	31,000	$36.60	$1,134,600
May 18	33,000	39.00	1,287,000
June 6	40,000	39.60	1,584,000
July 10	40,000	42.00	1,680,000
August 10	27,200	42.75	1,162,800
October 25	12,800	43.50	556,800
November 4	8,000	44.85	358,800
December 10	8,000	48.00	384,000
	200,000		$8,148,000

Sales:

April	16,000 units
May	16,000
June	20,000
July	24,000
August	28,000
September	28,000
October	18,000
November	10,000
December	8,000
Total units	168,000
Total sales	$10,000,000

The president of the company, Connie Kilmer, has asked for your advice on which inventory cost flow method should be used for the 32,000-unit physical inventory that was taken on December 31. The company plans to expand its product line in the future and uses the periodic inventory system.

Write a brief memo to Ms. Kilmer comparing and contrasting the LIFO and FIFO inventory cost flow methods and their potential impacts on the company's financial statements.

Case 7-5 Data Analytics: Out-of-stock items

Acme Auto Parts, Inc. sells automobile parts, maintenance items, and accessories to repair garages and service stations. A major focus of Acme Auto's business strategy is to provide customers with their ordered parts no later than 48 hours from when an order is received. Recently, Acme Auto has received complaints from customers about delays in receiving parts. The sales manager of Acme Auto has requested an analysis of customer orders for the week of November 11–15.

1. Prepare the following for the manager:
   a. A list of the total out-of-stock items by product from largest to smallest.
   b. A bar chart of the quantity of out-of-stock items by day of the week.
2. Explain how the sales manager can use the preceding information.

Go to CengageNOWv2 to complete this assignment.

The annual report (10-K) assignment for this chapter is in Appendix B: Nike Annual Report, Chapter 7.

Answers to Self-Examination Questions

1. **B** When a retailer sells inventory, the related cost is moved from the merchandise inventory account reported on the balance sheet to cost of goods on the income statement. Cost of goods sold is an expense account.
2. **A** The FIFO method (answer A) of costing is based on the assumption that costs should be charged against revenue in the order in which they were incurred (first-in, first-out).
3. **D** The FIFO method of costing is based on the assumption that costs should be charged against revenue in the order in which they were incurred (first-in, first-out). Thus, the most recent costs are assigned to inventory. The 35 units would be assigned a unit cost of $23 (answer D).
4. **B** When the price level is steadily rising, the earlier unit costs are lower than recent unit costs. Under the FIFO method (answer B), these earlier costs are matched against revenue to yield the highest possible net income.
5. **D** The understatement of inventory by $7,500 at the end of the year will cause the cost of goods sold for the year to be overstated by $7,500, the gross profit for the year to be understated by $7,500, next year's beginning inventory to be understated by $7,500, and the net income for the year to be understated by $7,500 (answer D).

Chapter 8

Long-Term Operating Assets

What's Covered:

Topics: Fixed Assets, Natural Resources, and Intangible Assets

Fixed Assets
- Nature (Obj. 1)
- Depreciation (Obj. 2)
- Repairs and improvements (Obj. 2)
- Disposal (Obj. 3)

Natural Resources
- Cost (Obj. 4)
- Depletion (Obj. 4)

Intangible Assets
- Patents, copyrights, trademarks, goodwill (Obj. 5)
- Amortization and impairment (Obj. 5)

Financial Reporting
- Income statement (Obj. 6)
- Balance sheet (Obj. 6)

Metric-Based Analysis
- Transactions:
  - Liquidity: Free cash flow (Obj. 1, 2, 3, 4, 5)
  - Profitability: Asset turnover (Obj. 1, 2, 3, 4, 5)
- Financial Statements:
  - Asset turnover (Obj. 7)

Learning Objectives

Obj.1 Define, classify, and account for the cost of fixed assets.

Obj.2 Compute depreciation using the straight-line and double-declining-balance methods.

Obj.3 Describe the accounting for the disposal of fixed assets.

Obj.4 Describe the accounting for depletion of natural resources.

Obj.5 Describe the accounting for intangible assets.

Obj.6 Describe the reporting of fixed assets, natural resources, and intangible assets on the income statement and balance sheet.

Obj.7 Describe and illustrate asset turnover in assessing a company's operating results.

Chapter Metrics

Use the following metrics to analyze transactions and financial statements:

TRANSACTIONS
- Liquidity: Free Cash Flow
- Profitability: Asset Turnover

FINANCIAL STATEMENTS
- Asset Turnover

Chipotle Mexican Grill Inc.

Jonathan Weiss/Shutterstock.com

Steve Ells is a graduate of Boulder High School, University of Colorado (majoring in Art History), and the Culinary Institute of America. After spending several years working as a cook in San Francisco, he returned to Colorado with a dream of opening a high-end Denver restaurant. In 1993, he opened a small restaurant serving burritos near the University of Denver with hopes of earning enough to finance his dream of a "high-end, fine-dining" restaurant. He never fulfilled his dream. Instead, this first restaurant was the start of what is now **Chipotle Mexican Grill (CMG)**.

Currently, Chipotle (pronounced chi-POAT-lay) has over 1,700 restaurants worldwide and has expanded its operations to include ShopHouse Southeast Asian Kitchen and Pizzeria Locale restaurants. Chipotle's overriding business philosophy is "Food With Integrity" using carefully selected, quality ingredients while avoiding genetically modified ingredients. Consistent with its philosophy of "a few things, thousands of ways," it serves a simple menu including burritos, burrito bowls (without a tortilla), tacos, and salads. In addition, Chipotle implemented a restaurateur training program for its "crew members" that emphasizes a high-energy, conscientious, and motivated employee environment.

Within the United States, a new Chipotle restaurant costs approximately $800,000 to start. To finance its early expansion, Ells solicited funding from **McDonald's Corp. (MCD)**, which at the time was attempting to diversify its operations. In 2006 Chipotle offered its stock to the public and McDonald's sold its shares. In the coming years, Chipotle plans to open hundreds of new restaurants.

This chapter discusses the accounting for the costs of fixed assets, such as Chipotle's restaurants. In addition, methods of depreciating fixed asset costs are discussed. Finally, the accounting for the disposal of fixed assets as well as the accounting for natural resources and intangible assets, such as the trademark "Chipotle," are discussed.

Sources: Chipotle Mexican Grill 10-K; "Steve Ells, Chipotle Founder, Reflects on McDonald's, GMOs And The First 20 Years of His Chain," Joe Satran, Huffingtonpost.com, July 12, 2013; https://chipotle.com/company.

Nature of Fixed Assets

Objective 1
Define, classify, and account for the cost of fixed assets.

Fixed assets are long-term or relatively permanent assets such as equipment, machinery, buildings, and land. Other descriptive titles for fixed assets are *plant assets* or *property, plant, and equipment*. Fixed assets have the following characteristics:

- They exist physically and thus are *tangible* assets.
- They are owned and used by the company in its normal operations.
- They are not offered for sale as part of normal operations.

Exhibit 1 shows the percent of fixed assets to total assets for some select companies. As shown in Exhibit 1, fixed assets are often a significant portion of the total assets of a company.

Exhibit 1
Fixed Assets as a Percent of Total Assets—Selected Companies

	Fixed Assets as a Percent of Total Assets
Alcoa Corporation (AA)	54%
Exxon Mobil Corporation (XOM)	72
Hyatt Hotels Corporation (H)	47
The Kroger Co. (KR)	57
Starbucks Corporation (SBUX)	33
Target Corporation (TGT)	67
United Parcel Service, Inc. (UPS)	58
Verizon Communications Inc. (VZ)	39
Walmart Inc. (WMT)	54

Chipotle Connection

On a recent balance sheet, property, plant, and equipment made up 29% of Chipotle's total assets.

Classifying Costs

A cost that has been incurred may be classified as a fixed asset, an investment, or an expense. Exhibit 2 shows how to determine the proper classification of a cost and thus how it should be recorded.

Exhibit 2
Classifying Costs

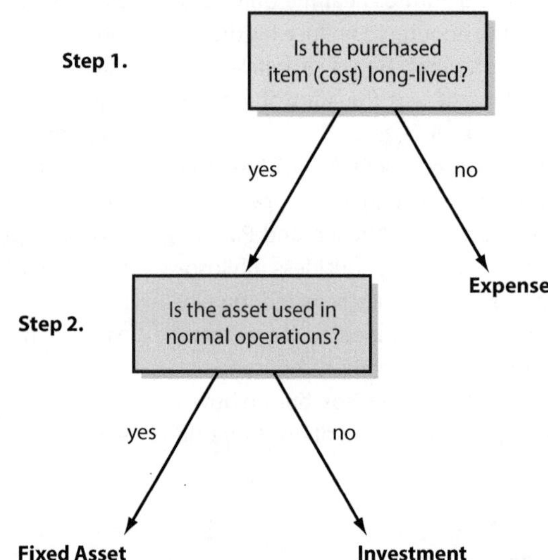

As shown in Exhibit 2, classifying a cost involves the following steps:

Step 1. Is the purchased item (cost) long-lived?
If *yes*, the cost of the item is classified as an asset on the balance sheet as either a fixed asset or an investment. Proceed to Step 2.
If *no*, the item is classified and recorded as an *expense*.

Step 2. Is the asset used in normal operations?
If *yes*, the asset is classified and recorded as a *fixed asset*.
If *no*, the asset is classified and recorded as an *investment*.

Costs that are classified and recorded as fixed assets include the purchase of land, buildings, or equipment. Such assets normally last more than a year and are used in normal operations. However, standby equipment for use during peak periods or when other equipment breaks down is still classified as a fixed asset even though it is not used very often. In contrast, fixed assets that have been abandoned or are no longer used in operations are not fixed assets.

Although fixed assets may be sold, they should not be offered for sale as part of normal operations. For example, cars and trucks offered for sale by an automotive dealership are not fixed assets of the dealership. On the other hand, a tow truck used in the normal operations of the dealership is a fixed asset of the dealership.

Investments are long-lived assets that are not used in the normal operations and are held for future resale. Such assets are reported on the balance sheet in a section entitled *Investments*. For example, undeveloped land acquired for future resale would be classified and reported as an investment.

The Cost of Fixed Assets

The costs of acquiring fixed assets include all amounts spent to get the asset in place and ready for use. For example, freight costs and the costs of installing equipment are part of the asset's total cost.

Exhibit 3 summarizes some of the common costs of acquiring fixed assets. These costs are recorded by increasing the related fixed asset account, such as Building, Machinery and Equipment, Land,[1] and Land Improvements.

Exhibit 3 Costs of Acquiring Fixed Assets

Building

- Architects' fees
- Engineers' fees
- Insurance costs incurred during construction
- Interest on money borrowed to finance construction
- Walkways to and around the building
- Sales taxes
- Repairs (purchase of existing building)
- Reconditioning (purchase of existing building)
- Modifying for use
- Permits from government agencies

Machinery & Equipment

- Sales taxes
- Freight
- Installation
- Repairs (purchase of used equipment)
- Reconditioning (purchase of used equipment)
- Insurance while in transit
- Assembly
- Modifying for use
- Testing for use
- Permits from government agencies

Land & Land Improvements

- Purchase price
- Sales taxes
- Permits from government agencies
- Broker's commissions
- Title fees
- Surveying fees
- Delinquent real estate taxes
- Removing unwanted buildings, less any salvage
- Grading and leveling
- Paving a public street bordering the land
- Trees and shrubs
- Paved parking areas
- Outdoor lighting
- Fences

Only costs necessary for preparing the fixed asset for use are included as a cost of the asset. Unnecessary costs that do not increase the asset's usefulness are recorded as an expense. For example, the following costs are recorded as an expense:

- Vandalism
- Mistakes in installation
- Uninsured theft
- Damage during unpacking and installing
- Fines for not obtaining proper permits from governmental agencies

To illustrate, assume that Southwest Needle Inc. purchased the following equipment on June 5 and that all costs were paid in cash.

Purchase price	$30,000
Freight costs (FOB shipping point)	1,100
Installation costs	2,750 *

* Includes cost of $900 incurred to repair equipment damaged during installation.

The equipment would be recorded at a cost of $32,950 ($30,000 + $1,100 + $2,750 − $900). The cost of the $900 damage incurred during installation is recorded as an expense.

1. As discussed here, land is assumed to be used only as a location or site and not for its mineral deposits or other natural resources.

The effects of purchasing the equipment on the financial statements are as follows:

Financial Statement Effects

BALANCE SHEET

	Assets		=	Liabilities	+	Stockholders' Equity
	Cash	**+ Equipment**	**=**			**Retained Earnings**
June 5.	(33,850)	32,950				(900)

STATEMENT OF CASH FLOWS

June 5. Investing	(32,950)
5. Operating	(900)

INCOME STATEMENT

June 5. Misc. expense	(900)

Transaction Metric Effects

The effects of transactions on liquidity and profitability metrics are also illustrated throughout this chapter. **Free cash flow** is used as the liquidity metric and is computed as follows:

Free Cash Flow = Operating Cash Flows – Investing Cash Flows

Operating cash flows (cash flows from operating activities) and investing cash flows (cash flows used for investing activities) are reported on the statement of cash flows. Free cash flow represents the cash available after maintaining and expanding current operating capacity.

Asset turnover is used as the profitability metric and is computed as follows:

$$\text{Asset Turnover} = \frac{\textbf{Sales}}{\textbf{Average Long-Term Operating Assets}}$$

Long-term operating assets consist of property, plant, and equipment (net of accumulated depreciation) plus natural resources and intangible assets. Asset turnover measures how efficiently a company is using its operating assets to generate sales. The higher the asset turnover the more efficient assets are being used.

The effects of purchasing the above equipment on the liquidity and profitability metrics are as follows:

LIQUIDITY

Free Cash Flow	$(33,850)

PROFITABILITY

Asset Turnover	Decrease

Since the equipment purchase increases investing cash flows, free cash flow decreases. Since equipment increases average long-term operating assets with no increase in sales, asset turnover decreases.

A company may incur costs associated with constructing a fixed asset such as a new building. The direct costs incurred in the construction, such as labor and materials, should be capitalized by increasing an account entitled Construction in Progress. When the construction is complete, the costs are reclassified by decreasing Construction in Progress and increasing the proper fixed asset account such as Building. For some companies, construction in progress can be significant.

Fixed Asset Leases

A **lease** is a contract for the use of an asset for a period of time. Leases are often used in business. For example, automobiles, computers, medical equipment, buildings, and airplanes are often leased.

The two parties to a lease contract are as follows:

- The *lessor* is the party who owns the asset.
- The *lessee* is the party to whom the rights to use the asset are granted by the lessor.

Under a lease contract, the lessee pays rent on a periodic basis for the lease term. An advantage of leasing an asset is that the lessee has use of the asset without having to buy the asset. In addition, the lessor may be responsible for expenses, such as maintenance and repair costs. Finally, the risk that the asset may become obsolete is mitigated.

The accounting for leases is complex.[2] For some long-term leases, generally accepted accounting principles (GAAP) require the recording of assets and liabilities. However, most short-term leases, called operating leases, require monthly payments that are recorded as Rent Expense. In earlier chapters and throughout the remainder of this text, we assume that all lease (rental) agreements are short-term and record lease payments as Rent Expense. Regardless of the type of lease, lease terms, such as renewal options, are normally disclosed in the notes to the financial statements.

Chipotle leases its main office in Denver as well as almost all the properties on which its restaurants are located. The lease terms are from five to ten years with two or more five-year renewal extensions.

Accounting for Depreciation

Objective 2
Compute depreciation using the straight-line and double-declining-balance methods.

Fixed assets, with the exception of land, lose their ability, over time, to provide services. Thus, the cost of fixed assets such as equipment and buildings should be recorded as an expense over their useful lives. This periodic recording of the cost of fixed assets as an expense is called **depreciation**. Because land has an unlimited life, it is not depreciated.[3]

The adjustment to record depreciation was illustrated in earlier chapters. This adjustment increases *Depreciation Expense* and a *contra asset* account entitled *Accumulated Depreciation* or *Allowance for Depreciation*. The use of a contra asset account allows the original cost to remain unchanged in the fixed asset account.

Depreciation can be caused by physical or functional factors.

- *Physical depreciation* factors include wear and tear during use or from exposure to weather.
- *Functional depreciation* factors include obsolescence and changes in customer needs that cause the asset to no longer provide services for which it was intended. For example, equipment may become obsolete due to changing technology.

Two common misunderstandings that exist about *depreciation* as used in accounting include:

- Depreciation does not measure a decline in the market value of a fixed asset. Instead, depreciation is an allocation of a fixed asset's cost to expense over the asset's useful life. Thus, the **book value of a fixed asset** (cost less accumulated depreciation) usually

2. Accounting Standards Update, *Leases (Topic 842)*, Financial Accounting Standards Board, 2016.
3. Land on which natural resources are extracted is discussed later in this chapter.

does not agree with the asset's market value. This is justified in accounting because a fixed asset is for use in a company's operations rather than for resale.

- Depreciation does not provide cash to replace fixed assets as they wear out. This misunderstanding may occur because depreciation, unlike most expenses, does not require an outlay of cash when it is recorded.

Factors in Computing Depreciation Expense

Three factors determine the depreciation expense for a fixed asset. These three factors are as follows:

- The asset's initial cost
- The asset's expected useful life
- The asset's estimated residual value

The **initial cost of a fixed asset** is the purchase price of the asset plus all costs to obtain and ready it for use. This initial cost is determined using the concepts discussed and illustrated earlier in this chapter.

The **expected useful life** of a fixed asset is estimated at the time the asset is placed into service. Estimates of expected useful lives are available from industry trade associations. The Internal Revenue Service also publishes guidelines for useful lives, which may be helpful for financial reporting purposes. However, it is not uncommon for different companies to use a different useful life for similar assets.

Chipotle uses estimated useful lives of 4–7 years for furniture and fixtures, and 3–10 years for equipment.

The **residual value of a fixed asset** is the estimated value of the asset at the end of its useful life. It is estimated at the time the asset is placed into service. Residual value is sometimes referred to as *scrap value*, *salvage value*, or *trade-in value*.

The difference between a fixed asset's initial cost and its residual value is called the asset's **depreciable cost**. The depreciable cost is the amount of the asset's cost that is allocated over its useful life as depreciation expense. If a fixed asset has no residual value, then its entire cost should be allocated to depreciation.

To illustrate, assume a used delivery van was purchased on January 1, details of which are given as follows:

Initial cost	$24,000
Expected useful life	5 years
Estimated residual value	$2,000

Exhibit 4 shows the relationship among the van's initial cost, residual value, depreciable cost, expected useful life, and depreciation expense.

The two depreciation methods often used are:

1. Straight-line
2. Double-declining-balance

It is not necessary that a company use one method of computing depreciation for all of its fixed assets. For example, a company may use one method for depreciating equipment and another method for depreciating buildings. A company may also use different methods for determining income and property taxes.

Exhibit 4 Depreciation

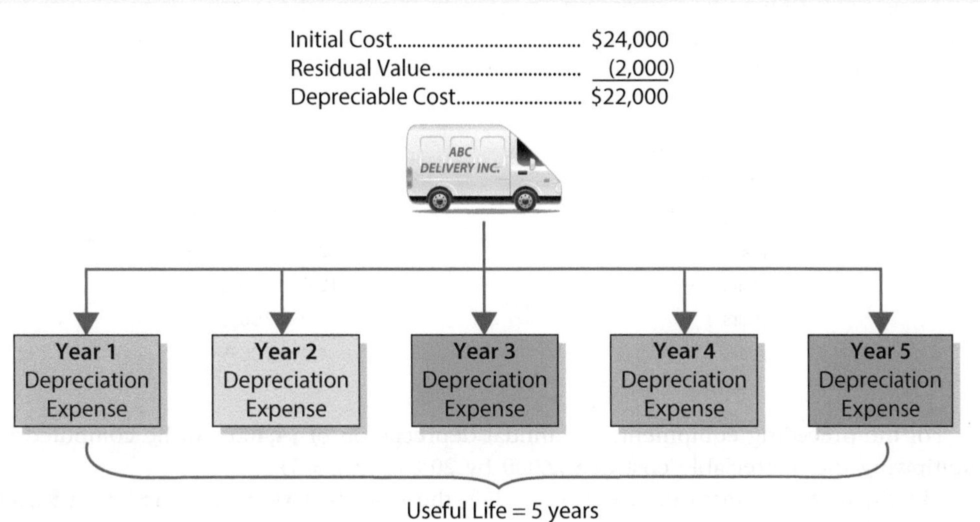

Straight-Line Method

The **straight-line method** provides for the same amount of depreciation expense for each year of the asset's useful life. The straight-line method is the most widely used depreciation method.

To illustrate, assume that the van was purchased on January 1 with details as follows:

Initial cost	$24,000
Expected useful life	5 years
Estimated residual value	$2,000

The annual straight-line depreciation of $4,400 is computed as follows:

$$\textbf{Annual Depreciation} = \frac{\textbf{Cost} - \textbf{Residual Value}}{\textbf{Useful Life}} = \frac{\$24{,}000 - \$2{,}000}{5 \textbf{ Years}} = \$4{,}400$$

The straight-line method reports the same amount of depreciation expense each year, as illustrated in Exhibit 5.

Exhibit 5 Straight-Line Method

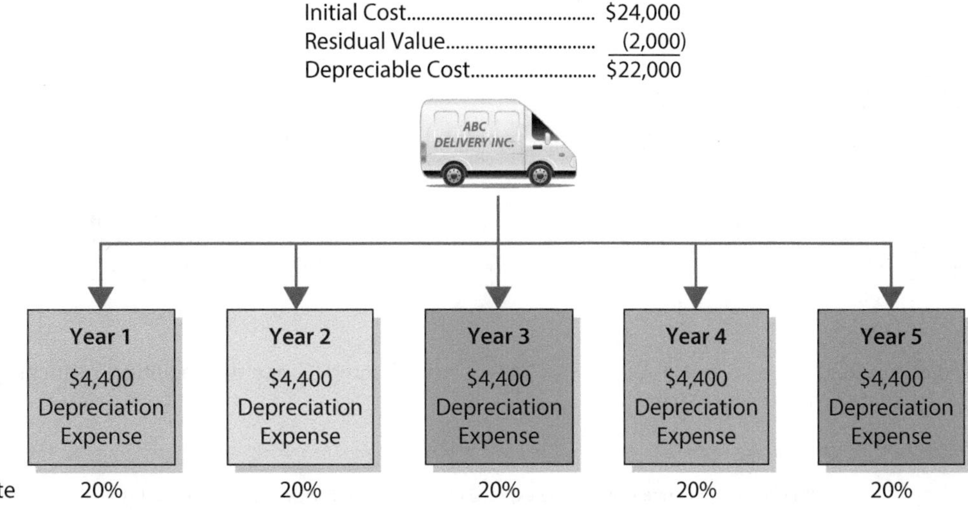

Computing straight-line depreciation may be simplified by converting the annual depreciation to a percentage of depreciable cost.[4] The straight-line percentage is determined by dividing 100% by the number of years of expected useful life, as follows:

Expected Years of Useful Life	Straight-Line Percentage
5 years	20.0% (100% ÷ 5)
8 years	12.5% (100% ÷ 8)
10 years	10.0% (100% ÷ 10)
20 years	5.0% (100% ÷ 20)
25 years	4.0% (100% ÷ 25)

For the preceding equipment, the annual depreciation of $4,400 can be computed by multiplying the depreciable cost of $22,000 by 20% (100% ÷ 5).

The financial statement effects of recording the van's first year depreciation of $4,400 on December 31 are as follows:

Financial Statement Effects

BALANCE SHEET

	Assets			=	Liabilities	+	Stockholders' Equity
	Equipment	**–**	**Acc. Depr.— Equip.**	**=**			**Retained Earnings**
Dec. 31.			(4,400)				(4,400)

STATEMENT OF CASH FLOWS

INCOME STATEMENT

Dec. 31. Depr. expense	(4,400)

The book value of the van at the end of the first year is $19,600 as follows:

Equipment	$24,000
Accumulated depreciation	(4,400)
Book value	$19,600

Transaction Metric Effects

The effects of the depreciation on the liquidity and profitability metrics are as follows:

LIQUIDITY

Free Cash Flow	No Effect

PROFITABILITY

Asset Turnover	Increase

Since depreciation does not affect cash, free cash flow is not affected. Since depreciation reduces the book value of the van, the asset turnover increases.

4. The depreciation rate may also be expressed as a fraction. For example, the annual straight-line rate for an asset with a three-year useful life is 1/3.

As illustrated, the straight-line method is simple to use. When an asset's revenues are about the same from period to period, straight-line depreciation provides a good matching of depreciation expense with the revenues generated by the asset.

Chipotle uses the straight-line method of depreciation. *Chipotle Connection*

Double-Declining-Balance Method

The **double-declining-balance method** provides for a declining periodic expense over the expected useful life of the asset. The double-declining-balance method is applied in three steps.

Step 1. Determine the straight-line percentage using the expected useful life.

Step 2. Determine the double-declining-balance rate by multiplying the straight-line rate from Step 1 by two.

Step 3. Compute the depreciation expense by multiplying the double-declining-balance rate from Step 2 by the book value of the asset.

To illustrate, the van purchased in the preceding example is used to compute double-declining-balance depreciation. For the first year, the depreciation is $9,600, determined as follows:

Step 1. Straight-line percentage = 20% (100% ÷ 5)

Step 2. Double-declining-balance rate = 40% (20% × 2)

Step 3. Depreciation expense = $9,600 ($24,000 × 40%)

For the first year, the book value of the equipment is its initial cost of $24,000. After the first year, the book value (cost minus accumulated depreciation) declines and thus the depreciation also declines. The double-declining-balance depreciation for the full five-year life of the equipment is as follows:

Year	Cost	Acc. Depr. at Beginning of Year	Book Value at Beginning of Year		Double-Declining-Balance Rate	Depreciation for Year	Book Value at End of Year
1	$24,000		$24,000.00	×	40%	$9,600.00	$14,400.00
2	24,000	$ 9,600.00	14,400.00	×	40%	5,760.00	8,640.00
3	24,000	15,360.00	8,640.00	×	40%	3,456.00	5,184.00
4	24,000	18,816.00	5,184.00	×	40%	2,073.60	3,110.40
5	24,000	20,889.60	3,110.40	×	—	1,110.40	2,000.00

When the double-declining-balance method is used, the estimated residual value is *not* considered. However, the asset should not be depreciated below its estimated residual value. In the above example, the estimated residual value was $2,000. Therefore, the depreciation for the fifth year is $1,110.40 ($3,110.40 − $2,000.00) instead of $1,244.16 (40% × $3,110.40).

Exhibit 6 illustrates the depreciation expense and book value of the van over its five-year life using the double-declining-balance method. As shown in Exhibit 6, the double-declining-balance method has higher depreciation in the first year of the asset's life, followed by declining depreciation amounts. For this reason, the double-declining-balance method is called an **accelerated depreciation method**.

Exhibit 6 Double-Declining-Balance Method

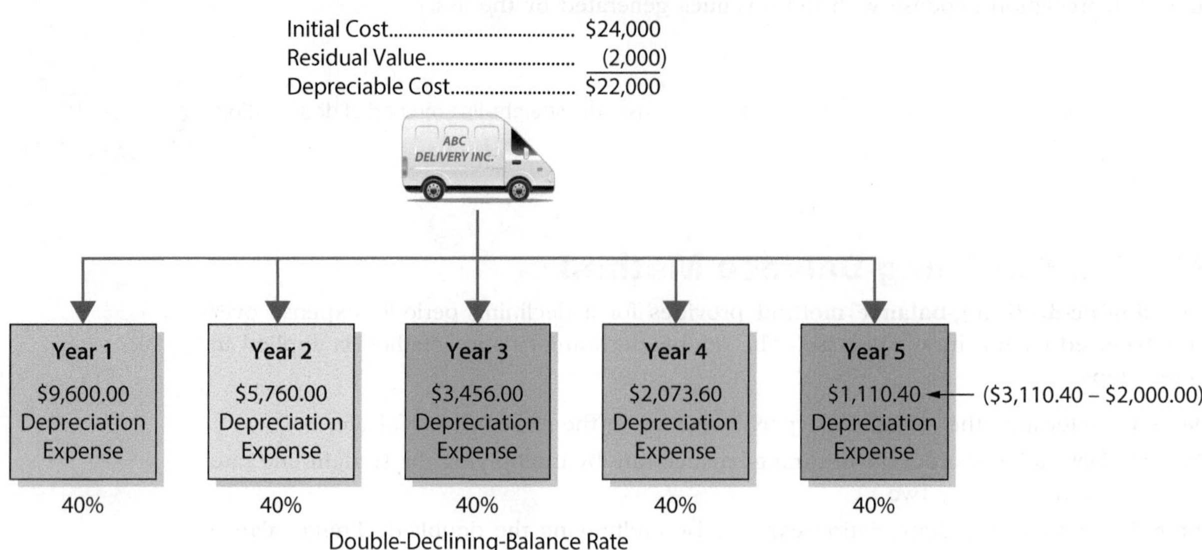

Except for the amount of depreciation, the effects of recording double-declining-balance depreciation on the financial statements are the same as those illustrated for the straight-line method. The liquidity and profitability metric effects are also the same.

An asset's revenues are often greater in the early years of its use than in later years. In such cases, the double-declining-balance method provides a good matching of depreciation expense with the asset's revenues.

Comparing Depreciation Methods

The depreciation methods are summarized in Exhibit 7. Both methods allocate a portion of the total cost of an asset to an accounting period, while never depreciating an asset below its residual value. The straight-line method provides for the same periodic amounts of depreciation expense over the life of the asset. The double-declining-balance method provides for a higher depreciation amount in the first year of the asset's use, followed by declining amounts.

Exhibit 7 Summary of Depreciation Methods

Method	Useful Life	Depreciable Cost	Depreciation Rate	Depreciation Expense
Straight-line	Years	Cost less residual value	Straight-line rate*	Constant
Double-declining-balance	Years	Declining book value, but not below residual value	Straight-line rate * × 2	Declining

*Straight-Line Rate = (100% ÷ Useful Life)

Exhibit 8 illustrates depreciation expense for each depreciation method over the five-year life of the van.

Exhibit 8
Comparing Depreciation Methods

Year	Depreciation Expense	
	Straight-Line Method	Double-Declining-Balance Method
1	$ 4,400.00*	$ 9,600.00 ($24,000 × 40%)
2	4,400.00	5,760.00 ($14,400 × 40%)
3	4,400.00	3,456.00 ($8,640 × 40%)
4	4,400.00	2,073.60 ($5,184 × 40%)
5	4,400.00	1,110.40**
Total	$22,000.00	$22,000.00

*$4,400 = ($24,000 − $2,000) ÷ 5 years
**$3,110.40 − $2,000.00 because the equipment cannot be depreciated below its residual value.

Partial Year Depreciation

A fixed asset may be purchased and placed in service other than the first month of an accounting period. In such cases, depreciation is prorated based on the month the asset is placed in service. For example, assume an asset is placed in service on March 1. For an accounting period ending December 31, depreciation would be computed (prorated) for 10 months (March 1 to December 31).

Assets may also be placed in service other than the first day of a month. In such cases, assets placed in service during the first half of a month are normally treated as having been purchased on the first day of *that* month. Likewise, asset purchases during the second half of a month are treated as having been purchased on the first day of *the next* month.

Straight-Line Method Under the straight-line method, depreciation is prorated based on the number of months the asset is in service. To illustrate, assume the van in the preceding illustration was purchased on October 1 instead of January 1. The first-year depreciation would be based upon three months (October, November, and December). Thus, the first-year depreciation would be $1,100, computed as follows:

$$\text{Annual Depreciation} = (\$22{,}000 - \$2{,}000) \div 5 \text{ years} = \$4{,}400$$
$$\text{First-Year Depreciation} = \$4{,}400 \times (3 \div 12) = \$1{,}100$$

The second year's depreciation would be for a full year and would be $4,400.

Double-Declining-Balance Method Like the straight-line method, if an asset is used for only part of a year, the annual double-declining-balance depreciation is prorated based on the number of months the asset is in service. To illustrate, assume the van was purchased on October 1 instead of January 1. The first-year depreciation would be based upon three months (October, November, and December). First-year depreciation would be $2,400, computed as follows:

$$\text{Double-Declining Balance Rate} = (100 \div 5) \times 2 = 40\%$$
$$\text{First-Year Annual Depreciation} = \$24{,}000 \times 40\% = \$9{,}600$$
$$\text{First-Year Partial Depreciation} = \$9{,}600 \times (3 \div 12) = \$2{,}400$$

The second-year depreciation would be computed by multiplying the book value on January 1 of the second year by the double-declining-balance rate. To illustrate, assume partial depreciation on the van of $2,400 was recorded on December 31. Thus, the book value of the van on January 1 of the second year is $21,600 ($24,000 − $2,400). The second-year depreciation of $8,640 is computed as follows:

$$\text{Second-Year Annual Depreciation} = \$21{,}600 \times 40\% = \$8{,}640$$

Maintenance, Repair, and Improvement Costs

After a fixed asset has been purchased and placed into service, additional costs are often incurred. These costs include the following:

- Routine maintenance and repairs
- Extraordinary repairs
- Improvements

Routine maintenance and repair costs are often referred to as **revenue expenditures**. This is because these costs primarily benefit the current period. Extraordinary repairs and improvement costs are often referred to as **capital expenditures**. The benefits of these costs normally extend to multiple periods.

Routine Maintenance and Repairs Costs related to the routine maintenance and repairs are recorded as a revenue expenditure by increasing the repairs and maintenance expense account.

Extraordinary Repairs Costs incurred to extend the asset's useful life are recorded as a capital expenditure by decreasing the asset's accumulated depreciation account.

Improvements Costs incurred to improve the asset are recorded as a capital expenditure by increasing the fixed asset account.

To illustrate, assume that on January 8 of Year 2, the van used in the preceding examples incurred the following costs:

Tune-up engine and oil change	$ 300
Repaired transmission	900
Installed new hydraulic lift	1,500

The tune-up and oil change costs of $300 are recorded as an increase to Repairs and Maintenance Expense. The cost of repairing the transmission of $900 is recorded as a decrease in Accumulated Depreciation. The cost of installing the new hydraulic lift of $1,500 is recorded as an increase to the fixed asset account Delivery Van.[5]

The effects on the financial statements of incurring the preceding costs are as follows:

Financial Statement Effects

BALANCE SHEET

	Assets			= Liabilities +	Stockholders' Equity
	Cash +	**Delivery Van**	– **Acc. Depr.— Delivery Van**	=	**Retained Earnings**
Jan. 8.	(2,700)	1,500	900		(300)

STATEMENT OF CASH FLOWS

Jan. 8. Investing	(2,400)
8. Operating	(300)

INCOME STATEMENT

Jan. 8. Repairs & maint. exp.	(300)

5. The costs of installing the lift (increase in Delivery Van) and repairing the transmission (decrease in Acc. Depr.) will change (revise) the depreciation expense in future years.

Transaction Metric Effects

The effects of the costs on liquidity and profitability metrics are as follows:

LIQUIDITY	
Free Cash Flow	$(2,700)

PROFITABILITY	
Asset Turnover	Decrease

Since the operating cash flows decrease by $300 and the investing cash flows increase by $2,400, the free cash flow decreases by $2,700. Since the costs of the lift and transmission increase the book value of the van, asset turnover will decrease.

Chipotle Connection

In its financial statements, **Chipotle** reports that "expenditures for major renewals or improvements are capitalized *(treated as capital expenditures)* while expenditures for minor replacements, maintenance, and repairs are expensed (treated as revenue expenditures) as incurred."

The accounting for revenue and capital expenditures is summarized in Exhibit 9.

Exhibit 9
Revenue and Capital Expenditures

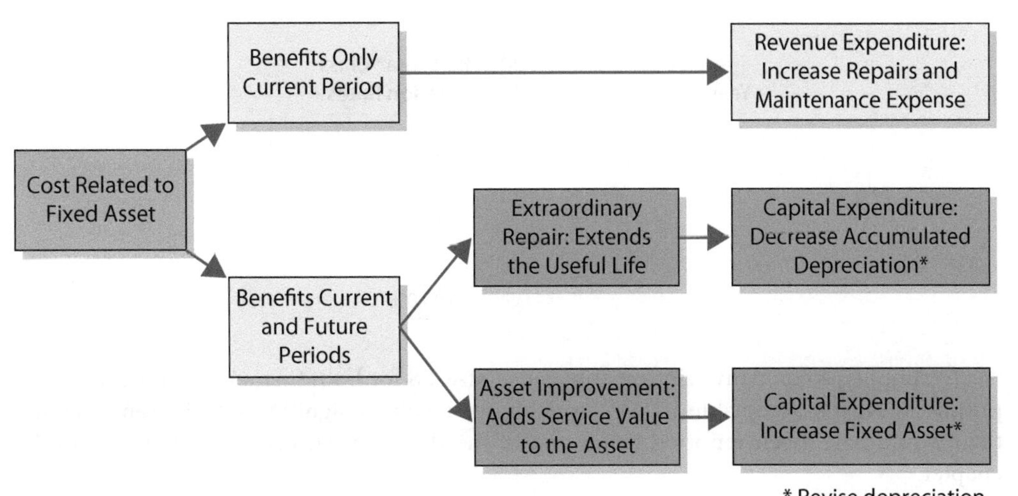

Using Data Analytics

Maintaining Equipment

Maintaining equipment is a critical activity for capital-intensive companies like **United Parcel Services (UPS)**. As one of the world's largest package delivery companies, UPS operates over 500 aircraft and approximately 125,000 delivery cars, vans, trucks, and motorcycles. As a result, UPS employs over 4,000 aircraft and auto mechanics and spends millions of dollars on repairs and maintenance each year.

For UPS, scheduling preventive maintenance and avoiding equipment breakdowns is an integral part of its operations. Some of UPS's maintenance activities are mandated by regulatory authorities. For example, the Federal Aviation Administration (FAA) regulates UPS's maintenance and inspection of its aircraft. However, UPS has more discretion over scheduling and maintaining its 125,000 cars, vans, trucks, and motorcycles.

Data analytics can be useful to companies like UPS in scheduling maintenance and deciding when to replace its cars, vans, trucks, and motorcycles. For example, UPS could use data analytics to prepare an analysis of breakdowns and repair costs by type of delivery vehicle. This might show that trucks break down more frequently and have more costly repairs than vans. This might result in UPS replacing some of its trucks with vans. Likewise, an analysis of breakdowns by geographic area might show more breakdowns for delivery vehicles in hot climates such as Arizona. This might result in UPS scheduling more frequent oil changes and tire replacements in these areas.

See Case 8-5 for a homework assignment using data analytics.

Depreciation for Federal Income Tax

The Internal Revenue Code uses the *Modified Accelerated Cost Recovery System (MACRS)* to compute depreciation for tax purposes. MACRS has eight classes of useful lives and depreciation rates for each class. Two of the most common classes are the five-year class and the seven-year class.[6] The five-year class includes automobiles and light-duty trucks. The seven-year class includes most machinery and equipment. Depreciation for these two classes is similar to that computed using the double-declining-balance method.

In using the MACRS rates, residual value is ignored. Also, all fixed assets are assumed to be put in and taken out of service in the middle of the year. For the five-year-class of assets, depreciation is spread over six years, as follows:

Year	MACRS 5-Year-Class Depreciation Rates
1	20.0%
2	32.0
3	19.2
4	11.5
5	11.5
6	5.8
	100.0%

To simplify, a company will sometimes use MACRS for both financial statement and tax purposes. This is acceptable if MACRS does not result in significantly different amounts than would have been reported using one of the depreciation methods discussed in this chapter.

Integrity, Objectivity, and Ethics in Business

Capital Crime

One of the largest alleged accounting frauds in history involved the improper accounting for capital expenditures. WorldCom, the second largest telecommunications company in the United States at the time, improperly treated maintenance expenditures on its telecommunications network as capital expenditures. As a result, the company had to restate its prior years' earnings downward by nearly $4 billion to correct this error. The company declared bankruptcy within months of disclosing the error, and the CEO was sentenced to 25 years in prison.

6. Real estate is in either a 27½-year or a 31½-year class and is depreciated by the straight-line method.

Disposal of Fixed Assets

Objective 3
Describe the accounting for the disposal of fixed assets.

Fixed assets that are no longer useful may be discarded or sold.[7] In such cases, the fixed asset is removed from the accounts. Just because a fixed asset is fully depreciated, however, does not mean that it should be removed from the accounts.

If a fixed asset is still being used, its cost and accumulated depreciation should remain in the records even if the asset is fully depreciated. This maintains accountability. If the asset was removed from the records, the accounts would contain no evidence of the continued existence of the asset. In addition, cost and accumulated depreciation data on such assets are often needed for property tax and income tax reports.

Discarding Fixed Assets

If a fixed asset is no longer used and has no residual value, it is discarded. To illustrate, assume that fully depreciated equipment acquired at a cost of $25,000 is discarded on February 14, 20Y7. The effect on the accounts and financial statements is as follows:

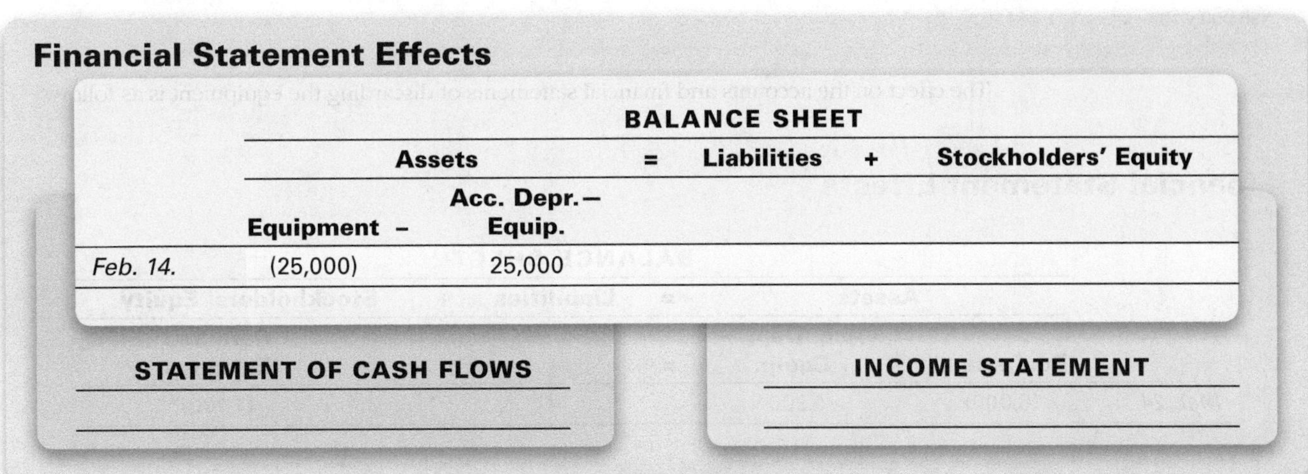

Financial Statement Effects

BALANCE SHEET

	Assets		=	Liabilities	+	Stockholders' Equity
	Equipment –	Acc. Depr.—Equip.				
Feb. 14.	(25,000)	25,000				

STATEMENT OF CASH FLOWS

INCOME STATEMENT

Transaction Metric Effects

The effects of discarding the asset on liquidity and profitability metrics are as follows:

LIQUIDITY	
Free Cash Flow	No Effect

PROFITABILITY	
Asset Turnover	No Effect

Since there are no cash flows related to the transaction, there is no effect on free cash flow. Since the equipment was fully depreciated, discarding the asset has no effect on asset turnover.

If an asset has not been fully depreciated, depreciation should be recorded before removing the asset from the accounting records. To illustrate, assume that equipment costing $6,000 with no estimated residual value is depreciated at a straight-line rate of 10%. On December 31, 20Y6, the accumulated depreciation balance, after adjusting entries, is $4,750. On March 24, 20Y7, the asset is removed from service and discarded. The effect

7. The accounting for the exchange of fixed assets is described and illustrated in advanced accounting courses.

of recording the depreciation for the three months of 20Y7 before the asset is discarded is as follows:

Financial Statement Effects

BALANCE SHEET

	Assets			=	Liabilities	+	Stockholders' Equity
	Equipment	–	**Acc. Depr.— Equip.**	=			**Retained Earnings**
Mar. 24.			(150)*				(150)

STATEMENT OF CASH FLOWS

INCOME STATEMENT

Mar. 24. Depr. expense (150)

*($6,000 x 10%) x (3 ÷ 12) = $150

The effect on the accounts and financial statements of discarding the equipment is as follows:

Financial Statement Effects

BALANCE SHEET

	Assets			=	Liabilities	+	Stockholders' Equity
	Equipment	–	**Acc. Depr.— Equip.**	=			**Retained Earnings**
Mar. 24.	(6,000)		4,900*				(1,100)

STATEMENT OF CASH FLOWS

INCOME STATEMENT

Mar. 24. Loss on disposal of equip. (1,100)

*$4,750 + $150 = $4,900

The loss of $1,100 is recorded because the balance of the accumulated depreciation account ($4,900) is less than the balance in the equipment account ($6,000). Losses on the discarding of fixed assets are nonoperating items and are normally reported in the "Other expense (loss)" section of the income statement.

Transaction Metric Effects

The effects of updating depreciation and discarding the asset on liquidity and profitability metrics are as follows:

LIQUIDITY	
Free Cash Flow	No Effect

PROFITABILITY	
Asset Turnover	Increase

Since there are no cash flows, there is no effect on free cash flow. After updating depreciation, the equipment has a book value of $1,100 ($6,000 – $4,900). Discarding the equipment reduces the operating assets and increases asset turnover.

Selling Fixed Assets

The entry to record the sale of a fixed asset is similar to the entries for discarding an asset. The only difference is that the receipt of cash is also recorded. If the selling price is more than the book value of the asset, a gain is recorded. If the selling price is less than the book value, a loss is recorded.

To illustrate, assume that equipment is purchased at a cost of $10,000 with no estimated residual value and is depreciated at a straight-line rate of 10%. The equipment is sold for cash on October 12 of the eighth year of its use. The balance of the accumulated depreciation account as of the preceding December 31 is $7,000. The effect on the accounts and financial statements of updating depreciation for the nine months of the current year is as follows:

Financial Statement Effects

BALANCE SHEET

	Assets		=	Liabilities	+	Stockholders' Equity
	Equipment –	Acc. Depr.—Equip.	=			Retained Earnings
Oct. 12.		(750)*				(750)

STATEMENT OF CASH FLOWS

INCOME STATEMENT	
Oct. 12. Depr. exp.—equip.	(750)

*($10,000 x 10%) x (9 ÷ 12) = $750

After the current depreciation is recorded, the book value of the asset is $2,250 ($10,000 − $7,750). The effect of the sale, assuming three different selling prices, is as follows:

Sold at book value, for $2,250. No gain or loss.

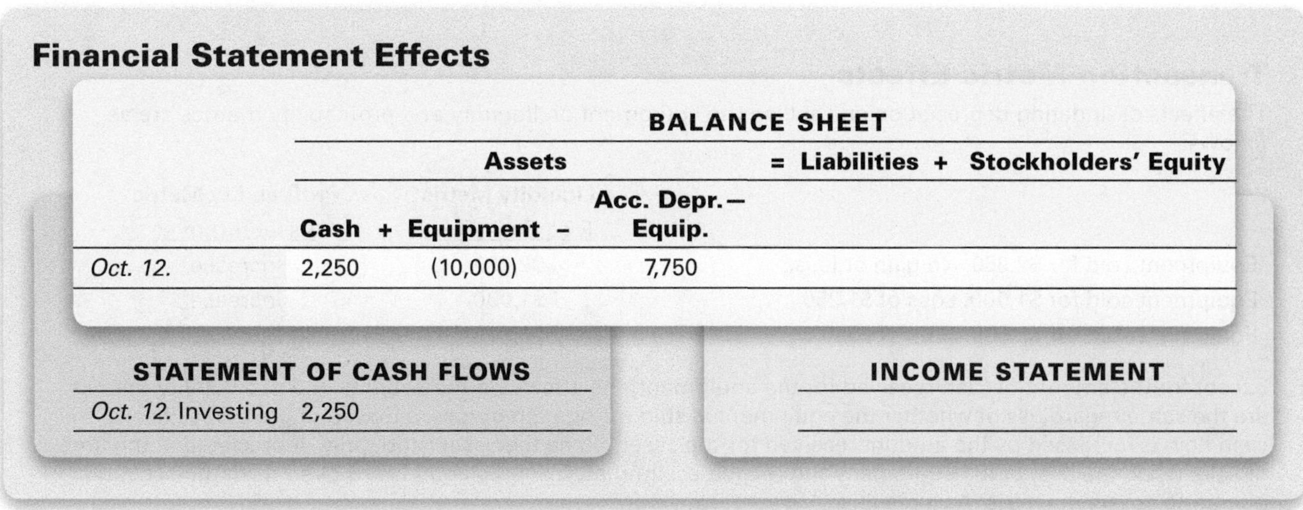

Financial Statement Effects

BALANCE SHEET

	Assets			= Liabilities + Stockholders' Equity
	Cash +	Equipment –	Acc. Depr.—Equip.	
Oct. 12.	2,250	(10,000)	7,750	

STATEMENT OF CASH FLOWS	
Oct. 12. Investing	2,250

INCOME STATEMENT

Sold below book value, for $1,000. Loss of $1,250.

Financial Statement Effects

BALANCE SHEET

	Assets				= Liabilities + Stockholders' Equity
	Cash	+ Equipment	– Acc. Depr.—Equip.	=	Retained Earnings
Oct. 12.	1,000	(10,000)	7,750		(1,250)

STATEMENT OF CASH FLOWS

Oct. 12. Investing 1,000

INCOME STATEMENT

Oct. 12. Loss on disposal of equip. (1,250)

Sold above book value, for $2,800. Gain of $550.

Financial Statement Effects

BALANCE SHEET

	Assets				= Liabilities + Stockholders' Equity
	Cash	+ Equipment	– Acc. Depr.—Equip.	=	Retained Earnings
Oct. 12.	2,800	(10,000)	7,750		550

STATEMENT OF CASH FLOWS

Oct. 12. Investing 2,800

INCOME STATEMENT

Oct. 12. Gain on disposal of equip. 550

Transaction Metric Effects

The effects of updating depreciation and selling the equipment on liquidity and profitability metrics are as follows:

	Liquidity Metric Free Cash Flow	Profitability Metric Asset Turnover
Equipment sold for $2,250. No gain or loss.	$2,250	Increase
Equipment sold for $1,000. Loss of $1,250.	$1,000	Increase
Equipment sold for $2,800. Gain of $550.	$2,800	Increase

Except for the amount of cash received for the equipment, the effects on the liquidity and profitability metrics are the same regardless of whether the equipment is sold for no gain or loss, a loss, or a gain. Specifically, free cash flow is increased by the amount received for the asset. Since the asset is not fully depreciated at the time of sale, when the cost of the equipment and related accumulated depreciation is removed from the accounts, operating assets decrease. As a result, the asset turnover increases.

In notes to its financial statements, **Chipotle** stated the following: "Upon retirement or disposal of assets, the accounts are relieved of cost and accumulated depreciation and any related gain or loss is reflected in loss on disposal ... of assets in the ... statement of income."

Chipotle Connection

Natural Resources

Objective 4

Describe the accounting for depletion of natural resources.

Some businesses own natural resources, such as timber, minerals, or oil. The characteristics of natural resources are as follows:

- Naturally Occurring: This is an asset created through natural growth or naturally through the passage of time. For example, timber is a natural resource naturally occurring over time.
- Removed for Sale: The asset is consumed by removing it from its land source. For example, timber is removed for use when it is harvested, and minerals are removed when they are mined.
- Removed and Sold over More Than One Year: The natural resource is removed and sold over a period of more than one year.

Natural resources are classified as a type of long-term asset. The cost of a natural resource includes the cost of obtaining and preparing it for use. For example, legal fees incurred in purchasing a natural resource are included as part of its cost.

As natural resources are harvested or mined and then sold, an expense account is increased for a portion of the cost of the resource removed. This expense is called **depletion expense**.

Depletion is determined as follows[8]:

Step 1. Determine the depletion rate as:

$$\textbf{Depletion Rate} = \frac{\textbf{Cost of Resource}}{\textbf{Estimated Total Units of Resource}}$$

Step 2. Multiply the depletion rate by the quantity extracted from the resource during the period.

$$\textbf{Depletion Expense} = \textbf{Depletion Rate} \times \textbf{Quantity Removed}$$

To illustrate, assume that Karst Company purchased mining rights as follows:

Cost of mineral deposit	$400,000
Estimated total units of resource	1,000,000 tons
Tons mined during year	90,000 tons

The depletion expense of $36,000 for the year is computed as follows:

Step 1.

$$\text{Depletion Rate} = \frac{\text{Cost of Resource}}{\text{Estimated Total Units of Resource}}$$

$$= \frac{\$400{,}000}{1{,}000{,}000 \text{ Tons}} = \$0.40 \text{ per Ton}$$

Step 2.

$$\text{Depletion Expense} = \$0.40 \text{ per Ton} \times 90{,}000 \text{ Tons} = \$36{,}000$$

8. It is assumed that there is no significant residual value left after all the natural resource is extracted.

The effect of the depletion on the accounts and financial statements is as follows:

Financial Statement Effects

BALANCE SHEET

	Assets		=	Liabilities	+	Stockholders' Equity
	Mineral Deposit	– –Acc. Depletion	=			Retained Earnings
Dec. 31.		(36,000)				(36,000)

STATEMENT OF CASH FLOWS

INCOME STATEMENT

Dec. 31. Depletion exp.	(36,000)

Like the accumulated depreciation account, Accumulated Depletion is a *contra asset* account. It is reported on the balance sheet as a deduction from the cost of the mineral deposit.

Transaction Metric Effects

The effects of depletion on the liquidity and profitability metrics are as follows:

LIQUIDITY	
Free Cash Flow	No Effect

PROFITABILITY	
Asset Turnover	Increase

Depletion has no effect on free cash flow. Depletion decreases operating assets, which increases asset turnover.

Objective 5
Describe the accounting for intangible assets.

Intangible Assets

Long-term assets that are used in the operations of the business but do not exist physically are called intangible assets. **Intangible assets** may be acquired through innovative, creative activities or from purchasing the rights from another company. Examples of intangible assets include patents, copyrights, trademarks, and goodwill.

The accounting for intangible assets is similar to the accounting for fixed assets. The major issues are:

- Determining the initial cost
- Determining the **amortization**, which is the amount of cost to transfer to expense

Amortization results from the passage of time or a decline in the usefulness of the intangible asset.

Patents

Manufacturers may acquire exclusive rights to produce and sell goods with one or more unique features. Such rights are granted by **patents**, which the federal government issues to inventors. These rights continue in effect for 20 years. A business may purchase patent rights from others, or it may obtain patents developed by its own research and development.

The initial cost of a purchased patent, including any legal fees, is recorded by increasing an asset account. This cost is written off, or amortized, over the years of the patent's expected useful life. The expected useful life of a patent may be less than its legal life. For example, a patent may become worthless due to changing technology or consumer tastes.

Patent amortization is normally computed using the straight-line method. The amortization is recorded by increasing an amortization expense account and decreasing the patents account. A separate contra asset account is usually *not* used for intangible assets.

To illustrate, assume that at the beginning of its fiscal year, a company acquires patent rights for $100,000. Although the patent will not expire for 14 years, its remaining useful life is estimated as five years. Thus, the annual patent amortization expense is $20,000 ($100,000 ÷ 5 years). The effect of amortizing the patent at the end of the fiscal year is as follows:

Financial Statement Effects

BALANCE SHEET

	Assets	=	**Liabilities**	+	**Stockholders' Equity**
	Patents	=			**Retained Earnings**
Dec. 31.	(20,000)				(20,000)

STATEMENT OF CASH FLOWS

INCOME STATEMENT

Dec. 31. Amortization exp.—patents	(20,000)

Transaction Metric Effects

The effects of amortizing the patent on the liquidity and profitability metrics are as follows:

LIQUIDITY	
Free Cash Flow	No Effect

PROFITABILITY	
Asset Turnover	Increase

Amortizing the patent has no effect on free cash flow. Amortizing the patent decreases operating assets, which increases asset turnover.

Some companies develop their own patents through research and development. In such cases, any *research and development costs* are usually recorded as current operating expenses in the period in which they are incurred. This accounting for research and development costs is justified on the basis that any future benefits from research and development are highly uncertain.

Copyrights and Trademarks

The exclusive right to publish and sell a literary, artistic, or musical composition is granted by a **copyright**. Copyrights are issued by the federal government and extend for 70 years beyond the author's death. The costs of a copyright include all costs of creating the work plus any other costs of obtaining the copyright. A copyright that is purchased is recorded at the price paid for it. Copyrights are amortized over their estimated useful lives.

A **trademark** is a name, term, or symbol used to identify a business and its products. Most businesses identify their trademarks with the symbol ® in their advertisements and on their products.

Under federal law, businesses can protect their trademarks by registering them for 10 years and renewing the registration for 10-year periods. Like a copyright, the legal costs of registering a trademark are recorded as an asset.

If a trademark is purchased from another business, its cost is recorded as an asset. In such cases, the cost of the trademark is considered to have an indefinite useful life. Thus, trademarks are not amortized. Instead, trademarks are reviewed periodically for impaired value. When a trademark is impaired, the trademark should be written down and a loss recognized.

Chipotle Connection

A number of names, designs, and logos are trademarks of **Chipotle** including the following: Chipotle, Chipotle Mexican Grill, Food With Intregity, and Responsibly Raised.

Goodwill

Goodwill refers to an intangible asset of a business that is created from such favorable factors as location, product quality, reputation, and managerial skill. Goodwill allows a business to earn a greater rate of return than normal.

Generally accepted accounting principles (GAAP) allow goodwill to be recorded only if it is objectively determined by a transaction. An example of such a transaction is the purchase of a business at a price in excess of the fair value of its net assets (assets – liabilities). The excess is recorded as goodwill and reported as an intangible asset.

On a recent balance sheet, **Chipotle** reported goodwill of $21,939,000.

Unlike patents and copyrights, goodwill is not amortized. However, a loss should be recorded if the future prospects of the purchased firm become impaired. This loss would normally be disclosed in the Other expense section of the income statement.

International Connection

Development Costs Under IFRS

In the United States, research and development costs must be expensed in the period in which they are incurred. IFRS, however, allow certain development costs to be recorded as an asset if specific criteria are met. Included in the criteria are the technical feasibility of completing the development of the intangible asset and whether the company intends to use or sell the asset. Whether development costs are recorded as an asset or expensed could have a significant impact on the financial statements.

To illustrate, assume that on December 31 FaceCard Company has determined that $250,000 of the goodwill created from the purchase of Electronic Systems is impaired. The effect on the accounts and financial statements is as follows:

Financial Statement Effects

BALANCE SHEET

	Assets	=	Liabilities	+	Stockholders' Equity
	Goodwill	=			Retained Earnings
Dec. 31.	(250,000)				(250,000)

STATEMENT OF CASH FLOWS

INCOME STATEMENT

Dec. 31. Loss from impaired goodwill	(250,000)

Transaction Metric Effects

The effects of the impaired goodwill on liquidity and profitability metrics are as follows:

LIQUIDITY	
Free Cash Flow	No Effect

PROFITABILITY	
Asset Turnover	Increase

The impairment of the goodwill has no effect on free cash flow. Recording the impairment decreases operating assets, which increases asset turnover.

In recent financial statements, **Chipotle** noted that the goodwill reported on its balance sheet is not impaired.

Chipotle Connection

Integrity, Objectivity, and Ethics in Business

When Does Goodwill Become Worthless?

The timing and amount of goodwill write-offs can be very subjective. Managers and their accountants should fairly estimate the value of goodwill and record goodwill impairment when it occurs. It would be unethical to delay a write-down of goodwill when it is determined that the asset is impaired.

Exhibit 10 summarizes the characteristics of intangible assets.

Exhibit 10
Comparison of Intangible Assets

Intangible Asset	Description	Amortization Period	Periodic Expense
Patent	Exclusive right to benefit from an innovation	Estimated useful life not to exceed legal life	Amortization expense
Copyright	Exclusive right to benefit from a literary, artistic, or musical composition	Estimated useful life not to exceed legal life	Amortization expense
Trademark	Exclusive use of a name, term, or symbol	None	Impairment loss if fair value less than carrying value (impaired)
Goodwill	Excess of purchase price of a business over the fair value of its net assets (assets – liabilities)	None	Impairment loss if fair value less than carrying value (impaired)

Financial Reporting for Fixed Assets and Intangible Assets

Objective 6
Describe the reporting of fixed assets, natural resources, and intangible assets on the income statement and balance sheet.

On the income statement, depreciation and amortization expense should be reported separately or disclosed in a note. A description of the methods used in computing depreciation should also be reported.

In the balance sheet, each class of fixed assets should be disclosed on the face of the statement or in the notes. The related accumulated depreciation should also be disclosed, either by class or in total. The fixed assets may be shown at their *book value* (cost less accumulated depreciation), which can also be described as their *net* amount.

If there are many classes of fixed assets, a single amount may be presented in the balance sheet, supported by a note with a separate listing. Fixed assets may be reported under the more descriptive caption of property, plant, and equipment.

The cost of mineral rights or ore deposits is normally shown as part of the fixed assets section of the balance sheet. The related accumulated depletion should also be disclosed. In some cases, the mineral rights are shown net of depletion on the face of the balance sheet, accompanied by a note that discloses the amount of the accumulated depletion.

Intangible assets are usually reported on the balance sheet in a separate section immediately following fixed assets. The balance of each major class of intangible assets should be disclosed at an amount net of amortization taken to date. Exhibit 11 is a partial balance sheet that shows the reporting of fixed assets and intangible assets.

Exhibit 11
Fixed Assets and Intangible Assets on the Balance Sheet

Assets					
Total current assets					$ 462,500
Property, plant, and equipment:	Cost	Acc. Depr.	Book Value		
Land	$ 30,000	—	$ 30,000		
Buildings	110,000	$ 26,000	84,000		
Factory equipment	650,000	192,000	458,000		
Office equipment	120,000	13,000	107,000		
	$ 910,000	$ 231,000		$ 679,000	
Mineral deposits:	Cost	Acc. Depl.	Book Value		
Alaska deposit	$1,200,000	$ 800,000	$ 400,000		
Wyoming deposit	750,000	200,000	550,000		
	$1,950,000	$ 1,000,000		950,000	
Total property, plant, and equipment					1,629,000
Intangible assets:					
Patents				$ 75,000	
Goodwill				50,000	
Total intangible assets					125,000

Hub-and-Spoke or Point-to-Point?

Business Insight

Southwest Airlines Co. (LUV) uses a simple fare structure, featuring low, unrestricted, unlimited, everyday coach fares. These fares are made possible by Southwest's use of a point-to-point, rather than a hub-and-spoke, business approach. **United Airlines, Inc. (UAL)**, **Delta Air Lines (DAL)**, and **American Airlines Group Inc. (AAL)** employ a hub-and-spoke approach in which an airline establishes major hubs that serve as connecting links to other cities. For example, Delta has established major connecting hubs in Atlanta and Salt Lake City. In contrast, Southwest focuses on point-to-point service between select cities. As a result, Southwest minimizes connections, delays, and total trip time. Southwest also focuses on serving conveniently located satellite or downtown airports, such as Dallas Love Field, Houston Hobby, and Chicago Midway. Because these airports are normally less congested than hub airports, Southwest is better able to maintain high employee productivity and reliable on-time performance. This operating approach permits the company to achieve high utilization of its fixed assets. For example, aircraft are scheduled to minimize time spent at the gate, thereby reducing the number of aircraft and gate facilities that would otherwise be required.

AP Images/MATT SLOCUM

Objective 7
Describe and illustrate asset turnover in assessing a company's operating results.

Metric-Based Analysis: Asset Turnover

Long-term fixed, operating assets, such as property, plant, and equipment are a large percent of total assets for many companies. For example, on a recent balance sheet almost 50% of **Delta Air Lines'** total assets are composed of property, plant, and equipment. For such companies, maximizing the use of these assets to generate sales is an important operating objective.

One metric that measures how efficiently a company is using its operating assets to generate sales is **asset turnover**. Asset turnover computes the sales revenue generated for each dollar invested in long-term operating assets. Normally, a high or increasing fixed asset turnover is considered favorable. It is computed as follows:

$$\textbf{Asset Turnover} = \frac{\textbf{Sales}}{\textbf{Average of Long-Term Operating Assets}}$$

Long-term operating assets consist of property, plant, and equipment (net of accumulated depreciation) plus natural resources and intangible assets.

To illustrate, assume the following data (in millions) adapted from recent financial statements for Delta Air Lines.

	Year 2	Year 1
Sales	$47,007	$44,438
Operating assets (average for year):		
Property, plant, equipment	35,633	30,446
Intangibles	14,778	14,626

The asset turnover (rounded to two decimal places) for Delta Air Lines is computed as follows:

	Year 2	Year 1
Asset turnover:		
$47,007 ÷ ($35,633 + $14,778)	0.93	
$44,438 ÷ ($30,466 + $14,626)		0.99

Delta Air Lines' asset turnover decreased from 0.99 in Year 1 to 0.93 in Year 2. Thus, Delta's efficiency in generating sales from its assets decreased between years. This may be due to increasing price (fare) pressures from competing airlines, including **United Airlines (UAL)** and **Southwest Airlines (LUV)**.

For two recent years, **Chipotle** generated an average revenue of $0.72 per dollar of invested long-term operating assets.

Key Points

1. Define, classify, and account for the cost of fixed assets.

Fixed assets are long-term tangible assets that are owned by the business and are used in the normal operations of the business. Examples of fixed assets are equipment, buildings, and land. The initial cost of a fixed asset includes all amounts spent to get the asset in place and ready for use. For example, sales tax, freight, insurance in transit, and installation costs are all included in the cost of a fixed asset. Rather than purchase an asset, a company (lessee) may lease the asset from a lessor.

2. Compute depreciation using the straight-line and double-declining-balance methods.

In computing depreciation, three factors need to be considered: (1) the fixed asset's initial cost, (2) the useful life of the asset, and (3) the residual value of the asset.

The straight-line method spreads the initial cost less the residual value equally over the asset's useful life. The double-declining-balance method is applied by multiplying the declining book value of the asset by twice the straight-line rate.

When an asset is purchased during the year, annual depreciation must be prorated based upon the month the asset is placed in service. After an asset is placed in service, maintenance, repair, and improvement costs may be incurred. Routine maintenance and repair costs, called revenue expenditures, are recorded as expenses when incurred. Extraordinary repairs and improvement costs, called capital expenditures, are recorded as decreases in accumulated depreciation (extraordinary repairs) or as increases to the asset (improvements).

3. Describe the accounting for the disposal of fixed assets.

The recording of disposals of fixed assets will vary. In all cases, however, any depreciation for the current period should be recorded, and the book value of the asset removed from the accounts. For assets retired from service, a loss may be recorded for any remaining book value of the asset. When a fixed asset is sold, the book value is removed and the cash received is also recorded. If the selling price is more than the book value of the asset, the transaction results in a gain. If the selling price is less than the book value, there is a loss.

4. Describe the accounting for depletion of natural resources.

The amount of periodic depletion is computed by multiplying the quantity of minerals extracted during the period by a depletion rate. The depletion rate is computed by dividing the cost of the mineral deposit by its estimated size. Recording depletion increases a depletion expense account and an accumulated depletion account.

5. Describe the accounting for intangible assets.

Long-term assets that are without physical attributes but are used in the business are classified as intangible assets. Examples of intangible assets are patents, copyrights, trademarks, and goodwill. The initial cost of an intangible asset should be recorded by increasing an asset account. For patents and copyrights, this cost should be written off, or amortized, over the years of the asset's expected usefulness by increasing an expense account and decreasing the intangible asset account. Trademarks and goodwill are not amortized but are written down only on impairment.

6. Describe the reporting of fixed assets, natural resources, and intangible assets on the income statement and balance sheet.

The amount of depreciation expense and the method or methods used in computing depreciation should be disclosed in the financial statements. In addition, each major class of fixed assets should be disclosed, along with the related accumulated depreciation. Intangible assets are usually presented in the balance sheet in a separate section immediately following fixed assets. Each major class of intangible assets should be disclosed at an amount net of the amortization recorded to date.

7. Metric-Based Analysis: Describe and illustrate asset turnover in assessing a company's operating results.

The asset turnover is a measure of a company's use of its long-term operating assets to generate sales. It is computed by dividing sales by the average long-term operating assets for the period.

Key Terms

Accelerated depreciation method (317)
Amortization (328)
Asset turnover (312, 334)
Book value of a fixed asset (313)
Capital expenditures (320)
Copyright (330)
Depletion expense (327)
Depreciable cost (314)
Depreciation (313)
Double-declining-balance method (317)
Expected useful life (314)
Fixed assets (309)
Free cash flow (312)
Goodwill (330)
Initial cost of a fixed asset (314)
Intangible assets (328)
Lease (313)
Patents (328)
Residual value (314)
Revenue expenditures (320)
Straight-line method (315)
Trademark (330)

Illustrative Problem

McCollum Company, a furniture wholesaler, acquired new equipment at a cost of $150,000 at the beginning of the fiscal year. The equipment has an estimated life of 5 years and an estimated residual value of $12,000. Ellen McCollum, the president, has requested information regarding alternative depreciation methods.

Instructions

Determine the annual depreciation for each of the 5 years of estimated useful life of the equipment, the accumulated depreciation at the end of each year, and the book value of the equipment at the end of each year by (a) the straight-line method and (b) the double-declining-balance method.

Solution

	Year	Depreciation Expense	Accumulated Depreciation, End of Year	Book Value, End of Year
a.	1	$27,600*	$ 27,600	$122,400
	2	27,600	55,200	94,800
	3	27,600	82,800	67,200
	4	27,600	110,400	39,600
	5	27,600	138,000	12,000

*$27,600 = ($150,000 − $12,000) ÷ 5

	Year	Depreciation Expense	Accumulated Depreciation, End of Year	Book Value, End of Year
b.	1	$60,000**	$ 60,000	$ 90,000
	2	36,000	96,000	54,000
	3	21,600	117,600	32,400
	4	12,960	130,560	19,440
	5	7,440***	138,000	12,000

**$60,000 = $150,000 × 40%

***The asset is not depreciated below the estimated residual value of $12,000.

Self-Examination Questions

(Answers appear at the end of the chapter.)

1. Which of the following expenditures incurred in connection with acquiring machinery is a proper addition to the asset account?
   A. Freight
   B. Installation costs
   C. Both A and B
   D. Neither A nor B

2. What is the amount of depreciation, using the double-declining-balance method (twice the straight-line rate), for the second year of use for equipment costing $9,000, with an estimated residual value of $600 and an estimated life of 3 years?
   A. $6,000 C. $2,000
   B. $3,000 D. $400

3. An example of an accelerated depreciation method is:
   A. Straight-line
   B. Double-declining-balance
   C. Units-of-activity
   D. Depletion balance

4. Hyde Inc. purchased mineral rights estimated at 2,500,000 tons near Great Falls, Montana, for $3,600,000 on August 7, 20Y4. During the remainder of the year, Hyde mined 175,000 tons of ore. What is the depletion expense for 20Y4?
   A. $121,528 C. $1,500,000
   B. $252,000 D. $3,600,000

5. Which of the following is an example of an intangible asset?
   A. Patents C. Copyrights
   B. Goodwill D. All of the above

Class Discussion Questions

1. Which of the following qualities are characteristic of fixed assets? (a) tangible, (b) capable of repeated use in the normal operations of the business, (c) not held for sale in the normal course of business, (d) not used in the operations of the business, (e) useful life must be greater than 10 years.

2. Enterprise Supplies Co. has a fleet of automobiles and trucks for use by salespersons and for delivery of office supplies and equipment. Bizarro Auto Sales Co. has automobiles and trucks for sale. Under what caption would the automobiles and trucks be reported on the balance sheet of (a) Enterprise Supplies Co. and (b) Bizarro Auto Sales Co.?

3. The Stone Store Co. acquired an adjacent vacant lot with the hope of selling it in the future at a gain. The lot is not intended to be used in The Stone Store's business operations. Where should such real estate be listed on the balance sheet?

4. Lanier Company solicited bids from several contractors to construct an addition to its office building. The lowest bid received was for $600,000. Lanier Company decided to construct the addition itself at a cost of $475,000. What amount should be recorded in the building account?

5. Are the amounts at which fixed assets are reported on the balance sheet their approximate market values as of the balance sheet date? Discuss.

6. a. Does the recognition of depreciation in the accounts provide a special cash fund for the replacement of fixed assets? Explain.
   b. Describe the nature of depreciation as the term is used in accounting.

7. Backyard Company purchased a machine that has a manufacturer's suggested life of 30 years. The company plans to use the machine on a special project that will last 18 years. At the completion of the project, the machine will be sold. Over how many years should the machine be depreciated?

8. Is it necessary for a business to use the same method of computing depreciation (a) for all classes of its depreciable assets and (b) in the financial statements and in determining income taxes?

9. Distinguish between the accounting for capital expenditures and revenue expenditures.

10. Immediately after a used truck is acquired, a new motor is installed and the tires are replaced at a total cost of $4,300. Is this a capital expenditure or a revenue expenditure?

11. Classify each of the following expenditures as either a revenue or capital expenditure: (a) installation of a video messaging system on a semitrailer, (b) changing oil in a delivery truck, (c) purchase of a color copier.

12. a. Under what conditions is the use of an accelerated depreciation method most appropriate?
    b. Why is an accelerated depreciation method often used for income tax purposes?
    c. What is the Modified Accelerated Cost Recovery System (MACRS), and under what conditions is it used?

13. For some of the fixed assets of a business, the balance in Accumulated Depreciation is exactly equal to the cost of the asset. (a) Is it permissible to record additional depreciation on the assets if they are still useful to the company? Explain. (b) When should the cost and the accumulated depreciation be removed from the accounts?

14. How is depletion determined?

15. a. Over what period of time should the cost of a patent acquired by purchase be amortized?
    b. In general, what is the required accounting treatment for research and development costs?
    c. How should goodwill be amortized?

Exercises

E8-1 Costs of acquiring fixed assets — Obj. 1

Boots Young owns and operates Kinetic Printing. During August, Kinetic Printing incurred the following costs in acquiring two printing presses. One printing press was new, and the other was used by a business that recently filed for bankruptcy.

Costs related to new printing press:

1. Fee paid to factory representative for installation
2. Freight
3. Insurance while in transit
4. New parts to replace those damaged in unloading
5. Sales tax on purchase price
6. Special foundation

Costs related to used printing press:

7. Amount paid to attorney to review purchase agreement
8. Freight
9. Installation
10. Repair of vandalism during installation
11. Replacement of worn-out parts
12. Repair of damage incurred in reconditioning the press

a. Indicate which costs incurred in acquiring the new printing press should be recorded as an increase to the asset account.

b. Indicate which costs incurred in acquiring the used printing press should be recorded as an increase to the asset account.

Obj. 1

E8-2 Determine cost of land

Snowy Ridges Ski Co. has developed a tract of land into a ski resort. The company has cut the trees, cleared and graded the land and hills, and constructed ski lifts. (a) Should the tree cutting, land clearing, and grading costs of constructing the ski slopes be recorded as an increase in the land account? (b) If such costs are recorded as an increase in Land, should they be depreciated?

Obj. 1

✔ $299,000

SHOW ME HOW

E8-3 Determine cost of land

Village Delivery Company purchased a lot to construct a new warehouse for $287,500, paying $100,000 in cash and giving a short-term note for the remainder. Legal fees paid in connection with the purchase were $3,000, delinquent taxes assumed were $2,050, and fees paid to remove an old building from the land were $7,750. Materials salvaged from the demolition of the building were sold for $1,300. A contractor was paid $450,000 to construct a new warehouse. Determine the cost of the land to be reported on the balance sheet.

Obj. 2

E8-4 Nature of depreciation

Custer Construction Co. reported $8,300,000 for equipment and $4,950,000 for accumulated depreciation—equipment on its balance sheet.

Does this mean (a) that the replacement cost of the equipment is $8,300,000 and (b) that $4,950,000 is set aside in a special fund for the replacement of the equipment? Explain.

Obj. 2

✔ c. 10%

E8-5 Straight-line depreciation rates

Convert each of the following estimates of useful life to a straight-line depreciation rate, stated as a percentage, assuming that the residual value of the fixed asset is to be ignored: (a) 4 years, (b) 8 years, (c) 10 years, (d) 20 years, (e) 25 years, (f) 40 years, and (g) 50 years.

E8-6 Straight-line depreciation

Obj. 2

A refrigerator used by a restaurant has a cost of $45,000, an estimated residual value of $7,500, and an estimated useful life of 15 years. What is the amount of the annual depreciation computed by the straight-line method?

E8-7 Depreciation by two methods

Obj. 2

✔ a. First Year, $18,000

A piece of heavy equipment acquired on January 1 at a cost of $360,000 has an estimated useful life of 20 years. Assuming that it will have no residual value, determine the depreciation for each of the first 2 years ending December 31 by (a) the straight-line method and (b) the double-declining-balance method.

E8-8 Depreciation by two methods

Obj. 2

✔ a. $7,775

Equipment acquired at the beginning of the fiscal year at a cost of $160,000 has an estimated residual value of $4,500 and an estimated useful life of 20 years. Determine the following: (a) the amount of annual depreciation by the straight-line method and (b) the amount of depreciation for the first and second years computed by the double-declining-balance method.

E8-9 Partial-year depreciation

Obj. 2

✔ a. 20Y5, $900

Sandblasting equipment acquired at a cost of $42,000 has an estimated residual value of $6,000 and an estimated useful life of 10 years. It was placed in service on October 1 of the current fiscal year, which ends on December 31, 20Y5. Determine the depreciation for 20Y5 and for 20Y6 by (a) the straight-line method and (b) the double-declining-balance method.

E8-10 Capital and revenue expenditures

Obj. 2

Retrograde Delivery Co. incurred the following costs related to trucks and vans used in operating its delivery service:

1. Changed the oil and greased the joints of all the trucks and vans.
2. Changed the radiator fluid on a truck that had been in service for the past four years.
3. Installed a hydraulic lift to a van.
4. Installed security systems on four of the newer trucks.
5. Overhauled the engine on one of the trucks purchased four years ago.
6. Rebuilt the transmission on one of the vans that had been driven 50,000 miles. The van was no longer under warranty.
7. Removed a two-way radio from one of the trucks and installed a new radio with Bluetooth capability.
8. Repaired a flat tire on one of the vans.
9. Replaced a truck's suspension system with a new suspension system that allows for the delivery of heavier loads.
10. Tinted the back and side windows of one of the vans to discourage theft of contents.

Classify each of the costs as a capital expenditure or a revenue expenditure.

Obj. 2

E8-11 Capital and revenue expenditures

Debra Bundy owns and operates DB Transport Co. During the past year, Debra incurred the following costs related to an 18-wheel truck:

1. Changed engine oil.
2. Installed a television in the sleeping compartment of the truck.
3. Installed a wind deflector on top of the cab to increase fuel mileage.
4. Modified the factory-installed turbo charger with a special-order kit designed to add 50 more horsepower to the engine performance.
5. Removed the old GPS navigation system and replaced it with a newer model.
6. Replaced fog and cab light bulbs.
7. Replaced a headlight that had burned out.
8. Replaced a shock absorber that had worn out.
9. Replaced the hydraulic brake system that had begun to fail during her latest trip through the Rocky Mountains.
10. Replaced the old radar detector with a newer model that detects additional frequencies now used by many of the state patrol radar guns. The detector is wired directly into the cab, so that it is partially hidden. In addition, Debra fastened the detector to the truck with a locking device that prevents its removal.

Classify each of the costs as a capital expenditure or a revenue expenditure.

Obj. 2

EXCEL ONLINE

E8-12 Book value of fixed assets

The following data (in millions) were adapted from recent annual reports of United Parcel Service, Inc. (UPS). UPS provides delivery and freight services throughout the world.

	Year 2	Year 1
Vehicles	$10,613	$ 9,820
Aircraft	19,045	17,499
Land	2,087	2,000
Building and improvements	9,944	9,131
Equipment	16,055	13,926
Construction in progress	1,983	2,112
Less accumulated depreciation	(29,245)	(27,912)

a. Compute the net property, plant, and equipment (book value) for Years 1 and 2.

b. Compare Years 1 and 2; comment on changes between years.

Obj. 3

SHOW ME HOW

✔ a. $430,000

E8-13 Sale of asset

Equipment acquired on January 9, 20Y3, at a cost of $560,000, has an estimated useful life of 20 years, an estimated residual value of $40,000, and is depreciated by the straight-line method.

a. What was the book value of the equipment at the end of the fifth year, December 31, 20Y7?

b. Assuming that the equipment was sold on July 1, 20Y8, for $400,000, illustrate the effects on the accounts and financial statements of (1) depreciation for the six months until the sale date and (2) the sale of the equipment.

Obj. 3

SHOW ME HOW

✔ a. $25,000

E8-14 Disposal of fixed asset

Equipment acquired on January 3, 20Y1, at a cost of $140,000, has an estimated useful life of 5 years and an estimated residual value of $15,000.

a. What was the annual amount of depreciation for the years 20Y1, 20Y2, and 20Y3, using the straight-line method of depreciation?

b. What was the book value of the equipment on January 1, 20Y4?

c. Assuming that the equipment was sold on January 2, 20Y4, for $63,500, illustrate the effects on the accounts and financial statements of the sale.

d. Assuming that the equipment was sold on January 2, 20Y4, for $71,000 instead of $63,500, illustrate the effects on the accounts and financial statements of the sale.

E8-15 Recording depletion

Obj. 4

✔ a. $6,750,000

Quavo Mining Co. acquired mineral rights for $36,000,000. The mineral deposit is estimated at 80,000,000 tons. During the current year, 15,000,000 tons were mined and sold.

a. Determine the amount of depletion expense for the current year.

b. Illustrate the effects on the accounts and financial statements of the depletion expense.

E8-16 Recording amortization

Obj. 5

✔ a. $223,500

SHOW ME HOW

Dovetail Technologies Company acquired patent rights on January 6, 20Y5, for $1,500,000. The patent has a useful life of 8 years. On January 7, 20Y6, Dovetail Technologies successfully defended the patent in a lawsuit at a cost of $252,000.

a. Determine the patent amortization expense for the current year ended December 31, 20Y6.

b. Illustrate the effects on the accounts and financial statements to recognize the amortization.

E8-17 Goodwill impairment

Obj. 5

SHOW ME HOW

On January 1, 20Y3, The Simmons Group, Inc., purchased the assets of NWS Insurance Co. for $36,000,000, a price reflecting an $8,000,000 goodwill premium. On December 31, 20Y9, The Simmons Group determined that the goodwill from the NWS acquisition was impaired and had a value of only $2,300,000.

a. Determine the book value of the goodwill on December 31, 20Y9, prior to making the impairment adjustment.

b. Illustrate the effects on the accounts and financial statements of the December 31, 20Y9, adjustment for the goodwill impairment.

E8-18 Book value of fixed assets

Obj. 6

Apple, Inc. (AAPL), designs, manufactures, and markets personal computers (iPad™) and related software. Apple also manufactures and distributes music players (iPod™) along with related accessories and services, including the online distribution of third-party music. The following information was adapted from a recent annual report of Apple:

Property, Plant, and Equipment (in millions):

	Year 2	Year 1
Land and buildings	$ 17,085	$ 16,216
Machinery, equipment, and internal-use software	69,797	65,982
Leasehold improvements	9,075	8,205
Accumulated depreciation and amortization	(58,579)	(49,099)

a. Compute the book value of the fixed assets for Years 1 and 2 and explain the differences, if any.

b. Would you normally expect the book value of fixed assets to increase or decrease during the year?

Obj. 6

E8-19 Balance sheet presentation

List the errors you find in the following partial balance sheet:

CHICO COMPANY
Balance Sheet
December 31, 20Y7

Assets

	Replacement Cost	Accumulated Depreciation	Book Value	
Total current assets				$350,000
Property, plant, and equipment:				
Land	$ 250,000	$ 20,000	$230,000	
Buildings	400,000	150,000	250,000	
Factory equipment	330,000	175,200	154,800	
Office equipment	72,000	48,000	24,000	
Patents	48,000	—	48,000	
Goodwill	90,000	3,000	87,000	
Total property, plant, and equipment	$1,190,000	$396,200		793,800

Problems

Obj. 1

✔ Land, $473,500

P8-1 Allocate payments and receipts to fixed asset accounts

The following payments and receipts are related to land, land improvements, and buildings acquired for use in a wholesale apparel business. The receipts are identified by an asterisk.

a. Architect's and engineer's fees for plans and supervision	$ 80,000
b. Cost of filling and grading land	30,000
c. Cost of removing building purchased with land in (e)	10,000
d. Cost of paving parking lot to be used by customers	25,000
e. Cost of real estate acquired as a plant site: Land ($375,000) and Building ($25,000)	400,000
f. Cost of repairing windstorm damage during construction	5,000
g. Cost of repairing vandalism damage during construction	1,800
h. Cost of trees and shrubbery planted	12,000
i. Delinquent real estate taxes on property, assumed by purchaser	20,000
j. Fee paid to attorney for title search	3,000
k. Finder's fee paid to real estate agency	4,000
l. Interest incurred on building loan during construction	40,000
m. Money borrowed to pay building contractor	775,000*
n. Payment to building contractor for new building	750,000
o. Proceeds from insurance company for windstorm and vandalism damage	3,600*
p. Premium on one-year insurance policy during construction	7,500
q. Proceeds from sale of salvage materials from old building	4,000*
r. Refund of premium on insurance policy (p) canceled after 10 months	1,250*
s. Special assessment paid to city for extension of water main to the property	10,500

Instructions

1. Assign each payment and receipt to Land (unlimited life), Land Improvements (limited life), Building, or Other Accounts. Indicate receipts by an asterisk. Identify each item by letter and list the amounts in columnar form, as follows:

Item	Land	Land Improvements	Building	Other Accounts

2. Determine the increases to Land, Land Improvements, and Building.
3. The costs assigned to the land, which is used as a plant site, will not be depreciated, while the costs assigned to land improvements will be depreciated. Explain this seemingly contradictory application of the concept of depreciation.

P8-2 Compare two depreciation methods

Obj. 2

✔ a. 20Y4: straight-line depreciation, $45,250

Bayside Coatings Company purchased waterproofing equipment on January 2, 20Y4, for $190,000. The equipment was expected to have a useful life of 4 years and a residual value of $9,000.

Instructions

Determine the amount of depreciation expense for the years ended December 31, 20Y4, 20Y5, 20Y6, and 20Y7, by (a) the straight-line method and (b) the double-declining-balance method. Also determine the total depreciation expense for the four years by each method. The following columnar headings are suggested for recording the depreciation expense amounts:

	Depreciation Expense	
Year	Straight-Line Method	Double-Declining-Balance Method

P8-3 Depreciation by two methods; partial years

Obj. 2

✔ a. 20Y5, $2,550

Knife Edge Company purchased tool sharpening equipment on July 1, 20Y5, for $16,200. The equipment was expected to have a useful life of 3 years and a residual value of $900.

Instructions

Determine the amount of depreciation expense for the years ended December 31, 20Y5, 20Y6, 20Y7, and 20Y8, by (a) the straight-line method and (b) the double-declining-balance method.

P8-4 Depreciation by two methods; sale of fixed asset

Obj. 2, 3

✔ 1. b. Year 1, $70,000 depreciation expense

New tire retreading equipment, acquired at a cost of $140,000 at the beginning of a fiscal year, has an estimated useful life of 4 years and an estimated residual value of $10,000. The manager requested information regarding the effect of alternative methods on the amount of depreciation expense each year. On the basis of the data presented to the manager, the double-declining-balance method was selected.

In the first week of the fourth year, the equipment was sold for $23,300.

Instructions

1. Determine the annual depreciation expense for each of the estimated 4 years of use, the accumulated depreciation at the end of each year, and the book value of the equipment at the end of each year by (a) the straight-line method and (b) the double-declining-balance method. The following columnar headings are suggested for each schedule:

Year	Depreciation Expense	Accumulated Depreciation, End of Year	Book Value, End of Year

2. Illustrate the effects on the accounts and financial statements of the sale.
3. Illustrate the effects on the accounts and financial statements of the sale, assuming a sales price of $15,250 instead of $23,300.

Obj. 4, 5

✔ 1. b. $57,500

P8-5 Amortization and depletion entries

Data related to the acquisition of timber rights and intangible assets of Gemini Company during the current year ended December 31 are as follows:

a. On December 31, Gemini Company determined that $3,000,000 of goodwill was impaired.
b. Governmental and legal costs of $920,000 were incurred by Gemini Company on June 30 in obtaining a patent with an estimated economic life of 8 years. Amortization is to be for one-half year.
c. Timber rights on a tract of land were purchased for $1,350,000 on March 6. The stand of timber is estimated at 15,000,000 board feet. During the current year, 3,300,000 board feet of timber were cut and sold.

Instructions

1. Determine the amount of the amortization, depletion, or impairment for the current year for each of the foregoing items.
2. Illustrate the effects on the accounts and financial statements of the adjustments for each item.

Metric-Based Analysis

Obj. 1

MBA 8-1 Purchase of land

Using the data from E8-3, indicate the effects of purchasing the land on the liquidity metric free cash flow and profitability metric asset turnover. Assume all costs were paid in cash and cash was received for the salvaged materials.

Obj. 2

MBA 8-2 Comparing depreciation methods

Use the data from E8-9 to answer each of the following:

1. Using the integrated financial statement framework, indicate the effects (increase or decrease) of using double-declining-balance depreciation rather than straight-line depreciation on accumulated depreciation, retained earnings, and depreciation expense at the beginning of the asset's useful life.
2. Indicate the effects (increase, decrease, or no effect) of using double-declining-balance depreciation rather than straight-line depreciation on the liquidity metric free cash flow and profitability metric asset turnover at the beginning of the asset's useful life.

Obj. 3

MBA 8-3 Disposal of fixed assets

Using the data from E8-4, indicate the effects on the liquidity metric free cash flow and profitability metric asset turnover for each of the following:

1. The equipment was sold in the first week of the fourth year for $23,300.
2. The equipment was sold in the first week of the fourth year for $15,250 instead of $23,300.
3. The equipment was sold at the end of four years for its estimated residual value of $10,000.
4. The equipment was discarded at the end of its useful life with no residual value. The balance of the equipment and its related accumulated depreciation is $140,000.

MBA 8-4 Depletion, patent amortization, goodwill impairment

Obj. 4, 5

Using the data from P8-5, indicate the effects on the liquidity metric free cash flow and profitability metric asset turnover for each of the following:

- Impaired goodwill
- Patent amortization
- Natural resource depletion

MBA 8-5 Asset turnover

Obj. 7

United Continental Holdings, Inc. (UAL) operates passenger service throughout the world. The following data (in millions) were adapted from a recent financial statement of United.

Sales (revenue)	$43,259
Average property, plant, and equipment	31,629
Average intangible assets	7,607

1. Compute the asset turnover. Round to two decimal places.
2. Compare the results from part (1) with Delta's asset turnover of 0.93.

MBA 8-6 Asset turnover

Obj. 7

Southwest Airlines (LUV) operates passenger services throughout the United States. The following data (in millions) were adapted from a recent financial statement of Southwest.

Sales (revenue)	$22,428
Average property, plant, and equipment	18,950
Average intangible assets	1,318

1. Compute the asset turnover. Round to two decimal places.
2. Compare the results from part (1) with the asset turnover calculated for United in MBA 8-5 and Delta's asset turnover of 0.93.

MBA 8-7 Asset turnover

Obj. 7

JetBlue Airways Corporation (JBLU) operates passenger services throughout the United States. The following data (in millions) were adapted from recent financial statements of JetBlue.

	Year 2	Year 1
Sales	$8,094	$7,658
Operating assets (average for year):		
Property, plant, and equipment	8,921	8,182

1. Compute the asset turnover for Years 1 and 2. Round to two decimal places.
2. Comment on the asset turnover results from part (1).

MBA 8-8 Asset turnover

Obj. 7

1. Compare the asset turnover ratios for Delta Air Lines (see the chapter illustration), United (MBA 8-5), Southwest (MBA 8-6), and JetBlue (MBA 8-7). Use Year 2 of Delta and JetBlue for your comparison.
2. Comment on the results from part (1).

Obj. 7

MBA 8-9 Asset turnover

Marriott International Inc. (MAR) and Hilton Wordwide Holdings Inc. (HLT) operate hotels worldwide. The following data (in millions) were adapted from recent financial statements of Marriott and Hilton.

	Marriott	Hilton
Sales (revenue)	$20,972	$9,452
Average property, plant, and equipment	2,374	807
Average intangible assets	17,554	11,275

1. Compute the asset turnover for Marriott and Hilton. Round to two decimal places.
2. Comment on the asset turnover results from part (1).

Cases

Case 8-1 Ethics and professional conduct in business

ETHICS

Rowel Baylon, CPA, is an assistant to the controller of Arches Consulting Co. In his spare time, Rowel also prepares tax returns and performs general accounting services for clients. Frequently, Rowel performs these services after his normal working hours, using Arches Consulting Co.'s computers and laser printers. Occasionally, Rowel's clients will call him at the office during regular working hours.

Discuss whether Rowel is performing in a professional manner.

Case 8-2 Financial vs. tax depreciation

The following is an excerpt from a conversation between two employees of Linquest Technologies, Don Corbet and Rita Shevlin. Don is the accounts payable clerk, and Rita is the cashier.

Don: Rita, could I get your opinion on something?

Rita: Sure, Don.

Don: Do you know Margaret, the fixed assets clerk?

Rita: I know who she is, but I don't know her real well. Why?

Don: Well, I was talking to her at lunch last Tuesday about how she liked her job, etc. You know, the usual ... and she mentioned something about having to keep two sets of books ... one for taxes and one for the financial statements. That can't be good accounting, can it? What do you think?

Rita: Two sets of books? It doesn't sound right.

Don: It doesn't seem right to me either. I was always taught that you had to use generally accepted accounting principles. How can there be two sets of books? What could be the difference between the two?

How would you respond to Rita and Don if you were Margaret?

Case 8-3 Effect of depreciation on net income

Einstein Construction Co. specializes in building replicas of historic houses. Bree Andrus, president of Einstein Construction, is considering the purchase of various items of equipment on July 1, 20Y2, for $300,000. The equipment would have a useful life of 5 years and no residual value. In the past, all equipment has been leased. For tax purposes, Bree is considering depreciating the equipment by the straight-line method. She discussed the matter with her CPA and learned that although the straight-line method could be elected, it was to her advantage to use the Modified Accelerated Cost Recovery System (MACRS) for tax purposes. She asked for your advice as to which method to use for tax purposes.

1. Compute depreciation for each of the years (20Y2, 20Y3, 20Y4, 20Y5, 20Y6, and 20Y7) of useful life by (a) the straight-line method and (b) MACRS. In using the straight-line method, one-half year's depreciation should be computed for 20Y2 and 20Y7. Use the MACRS rates presented in the chapter.
2. Assuming that income before depreciation and income tax is estimated to be $800,000 uniformly per year and that the income tax rate is 40%, compute the net income for each of the years 20Y2, 20Y3, 20Y4, 20Y5, 20Y6, and 20Y7 if (a) the straight-line method is used and (b) MACRS is used.
3. What factors would you present for Bree's consideration in the selection of a depreciation method?

Case 8-4 Ethics and professional conduct in business

The following is an excerpt from a conversation between the chief executive officer, Kim Jenkins, and the chief financial officer, Steve Mueller, of Quatro Group Inc.:

Kim: Steve, as you know, the auditors are coming in to audit our year-end financial statements pretty soon. Do you see any problems on the horizon?

Steve: Well, you know about our "famous" Scher Company acquisition from a couple of years ago. We booked $9,000,000 of goodwill from that acquisition, and the accounting rules require us to recognize any impairment of goodwill.

Kim: Uh-oh.

Steve: Yeah, right. We had to shut the old Scher Company operations down this year because those products were no longer selling. Thus, our auditor is going to insist that we write off the $9,000,000 of goodwill to reflect the impaired value.

Kim: We can't have that—at least not this year! Do everything you can to push back on this one. We just can't take that kind of a hit this year. The most we could stand is $5,000,000. Steve, keep the write-off to $5,000,000 and promise anything in the future. Then we'll deal with that down the road.

How should Steve respond to Kim?

Case 8-5 Equipment maintenance, downtime, and costs

Inject Solutions, LLC is a provider of finished plastic molding injection products to different industries. Inject Solutions works primarily with customers in the automobile, medical devices, and consumer toy manufacturing industries. With a fleet of 13 injection molding machines, Inject Solutions produces custom components for large manufacturers to use in their finished products. Inject Solutions has been operating 24-7 trying to meet its customer demands. As a result, the production supervisor for Inject Solutions, Natalie Ritter, wants an analysis of maintenance, downtime, and related costs.

1. Using the dataset for Inject Solutions, provide the following analyses for Natalie:
   a. Number of unplanned shutdowns by machine type
   b. Scheduled maintenance cost, shutdown repair cost, and total maintenance cost by product
2. How might Natalie Ritter use the preceding analyses?

Go to CengageNOWv2 to complete this assignment.

The annual report (10-K) assignment for this chapter is in Appendix B: Nike Annual Report, Chapter 8.

Answers to Self-Examination Questions

1. **C** All amounts spent to get a fixed asset (such as machinery) in place and ready for use are proper additions to the asset account. In the case of machinery acquired, the freight (answer A) and the installation costs (answer B) are both (answer C) proper charges to the machinery account.

2. **C** The periodic charge for depreciation under the double-declining-balance method for the second year is determined by first computing the depreciation charge for the first year. The depreciation for the first year of $6,000 (answer A) is computed by multiplying the cost of the equipment, $9,000, by 2/3 (the straight-line rate of 1/3 multiplied by 2). The depreciation for the second year of $2,000 (answer C) is then determined by multiplying the book value at the end of the first year, $3,000 (the cost of $9,000 minus the first-year depreciation of $6,000), by 2/3. The third year's depreciation is $400 (answer D). It is determined by multiplying the book value at the end of the second year, $1,000, by 2/3, thus yielding $667. However, the equipment cannot be depreciated below its residual value of $600; thus, the third-year depreciation is $400 ($1,000 − $600).

3. **B** A depreciation method that provides for a higher depreciation amount in the first year of the use of an asset and a gradually declining periodic amount thereafter is called an accelerated depreciation method. The double-declining-balance method (answer B) is an example of such a method.

4. **B** $252,000. The depletion expense is determined by first computing a depletion rate. For Hyde Inc., the depletion rate is $1.44 per ton ($3,600,000/2,500,000 tons). The depletion rate of $1.44 per ton is then multiplied by the number of tons mined during the year, or 175,000 tons, to determine the depletion expense of $252,000 (175,000 tons × $1.44).

5. **D** Long-lived assets that are useful in operations, not held for sale, and without physical qualities are called intangible assets. Patents, goodwill, and copyrights are examples of intangible assets (answer D).

Chapter

9 Liabilities

What's Covered:

Topics: Liabilities

Financing Corporations
- Short-term debt (Obj. 1)
- Long-term debt (Obj. 1)
- Equity (Obj. 1)
- Earnings per share (Obj. 1)

Current Liabilities
- Accounts payable and accruals (Obj.2)
- Notes payable (Obj. 2)
- Payroll (Obj. 2)

Long-Term Liabilities
- Bonds (Obj. 3)

Contingent Liabilities
- Probable and estimable (Obj. 4)
- Probable and not estimable (Obj. 4)
- Reasonably possible (Obj. 4)
- Remote (Obj. 4)

Reporting Liabilities
- Balance sheet (Obj. 5)

Metric-Based Analysis
- Transactions:
  - Solvency: Net assets (Obj. 2, 3, 4)
  - Profitability: Earnings per share (Obj. 2, 3, 4)
- Financial Statements
  - Debt ratio (Obj. 6)

Learning Objectives

Obj. 1 Describe how corporations finance their operations and its impact on earnings per share.

Obj. 2 Describe and illustrate the accounting for current liabilities, notes payable, and payroll.

Obj. 3 Describe the accounting for bonds payable.

Obj. 4 Describe types of contingent liabilities and the related accounting.

Obj. 5 Describe and illustrate the reporting of liabilities on the balance sheet.

Obj. 6 Describe and illustrate the use of the debt ratio to assess a company's risk of insolvency.

Chapter Metrics

Use the following metrics to analyze transactions and financial statements.

TRANSACTIONS

Solvency*: Net Assets

Profitability: Earnings per Share

FINANCIAL STATEMENTS

Debt Ratio

*As will be discussed, a solvency rather than a liquidity metric is used in this chapter.

©Robert Mullan/Getty Images

Starbucks Corporation

Buying goods on credit is essential for businesses to run efficiently. The use of credit makes transactions more convenient and improves buying power. For individuals, the most common form of short-term credit is a credit card. Credit cards allow individuals to purchase items before they are paid for, while removing the need for individuals to carry large amounts of cash. They also provide documentation of purchases through a monthly credit card statement.

Short-term credit is used by *businesses* to make purchasing items more convenient. It also gives the business control over the payment for goods and services. When **Starbucks Corporation (SBUX)** opened its first coffee shop in 1971, it relied on short-term trade credit, or accounts payable, to purchase ingredients for its coffee shop in Seattle's historic Pike Place Market. Today, Starbucks still relies on accounts payable and short-term trade credit, which also gives it control over cash payments by separating the purchase function from the payment function. Thus, the employee responsible for purchasing the ingredients is separated from the employee responsible for paying for the purchase. This separation of duties can help prevent unauthorized purchases or payments.

In addition to accounts payable, Starbucks has liabilities related to payroll, notes, and contingencies. This chapter describes and illustrates the accounting for each of these liabilities.

Objective 1
Describe how corporations finance their operations and its impact on earnings per share.

Financing Corporations

Corporations finance their operations using the following sources:

- Short-term debt
- Long-term debt
- Equity

Short-term debt includes the purchasing of goods and services on account as well as issuing short-term notes payable. Long-term debt includes issuing long-term notes payable or bonds payable. A **bond** is a form of an interest-bearing note requiring periodic interest payments with the face amount due at the maturity date.

Equity includes issuing common stock and preferred stock. Preferred stock has preference to (is paid) dividends before common stock.

Starbucks Connection

Starbucks reported more than $11,167 million of long-term debt on a recent financial statement. In addition to financing its operations with long-term debt, Starbucks also has common stock outstanding and is authorized to issue preferred stock.

A factor influencing whether a company's operations should be financed with debt or equity is the impact of the financing decision on the company's earnings per share (EPS). **Earnings per share (EPS)** measures the income earned for each share of common stock outstanding. It is computed as follows:

$$\textbf{Earnings per Share} = \frac{\textbf{Net Income} - \textbf{Preferred Dividends}}{\textbf{Number of Common Shares Outstanding}}$$

Starbucks Connection

Starbucks reported earnings per share of $2.95 on a recent income statement. Starbucks is authorized to issue preferred stock, but no preferred stock is outstanding. Thus, no preferred dividends are deducted in computing its earnings per share.

To illustrate the effects of financing with debt or equity, assume that Reedy Corporation needs to raise $4,000,000 to begin its operations. Reedy Corporation is considering the three financing alternatives shown in Exhibit 1.

Exhibit 1
Reedy Corporation Financing Alternatives

	Alternative One		Alternative Two		Alternative Three	
	Amount	**Percent**	**Amount**	**Percent**	**Amount**	**Percent**
Issue 12% bonds	—	0%	—	0%	$2,000,000	50%
Issue preferred 9% stock, $50 par value	—	0	$2,000,000	50	1,000,000	25
Issue common stock, $10 par value	$4,000,000	100	2,000,000	50	1,000,000	25
Total amount of financing	$4,000,000	100%	$4,000,000	100%	$4,000,000	100%

Each alternative in Exhibit 1 finances a percent of the corporation's operations with common stock. However, this percent varies from 100% (Alternative One) to 25% (Alternative Three). The par value of a stock in Exhibit 1 is the dollar amount assigned to each share of stock. For example, in Alternative One Reedy issues 400,000 shares of common stock with a par value of $10 per share for a total of $4,000,000 (400,000 shares × $10 per share).[1]

Assume that during its first year of operations, Reedy Corporation earned income of $800,000 before interest and income taxes. Also, assume that the bonds were issued at their face amount and an income tax rate of 40%. The effect on earnings per share of financing Reedy's operations with each of the Exhibit 1 alternatives is shown in Exhibit 2.

Exhibit 2
Earnings per Share with Earnings of $800,000*

	Alternative One	Alternative Two	Alternative Three
12% bonds	—	—	$2,000,000
Preferred 9% stock, $50 par	—	$2,000,000	1,000,000
Common stock, $10 par	$4,000,000	2,000,000	1,000,000
Total	$4,000,000	$4,000,000	$4,000,000
Earnings before interest and income tax	$ 800,000	$ 800,000	$ 800,000
Deduct interest on bonds	—	—	(240,000)[a]
Income before income tax	$ 800,000	$ 800,000	$ 560,000
Deduct income tax	(320,000)[b]	(320,000)[b]	(224,000)[b]
Net income	$ 480,000	$ 480,000	$ 336,000
Dividends on preferred stock	—	(180,000)[c]	(90,000)[c]
Available for dividends on common stock	$ 480,000	$ 300,000	$ 246,000
Shares of common stock outstanding	÷ 400,000[d]	÷ 200,000[d]	÷ 100,000[d]
Earnings per share on common stock	$ 1.20	$ 1.50	$ 2.46

[a]$2,000,000 bonds × 12%
[b]Income before income tax × 40%
[c]Preferred stock × 9%
[d]Common stock ÷ $10 par value per share
*Earnings before interest and taxes

Exhibit 2 indicates that when earnings are $800,000, Alternative Three has the highest earnings per share. Thus, Alternative Three is most attractive for common shareholders. This is because $800,000 of income is enough to pay the bondholders their interest and the preferred shareholder their dividends.

For income more than $800,000, the earnings per share for each of the alternatives is even greater, with Alternative Three still generating the highest earnings per share.

1. In Chapter 10, we discuss the issuance of stock for amounts other than par value.

However, lowering the income will have the opposite effect. For example, if income is lowered to $440,000 Alternatives One and Two become more attractive to common stockholders. This is shown in Exhibit 3.

Exhibit 3
Earnings per Share with Earnings of $440,000*

	Alternative One	Alternative Two	Alternative Three
12% bonds	—	—	$2,000,000
Preferred 9% stock, $50 par	—	$2,000,000	1,000,000
Common stock, $10 par	$4,000,000	2,000,000	1,000,000
Total	$4,000,000	$4,000,000	$4,000,000
Earnings before interest and income tax	$ 440,000	$ 440,000	$ 440,000
Deduct interest on bonds	—	—	(240,000)
Income before income tax	$ 440,000	$ 440,000	$ 200,000
Deduct income tax	(176,000)	(176,000)	(80,000)
Net income	$ 264,000	$ 264,000	$ 120,000
Dividends on preferred stock	—	(180,000)	(90,000)
Available for dividends on common stock	$ 264,000	$ 84,000	$ 30,000
Shares of common stock outstanding	÷ 400,000	÷ 200,000	÷ 100,000
Earnings per share on common stock	$ 0.66	$ 0.42	$ 0.30

*Earnings before interest and taxes

In Exhibit 3, earnings per share is lowest for Alternative Three because the income must first be used to pay bond interest and preferred stock dividends. What's left then becomes available to common stockholders.

In addition to earnings per share, a corporation should consider other factors in deciding among the financing plans. For example, if bonds are issued, periodic interest and the face value of the bonds at maturity must be paid. If these payments are not made, the bondholders could seek court action and force the company into bankruptcy. In contrast, a corporation is not legally obligated to pay dividends on preferred or common stock.

Objective 2
Describe and illustrate the accounting for current liabilities, notes payable, and payroll.

Current Liabilities

Liabilities are debts owed to others called **creditors**. Liabilities that are to be paid out of current assets and are due within a short time are reported as **current liabilities** on the balance sheet. Liabilities due beyond one year are classified as **long-term liabilities**. When a long-term liability becomes due within one year, it is reclassified as a current liability.

Accounts Payable and Accruals

Accounts payable transactions have been described and illustrated in earlier chapters. These transactions involve a variety of purchases on account, including the purchase of merchandise and supplies. Accruals have also been described and illustrated in earlier chapters. Accrued liabilities are an obligation to pay current assets in the future. Accrued liabilities are normally recorded at the end of an accounting period as part of the adjustment process. For example, wages due employees at the end of the period are recorded as an expense (Wages Expense) and an accrued liability (Wages Payable). For many companies, accounts payable and accrued liabilities make up most of their current liabilities.

Starbucks Connection

In the "Current liabilities" section of a recent balance sheet, **Starbucks** reported accounts payable of $1,190 million and accrued liabilities of $1,754 million.

Notes Payable

Notes payable are often issued to:

1. Satisfy an account payable
2. Purchase merchandise or other assets

The issuer of the note is called the borrower, while the party receiving the note is called the lender. The lender accounts for the note as a note receivable, which was described and illustrated in Chapter 6.[2]

To illustrate the effects on the accounts and financial statements of issuing a note to satisfy an account payable, assume the following:

Face value of note:	$1,000
Interest rate:	6%
Date of note:	August 1, 20Y5
Term of note:	90 days
Due date of note:	October 30

The effects on the accounts and financial statements of issuing and paying the note are as follows:

Issued a 90-day, 6%, $1,000 note on account on August 1.

Financial Statement Effects

BALANCE SHEET

	Assets =	Liabilities		+ Stockholders' Equity
		Accounts Payable	+ Notes Payable	
Aug. 1.		(1,000)	1,000	

STATEMENT OF CASH FLOWS

INCOME STATEMENT

Paid note on October 30, including interest of $15($1,000 × 6% × 90/360).

Financial Statement Effects

BALANCE SHEET

	Assets	=	Liabilities	+	Stockholders' Equity
	Cash	=	Notes Payable	+	Retained Earnings
Oct. 30.	(1,015)		(1,000)		(15)

STATEMENT OF CASH FLOWS

Oct. 30. Operating	(1,015)

INCOME STATEMENT

Oct. 30. Interest expense	(15)

2. The effects on the accounts and financial statements of a lender who accepts a note is exactly opposite that for the issuer of the note.

The interest expense is reported in the "Other expense" section of the income statement for the year ended December 31, 20Y5. If the accounting period ends before the maturity date of the note, interest expense to the end of the period is recorded by an adjustment.

The current portion of notes payable is reported as a current liability on the balance sheet. Notes due beyond one year are reported as part of long-term liabilities on the balance sheet with supplemental information, such as maturity dates and interest rates, disclosed in the notes to the financial statements.

Starbucks Connection

On a recent balance sheet, **Starbucks** reported notes payable of $11,167 as a long-term liability. Notes to the financial statements disclosed the face values, maturity dates, and interest rates of the various notes. None of the notes were due within one year.

The transaction metric effects of issuing and paying the note payable are also illustrated. Earnings per share (EPS) is used as the profitability metric. Since this chapter focuses on total liabilities, current as well as long-term, the solvency metric rather than a liquidity metric is used. **Net assets** (Total assets − Total liabilities) is used as the solvency metric. A company is said to be **insolvent** if it cannot pay its liabilities as they become due or if its total liabilities exceed its total assets.

Transaction Metric Effects

The effects of issuing and paying the $1,000 note payable, including interest, on solvency and profitability metrics are as follows:

SOLVENCY	
Net Assets	
Issuing note payable	No Effect
Paying note payable	$(15)

PROFITABILITY	
Earnings per Share	
Issuing note payable	No Effect
Paying note payable	Decreases

Since the note payable was issued to satisfy an account payable, there is no effect on liabilities and net assets. Likewise, issuing the note payable has no effect on revenue, expenses, and earnings per share. Paying the note payable at its maturity decreases assets by $1,015 and liabilities by $1,000. Thus, net assets decrease by $15, the amount of the interest expense. The interest expense decreases earnings, thus, decreasing earnings per share.

Payroll

The term **payroll** refers to the amount paid to employees for the services they provide during a period. Payroll can include salaries or wages. The rate of salary is normally expressed in terms of a month or a year. *Wages* refers to payment for manual labor, both skilled and unskilled. The rate of wages is normally stated on an hourly or a weekly basis.

The total earnings of an employee for a payroll period, including bonuses and overtime pay, is called **gross pay**. From this amount is subtracted one or more deductions to arrive at the net pay. **Net pay** is the amount the employer must pay the employee. The deductions for federal income taxes are usually the largest deduction. Deductions may also be required for state or local income taxes. Still other deductions may be made for FICA tax, medical insurance, contributions to pensions, and items authorized by individual employees.

The FICA tax withheld from employees contributes to two federal programs. The first program, called *Social Security*, is for old age, survivors, and disability insurance (OASDI). The second program, called *Medicare*, is health insurance for senior citizens. The FICA tax rate and the amounts subject to the tax are established annually by law.[3]

3. The social security tax portion of the Federal Insurance Conributions Act (FICA) tax is limited to a specific amount of the annual compensation for each individual. The Medicare portion is not subject to a limitation. To simplify, it is assumed that all compensation is within the social security limitation. By doing so, we express social security and Medicare as a single assumed rate of 7.5%. Two other employer payroll taxes are Federal Unemployment Taxes (FUTA) and State Unemployment Taxes (SUTA). The maximum FUTA rate is 6.0% and is subject to an annual compensation limit per individual. SUTA rates vary by state and are also subject to an annual compensation limit per individual.

To illustrate recording payroll, assume that McDermott Co. had a gross payroll of $13,800 for the week ending April 11. Assume that the FICA tax was 7.5% of the gross payroll and that federal and state withholding were $1,655 and $280, respectively. The effects on the accounts and financial statements of McDermott Co. of paying employees for the week ending April 11 are as follows:

Financial Statement Effects

BALANCE SHEET

	Assets =	Liabilities		+	Stockholders' Equity
	Cash =	FICA Tax Payable	+ Employee Federal Income Tax Payable	+ Employee State Income Tax Payable +	Retained Earnings
Apr. 11.	(10,830)*	1,035**	1,655	280	(13,800)

STATEMENT OF CASH FLOWS

Apr. 11. Operating	(10,830)

INCOME STATEMENT

Apr. 11. Wages and salary exp.	(13,800)

*$13,800 − $1,035 − $ 1,655 − $280 = $10,830
**$13,800 × 7.5% = $1,035

Transaction Metric Effects

The effects of paying the employees on the solvency and profitability metrics are as follows:

SOLVENCY

Net Assets	$(13,800)

PROFITABILITY

Earnings per Share	Decreases

Net assets decrease by $13,800 [−$10,830 − $1,035 − $1,655 − $280]. The increase in payroll tax expense decreases net income, thus, decreasing earnings per share (EPS).

The FICA, federal, and state taxes withheld from the employees' earnings are not expenses to the employer. Rather, these amounts are withheld on the behalf of employees. These amounts must be remitted periodically to the state and federal agencies.

Most employers are subject to federal and state payroll taxes. Such taxes are an operating expense of the business. For example, employers are required to match employees' contributions to Social Security and Medicare. In addition, most businesses must pay federal and state unemployment taxes.

The Federal Unemployment Tax Act (FUTA) provides for temporary payments to those who become unemployed as a result of layoffs or other causes beyond their control. The FUTA tax rate and maximum earnings of each employee subject to the tax are established annually by law.

State Unemployment Tax Acts (SUTA) provide for payments to unemployed workers. The amounts paid as benefits are obtained, for the most part, from a tax on employers only. The employment experience and the status of each employer's tax account are reviewed annually, and the tax rates are adjusted accordingly by each state.

The employer's payroll taxes become liabilities when the related payroll is *recorded*. The prior payroll information of McDermott Co. indicates that the amount of FICA tax withheld is $1,035 on April 11. Since the employer must match the employees' FICA contributions, the employer's social security payroll tax will also be $1,035. Furthermore, assume that the FUTA and SUTA taxes are $145 and $25, respectively. The effects on the accounts and financial statements of McDermott Co. of recording the employer's payroll tax liabilities for the week are as follows:

Financial Statement Effects

BALANCE SHEET

	Assets =	Liabilities			+ Stockholders' Equity
		FICA Tax Payable +	FUTA Tax Payable +	SUTA Tax Payable +	Retained Earnings
Apr. 11.		1,035	145	25	(1,205)

STATEMENT OF CASH FLOWS

INCOME STATEMENT

Apr. 11. Payroll tax exp.	(1,205)

Payroll tax liabilities are paid to appropriate taxing authorities on a quarterly basis by decreasing Cash and the related taxes payable.

Transaction Metric Effects

The effects of recording the employer's payroll tax liabilities on the solvency and profitability metrics are as follows:

SOLVENCY	
Net Assets	$(1,205)

PROFITABILITY	
Earnings per Share	Decreases

Net assets decrease by the total of the payroll tax liabilities of $1,205. The increase in payroll tax expense decreases earnings, thus decreasing earnings per share.

Employee Fringe Benefits

Many companies provide their employees benefits in addition to salary and wages earned. Such fringe benefits may include vacation, medical, and retirement benefits.

The cost of employee fringe benefits is recorded as an expense by the employer. To match revenues and expenses, the estimated cost of **fringe benefits** is recorded as an expense during the period in which the employees earn the benefits.

Vacation Pay Most employers provide employees vacations, sometimes called *compensated absences*. The liability to pay for employee vacations could be accrued at the end of each pay period. However, many companies wait and record an adjustment for accrued vacation at the end of the year.

To illustrate, assume that employees earn one day of vacation for each month worked. The estimated vacation pay for the year ending December 31 is $325,000. The effects of the adjustment for the accrued vacation of $325,000 on the accounts and financial statements are as follows:

Financial Statement Effects

BALANCE SHEET

	Assets	=	Liabilities	+	Stockholders' Equity
			Vacation Pay Payable		Retained Earnings
Dec. 31.			325,000		(325,000)

STATEMENT OF CASH FLOWS

INCOME STATEMENT

Dec. 31. Vacation pay expense	(325,000)

Transaction Metric Effects

The effects of the adjustment for accrued vacation pay on the solvency and profitability metrics are as follows:

SOLVENCY

Net Assets	$(325,000)

PROFITABILITY

Earnings per Share	Decreases

Net assets decrease by $325,000 and expenses increase by $325,000. Since expenses increased, earnings per share decreases.

Employees may be required to take all their vacation time within one year. In such cases, any accrued vacation pay will be paid within one year. Thus, the vacation pay payable is reported as a current liability on the balance sheet. If employees are allowed to accumulate their vacation pay, the estimated vacation pay payable that will *not* be taken within a year is reported as a long-term liability.

When employees take vacations, the liability for vacation pay, Vacation Pay Payable, is decreased. Salaries or Wages Payable and the other related payroll accounts for taxes and withholdings are increased.

Pensions A **pension** is a cash payment to retired employees. Pension rights are accrued by employees as they work, based on the employer's pension plan. Two basic types of pension plans are defined contribution and defined benefit plans.[4]

In a **defined contribution plan**, the company invests contributions on behalf of the employee during the employee's working years. Normally, the employee and employer contribute to the plan. The employee's pension depends on the total contributions and the investment returns earned on those contributions.

4. The accounting for pensions is complex due to the uncertainties of estimating future pension liabilities. These estimates depend on such factors as employee life expectancies, employee turnover, expected employee compensation levels, and investment income on pension contributions. Additional accounting and disclosures related to pensions are covered in advanced accounting courses.

One of the more popular defined contribution plans is the 401k plan. Under this plan, employees contribute a portion of their gross pay to investments, such as mutual funds. A 401k plan offers employees the following two advantages:

1. The employee contribution is deducted before taxes.
2. The contributions and related earnings are not taxed until withdrawn at retirement.

In many cases, the employer matches some portion of the employee's contribution. The employer's cost increases Pension Expense. To illustrate, assume that Heaven Scent Perfumes Company contributes 10% of employee monthly salaries to an employee 401k plan. Assuming $500,000 of monthly salaries, the effects of the monthly contribution on the accounts and financial statements are as follows:

Financial Statement Effects

BALANCE SHEET

	Assets	=	Liabilities	+	Stockholders' Equity
	Cash				Retained Earnings
Dec. 31.	(50,000)				(50,000)

STATEMENT OF CASH FLOWS

Dec.31. Operating	(50,000)

INCOME STATEMENT

Dec. 31. Pension expense	(50,000)

Transaction Metric Effects

The effects of the monthly contribution to employee 401k plan on the solvency and profitability metrics are as follows:

SOLVENCY

Net Assets	$(50,000)

PROFITABILITY

Earnings per Share	Decreases

Net assets decrease by $50,000 and expenses increase by $50,000. Since expenses increased, earnings per share decreases.

Starbucks Connection

In a recent year, **Starbucks** disclosed that it made matching contributions of $122.1 million to its employee defined contribution plan. The plan is voluntary for employees.

In a **defined benefit plan**, the employer is obligated to pay for (fund) the employee's future pension benefits. The employee's annual pension is based on a formula, which includes such factors as the employee's years of service, age, and past salary. Many companies are replacing their defined benefit plans with defined contribution plans.

The annual pension cost of a defined benefit plan increases Pension Expense. The amount contributed (funded) by the employer decreases Cash and any unfunded amount increases Unfunded Pension Liability.

To illustrate, assume that the defined benefit plan of Hinkle Co. requires an annual pension cost of $80,000. This annual contribution is based on estimates of Hinkle's future pension liabilities.

On December 31, Hinkle pays $60,000 to the pension fund. The effects of the annual pension cost and related contribution on the accounts and financial statements are as follows:

Financial Statement Effects

BALANCE SHEET

	Assets	=	Liabilities	+	Stockholders' Equity
	Cash		**Unfunded Pension Liability**		**Retained Earnings**
Dec. 31.	(60,000)		20,000		(80,000)

STATEMENT OF CASH FLOWS

Dec.31. Operating	(60,000)

INCOME STATEMENT

Dec. 31. Pension expense	(80,000)

Transaction Metric Effects

The effects of the annual pension cost and related contribution on the solvency and profitability metrics are as follows:

SOLVENCY

Net Assets	$(80,000)

PROFITABILITY

Earnings per Share	Decreases

Cash decreases by $60,000 and liabilities increase by $20,000, thus net assets decrease by $80,000. Expenses increase by $80,000. Since expenses increased, earnings per share decreases.

Other Postretirement Benefits Employees may earn rights to other postretirement benefits from their employer. Such benefits may include dental care, eye care, medical care, life insurance, tuition assistance, tax services, and legal services.

The accounting for other postretirement benefits is similar to that of defined benefit pension plans. The estimate of the annual benefits expense is recorded by increasing Postretirement. Benefits Expense. If the benefits are fully funded, Cash is decreased for the same amount. If the benefits are not fully funded, a postretirement benefits plan liability account is also increased.

The financial statements should disclose the nature of the postretirement benefits liabilities. These disclosures are usually included as notes to the financial statements. Additional accounting and disclosures for postretirement benefits are covered in advanced accounting courses.

Integrity, Objectivity, and Ethics in Business

A Résumé Padding

Misrepresenting your accomplishments on your résumé could come back to haunt you. In one case, the chief financial officer (CFO) of **Veritas Software** was forced to resign his position when it was discovered that he had lied about earning an MBA from Stanford University, when in actuality he had earned only an undergraduate degree from Idaho State University.

Source: Reuters News Service, October 4, 2002.

Objective 3
Describe the accounting for bonds payable.

Bonds

Many large corporations finance their long-term operations through the issuance of bonds. A **bond** is simply a form of an interest-bearing note. Like a note, a bond requires periodic interest payments, with the face amount payable at the maturity date.

A corporation that issues bonds enters into a contract, called a **bond indenture** or trust indenture, with the bondholders. A bond issue is normally divided into a number of individual bonds. Usually, the face value of each bond, called the *principal*, is $1,000 or a multiple of $1,000. The interest on bonds may be payable annually, semiannually, or quarterly. Most bonds pay interest semiannually.

The prices of bonds are quoted on bond exchanges as a percentage of the bonds' face value. Thus, investors could purchase or sell bonds quoted at 109⅞ for $1,098.75. Likewise, bonds quoted at 98 could be purchased or sold for $980.

When a corporation issues bonds, the price that buyers are willing to pay for the bonds depends on these three factors:

1. The face amount of the bonds due at the maturity date
2. The periodic interest to be paid on the bonds
3. The market rate of interest

The periodic interest to be paid on the bonds is identified in the bond indenture and is expressed as a percentage of the face amount of the bond. This percentage or rate of interest is called the **contract rate** or *coupon rate*. The **market rate of interest**, sometimes called the *effective rate of interest*, is determined by transactions between buyers and sellers of similar bonds. If the contract rate of interest is the same as the market rate of interest, the bonds sell for their face amount.

To illustrate, assume that on January 1 a corporation issues for cash $100,000 of 6%, 5-year bonds, with interest of $3,000 payable semiannually. The market rate of interest at the time the bonds are issued is 6%. Since the contract rate and the market rate of interest are the same, the bonds will sell at their face amount. The effects on the accounts and financial statements of issuing the bonds, paying the semiannual interest, and paying off the bonds at the maturity date are shown as follows.

Issued $100,000 of bonds payable at face amount on January 1.

Financial Statement Effects

BALANCE SHEET

	Assets	=	Liabilities	+	Stockholders' Equity
	Cash	=	Bonds Payable		
Jan. 1.	100,000		100,000		

STATEMENT OF CASH FLOWS

Jan. 1. Financing	100,000

INCOME STATEMENT

Paid semiannual interest on June 30. (Interest: $100,000 × 0.06 × ½ = $3,000)

Financial Statement Effects

BALANCE SHEET

	Assets	=	Liabilities	+	Stockholders' Equity
	Cash	**=**			**Retained Earnings**
June 30.	(3,000)				(3,000)

STATEMENT OF CASH FLOWS	
June 30. Operating	(3,000)

INCOME STATEMENT
June 30. Interest expense (3,000)

Paid face value of $100,000 bond at maturity.

BALANCE SHEET

	Assets	=	Liabilities	+	Stockholders' Equity
	Cash	**=**	**Bonds Payable**		
Dec. 31.	(100,000)		(100,000)		

STATEMENT OF CASH FLOWS	
Dec. 31. Financing	(100,000)

INCOME STATEMENT

Transaction Metric Effects

The effects of the bond payable transactions on the solvency and profitability metrics are as follows:

SOLVENCY	
Net Assets	
Issuing bonds payable	No Effect
Paying interest	$(3,000)
Paying face value of bonds	No Effect

PROFITABILITY	
Earnings per Share	
Issuing bonds payable	No Effect
Paying interest	Decreases
Paying face value of bonds	No Effect

Issuing bonds payable increases assets and liabilities by $100,000 and, thus, has no effect on net assets. Since revenue and expenses are unaffected by issuing bonds payable, there is no effect on the earnings per share (EPS). Paying interest decreases assets and increases expenses but does not change liabilities. Thus, paying interest decreases net assets by $3,000 and decreases earnings per share. Paying the face value of the bonds at their maturity has no effect on net assets or earnings per share.

The market and contract rates of interest determine whether the selling price of a bond will be equal to, less than, or more than the bond's face amount. The relationship between the market rate of interest, the contract rate, and the selling price of a bond is shown in Exhibit 4.

Exhibit 4
Selling Price of a Bond

Market Rate = Contract Rate
Selling Price = Face Value of Bonds

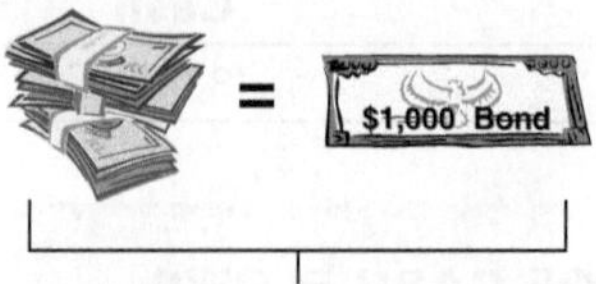

No Discount or Premium on Bonds Payable

Market Rate > Contract Rate
Selling Price < Face Value of Bonds

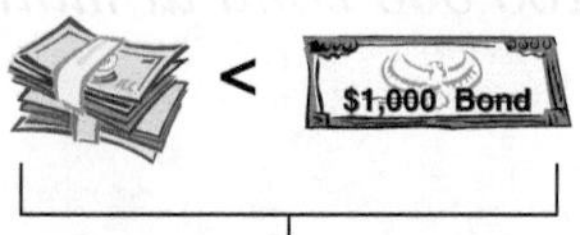

Discount on Bonds Payable

Market Rate < Contract Rate
Selling Price > Face Value of Bonds

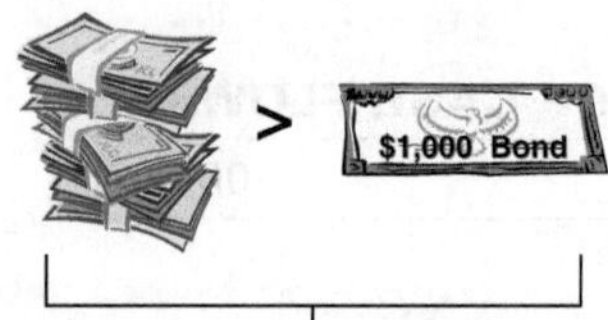

Premium on Bonds Payable

If the market rate of interest equals the bond's contract rate, a bond will sell at its face value. If the market rate of interest is more than the contract rate, the bond will sell at a discount. This is because investors can earn more interest elsewhere. By purchasing the bond at a discount, the investor increases the effective rate of interest on the investment to the equivalent of the market rate.

If the market rate is less than the contract rate, the bond will sell at a premium. This is because the investor demand for the bonds will be high and, as a result, the price of the bonds will be bid up. The price of the bonds will increase until the effective rate of the bonds is equivalent to the market rate.

Generally accepted accounting principles require that the interest expense reported on the income statement be adjusted for any discount or premium that was incurred when the bond was sold. The adjustment for a discount on bonds payable increases Interest Expense over the life of the bond. The adjustment for a premium on bonds payable decreases Interest Expense over the life of the bond.[5]

5. The amortization of bond discounts and premiums is discussed in advanced accounting courses.

Contingent Liabilities

Objective 4

Describe types of contingent liabilities and the related accounting.

Some liabilities may arise from past transactions if certain events occur in the future. These *potential* liabilities are called **contingent liabilities**.

The accounting for contingent liabilities depends on the following two factors:

1. Likelihood of occurring
2. Measurement

The likelihood of the potential liability occurring is classified as *probable*, *reasonably possible*, or *remote*. The ability to measure the potential liability is classified as *estimable* or *not estimable*.

Probable and Estimable

If a contingent liability is *probable* and the amount of the liability can be *reasonably estimated*, it is recorded and disclosed. The liability is recorded by increasing an expense and a liability.

To illustrate, assume that during June a company sold a product for $60,000 that includes a 36-month warranty for repairs. The average cost of repairs over the warranty period is 5% of the sales price.

Warranty expense of $3,000 ($60,000 × 5%) is recorded by increasing Warranty Expense and increasing Product Warranty Payable. In doing so, the warranty expense is recorded in the same period in which the related product sale is recorded. In other words, the warranty expense is matched with the related revenue (sales). When a defective product is repaired, the repair costs are recorded by decreasing Product Warranty Payable and decreasing Cash, Supplies, or other appropriate accounts.

Probable and Not Estimable

A contingent liability may be probable but cannot be estimated. In this case, the contingent liability is disclosed in the notes to the financial statements. For example, a company may have accidentally polluted a local river by dumping waste products. At the end of the period, the cost of the cleanup and any fines may not be able to be estimated.

Reasonably Possible

A contingent liability may be only possible. For example, a company may have lost a lawsuit for infringing on another company's patent rights. However, the verdict is under appeal and the company's lawyers feel that the verdict will be reversed or significantly reduced. In this case, the contingent liability is disclosed in the notes to the financial statements.

Remote

A contingent liability may be remote. For example, a ski resort may be sued for injuries incurred by skiers. In most cases, the courts have found that a skier accepts the risk of injury when participating in the activity of skiing. Thus, unless the ski resort is grossly negligent, the resort will not incur a liability for ski injuries. In such cases, no disclosure needs to be made in the notes to the financial statements.

The accounting for contingencies is summarized in Exhibit 5.

Exhibit 5 Accounting for Contingent Liabilities

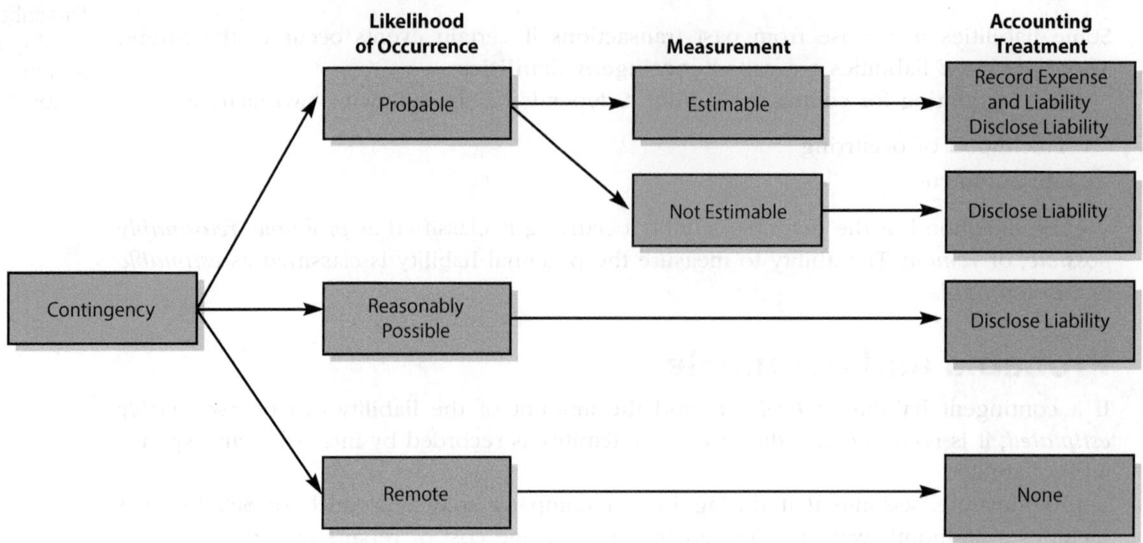

Disclosure of Contingent Liabilities

Common examples of contingent liabilities disclosed in notes to the financial statements are litigation, environmental matters, guarantees, and contingencies from the sale of receivables.

Professional judgment is necessary in distinguishing among classes of contingent liabilities. This is especially the case when distinguishing between probable and reasonably possible contingent liabilities.

Starbucks Connection

Starbucks leases (rents) space for its retail stores, distribution and warehouse facilities, and office space. Some of the retail store leases provide for contingent rent based upon a percentage of sales. In notes to recent financial statements, Starbucks disclosed the following related to its contingent rent:

> *Certain leases provide for contingent rent, which is determined as a percentage of gross sales in excess of specified levels. We record a contingent rent liability in accrued occupancy costs within accrued liabilities on our consolidated balance sheets and the corresponding rent expense when we determine that achieving the specified levels during the fiscal year is probable.*

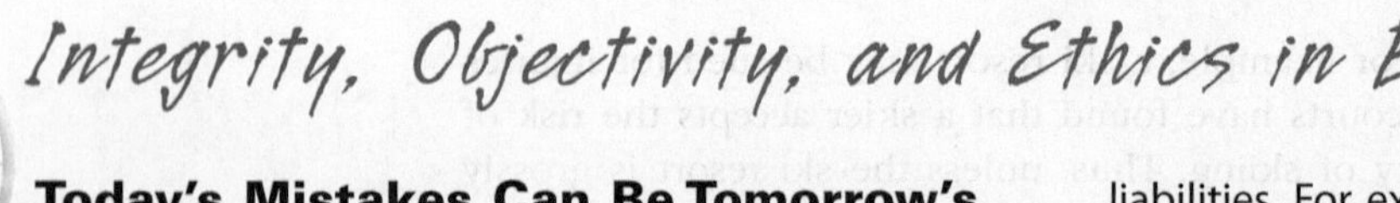

Integrity, Objectivity, and Ethics in Business

Today's Mistakes Can Be Tomorrow's Liability

Environmental and public health claims are quickly growing into some of the largest contingent liabilities facing companies. As a result, managers must be careful that today's decisions do not become tomorrow's liabilities. For example, tobacco, asbestos, and environmental cleanup claims have reached billions of dollars and have led to a number of corporate bankruptcies.

Durabla Manufacturing Co., which produced sealing products, had over 100,000 asbestos lawsuits filed against it. As a result, Durabla filed for bankruptcy.

Reporting Liabilities

Objective 5
Describe and illustrate the reporting of liabilities on the balance sheet.

Liabilities that are expected to be paid within one year are presented in the "Current liabilities" section of the balance sheet. Thus, any notes or bonds payable maturing within one year are reported as current liabilities. The detailed descriptions, including terms, due dates, and interest rates for notes or bonds, are reported either on the balance sheet or in a note. Also, the fair market value of notes or bonds is disclosed.

Starbucks Connection

The reporting of **Starbucks Corporation**'s current liabilities and long-term debt is as follows:

Starbucks Corporation
Balance Sheet
September 29
(in millions)

Current liabilities:		
Accounts payable	$ 1,189.7	
Accrued liabilities	1,753.7	
Accrued payroll and benefits	664.6	
Income taxes payable	1,291.7	
Store value card liability	1,269.0	
Current portion of long-term debt	—	
Total current liabilities		$ 6,168.7
Long-term liabilities:		
Long-term debt	$11,167.0	
Deferred (unearned) revenue	6,744.4	
Other long-term liabilities	1,370.5	
Total long-term liabilities		19,281.9
Total liabilities		$25,450.6

Notes (excerpts)

Long-Term Debt
Components of long-term debt including the associated interest rates and related fair values by calendar maturity (in millions, except interest rates):

			Interest	
Issuance	**Face Value**	**Fair Value**	**Contract Rate**	**Effective Rate**
...	...	...	...	...
August 2025 notes	$ 1,250	$1,351	3.800%	3.721%
June 2026 notes	$500	$502	2.450%	2.511%
...	...	...	...	...
November 2048 notes	$1,000	$1,160	4.500%	4.504%
May 2049 notes	$1,000	$1,165	4.450%	4.433%
Total	$11,167	$12,033		

Contingent liabilities that are probable but cannot be reasonably estimated or are only possible are also disclosed in the notes to the financial statements.

Using Data Analytics

Supplier (Vendor) Relationships

Developing and maintaining reliable suppler (vendor) relationships is critical for most businesses. For example, manufacturers such as **Procter & Gamble (PG)** depend on suppliers (vendors) to furnish raw materials for its manufacturing facilities, which produce products such as Tide laundry detergent. A disruption or stoppage of raw materials could result in idle production facilities and lost sales.

Likewise, supplier relationships are essential for large retail chains such as **Costco (COST)**, **Walmart (WMT)**, and **Target (TGT)**. For example, Costco states the following in a recent annual report:

> *Suppliers may be unable to timely supply us with quality merchandise at competitive prices . . . resulting in adverse effects on our business, merchandise inventories, sales, and profit margins.*

Data analytics could be used by companies such as Costco to analyze and report on a variety of supplier (vendor) metrics, including average time to receive an order as well as the percent of back orders and returns. These analyses could then be used as a basis for developing supplier-buyer expectations and trusted, "win-win" relationships.

See Case 9-6 for a homework assignment using data analytics.

Objective 6

Describe and illustrate the use of the debt ratio to assess a company's risk of insolvency.

Financial Statement Metric-Analysis: Debt Ratio

The **debt ratio**, sometimes called the debt to assets ratio, is a useful solvency metric. It is normally expressed as a percent and is computed as follows:

$$\text{Debt Ratio} = \frac{\text{Total Liabilities}}{\text{Total Assets}}$$

The debt ratio measures the percent of the company's assets financed by debt. The debt ratio also may be used to measure how a company is using debt to generate income. However, the higher the debt ratio (financial leverage), the more risk a company is taking in managing its operations.

To illustrate, the following data (in millions) from recent financial statements of **Apple (AAPL)** and **Microsoft (MSFT)** are used.

	Assets	Total Liabilities	Stockholders' Equity
Apple	$338,516	$248,028	$ 90,488
Microsoft	286,556	184,226	102,330

The debt ratios (rounded to one decimal place) for Apple and Microsoft are as follows:

Apple:	73.3% ($248,028 ÷ $338,516)
Microsoft:	64.3% ($184,226 ÷ $286,556)

Apple and Microsoft finance over half of their operations using debt. Apple finances 73.3% of its assets using debt, while Microsoft finances 64.3% of its assets using debt. While Microsoft has slightly less risk of insolvency than Apple, both companies have strong operating results and generate significant cash flows from operations.

Exhibit 2 illustrates the effects of how issuing bonds can increase earnings per share. This use of debt to enhance the earnings of stockholders is called **financial leverage**. With over half of their operations financed by debt, Apple and Microsoft are using financial leverage to enhance earnings for their shareholders.

Key Points

1. Describe how corporations finance their operations and its impact on earnings per share.

A business must finance its operations through either debt or equity. Debt financing includes all liabilities owed by a business, including both current and long-term liabilities. A corporation may also finance its operations by issuing equity (common stock and preferred stock). The method of financing impacts earnings per share for common stock.

2. Describe and illustrate the accounting for current liabilities, notes payable, and payroll.

Liabilities that are to be paid out of current assets and are due within a short time, usually within one year, are called *current liabilities*. Most current liabilities arise from either receiving goods or services prior to making payment or receiving payment prior to delivering goods or services. Current liabilities can also arise from accruals, notes payable, and payroll. Wages and salaries payable and employee and employer payroll taxes are examples of liabilities arising from payroll.

3. Describe the accounting for bonds payable.

Many large corporations finance their operations through the issuance of bonds. A bond is simply a form of an interest-bearing note that requires periodic interest payments and the repayment of the face amount at the maturity date. When the contract rate of interest differs from the market rate of interest, bonds are issued at discounts or premiums. The amortization of discounts and premiums affects interest expense.

4. Describe types of contingent liabilities and the related accounting.

A contingent liability is a potential obligation that results from a past transaction but depends on a future event.

The accounting for contingent liabilities depends upon their likelihood of occurrence and the ability to measure the amount of the contingency. The accounting for contingent liabilities is summarized in Exhibit 5.

5. Describe and illustrate the reporting of liabilities on the balance sheet.

Liabilities that are expected to be paid within one year are presented in the "Current liabilities" section of the balance sheet. Notes or bonds payable not maturing within one year should be shown as long-term liabilities. The detailed descriptions including terms, due dates, and interest rates for notes or bonds should be reported either on the balance sheet or in an accompanying note. Also, the fair market value of notes or bonds should be disclosed. The notes should disclose any contingent liabilities that cannot be reasonably estimated or are only possible.

6. Metric-Based Analysis: Describe and illustrate the use of the debt ratio to assess a company's risk of insolvency.

The debt ratio indicates the percent of a company's operations that are financed by debt. The higher the ratio, the higher the financial leverage and more risk to creditors.

Key Terms

Bond (350, 359)
Bond indenture (360)
Contingent liabilities (363)
Contract rate (360)
Creditors (352)
Current liabilities (352)
Debt ratio (366)
Defined benefit plan (358)
Defined contribution plan (357)
Earnings per share (EPS) (350)
Financial leverage (367)
Fringe benefits (356)
Gross pay (354)
Insolvent (354)
Long-term liabilities (352)
Market rate of interest (360)
Net assets (354)
Net pay (354)
Payroll (354)
Pension (357)

Illustrative Problem

Three different plans for financing an $18,000,000 corporation are under consideration by its organizers. Under each of the following plans, the securities will be issued at their par or face amount, and the income rax rate is estimated at 40% of income

	Plan1	Plan 2	Plan 3
8% bonds	—	—	$ 9,000,000
Preferred 4% stock, $20 par	—	$9,000,000	4,500,000
Common stock, $10 par	$18,000,000	9,000,000	4,500,000
Total	$18,000,000	$18,000,000	$18,000,000

Instructions

1. Determine the earnings per share of common stock for each plan, assuming that the income before bond interest and income tax is $2,100,000.
2. Determine the earnings per share of common stock for each plan, assuming that the income before bond interest and income tax is $1,050,000.
3. Discuss the advantages and disadvantages of each plan.

Solution

1.	Plan1	Plan 2	Plan 3
Earnings before interest and income tax	$2,100,000	$2,100,000	$2,100,000
Deduct interest on bonds	0	0	(720,000)
Income before income tax	$2,100,000	$2,100,000	$1,380,000
Deduct income tax	(840,000)	(840,000)	(552,000)
Net income	$1,260,000	$1,260,000	$ 828,000
Dividends on preferred stock	0	(360,000)	(180,000)
Available for dividends on common stock	$1,260,000	$ 900,000	$ 648,000
Shares of common stock outstanding	÷1,800,000	÷ 900,000	÷ 450,000
Earnings per share on common stock	$ 0.70	$ 1.00	$ 1.44

2.	Plan1	Plan 2	Plan 3
Earnings before interest and income tax	$1,050,000	$1,050,000	$1,050,000
Deduct interest on bonds	0	0	(720,000)
Income before income tax	$1,050,000	$1,050,000	$ 330,000
Deduct income tax	(420,000)	(420,000)	(132,000)
Net income	$ 630,000	$ 630,000	$ 198,000
Dividends on preferred stock	0	(360,000)	(180,000)
Available for dividends on common stock	$ 630,000	$ 270,000	$ 18,000
Shares of common stock outstanding	÷1,800,000	÷ 900,000	÷ 450,000
Earnings per share on common stock	$ 0.35	$ 0.30	$ 0.04

3. The principal advantage of Plan 1 is that it involves only the issuance of common stock, which does not require a periodic interest payment or return of principal, and a payment of preferred dividends is not required. It is also more attractive to common shareholders than is Plan 2 or 3 if earnings before interest and income tax is $1,050,000. In this case, it has the largest EPS ($0.35). The principal disadvantage of Plan 1 is that, if earnings before interest and income tax is $2,100,000, it offers the lowest EPS ($0.70) on common stock.

   The principal advantage of Plan 3 is that less investment would need to be made by common shareholders. Also, it offers the largest EPS ($1.44) if earnings before interest and income tax is $2,100,000. Its principal disadvantage is that the bonds carry a fixed annual interest charge and require the repayment of principal. It also requires a dividend payment to preferred stockholders before a common dividend can be paid. Finally, Plan 3 provides the lowest EPS ($0.04) if earnings before interest and income tax is $1,050,000.

   Plan 2 provides a middle ground in terms of the advantages and disadvantages described in the preceding paragraphs for Plans 1 and 3.

Self-Examination Questions

(Answers appear at the end of the chapter.)

1. A business issued a $5,000, 60-day, 12% note to the bank. The amount due at maturity is:
   A. $4,900
   B. $5,000
   C. $5,100
   D. $5,600

2. Which of the following taxes are employers usually not required to withhold from employees?
   A. Federal income tax
   B. Federal unemployment compensation tax
   C. FICA tax
   D. State and local income taxes

3. Employers do not incur an expense for which of the following payroll taxes?
   A. FICA tax
   B. Federal unemployment compensation tax
   C. State unemployment compensation tax
   D. Employees' federal income tax

4. An employee's rate of pay is $36 per hour, with time and a half for all hours worked in excess of 40 during a week. The employee worked 45 hours during the week. The amount of the employee's gross pay for the week is:
   A. $1,440
   B. $1,620
   C. $1,710
   D. $1,800

5. If a corporation plans to issue $1,000,000 of 7% bonds when the market rate for similar bonds is 6%, the bonds can be expected to sell at:
   A. Their face amount
   B. A premium
   C. A discount
   D. A price below their face amount

Class Discussion Questions

1. For most companies, what two types of transactions make up the largest percent of their current liabilities?
2. When are short-term notes payable issued?
3. For each of the following payroll-related taxes, indicate whether it generally applies to (1) employees only, (2) employers only, or (3) both employees and employers:
   a. Federal income tax
   b. Federal unemployment compensation tax
   c. Medicare tax
   d. Social security tax
   e. State unemployment compensation tax
4. To match revenues and expenses properly, should the expense for employee vacation pay be recorded in the period during which the vacation privilege is earned or during the period in which the vacation is taken?
5. Identify the two distinct obligations incurred by a corporation when issuing bonds.

6. A corporation issues $40,000,000 of 6% bonds when the market rate of interest was 8%.
   a. Was the amount of cash received from the sale of the bonds more or less than $40,000,000?
   b. Identify the following amounts related to the bond issue: (1) face amount, (2) market rate of interest, (3) contract rate of interest, and (4) maturity amount.
7. When should a contingent liability be recorded?
8. Assume Thomas Inc. has been selling a product over the past ten years with a 90-day warranty. When should the liability associated with a product warranty be recorded? Discuss.
9. Deere & Company (DE), a company well known for manufacturing farm equipment, reported more than $1,200 million of product warranties in recent financial statements. How would costs of repairing a defective product be recorded?
10. Delta Air Lines' (DAL) SkyMiles program allows frequent flyers to earn credit toward free tickets and other amenities.
    a. Does Delta Air Lines have a contingent liability for award redemption by its SkyMiles members?
    b. When should a contingent liability be recorded?

Exercises

Obj. 1

✔ a. $0.60

E9-1 Effect of financing on earnings per share

BSF Co., which produces and sells skiing equipment, is financed as follows:

Bonds payable, 8% (issued at face amount)	$7,500,000
Preferred 2% stock, $10 par	7,500,000
Common stock, $50 par	7,500,000

Income tax is estimated at 40% of income.

Determine the earnings per share of common stock, assuming that the income before bond interest and income tax is (a) $1,000,000, (b) $3,000,000, and (c) $4,500,000.

Obj. 1

E9-2 Evaluate alternative financing plans

Based on the data in Exercise E9-1, discuss factors other than earnings per share that should be considered in evaluating such financing plans.

Obj. 2, 5

SHOW ME HOW

✔ Total current liabilities, $392,800

E9-3 Current liabilities

By the Month Inc. sold 32,000 annual magazine subscriptions for $10 during December 20Y4. These new subscribers will receive monthly issues, beginning in January 20Y5. By the Month Inc. issued a $96,000, 180-day, 5% note payable on December 1, 20Y4. On March 31, 20Y5, By the Month Inc. had accounts payable of $43,000 and accrued wages payable of $12,200.

Prepare the "Current liabilities" section of the balance sheet for By the Month Inc. on March 31, 20Y5.

Obj. 2

SHOW ME HOW

E9-4 Notes payable

A business issued a 90-day, 5% note for $60,000 to a creditor for an accounts payable. Illustrate the effects on the accounts and financial statements of recording (a) the issuance of the note and (b) the payment of the note at maturity, including interest.

E9-5 Compute payroll

Obj. 2

✔ b. Net pay, $687.90

An employee earns $24 per hour and 1.5 times that rate for all hours in excess of 40 hours per week. Assume that the employee worked 43 hours during the week. Assume that the FICA tax rate is 7.5% and that federal income tax of $300 was withheld.

a. Determine the gross pay for the week.

b. Determine the net pay for the week.

E9-6 Summary payroll data

Obj. 2

✔ (3) Total earnings, $840,000

In the following summary of data for a payroll period, some amounts have been intentionally omitted:

Earnings:	
1. At regular rate	?
2. At overtime rate	$120,000
3. Total earnings	?
Deductions:	
4. FICA tax	63,000
5. Income tax withheld	200,000
6. Medical insurance	37,000
7. Union dues	?
8. Total deductions	315,000
9. Net amount paid	525,000
Accounts increased:	
10. Wages	400,000
11. Sales Salaries	?
12. Office Salaries	150,000

Compute the amounts omitted in lines (1), (3), (7), and (11).

E9-7 Recording payroll taxes

Obj. 2

According to a summary of the payroll of PJW Co., $90,000 in earnings were subject to the 7.5% FICA tax. Also, $30,000 in earnings were subject to state and federal unemployment taxes.

a. Compute the employer's payroll taxes, using the following rates: state unemployment, 2.7%; federal unemployment, 0.8%.

b. Illustrate the effects on the accounts and financial statements of recording the accrual of payroll taxes.

E9-8 Accrued vacation pay

Obj. 2

ProTech Inc. provides its employees with varying amounts of vacation per year, depending on the length of employment. The estimated amount of the current year's vacation pay is $432,000. Illustrate the effects on the accounts and financial statements of the adjustment required on January 31, the end of the first month of the current year, to record the accrued vacation pay.

E9-9 Pension liability and payment

Obj. 2

Yuri Co. operates a chain of gift shops. The company maintains a defined contribution pension plan for its employees. The plan requires quarterly installments to be paid to the funding agent, Whims Funds, by the fifteenth of the month following the end of each quarter. Assume that the pension cost is $365,000 for the quarter ended December 31.

a. Illustrate the effects on the accounts and financial statements of the accrued pension liability on December 31.

b. Illustrate the effects on the accounts and financial statements of the payment to the funding agent on January 15.

c. How does a defined contribution plan differ from a defined benefit plan?

Obj. 2

E9-10 Unfunded pension liability

In a recent year's financial statements, Procter & Gamble (PG) showed an unfunded pension liability of $5,655 million and a periodic pension cost of $139 million. Explain the meaning of the $5,655 million unfunded pension liability and the $139 million periodic pension cost.

Obj. 3

E9-11 Bond price

CVS Caremark Corp. (CVS) 5.3% bonds due in 2043, sold for 131.951. Were the bonds selling at a premium or at a discount? Explain.

Obj. 3

SHOW ME HOW

E9-12 Issuing bonds

Cyber Tech Inc. produces and distributes fiber optic cable for use by telecommunications companies. Cyber Tech Inc. issued $50,000,000 of 20-year, 6% bonds on March 1 at their face amount, with interest payable on March 1 and September 1. The fiscal year of the company is the calendar year. Illustrate the effects on the accounts and financial statements of recording the following selected transactions for the current year:

Mar. 1. Issued the bonds for cash at their face amount.

Sept. 1. Paid the interest on the bonds.

Dec. 31. Recorded accrued interest for four months.

Obj. 4

SHOW ME HOW

EXCEL ONLINE

E9-13 Accrued product warranty

A Wrinkle in Time Inc. warrants its products for one year. The estimated product warranty is 1% of sales. Assume that sales were $625,000 for March. In April, a customer received warranty repairs requiring $375 of parts.

a. Determine the warranty liability at March 31, the end of the first month of the current fiscal year.

b. What accounts are decreased for the warranty work provided in April?

Obj. 4

E9-14 Accrued product warranty

Ford Motor Company (F) disclosed the following estimated product warranty payable for two recent years.

	December 31,	
	Year 2	Year 1
	(in millions)	
Product warranty payable	$5,702	$5,137

Ford's sales in its automotive sector were $143,599 million in Year 2 and $148,294 million in Year 1. Assume that the total paid on warranty claims during Year 2 was $4,360 million.

a. Illustrate the effects on the accounts and financial statements for the Year 2 product warranty expense.

b. Explain the $565 ($5,702 − $5,137) million increase in the total warranty liability from Year 1 to Year 2.

E9-15 Contingent liabilities

Obj. 4

Several months ago, Cinnabar Chemical Company experienced a hazardous materials spill at one of its plants. As a result, the Environmental Protection Agency (EPA) fined the company $1,000,000. The company is contesting the fine. In addition, an employee is seeking $150,000 damages related to injuries sustained while cleaning up the spill. Lastly, a homeowner has sued the company for $100,000. The homeowner lives 6 miles from the plant but believes that the incident has reduced the home's resale value by $100,000.

Cinnabar's legal counsel believes that it is probable that the EPA fine will stand. In addition, counsel indicates that an out-of-court settlement of $75,000 has recently been reached with the employee. The final papers will be signed next week. Counsel believes that the homeowner's case is much weaker and will be decided in favor of Cinnabar. Other litigation related to the spill is possible, but the damage amounts are uncertain.

a. Illustrate the effects of the contingent liabilities associated with the hazardous materials spill on the accounts and financial statements.

b. Prepare a note disclosure relating to this incident.

E9-16 Contingent liabilities

Obj. 4

The following note accompanied the financial statements for Goodyear Tire and Rubber Company (GT):

> ***We have recorded liabilities totaling $293 million, including related legal fees expected to be incurred, for potential product liability and other tort claims, including asbestos claims.... General and product liability and other litigation liabilities are recorded based on management's assessment that a loss arising from these matters is probable.... Typically, these lawsuits have been brought against multiple defendants in Federal and state courts.***

a. Illustrate the effects on the accounts and financial statements of recording the contingent liability of $293,000,000.

b. Why was the contingent liability recorded?

Problems

P9-1 Effect of financing on earnings per share

Obj. 1

✔ 1. Plan 3: $1.72

Three different plans for financing a $5,000,000 corporation are under consideration by its organizers. Under each of the following plans, the securities will be issued at their par or face amount, and the income tax rate is estimated at 40% of income.

	Plan 1	Plan 2	Plan 3
8% bonds	—	—	$2,500,000
Preferred 4% stock, $100 par	—	$2,500,000	1,250,000
Common stock, $5 par	$5,000,000	2,500,000	1,250,000
Total	$5,000,000	$5,000,000	$5,000,000

Instructions

1. Determine for each plan the earnings per share of common stock, assuming that the income before bond interest and income tax is $1,000,000.
2. Determine for each plan the earnings per share of common stock, assuming that the income before bond interest and income tax is $300,000.
3. Discuss the advantages and disadvantages of each plan.

Obj. 2, 4

P9-2 Notes payable; contingent liability

The following items were selected from among the transactions completed by Sherwood Co. during the current year:

Mar. 31. Issued a 30-day, 8% note for $225,000 to Kirkwood Co., on account.

Apr. 30. Paid Kirkwood Co. the amount owed on the note of March 31.

June 1. Borrowed $600,000 from Triple Creek Bank, issuing a 45-day, 6% note.

July 16. Paid Triple Creek Bank the amount owed on the note of June 1.

Dec. 22. Settled a product liability lawsuit with a customer for $40,000, payable in January. Record the litigation settlement as a loss with a related litigation claims payable account.

Instructions

1. Illustrate the effects on the accounts and financial statements of recording each of the preceding transactions.
2. Illustrate the effects on the accounts and financial statements of an end-of-year adjustment for accrued warranty costs of $65,000.

Obj. 2

✔ 1. $3,375

P9-3 Payroll and payroll taxes

The following information about the payroll for the week ended September 15 was obtained from the records of Simkins Mining Co.:

Salaries and wages:		Deductions:	
Sales salaries	$15,000	Income tax withheld	$8,500
Employee wages	20,000	U.S. savings bonds	1,000
Office salaries	10,000	Group insurance	3,000
	$45,000		

Tax rates assumed:

FICA tax, 7.5% of employee annual earnings

State unemployment (employer only), 4.2%

Federal unemployment (employer only), 0.8%

Instructions

1. For the September 15 payroll, determine the employee FICA tax payable.
2. Illustrate the effects on the accounts and financial statements of paying the September 15 payroll.
3. Determine the following amounts for the employer payroll taxes related to the September 15 payroll: (a) FICA tax payable, (b) state unemployment tax payable, and (c) federal unemployment tax payable. Assume all salaries and wages are subject to state and federal unemployment taxes.
4. Illustrate the effects on the accounts and financial statements of recording the liability for the September 15 employer payroll taxes.

Obj. 3

P9-4 Bonds payable

Beaufort Vaults Corporation produces and sells burial vaults. On July 1, 20Y3, Beaufort Vaults Corporation issued $25,000,000 of 10-year, 8% bonds at par. Interest on the bonds is payable semiannually on December 31 and June 30. The fiscal year of the company is the calendar year.

Instructions

1. Illustrate the effects of the issuance of the bonds on July 1, 20Y3, on the accounts and financial statements.
2. Illustrate the effects of the first semiannual interest payment on December 31, 20Y3, on the accounts and financial statements.
3. Illustrate the effects of the payment of the face value of bonds at maturity on the accounts and financial statements.
4. If the market rate of interest had been 7% on July 1, 20Y3, would the bonds have sold at a discount or premium?
5. If the market rate of interest had been 10% on July 1, 20Y3, would the bonds have sold at a discount or premium?

Metric-Based Analysis

MBA 9-1 Notes payable transactions — Obj. 2

Using the data from E9-4, indicate the effects on net assets and earnings per share (EPS) of each of the following:

1. Issuing the notes payable.
2. Paying the note at maturity, including interest.

MBA 9-2 Recording payroll and payroll taxes — Obj. 2

Using the data from P9-3, indicate the effects on net assets and EPS of each of the following:

1. Recording and paying the payroll.
2. Recording the employer payroll taxes.
3. Paying the employee and employer payroll taxes.

MBA 9-3 Bonds payable transactions — Obj. 3

Using the data from P9-4, indicate the effects on net assets and EPS of each of the following:

1. Issuing the bonds payable on July 1, 20Y3.
2. Paying interest on December 31, 20Y3.
3. Paying the face value of the bonds at maturity.

MBA 9-4 Debt ratios — Obj. 6

The Ford Motor Company (F) designs, manufactures, markets, and sells cars, trucks, and sport utility vehicles (SUVs). Ford is a major competitor of General Motors Company (GM). The following data (in millions) were adapted from recent financial statements of Ford Motor Company:

	Year 2	Year 1
Total assets	$258,537	$256,540
Total liabilities	225,352	220,608
Total stockholders' equity	33,185	35,932

1. Compute the debt ratio for Years 1 and 2. Round to one decimal place.
2. Given your answer to part (1), what is the ratio of stockholders' equity to total assets for Years 1 and 2? Round to one decimal place.
3. Are Ford's operations financed primarily with debt or equity?
4. Comparing Years 1 and 2, should creditors feel more or less safe in Year 2?

Obj. 6

MBA 9-5 Debt ratios

General Motors Company (GM) manufactures and sells cars, trucks, and sport utility vehicles (SUVs) under the brand names Buick, Cadillac, Chevrolet, and GMC. General Motors is a major competitor of Ford Motor Company (F). The following data (in millions) were adapted from recent financial statements of General Motors:

	Year 2	Year 1
Total assets	$228,037	$227,339
Total liabilities	186,245	188,479
Total stockholders' equity	41,792	38,860

1. Compute the debt ratio for Years 1 and 2. Round to one decimal place.
2. Given your answer to part (1), what is the ratio of stockholders' equity to total assets? Round to one decimal place.
3. Are General Motor's operations financed primarily with debt or equity?

MBA 9-6 Debt ratios

1. Compare the debt ratios of Ford Motor Company and General Motors Company using your results from MBA 9-4 and MBA 9-5.
2. Comment on the results from part (1)

Obj. 6

MBA 9-7 Debt ratios

Alphabet (GOOG) is a technology company that offers users Internet search and e-mail services. Google also developed the Android operating system for use with cell phones and other mobile devices. The following data (in millions) were adapted from a recent financial statement of Alphabet:

	Year 2	Year 1
Total assets	$275,909	$232,792
Total liabilities	74,467	55,164
Total stockholders' equity	201,442	177,628

1. Compute the debt ratio for Years 1 and 2. Round to one decimal place.
2. Given your answer to part (1), what is the ratio of stockholders' equity to total assets? Round to one decimal place.
3. Compute the ratio of liabilities to stockholders' equity. Round to one decimal place.
4. Are Google's operations financed primarily with debt or equity?
5. Comparing Years 1 and 2, should creditors feel more or less safe in Year 2?

MBA 9-8 Debt ratios

Obj. 6

Twitter, Inc. (TWTR) is a technology company that provides a platform for users to express themselves and conduct conversations in real time. The following data (in millions) were adapted from recent financial statements of Twitter:

	Year 2	Year 1
Total assets	$12,703	$10,163
Total liabilities	3,999	3,357
Total stockholders' equity	8,704	6,806

1. Compute the debt ratio for Years 1 and 2. Round to one decimal place.
2. Compute the ratio of liabilities to stockholders' equity. Round to one decimal place.
3. Are Twitter's operations financed primarily with debt or equity?
4. Compare Twitter's debt ratios for Years 1 and 2. Should creditors feel more or less safe in Year 2?
5. Would you expect Twitter's debt ratios to be similar to Alphabet's in MBA 9-7?
6. Would you expect Twitter's debt ratio to be similar, larger, or smaller than Amazon.com's debt ratios?

Cases

Case 9-1 Ethics and professional conduct in business

ETHICS

Jas Carillo was discussing summer employment with Maria Perez, president of Valparaiso Construction Service:

Maria: I'm glad that you're thinking about joining us for the summer. We could certainly use the help.

Jas: Sounds good. I enjoy outdoor work, and I could use the money to help with next year's school expenses.

Maria: I've got a plan that can help you out on that. As you know, I'll pay you $8 per hour; but in addition, I'd like to pay you with cash. Since you're only working for the summer, it really doesn't make sense for me to go to the trouble of formally putting you on our payroll system. In fact, I do some jobs for my clients on a strictly cash basis, so it would be easy to just pay you that way.

Jas: Well, that's a bit unusual, but I guess money is money.

Maria: Yeah, not only that, it's tax-free!

Jas: What do you mean?

Maria: Didn't you know? Any money that you receive in cash is not reported to the IRS; therefore, the IRS doesn't know about the income—hence, it's the same as tax-free earnings.

1. Why does Maria Perez want to conduct business transactions using cash (not check or credit card)?
2. How should Jas respond to Maria's suggestion?

Case 9-2 Payroll bonus

ETHICS

Tonya Latirno is a staff accountant for Cannally and Kennedy, a local CPA firm. For the past 10 years, the firm has given employees a year-end bonus equal to two weeks' salary. On November 15, the firm's management team announced that there would be no annual bonus this year. Because of the firm's long history of giving a year-end bonus, Tonya and her co-workers had come to expect the bonus and felt that Cannally and Kennedy had breached an implicit agreement by discontinuing the bonus. As a result, Tonya decided that she would make up for the lost bonus by working an extra six hours of overtime per week for the rest of the year. Cannally and Kennedy's policy is to pay overtime at 150% of straight time.

Tonya's supervisor was surprised to see overtime being reported, because there are generally very little additional or unusual client service demands at the end of the calendar year. However, the overtime was not questioned, because employees are on the "honor system" in reporting their work hours.

1. Is Cannally and Kennedy acting in an ethical manner by eliminating the bonus? Explain your answer.
2. Is Tonya behaving ethically by making up the bonus with unnecessary overtime? Why?

Case 9-3 Contingent liability

WBM Motorworks is a manufacturer of high-end touring and off-road motorcycles. On November 30, the company was sued by a customer who was injured when the front shock absorber on the WBM Series 3 motorcycle cracked during use. The company conducted a preliminary investigation into the matter during December and found evidence of a manufacturing defect in the shock absorber. While it is uncertain whether the manufacturing defect is the source of the product failure, the company has voluntarily recalled the front shock absorbers on the Series 3 motorcycles. The company is uncertain how the lawsuit will be resolved. Similar lawsuits against other manufacturers have been settled for approximately $2,000,000.

Write a brief memo to the president of WBM Motorworks, U. D. Mach III, discussing how the lawsuit might be reported in the financial statements.

Case 9-4 Pension expense

The annual examination of Felton Company's financial statements by its external public accounting firm (auditors) is nearing completion. The following conversation took place between the controller of Felton Company (Francie) and the audit manager from the public accounting firm (Sumana):

Sumana: You know, Francie, we are about to wrap up our audit for this fiscal year. Yet, there is one item still to be resolved.

Francie: What's that?

Sumana: Well, as you know, at the beginning of the year, Felton began a defined benefit pension plan. This plan promises your employees an annual payment when they retire, using a formula based on their salaries at retirement and their years of service. I believe that a pension expense should be recognized this year, equal to the amount of pension earned by your employees.

Francie: Wait a minute. I think you have it all wrong. The company doesn't have a pension expense until it actually pays the pension in cash when the employee retires. After all, some of these employees may not reach retirement, and if they don't, the company doesn't owe them anything.

Sumana: You're not really seeing this the right way. The pension is earned by your employees during their working years. You actually make the payment much later—when they retire. It's like one long accrual—much like incurring wages in one period and paying them in the next. Thus, I think you should recognize the expense in the period the pension is earned by the employees.

Francie: Let me see if I've got this straight. I should recognize an expense this period for something that may or may not be paid to the employees in 20 or 30 years, when they finally retire. How am I supposed to determine what the expense is for the current year? The amount of the final retirement depends on many uncertainties: salary levels, employee longevity, mortality rates, and interest earned on investments to fund the pension. I don't think an amount can be determined even if I accepted your arguments.

Evaluate Sumana's position. Is she right, or is Francie correct?

Case 9-5 Financing business expansion

You hold a 30% common stock interest in the family-owned business, a vending machine company. Your sister, who is the manager, has proposed an expansion of plant facilities at an expected cost of $6,000,000. Two alternative plans have been suggested as methods of financing the expansion. Each plan is briefly described as follows:

Plan 1. Issue $6,000,000 of 15-year, 8% bonds at face amount.

Plan 2. Issue an additional 100,000 shares of $20 par common stock at $25 per share, and $3,500,000 of 15-year, 8% bonds at face amount.

The balance sheet as of the end of the previous fiscal year is as follows:

MOJAVE OASIS, INC.
Balance Sheet
December 31, 20Y6

Assets	
Current assets	$10,000,000
Property, plant, and equipment	15,000,000
Total assets	$25,000,000
Liabilities and Stockholders' Equity	
Liabilities	$ 7,000,000
Common stock, $20	8,000,000
Paid-in capital in excess of par	300,000
Retained earnings	9,700,000
Total liabilities and stockholders' equity	$25,000,000

Net income has remained relatively constant over the past several years. The expansion program is expected to increase yearly income before bond interest and income tax from $900,000 in the previous year to $1,200,000 for this year. Your sister has asked you, as the company treasurer, to prepare an analysis of each financing plan.

1. Prepare a table indicating the expected earnings per share on the common stock under each plan. Assume an income tax rate of 25%.
2. a. Discuss the factors that should be considered in evaluating the two plans.
   b. Which plan offers the greater benefit to the present stockholders? Give reasons for your opinion.

Case 9-6 Data Analytics: Supplier (vendor) analyses

Corwin LTD is a business supply company in Phoenix, Arizona. Corwin's current liabilities consist almost entirely of accounts payables to its suppliers (vendors). In an effort to better understand its accounts payable and supplier relationships, management has asked you to analyze one month's purchasing data.

1. Using the dataset for Corwin LTD, perform analyses to answer the following questions:
   a. How many days on average does it take to receive an order from each supplier?
   b. How many partial orders do we receive from each supplier?
   c. How many orders do we return from each supplier?
   d. How many orders are back-ordered from each supplier?
2. How can Corwin LTD use these analyses to improve or change its supplier relationships?

Go to CengageNOWv2 to complete this assignment.

The annual report (10-K) assignment for this chapter is in Appendix B: Nike Annual Report, Chapter 9.

Answers to Self-Examination Questions

1. **C** The maturity value is $5,100, determined as follows:

Face amount of note	$5,000
Plus interest ($5,000 × 0.12 × 60/360)	100
Maturity value	$5,100

2. **B** Employers are usually required to withhold a portion of their employees' earnings for payment of federal income taxes (answer A), FICA tax (answer C), and state and local income taxes (answer D). Generally, federal unemployment compensation taxes (answer B) are levied against the employer only and thus are not withheld from employee earnings.
3. **D** The employer incurs an expense for FICA tax (answer A), federal unemployment compensation tax (answer B), and state unemployment compensation tax (answer C). The employees' federal income tax (answer D) is not an expense of the employer. It is withheld from the employees' earnings.
4. **C** The amount of gross pay of $1,710 (answer C) is determined as follows:

   $1,710 = (40 hours × $36) + [(45 hrs. − 40 hrs.) × ($36 × 1.5)]

   $1,710 = $1,440 + (5 hrs. × $54) = $1,440 + $270
5. **B** Since the contract rate on the bonds is higher than the prevailing market rate, a rational investor would be willing to pay more than the face amount, or a premium (answer B), for the bonds. If the contract rate and the market rate were equal, the bonds could be expected to sell at their face amount (answer A). Likewise, if the market rate is higher than the contract rate, the bonds would sell at a price below their face amount (answer D) or at a discount (answer C).

Chapter 10 Stockholders' Equity

What's Covered:

Topics: Stockholders' Equity

Corporations
- Characteristics (Obj. 1)
- Forming (Obj. 1)

Contributed (Paid-In) Capital
- Common stock (Obj. 2)
- Preferred stock (Obj. 2)

Dividends and Stock Splits
- Cash dividends (Obj. 3)
- Stock dividends (Obj. 3)
- Stock splits (Obj. 3)

Treasury Stock
- Purchasing (Obj. 4)
- Selling (Obj. 4)

Reporting Stockholders' Equity
- Statement of stockholders' equity (Obj. 6)

Metric-Based Analysis
- Transactions:
  - Solvency: Net assets (Obj. 2, 3, 4)
  - Profitability: Earnings per share (Obj. 2, 3, 4)
- Financial Statements:
  - Price-earnings ratio (Obj. 7)

Learning Objectives

Obj. 1 Describe the nature of the corporate form of organization.

Obj. 2 Describe types of stock and illustrate the effects of issuing stock.

Obj. 3 Describe types of dividends and the effects of declaring and paying dividends.

Obj. 4 Describe the nature of stock splits and their effect on stockholders' equity.

Obj. 5 Describe and illustrate the nature and effects of treasury stock transactions.

Obj. 6 Describe and illustrate the reporting of stockholders' equity.

Obj. 7 Describe and illustrate the price-earnings ratio for assessing the current and future profitability of a company.

Chapter Metrics

Use the following metrics to analyze transactions and financial statements.

TRANSACTIONS

Solvency*: Net Assets

Profitability: Earnings per Share

FINANCIAL STATEMENTS

Price-Earnings Ratio

*As will be discussed, a solvency rather than a liquidity metric is used in this chapter.

© SiliconValleyStock/ Alamy Stock Photo

Alphabet Inc.

If you purchase a share of stock from **Alphabet Inc. (GOOG)**, you own a small interest in a company that includes businesses such as Google, Android, and YouTube. You may request an Alphabet stock certificate as an indication of your ownership.

Alphabet's largest segment, Google, is one of the most visible names on the Internet. Many of us cannot visit the Web without using Google to power a search or to retrieve our e-mail using Google's Gmail. Yet Google's Internet tools are free to online browsers. The Google segment generates 99% of Alphabet's revenues, with most of this revenue coming from online advertising.

Purchasing a share of stock from Alphabet may be a great gift idea for the "hard-to-shop-for person." However, a stock certificate represents more than just a picture that you can frame. In fact, the stock certificate is a document that reflects legal ownership of the future financial prospects of Alphabet. In addition, as a shareholder, it represents your claim against the assets and earnings of the corporation.

If you are purchasing Alphabet stock as an investment, you should analyze Alphabet's financial statements and management's plans for the future. For example, Alphabet first offered its stock to the public on August 19, 2004, for $100 per share. Alphabet's stock has sold for more than $1,500 per share, even though it pays no dividends. In addition, Alphabet recently expanded into developing and offering free software platforms for mobile devices such as cell phones. For example, your cell phone may use the Android™ operating system. So, should you purchase Alphabet stock?

This chapter describes and illustrates the nature of corporations, including the accounting for stock and dividends. This discussion will aid you in making decisions such as whether or not to buy stock in a company.

Objective 1
Describe the nature of the corporate form of organization.

Nature of a Corporation

Most large businesses are organized as corporations. As a result, corporations generate more than 90% of the total business dollars in the United States. In contrast, most small businesses are organized as proprietorships, partnerships, or limited liability companies.

Characteristics of a Corporation

A *corporation* is a legal entity, distinct and separate from the individuals who create and operate it. As a legal entity, a corporation may acquire, own, and dispose of property in its own name. It may also incur liabilities and enter into contracts. Most importantly, it can sell shares of ownership, called **stock**. This characteristic gives corporations the ability to raise large amounts of capital.

The **stockholders** or *shareholders* who own the stock own the corporation. They can buy and sell stock without affecting the corporation's operations or continued existence. Corporations whose shares of stock are traded in public markets are called *public corporations*. Corporations whose shares are not traded publicly are usually owned by a small group of investors and are called *nonpublic* or *private corporations*.

The stockholders of a corporation have *limited liability*. This means that creditors usually may not go beyond the assets of the corporation to satisfy their claims. Thus, the financial loss that a stockholder may suffer is limited to the amount invested.

The stockholders control a corporation by electing a *board of directors*. This board meets periodically to establish corporate policies. It also selects the chief executive officer (CEO) and other major officers to manage the corporation's day-to-day affairs. Exhibit 1 shows the organizational structure of a corporation.

As a separate entity, a corporation is subject to taxes. For example, corporations must pay federal income taxes on their income.[1] Thus, corporate income that is distributed to stockholders in the form of *dividends* has already been taxed. In turn, stockholders must pay income taxes on the dividends they receive. This *double taxation* of corporate earnings is a major disadvantage of the corporate form. The advantages and disadvantages of the corporate form are listed in Exhibit 2.

1. A majority of states also require corporations to pay income taxes.

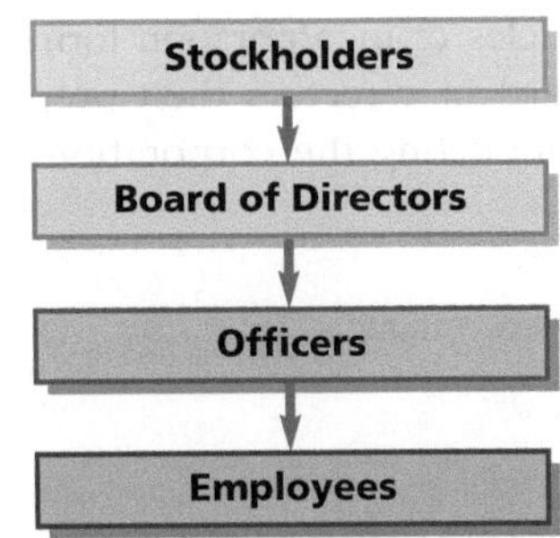

Exhibit 1 Organizational Structure of a Corporation

Exhibit 2 Advantages and Disadvantages of the Corporate Form

Advantages	Explanation
Separate legal existence	A corporation exists separately from its owners.
Continuous life	A corporation's life is separate from its owners; therefore, it exists indefinitely.
Raising large amounts of capital	The corporate form is suited for raising large amounts of money from shareholders.
Ownership rights are easily transferable	A corporation sells shares of ownership, called *stock*. The stockholders of a public company can transfer their shares of stock to other stockholders through stock markets, such as the New York Stock Exchange.
Limited liability	A corporation's creditors usually may not go beyond the assets of the corporation to satisfy their claims. Thus, the financial loss that a stockholder may suffer is limited to the amount invested.
Disadvantages	**Explanation**
Owner is separate from management	Stockholders control management through a board of directors. The board of directors should represent shareholder interests; however, the board is may be more closely tied to management than to shareholders. As a result, the board of directors and management may not always behave in the best interests of stockholders.
Double taxation of dividends	As a separate legal entity, a corporation is subject to taxation. Thus, net income distributed as dividends will be taxed once at the corporation level, and then again at the individual level.
Regulatory costs	Corporations must satisfy many requirements, such as those required by the Sarbanes-Oxley Act.

Forming a Corporation

The first step in forming a corporation is to file an *application of incorporation* with the state. State incorporation laws differ, and corporations often organize in those states with the more favorable laws. For this reason, more than half of the largest companies are incorporated in Delaware. Exhibit 3 lists some corporations, their states of incorporation, and the location of their headquarters.

Exhibit 3 Examples of Corporations and Their States of Incorporation

Corporation	State of Incorporation	Headquarters
Caterpillar Inc. (CAT)	Delaware	Peoria, IL
Delta Air Lines, Inc. (DAL)	Delaware	Atlanta, GA
The Dow Chemical Company (DOW)	Delaware	Midland, MI
Alphabet Inc. (GOOG)	Delaware	Mountain View, CA
General Electric Company (GE)	New York	Fairfield, CT
The Home Depot (HD)	Delaware	Atlanta, GA
Kellogg Company (K)	Delaware	Battle Creek, MI
Reynolds American Inc. (RAI)	Delaware	Winston-Salem, NC
Starbucks Corporation (SBUX)	Washington	Seattle, WA
3M Company (MMM)	Delaware	St. Paul, MN
Walt Disney Company (DIS)	Delaware	Burbank, CA
Whirlpool Corporation (WHR)	Delaware	Benton Harbor, MI

After the application of incorporation has been approved, the state grants a *charter* or *articles of incorporation*. The articles of incorporation formally create the corporation.[2] The corporate management and board of directors then prepare a set of *bylaws*, which are the rules and procedures for conducting the corporation's affairs.

Alphabet Connection

Some excepts from **Alphabet**'s bylaws follow:

ARTICLE I—CORPORATE OFFICES

1.1 REGISTERED OFFICE.
The registered office of Alphabet Inc. shall be fixed in the corporation's certificate of incorporation. …

1.2 OTHER OFFICES.
The corporation's Board of Directors (the "Board") may at any time establish other offices at any place or places where the corporation is qualified to do business.

ARTICLE II—MEETINGS OF STOCKHOLDERS

2.2 ANNUAL MEETING.
The annual meeting of stockholders shall be held each year on a date and at a time designated by the Board. At the annual meeting, directors shall be elected and any other proper business may be transacted.

2.4 NOTICE OF STOCKHOLDERS' MEETINGS.
All notices of meetings of stockholders shall be sent … not less than ten (10) nor more than sixty (60) days before the date of the meeting to each stockholder entitled to vote at such meeting. … The notice shall specify the place, if any, date and hour of the meeting, the means of remote communication, if any, by which stockholders and proxy holders may be deemed to be present in person and vote at such meeting. …

2.8 ADMINISTRATION OF THE MEETING.
Meetings of stockholders shall be presided over by the chairman of the Board. …

ARTICLE V—OFFICERS

5.1 OFFICERS.
The officers of the corporation shall be a chief executive officer and a secretary. The corporation may also have, at the discretion of the Board, a chairman of the Board, a vice chairman of the Board, one or more presidents, a chief financial officer, a treasurer, one or more vice presidents, one or more assistant vice presidents, one or more assistant treasurers, one or more assistant secretaries, and any such other officers as may be appointed in accordance with the provisions of these bylaws.

5.6 CHAIRMAN OF THE BOARD.
The chairman of the Board shall be a member of the Board and, if present, preside at meetings of the Board. …

5.7 CHIEF EXECUTIVE OFFICER.
Subject to the control of the Board, … the chief executive officer shall have general supervision, direction, and control of the business and affairs of the corporation. … The chief executive officer shall … preside at all meetings of the stockholders.

5.11 CHIEF FINANCIAL OFFICER.
The chief financial officer shall keep and maintain … adequate and correct books and records of accounts of the properties and business transactions of the corporation, including accounts of its assets, liabilities, receipts, disbursements, gains, losses, capital, retained earnings and shares. …

5.12 TREASURER.
The treasurer shall deposit all moneys and other valuables in the name and to the credit of the corporation. …

Source: https://abc.xyz/investor/other/bylaws.html

2. The articles of incorporation may also restrict a corporation's activities in certain areas, such as owning certain types of real estate, conducting certain types of business activities, or purchasing its own stock.

Costs may be incurred in organizing a corporation. These costs include legal fees, taxes, state incorporation fees, license fees, and promotional costs. Such costs are recorded as an organizational expense.

Contributed (Paid-In) Capital

Objective 2
Describe types of stock and illustrate the effects of issuing stock.

The two main sources of stockholders' equity are paid-in capital and retained earnings. The main source of paid-in capital is from issuing stock to investors.

In recent financial statements, **Alphabet** reported paid-in capital of over $40 billion.

Alphabet Connection

Characteristics of Stock

The number of shares of stock that a corporation is *authorized* to issue is stated in its charter. The term *issued* refers to the shares issued to the stockholders. A corporation may reacquire some of the stock that it has issued. The stock remaining in the hands of stockholders is then called **outstanding stock**. The relationship between authorized, issued, and outstanding stock is shown in Exhibit 4.

Exhibit 4
Authorized, Issued, and Outstanding Stock

Number of shares authorized, issued, and outstanding

Upon request, corporations may issue stock certificates to stockholders to document their ownership. Printed on a stock certificate is the name of the company, the name of the stockholder, and the number of shares owned. The stock certificate may also indicate a dollar amount assigned to each share of stock, called **par value**. Stock may be issued without par, in which case it is called *no-par stock*. In some states, the board of directors of a corporation is required to assign a **stated value** to no-par stock.

Corporations have limited liability, and thus, creditors have no claim against stockholders' personal assets. To protect creditors, however, some states require corporations to maintain a minimum amount of paid-in capital. This minimum amount, called *legal capital,* usually includes the par or stated value of the shares issued.

The major rights that accompany ownership of a share of stock are as follows:

- The right to vote in matters concerning the corporation.
- The right to share in distributions of earnings.
- The right to share in assets upon liquidation.

These stock rights normally vary with the class of stock.

Types of Stock

When only one class of stock is issued, it is called **common stock**. Each share of common stock has equal rights. Recently, many public companies have begun issuing different classes of common stock with different rights.

Alphabet has three classes of common stock outstanding. Class A has one vote per share; Class B has ten votes per share; and Class C has no voting rights. The current executive chairman and the two original founders own 84.3% of the Class B stock and control over 50% of the voting power of the outstanding common stock.

A corporation may also issue one or more classes of stock with various preference rights such as a preference to dividends. Such a stock is called a **preferred stock**. The dividend rights of preferred stock are stated either as dollars per share or as a percent of par. For example, a $50 par value preferred stock with a $4 per share dividend may be described as either:[3]

Preferred $4 stock, $50 par
or
Preferred 8% stock, $50 par

As shown in Exhibit 5, preferred stockholders have first rights (preference) to any dividends, and thus, they have a greater chance of receiving dividends than common stockholders. However, since dividends are normally based on earnings, a corporation cannot guarantee dividends even to preferred stockholders.

Exhibit 5
Dividend Preferences

Alphabet Connection

Alphabet has 100,000,000 shares of authorized preferred stock with a par of $0.001, which are convertible to common stock. However, there are no shares of preferred stock issued or outstanding.

The payment of dividends is authorized by the corporation's board of directors. When authorized, the directors are said to have *declared* a dividend.

Cumulative preferred stock has a right to receive regular dividends that were not declared (paid) in prior years. Noncumulative preferred stock does not have this right.

3. In some cases, preferred stock may receive additional dividends if certain conditions are met. Such stock, called *participating preferred stock*, is not often issued.

Cumulative preferred stock dividends that have not been paid in prior years are said to be **in arrears**. Any preferred dividends in arrears must be paid before any common stock dividends are paid. In addition, any dividends in arrears are normally disclosed in notes to the financial statements.

To illustrate, assume that a corporation has issued the following preferred and common stock:

1,000 shares of cumulative preferred $4 stock, $50 par
4,000 shares of common stock, $15 par

The corporation was organized on January 1 of 20Y1 and paid no dividends in 20Y1 and 20Y2. In 20Y3, the corporation paid $22,000 in dividends, of which $12,000 was paid to preferred stockholders and $10,000 was paid to common stockholders, computed as shown in Exhibit 6.

Exhibit 6 Preferred Dividends in Arrears

Total dividends paid		$ 22,000
Preferred stockholders:		
20Y1 dividends in arrears (1,000 shares × $4)	$4,000	
20Y2 dividends in arrears (1,000 shares × $4)	4,000	
20Y3 dividend (1,000 shares × $4)	4,000	
Total preferred dividends paid		(12,000)
Dividends available to common stockholders		$ 10,000

As a result, preferred stockholders received $12.00 per share ($12,000 ÷ 1,000 shares) in dividends, while common stockholders received $2.50 per share ($10,000 ÷ 4,000 shares).

In addition to dividend preference, preferred stock may be given preferences to assets if the corporation goes out of business and is liquidated. However, claims of creditors must be satisfied first. Preferred stockholders are then next in line to receive any remaining assets, followed by the common stockholders.

You Have No Vote

Business Insight

An emerging trend in technology companies is using multiple classes of stock to concentrate voting control of the company to the founders. For example, Mark Zuckerberg, the founder and CEO of **Facebook (FB)**, owns Class B shares of Facebook. The public owns Class A shares. The Class B shares grant ten votes for every one vote granted by the Class A shares. As a result, Zuckerberg controls the voting rights of Facebook's common stock. Other companies using multiple classes of stock in this way include **Alphabet (GOOG)**, **Groupon (GRPN)**, **Zynga (ZNGA)**, and **Yelp! (YELP)**.

While becoming prevalent among technology companies, using multiple classes of stock is not a new idea. **The Hershey Company (HSY)** has had two classes of stock since becoming a public company in 1927. The Hershey Trust Company, which oversees the Hershey School for orphans, has voting control of The Hershey Company by holding super voting shares.

The argument in favor of super voting rights is that the founders can concentrate on the long-term goals of the company without concern for possibly more short-term goals of public shareholders. The argument in opposition is that concentrating control among the founders can eliminate or reduce the public shareholders' ability to hold management accountable.

Issuance of Stock

Because different classes of stock have different rights, a separate account is used for recording the amount of each class of stock issued to investors. For example, assume that a corporation is authorized to issue 10,000 shares of $100 par preferred stock and 100,000 shares of $20 par common stock. The corporation issued 5,000 shares of preferred stock and 50,000 shares of common stock at par for cash. The effects on the accounts and financial statements of issuing the stock are as follows:

Financial Statement Effects

BALANCE SHEET

Assets	=	Liabilities	+	Stockholders' Equity		
Cash	=			Preferred Stock	+	Common Stock
1,500,000				500,000		1,000,000

STATEMENT OF CASH FLOWS

Financing	1,500,000

INCOME STATEMENT

Transaction Metric Effects

Like Chapter 9, this chapter uses **net assets** (Total Assets − Total Liabilities) as a solvency metric. Likewise, **earnings per share** [(Net Income − Preferred Dividends) ÷ Number of Common Shares Outstanding] is used as the profitability metric. The effects of issuing the preferred and common stock on the solvency and profitability metrics are as follows:

SOLVENCY

Net Assets	$1,500,000

PROFITABILITY

Earnings per Share	Decreases

Net assets increase by $1,500,000. Since the number of common stock shares outstanding increases, earnings per share decreases.

Some states prohibit the issuance of stock below its par value. Other states require a corporation to maintain a minimum amount of paid-in capital equal to the par value of its shares. For this reason, most corporations issue stock with very low par values. As a result, stock is normally issued for a price that is more than its par. In this case, stock is said to be sold at a premium. For example, if stock with a par value of $50 is issued for a price of $60, the stock is sold at a premium of $10.

The par value of **Alphabet**'s stock is $0.001 per share.

When stock is issued at a premium, Cash is increased for the amount received. Common Stock or Preferred Stock is increased for the par amount. The excess of the amount paid over par is part of the paid-in capital. An account entitled **Paid-In Capital in Excess of Par** is increased for this amount.

To illustrate, assume that Caldwell Company issues 2,000 shares of $1 par common stock for cash at $55 per share on November 1. The effects on the accounts and financial statements are as follows:

Financial Statement Effects

BALANCE SHEET

	Assets	=	Liabilities	+	Stockholders' Equity		
	Cash	=			Common Stock	+	Paid-In Capital in Excess of Par
Nov. 1.	110,000				2,000		108,000

STATEMENT OF CASH FLOWS

Nov. 1. Financing	110,000

INCOME STATEMENT

Transaction Metric Effects

The effecs of issuing common stock on the solvency and profitability metrics are as follows:

SOLVENCY

Net Assets	$110,000

PROFITABILITY

Earnings per Share	Decreases

Issuing common stock increases assets and equity with no change in liabilities. Thus, net assets increase by $110,000. Revenues and expenses are not affected, but the number of common shares outstanding increases. As a result, the earnings per share (EPS) decreases.

When stock is issued in exchange for assets other than cash, such as land, buildings, and equipment, the assets acquired are recorded at their fair market value. If this value cannot be objectively determined, the fair market price of the stock issued may be used.

In most states, both preferred and common stock may be issued without a par value. When no-par stock is issued, the entire proceeds are recorded in the stock account. In some states, no-par stock may be assigned a *stated value* per share. The stated value is recorded like a par value, and the excess of the amount received over the stated value is recorded in Paid-In Capital in Excess of Stated Value.

To illustrate, assume that on January 9, a corporation issues 10,000 shares of no-par common stock at $40 a share. On June 27, the corporation issues an additional

2,000 shares at $36. The effects on the accounts and financial statements of issuing the no-par stock on January 9 and June 27 are as follows:

Financial Statement Effects

BALANCE SHEET

	Assets	=	Liabilities	+	Stockholders' Equity
	Cash	**=**			**Common Stock**
Jan. 9.	400,000				400,000
June 27.	72,000				72,000

STATEMENT OF CASH FLOWS

Jan. 9. Financing	400,000
June 27. Financing	72,000

INCOME STATEMENT

Assume that in the preceding example, the no-par stock had been assigned a stated value per share of $25. The effects on the accounts and financial statements of issuing the no-par stock with a stated value of $25 on January 9 and June 27 are as follows:

Financial Statement Effects

BALANCE SHEET

	Assets	=	Liabilities	+	Stockholders' Equity		
	Cash	**=**			**Common Stock**	**+**	**Paid-In Capital in Excess of Stated Value**
Jan. 9.	400,000				250,000*		150,000
June 27.	72,000				50,000**		22,000

STATEMENT OF CASH FLOWS

Jan. 9. Financing	400,000
June 27. Financing	72,000

INCOME STATEMENT

* 10,000 shares × $25 stated value
** 2,000 shares × $25 stated value

Transaction Metric Effects

The effects on the solvency and proifitability metrics of issuing the no-par common stock with and without stated value are the same.

SOLVENCY

Net Assets	$472,000

PROFITABILITY

Earnings per Share	Decreases

Net assets increase by $472,000. Since the number of common stock shares outstanding increases, earnings per share decreases.

Dividends

Objective 3
Describe types of dividends and the effects of declaring and paying dividends.

When a board of directors declares a cash dividend, it authorizes the distribution of cash to stockholders. When a board of directors declares a stock dividend, it authorizes the distribution of its stock. In both cases, declaring a dividend decreases the retained earnings of the corporation.[4]

Cash Dividends

A cash distribution of earnings by a corporation to its shareholders is a **cash dividend**. Although dividends may be paid in other assets, cash dividends are the most common.

Three conditions for a cash dividend are as follows:

1. Sufficient retained earnings
2. Sufficient cash
3. Formal action by the board of directors

There must be a sufficient (large enough) balance in Retained Earnings to declare a cash dividend. However, a large Retained Earnings balance does not mean that there is cash available to pay dividends. This is because the balances of Cash and Retained Earnings are often unrelated.

Even if there are sufficient retained earnings and cash, a corporation's board of directors is not required to pay dividends. Nevertheless, many corporations pay quarterly cash dividends to make their stock more attractive to investors. *Special* or *extra* dividends may also be paid when a corporation experiences higher than normal profits.

Three dates included in a dividend announcement are as follows:

1. Date of declaration
2. Date of record
3. Date of payment

The *date of declaration* is the date the board of directors formally authorizes the payment of the dividend. On this date, the corporation incurs the liability to pay the amount of the dividend.

The *date of record* is the date the corporation uses to determine which stockholders will receive the dividend. During the period of time between the date of declaration and the date of record, the stock price is quoted as selling *with-dividends*. This means that any investors purchasing the stock before the date of record will receive the dividend.

The *date of payment* is the date the corporation will pay the dividend to the stockholders who owned the stock on the date of record. During the period of time between the record date and the payment date, the stock price is quoted as selling *ex-dividends*. This means that since the date of record has passed, any new investors will not receive the dividend.

To illustrate, assume that on *December 1*, Hiber Corporation's board of directors declares the cash dividends of $42,500 as shown in Exhibit 7. The date of record is *January 10*, and the date of payment is *February 2*.

4. In rare cases, when a corporation is reducing its operations or going out of business, a dividend may be a distribution of paid-in capital. Such a dividend is called a liquidating dividend.

Exhibit 7
Cash Dividend Dates

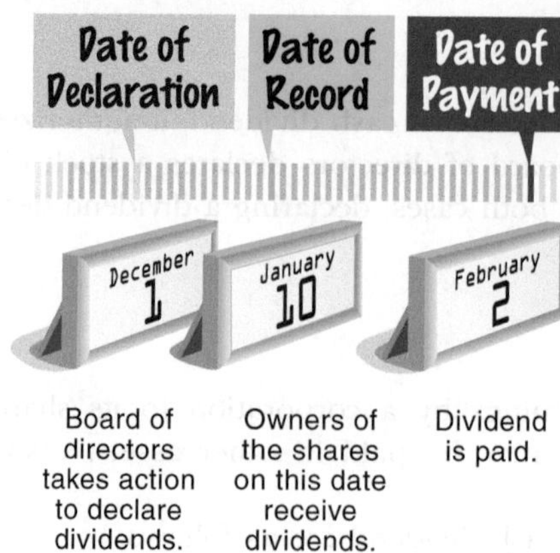

The effects of the declaration of the dividend on the accounts and financial statements are as follows:

Financial Statement Effects

BALANCE SHEET

	Assets	=	Liabilities	+	Stockholders' Equity
			Dividends Payable	+	**Retained Earnings**
Dec. 1.			42,500		(42,500)

STATEMENT OF CASH FLOWS

INCOME STATEMENT

Note that the date of record, January 10, does not affect the accounts or the financial statements, since this date merely determines which stockholders will receive the dividend. The payment of the dividend on February 2 decreases Cash and Dividends Payable.

The effects of the payment of the cash dividend on the accounts and financial statements are as follows:

Financial Statement Effects

BALANCE SHEET

	Assets	=	Liabilities	+	Stockholders' Equity
	Cash	=	**Dividends Payable**		
Feb. 2.	(42,500)		(42,500)		

STATEMENT OF CASH FLOWS

Feb. 2. Financing	(42,500)

INCOME STATEMENT

Transaction Metric Effects

The effects of declaring and paying a cash dividend on the solvency and profitability metrics are as follows:

SOLVENCY Net Assets	
Declaring cash dividend	$(42,500)
Paying cash dividend	No Effect

PROFITABILITY Earnings per Share	
Declaring cash dividend	No Effect
Paying cash dividend	No Effect

Declaring the cash dividend increases a liability and, thus, decreases net assets by $42,500. Payment of the cash dividend decreases cash and decreases a liability by $42,500 and thus, has no effect on net assets. Since revenue and expenses are unaffected by dividends, there is no effect on earnings per share of declaring or paying a cash dividend.

A corporation may purchase and hold its own stock, called treasury stock. If the corporation declares a cash dividend, the dividends are not paid on the treasury shares. To do so would place the corporation in the position of earning income through dealing with itself. For example, assume a corporation with 100,000 shares of outstanding common stock holds 5,000 of its shares as treasury stock. Declaration of a $0.30 per share cash dividend results in paying dividends of $28,500 [(100,000 shares − 5,000 shares) × $0.30] rather than $30,000 (100,000 shares × $0.30).

Alphabet has never declared or paid a cash dividend.

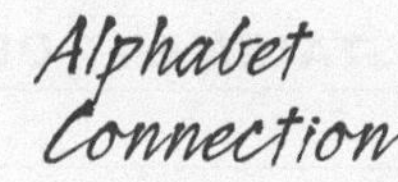

Stock Dividends

A **stock dividend** is a distribution of shares of stock to stockholders. Stock dividends are normally declared only on common stock and issued to common stockholders.

The effect of a stock dividend on the stockholders' equity of the issuing corporation is to transfer retained earnings to paid-in capital. For public corporations, the amount transferred from the retained earnings account to the paid-in capital account is normally the fair value (market price) of the shares issued in the stock dividend.[5]

Integrity, Objectivity, and Ethics in Business

The Professor Who Knew Too Much

A major Midwestern university released a quarterly "American Customer Satisfaction Index" based on its research of customers of popular U.S. products and services. Before the release of the index to the public, the professor in charge of the research bought and sold stocks of some of the companies in the report. The professor was quoted as saying that he thought it was important to test his theories of customer satisfaction with "real" [his own] money.

Is this proper or ethical? Apparently, the dean of the Business School didn't think so. In a statement to the press, the dean stated: "I have instructed anyone affiliated with the (index) not to make personal use of information gathered in the course of producing the quarterly index, prior to the index's release to the general public, and they [the researchers] have agreed."

Sources: Jon E. Hilsenrath and Dan Morse, "Researcher Uses Index to Buy, Short Stocks," *The Wall Street Journal*, February 18, 2003; and Jon E. Hilsenrath, "Satisfaction Theory: Mixed Results," *The Wall Street Journal*, February 19, 2003.

5. The use of fair market value is justified as long as the number of shares issued for the stock dividend is small (less than 25% of the shares outstanding).

To illustrate, assume that the stockholders' equity accounts of Hendrix Corporation as of December 15 are as follows:

Common Stock, $20 par (2,000,000 shares issued)	$40,000,000
Paid-In Capital in Excess of Par—Common Stock	9,000,000
Retained Earnings	26,600,000

On August 5, Hendrix Corporation declares a stock dividend of 5% or 100,000 shares (2,000,000 shares × 5%) to be issued on September 30 to stockholders of record on August 31. The market price of the stock on August 5 (the date of declaration) is $31 per share.

The effects of the declaration of the stock dividend on the accounts and financial statements of Hendrix Corporation are as follows:

Financial Statement Effects

BALANCE SHEET

	Assets	=	Liabilities	+	Stockholders' Equity		
					Retained Earnings	**Stock Dividends Distributable**	**Paid-In Capital in Excess of Stated Value**
Aug. 5.					(3,100,000)*	2,000,000**	1,100,000***

STATEMENT OF CASH FLOWS

INCOME STATEMENT

* (2,000,000 shares × 5%) × $31 market value per share
** 100,000 shares × $20 par value per share
*** $3,100,000 – $2,000,000

As with cash dividends, the August 31 date of record does not affect the accounts or financial statements. When the common stock is distributed on September 30, Stock Dividends Distributable is decreased and Common Stock is increased as follows:

Financial Statement Effects

BALANCE SHEET

	Assets	=	Liabilities	+	Stockholders' Equity	
					Stock Dividends Distributable	**Common Stock**
Sept. 30.					(2,000,000)	2,000,000

STATEMENT OF CASH FLOWS

INCOME STATEMENT

Transaction Metric Effects

The effects of declaring and distributing the stock dividend on the solvency and profitability metrics are as follows:

SOLVENCY	
Net Assets	No Effect

PROFITABILITY	
Earnings per Share	Decreases

The stock dividend does not affect asset or liabilities, and thus there is no effect on net assets. Since the number of common stock shares outstanding increases, earnings per share decreases.

As the preceding example shows, a stock dividend does not change the assets, liabilities, or *total* stockholders' equity of a corporation. Likewise, a stock dividend does not change an individual stockholder's proportionate interest (equity) in the corporation.

To illustrate, assume a stockholder owns 1,000 of a corporation's 10,000 shares outstanding. If the corporation declares a 6% stock dividend, the stockholder's proportionate interest will not change, as shown in Exhibit 8.

Exhibit 8
Effects of Stock Dividend

	Before Stock Dividend	After Stock Dividend
Total shares issued	10,000	10,600 [10,000 + (10,000 × 6%)]
Number of shares owned	1,000	1,060 [1,000 + (1,000 × 6%)]
Proportionate ownership	10% (1,000÷10,000)	10% (1,060 ÷ 10,600)

Stock Splits

Objective 4
Describe the nature of stock splits and their effect on stockholders' equity.

A **stock split** is a process by which a corporation reduces the par or stated value of its common stock and issues a proportionate number of additional shares. A stock split applies to all common shares including the unissued, issued, and treasury shares.

A major objective of a stock split is to reduce the market price per share of the stock. This, in turn, attracts more investors to the stock and broadens the types and numbers of stockholders.

To illustrate, assume that Rojek Corporation has 10,000 shares of $100 par common stock outstanding with a current market price of $150 per share. The board of directors declares the following stock split:

1. Each common shareholder will receive 5 shares for each share held. This is called a 5-for-1 stock split. As a result, 50,000 shares (10,000 shares × 5) will be outstanding.
2. The par of each share of common stock will be reduced to $20 ($100÷5).

The par value of the common stock outstanding before and after the stock split is as follows:

	Before Split	After Split
Number of shares	10,000	50,000
Par value per share	× $100	× $20
Total	$1,000,000	$1,000,000

Exhibit 9 shows that each Rojek Corporation shareholder owns the same total par amount of stock before and after the stock split. For example, a stockholder who owned 4 shares of $100 par stock before the split (total par of $400) would own 20 shares of $20 par stock after the split (total par of $400). Only the number of shares and the par value per share have changed.

Since there are more shares outstanding after the stock split, the market price of the stock should decrease. For example, in the preceding example, there would be 5 times as many shares outstanding after the split. Thus, the market price of the stock would be expected to fall from $150 to about $30 ($150÷5).

Stock splits do not affect any financial statement accounts, since only the par (or stated) value and number of shares outstanding have changed. However, the details of stock splits are normally disclosed in the notes to the financial statements.

Exhibit 9
Stock Split Before and After

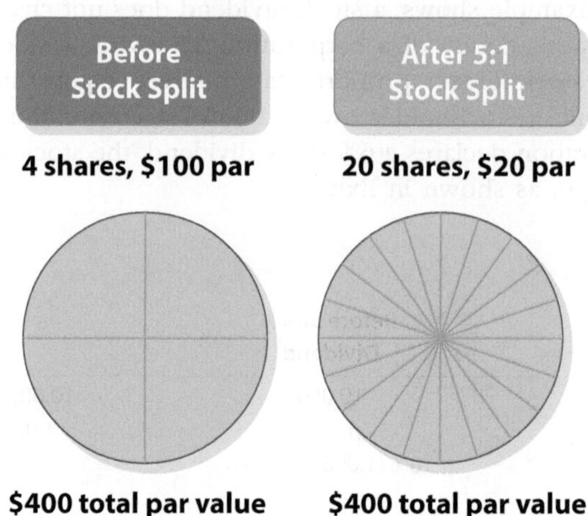

Transaction Metric Effects

The effects of declaring a stock split on the solvency and profitability metrics are as follows:

SOLVENCY	
Net Assets	No Effect

PROFITABILITY	
Earnings per Share	Decreases

Since stock splits do not affect assets, liabilities, revenues, or expenses, the solvency metric is not affected. Since a stock split increases the number of shares of common stock outstanding, the profitability metric earnings per share decreases.

Objective 5
Describe and illustrate the nature and effects of treasury stock transactions.

Treasury Stock

Treasury stock is stock that a corporation has issued and then reacquired. A corporation may reacquire (purchase) its own stock for a variety of reasons including the following:

- To provide shares for resale to employees
- To reissue as bonuses to employees
- To support the market price of the stock when the corporation feels the stock is undervalued by the market

The purchase of treasury stock increases Treasury Stock and decreases Cash by the cost of the repurchased shares. To illustrate, assume that, on February 6, Hoffman Inc. purchases

10,000 shares of its outstanding common stock at $15 per share for $150,000. The effects of the treasury stock purchase on the accounts and financial statements are as follows:

Financial Statement Effects

BALANCE SHEET

	Assets	=	Liabilities	+	Stockholders' Equity
	Cash	=			Treasury Stock
Feb. 6.	(150,000)				(150,000)

STATEMENT OF CASH FLOWS	
Feb. 6. Financing	(150,000)

INCOME STATEMENT

Transaction Metric Effects

The effects of purchasing treasury stock on the solvency and profitability metrics are as follows:

SOLVENCY	
Net Assets	$(150,000)

PROFITABILITY	
Earnings per Share	Increases

Purchasing $150,000 of treasury stock decreases cash and stockholders' equity. Thus, net assets decreases by $150,000. Since the number of shares of common stock outstanding decreases while revenue and expenses are unaffected, earnings per share increases. Public corporations often purchase treasury stock and, in doing so, increase their earnings per share.

A corporation may purchase treasury stock because it feels the stock is undervalued. If the corporation later resells the stock at a higher price, Cash is increased, Treasury Stock is decreased for its cost, and any difference increases Paid-In Capital from Sale of Treasury Stock.[6]

To illustrate, assume that on July 12 Hoffman Inc. sells 6,000 shares of its treasury stock purchased on February 6 for $20 per share. The effects of selling the treasury stock on the accounts and financial statements of Hoffman Inc. are as follows:

Financial Statement Effects

BALANCE SHEET

	Assets	=	Liabilities	+	Stockholders' Equity		
	Cash	=			Treasury Stock	+	Paid-In Capital from Sale of Treasury Stock
July 12.	120,000				90,000*		30,000**

STATEMENT OF CASH FLOWS	
July 12. Financing	120,000

INCOME STATEMENT

* 6,000 shares × $15 cost per share
** 6,000 shares × ($20 selling price per share − $15 cost per share)

6. The selling of treasury stock at a lower price is unusual and for this reason is not illustrated.

Transaction Metric Effects

The effects of selling the treasury stock on the solvency and profitability metrics are as follows:

SOLVENCY	
Net Assets	$120,000

PROFITABILITY	
Earnings per Share	Decreases

Since cash increases with no change in liabilities, net assets increase by $120,000. Since the number of common stock shares outstanding increases, earnings per share decreases.

No dividends are paid on shares of treasury stock. To do so would result in the corporation earning dividend revenue from itself.

At the end of the year, the balance of the treasury stock account is reported as a reduction of stockholders' equity while the balance of Paid-In Capital from Sale of Treasury Stock increases stockholders' equity.

Alphabet Connection

In a recent year, **Alphabet** purchased 15.3 million shares of its Class C common stock for $18.4 billion.

Objective 6

Describe and illustrate the reporting of stockholders' equity.

Reporting Stockholders' Equity

The "Stockholders' Equity" section of the balance sheet normally reports contributed capital followed by retained earnings and treasury stock. Each class of stock, paid-in capital in excess of par, paid-in capital from treasury stock, and total contributed capital is reported. This is followed by reporting retained earnings and total stockholders' equity before the effects of treasury stock. Since treasury stock reduces stockholders' equity, it is deducted to arrive at total stockholders' equity. Exhibit 10 illustrates the reporting of stockholders' equity on the balance sheet.

A separate statement of stockholders' equity should report changes in preferred stock, common stock, paid-in capital, retained earnings, and treasury stock. An example of a statement of stockholders' equity is shown in Exhibit 11.

Exhibit 10 Partial Balance Sheet with Stockholders' Equity

Bergstom Corporation
Balance Sheet
December 31, 20Y8

^^

Stockholders' Equity

Contributed capital:		
Preferred 10% stock, $50 par (20,000 shares authorized and issued)	$1,000,000	
Common stock, $20 par (250,000 shares authorized, 100,000 shares issued)	2,000,000	
Paid-in capital in excess of par	400,000	
Paid-in capital from treasury stock	120,000	
Total contributed capital	$3,520,000	
Retained earnings	4,580,500	
Total	$8,100,500	
Deduct treasury stock (1,000 shares at cost)	(75,000)	
Total stockholders' equity		8,025,500

Exhibit 11 Statement of Stockholders' Equity

Bergstom Corporation
Statement of Stockholders' Equity
For the Year Ended December 31, 20Y8

	Preferred Stock	Common Stock	Paid-In Capital in Excess of Par—Common Stock	Paid-In Capital from Treasury Stock	Retained Earnings	Treasury (Common) Stock	Total
Balance, January 1	$1,000,000	$1,750,000	$350,000	$120,000	$3,900,500	$(45,000)	$7,075,500
Net income					860,000		860,000
Dividends on preferred stock					(100,000)		(100,000)
Dividends on common stock					(80,000)		(80,000)
Issuance of additional common stock		250,000	50,000				300,000
Purchase of treasury stock						(30,000)	(30,000)
Balance, December 31	$1,000,000	$2,000,000	$400,000	$120,000	$ 4,580,500	$(75,000)	$8,025,500

Alphabet Connection

For a recent year, the stockholders' equity section of **Alphabet**'s balance sheet for December 31 and its statement of stockholders' equity for the year ended December 31 are as follows:

Stockholders' Equity
(in millions)

Class A, B, and C common stock, $0.001 par value per share	$ 50,552
Retained earnings	152,122
Other equity items*	(1,232)
Total stockholders' equity	$201,442

* Includes accumulated other comprehensive loss, which is discussed in Appendix A, Topic 4, *Reporting Unusual Items and Comprehensive Income.*

Alphabet Inc.
Statement of Stockholders' Equity
For the Year Ended December 31
(in millions)

	Common Stock and Paid-In Capital	Retained Earnings	Other	Total
Balances, January 1	$45,049	$134,885	$(2,306)	$177,628
Common stock issued	202			202
Purchase of treasury stock	(1,294)	(17,102)		(18,396)
Net income		34,343		34,343
Other*	6,595	(4)	1,074	7,665
Balances, December 31	$50,552	$152,122	$(1,232)	$201,442

* Includes topics discussed in advanced accounting courses.

International Connection

Reporting Liabilities and Stockholders' Equity Under IFRS

In the United States, liabilities are reported in the order that they will become due, with current liabilities reported first followed by long-term liabilities. On the balance sheet, stockholders' equity is reported after liabilities. Typically, companies reporting under IFRS report stockholders' equity before liabilities on the balance sheet. In addition, long-term liabilities are reported before current liabilities. That is, liabilities are reported in the reverse order in which they become due, with liabilities due within one year reported last.

Using Data Analytics

Use of Financial Leverage

Companies can use financial leverage to increase their profitability and earnings per share. The objective of financial leverage is to use borrowed money (debt) to increase earnings to common stockholders (equity holders). Financial leverage is based upon the principle that a company can borrow money at a lower cost than it earns on its operations. For example, assume a company can earn a 15% return on its operations and borrow funds at 5%. By borrowing money, the company can increase profits to its equity holders.

While financial leverage can improve profits, too much debt can result in financial distress. For example, if a company's return on its operations falls below the interest on its debt, it may be forced into bankruptcy and/or insolvency.

The debt-to-equity ratio is a common measure of a company's use of financial leverage, computed as follows:

$$\text{Debt-to-Equity Ratio} = \frac{\text{Total Liabilities}}{\text{Total Stockholders' Equity}}$$

The higher the debt-to-equity ratio, the more the company is using financial leverage to enhance its profitability and the higher the risk to equity holders. The debt-to-equity ratios of some well-known companies are as follows:

Apple Inc. (AAPL)	2.7
Caterpillar Inc. (CAT)	4.4
Deere & Company (DE)	5.4
Exxon Mobil Corporation (XOM)	0.9
General Electric Company (GE)	8.4
The Procter & Gamble Company (PG)	1.4
Walmart Inc. (WMT)	2.2

Investors can use publicly available databases and data analytics to compute the debt-to-equity ratio across companies and industries. Using these results and the current economic environment, an investor could evaluate a company's use of financial leverage and the related risk of investing in the company.

Financial Statement Metric-Analysis: Price-Earnings Ratio

Objective 7
Describe and illustrate the price-earnings ratio for assessing the current and future profitability of a company.

The market's assessment of the future earnings potential of a company is indicated by the **price-earnings ratio**. The price-earnings ratio, sometimes called the earnings multiple, is computed as follows:

$$\textbf{Price-Earnings Ratio} = \frac{\textbf{Market Price per Share of Common Stock}}{\textbf{Earnings per Share of Common Stock}}$$

The higher a company's price-earnings ratio, the more favorable the market's assessment of the future earnings potential and growth of the company. A price-earnings ratio of less than 10 is often interpreted as indicating a company that has declining earnings or is undervalued. A price-earnings ratio of over 25 usually indicates an expanding company with high earnings potential or a company that is overvalued.

Price-earnings ratios are often compared over time or with other companies within the same industry. To illustrate, earnings per share (EPS) of common stock and stock prices of **Apple Inc. (AAPL)** and **Microsoft Corporation (MSFT)** for three years are as follows:

	Year 3	Year 2	Year 1
Apple Inc.:			
Earnings per share	$ 11.97	$ 12.01	$ 9.27
Common stock price at end of year*	223.97	224.79	154.12
Microsoft:			
Earnings per share	$ 5.11	$ 2.15	$ 3.29
Common stock price at end of year*	133.96	98.61	68.93

* Adjusted for dividends and stock splits.

The price-earnings ratios (P/E) for each year (rounded to one decimal place) are as follows:

	Year 3	Year 2	Year 1
Apple Inc.:			
$223.97 ÷ $11.97	18.7		
$224.79 ÷ $12.01		18.7	
$154.12 ÷ $9.27			16.6
Microsoft:			
$133.96 ÷ $5.11	26.2		
$98.61 ÷ $2.15		45.9	
$68.93 ÷ $3.29			21.0

The P/E for Apple improved from 16.6 in Year 1 to 18.7 in Year 2 and Year 3. The P/E for Microsoft improved from 21.0 in Year 1 to 45.9 in Year 2, which indicates a significant change in the market's expectations for future earnings and growth. In Year 3, Microsoft's P/E declined to 26.2, which is still higher than Year 1.

Overall, Microsoft's P/Es are higher in all three years than Apple's. This suggests that the market has a more favorable outlook for Microsoft than for Apple. This is due to Microsoft's push for cloud computing and a move toward a subscription model for its business.

Key Points

1. Describe the nature of the corporate form of organization.

Corporations have a separate legal existence, transferable units of stock, unlimited life, and limited stockholders' liability. The advantages and disadvantages of the corporate form are summarized in Exhibit 2. Costs incurred in organizing a corporation are recorded as organizational expense.

2. Describe types of stock and illustrate the effects of issuing stock.

The main source of paid-in capital is from issuing common and preferred stock. Because different classes of stock have different rights, a separate account is used for recording each class of stock. When stock is issued at its par value, Cash is increased and the class of stock issued is increased. When stock is issued at a premium, Cash is increased for the amount received, Common Stock or Preferred Stock is increased for the par amount, and Paid-In Capital in Excess of Par is increased for the difference. When no-par stock is issued, the stock account is increased for the entire proceeds. If no-par stock is assigned a stated value per share, Paid-In Capital in Excess of Stated Value is increased for the excess of the proceeds over the stated value.

3. Describe types of dividends and the effects of declaring and paying dividends.

A corporation may declare cash or stock dividends. When a cash dividend is declared, Retained Earnings is decreased and Dividends Payable is increased. When the dividends are paid, Cash and Dividends Payable decrease. When a stock dividend is declared, Retained Earnings is decreased by the fair (market) value of the stock to be issued. Stock Dividends Distributable is increased for the par or stated value of the common stock to be issued and Paid-In Capital in Excess of Par—Common Stock is increased for the difference. When the stock is issued, Stock Dividends Distributable is decreased and Common Stock is increased for the par or stated value of the stock issued.

4. Describe the nature of stock splits and their effect on stockholders' equity.

Corporations sometimes reduce the par or stated value of their common stock and issue a proportionate number of additional shares in what is called a *stock split*. Since a stock split changes only the par or stated value and the number of shares outstanding, it is not recorded. However, the details of stock splits are normally disclosed in the notes to the financial statements.

5. Describe and illustrate the nature and effects of treasury stock transactions.

When a corporation buys its own stock, Treasury Stock is increased for its cost, and Cash is decreased. If the stock is resold, Cash is increased, Treasury Stock is decreased for its cost, and Paid-In Capital from Sale of Treasury Stock is increased for any difference between the cost and the selling price. Treasury stock is reported as a deduction from stockholders' equity.

6. Describe and illustrate the reporting of stockholders' equity.

The stockholders' equity section of the balance sheet normally reports paid-in capital followed by retained earnings and treasury stock. Each class of stock, paid-in capital in excess of par, paid-in capital from treasury stock, and total paid-in capital is reported. This is followed by reporting retained earnings and total stockholders' equity before the effects of treasury stock. Since treasury stock reduces stockholders' equity, it is deducted to arrive at total stockholders' equity. Exhibit 10 illustrates the reporting of stockholders' equity on the balance sheet. Most corporations report a separate statement of stockholders' equity showing the changes in the various stockholder equity accounts as illustrated in Exhibit 11.

7. Metric-Based Analysis: Describe and illustrate the price-earnings ratio for assessing the current and future profitability of a company.

The price-earnings ratio measures the market's assessment of the future earnings potential of the company. It is computed as the market price per share of common stock divided by the earnings per share of common stock. The higher the priceearnings ratio, the greater the market's expectations of future earnings.

Key Terms

Cash dividend (391)
Common stock (386)
Cumulative preferred stock (386)
Earnings per share (EPS) (388)
In arrears (387)
Net assets (388)
Outstanding stock (385)
Paid-In Capital in Excess of Par (389)
Par value (385)
Preferred stock (386)
Price-earnings ratio (400)
Stated value (385)
Stock (382)
Stock dividend (393)
Stock split (395)
Stockholders (382)
Treasury stock (396)

Illustrative Problem

Diamondback Welding & Fabrication Corporation sells and services pipe welding equipment in Illinois. The following selected accounts appear in the ledger of Diamondback Welding & Fabrication at the beginning of the current year:

Preferred 2% Stock, $80 par (100,000 shares authorized, 60,000 shares issued)	$ 4,800,000
Paid-In Capital in Excess of Par—Preferred Stock	210,000
Common Stock, $9 par (3,000,000 shares authorized, 1,750,000 shares issued)	15,750,000
Paid-In Capital in Excess of Par—Common Stock	1,400,000
Retained Earnings	52,840,000

During the year, the corporation completed the following transactions affecting the stockholders' equity.

Feb. 6. Purchased 87,500 shares of treasury common for $8 per share.

Apr. 12. Sold 55,000 shares of treasury common for $11 per share.

May 22. Issued 20,000 shares of preferred 2% stock at $84.

Aug. 31. Issued 400,000 shares of common stock at $13, receiving cash.

Oct. 16. Declared cash dividends of $1.60 per share on preferred stock and $0.05 per share on common stock.

Dec. 15. Paid the cash dividends.

Instructions

1. Illustrate the effects on the accounts and financial statements of the preceding transactions.
2. Prepare the "Stockholders' Equity" section of the balance sheet on December 31. Assume Diamondback Welding & Fabrication Corporation had net income of $500,000 for the year.

Solution

1.

Financial Statement Effects

BALANCE SHEET

	Assets	=	Liabilities	+	Stockholders' Equity
	Cash				Treasury Stock
Feb. 6.	(700,000)				(700,000)*

STATEMENT OF CASH FLOWS	
Feb. 6. Financing	(700,000)

INCOME STATEMENT

* 87,500 shares × $8

Financial Statement Effects

BALANCE SHEET

	Assets	=	Liabilities	+	Stockholders' Equity	
	Cash				Treasury Stock	Paid-In Capital from Sale of Treasury Stock
Apr. 12.	605,000*				440,000**	165,000

STATEMENT OF CASH FLOWS	
Apr. 12. Financing	605,000

INCOME STATEMENT

* 55,000 shares × $11
** 55,000 shares × $8

Financial Statement Effects

BALANCE SHEET

	Assets	=	Liabilities	+	Stockholders' Equity	
	Cash				Preferred Stock	Paid-In Capital in Excess of Par—Preferred Stock
May 22.	1,680,000*				1,600,000**	80,000

STATEMENT OF CASH FLOWS	
May 22. Financing	1,680,000

INCOME STATEMENT

* 20,000 shares × $84
** 20,000 shares × $80

Financial Statement Effects

BALANCE SHEET

	Assets	=	Liabilities	+	Stockholders' Equity	
	Cash				**Common Stock**	**Paid-In Capital in Excess of Par—Common Stock**
Aug. 31.	5,200,000*				3,600,000**	1,600,000

STATEMENT OF CASH FLOWS

Aug. 31. Financing 5,200,000

INCOME STATEMENT

* 400,000 shares × $13
** 400,000 shares × $9

Financial Statement Effects

BALANCE SHEET

	Assets	=	Liabilities	+	Stockholders' Equity
			Dividends Payable		**Retained Earnings**
Oct. 16.			233,875*		(233,875)

STATEMENT OF CASH FLOWS

INCOME STATEMENT

* Computation of cash dividends:

	Outstanding Shares of Stock	
	Preferred Stock	Common Stock
Beginning of year	60,000	1,750,000
Feb. 6 Purchased treasury stock		(87,500)
Apr. 12 Sold treasury stock		55,000
May 22 Issued preferred stock	20,000	
Aug. 31 Issued common stock		400,000
Shares outstanding on Oct.16	80,000	2,117,500
Cash dividends per share	×$1.60	×$0.05
Dividends declared on Oct.16	$128,000	$ 105,875
Total dividends	$233,875	

Financial Statement Effects

BALANCE SHEET

	Assets	=	Liabilities	+	Stockholders' Equity
	Cash		Dividends Payable		
Dec. 15.	(233,875)		(233,875)		

STATEMENT OF CASH FLOWS

Dec.15.	Financing	(233,875)

INCOME STATEMENT

2.

Stockholder's Equity

Contributed capital:	
Preferred 2% stock, $80 par (100,000 shares authorize, 80,000 shares issued)	$ 6,400,000
Paid-in capital in excess of par—preferred stock	290,000
Common stock, $9 par (3,000,000 shares authorized, 2,117,500 shares issued)	19,057,500
Paid-in capital in excess of par—common stock	3,000,000
Paid-in capital from sale of treasury stock	165,000
Total contributed capital	$ 28,912,500
Retained earnings	53,106,125*
Total	$82,018,625
Deduct treasury stock (32,500 shares at $8)	(260,000)
Total stockholder's equity	$ 81,758,625

* $52,840,000 + $500,000 − $233,875

Self-Examination Questions

(Answers appear at the end of the chapter.)

1. Which of the following is a disadvantage of the corporate form of organization?
   A. Limited liability
   B. Continuous life
   C. Owner is separate from management
   D. Ability to raise capital

2. Paid-in capital for a corporation may arise from which of the following sources?
   A. Issuing preferred stock
   B. Issuing common stock
   C. Selling the corporation's treasury stock
   D. All of the above

3. The "Stockholders' Equity" section of the balance sheet may include:
   A. common stock.
   B. stock dividends distributable.
   C. preferred stock.
   D. all of the above.

4. If a corporation reacquires its own stock, the stock is listed on the balance sheet in the:
   A. "Current assets" section.
   B. "Long-term liabilities" section.
   C. "Stockholders' Equity" section.
   D. "Investments" section.

5. A corporation has issued 25,000 shares of $100 par common stock and holds 3,000 of these shares as treasury stock. If the corporation declares a $2-per-share cash dividend, what amount will be recorded as cash dividends?
   A. $22,000
   B. $25,000
   C. $44,000
   D. $50,000

Class Discussion Questions

1. Of two corporations organized at approximately the same time and engaged in competing businesses, one issued $75 par common stock, and the other issued $1 par common stock. Do the par designations provide any indication as to which stock is preferable as an investment? Explain.
2. A stockbroker advises a client to buy preferred stock, saying "With that type of stock, you will never have to worry about losing the dividends." Is the broker right?
3. When a corporation issues stock at a premium, is the premium income? Explain.
4. A corporation with preferred stock and common stock outstanding has a substantial balance in its retained earnings account at the beginning of the current fiscal year. Although net income for the current year is sufficient to pay the preferred dividend of $150,000 each quarter and a common dividend of $40,000 each quarter, the board of directors declares dividends only on the preferred stock. Suggest possible reasons that the board did not declare dividends on the common stock.
5. An owner of 300 shares of Colorado Spring Company common stock receives a stock dividend of 6 shares.
   a. What is the effect of the stock dividend on the stockholder's proportionate interest (equity) in the corporation?
   b. How does the total equity of 306 shares compare with the total equity of 300 shares before the stock dividend?
6. a. Where should a declared but unpaid cash dividend be reported on the balance sheet?
   b. Where should a declared but unissued stock dividend be reported on the balance sheet?
7. What is the primary purpose of a stock split?
8. How do a stock split and a stock dividend differ and what do they have in common?
9. a. In what respect does treasury stock differ from unissued stock?
   b. How should treasury stock be presented on the balance sheet?
10. A corporation reacquires 18,000 shares of its own $50 par common stock for $2,250,000, recording it at cost.
    a. What effect does this transaction have on revenue or expense of the period?
    b. What effect does the purchase of the treasury stock have on stockholders' equity?
    c. What effect does the selling of the treasury stock for $2,400,000 have on the corporation's revenue?
    d. What effect does the selling of the treasury stock for $2,400,000 have on the corporation's stockholders' equity?

Exercises

E10-1 Dividends per share

Obj. 2

Zero Calories Company has 15,000 shares of cumulative preferred 1% stock, $50 par and 100,000 shares of $10 par common stock. The following amounts were distributed as dividends:

20Y1	$ 28,500
20Y2	6,000
20Y3	110,000

Determine the dividends per share for preferred and common stock for each year.

E10-2 Dividends per share

Obj. 2

SHOW ME HOW

EXCEL ONLINE

Seventy-Two Inc., a developer of radiology equipment, has stock outstanding as follows: 60,000 shares of cumulative preferred 2% stock, $60 par and 300,000 shares of $20 par common. During its first four years of operations, the following amounts were distributed as dividends: first year, $51,000; second year, $105,000; third year, $81,000; fourth year, $120,000. Determine the dividends per share on each class of stock for each of the four years.

Obj. 2

E10-3 Issuing par stock

SHOW ME HOW

On January 29, The Stone Store Inc., a granite contractor, issued 150,000 shares of $20 par common stock for cash at $46 per share, and on May 31, it issued 200,000 shares of $8 par, noncumulative preferred stock for cash at $12 per share.

a. Illustrate the effects on the accounts and financial statements of the January 29 and May 31 transactions.

b. What is the total amount invested (total paid-in capital) by all stockholders as of May 31?

Obj. 2

E10-4 Issuing stock for assets other than cash

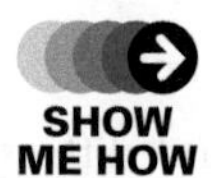
SHOW ME HOW

On August 7, Level Up Corporation, a wholesaler of hydraulic lifts, acquired land in exchange for 10,000 shares of $5 par common stock with a current market price of $7. Illustrate the effects on the accounts and financial statements of the purchase of the land.

Obj. 2

E10-5 Issuing no-par stock

SHOW ME HOW

On May 15, Helena Carpet Inc., a carpet wholesaler, issued for cash 750,000 shares of no-par common stock (with a stated value of $1.50) at $4, and on June 30, it issued for cash 17,500 shares of preferred stock, $50 par at $60.

a. Illustrate the effects on the accounts and financial statements of the May 15 and June 30 transactions

b. What is the total amount of paid-in capital from the May 15 and June 30 transactions?

Obj. 3

E10-6 Cash dividends

The date of declaration, date of record, and date of payment in connection with a cash dividend of $600,000 on a corporation's common stock are January 1, March 15, and June 14, respectively. Illustrate the effects on the accounts and financial statements for each date.

Obj. 3

E10-7 Stock dividends

SHOW ME HOW

Healthy Life Co. is an HMO for businesses in the Fresno area. The following account balances appear on Healthy Life's balance sheet as of January 1: Common Stock (3,000,000 shares authorized; 2,200,000 shares issued), $15 par, $33,000,000; Paid-In Capital in Excess of Par—Common Stock, $9,000,000; and Retained Earnings, $89,550,000.

The board of directors declared a 5% stock dividend on June 1. The market price of the stock was $18 per share on June 1 for stockholders of record July 15 to be distributed on August 15. No other stock transactions occurred during the year.

a. Illustrate the effects of the declaration and distribution of the stock dividend on the accounts and financial statements of Healthy Life Co.

b. Determine the following amounts before the stock dividend was declared on June 1: (1) total paid-in capital, (2) total retained earnings, and (3) total stockholders' equity.

c. Determine the following amounts after the stock dividend was declared and distributed on August 15: (1) total paid-in capital, (2) total retained earnings, and (3) total stockholders' equity.

E10-8 Effect of cash dividend, stock split, and stock dividend

Obj. 3, 4

Indicate whether the following actions would (+) increase, (−) decrease, or (0) not affect Ballistic Scientific Inc.'s total assets, liabilities, and stockholders' equity:

	Assets	Liabilities	Stockholders' Equity
(1) Declaring a cash dividend	______	______	______
(2) Paying the cash dividend declared in (1)	______	______	______
(3) Authorizing and issuing stock certificates in a stock split	______	______	______
(4) Declaring a stock dividend	______	______	______
(5) Issuing stock certificates for the stock dividend declared in (4)	______	______	______

E10-9 Effect of stock split

Obj. 4

Audrey's Restaurant Corporation wholesales ovens and ranges to restaurants throughout the Northwest. Audrey's Restaurant Corporation, which had 50,000 shares of common stock outstanding, declared a 6-for-1 stock split.

a. What will be the number of shares outstanding after the split?

b. If the common stock had a market price of $540 per share before the stock split, what would be an approximate market price per share after the split?

E10-10 Treasury stock transactions

Obj. 5

Blue Moon Water Supply Inc. bottles and distributes spring water. On July 17 of the current year, Blue Moon Water Supply reacquired 35,000 shares of its common stock at $60 per share. Blue Moon had not previously purchased any treasury shares.

a. What is the balance of Treasury Stock on December 31 of the current year?

b. Where will the balance of Treasury Stock be reported on the balance sheet?

c. For what reasons might Blue Moon Water Supply have purchased the treasury stock?

E10-11 Treasury stock transactions

Obj. 5

Sun Dance Gardens Inc. develops and produces spraying equipment for lawn maintenance and industrial uses. On June 3 of the current year, Sun Dance Gardens Inc. reacquired 28,000 shares of its common stock at $37 per share. Sun Dance had not previously purchased any treasury shares.

a. What is the balance of Treasury Stock on December 31 of the current year?

b. How will the balance in Treasury Stock be reported on the balance sheet?

c. Assume that Sun Dance Gardens sold 10,000 shares of its treasury stock at $40 on November 2. What accounts would be affected by the sale of the treasury stock?

E10-12 Treasury stock transactions

Obj. 5

Banff Water Inc. bottles and distributes spring water. On April 2 of the current year, Banff Water Inc. reacquired 30,000 shares of its common stock at $33 per share. Banff had not previously purchased any treasury shares.

a. What is the balance of Treasury Stock on December 31 of the current year?

b. Where will the balance of Treasury Stock be reported on the balance sheet?

c. For what reasons might Banff Water Inc. have purchased the treasury stock?

d. Assume that on January 25 of the following year, Banff Water Inc. sold 20,000 shares of its treasury stock for $40 per share. Illustrate the effects on the accounts and financial statements of the sale of the treasury stock.

Obj. 6

SHOW ME HOW

✔ Total stockholders' equity, $15,055,000

E10-13 "Stockholders' Equity" section of balance sheet

The following accounts and their balances appear in the ledger of Young Properties Inc. on November 30 of the current year:

Common Stock, $40 par	$ 3,000,000
Paid-In Capital in Excess of Par	450,000
Paid-In Capital from Treasury Stock	125,000
Retained Earnings	12,000,000
Treasury Stock	520,000

Prepare the "Stockholders' Equity" section of the balance sheet as of November 30. There are 100,000 common shares authorized, and 10,000 previously issued shares have been reacquired.

Obj. 6

✔ Total stockholders' equity, $22,818,000

10-14 "Stockholders' Equity" section of balance sheet

Premium Imports Inc. retails racing products for BMWs, Porsches, and Ferraris. The following accounts and their balances appear in the ledger of Premium Imports Inc. on November 30, the end of the current fiscal year:

Common Stock, $8 par	$ 3,200,000
Paid-In Capital in Excess of Par—Common Stock	700,000
Paid-In Capital in Excess of Par—Preferred Stock	182,000
Paid-In Capital from Treasury Stock—Common	150,000
Preferred 2% Stock, $80 par	2,080,000
Retained Earnings	17,250,000
Treasury Stock—Common	744,000

Shares authorized are 40,000 of preferred and 500,000 shares of common stock. There are 62,000 shares of common stock held as treasury stock.

Prepare the "Stockholders' Equity" section of the balance sheet as of November 30.

Problems

Obj. 2

✔ 1. Preferred dividends in Year 2: $44,000

P10-1 Dividends on preferred and common stock

Yukon Bike Corp. manufactures mountain bikes and distributes them through retail outlets in Canada, Montana, Idaho, Oregon, and Washington. Yukon Bike Corp. declared the following annual dividends over a six-year period ending December 31 of each year: Year 1, $28,000; Year 2, $44,000; Year 3, $48,000; Year 4, $60,000; Year 5, $76,000; and Year 6, $140,000. During the entire period, the outstanding stock of the company was composed of 40,000 shares of 2% noncumulative preferred stock, $65 par, and 50,000 shares of common stock, $1 par.

Instructions

1. Determine the total dividends and the per-share dividends declared on each class of stock for each of the six years. Assume that preferred dividends are paid before any common dividends. Summarize the data in tabular form, using the following column headings:

	Total	Preferred Dividends		Common Dividends	
Year	**Dividends**	**Total**	**Per Share**	**Total**	**Per Share**
Year 1	$ 28,000				
Year 2	44,000				
Year 3	48,000				
Year 4	60,000				
Year 5	76,000				
Year 6	140,000				

2. Calculate the average annual dividend per share for each class of stock for the six-year period.
3. Assuming that the preferred stock was sold at $57.50 and common stock was sold at $5.00 at the beginning of the six-year period, calculate the average annual percentage return on initial shareholders' investment, based on the average annual dividend per share (a) for preferred stock and (b) for common stock.

P10-2 Stock transactions for corporate expansion

Obj. 2

Vaga Optics produces medical lasers for use in hospitals. The following accounts and their balances appear in the ledger of Vaga Optics on December 31 of the current year:

Preferred 2% Stock, $120 par (50,000 shares authorized, 25,000 shares issued)	$ 3,000,000
Paid-In Capital in Excess of Par—Preferred Stock	400,000
Common Stock, $75 par (500,000 shares authorized, 300,000 shares issued)	22,500,000
Paid-In Capital in Excess of Par—Common Stock	540,000
Retained Earnings	55,000,000

At the annual stockholders' meeting on January 31, the board of directors presented a plan for modernizing and expanding plant operations at a cost of approximately $9,500,000. The plan provided (a) that the corporation borrow $4,500,000, (b) that 20,000 shares of the unissued preferred stock be issued through an underwriter, and (c) that a building, valued at $1,200,000, and the land on which it is located, valued at $900,000, be acquired in accordance with preliminary negotiations by the issuance of 27,400 shares of common stock. The plan was approved by the stockholders and accomplished by the following transactions:

Mar. 8. Borrowed $4,500,000 from Conrad National Bank, giving a 6% mortgage note.
13. Issued 20,000 shares of preferred stock, receiving $130 per share in cash.
26. Issued 27,400 shares of common stock in exchange for land and a building, according to the plan.

No other expansion-related transactions occurred during March.

Instructions

Illustrate the effects on the accounts and financial statements of each of the preceding transactions.

Obj. 2, 3, 5, 6

P10-3 Stock transactions

Parks Construction Inc. had the following selected account balances as of January 1, the beginning of the current accounting period (year):

Preferred Noncumulative 2% Stock, $100 par (100,000 shares authorized, 80,000 shares outstanding)	$ 8,000,000
Paid-In Capital in Excess of Par—Preferred Stock	440,000
Common Stock, $5 par (5,000,000 shares authorized, 4,000,000 shares outstanding)	20,000,000
Paid-In Capital in Excess of Par—Common Stock	2,280,000
Retained Earnings	115,400,000

During the year ended December 31, Parks Construction Inc. completed the following transactions affecting stockholders' equity.

Mar. 10. Issued 200,000 shares of common stock at $12 per share, receiving cash.

Apr. 8. Issued 8,000 shares of preferred 2% stock at $115 per share.

Aug. 22. Purchased 175,000 shares of treasury common for $10 per share.

Sept. 19. Sold 110,000 shares of treasury common for $14 per share.

30. Declared cash dividends of $2.00 per share on preferred stock and $0.08 per share on common stock.

Nov. 15. Paid the cash dividends.

Instructions

1. Illustrate the effects on the accounts and financial statements of the preceding transactions.
2. Prepare the "Stockholders' Equity" section of the balance sheet on December 31. Assume Parks Construction Inc. had net income of $750,000 for the year.

Obj. 2, 3, 4, 5

P10-4 Stock transactions

Selected transactions completed by Primo Discount Corporation during the current fiscal year are as follows:

Jan. 9. Split the common stock 3 for 1 and reduced the par from $75 to $25 per share. After the split, there were 1,200,000 common shares outstanding.

Feb. 28. Purchased 40,000 shares of the corporation's own common stock at $28 per share, recording the stock at cost.

May 1. Declared semiannual dividends of $0.80 per share on 75,000 shares of preferred stock and $0.12 per share on the common stock to stockholders of record on June 1, payable on July 10.

July 10. Paid the cash dividends.

Sept. 7. Sold 30,000 shares of treasury stock for $34 per share, receiving cash.

Oct. 1. Declared semiannual dividends of $0.80 per share on the preferred stock and $0.12 per share on the common stock (before the stock dividend).

1. In addition to cash dividends, a 2% common stock dividend was declared on the common stock outstanding. The fair market value of the common stock is estimated at $36.

Dec. 1. Paid the cash dividends and issued the certificates for the common stock dividend.

Instructions

Illustrate the effects on the accounts and financial statements of the preceding transactions.

Metric-Based Analysis

MBA 10-1 Stock transactions

Obj. 2

Using the data from E10-3, indicate the effects on net assets and EPS for the January 29 and May 31 transactions.

MBA 10-2 Dividends

Obj. 3

Using the data from E10-6, indicate the effects on net assets and EPS for the following dates:

1. January 1 (date of declaration)
2. March 15 (date of record)
3. June 14 (date of payment)

MBA 10-3 Treasury stock purchase

Obj. 5

Using the data from E10-12, indicate the effects on net assets and EPS for the following transactions:

1. Purchasing the treasury stock on April 2.
2. Selling the treasury stock on January 25 of the following year.

MBA 10-4 Stock transactions

Obj. 2, 3, 5, 6

Using the data from P10-3, indicate the effects on net assets and EPS for each of the transactions.

MBA 10-5 Stock split

Obj. 4

Using the data from E10-9, indicate the effects on net assets and EPS of the stock split.

MBA 10-6 Price-earnings ratios

Obj. 7

The Home Depot, Inc. (HD) operates over 2,200 home improvement retail stores and is a competitor of Lowe's (LOW). For two recent years, The Home Depot's earnings per share and related end-of-year stock price were as follows:

	Year 2	Year 1
Earnings per share	$ 10.29	$ 9.78
End-of-year stock price	231.54	186.43

1. Compute the price-earnings ratio for Year 2. Round to one decimal place.
2. Compute the price-earnings ratio for Year 1. Round to one decimal place.
3. Compare the results of parts (1) and (2) and comment.

Obj. 7

MBA 10-7 Price-earnings ratios

Lowe's Companies Inc. (LOW) operates over 1,800 home improvement retail stores and is a competitor of The Home Depot (HD). For two recent years, Lowe's Companies Inc.'s earnings per share and related end-of-year stock price were as follows:

	Year 2	Year 1
Earnings per share	$ 5.49	$ 2.84
End-of-year stock price	116.24	97.11

1. Compute the price-earnings ratio for Year 2. Round to one decimal place.
2. Compute the price-earnings ratio for Year 1. Round to one decimal place.
3. Compare the results of parts (1) and (2) and comment.
4. Compare the price-earnings ratios of Lowe's and The Home Depot (MBA 10-6) for Year 2. Comment on any differences.

Obj. 7

MBA 10-8 Price-earnings ratios

Alphabet (GOOG) is a technology company that offers users Internet search and e-mail services. Google also developed the Android operating system for use with cell phones and other mobile devices. For two recent years, Alphabet's earnings per share and related end-of-year stock price were as follows:

	Year 2	Year 1
Earnings per share	$ 49.59	$ 44.22
End-of-year stock price	1,337.02	1,035.61

1. Compute the price-earnings ratio for Year 2. Round to one decimal place.
2. Compute the price-earnings ratio for Year 1. Round to one decimal place.
3. Compare the results of parts (1) and (2) and comment.

Obj. 7

MBA 10-9 Price-earnings ratios

For each of the following companies, indicate whether you think the price-earnings ratio is above 10.

	Price-Earnings Ratio Above 10 (Yes, No)
Alphabet (GOOG)	
Amazon.com (AMZN)	
Bank of America Corporation (BAC)	
Dell	
HP (formerly Hewlett-Packard) (HPQ)	
McDonald's (MCD)	
Nike (NKE)	
Walmart (WMT)	

Cases

Case 10-1 Employee stock purchases

Tommy Gunn is a division manager for K-Cern Inc., a small pharmaceutical company. Tommy's division has been working on a new drug that has the potential to revolutionize the treatment of skin cancer. Once the drug is proven to be effective in clinical trials, it will be approved for sale by the government and patented by the company. Because of the potential market for this drug, it is highly likely that the company's revenues and net income will increase significantly when it is approved. Tommy recently saw an internal company memo indicating that the drug passed its final clinical trial and that the company has received government approval to sell the drug. The company will issue a press release announcing this news in the next two days, and this announcement is expected to result in a dramatic increase in the company's stock price. Tommy knows that there is "free money" to be made if he invests in the stock before the announcement is made. However, K-Cern has a strict policy against employee purchases of company stock outside of established employee stock purchase plans. To get around this rule, Tommy asks his father to purchase the stock for him. The next morning, Tommy's father purchases the stock with the understanding that he will split the profits with Tommy.

Is Tommy behaving ethically? Why or why not?

Case 10-2 Establishing par value of common stock

Lou Hoskins and Shirley Crothers are organizing Red Lodge Metals Unlimited Inc. to undertake a high-risk gold mining venture in Canada. Lou and Shirley tentatively plan to request authorization for 400,000,000 shares of common stock to be sold to the general public. Lou and Shirley have decided to establish par of $0.03 per share in order to appeal to a wide variety of potential investors. Lou and Shirley believe that investors would be more willing to invest in the company if they received a large quantity of shares for what might appear to be a "bargain" price.

Discuss whether Lou and Shirley are behaving in a professional manner.

Case 10-3 Issuing stock

Sahara Unlimited Inc. began operations on January 2, 20Y4, with the issuance of 250,000 shares of $8 par common stock. The sole stockholders of Sahara Unlimited Inc. are Karina Takemoto and Dr. Noah Grove, who organized Sahara Unlimited Inc. with the objective of developing a new flu vaccine. Dr. Grove claims that the flu vaccine, which is nearing the final development stage, will protect individuals against 80% of the flu types that have been medically identified. To complete the project, Sahara Unlimited Inc. needs $25,000,000 of additional funds. The banks have been unwilling to loan the funds because of the lack of sufficient collateral and the riskiness of the business. The following is a conversation between Karina Takemoto, the chief executive officer of Sahara Unlimited Inc., and Dr. Noah Grove, the leading researcher:

Karina: What are we going to do? The banks won't loan us any more money, and we've got to have $25 million to complete the project. We are so close! It would be a disaster to quit now. The only thing I can think of is to issue additional stock. Do you have any suggestions?

Noah: I guess you're right. But if the banks won't loan us any more money, how do you think we can find any investors to buy stock?

Karina: I've been thinking about that. What if we promise the investors that we will pay them 2% of sales until they have received an amount equal to what they paid for the stock?

Noah: What happens when we pay back the $25 million? Do the investors get to keep the stock? If they do, it'll dilute our ownership.

Karina: How about, if after we pay back the $25 million, we make them turn in their stock for what they paid for it? Plus, we could pay them an additional $50 per share. That's a $50 profit per share for the investors.

Noah: It could work. We get our money, but don't have to pay any interest or dividends until we start generating sales. At the same time, the investors could get their money back plus $50 per share.

Karina: We'll need current financial statements for the new investors. I'll get our accountant working on them and contact our attorney to draw up a legally binding contract for the new investors. Yes, this could work.

In late 20Y4, the attorney and the various regulatory authorities approved the new stock offering, and shares of common stock were privately sold to new investors for $25,000,000.

In preparing financial statements for 20Y4, Karina Takemoto and Glenn Bergum, the controller for Sahara Unlimited Inc., have the following conversation:

Glenn: Karina, I've got a problem.

Karina: What's that, Glenn?

Glenn: Issuing common stock to raise that additional $25 million was a great idea. But ...

Karina: But what?

Glenn: I've got to prepare the 20Y4 annual financial statements, and I am not sure how to classify the common stock.

Karina: What do you mean? It's common stock.

Glenn: I'm not so sure. I called the auditor and explained how we are contractually obligated to pay the new stockholders 2% of sales until they receive what they paid for the stock. Then, we may be obligated to pay them $50 per share.

Karina: So ...

Glenn: So the auditor thinks that we should classify the additional issuance of $25 million as debt, not stock! And, if we put the $25 million on the balance sheet as debt, we will violate our other loan agreements with the banks. And, if these agreements are violated, the banks may call in all our debt immediately. If they do that, we are in deep trouble. We'll probably have to file for bankruptcy. We just don't have the cash to pay off the banks.

1. Discuss the arguments for and against classifying the issuance of the $25 million of stock as debt.
2. What do you think might be a practical solution to this classification problem?

Case 10-4 Preferred stock vs. bonds

Living Smart Inc. has decided to expand its operations to owning and operating long-term health care facilities. The following is an excerpt from a conversation between the chief executive officer, Mark Vierra, and the vice president of finance, Jolin Kilcup.

Mark: Jolin, have you given any thought to how we're going to finance the acquisition of St. George Health Care?

Jolin: Well, the two basic options, as I see it, are to issue either preferred stock or bonds. The equity market is a little depressed right now. The rumor is that the Federal Reserve Bank may increase the interest rates either this month or next.

Mark: Yes, I've heard the rumor. The problem is that we can't wait around to see what's going to happen. We'll have to move on this next week if we want any chance to complete the acquisition of St. George.

Jolin: Well, the bond market is strong right now. Maybe we should issue debt this time around.

Mark: That's what I would have guessed as well. St. George's financial statements look pretty good, except for the volatility of its income and cash flows. But that's characteristic of the industry.

Discuss the advantages and disadvantages of issuing preferred stock versus bonds.

The annual report (10-K) assignment for this chapter is in Appendix B: Nike Annual Report, Chapter 10.

Answers to Self-Examination Questions

1. **C** The separation of the owner from management (answer C) is a disadvantage of the corporate form of organization. This is because management may not always behave in the best interests of the owners. Limited liability (answer A), continuous life (answer B), and the ability to raise capital (answer D) are all advantages of the corporate form of organization.
2. **D** Paid-in capital is one of the two major subdivisions of the stockholders' equity of a corporation. It may result from many sources, including the issuance of preferred stock (answer A), the issuance of common stock (answer B), or the sale of a corporation's treasury stock (answer C).
3. **D** The "Stockholders' Equity" section of corporate balance sheets is divided into two principal subsections: (1) investments contributed by the stockholders and others and (2) net income retained in the business. Included as part of the investments by stockholders and others is the par of common stock (answer A), stock dividends distributable (answer B), and the par of preferred stock (answer C).
4. **C** Reacquired stock, known as treasury stock, should be listed in the "Stockholders' Equity" section (answer C) of the balance sheet. The price paid for the treasury stock is deducted from the total of all the stockholders' equity accounts.
5. **C** If a corporation that holds treasury stock declares a cash dividend, the dividends are not paid on the treasury shares. The corporation will record $44,000 (answer C) as cash dividends [(25,000 shares issued less 3,000 shares held as treasury stock) × $2-per-share dividend].

Chapter 11 Statement of Cash Flows

What's Covered

Statement of Cash Flows

Cash Flows
- Types of cash flows (Obj. 1)
- Direct method (Obj. 1)
- Indirect method (Obj. 1)
- Noncash transactions (Obj. 1)

Operating Activities—Indirect Method
- Net income (Obj. 2)
- Noncash expenses (Obj. 2)
- Gains and losses (Obj. 2)
- Current assets and liabilities (Obj. 2)

Investing Activities
- Land (Obj. 3)
- Buildings (Obj. 3)

Financing Activities
- Bonds payable (Obj. 4)
- Common stock (Obj. 4)
- Dividends and dividends payable (Obj. 4)

Reporting Cash Flows
- Preparing the statement of cash flows (Obj. 5)

Metric-Based Analysis
- Free cash flow (Obj. 6)
- Cash flow adequacy (Obj. 6)

Learning Objectives

Obj. 1 Describe the cash flow activities reported on the statement of cash flows.

Obj. 2 Prepare the "Cash flows from (used for) operating activities" section of the statement of cash flows using the indirect method.

Obj. 3 Prepare the "Cash flows from (used for) investing activities" section of the statement of cash flows.

Obj. 4 Prepare the "Cash flows from (used for) financing activities" section of the statement of cash flows.

Obj. 5 Prepare a statement of cash flows.

Obj. 6 Describe and illustrate the use of free cash flow and cash flow adequacy in evaluating a company's cash flow.

Chapter Metrics

Use the following metrics to analyze transactions and financial statements.

TRANSACTIONS*

Liquidity: N/A

Profitability: N/A

FINANCIAL STATEMENTS

Free Cash Flow

Cash Flow Adequacy

*There are no transactions in this chapter.

National Beverage Corp.

Source: National Beverage Corporation

Suppose you were to receive $100 from an event. Would it make a difference what the event was? Yes, it would! If you received $100 for your birthday, then it's a gift. If you received $100 as a result of working part time for a week, then it's the result of your effort. If you received $100 as a loan, then it's money that you will have to pay back in the future. If you received the $100 as a result of selling your iPod, then it's the result of selling an asset. Thus, the $100 received can be associated with different types of events, and these events have different meanings to you and different implications for your future. You would much rather receive a $100 gift than take out a $100 loan. Likewise, company stakeholders view inflows and outflows of cash differently, depending on their source.

Companies are required to report information about the events causing a change in cash over a period of time. This information is reported on the statement of cash flows. One such company is **National Beverage Corp. (FIZZ)**, which is an alternative beverage company, known for its innovative soft drinks, enhanced juices and waters, and fortified powders and supplements. You have probably seen the company's Shasta and Faygo soft drinks, or LaCroix, Everfresh, and Crystal Bay drinks at your local grocery or convenience store. As with any company, cash is important to National Beverage. Without cash, National Beverage would be unable to expand its brands, distribute its products, support extreme sports, or provide a return for its owners. Thus, its managers are concerned about the sources and uses of cash.

In previous chapters, we have used the income statement, balance sheet, statement of stockholders' equity, and other information to analyze the effects of management decisions on a business's financial position and operating performance. In this chapter, we focus on the events causing a change in cash by presenting the preparation and use of the statement of cash flows.

Reporting Cash Flows

Objective 1
Describe the cash flow activities reported on the statement of cash flows.

The **statement of cash flows** reports a company's cash inflows and outflows for a period.[1] The statement of cash flows provides useful information about a company's ability to do the following:

- Generate cash from operations
- Maintain and expand its operating capacity
- Meet its financial obligations
- Pay dividends

The statement of cash flows is used by managers in evaluating past operations and in planning future investing and financing activities. It is also used by external users such as investors and creditors to assess a company's profit potential and ability to pay its debt and pay dividends.

The statement of cash flows reports three types of cash flow activities, as follows:

1. **Cash flows from (used for) operating activities** are the cash flows from transactions that affect the net income of the company.

   Example: Purchase and sale of merchandise by a retailer.

2. **Cash flows from (used for) investing activities** are the cash flows from transactions that affect investments in the noncurrent assets of the company.

   Example: Purchase and sale of fixed assets, such as equipment and buildings.

3. **Cash flows from (used for) financing activities** are the cash flows from transactions that affect the debt and equity of the company.

   Example: Issuing or retiring equity and debt securities.

1. As used in this chapter, *cash* refers to cash and cash equivalents. Examples of cash equivalents include short-term, highly liquid investments, such as money market accounts, bank certificates of deposit, and U.S. Treasury bills.

The cash flows are reported on the statement of cash flows as follows:

Cash flows from (used for) operating activities	$XXX
Cash flows from (used for) investing activities	XXX
Cash flows from (used for) financing activities	XXX
Net increase (decrease) in cash	$XXX
Cash as of the beginning of the period	XXX
Cash as of the end of the period	$XXX

The ending cash on the statement of cash flows equals the cash reported on the company's balance sheet at the end of the year.

Exhibit 1 illustrates the sources (increases) and uses (decreases) of cash by each of the three cash flow activities. A *source* of cash causes the cash flow to increase and is called a *cash inflow*. A *use* of cash causes cash flow to decrease and is called a *cash outflow*.

Exhibit 1 Sources and Uses of Cash

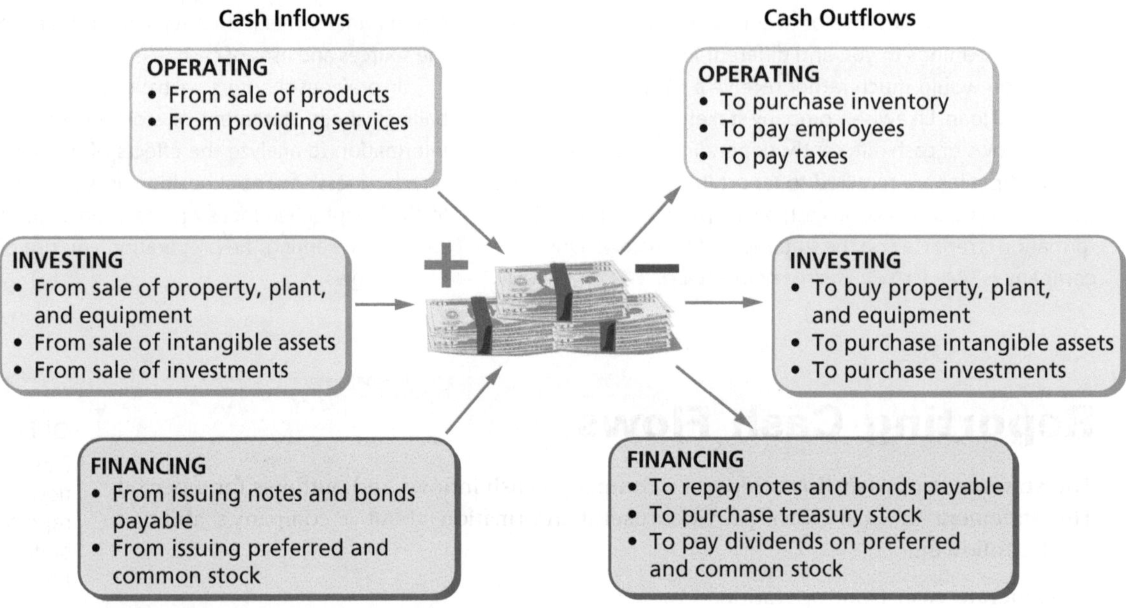

Cash Flows: Operating Activities

Cash flows from (used for) operating activities report the cash inflows and outflows from a company's day-to-day operations. Companies may select one of two alternative methods for reporting cash flows from operating activities on the statement of cash flows:

- The direct method
- The indirect method

Both methods result in the same amount of cash flows from operating activities. They differ in the way they report cash flows from operating activities.

The Direct Method The **direct method** reports operating cash inflows (receipts) and cash outflows (payments) as follows:

Cash flows from (used for) operating activities:		
Cash received from customers	$ XXX	
Cash paid for merchandise	(XXX)	
Cash paid for operating expenses	(XXX)	
Cash paid for interest	(XXX)	
Cash paid for income taxes	(XXX)	
Net cash flows from (used for) operating activities		$XXX

The primary operating cash inflow is cash received from customers. The primary operating cash outflows are cash payments for merchandise, operating expenses, interest, and income tax payments. The cash received from operating activities less the cash payments for operating activities is the net cash flows from operating activities.

The primary advantage of the direct method is that it *directly* reports cash receipts and cash payments for each operating activity on the statement of cash flows. Its primary disadvantage is that these data may not be readily available in the accounting records. Thus, the direct method is normally more costly to prepare and, as a result, is used infrequently in practice. For this reason, the direct method is described and illustrated in the Appendix following this chapter.

The Indirect Method The **indirect method** reports cash flows from operating activities by beginning with net income and adjusting it for revenues and expenses that do not involve the receipt or payment of cash, as follows:

Cash flows from (used for) operating activities:		
Net income	$XXX	
Adjustments to reconcile net income (loss) to net cash flows from (used for) operating activities	XXX	
Net cash flows from (used for) operating activities		$XXX

The adjustments to reconcile net income to net cash flows from operating activities include such items as depreciation and gains or losses on fixed assets. Changes in current operating assets and liabilities such as accounts receivable or accounts payable are also added or deducted, depending on their effect on cash flows. In effect, these additions and deductions adjust net income, which is reported on an accrual accounting basis, to cash flows from operating activities, which is a cash basis.

A primary advantage of the indirect method is that it reconciles the differences between net income and net cash flows from operations. In doing so, it shows how net income is related to the ending cash balance that is reported on the balance sheet.

Because the data are readily available, the indirect method is less costly to prepare than the direct method. As a result, the indirect method of reporting cash flows from operations is most commonly used in practice. The indirect method was illustrated in the Appendix, "Reconciliation: Net Cash Flows from (Used for) Operating Activities and Net Income," to Chapter 3.

National Beverage Corp. uses the indirect method of reporting the cash flows from operating activities in its statement of cash flows.

National Beverage Connection

Comparing the Direct and Indirect Methods Exhibit 2 illustrates the "Cash flows from (used for) operating activities" section of the statement of cash flows for Family Health Care, P.C. It shows the direct and indirect methods using the Family Health Care data from Chapter 3. As Exhibit 2 illustrates, both methods report the same amount of net cash flows used for operating activities of $(1,690).

Exhibit 2 Cash Flows Used for Operations: Direct and Indirect Methods—Family Health Care, P. C.

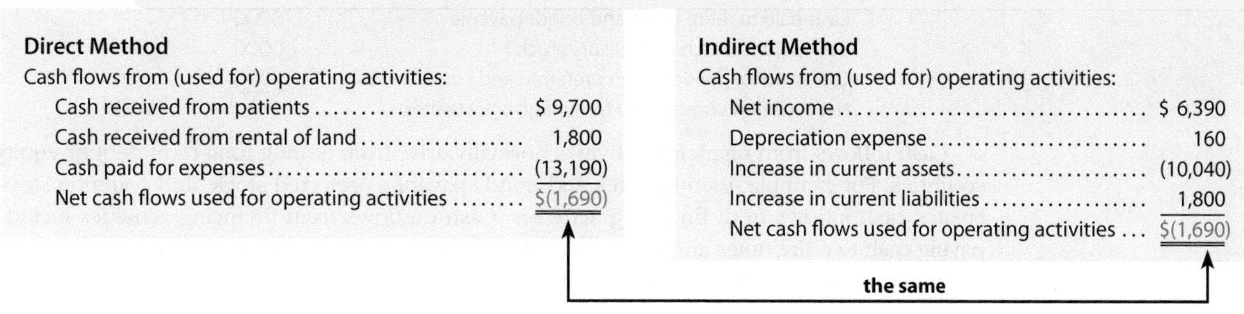

Direct Method

Cash flows from (used for) operating activities:	
Cash received from patients	$ 9,700
Cash received from rental of land	1,800
Cash paid for expenses	(13,190)
Net cash flows used for operating activities	$(1,690)

Indirect Method

Cash flows from (used for) operating activities:	
Net income	$ 6,390
Depreciation expense	160
Increase in current assets	(10,040)
Increase in current liabilities	1,800
Net cash flows used for operating activities	$(1,690)

For a recent year, **National Beverage Corp.** reported net cash provided by operating activities of $177,692,000.

National Beverage Connection

Business Insight

Cash Crunch!

Pier 1 Imports, Inc. (PIR), a home furnishings retailer recently filed for bankruptcy protection. The cash flows from operating activities for the three years prior to bankruptcy (in thousands) follow:

	Year 3	Year 2	Year 1
Cash provided (used for) operating activities	$(98,798)	$65,806	$117,738

As can be seen, cash flows from operating activities trended into negative territory during the three years prior to the firm's bankruptcy. Thus, when cash flows from operating activities are negative, it can lead to financial distress.

Cash Flows: Investing Activities

Cash flows from (used for) investing activities show the cash inflows and outflows related to changes in a company's long-term assets. Cash flows from (used for) investing activities are reported on the statement of cash flows as follows:

Cash flows from (used for) investing activities:		
Cash received from sale of property, plant, and equipment	$ XXX	
Cash received from sale of intangible assets	XXX	
Cash received from sale of investments	XXX	
Cash paid for purchase of property, plant, and equipment	(XXX)	
Cash paid for purchase of intangible assets	(XXX)	
Cash paid for purchase of investments	(XXX)	
Net cash flows from (used for) investing activities		$XXX

Cash inflows from investing activities normally arise from selling property, plant, and equipment; investments; and intangible assets. Cash outflows normally include payments to purchase these assets.

National Beverage Connection

For a recent year, **National Beverage Corp.** reported net cash flows used for investing activities of $23,881,000.

Cash Flows: Financing Activities

Cash flows from (used for) financing activities show the cash inflows and outflows related to changes in a company's long-term liabilities and stockholders' equity. Cash flows from (used for) financing activities are reported on the statement of cash flows as follows:

Cash flows from (used for) financing activities:		
Cash received from issuing notes and bonds payable	$ XXX	
Cash received from issuing preferred or common stock	XXX	
Cash paid to retire notes and bonds payable	(XXX)	
Cash paid to purchase treasury stock	(XXX)	
Cash paid for dividends on preferred and common stock	(XXX)	
Net cash flows from (used for) financing activities		$XXX

Cash inflows from financing activities normally arise from issuing long-term debt or equity securities. For example, issuing notes and bonds payable, preferred stock, and common stock creates cash inflows from financing activities. Cash outflows from financing activities include paying cash to retire notes and bonds payable, purchasing treasury stock, and paying dividends on preferred and common stock.

National Beverage Connection

For a recent year, **National Beverage Corp.** reported net cash flows used for financing activities of $5,493,000.

Growing Pains

Twitter, Inc. (TWTR) is a global social media platform used for real-time self-expression and conversation within the limits of 140-character tweets. The net cash flows from operating, investing, and financing activities for Twitter's first four years as a public company (in thousands) are as follows:

	Net Cash Provided by (Used for)			
	Operating Activities	Investing Activities	Financing Activities	Net Change for Year
Year 1	$ 1,398	$(1,306,066)	$1,942,176	$637,508
Year 2	81,796	(1,097,272)	1,691,722	676,246
Year 3	383,066	(902,421)	(62,998)	(582,353)
Year 4	763,055	(598,008)	(83,975)	81,072

Twitter significantly improved its cash flows from operations from Year 1 to Year 4. Twitter made significant investments in order to expand. This is shown by the net cash flows used in investing activities for Years 1 through 4. Since the net cash flows from operations were insufficient to fund this growth, the company obtained cash from financing activities. For example, Twitter received cash from stockholders in Year 1 and from creditors in Year 2, which was used to expand and provide future flexibility.

Noncash Investing and Financing Activities

A company may enter into transactions involving investing and financing activities that do not *directly* affect cash. For example, a company may issue common stock to retire long-term debt. Although this transaction does not directly affect cash, it does eliminate future cash payments for interest and for paying the bonds when they mature. Because such transactions *indirectly* affect cash flows, they are reported in a separate section of the statement of cash flows. This section usually appears at the bottom of the statement of cash flows.

Format of the Statement of Cash Flows

The statement of cash flows presents the cash flows generated from, or used for, the three activities previously discussed: operating, investing, and financing. These three activities are always reported in the same order, as shown in Exhibit 3.

Exhibit 3 Order of Reporting Statement of Cash Flows

Rundell Inc.
Statement of Cash Flows
For the Year Ended 20Y8

Cash flows from (used for) operating activities:		
(List of items, as illustrated in Exhibit 1)	$XXX	
Net cash flows from (used for) operating activities		$XXX
Cash flows from (used for) investing activities:		
(List of items, as illustrated in Exhibit 1)	$XXX	
Net cash flows from (used for) investing activities		XXX
Cash flows from (used for) financing activities:		
(List of items, as illustrated in Exhibit 1)	$XXX	
Net cash flows from (used for) financing activities		XXX
Net increase (decrease) in cash		$XXX
Cash as of the beginning of the period		XXX
Cash as of the end of the period		$XXX
Noncash investing and financing activities		$XXX

No Cash Flow per Share

Cash flow per share is sometimes reported in the financial press. As reported, cash flow per share is normally computed as *net cash flows from operating activities divided by the number of common shares outstanding*. However, such reporting may be misleading because of the following:

- Users may misinterpret cash flow per share as the per-share amount available for dividends. This would not be the case if the cash generated by operations is required for repaying loans or for reinvesting in the business.
- Users may misinterpret cash flow per share as equivalent to (or better than) earnings per share.

For these reasons, the financial statements, including the statement of cash flows, should not report cash flow per share.

Objective 2

Prepare the "Cash flows from (used for) operating activities" section of the statement of cash flows using the indirect method.

Cash Flows: Operating Activities

The indirect method of reporting cash flows from (used for) operating activities uses the logic that a change in any balance sheet account (including cash) can be analyzed in terms of changes in the other balance sheet accounts. Thus, by analyzing changes in noncash balance sheet accounts, any change in the cash account can be *indirectly* determined.

To illustrate, the accounting equation can be solved for cash as follows:

$$\text{Assets} = \text{Liabilities} + \text{Stockholders' Equity}$$
$$\text{Cash} + \text{Noncash Assets} = \text{Liabilities} + \text{Stockholders' Equity}$$
$$\text{Cash} = \text{Liabilities} + \text{Stockholders' Equity} - \text{Noncash Assets}$$

Therefore, any change in the cash account can be determined by analyzing changes in the liability, stockholders' equity, and noncash asset accounts as follows:

$$\textit{Change}\text{ in Cash} = \textit{Change}\text{ in Liabilities} + \textit{Change}\text{ in Stockholders' Equity} - \textit{Change}\text{ in Noncash Assets}$$

Under the indirect method, there is no order in which the balance sheet accounts must be analyzed. However, net income (or net loss) is the first amount reported on the statement of cash flows. Because net income (or net loss) is a component of any change in Retained Earnings, the first account normally analyzed is Retained Earnings.

To illustrate the indirect method, the income statement and comparative balance sheet for Rundell Inc., shown in Exhibit 4, are used. Other data supporting the income statement and balance sheet are presented as needed.[2]

Adjustments to Net Income

The net income of $108,000 reported by Rundell Inc. in Exhibit 4 does not equal the net cash flows from operating activities for the period. This is because net income is determined using the accrual method of accounting.

Under the accrual method of accounting, revenues and expenses are recorded at different times from when cash is received or paid. For example, merchandise may be sold on account and the cash received at a later date. Likewise, insurance premiums may be paid in the current period but expensed in a following period.

2. A spreadsheet (work sheet) used as an aid in assembling data for the statement of cash flows is presented in an online Appendix. This appendix illustrates the use of this spreadsheet in reporting cash flows from operating activities using the indirect method.

Exhibit 4 Income Statement and Comparative Balance Sheet

Rundell Inc.
Income Statement
For the Year Ended December 31, 20Y8

Sales		$1,180,000
Cost of goods sold		(790,000)
Gross profit		$ 390,000
Operating expenses:		
Depreciation expense	$ 7,000	
Other operating expenses	196,000	
Total operating expenses		(203,000)
Operating income		$ 187,000
Other revenue and expense:		
Gain on sale of land	$ 12,000	
Interest expense	(8,000)	4,000
Income before income tax		$ 191,000
Income tax expense		(83,000)
Net income		$ 108,000

Rundell Inc.
Comparative Balance Sheet
December 31, 20Y8 and 20Y7

	20Y8	20Y7	Increase (Decrease)
Assets			
Cash	$ 97,500	$ 26,000	$ 71,500
Accounts receivable (net)	74,000	65,000	9,000
Inventories	172,000	180,000	(8,000)
Land	80,000	125,000	(45,000)
Building	260,000	200,000	60,000
Accumulated depreciation—building	(65,300)	(58,300)	(7,000)*
Total assets	$618,200	$537,700	$ 80,500
Liabilities			
Accounts payable (merchandise creditors)	$ 43,500	$ 46,700	$ (3,200)
Accrued expenses payable (operating expenses)	26,500	24,300	2,200
Income taxes payable	7,900	8,400	(500)
Dividends payable	14,000	10,000	4,000
Bonds payable	100,000	150,000	(50,000)
Total liabilities	$191,900	$239,400	$(47,500)
Stockholders' Equity			
Common stock, $2 par	$ 24,000	$ 16,000	$ 8,000
Paid-in capital in excess of par	120,000	80,000	40,000
Retained earnings	282,300	202,300	80,000
Total stockholders' equity	$426,300	$298,300	$128,000
Total liabilities and stockholders' equity	$618,200	$537,700	$ 80,500

*There is a $7,000 increase to Accumulated Depreciation—Building, which is a contra asset account. As a result, the $7,000 increase in this account must be subtracted in summing to the increase in total assets of $80,500.

Thus, under the indirect method, adjustments to net income must be made to determine cash flows from operating activities. The typical adjustments to net income are shown in Exhibit 5.[3]

Exhibit 5
Adjustments to Net Income (Loss) Using the Indirect Method

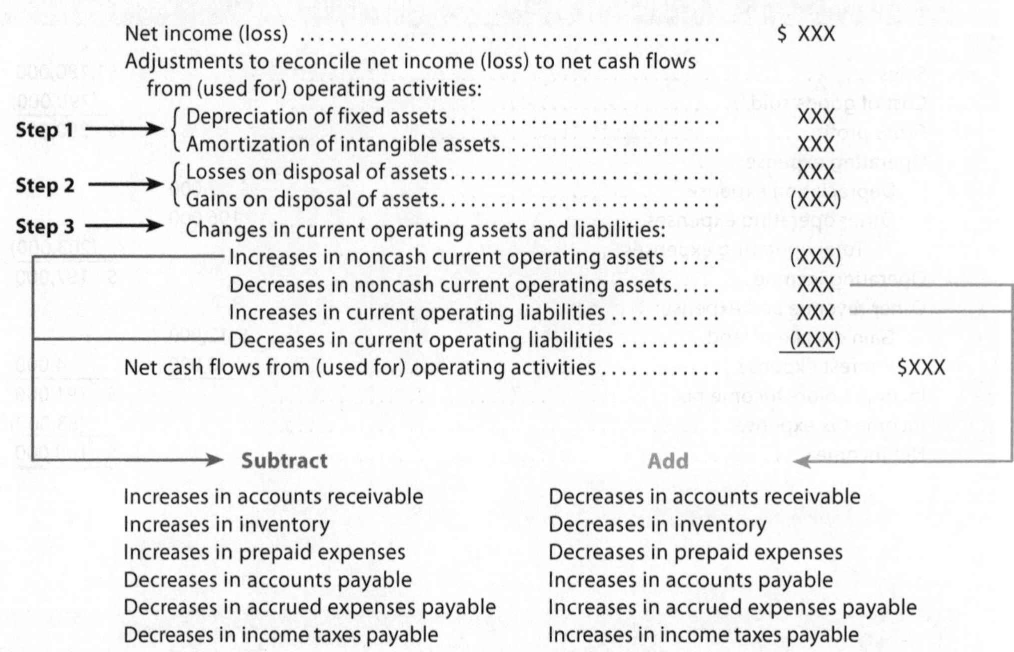

Net income is normally adjusted to cash flows from operating activities, using the following steps:

- Step 1. Expenses that do not affect cash are added. Such expenses decrease net income but do not involve cash payments.

  Example: Depreciation of fixed assets and amortization of intangible assets are added to net income.

- Step 2. Losses on the disposal of assets are added and gains on the disposal of assets are deducted. The disposal (sale) of assets is an investing activity rather than an operating activity. However, such losses and gains are reported as part of net income. Thus, to adjust net income to a cash basis, any *losses* on disposal of assets are *added* back to net income. Likewise, any *gains* on disposal of assets are *deducted* from net income.

  Example: Land costing $100,000 is sold for $90,000. The loss of $10,000 is added back to net income.

- Step 3. Changes in current operating assets and liabilities are added or deducted as follows:

  - Increases in noncash current operating assets are deducted.
  - Decreases in noncash current operating assets are added.
  - Increases in current operating liabilities are added.
  - Decreases in current operating liabilities are deducted.

3. Other items that also require adjustments to net income to obtain cash flows from operating activities include amortization of bonds payable discounts (add), losses on debt retirement (add), amortization of bonds payable premiums (deduct), and gains on retirement of debt (deduct). These topics are covered in advanced accounting courses.

Example: A sale of $10,000 on account increases sales, accounts receivable, and net income by $10,000. However, cash is not affected. Thus, the $10,000 increase in accounts receivable is deducted. Similar adjustments are required for the changes in the other current asset and liability accounts, such as inventory, prepaid expenses, accounts payable, accrued expenses payable, and income taxes payable, as shown in Exhibit 5.

National Beverage Connection

On a recent statement of cash flows, **National Beverage Corp.** reported changes in current asset and liability accounts for accounts receivable, inventories, accounts payable, and accrued liabilities.

The "Cash flows from (used for) operating activities" section of Rundell Inc.'s statement of cash flows is shown in Exhibit 6.

Exhibit 6
Net Cash Flows from Operating Activities—Indirect Method

	Cash flows from (used for) operating activities:		
	Net income	$108,000	
	Adjustments to reconcile net income to net cash flows from (used for) operating activities:		
Step 1 →	Depreciation	7,000	
Step 2 →	Gain on sale of land	(12,000)	
	Changes in current operating assets and liabilities:		
Step 3 →	Increase in accounts receivable	(9,000)	
	Decrease in inventories	8,000	
	Decrease in accounts payable	(3,200)	
	Increase in accrued expenses payable	2,200	
	Decrease in income taxes payable	(500)	
	Net cash flows from operating activities		$100,500

Rundell's net income of $108,000 is converted to net cash flows from operating activities of $100,500 as follows:

- Step 1. Add depreciation of $7,000.
  Analysis: The comparative balance sheet in Exhibit 4 indicates that Accumulated Depreciation—Building increased by $7,000 ($65,300 – $58,300). In addition, no buildings were sold during the year. Thus, depreciation for the year was $7,000.
- Step 2. Deduct the gain on the sale of land of $12,000.
  Analysis: The income statement in Exhibit 4 reports a gain of $12,000 from the sale of land. The proceeds, which include the gain, are reported in the investing section of the statement of cash flows.[4] Thus, the gain of $12,000 is deducted from net income in determining net cash flows from operating activities.
- Step 3. Add and deduct changes in current operating assets and liabilities excluding cash.
  Analysis: The increases and decreases in the current operating asset and current liability accounts excluding cash are as follows:

	December 31		Increase
Accounts	**20Y8**	**20Y7**	**(Decrease)**
Accounts Receivable (net)	$ 74,000	$ 65,000	$ 9,000
Inventories	172,000	180,000	(8,000)
Accounts Payable (merchandise creditors)	43,500	46,700	(3,200)
Accrued Expenses Payable (operating expenses)	26,500	24,300	2,200
Income Taxes Payable	7,900	8,400	(500)

4. The reporting of the proceeds (cash flows) from the sale of land as part of investing activities is discussed later in this chapter.

Accounts receivable (net): The $9,000 increase is deducted from net income. This is because the $9,000 increase in accounts receivable indicates that sales on account were $9,000 more than the cash received from customers. Thus, sales (and net income) includes $9,000 that was not received in cash during the year.

Inventories: The $8,000 decrease is added to net income. This is because the $8,000 decrease in inventories indicates that the cost of goods *sold* exceeds the cost of the merchandise *purchased* during the year by $8,000. In other words, the cost of goods sold includes $8,000 of merchandise from inventory that was not purchased (paid with cash) during the year.

Accounts payable (merchandise creditors): The $3,200 decrease is deducted from net income. This is because a decrease in accounts payable indicates that the cash *payments* to merchandise creditors exceed the merchandise *purchased on account* by $3,200. Therefore, the cost of goods sold is $3,200 less than the cash paid to merchandise creditors during the year.

Accrued expenses payable (operating expenses): The $2,200 increase is added to net income. This is because an increase in accrued expenses payable indicates that operating expenses exceed the cash payments for operating expenses by $2,200. In other words, operating expenses reported on the income statement include $2,200 that did not require a cash outflow during the year.

Income taxes payable: The $500 decrease is deducted from net income. This is because a decrease in income taxes payable indicates that taxes paid exceed the amount of taxes incurred during the year by $500. In other words, the amount reported on the income statement for income tax expense is less than the amount paid by $500.

Using Data Analytics

Data Analytics Software

There are a variety of software programs available for use in performing data analytics. Excel and Tableau are the most common software programs used to perform data analytics. Each program has its own advantages. For example, Excel is better for creating or revising data sets with computations on cell values. Tableau is better for filtering data and preparing data visualizations.*

A variety of companies offer other data analytics software, including the following:

- Alteryx (**www.alteryx.com**): Alteryx is a data blending and integration tool.
- Birst (**www.infor.com/products/birst**): Birst is a proprietary, cloud-based analytics platform that provides a networked analytics solution across a business.
- Looker (**www.looker.com**): Looker is a data visualization platform.
- Power BI (**https://powerbi.microsoft.com/en-us/**): Power BI is a data visualization platform.
- Qlik (**www.qlik.com/us/**): Qlik is an end-to-end analytics platform, combining integration and presentational features.
- SAS (**www.sas.com/en_us/home.html**): SAS is a statistical computing software package.
- ZoomData (**www.zoomdata.com**): ZoomData is a data visualization platform.

Almost all analytic processes also depend on open-sourced database systems or programming languages such as the following:

- PostgreSQL (**www.postgresql.org**): PostgreSQL is a relational (structured) database software.
- Python (**www.python.org**): Python is a programming language with strong support for data analytics.
- Apache Spark (**https://spark.apache.org**): Apache Spark is a data analytics engine software.
- MongoDB (**www.mongodb.com**): MongoDB is a NoSQL (unstructured) database software.

*Kevin Pan and Alan Blankley, "Excel vs. Tableau: See Your Data Differently," *Journal of Accountancy*, March 1, 2020.

Cash Flows: Investing Activities

Objective 3
Prepare the "Cash flows from (used for) investing activities" section of the statement of cash flows.

The "Cash flows from (used for) investing activities" section reports the cash inflows and outflows related to changes in a company's long-term assets. Rundell Inc.'s comparative balance sheet in Exhibit 4 lists land, building, and accumulated depreciation—building as long-term assets. Similar to preparing the "Cash flows from (used for) operating activities" section, each change in each long-term asset account is analyzed for its effect on cash flows from investing activities.

Land

The $45,000 ($125,000 – $80,000) decline in the land account of Rundell Inc. was from two transactions, as follows:

Jan. 1, 20Y8	Balance	$125,000
June 8	Sold land that cost $60,000 for $72,000	(60,000)
Oct. 12	Purchased additional land for $15,000	15,000
Dec. 31, 20Y8	Balance	$ 80,000

The June 8 transaction is the sale of land with a cost of $60,000 for $72,000 in cash. The $72,000 proceeds from the sale are reported in the "Cash flows from (used for) investing activities" section as follows:

Cash flows from (used for) investing activities:	
Cash received from sale of land	$72,000

The proceeds of $72,000 include the $12,000 gain on the sale of land and the $60,000 cost (book value) of the land. As shown in Exhibit 6, the $12,000 gain is deducted from net income in the "Cash flows from (used for) operating activities" section. This is so that the $12,000 cash inflow related to the gain is not included twice as a cash inflow.

The October 12 transaction is the purchase of land for cash of $15,000. This transaction is reported as an outflow of cash in the investing activities section as follows:

Cash flows from (used for) investing activities:	
Cash paid for purchase of land	$(15,000)

Building and Accumulated Depreciation—Building

The building account of Rundell Inc. increased by $60,000 ($260,000 – $200,000), and the accumulated depreciation—building account increased by $7,000 ($65,300 – $58,300), as follows:

		Building	Accumulated Depreciation—Building
Jan. 1, 20Y8	Balances	$200,000	$58,300
Dec. 27	Purchased building for cash	60,000	
Dec. 31	Depreciation for the year		7,000
Dec. 31, 20Y8	Balances	$260,000	$65,300

The purchase of a building for cash of $60,000 is reported as an outflow of cash in the "Cash flows from (used for) investing activities" section as follows:

Cash flows from (used for) investing activities:	
Cash paid for purchase of building	$(60,000)

The increase in the accumulated depreciation—building account represents depreciation expense for the year. This depreciation expense of $7,000 on the building was added to net income in determining cash flows from operating activities, as reported in Exhibit 6.

On a recent statement of cash flows, **National Beverage Corp.** reported cash used for purchases of property, plant, and equipment of $23,890,000 and cash received for selling property, plant, and equipment of $9,000 resulting in net cash used for investing activities of $23,881,000.

National Beverage Connection

Objective 4
Prepare the "Cash flows from (used for) financing activities" section of the statement of cash flows.

Cash Flows: Financing Activities

The "Cash flows from (used for) financing activities" section reports the cash inflows and outflows related to changes in a company's long-term liabilities and stockholders' equity. Rundell Inc.'s comparative balance sheet in Exhibit 4 reports changes in bonds payable, common stock, and paid-in capital in excess of par. In addition, dividends payable has changed, which impacts retained earnings. Each change must be analyzed to determine its effect on cash flows from financing activities.

Bonds Payable

The bonds payable account of Rundell Inc. decreased by $50,000 ($100,000 − $150,000), from retiring bonds by a cash payment for their face amount. The effect on the accounts and financial statements are as follows:

Jan. 1, 20Y8	Balance	$150,000
June 1	Retired (paid-off) $50,000 bonds at face value	(50,000)
Dec. 31, 20Y8	Balance	$100,000

This decrease is from retiring the bonds by a cash payment for their face amount. This cash outflow is reported in the financing activities section as follows:

Cash flows from (used for) financing activities:	
Cash paid to retire bonds payable.................	$(50,000)

Common Stock

The common stock account of Rundell Inc. increased by $8,000 ($24,000 − $16,000), and the paid-in capital in excess of par—common stock account increased by $40,000 ($120,000 − $80,000), as follows:

		Common Stock	Paid-In Capital in Excess of Par—Common Stock
Jan. 1, 20Y8	Balances	$16,000	$ 80,000
Nov. 1	Issued common stock for cash	8,000	40,000
Dec. 31, 20Y8	Balances	$24,000	$120,000

These increases were from issuing 4,000 shares of common stock for $12 per share. This cash inflow is reported in the financing activities section as follows:

Cash flows from (used for) financing activities:	
Cash received from sale of common stock.................	$48,000

Dividends and Dividends Payable

The retained earnings account of Rundell Inc. indicates cash dividends of $28,000 ($14,000 + $14,000) were declared during the year. However, only $24,000 ($10,000 + $14,000) of dividends were paid during the year, as follows:

Jan. 1, 20Y8	Balance	$10,000
Jan. 10	Paid cash dividends	(10,000)
June 30	Declared cash dividends	14,000
July 10	Paid cash dividends	(14,000)
Dec. 31	Declared cash dividends	14,000
Dec. 31, 20Y8	Balance	$14,000

Cash dividends paid during the year can also be computed by adjusting the dividends declared during the year for the change in the dividends payable account as follows:

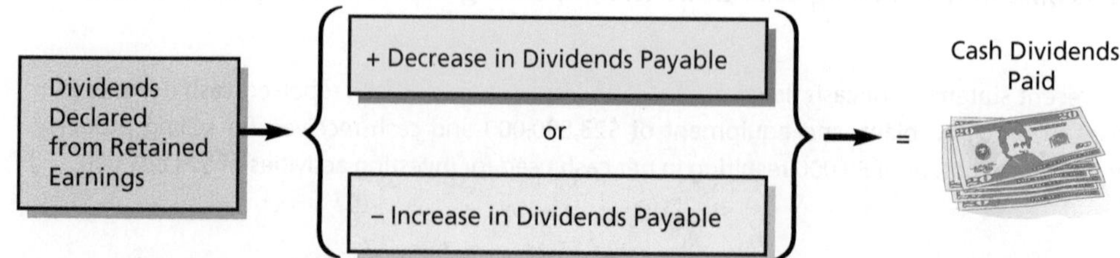

The cash dividends paid by Rundell Inc. during 20Y8 are $24,000, computed as follows:

Dividends declared ($14,000 + $14,000)	$28,000
Increase in Dividends Payable	(4,000)
Cash dividends paid	$24,000

Because dividend payments are a financing activity, the cash dividends paid of $24,000 are reported in the financing activities section of the statement of cash flows, as follows:

Cash flows from (used for) financing activities:	
Cash paid for dividends	$(24,000)

On a recent statement of cash flows, **National Beverage Corp.** reported cash used for the purchase of treasury stock of $6,233,000 and cash received from issuing stock of $740,000.

National Beverage Connection

Preparing the Statement of Cash Flows

Objective 5
Prepare a statement of cash flows.

The statement of cash flows for Rundell Inc., using the indirect method, is shown in Exhibit 7. The statement of cash flows indicates that cash increased by $71,500 during the year. The most significant increase in net cash flows ($100,500) was from operating activities. The most significant use of cash ($26,000) was for financing activities. The ending balance of cash on December 31, 20Y8, is $97,500. This ending cash balance is also reported on the December 31, 20Y8, balance sheet shown in Exhibit 4.

Exhibit 7 Statement of Cash Flows—Indirect Method

Rundell Inc.
Statement of Cash Flows
For the Year Ended December 31, 20Y8

Cash flows from (used for) operating activities:		
Net income	$108,000	
Adjustments to reconcile net income to net cash flows from (used for) operating activities:		
Depreciation	7,000	
Gain on sale of land	(12,000)	
Changes in current operating assets and liabilities:		
Increase in accounts receivable	(9,000)	
Decrease in inventories	8,000	
Decrease in accounts payable	(3,200)	
Increase in accrued expenses payable	2,200	
Decrease in income taxes payable	(500)	
Net cash flows from operating activities		$100,500
Cash flows from (used for) investing activities:		
Cash received from sale of land	$ 72,000	
Cash paid for purchase of land	(15,000)	
Cash paid for purchase of building	(60,000)	
Net cash flows used for investing activities		(3,000)
Cash flows from (used for) financing activities:		
Cash received from sale of common stock	$ 48,000	
Cash paid to retire bonds payable	(50,000)	
Cash paid for dividends	(24,000)	
Net cash flows used for financing activities		(26,000)
Net increase in cash		$ 71,500
Cash as of January 1, 20Y8		26,000
Cash as of December 31, 20Y8		$ 97,500

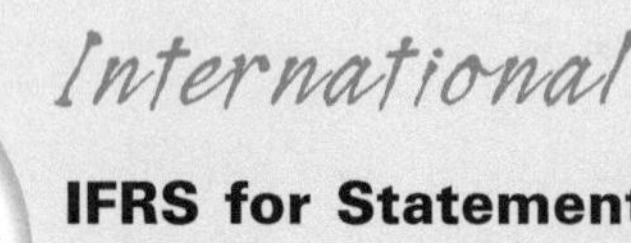

On a recent statement of cash flows, **National Beverage Corp.** reported net cash provided by operating activities of $177,692,000; net cash used for investing activities of $23,881,000; and net cash used for financing activities of $5,493,000 for a net increase in cash of $148,318,000 for the year.

International Connection

IFRS for Statement of Cash Flows

The statement of cash flows is required under International Financial Reporting Standards (IFRS). The statement of cash flows under IFRS is similar to that reported under U.S. GAAP in that the statement has separate sections for operating, investing, and financing activities. Like U.S. GAAP, IFRS also allows the use of either the indirect or direct method of reporting cash flows from operating activities. IFRS differs from U.S. GAAP in some minor areas, including:

- Interest paid can be reported as either an operating or a financing activity, while interest received can be reported as either an operating or an investing activity. In contrast, U.S. GAAP reports interest paid or received as an operating activity.
- Dividends paid can be reported as either an operating or a financing activity, while dividends received can be reported as either an operating or an investing activity. In contrast, U.S. GAAP reports dividends paid as a financing activity and dividends received as an operating activity.
- Cash flows to pay taxes are reported as a separate line in the operating activities, in contrast to U.S. GAAP, which does not require a separate line disclosure.

Metric-Based Analysis: Free Cash Flow and Cash Flow Adequacy

Objective 6
Describe and illustrate the use of free cash flow and cash flow adequacy in evaluating a company's cash flow.

A valuable tool for evaluating the liquidity of a business is free cash flow. **Free cash flow** measures the operating cash flow available to a company after it purchases the property, plant, and equipment (PP&E) necessary to maintain its current operations. Since the investments in PP&E necessary to maintain current operations cannot often be determined from financial statements, analysts estimate this amount using the cash used to purchase PP&E, as shown in the statement of cash flows. Thus, free cash flow is computed as follows:

Net cash flows from operating activities	XXX
Cash used to purchase property, plant, and equipment	(XXX)
Free cash flow	XXX

Positive free cash flow is considered favorable. A company that has free cash flow is able to fund growth and acquisitions, retire debt, purchase treasury stock, and pay dividends. A company with no free cash flow may have limited financial flexibility, potentially leading to liquidity problems. As one analyst notes, "Free cash flow gives the company firepower to reduce debt and ultimately generate consistent, actual income."

A second useful metric in evaluating a company's ability to meet its maturing debt obligations is the **cash flow adequacy ratio**. This metric is calculated as:

$$\textbf{Cash Flow Adequacy Ratio} = \frac{\textbf{Free Cash Flow}}{\textbf{Average Amount of Debt Maturing over the Next Five Years}}$$

The cash flow adequacy ratio is an indicator of the company's credit quality. Generally, a higher cash flow adequacy ratio signals that a company is a better credit risk than a company that must seek outside sources of capital to repay its debt obligations.

To illustrate, information from the annual reports of **Caterpillar Inc. (CAT)** for three recent years is as follows (in millions):

	Year 3	Year 2	Year 1
Net cash flows from operating activities	$6,912	$6,558	$5,706
Cash used to purchase property, plant, and equipment	1,056	1,276	898
Average amount of debt maturing over next five years	5,205.2	4,673.4	4,378.2

The free cash flow is computed for the three years as follows:

	Year 3	Year 2	Year 1
Net cash flows from operating activities	$6.912	$6,558	$5,706
Cash used to purchase property, plant, and equipment	(1,056)	(1,276)	(898)
Free cash flow	$5,856	$5,282	$4,808

As can be seen, free cash flow has increased across the three years. In Year 3, it is nearly 22% higher than in Year 1 [($5,856 − $4,808) ÷ $4,808]. The cash flow adequacy ratio is as follows (rounded to one decimal place):

	Year 3	Year 2	Year 1
Cash flow adequacy ratio	112.5%	113.0%	109.8%
	($5,856 ÷ $5,205.2)	($5,282 ÷ $4,673.4)	($4,808 ÷ $4,378.2)

The cash flow adequacy ratio increased from 109.8% in Year 1 to 113.0% in Year 2. From Year 2 to Year 3, the cash flow adequacy ratio decreased slightly to 112.5%. Overall, there was a 2.5% increase [(112.5% − 109.8%) ÷ 109.8%]. This increase is due mainly to the large increase in net cash flows from operations, which led to relatively higher free cash flow.

Appendix

Objective 7

Prepare a statement of cash flows using the direct method.

Preparing the Statement of Cash Flows—The Direct Method

The direct method reports cash flows from operating activities as follows:

Cash flows from (used for) operating activities:		
Cash received from customers	$ XXX	
Cash payments for merchandise	(XXX)	
Cash payments for operating expenses	(XXX)	
Cash payments for interest	(XXX)	
Cash payments for income taxes	(XXX)	
Net cash flows from (used for) operating activities		$XXX

The "Cash flows from (used for) investing activities" and "Cash flows from (used for) financing activities" sections of the statement of cash flows are exactly the same under both the direct and indirect methods. The amount of net cash flows from operating activities is also the same, but the manner in which it is reported is different.

Under the direct method, the income statement is adjusted to cash flows from operating activities as shown in Exhibit 8.

Exhibit 8

Converting Income Statement to Cash Flows from (Used for) Operating Activities Using the Direct Method

Income Statement	Adjusted to	Cash Flows from (Used for) Operating Activities
Sales	→	Cash received from customers
Cost of goods sold	→	Cash payments for merchandise
Operating expenses:		
Depreciation expense*	n/a	n/a
Other operating expenses	→	Cash payments for operating expenses
Gain (loss) on sale of land**	n/a	n/a
Interest expense	→	Cash payments for interest
Income tax expense	→	Cash payments for income taxes
Net income	→	Net cash flows from (used for) operating activities

* Depreciation does not affect cash and, thus, is not considered in the direct method.

** Gains (losses) on sales of property, plant, and equipment are reported as part of investing activities.

As shown in Exhibit 8, depreciation expense is not adjusted or reported as part of cash flows from operating activities. This is because deprecation expense does not involve a cash outflow. The gain on the sale of the land is also not adjusted and is not reported as part of cash flows from operating activities. This is because the cash flow from operating activities is determined directly, rather than by reconciling net income. The cash proceeds from the sale of the land are reported as an investing activity.

To illustrate the direct method, the income statement and comparative balance sheet for Rundell Inc., shown in Exhibit 4, are used.

Cash Received from Customers

The income statement (shown in Exhibit 4) of Rundell Inc. reports sales of $1,180,000. To determine the cash received from customers, the $1,180,000 is adjusted for any increase or decrease in accounts receivable. The adjustment is summarized in Exhibit 9.

Exhibit 9
Determining the Cash Received from Customers

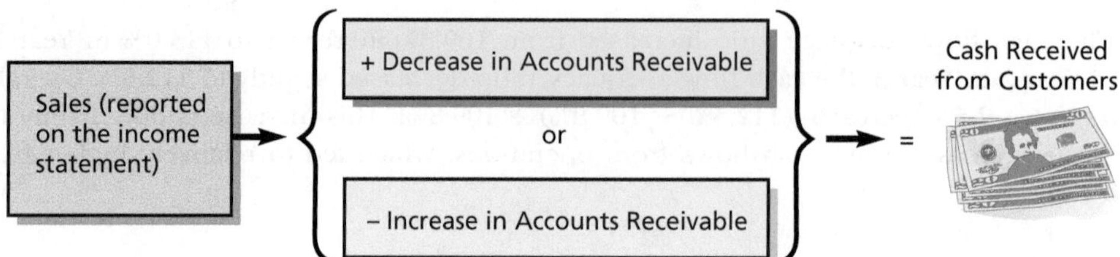

The cash received from customers is $1,171,000, computed as follows:

Sales	$1,180,000
Increase in accounts receivable	(9,000)
Cash received from customers	$1,171,000

The increase of $9,000 in accounts receivable (shown in Exhibit 4) during 20Y8 indicates that sales on account exceeded cash received from customers by $9,000. In other words, sales include $9,000 that did not result in a cash inflow during the year. Thus, $9,000 is deducted from sales to determine the cash received from customers.

Cash Payments for Merchandise

The income statement (shown in Exhibit 4) for Rundell Inc. reports cost of goods sold of $790,000. To determine the cash payments for merchandise, the $790,000 is adjusted for any increases or decreases in inventories and accounts payable. Assuming the accounts payable are owed to merchandise suppliers, the adjustment is summarized in Exhibit 10.

Exhibit 10
Determining the Cash Payments for Merchandise

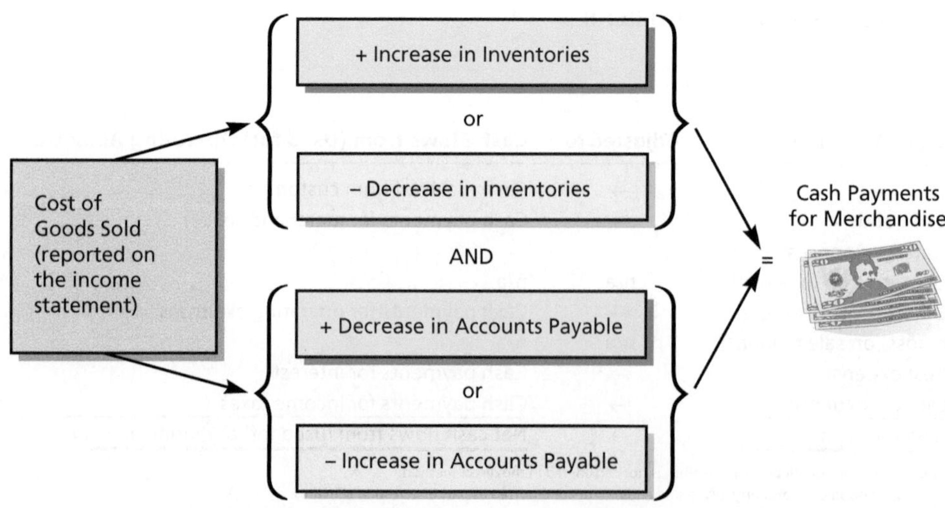

The cash payments for merchandise are $785,200, computed as follows:

Cost of goods sold	$790,000
Decrease in inventories	(8,000)
Decrease in accounts payable	3,200
Cash payments for merchandise	$785,200

The $8,000 decrease in inventories (from Exhibit 4) indicates that the merchandise sold exceeded the cost of the merchandise purchased by $8,000. In other words, the cost of goods sold includes $8,000 of merchandise sold from inventory that did not require a cash outflow during the year. Thus, $8,000 is deducted from the cost of goods sold in determining the cash payments for merchandise.

The $3,200 decrease in accounts payable (from Exhibit 4) indicates that cash payments for merchandise were $3,200 more than the purchases on account during 20Y8. Therefore, $3,200 is added to the cost of goods sold in determining the cash payments for merchandise.

Cash Payments for Operating Expenses

The income statement for Rundell Inc. (from Exhibit 4) reports total operating expenses of $203,000, which includes depreciation expense of $7,000. Because depreciation expense does not require a cash outflow, it is omitted from cash payments for operating expenses.

To determine the cash payments for operating expenses, the other operating expenses (excluding depreciation) of $196,000 ($203,000 − $7,000) are adjusted for any increases or decreases in prepaid expenses and accrued expenses payable. This adjustment is summarized in Exhibit 11.

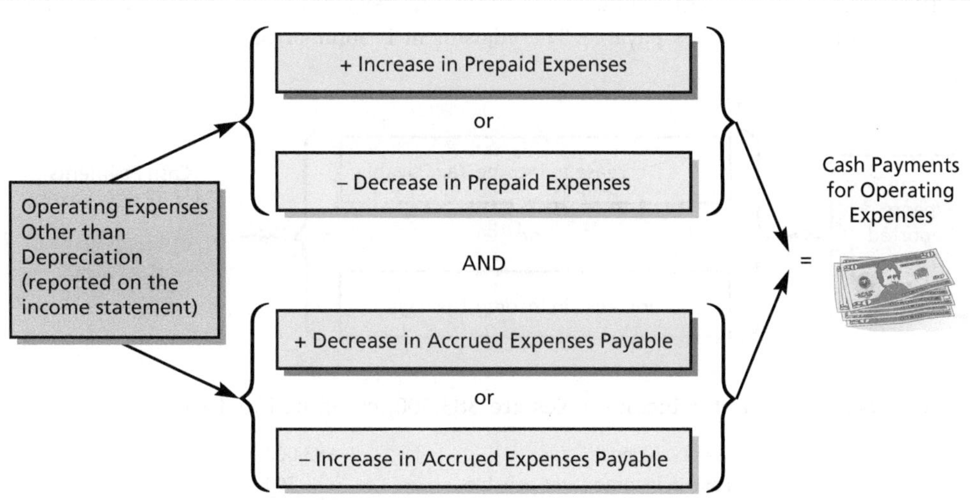

Exhibit 11 Determining the Cash Payments for Operating Expenses

Since Rundell Inc. has no prepaid expenses, the cash payments for operating expenses are $193,800, computed as follows:

Operating expenses other than depreciation	$196,000
Increase in accrued expenses payable	(2,200)
Cash payments for operating expenses	$193,800

The increase in accrued expenses payable (from Exhibit 4) indicates that the cash payments for operating expenses were $2,200 less than the amount reported for operating expenses during the year. Thus, $2,200 is deducted from the operating expenses in determining the cash payments for operating expenses.

Gain on Sale of Land

The income statement for Rundell Inc. (from Exhibit 4) reports a gain of $12,000 on the sale of land. The sale of land is an investing activity. Thus, the proceeds from the sale, which include the gain, are reported as part of the cash flows from investing activities.

Interest Expense

The income statement for Rundell Inc. (from Exhibit 4) reports interest expense of $8,000. To determine the cash payments for interest, the $8,000 is adjusted for any increases or decreases in interest payable. The adjustment is summarized in Exhibit 12.

Exhibit 12
Determining the Cash Payments for Interest

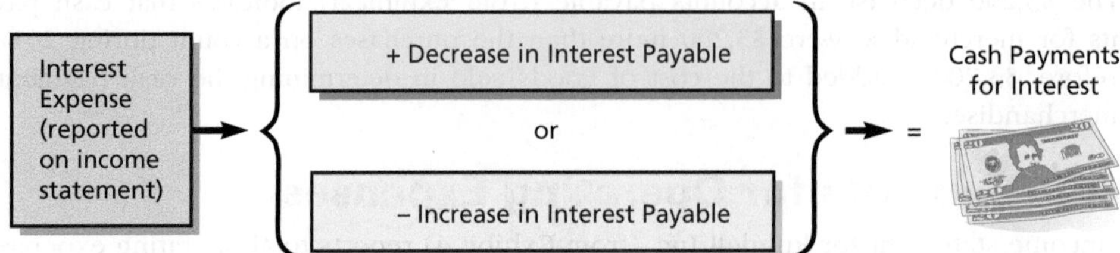

The comparative balance sheet of Rundell in Exhibit 4 indicates no interest payable. This is because the interest expense on the bonds payable is paid on June 1 and December 31. Because there is no interest payable, no adjustment of the interest expense of $8,000 is necessary.

Cash Payments for Income Taxes

The income statement for Rundell Inc. (from Exhibit 4) reports income tax expense of $83,000. To determine the cash payments for income taxes, the $83,000 is adjusted for any increases or decreases in income taxes payable. The adjustment is summarized in Exhibit 13.

Exhibit 13
Determining the Cash Payments for Income Taxes

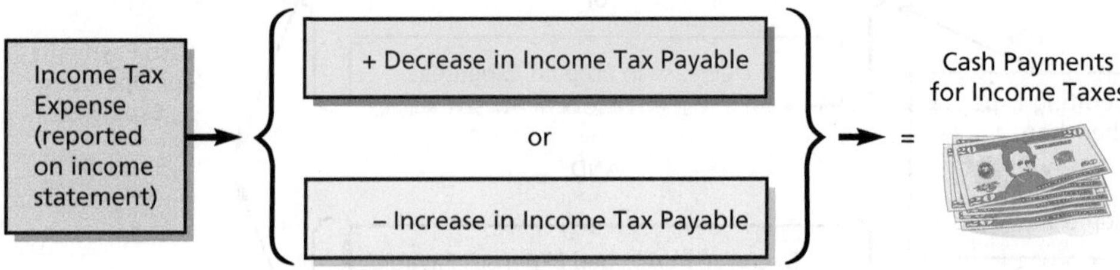

The cash payments for income taxes are $83,500, computed as follows:

Income tax expense	$83,000
Decrease in income taxes payable	500
Cash payments for income taxes	$83,500

The $500 decrease in income taxes payable (from Exhibit 4) indicates that the cash payments for income taxes were $500 more than the amount reported for income tax expense during 20Y8. Thus, $500 is added to the income tax expense in determining the cash payments for income taxes.

Reporting Cash Flows from (Used for) Operating Activities—Direct Method

The statement of cash flows for Rundell Inc., using the direct method for reporting cash flows from operating activities, is shown in Exhibit 14. The portions of the statement that differ from those prepared under the indirect method are highlighted.

Exhibit 14 also includes the separate schedule reconciling net income and net cash flows from operating activities. This schedule is included as part of the statement of cash flows when the direct method is used. This schedule is similar to the "Cash flows from (used for) operating activities" section prepared under the indirect method.

Exhibit 14 Statement of Cash Flows—Direct Method

Rundell Inc.
Statement of Cash Flows
For the Year Ended December 31, 20Y8

Cash flows from (used for) operating activities:		
Cash received from customers	$1,171,000	
Cash payments for merchandise	(785,200)	
Cash payments for operating expenses	(193,800)	
Cash payments for interest	(8,000)	
Cash payments for income taxes	(83,500)	
Net cash flows from operating activities		$100,500
Cash flows from (used for) investing activities:		
Cash received from sale of land	$ 72,000	
Cash paid for purchase of land	(15,000)	
Cash paid for purchase of building	(60,000)	
Net cash flows used for investing activities		(3,000)
Cash flows from (used for) financing activities:		
Cash received from sale of common stock	$ 48,000	
Cash paid to retire bonds payable	(50,000)	
Cash paid for dividends	(24,000)	
Net cash flows used for financing activities		(26,000)
Net increase in cash		$ 71,500
Cash as of January 1, 20Y8		26,000
Cash as of December 31, 20Y8		$ 97,500

Schedule Reconciling Net Income with Net Cash Flows from Operating Activities:	
Cash flows from (used for) operating activities:	
Net income	$108,000
Adjustments to reconcile net income to net cash flows from operating activities:	
Depreciation	7,000
Gain on sale of land	(12,000)
Changes in current operating assets and liabilities:	
Increase in accounts receivable	(9,000)
Decrease in inventories	8,000
Decrease in accounts payable	(3,200)
Increase in accrued expenses payable	2,200
Decrease in income taxes payable	(500)
Net cash flows from operating activities	$100,500

Key Points

1. Describe the cash flow activities reported on the statement of cash flows.

The statement of cash flows reports cash receipts and cash payments by three types of activities: operating activities, investing activities, and financing activities. The "Cash flows from (used for) operating activities" section reports the cash inflows and outflows from a company's day-to-day operations. The "Cash flows from (used for) investing activities" section reports the cash inflows and outflows related to changes in a company's long-term assets. The "Cash flows from (used for) financing activities" section reports the cash inflows and outflows related to changes in a company's long-term liabilities and stockholders' equity. Investing and financing for a business may be affected by transactions that do not involve cash. The effect of such transactions should be reported in a separate schedule accompanying the statement of cash flows.

2. Prepare the "Cash flows from (used for) operating activities" section of the statement of cash flows using the indirect method.

The indirect method reports cash flows from operating activities by adjusting net income for revenues and expenses that do not involve the receipt or payment of cash. Noncash expenses such as depreciation are added back to net income. Gains and losses on the disposal of assets are added to or deducted from net income. Changes in current operating assets and liabilities are added to or subtracted from net income, depending on their effect on cash.

3. Prepare the "Cash flows from (used for) investing activities" section of the statement of cash flows.

Cash flows from (used for) investing activities are reported below cash flows from (used for) operating activities on the statement of cash flows. The "Cash flows from (used for) investing activities" section reports the cash inflows and outflows related to changes in a company's long-term assets.

4. Prepare the "Cash flows from (used for) financing activities" section of the statement of cash flows.

Cash flows from (used for) financing activities are reported below cash flows from (used for) operating activities on the statement of cash flows. The "Cash flows from (used for) financing activities" section reports the cash inflows and outflows related to changes in a company's long-term liabilities and stockholders' equity.

5. Prepare a statement of cash flows.

The statement of cash flows reports cash flows from (used for) operating activities followed by cash flows from (used for) investing and financing activities. The result of summing the net cash flows from (used for) operating, investing, and financing activities is the net increase or decrease in cash for the period. Cash at the beginning of the period is added to determine the cash at the end of the period. This ending cash amount must agree with cash reported on the end-of-period balance sheet.

6. Metric-Based Analysis: Describe and illustrate the use of free cash flow and cash flow adequacy in evaluating a company's cash flow.

Free cash flow measures the operating cash flow available for a company to use after it purchases the property, plant, and equipment necessary to maintain its current operations. It is computed as net cash flows from operating activities minus cash used to purchase property, plant, and equipment. The cash flow adequacy ratio evaluates a company's ability to meet its maturing debt obligations. It is computed as free cash flow divided by average debt maturing over the next five years.

Key Terms

cash flow adequacy ratio (432)
cash flow per share (424)
cash flows from (used for) financing activities (419)
cash flows from (used for) investing activities (419)
cash flows from (used for) operating activities (419)
direct method (420)
free cash flow (432)
indirect method (421)
statement of cash flows (419)

Illustrative Problem

The comparative balance sheet of Dowling Company for December 31, 20Y5 and 20Y4, is as follows:

DOWLING COMPANY
Comparative Balance Sheet
December 31, 20Y5 and 20Y4

	20Y5	20Y4
Assets		
Cash	$ 140,350	$ 95,900
Accounts receivable (net)	95,300	102,300
Inventories	165,200	157,900
Prepaid expenses	6,240	5,860
Investments (long-term)	35,700	84,700
Land	75,000	90,000
Buildings	375,000	260,000
Accumulated depreciation—buildings	(71,300)	(58,300)
Machinery and equipment	428,300	428,300
Accumulated depreciation—machinery and equipment	(148,500)	(138,000)
Patents	58,000	65,000
Total assets	$1,159,290	$1,093,660
Liabilities and Stockholders' Equity		
Accounts payable (merchandise creditors)	$ 43,500	$ 46,700
Accrued expenses payable (operating expenses)	14,000	12,500
Income taxes payable	7,900	8,400
Dividends payable	14,000	10,000
Mortgage note payable, due in 10 years	40,000	0
Bonds payable	150,000	250,000
Common stock, $30 par	450,000	375,000
Paid-in capital in excess of par—common stock	66,250	41,250
Retained earnings	373,640	349,810
Total liabilities and stockholders' equity	$1,159,290	$1,093,660

The income statement for Dowling Company follows:

DOWLING COMPANY
Income Statement
For the Year Ended December 31, 20Y5

Sales		$1,100,000
Cost of goods sold		(710,000)
Gross profit		$ 390,000
Operating expenses:		
Depreciation expense	$ 23,500	
Patent amortization	7,000	
Other operating expenses	196,000	
Total operating expenses		(226,500)
Operating income		$ 163,500
Other revenue and expense:		
Gain on sale of investments	$ 11,000	
Interest expense	(26,000)	(15,000)
Income before income tax		$ 148,500
Income tax expense		(50,000)
Net income		$ 98,500

An examination of the accounting records revealed the following additional information applicable to 20Y5:

a. Land costing $15,000 was sold for $15,000.
b. A mortgage note was issued for $40,000.
c. A building costing $115,000 was constructed.
d. 2,500 shares of common stock were issued at $40 in exchange for the bonds payable.
e. Cash dividends declared were $74,670.

Instructions

1. Prepare a statement of cash flows, using the indirect method of reporting cash flows from (used for) operating activities.
2. (Appendix) Prepare a statement of cash flows, using the direct method of reporting cash flows from (used for) operating activities.

Solution

1.

DOWLING COMPANY
Statement of Cash Flows—Indirect Method
For the Year Ended December 31, 20Y5

Cash flows from (used for) operating activities:		
Net income	$ 98,500	
Adjustments to reconcile net income to net cash flows from (used for) operating activities:		
Depreciation	23,500	
Amortization of patents	7,000	
Gain on sale of investments	(11,000)	
Changes in current operating assets and liabilities:		
Decrease in accounts receivable	7,000	
Increase in inventories	(7,300)	
Increase in prepaid expenses	(380)	
Decrease in accounts payable	(3,200)	
Increase in accrued expenses payable	1,500	
Decrease in income taxes payable	(500)	
Net cash flows from operating activities		$115,120
Cash flows from (used for) investing activities:		
Cash received from sale of investments	$ 60,000[1]	
Cash received from sale of land	15,000	
Cash paid for construction of building	(115,000)	
Net cash flows used for investing activities		(40,000)
Cash flows from (used for) financing activities:		
Cash received from issuing mortgage note payable	$ 40,000	
Cash paid for dividends	(70,670)[2]	
Net cash flows used for financing activities		(30,670)
Net increase in cash		$ 44,450
Cash as of January 1, 20Y5		95,900
Cash as of December 31, 20Y5		$140,350

Schedule of Noncash Investing and Financing Activities:

Issued common stock to retire bonds payable	$100,000

[1] $60,000 = $11,000 gain + $49,000 (decrease in investments)
[2] $70,670 = $74,670 – $4,000 (increase in dividends)

2.

DOWLING COMPANY
Statement of Cash Flows—Direct Method
For the Year Ended December 31, 20Y5

Cash flows from (used for) operating activities:		
Cash received from customers[1]	$1,107,000	
Cash paid for merchandise[2]	(720,500)	
Cash paid for operating expenses[3]	(194,880)	
Cash paid for interest expense	(26,000)	
Cash paid for income tax[4]	(50,500)	
Net cash flows from operating activities		$115,120
Cash flows from (used for) investing activities:		
Cash received from sale of investments	$ 60,000[5]	
Cash received from sale of land	15,000	
Cash paid for construction of building	(115,000)	
Net cash flows used for investing activities		(40,000)
Cash flows from (used for) financing activities:		
Cash received from issuing mortgage note payable	$ 40,000	
Cash paid for dividends[6]	(70,670)	
Net cash flows used for financing activities		(30,670)
Net increase in cash		$ 44,450
Cash as of January 1, 20Y5		95,900
Cash as of December 31, 20Y5		$140,350

Schedule of Noncash Investing and Financing Activities:

Issued common stock to retire bonds payable	$100,000

Schedule Reconciling Net Income with Net Cash Flows from Operating Activities[7]

Computations:

[1]$1,100,000 + $7,000 = $1,107,000
[2]$710,000 + $3,200 + $7,300 = $720,500
[3]$196,000 + $380 − $1,500 = $194,880
[4]$50,000 + $500 = $50,500
[5]$60,000 = $11,000 gain + $49,000 (decrease in investments)
[6]$74,670 + $10,000 − $14,000 = $70,670
[7]The content of this schedule is the same as the "Cash flows from (used for) operating activities" section of part (1) of this solution and is not reproduced here for the sake of brevity.

Self-Examination Questions

(Answers appear at the end of the chapter.)

1. An example of a cash flow from an operating activity is:
   A. receipt of cash from the sale of stock.
   B. receipt of cash from the sale of bonds.
   C. payment of cash for dividends.
   D. receipt of cash from customers on account.

2. An example of a cash flow from an investing activity is:
   A. receipt of cash from the sale of equipment.
   B. receipt of cash from the sale of stock.
   C. payment of cash for dividends.
   D. payment of cash to acquire treasury stock.

3. An example of a cash flow for a financing activity is:
   A. receipt of cash from customers on account.
   B. receipt of cash from the sale of equipment.
   C. payment of cash for dividends.
   D. payment of cash to acquire land.
4. Which of the following methods of reporting cash flows from (used for) operating activities adjusts net income for revenues and expenses not involving the receipt or payment of cash?
   A. Direct method
   B. Purchase method
   C. Reciprocal method
   D. Indirect method
5. The net income reported on the income statement for the year was $55,000, and depreciation of fixed assets for the year was $22,000. The balances of the current asset and current liability accounts at the beginning and end of the year are as follows:

	End of Year	Beginning of Year
Cash	$ 65,000	$ 70,000
Accounts receivable	100,000	90,000
Inventories	145,000	150,000
Prepaid expenses	7,500	8,000
Accounts payable (merchandise creditors)	51,000	58,000

   The net cash flows from operating activities on the statement of cash flows using the indirect method is:
   A. $33,000.
   B. $55,000.
   C. $65,500.
   D. $77,000.

Class Discussion Questions

1. What is the principal disadvantage of the direct method of reporting cash flows from operating activities?
2. What are the major advantages of the indirect method of reporting cash flows from operating activities?
3. A corporation issued $2,000,000 of common stock in exchange for $2,000,000 of fixed assets. Where would this transaction be reported on the statement of cash flows?
4. A retail business, using the accrual method of accounting, owed merchandise creditors (accounts payable) $320,000 at the beginning of the year and $350,000 at the end of the year. How would the $30,000 increase be used to adjust net income in determining the amount of net cash flows from (used for) operating activities by the indirect method? Explain.
5. If salaries payable was $100,000 at the beginning of the year and $75,000 at the end of the year, should the $25,000 decrease be added to or deducted from income to determine the amount of net cash flows from (used for) operating activities by the indirect method? Explain.
6. A long-term investment in bonds with a cost of $500,000 was sold for $600,000 cash. (a) What was the gain or loss on the sale? (b) What was the effect of the transaction on cash flows? (c) How should the transaction be reported on the statement of cash flows if cash flows from (used for) operating activities are reported by the indirect method?
7. A corporation issued $2,000,000 of 20-year bonds for cash at 98. How would the transaction be reported on the statement of cash flows?
8. Fully depreciated equipment costing $50,000 was discarded. What was the effect of the transaction on cash flows if (a) $15,000 cash is received for the equipment, and (b) no cash is received for the equipment?
9. For the current year, Packers Company decided to switch from the indirect method to the direct method for reporting cash flows from (used for) operating activities on the statement of cash flows. Will the change cause the amount of net cash flows from operating activities to be larger, smaller, or the same as if the indirect method had been used? Explain.
10. Name five common major classes of operating cash receipts or operating cash payments presented on the statement of cash flows when the cash flows from (used for) operating activities are reported by the direct method.

Exercises

E11-1 Cash flows from operating activities—net loss

Obj. 1

In a recent year, J. C. Penney Company, Inc. (JCP) reported a net *loss* of $268 million from operations. However, on its statement of cash flows, it reported $428 million of net cash flows from operating activities.

Explain this apparent contradiction between the loss and the positive cash flows.

E11-2 Effect of transactions on cash flows

Obj. 1

✔ b. Cash receipt, $800,000

State the effect (cash receipt or cash payment and amount) of each of the following transactions, considered individually, on cash flows:

a. Retired $400,000 of bonds for $407,000.
b. Sold 20,000 shares of $5 par common stock for $40 per share.
c. Sold equipment with a book value of $76,200 for $82,800.
d. Purchased land for $625,000 cash.
e. Purchased a building by paying $50,000 cash and issuing a $500,000 mortgage note payable.
f. Sold a new issue of $400,000 of bonds at 99.
g. Purchased 10,000 shares of $10 par common stock as treasury stock at $18.50 per share.
h. Paid dividends of $1.75 per share. There were 1,000,000 shares issued and 180,000 shares of treasury stock.

E11-3 Classifying cash flows

Obj. 1

Identify the type of cash flow activity for each of the following events (operating, investing, or financing):

a. Net income
b. Paid cash dividends
c. Issued common stock
d. Issued bonds
e. Redeemed bonds
f. Sold long-term investments
g. Purchased treasury stock
h. Sold equipment
i. Issued preferred stock
j. Purchased buildings
k. Purchased patents

E11-4 Cash flows from (used for) operating activities—indirect method

Obj. 2

Indicate whether each of the following would be added to or deducted from net income in determining net cash flows from operating activities by the indirect method:

a. Decrease in inventory
b. Increase in accounts receivable
c. Increase in accounts payable
d. Loss on retirement of long-term debt
e. Depreciation of fixed assets
f. Decrease in notes receivable due in 60 days from customers
g. Increase in salaries payable
h. Decrease in prepaid expenses
i. Amortization of patent
j. Increase in notes payable due in 120 days to vendors
k. Gain on disposal of fixed assets

Obj. 1, 2

✔ Net cash flows from operating activities, $148,250

SHOW ME HOW

EXCEL ONLINE

E11-5 Cash flows from (used for) operating activities—indirect method

The net income reported on the income statement for the current year was $106,800. Depreciation recorded on store equipment for the year amounted to $41,700. Balances of the current asset and current liability accounts at the beginning and end of the year are as follows:

	End of Year	Beginning of Year
Cash	$24,100	$19,700
Accounts receivable (net)	65,000	54,000
Inventories	47,200	52,000
Prepaid expenses	3,250	6,000
Accounts payable (merchandise creditors)	23,400	18,500
Wages payable	4,700	6,400

a. Prepare the "Cash flows from (used for) operating activities" section of the statement of cash flows, using the indirect method.

b. Briefly explain why net cash flows from operating activities is different than net income.

Obj. 1, 2

✔ Net cash flows from operating activities, $307,640

SHOW ME HOW

E11-6 Cash flows from (used for) operating activities—indirect method

The net income reported on the income statement for the current year was $222,000. Depreciation recorded on equipment and a building amounted to $98,400 for the year. Balances of the current asset and current liability accounts at the beginning and end of the year are as follows:

	End of Year	Beginning of Year
Cash	$ 75,900	$ 84,610
Accounts receivable (net)	82,150	89,120
Inventories	181,600	175,900
Prepaid expenses	4,450	5,100
Accounts payable (merchandise creditors)	98,370	115,000
Salaries payable	6,500	4,550

a. Prepare the "Cash flows from (used for) operating activities" section of the statement of cash flows, using the indirect method.

b. If the direct method had been used, would the net cash flows from operating activities have been the same? Explain.

Obj. 1, 2

✔ Net cash flows from operating activities, $525,410

SHOW ME HOW

EXCEL ONLINE

E11-7 Cash flows from (used for) operating activities—indirect method

The income statement disclosed the following items for the year:

Depreciation expense	$ 57,600
Gain on disposal of equipment	33,600
Net income	508,000

The changes in the current asset and liability accounts for the year are as follows:

	Increase (Decrease)
Accounts receivable	$ 8,960
Inventory	(5,120)
Prepaid insurance	(1,920)
Accounts payable	(6,080)
Income taxes payable	1,410
Dividends payable	2,200

a. Prepare the "Cash flows from (used for) operating activities" section of the statement of cash flows, using the indirect method.

b. Briefly explain why net cash flows from operating activities is different than net income.

E11-8 Reporting changes in equipment on statement of cash flows

Obj. 3

An analysis of the financial statements indicates that office equipment, which cost $280,000 and on which accumulated depreciation totaled $153,900 on the date of sale, was sold for $108,200 during the year. Using this information, indicate the items to be reported on the statement of cash flows.

E11-9 Reporting changes in equipment on statement of cash flows

Obj. 3

An analysis of the financial statements indicates that delivery equipment, which cost $75,000 and on which accumulated depreciation totaled $54,000 on the date of sale, was sold for $26,900 during the year. Using this information, indicate the items to be reported on the statement of cash flows.

E11-10 Reporting land transactions on statement of cash flows

Obj. 3

On the basis of the following transactions in the land account, indicate the items to be reported on the statement of cash flows:

Jan. 1	Balance	$925,000
Mar. 12	Purchased land for cash	142,400
Oct. 4	Sold land for $102,700 cash	(89,400)
Dec. 31	Balance	$978,000

E11-11 Determining cash payments to stockholders

Obj. 4

SHOW ME HOW

EXCEL ONLINE

The board of directors declared cash dividends totaling $1,200,000 during the current year. The comparative balance sheet indicates dividends payable of $250,000 at the beginning of the year and $100,000 at the end of the year. What was the amount of cash payments to stockholders during the year?

E11-12 Reporting stockholders' equity items on statement of cash flows

Obj. 4

On the basis of the following transactions in the stockholders' equity accounts, indicate the items, exclusive of net income, to be reported on the statement of cash flows. There were no unpaid dividends at either the beginning or the end of the year.

		Common Stock	Paid-In Capital in Excess of Par—Common Stock	Retained Earnings
Jan. 1	Balances	$4,800,000	$ 360,000	$2,000,000
Apr. 2	Issued 30,000 shares of stock for cash	1,200,000	720,000	
June 30	Declared and distributed 5% stock dividend	300,000	150,000	(450,000)
Dec. 30	Paid cash dividend			(315,000)
31	Net Income			1,000,000
31	Balances	$6,300,000	$1,230,000	$2,235,000

E11-13 Reporting land acquisition for cash and mortgage note on statement of cash flows

Obj. 3, 4

On the basis of the following transactions in the land account, indicate the items to be reported on the statement of cash flows:

Jan. 1	Balance	$156,000
Feb. 10	Purchased land for cash	246,000
Oct. 4	Purchased land with long-term mortgage note	324,000
Dec. 31	Balance	$726,000

Obj. 4

E11-14 Reporting issuance and retirement of long-term debt

On the basis of the following transactions and adjustment to the the bonds payable and discount on bonds payable accounts, indicate the items to be reported in the "Cash flows from (used for) financing activities" section of the statement of cash flows, assuming no gain or loss on retiring the bonds:

			Bonds Payable	Discount on Bonds Payable
Jan.	1	Balances	$ 750,000	$33,750
	2	Retire $150,000 face value bonds for $138,000 cash	(150,000)	(12,000)
June	30	Issue $450,000 face value bonds for $420,000 cash	450,000	30,000
Dec.	31	Amortize discount		(2,625)
	31	Balances	$1,050,000	$49,125

Obj. 2, 3, 4

✔ Net income, $341,770

SHOW ME HOW

E11-15 Determining net income from net cash flows from operating activities

Curwen Inc. reported net cash flows from operating activities of $357,500 on its statement of cash flows for the year ended December 31. The following information was reported in the "Cash flows from (used for) operating activities" section of the statement of cash flows, using the indirect method:

Decrease in income taxes payable	$ 7,700
Decrease in inventories	19,140
Depreciation	29,480
Gain on sale of investments	13,200
Increase in accounts payable	5,280
Increase in prepaid expenses	2,970
Increase in accounts receivable	14,300

a. Determine the net income reported by Curwen Inc. for the year ended December 31.

b. Briefly explain why Curwen's net income is different than net cash flows from operating activities.

Obj. 2

✔ Net cash flows from operating activities, $58,020

EXCEL ONLINE

E11-16 Cash flows from (used for) operating activities—indirect method

Selected data (in thousands) derived from the income statement and balance sheet of Cardinas Corp. for a recent year are as follows:

Income statement data:	
Net income	$49,311
Gain on disposal of property	1,188
Depreciation expense	11,580
Other items involving noncash expenses	1,383
Balance sheet data:	
Increase in accounts receivable	1,746
Decrease in inventory	990
Increase in prepaid expenses	605
Decrease in accounts payable	710
Decrease in accrued and other current liabilities	995

a. Prepare the "Cash flows from (used for) operating activities" section of the statement of cash flows, using the indirect method for Cardinas Corp.

b. Interpret your results in part (a).

E11-17 Statement of cash flows—indirect method

Obj. 2, 3, 4, 5

✔ Net cash flows from operating activities, $38

SHOW ME HOW

The comparative balance sheet of Olson-Jones Industries Inc. for December 31, 20Y2 and 20Y1, is as follows:

	Dec. 31, 20Y2	Dec. 31, 20Y1
Assets		
Cash	$183	$ 14
Accounts receivable (net)	55	49
Inventories	117	99
Land	250	330
Equipment	205	175
Accumulated depreciation—equipment	(68)	(42)
Total assets	$742	$625
Liabilities and Stockholders' Equity		
Accounts payable (merchandise creditors)	$ 51	$ 37
Dividends payable	5	—
Common stock, $1 par	125	80
Paid-in capital in excess of par—common stock	85	70
Retained earnings	476	438
Total liabilities and stockholders' equity	$742	$625

The following additional information is taken from the records:

a. Land was sold for $120.

b. Equipment was acquired for cash.

c. There were no disposals of equipment during the year.

d. The common stock was issued for cash.

e. There was a $62 increase to Retained Earnings for net income.

f. There was a $24 decrease to Retained Earnings for cash dividends declared.

a. Prepare a statement of cash flows, using the indirect method of presenting cash flows from (used for) operating activities.

b. Was Olson-Jones's net cash flows from operating activities more or less than net income? What is the source of this difference?

E11-18 Statement of cash flows—indirect method

Obj. 2, 3, 4, 5

List the errors you find in the following statement of cash flows. The cash balance at the beginning of the year was $240,000. All other amounts are correct, except the cash balance at the end of the year.

SHASTA INC.
Statement of Cash Flows
For the Year Ended December 31, 20Y9

Cash flows from (used for) operating activities:		
Net income	$ 360,000	
Adjustments to reconcile net income to net cash flows from (used for) operating activities:		
Depreciation	100,800	
Gain on sale of investments	17,280	
Changes in current operating assets and liabilities:		
Increase in accounts receivable	27,360	
Increase in inventories	(36,000)	
Increase in accounts payable	(3,600)	
Decrease in accrued expenses payable	(2,400)	
Net cash flows from operating activities		$ 463,440
Cash flows from (used for) investing activities:		
Cash received from sale of investments	$ 240,000	
Cash paid for purchase of land	(259,200)	
Cash paid for purchase of equipment	(432,000)	
Net cash flows used for investing activities		(415,200)

(Continued)

Cash flows from (used for) financing activities:		
Cash received from sale of common stock	$ 312,000	
Cash paid for dividends	(132,000)	
Net cash flows from financing activities		180,000
Net increase in cash		$ 47,760
Cash as of December 31, 20Y9		192,240
Cash as of January 1, 20Y9		$ 240,000

Obj. 7

✔ a. $801,900

E11-19 Appendix Cash flows from (used for) operating activities—direct method

The cash flows from (used for) operating activities are reported by the direct method on the statement of cash flows. Determine the following:

a. If sales for the current year were $753,500 and accounts receivable decreased by $48,400 during the year, what was the amount of cash received from customers?

b. If income tax expense for the current year was $50,600 and income tax payable decreased by $5,500 during the year, what was the amount of cash payments for income taxes?

c. Briefly explain why the cash received from customers in (a) is different than sales.

Obj. 7

✔ a. $1,025,800

E11-20 Appendix Determining selected amounts for cash flows from (used for) operating activities—direct method

Selected data taken from the accounting records of Ginis Inc. for the current year ended December 31 are as follows:

	Balance, December 31	Balance, January 1
Accrued expenses payable (operating expenses)	$ 12,650	$ 14,030
Accounts payable (merchandise creditors)	96,140	105,800
Inventories	178,020	193,430
Prepaid expenses	7,360	8,970

During the current year, the cost of goods sold was $1,031,550, and the operating expenses other than depreciation were $179,400. The direct method is used for presenting the cash flows from (used for) operating activities on the statement of cash flows.

Determine the amount reported on the statement of cash flows for (a) cash payments for merchandise and (b) cash payments for operating expenses.

Obj. 7

✔ Net cash flows from operating activities, $96,040

E11-21 Appendix Cash flows from (used for) operating activities—direct method

The income statement of Booker T Industries Inc. for the current year ended June 30 is as follows:

Sales		$ 511,000
Cost of goods sold		(290,500)
Gross profit		$ 220,500
Operating expenses:		
Depreciation expense	$ 39,200	
Other operating expenses	105,000	
Total operating expenses		(144,200)
Income before income tax		$ 76,300
Income tax expense		(21,700)
Net income		$ 54,600

Changes in the balances of selected accounts from the beginning to the end of the current year are as follows:

	Increase (Decrease)
Accounts receivable (net)	$(11,760)
Inventories	3,920
Prepaid expenses	(3,780)
Accounts payable (merchandise creditors)	(7,980)
Accrued expenses payable (operating expenses)	1,260
Income tax payable	(2,660)

a. Prepare the "Cash flows from (used for) operating activities" section of the statement of cash flows, using the direct method.

b. What does the direct method show about a company's cash flows from operating activities that is not shown using the indirect method?

E11-22 Appendix Cash flows from (used for) operating activities—direct method

Obj. 7
✔ Net cash flows from operating activities, $123,860

The income statement for Rhino Company for the current year ended June 30 and balances of selected accounts at the beginning and the end of the year are as follows:

Sales		$ 445,500
Cost of goods sold		(154,000)
Gross profit		$ 291,500
Operating expenses:		
Depreciation expense	$ 38,500	
Other operating expenses	115,280	
Total operating expenses		(153,780)
Income before income tax		$ 137,720
Income tax expense		(39,600)
Net income		$ 98,120

	End of Year	Beginning of Year
Accounts receivable (net)	$36,300	$31,240
Inventories	92,400	80,300
Prepaid expenses	14,520	15,840
Accounts payable (merchandise creditors)	67,540	62,700
Accrued expenses payable (operating expenses)	19,140	20,900
Income tax payable	4,400	4,400

Prepare the "Cash flows from (used for) operating activities" section of the statement of cash flows, using the direct method.

Problems

Obj. 2, 3, 4, 5

✔ Net cash flows from operating activities, $490,000

SHOW ME HOW

P11-1 Statement of cash flows—indirect method

The comparative balance sheet of Livers Inc. for December 31, 20Y3 and 20Y2, is shown as follows:

	Dec. 31, 20Y3	Dec. 31, 20Y2
Assets		
Cash	$ 155,000	$ 150,000
Accounts receivable (net)	450,000	400,000
Inventories	770,000	750,000
Investments	0	100,000
Land	500,000	0
Equipment	1,400,000	1,200,000
Accumulated depreciation—equipment	(600,000)	(500,000)
Total assets	$2,675,000	$2,100,000
Liabilities and Stockholders' Equity		
Accounts payable (merchandise creditors)	$ 340,000	$ 300,000
Accrued expenses payable (operating expenses)	45,000	50,000
Dividends payable	30,000	25,000
Common stock, $4 par	700,000	600,000
Paid-in capital in excess of par—common stock	200,000	175,000
Retained earnings	1,360,000	950,000
Total liabilities and stockholders' equity	$2,675,000	$2,100,000

Additional data obtained from an examination of the accounts in the ledger for 20Y3 are as follows:

a. The investments were sold for $175,000 cash.

b. Equipment and land were acquired for cash.

c. There were no disposals of equipment during the year.

d. The common stock was issued for cash.

e. There was a $500,000 increase to Retained Earnings for net income.

f. There was a $90,000 decrease to Retained Earnings for cash dividends declared.

Instructions

Prepare a statement of cash flows, using the indirect method of presenting cash flows from (used for) operating activities.

Obj. 2, 3, 4, 5

✔ Net cash flows from operating activities, $350,000

SHOW ME HOW

P11-2 Statement of cash flows—indirect method

The comparative balance sheet of Yellow Dog Enterprises Inc. at December 31, 20Y8 and 20Y7, is as follows:

	Dec. 31, 20Y8	Dec. 31, 20Y7
Assets		
Cash	$ 95,000	$ 110,000
Accounts receivable (net)	260,000	280,000
Inventories	520,000	450,000
Prepaid expenses	15,000	5,000
Equipment	1,130,000	800,000
Accumulated depreciation—equipment	(235,000)	(190,000)
Total assets	$1,785,000	$1,455,000
Liabilities and Stockholders' Equity		
Accounts payable (merchandise creditors)	$ 100,000	$ 75,000
Mortgage note payable	0	500,000
Common stock, $10 par	500,000	200,000
Paid-in capital in excess of par—common stock	400,000	100,000
Retained earnings	785,000	580,000
Total liabilities and stockholders' equity	$1,785,000	$1,455,000

Additional data obtained from the income statement and from an examination of the accounts in the ledger for 20Y8 are as follows:

a. Net income, $250,000.

b. Depreciation reported on the income statement, $135,000.

c. Equipment was purchased at a cost of $420,000 and fully depreciated equipment costing $90,000 was discarded, with no salvage realized.

d. The mortgage note payable was not due for six years, but the terms permitted earlier payment without penalty.

e. 30,000 shares of common stock were issued at $20 for cash.

f. Cash dividends declared and paid, $45,000.

Instructions

Prepare a statement of cash flows, using the indirect method of presenting cash flows from (used for) operating activities.

P11-3 Statement of cash flows—indirect method

Obj. 2, 3, 4, 5

✔ **Net cash flows used for operating activities, $(169,600)**

The comparative balance sheet of Whitman Co. at December 31, 20Y2 and 20Y1, is as follows:

	Dec. 31, 20Y2	Dec. 31, 20Y1
Assets		
Cash	$ 918,000	$ 964,800
Accounts receivable (net)	828,900	761,940
Inventories	1,268,460	1,162,980
Prepaid expenses	29,340	35,100
Land	315,900	479,700
Buildings	1,462,500	900,900
Accumulated depreciation—buildings	(408,600)	(382,320)
Equipment	512,280	454,680
Accumulated depreciation—equipment	(141,300)	(158,760)
Total assets	$4,785,480	$4,219,020
Liabilities and Stockholders' Equity		
Accounts payable (merchandise creditors)	$ 922,500	$ 958,320
Bonds payable	270,000	0
Common stock, $25 par	317,000	117,000
Paid-in capital in excess of par—common stock	758,000	558,000
Retained earnings	2,517,980	2,585,700
Total liabilities and stockholders' equity	$4,785,480	$4,219,020

Transactions and adjustments affecting the noncurrent asset, noncurrent liability, and stockholders' equity accounts for 20Y2 are as follows:

		Land
Jan. 1 20Y2	Balance	$479,700
Apr. 20	Sold land for $151,200 cash	(163,800)
Dec. 31, 20Y2	Balance	$315,900

		Buildings	Accumulated Depreciation—Buildings
Jan. 1, 20Y2	Balances	$ 900,900	$382,320
Apr. 20	Acquired building for cash	561,600	
Dec. 31	Depreciation for the year		26,280
Dec. 31, 20Y2	Balances	$1,462,500	$408,600

		Equipment	Accumulated Depreciation—Equipment
Jan. 1, 20Y2	Balances	$454,680	$158,760
Jan. 26	Discarded equipment, no salvage	(46,800)	(46,800)
Aug. 11	Purchased equipment for cash	104,400	
Dec. 31	Depreciation for the year		29,340
Dec. 31, 20Y2	Balances	$512,280	$141,300

		Bonds Payable
Jan. 1 20Y2	Balance	$ 0
May 1	Issued 20-year bonds for face value	270,000
Dec. 31, 20Y2	Balance	$270,000

		Common Stock, $25 par	Paid-In Capital in Excess of Par—Common Stock
Jan. 1, 20Y2	Balances	$117,000	$558,000
Dec. 7	Issued 8,000 shares of common stock for$50 per share	200,000	200,000
Dec. 31, 20Y2	Balances	$317,000	$758,000

		Retained Earnings
Jan. 1 20Y2	Balance	$2,585,700
Dec. 31	Net loss	(35,320)
Dec. 31	Declared and paid cash dividends	(32,400)
Dec. 31, 20Y2	Balance	$2,517,980

Instructions

Prepare a statement of cash flows, using the indirect method of presenting cash flows from (used for) operating activities.

Obj. 2, 3, 4, 5

✔ Net cash flows from operating activities, $52,120

P11-4 Statement of cash flows—indirect method

The comparative balance sheet of TechSource for December 31, 20Y7 and 20Y6, is shown as follows:

TECHSOURCE
Comparative Balance Sheets
December 31, 20Y7 and 20Y6

	20Y7	20Y6	Changes Increase (Decrease)
Assets			
Current assets:			
Cash	$ 52,650	$ 36,200	$ 16,450
Accounts receivable	91,080	53,000	38,080
Inventory	62,150	59,700	2,450
Estimated returns inventory	5,300	4,300	1,000
Office supplies	480	600	(120)
Prepaid insurance	2,650	3,000	(350)
Total current assets	$214,310	$ 156,800	$ 57,510
Property, plant, and equipment:			
Land	$ 20,000	$ 20,000	$ 0
Store equipment	27,100	20,000	7,100
Accumulated depreciation—store equipment	(5,700)	(2,600)	(3,100)
Office equipment	15,570	10,000	5,570
Accumulated depreciation—office equipment	(4,720)	(2,230)	(2,490)
Total property, plant, and equipment	$ 52,250	$ 45,170	$ 7,080
Total assets	$266,560	$ 201,970	$ 64,590
Liabilities			
Current liabilities:			
Accounts payable	$ 12,466	$ 5,216	$ 7,250
Customer refunds payable	7,954	7,454	500
Estimated coupons payable	2,000	1,600	400
Notes payable (current portion)	5,000	5,000	0
Salaries payable	1,140	1,500	(360)
Unearned rent	1,800	2,400	(600)
Total current liabilities	$ 30,360	$ 23,170	$ 7,190
Notes payable	20,000	25,000	(5,000)
Total liabilities	$ 50,360	$ 48,170	$ 2,190

Stockholders' Equity			
Common stock	$ 25,000	$ 25,000	$ 0
Retained earnings	191,200	128,800	62,400
Total stockholders' equity	$216,200	$ 153,800	$ 62,400
Total liabilities and stockholders' equity	$266,560	$ 201,970	$ 64,590

Additional data obtained from an examination of the accounts in the ledger for 20Y7 are as follows:

a. Store equipment was acquired for $7,100 cash

b. Office equipment was acquired for $5,570 cash.

c. Principal relating to the notes payable of $5,000 was paid.

d. There was a $80,400 increase in Retained Earnings for net income.

e. There was a $18,000 decrease in Retained Earnings for cash dividends declared.

Instructions

Prepare a statement of cash flows, using the indirect method of presenting cash flows from (used for) operating activities.

P11-5 Appendix Statement of cash flows—direct method

Obj. 7

✔ Net cash flows from operating activities, $293,600

The comparative balance sheet of Canace Products Inc. for December 31, 20Y6 and 20Y5, is as follows:

	Dec. 31, 20Y6	Dec. 31, 20Y5
Assets		
Cash	$ 643,400	$ 679,400
Accounts receivable (net)	566,800	547,400
Inventories	1,011,000	982,800
Investments	0	240,000
Land	520,000	0
Equipment	880,000	680,000
Accumulated depreciation	(244,400)	(200,400)
Total assets	$3,376,800	$2,929,200
Liabilities and Stockholders' Equity		
Accounts payable (merchandise creditors)	$ 771,800	$ 748,400
Accrued expenses payable (operating expenses)	63,400	70,800
Dividends payable	8,800	6,400
Common stock, $2 par	56,000	32,000
Paid-in capital in excess of par—common stock	408,000	192,000
Retained earnings	2,068,800	1,879,600
Total liabilities and stockholders' equity	$3,376,800	$2,929,200

The income statement for the year ended December 31, 20Y6, is as follows:

Sales		$ 5,980,000
Cost of goods sold		(2,452,000)
Gross profit		$ 3,528,000
Operating expenses:		
Depreciation expense	$ 44,000	
Other operating expenses	3,100,000	
Total operating expenses		(3,144,000)
Operating income		$ 384,000
Other expense:		
Loss on sale of investments		(64,000)
Income before income tax		$ 320,000
Income tax expense		(102,800)
Net income		$ 217,200

Additional data obtained from an examination of the accounts in the ledger for 20Y6 are as follows:

a. Equipment and land were acquired for cash.

b. There were no disposals of equipment during the year.

c. The investments were sold for $176,000 cash.

d. The common stock was issued for cash.

e. There was a $28,000 decrease in Retained Earnings for cash dividends declared.

Instructions

Prepare a statement of cash flows, using the direct method of presenting cash flows from (used for) operating activities.

Obj. 7

✔ **Net cash flows from operating activities, $490,000**

P11-6 Appendix Statement of cash flows—direct method applied to P11-1

The comparative balance sheet of Livers Inc. for December 31, 20Y3 and 20Y2, is as follows:

	Dec. 31, 20Y3	Dec. 31, 20Y2
Assets		
Cash	$ 155,000	$ 150,000
Accounts receivable (net)	450,000	400,000
Inventories	770,000	750,000
Investments	0	100,000
Land	500,000	0
Equipment	1,400,000	1,200,000
Accumulated depreciation—equipment	(600,000)	(500,000)
Total assets	$2,675,000	$2,100,000
Liabilities and Stockholders' Equity		
Accounts payable (merchandise creditors)	$ 340,000	$ 300,000
Accrued expenses payable (operating expenses)	45,000	50,000
Dividends payable	30,000	25,000
Common stock, $4 par	700,000	600,000
Paid-in capital in excess of par—common stock	200,000	175,000
Retained earnings	1,360,000	950,000
Total liabilities and stockholders' equity	$2,675,000	$2,100,000

The income statement for the year ended December 31, 20Y3, is as follows:

Sales		$ 3,000,000
Cost of goods sold		(1,400,000)
Gross profit		$ 1,600,000
Operating expenses:		
Depreciation expense	$100,000	
Other operating expenses	950,000	
Total operating expenses		(1,050,000)
Operating income		$ 550,000
Other revenue:		
Gain on sale of investments		75,000
Income before income tax		$ 625,000
Income tax expense		(125,000)
Net income		$ 500,000

Additional data obtained from an examination of the accounts in the ledger for 20Y3 are as follows:

a. The investments were sold for $175,000 cash.

b. Equipment and land were acquired for cash.

c. There were no disposals of equipment during the year.

d. The common stock was issued for cash.

e. There was a $90,000 decrease in Retained Earnings for cash dividends declared.

Instructions

Prepare a statement of cash flows, using the direct method of presenting cash flows from (used for) operating activities.

Metric-Based Analysis

MBA 11-1 Free cash flow

Obj. 7

The Priceline Group Inc. (PCLN) is a leading provider of online travel reservation services, including brand names Priceline, KAYAK, and OpenTable. Selected cash flow information from the statement of cash flows for three recent years is as follows (in millions):

	Year 3	Year 2	Year 1
Net cash provided by operating activities	$ 4,865	$5,338	$ 4,662
Net cash provided by (used for) investing activities	7,050	2,215	(4,202)
Net cash used for financing activities	(8,220)	(7,431)	(79)
Additions to property, plant, and equipment	(368)	(442)	(288)
Repurchase common stock	(8,187)	(5,971)	(1,828)
Acquisitions and investments	(9)	(273)	(553)

1. Determine the net change in cash for each year.
2. Determine the free cash flow for each year.
3. How is the free cash flow being used based on the data provided?
4. Which is better for measuring the cash flow available for investment, dividends, debt repayments, and stock repurchases: the change in cash for the period or the free cash flow? Explain.

MBA 11-2 Free cash flow

Obj. 4

Aeropostale, Inc. (AROPQ) is a specialty retailer of casual apparel and accessories for teens. Recently, the company declared bankruptcy to provide financial protection while attempting to reorganize its operations. Annual report information for the three most recent years prior to the bankruptcy are as follows (in millions):

	Year 3	Year 2	Year 1
Net cash flows used for operating activities	$ (68)	$ (56)	$ (38)
Cash used to purchase property, plant, and equipment	(16)	(24)	(84)

1. Determine the free cash flow.
2. Did the free cash flow information indicate financial stress? Explain.

MBA 11-3 Free cash flow and cash flow adequacy

Obj. 6

Amazon.com, Inc. (AMZN) is one of the largest Internet retailers in the world. **Best Buy Co., Inc. (BBY)** is a leading retailer of consumer electronics and media products in the United States, while **Walmart, Inc. (WMT)** is the leading retailer in the United States. Amazon, Best Buy, and Walmart compete in similar markets. Best Buy and Walmart sell through both traditional retail stores and the Internet, while Amazon sells only through the Internet. Sales and cash flow information from recent annual reports for all three companies is as follows (in millions):

	Amazon	Best Buy	Walmart
Average debt maturing over the next five years	$ 1,814	$ 133	$ 4,044
Net cash flows from operating activities	38,514	2,565	25,255
Purchases of property, plant, and equipment	(16,861)	(743)	(10,705)

1. Determine the free cash flow for all three companies.
2. Compute the cash flow adequacy ratio for all three companies. Round to one decimal place.
3. How does Amazon compare to the other two companies with respect to generating free cash flow?

Obj. 4

MBA 11-4 Free cash flow and cash flow adequacy ratio

Financial information for **Apple Inc. (AAPL)**, **The Coca-Cola Company (KO)**, and **Verizon Communications (VZ)** follows (in millions):

	Apple	Coca-Cola	Verizon
Average debt maturing over the next five years	$ 9,575	$ 3,576	$ 7,341
Net cash flows from operating activities	69,391	10,471	35,746
Cash used to purchase property, plant, and equipment	(10,495)	(2,054)	(17,939)

1. Compute the free cash flow for each company.
2. Compute the cash flow adequacy ratio for each company. Round percentages to one decimal place.
3. Which company has the greatest free cash flow?
4. Which company has the highest cash flow adequacy ratio?
5. How does Verizon differ from the other two companies?

Cases

ETHICS

Case 11-1 Cash flow per share

Head Donuts Inc. is a retailer of designer headphones, earphones, and hands-free audio devices. Polly Ester, the company president, is reviewing the company's financial statements after the close of the fiscal year and is troubled that earnings decreased by 10%. She shares her concerns with the company's chief accountant, Lucas Simmons, who points out that the drop in earnings was balanced by a 20% increase in net cash flows from operating activities. Polly is encouraged by the increase in net cash flows from operating activities, but is worried that investors might miss this information because it is "buried" in the statement of cash flows. To make it easier for investors to find this information, she instructs Lucas to include an operating cash flow per share number on the face of the income statement, directly below earnings per share. While Lucas is concerned about using such an unconventional financial reporting tactic, he agrees to include the information on the income statement.

Is Lucas behaving in an ethical and professional manner? Explain your answer.

Case 11-2 Financial condition

Tidewater Inc., a retailer, provided the following financial information for its most recent fiscal year:

Net income	$ 945,000
Return on invested capital	8%
Cash flows used for operating activities	$(1,428,000)
Cash flows from investing activities	$600,000
Cash flows from financing activities	$900,000

The company's "Cash flows from (used for) operating activities" section is as follows:

Net income	$ 945,000
Depreciation	210,000
Increase in accounts receivable	(1,134,000)
Increase in inventory	(1,260,000)
Decrease in accounts payable	(189,000)
Net cash flows used for operating activities	$(1,428,000)

An examination of the financial statements revealed the following additional information:

- Revenues increased during the year as a result of an aggressive marketing campaign aimed at increasing the number of new "Tidewater Card" credit card customers. This is the company's branded credit card, which can only be used at Tidewater stores. The credit card balances are accounts receivable on Tidewater's balance sheet.
- Some suppliers have made their merchandise available at a deep discount. As a result, the company purchased large quantities of these goods in an attempt to improve the company's profitability.
- In recent years, the company has struggled to pay its accounts payable on time. The company has improved on this during the past year and is nearly caught up on overdue payables balances.
- The company reported net losses in each of the two prior years.

Write a brief memo to your instructor evaluating the financial condition of Tidewater Inc.

Case 11-3 Using the statement of cash flows

You are considering an investment in a new start-up company, Giraffe Inc., an Internet service provider. A review of the company's financial statements reveals a negative retained earnings. In addition, it appears as though the company has been running a negative cash flow from operating activities since the company's inception.
How is the company staying in business under these circumstances? Could this be a good investment?

Case 11-4 Free cash flow and cash flow adequacy

Brees Inc. and Brady Company supply sports equipment to various college and professional teams. Information for each company is as follows:

	Brees Inc.	Brady Company
Net cash flows from operating activities	$2,475,000	$1,639,000
Purchases of property, plant, and equipment	1,442,000	937,000
Average debt maturing over the next five years	985,000	1,212,000

1. Compute the free cash flow and cash flow adequacy ratio for each company. Round ratios to one decimal place.
2. What information do these metrics provide with regard to the two companies?

The annual report (10-K) assignment for this chapter is in Appendix B: Nike Annual Report, Chapter 11.

Answers to Self-Examination Questions

1. **D** Cash flows from operating activities affect transactions that enter into the determination of net income, such as the receipt of cash from customers on account (answer D). Receipts of cash from the sale of stock (answer A) and the sale of bonds (answer B) and payments of cash for dividends (answer C) are cash flows from or used for financing activities.

2. **A** Cash flows from investing activities include receipts from the sale of noncurrent assets, such as equipment (answer A). Receipts of cash from the sale of stock (answer B) and payments of cash for dividends (answer C) and to acquire treasury stock (answer D) are cash flows from or used for financing activities.

3. **C** Payment of cash for dividends (answer C) is an example of a financing activity. The receipt of cash from customers on account (answer A) is an operating activity. The receipt of cash from the sale of equipment (answer B) and the payment of cash to acquire land (answer D) are examples of investing activities.

4. **D** The indirect method (answer D) reports cash flows from (used for) operating activities by beginning with net income and adjusting it for revenues and expenses not involving the receipt or payment of cash.

5. **C** The "Cash flows from (used for) operating activities" section of the statement of cash flows would report net cash flows from operating activities of $65,500, determined as follows:

Cash flows from (used for) operating activities:		
Net income	$ 55,000	
Adjustments to reconcile net income to net cash flows from (used for) operating activities:		
Depreciation expense	22,000	
Changes in current operating assets and liabilities:		
Increase in accounts receivable	(10,000)	
Decrease in inventories	5,000	
Decrease in prepaid expenses	500	
Decrease in accounts payable	(7,000)	
Net cash flows from operating activities		$65,500

Chapter **12**

Metric-Based Analysis of Financial Statements

What's Covered:

Topics: Metric-Based Analysis of Financial Statements

Analysis of Financial Statements
- Usefulness of financial statements (Obj. 1)
- Methods of analysis (Obj. 1)

Global Analysis
- Horizontal analysis (Obj. 2)
- Vertical analysis (Obj. 2)
- Common-sized statements (Obj. 2)

Component Analysis: Liquidity
- Current position (Obj. 3)
- Accounts receivable (Obj. 3)
- Inventory (Obj. 3)

Component Analysis: Solvency
- Debt ratio (Obj. 4)
- Liabilities to stockholders' equity (Obj. 4)
- Fixed assets to long-term liabilities (Obj. 4)
- Times interest earned (Obj. 4)

Component Analysis: Profitability
- Asset turnover (Obj. 5)
- Return on total assets (Obj. 5)
- Return on stockholders' equity (Obj. 5)
- Return on common stockholders' equity (Obj. 5)
- Earnings per share (Obj. 5)
- Price-earnings ratio (Obj. 5)
- Dividends per share (Obj. 5)
- Dividend yield (Obj. 5)

Corporate Annual Reports
- Management analysis (Obj. 6)
- Internal control report (Obj. 6)
- Audit report (Obj. 6)

Learning Objectives

Obj.1 Describe the usefulness of financial statements and methods of analysis.

Obj.2 Describe and illustrate global analysis of financial statements.

Obj.3 Describe and illustrate metrics used to analyze liquidity.

Obj.4 Describe and illustrate metrics used to analyze solvency.

Obj.5 Describe and illustrate metrics used to analyze profitability.

Obj.6 Describe the corporate annual reports.

Chapter Metrics

This chapter uses a variety of metrics to analyze financial statements to assess a company's liquidity, solvency, and profitability.

NIKE

Rose Carson/ Shutterstock.com

Nike Connection

"Just do it." These three words identify one of the most recognizable brands in the world, **Nike (NKE)**. While this phrase inspires athletes to "compete and achieve their potential," it also defines the company.

Nike began in 1964 as a partnership between University of Oregon track coach Bill Bowerman and one of his former student-athletes, Phil Knight. The two began by selling shoes imported from Japan out of the back of Knight's car to athletes at track and field events. As sales grew, the company opened retail outlets and began to develop its own shoes. In 1971, the company, originally named Blue Ribbon Sports, commissioned a graphic design student at Portland State University to develop the Nike Swoosh logo for a fee of $35. In 1978, the company changed its name to Nike, and in 1980, it sold its first shares of stock to the public.

Nike would have been a great company in which to have invested. If you had invested in Nike's common stock back in 1990, you would have paid $5 per share. Recently, Nike's stock sold for over $85 per share. Unfortunately, you can't invest using hindsight.

How then should you select companies in which to invest? Like any significant purchase, you should do some research to guide your investment decision. If you were buying a car, for example, you might go to the *Consumer Reports* or *Car and Driver* Web sites to obtain reviews, ratings, prices, specifications, options, and fuel economy across a number of vehicles. In deciding whether to invest in a company, you can use financial analysis to gain insight into a company's past performance and future prospects. This chapter describes and illustrates metrics and analyses to assist you in making investment decisions such as whether or not to invest in Nike's stock.

Source: http://www.nikebiz.com/.

Objective 1
Describe the usefulness of financial statements and methods of analysis.

Analysis of Financial Statements

The objective of financial statements is to provide useful information to a company's stakeholders about the company's financial condition and performance. A company's stakeholders include a wide range of potential users including creditors, investors, managers, employees, suppliers, customers, and government agencies. Because of the wide range of potential users, the financial statements illustrated throughout this text are often referred to as **general-purpose financial statements**.

Usefulness of Financial Statements

A company's financial condition and performance are normally analyzed and interpreted by focusing upon the following characteristics:

- Liquidity
- Solvency
- Profitability

Liquidity is the ability to convert assets to cash. Short-term creditors such as suppliers and banks often focus on a company's liquidity as a means of evaluating the ability of the company to pay its accounts payable and short-term debt. The current assets and liabilities reported on the balance sheet provide useful information on a company's liquidity.

Solvency is the ability of a company to pay its debts as they become due over a long period of time. Long-term creditors, such as banks and bondholders, focus on a company's solvency as a means of evaluating whether the company will continue to make its periodic interest payments and will be able to repay its loans at their maturity. The relationship among assets, liabilities, and equity reported on the balance sheet provides useful information on solvency. In addition, the income statement and statement of cash flows provide useful information on the ability of the company to generate cash to pay periodic interest and loans at maturity.

Profitability is the ability of a company to generate net income related to its invested assets. Stockholders, managers, and employees focus on profitability in evaluating whether a company's stock price will increase, whether the company will pay dividends, and whether the company will continue in business. The income statement and balance sheet provide useful information on the ability of a company to generate profits from its assets.

Methods of Analysis

Financial statements may be analyzed using a variety of methods and metrics. In this chapter, we focus upon the following two methods of analysis:

1. **Global analysis**, which computes changes in amounts, percentages of amounts, and percentage changes in amounts for each financial statement.
2. **Component analysis**, which computes metrics for liquidity, solvency, and profitability for components of financial statements.

Financial statement analysis is most effective when both methods of analyses are used and when results are compared over time and with competitors.

Global Analysis

Objective 2
Describe and illustrate global analysis of financial statements.

Users analyze a company's financial statements using a variety of analytical methods. Three such methods are as follows:

1. Horizontal analysis
2. Vertical analysis
3. Common-sized statements

Horizontal Analysis

The percentage analysis of increases and decreases in related items in comparative financial statements is called **horizontal analysis**. Each item on the most recent statement is compared with the related item on one or more earlier statements in terms of the following:

1. *Amount* of increase or decrease
2. *Percent* of increase or decrease

When comparing statements, the earlier statement is normally used as the base for computing increases and decreases.

Exhibit 1 illustrates horizontal analysis for the December 31, 20Y6 and 20Y5 balance sheets of Mooney Company. In Exhibit 1, the December 31, 20Y5, balance sheet (the earliest year presented) is used as the base.

Exhibit 1 indicates that total assets decreased by $91,000 (7.4%), liabilities decreased by $133,000 (30.0%), and stockholders' equity increased by $42,000 (5.3%).

Exhibit 1 Comparative Balance Sheet—Horizontal Analysis

Mooney Company
Comparative Balance Sheet
December 31, 20Y6 and 20Y5

	Dec. 31, 20Y6	Dec. 31, 20Y5	Increase (Decrease) Amount	Increase (Decrease) Percent
Assets				
Current assets	$ 550,000	$ 533,000	$ 17,000	3.2%
Long-term investments	95,000	177,500	(82,500)	(46.5)%
Property, plant, and equipment (net)	444,500	470,000	(25,500)	(5.4)%
Intangible assets	50,000	50,000	—	—
Total assets	$1,139,500	$1,230,500	$ (91,000)	(7.4)%
Liabilities				
Current liabilities	$ 210,000	$ 243,000	$ (33,000)	(13.6)%
Long-term liabilities	100,000	200,000	(100,000)	(50.0)%
Total liabilities	$ 310,000	$ 443,000	$(133,000)	(30.0)%
Stockholders' Equity				
Preferred 6% stock, $100 par	$ 150,000	$ 150,000	—	—
Common stock, $10 par	500,000	500,000	—	—
Retained earnings	179,500	137,500	$ 42,000	30.5%
Total stockholders' equity	$ 829,500	$ 787,500	$ 42,000	5.3%
Total liabilities and stockholders' equity	$1,139,500	$1,230,500	$ (91,000)	(7.4)%

The balance sheets in Exhibit 1 may be expanded or supported by a separate schedule that includes the individual asset and liability accounts. For example, Exhibit 2 is a supporting schedule of Mooney's current asset accounts.

Exhibit 2 indicates that while cash, temporary investments, and prepaid expenses increased, accounts receivable and inventories decreased. The decrease in accounts receivable could be caused by improved collection policies. The decrease in inventories could be caused by increased sales.

Exhibit 2 Comparative Schedule of Current Assets—Horizontal Analysis

Mooney Company
Comparative Schedule of Current Assets
December 31, 20Y6 and 20Y5

	Dec. 31, 20Y6	Dec. 31, 20Y5	Increase (Decrease) Amount	Increase (Decrease) Percent
Cash	$ 90,500	$ 64,700	$ 25,800	39.9%
Temporary investments	75,000	60,000	15,000	25.0%
Accounts receivable (net)	115,000	120,000	(5,000)	(4.2)%
Inventories	264,000	283,000	(19,000)	(6.7)%
Prepaid expenses	5,500	5,300	200	3.8%
Total current assets	$550,000	$533,000	$ 17,000	3.2%

On a recent balance sheet, Nike reported an increase in current assets of 9.2%. *Nike Connection*

Exhibit 3 illustrates horizontal analysis for the 20Y6 and 20Y5 income statements of Mooney Company. Exhibit 3 indicates an increase in sales of $298,000, or 24.8%. However, the percentage increase in sales of 24.8% was accompanied by an even greater percentage increase in the cost of goods (merchandise) sold of 27.2%.[1] Thus, gross profit increased by only 19.7% rather than by the 24.8% increase in sales.

Exhibit 3 Comparative Income Statement—Horizontal Analysis

Mooney Company
Comparative Income Statement
For the Years Ended December 31, 20Y6 and 20Y5

			Increase (Decrease)	
	20Y6	**20Y5**	**Amount**	**Percent**
Sales	$ 1,498,000	$1,200,000	$ 298,000	24.8%
Cost of goods sold	(1,043,000)	(820,000)	223,000	27.2%
Gross profit	$ 455,000	$ 380,000	$ 75,000	19.7%
Selling expenses	$ (191,000)	$ (147,000)	$ 44,000	29.9%
Administrative expenses	(104,000)	(97,400)	6,600	6.8%
Total operating expenses	$ (295,000)	$ (244,400)	$ 50,600	20.7%
Operating income	$ 160,000	$ 135,600	$ 24,400	18.0%
Other revenue and expense:				
Other revenue	8,500	11,000	(2,500)	(22.7)%
Other expense (interest)	(6,000)	(12,000)	(6,000)	(50.0)%
Income before income tax	$ 162,500	$ 134,600	$ 27,900	20.7%
Income tax expense	(71,500)	(58,100)	13,400	23.1%
Net income	$ 91,000	$ 76,500	$ 14,500	19.0%

Exhibit 3 also indicates that selling expenses increased by 29.9%. Thus, the 24.8% increase in sales could have been caused by an advertising campaign, which increased selling expenses. Administrative expenses increased by only 6.8%, total operating expenses increased by 20.7%, and operating income increased by 18.0%. Interest expense decreased by 50.0%. This decrease was probably caused by the 50.0% decrease in long-term liabilities (Exhibit 1). Overall, net income increased by 19.0%, a favorable result.

On a recent income statement, Nike reported an increase in sales of 7.5%, an increase in gross profit of 9.5%, and an increase in net income of 108.4%.

Exhibit 4 illustrates horizontal analysis of Mooney Company's retained earnings. Horizontal analysis of the statement of stockholders' equity is not illustrated because there were no changes in preferred or common stock during 20Y6.[2] The 20Y6 ending balance of retained earnings increased by 30.5%. This increase was due to a 19.0% increase in net income, which was partially offset by a 33.3% increase in dividends to common stockholders.

1. The term *cost of goods sold* is often used in practice in place of *cost of merchandise sold*. Such usage is followed in this chapter.
2. Horizontal analysis can also be prepared for the statement of cash flows, which is discussed in accounting and finance courses.

Exhibit 4 Comparative Analysis of Retained Earnings—Horizontal Analysis

Mooney Company
Comparative Retained Earnings
For the Year Ended December 31, 20Y6 and 20Y5

	Retained Earnings			
			Increase (Decrease)	
	20Y6	20Y5	Amount	Percent
Balances, Jan. 1	$137,500	$100,000	$37,500	37.5%
Net income	91,000	76,500	14,500	19.0%
Dividends:				
Preferred stock	(9,000)	(9,000)	0	0.0%
Common stock	(40,000)	(30,000)	(10,000)	33.3%
Balances, Dec. 31	$179,500	$137,500	$42,000	30.5%

Vertical Analysis

The percentage analysis of the relationship of each component in a financial statement to a total within the statement is called **vertical analysis**. Although vertical analysis is applied to a single statement, it may be applied to the same statement over time. This enhances the analysis by showing how the percentages of each item have changed.

In vertical analysis of the balance sheet, the percentages are computed as follows:

1. Each asset item is stated as a percent of the total assets.
2. Each liability and stockholders' equity item is stated as a percent of the total liabilities and stockholders' equity.

Exhibit 5 illustrates the vertical analysis of the December 31, 20Y6 and 20Y5, balance sheets of Mooney Company. Exhibit 5 indicates that current assets increased from 43.3% to 48.3% of total assets. Long-term investments decreased from 14.4% to 8.3% of total assets. Stockholders' equity increased from 64.0% to 72.8% with a comparable decrease in liabilities.

Nike Connection On a recent balance sheet, Nike reported that current assets were 69.7% of total assets.

In a vertical analysis of the income statement, each item is stated as a percent of sales. Exhibit 6 illustrates the vertical analysis of the 20Y6 and 20Y5 income statements of Mooney Company.

Exhibit 6 indicates a decrease of the gross profit rate from 31.7% in 20Y5 to 30.4% in 20Y6. Although this is only a 1.3 percentage points (31.7% − 30.4%) decrease, in dollars of potential gross profit, it represents a change of $75,000. Thus, a small percentage change can have a large dollar effect.

Nike Connection On a recent income statement, Nike reported that gross profit was 44.7% of sales, and sales and administrative expenses were 32.5% of sales.

Exhibit 5 Comparative Balance Sheet—Vertical Analysis

Mooney Company Comparative Balance Sheet December 31, 20Y6 and 20Y5	Dec. 31, 20Y6		Dec. 31, 20Y5	
	Amount	Percent	Amount	Percent
Assets				
Current assets	$ 550,000	48.3%	$ 533,000	43.3%
Long-term investments	95,000	8.3	177,500	14.4
Property, plant, and equipment (net)	444,500	39.0	470,000	38.2
Intangible assets	50,000	4.4	50,000	4.1
Total assets	$1,139,500	100.0%	$1,230,500	100.0%
Liabilities				
Current liabilities	$ 210,000	18.4%	$ 243,000	19.7%
Long-term liabilities	100,000	8.8	200,000	16.3
Total liabilities	$ 310,000	27.2%	$ 443,000	36.0%
Stockholders' Equity				
Preferred 6% stock, $100 par	$ 150,000	13.2%	$ 150,000	12.2%
Common stock, $10 par	500,000	43.9	500,000	40.6
Retained earnings	179,500	15.7	137,500	11.2
Total stockholders' equity	$ 829,500	72.8%	$ 787,500	64.0%
Total liabilities and stockholders' equity	$1,139,500	100.0%	$1,230,500	100.0%

Exhibit 6 Comparative Income Statement—Vertical Analysis

Mooney Company Comparative Income Statement For the Years Ended December 31, 20Y6 and 20Y5	20Y6		20Y5	
	Amount	Percent	Amount	Percent
Sales	$ 1,498,000	100.0%	$1,200,000	100.0%
Cost of goods sold	(1,043,000)	(69.6)	(820,000)	(68.3)
Gross profit	$ 455,000	30.4%	$ 380,000	31.7%
Selling expenses	$ (191,000)	(12.8)%	$ (147,000)	(12.3)%
Administrative expenses	(104,000)	(6.9)	(97,400)	(8.1)
Total operating expenses	$ (295,000)	(19.7)%	$ (244,400)	(20.4)%
Operating income	$ 160,000	10.7%	$ 135,600	11.3%
Other revenue and expense:				
Other revenue	8,500	0.6	11,000	0.9
Other expense (interest)	(6,000)	(0.4)	(12,000)	(1.0)
Income before income tax	$ 162,500	10.9%	$ 134,600	11.2%
Income tax expense	(71,500)	(4.8)	(58,100)	(4.8)
Net income	$ 91,000	6.1%	$ 76,500	6.4%

Common-Sized Statements

On a **common-sized statement**, all items are expressed as percentages with no dollar amounts shown. Common-sized statements are often useful for comparing one company with another or for comparing a company with industry averages.

Exhibit 7 illustrates common-sized income statements for Mooney Company and Lowell Corporation.

Exhibit 7 Common-Sized Income Statement

	Mooney Company	Lowell Corporation
Sales	100.0%	100.0%
Cost of goods sold	(69.6)	(70.0)
Gross profit	30.4%	30.0%
Selling expenses	(12.8)%	(11.5)%
Administrative expenses	(6.9)	(4.1)
Total operating expenses	(19.7)%	(15.6)%
Operating income	10.7%	14.4%
Other revenue and expense:		
Other revenue	0.6	0.6
Other expense (interest)	(0.4)	(0.5)
Income before income tax	10.9%	14.5%
Income tax expense	(4.8)	(5.5)
Net income	6.1%	9.0%

Exhibit 7 indicates that Mooney Company has a slightly higher rate of gross profit (30.4%) than Lowell Corporation (30.0%). However, Mooney has a higher percentage of selling expenses (12.8%) and administrative expenses (6.9%) than does Lowell (11.5% and 4.1%, respectively). As a result, the operating income of Mooney (10.7%) is less than that of Lowell (14.4%).

The unfavorable difference of 3.7 (14.4% − 10.7%) percentage points in operating income would concern the managers and other stakeholders of Mooney. The underlying causes of the difference should be investigated and possibly corrected. For example, Mooney Company may decide to outsource some of its administrative duties so that its administrative expenses are more comparative to those of Lowell Corporation.

Using Data Analytics

Databases

Data analytics can be used to analyze a company's financial statements by extracting and transforming information from a variety of publicly available databases. Databases available for analyzing companies include the following:

- SimFin (**https://simfin.com/**) covers over 2,700 companies and has over 300,000 financial statements uploaded. SimFin allows the user to download data sets and filter/screen companies by over 70 ratios and metrics. The user can also download data and search results in Excel.
- Securities and Exchange Commission (SEC) (**www.sec.gov/edgar/searchedgar/companysearch.html**) provides access to company filings with the SEC. Included in this database are 10-K filings of annual reports and 10-Q filings of quarterly financial statements.
- Yahoo! Finance (**https://finance.yahoo.com/**) allows searches for company financial and market data. The company data includes a company profile, key statistics (including ratios), analysis (including revenue and earnings estimates as well as analyst recommendations), and financial statements.
- MSN Money (**www.msn.com/en-us/money/**) allows company searches by quotation, which provides a company summary, financial statements, and analysis (key statistics and other metrics).

Component Analysis: Liquidity Metrics

Objective 3
Describe and illustrate metrics used to analyze liquidity.

Liquidity is the ability of a company to convert assets into cash, which affects its ability to pay short-term debts such as accounts payable. The following three types of metrics are commonly used to assess liquidity:

1. Current position metrics
2. Accounts receivable metrics
3. Inventory metrics

Current Position Analysis

A company's ability to pay its current liabilities is called **current position analysis**. It is of special interest to short-term creditors and includes the computation and analysis of the following:

- Working capital
- Current ratio
- Quick ratio

Working Capital A company's **working capital** is computed as follows:

Working Capital = Current Assets − Current Liabilities

To illustrate, the working capital for Mooney Company for 20Y6 and 20Y5 is computed as follows:

	20Y6	20Y5
Current assets	$550,000	$533,000
Less current liabilities	(210,000)	(243,000)
Working capital	$340,000	$290,000

The working capital is used to evaluate a company's ability to pay current liabilities. A company's working capital is often monitored monthly, quarterly, and yearly by creditors and other debtors. However, it is difficult to use working capital to compare companies of different sizes. For example, working capital of $250,000 may be adequate for a local hardware store, but it would be inadequate for **The Home Depot (HD)**.

Current Ratio The **current ratio**, sometimes called the *working capital ratio*, is computed as follows:

$$\textbf{Current Ratio} = \frac{\textbf{Current Assets}}{\textbf{Current Liabilities}}$$

To illustrate, the current ratio for Mooney Company for 20Y6 and 20Y5 is computed as follows:

	20Y6	20Y5
Current assets	$550,000	$533,000
Current liabilities	$210,000	$243,000
Current ratio	2.6 ($550,000 ÷ $210,000)	2.2 ($533,000 ÷ $243,000)

The current ratio is a more reliable indicator of the ability to pay current liabilities than is working capital. To illustrate, assume that as of December 31, 20Y6, the working capital of a competitor is much greater than $340,000, but its current ratio is only 1.3. Considering these facts alone, Mooney Company, with its current ratio of 2.6, is in a more favorable position to obtain short-term credit than the competitor, which has the greater amount of working capital.

Quick Ratio One limitation of working capital and the current ratio is that they do not consider the makeup of the current assets. Because of this, two companies may have the same working capital and current ratios but differ significantly in their ability to pay their current liabilities.

To illustrate, the current assets and liabilities for Mooney Company and Wendt Corporation as of December 31, 20Y6, are as follows:

	Mooney Company	Wendt Corporation
Current assets:		
Cash	$ 90,500	$ 45,500
Temporary investments	75,000	25,000
Accounts receivable (net)	115,000	90,000
Inventories	264,000	380,000
Prepaid expenses	5,500	9,500
Total current assets	$550,000	$550,000
Total current assets	$550,000	$550,000
Less current liabilities	(210,000)	(210,000)
Working capital	$340,000	$340,000
Current ratio ($550,000 ÷ $210,000)	2.6	2.6

Mooney and Wendt both have a working capital of $340,000 and current ratios of 2.6. Wendt, however, has more of its current assets in inventories. These inventories must be sold and the receivables collected before all the current liabilities can be paid. This takes time. In addition, if the market for its product declines, Wendt may have difficulty selling its inventory. This, in turn, could impair its ability to pay its current liabilities.

In contrast, Mooney's current assets contain more cash, temporary investments, and accounts receivable, which can easily be converted to cash. Thus, Mooney is in a stronger current position than Wendt to pay its current liabilities.

A ratio that measures the "instant" debt-paying ability of a company is the **quick ratio**, sometimes called the *acid-test ratio*. The quick ratio is computed as follows:

$$\textbf{Quick Ratio} = \frac{\textbf{Quick Assets}}{\textbf{Current Liabilities}}$$

Quick assets are cash and other current assets that can be easily converted to cash. Quick assets normally include cash, temporary investments, and receivables.

To illustrate, the quick ratio for Mooney Company is computed as follows:

	20Y6	20Y5
Quick assets:		
Cash	$ 90,500	$ 64,700
Temporary investments	75,000	60,000
Accounts receivable (net)	115,000	120,000
Total quick assets	$280,500	$244,700
Current liabilities	$210,000	$243,000
Quick ratio	1.3*	1.0**

*1.3 = $280,500 ÷ $210,000
**1.0 = $244,700 ÷ $243,000

Nike Connection

On a recent balance sheet, Nike reported working capital of $8,659 million, a current ratio of 2.1, and a quick ratio of 1.1.

Accounts Receivable Metrics

A company's accounts receivable metrics reflect the efficiency of collecting accounts receivable. These metrics include the following:

- Accounts receivable turnover
- Days' sales in receivables

Collecting accounts receivable as quickly as possible improves a company's liquidity. In addition, the cash collected from receivables may be used to improve or expand operations. Quick collection of receivables also reduces the risk of uncollectible accounts.

Accounts Receivable Turnover The **accounts receivable turnover** is computed as follows:

$$\textbf{Accounts Receivable Turnover} = \frac{\textbf{Sales}^3}{\textbf{Average Accounts Receivable}}$$

To illustrate, the accounts receivable turnover for Mooney Company for 20Y6 and 20Y5 is computed as follows:

	20Y6	20Y5
Sales	$ 1,498,000	$1,200,000
Accounts receivable (net):		
Beginning of year	$ 120,000	$ 140,000
End of year	115,000	120,000
Total	$ 235,000	$ 260,000
Average accounts receivable	$117,500 ($235,000 ÷ 2)	$130,000 ($260,000 ÷ 2)
Accounts receivable turnover	12.7 ($1,498,000 ÷ $117,500)	9.2 ($1,200,000 ÷ $130,000)

The increase in Mooney's accounts receivable turnover from 9.2 to 12.7 indicates that the collection of receivables has improved during 20Y6. This may be due to a change in how credit is granted, collection practices, or both.

For Mooney Company, the average accounts receivable was computed using the accounts receivable balance at the beginning and the end of the year. When sales are seasonal and thus vary throughout the year, monthly balances of receivables are often used. Also, if sales on account include notes receivable as well as accounts receivable, notes and accounts receivable are normally combined for analysis.

Days' Sales in Receivables The **days' sales in receivables** is computed as follows:

$$\textbf{Days' Sales in Receivables} = \frac{\textbf{Average Accounts Receivable}}{\textbf{Average Daily Sales}}$$

where

$$\textbf{Average Daily Sales} = \frac{\textbf{Sales}}{\textbf{365 days}}$$

3. If known, credit sales should be used in the numerator. Because credit sales are not normally known by external users, sales is used in the numerator.

To illustrate, the days' sales in receivables (rounded to nearest day) for Mooney Company is computed as follows:

	20Y6	20Y5
Average accounts receivable	$117,500 ($235,000 ÷ 2)	$130,000 ($260,000 ÷ 2)
Average daily sales	$4,104 ($1,498,000 ÷ 365)	$3,288 ($1,200,000 ÷ 365)
Days' sales in receivables	29 ($117,500 ÷ $4,104)	40 ($130,000 ÷ $3,288)

The days' sales in receivables is an estimate of the time (in days) that the accounts receivable have been outstanding. The days' sales in receivables is often compared with a company's credit terms to evaluate the efficiency of the collection of receivables.

To illustrate, if Mooney's credit terms are 2/10, n/30, then Mooney was very *inefficient* in collecting receivables in 20Y5. In other words, receivables should have been collected in 30 days or less but were being collected in 40 days. Although collections improved during 20Y6 to 29 days, there is probably still room for improvement.

Days' sales in receivables and accounts receivable turnover are related. Specifically, days' sales in receivables can be computed by dividing 365 days by the accounts receivable turnover. To illustrate, Mooney Company's 20Y6 days' sales in receivable is computed as 29 days (365 days ÷ 12.7).

In recent financial statements, Nike reported an accounts receivable turnover of 10.1 and days' sales in receivables of 36.2 days.

Inventory Metrics

A company's inventory metrics reflect the efficiency of purchasing and selling inventory. These metrics include the following:

- Inventory turnover
- Days' sales in inventory

Excess inventory decreases liquidity by tying up funds (cash) in inventory. In addition, excess inventory increases insurance expense, property taxes, storage costs, and other related expenses. These expenses further reduce funds that could be used elsewhere to improve or expand operations.

Excess inventory also increases the risk of losses because of price declines or obsolescence of the inventory. On the other hand, a company should keep enough inventory in stock so that it doesn't lose sales because of lack of inventory.

Inventory Turnover The **inventory turnover** is computed as follows:

$$\text{Inventory Turnover} = \frac{\text{Cost of Goods Sold}}{\text{Average Inventory}}$$

Business Insight

Flying Off the Shelves

Two companies with a fast inventory turnover relative to their industries are Apple Inc. (AAPL) and Costco Wholesale Corporation (COST):

	Inventory Turnover	Industry	Industry Average
Apple	39.4	Technology	5.4
Costco	11.7	Retail	10.9

Apple turns over its inventory over 39 times per year. There are two primary reasons for this performance. First, Apple does not manufacture its products, but contracts their manufacture to others. Thus, Apple has little inventory related to manufacturing. Second, the Apple Store inventory moves very quickly due to the popularity of its products. Costco is one of the most effective companies within the retail industry for inventory turns. This is because Costco employs a club warehouse model that stocks a minimum variety of highly popular products. Products that don't sell quickly are removed from its offerings.

To illustrate, the inventory turnover for Mooney Company for 20Y6 and 20Y5 is computed as follows:

	20Y6	20Y5
Cost of goods sold	$1,043,000	$820,000
Inventories:		
Beginning of year	$ 283,000	$311,000
End of year	264,000	283,000
Total	$ 547,000	$594,000
Average inventory	$273,500 ($547,000 ÷ 2)	$297,000 ($594,000 ÷ 2)
Inventory turnover	3.8 ($1,043,000 ÷ $273,500)	2.8 ($820,000 ÷ $297,000)

The increase in Mooney's inventory turnover from 2.8 to 3.8 indicates that the management of inventory has improved in 20Y6. The inventory turnover improved because of an increase in the cost of goods sold, which indicates more sales, and a decrease in the average inventories.

What is considered a good inventory turnover varies by type of inventory, companies, and industries. For example, grocery stores have a higher inventory turnover than jewelers or furniture stores. Likewise, within a grocery store, perishable foods have a higher turnover than the soaps and cleansers.

Days' Sales in Inventory The **days' sales in inventory** is computed as follows:

$$\textbf{Days' Sales in Inventory} = \frac{\textbf{Average Inventory}}{\textbf{Average Daily Cost of Goods Sold}}$$

where

$$\textbf{Average Daily Cost of Goods Sold} = \frac{\textbf{Cost of Goods Sold}}{\textbf{365 days}}$$

To illustrate, the days' sales in inventory (rounded to nearest day) for Mooney Company is computed as follows:

	20Y6	20Y5
Average inventory	$273,500 ($547,000 ÷ 2)	$297,000 ($594,000 ÷ 2)
Average daily cost of goods sold	$2,858 ($1,043,000 ÷ 365)	$2,247 ($820,000 ÷ 365)
Days' sales in inventory	96 ($273,500 ÷ $2,858)	132 ($297,000 ÷ $2,247)

The days' sales in inventory is a rough measure of the length of time it takes to purchase, sell, and replace the inventory. Mooney's days' sales in inventory improved from 132 days to 96 days during 20Y6. This is a major improvement in managing inventory.

Days' sales in inventory and inventory turnover are related. Specifically, days' sales in inventory can be computed by dividing 365 days by the inventory turnover. To illustrate, Mooney Company's 20Y6 days' sales in inventory is computed as 96 days (365 days ÷ 3.8).

Nike Connection

In recent financial statements, Nike reported an inventory turnover of 4.0 and days' sales in inventory of 91.8 days.

Objective 4
Describe and illustrate metrics used to analyze solvency.

Component Analysis: Solvency Metrics

Solvency is the ability of a company to pay its debts as they become due over a long period of time, which includes the company's ability to pay interest and loans as they mature. Metrics used to assess solvency include the following:

- Net assets
- Debt ratio
- Ratio of liabilities to stockholders' equity
- Ratio of fixed assets to long-term liabilities
- Times interest earned

Net Assets

A company's **net assets**, which equals the company's stockholders' equity, is computed as follows:

$$\textbf{Net Assets} = \textbf{Total Assets} - \textbf{Total Liabilities}$$

To illustrate, the net assets for Mooney Company for 20Y6 and 20Y5 are as follows:

	20Y6	20Y5
Total assets	$1,139,500	$1,230,500
Total liabilities	(310,000)	(443,000)
Net assets	$ 829,500	$ 787,500

Mooney's net assets increased $42,500 during 20Y6, which provides creditors an additional assurance that liabilities will be paid.

Debt Ratio

The **debt ratio**, sometimes called the debt to assets ratio, is computed as follows:

$$\textbf{Debt Ratio} = \frac{\textbf{Total Liabilities}}{\textbf{Total Assets}}$$

To illustrate, the debt ratio for Mooney Company is computed as follows:

	20Y6	20Y5
Total liabilities	$310,000	$443,000
Total assets	$1,139,500	$1,230,500
Debt ratio	27.2% ($310,000 ÷ $1,139,500)	36.0% ($443,000 ÷$1,230,500)

Mooney's debt ratio decreased from 36.0% to 27.2% during 20Y6. This indicates Mooney decreased the percentage of its assets financed by debt. This provides creditors an additional assurance that liabilities will be paid.

Ratio of Liabilities to Stockholders' Equity

Like the debt ratio, the **ratio of liabilities to stockholders' equity** measures how much of the company is financed by debt and equity. It is computed as follows:

$$\textbf{Ratio of Liabilities to Stockholders' Equity} = \frac{\textbf{Total Liabilities}}{\textbf{Total Stockholders' Equity}}$$

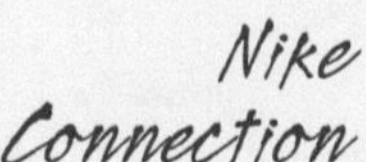

In recent financial statements, Nike reported a debt ratio of 61.9% and a ratio of liabilities to stockholders' equity of 1.6.

To illustrate, the ratio of liabilities to stockholders' equity for Mooney Company is computed as follows:

	20Y6	20Y5
Total liabilities	$310,000	$443,000
Total stockholders' equity	$829,500	$787,500
Ratio of liabilities to stockholders' equity	37.4% ($310,000 ÷ $829,500)	56.3% ($443,000 ÷ $787,500)

Mooney's ratio of liabilities to stockholders' equity decreased from 56.3% to 37.4% during 20Y6. This is an improvement and indicates that Mooney's creditors have an adequate assurance that liabilities will be paid.

Ratio of Fixed Assets to Long-Term Liabilities

The **ratio of fixed assets to long-term liabilities** provides a measure of whether noteholders or bondholders will be paid. Since fixed assets are often pledged as security for long-term notes and bonds, it is computed as follows:

$$\textbf{Ratio of Fixed Assets to Long-Term Liabilities} = \frac{\textbf{Fixed Assets (net)}}{\textbf{Long-Term Liabilities}}$$

To illustrate, the ratio of fixed assets to long-term liabilities for Mooney Company is computed as follows:

	20Y6	20Y5
Fixed assets (net)	$444,500	$470,000
Long-term liabilities	$100,000	$200,000
Ratio of fixed assets to long-term liabilities	4.4 ($444,500 ÷ $100,000)	2.4 ($470,000 ÷ $200,000)

During 20Y6, Mooney's ratio of fixed assets to long-term liabilities increased from 2.4 to 4.4. This increase was due primarily to Mooney paying off one-half of its long-term liabilities in 20Y6 and would be viewed as a positive change by creditors.

Times Interest Earned

Times interest earned, sometimes called the *fixed charge coverage ratio*, measures the risk that interest payments will not be made if earnings decrease. It is computed as as follows:

$$\textbf{Times Interest Earned} = \frac{\textbf{Income Before Income Tax + Interest Expense}}{\textbf{Interest Expense}}$$

Interest expense is paid before income taxes. In other words, interest expense is deducted in determining taxable income and, thus, income tax. For this reason, income *before taxes* is used in computing the times interest earned.

The *higher* the ratio, the more likely interest payments will be paid if earnings decrease. To illustrate, the times interest earned for Mooney Company is computed as follows:

	20Y6	20Y5
Income before income tax	$162,500	$134,600
Add interest expense	6,000	12,000
Amount available to pay interest	$168,500	$146,600
Times interest earned	28.1 ($168,500 ÷ $6,000)	12.2 ($146,600 ÷ $12,000)

The times interest earned ratio improved from 12.2 to 28.1 during 20Y6. This indicates that Mooney Company has sufficient earnings to pay interest expense.

The times interest earned ratio can be adapted for use with dividends on preferred stock. In this case, *times preferred dividends earned* is computed as follows:

$$\textbf{Times Preferred Dividends Earned} = \frac{\textbf{Net Income}}{\textbf{Preferred Dividends}}$$

Business Insight

Liquidity Crunch

Pier 1 Imports (PIR), a retailer specializing in home furnishings and decor, filed for bankruptcy protection. Information on the company's liquidity and solvency for the three years prior to bankruptcy follows:

	Year 3	Year 2	Year 1
Liquidity measures:			
Working capital (in thousands)	$204,062	$316,633	$318,685
Current ratio	1.8	2.3	2.1
Quick ratio	0.3	0.6	0.6
Solvency measures:			
Ratio of liabilities to stockholders' equity	6.3	1.8	1.9
Ratio of fixed assets to long-term liabilities	0.5	0.7	0.7

The data show that the company's liquidity and solvency measures deteriorated in the years prior to the firm's bankruptcy. All three of the company's liquidity measures declined significantly during the three-year period, indicating a growing risk that the company would not be able to repay its current liabilities. The ratio of liabilities to stockholders' equity also increased significantly during this period, indicating that the company might not be able to repay its long-term debts. Finally, the ratio of fixed assets to long-term liabilities began to deteriorate in Year 3, indicating that fewer assets would be available to secure the company's long-term liabilities.

Since dividends are paid after taxes, net income is used in computing the times preferred dividends earned. The *higher* the ratio, the more likely preferred dividend payments will be paid if earnings decrease.

To illustrate, times preferred dividends earned for Mooney Company is computed as follows:

	20Y6	20Y5
Net income	$91,000	$76,500
Preferred dividends	9,000	9,000
Times preferred dividends earned	10.1 ($91,000 ÷ $9,000)	8.5 ($76,500 ÷ $9,000)

During 20Y6, Mooney's times preferred dividends earned increased from 8.5 in 20Y5 to 10.1 in 20Y6. This provides preferred stockholders greater likelihood that preferred dividends will be paid.

Objective 5
Describe and illustrate metrics used to analyze profitability.

Component Analysis: Profitability Metrics

Profitability analysis focuses on the ability of a company to earn profits. This ability is reflected in the company's operating results, as reported on its income statement. The ability to earn profits also depends on the assets the company has available for use in its operations, as reported on its balance sheet. Thus, income statement and balance sheet relationships are often used in evaluating profitability.

Common profitability analyses include the following:

- Asset turnover
- Return on total assets
- Return on stockholders' equity
- Return on common stockholders' equity
- Earnings per share on common stock

- Price-earnings ratio
- Dividends per share
- Dividend yield

Asset Turnover

The **asset turnover** measures how effectively a company uses its long-term operating assets to generate sales. It is computed as follows:

$$\textbf{Asset Turnover} = \frac{\textbf{Sales}}{\textbf{Average Long-Term Operating Assets}}$$

A company's long-term operating assets consist of property, plant, and equipment (net of accumulated depreciation) plus natural resources and intangible assets.

To illustrate, the asset turnover for Mooney Company is computed as follows:

	20Y6	20Y5
Sales	$1,498,000	$1,200,000
Long-term operating assets:		
Beginning of year	$ 520,000[1]	$ 450,000
End of year	494,500[2]	520,000
Total	$1,014,500	$ 970,000
Average long-term operating assets	$507,250 ($1,014,500 ÷ 2)	$485,000 ($970,000 ÷ 2)
Asset turnover	3.0 ($1,498,000 ÷ $507,250)	2.5 ($1,200,000 ÷ $485,000)

1. $470,000 + $50,000
2. $444,500 + $50,000

The asset turnover indicates that Mooney's use of its operating assets has improved in 20Y6. This was primarily due to the increase in sales in 20Y6.

Return on Total Assets

The **return on total assets** measures the profitability of total assets, without considering how the assets are financed. In other words, this rate is not affected by the portion of assets financed by creditors or stockholders. It is computed as follows:

$$\textbf{Return on Total Assets} = \frac{\textbf{Net Income + Interest Expense}}{\textbf{Average Total Assets}}$$

The return on total assets is computed by adding interest expense to net income. By adding interest expense to net income, the effect of whether the assets are financed by creditors (debt) or stockholders (equity) is eliminated. Because net income includes any income earned from long-term investments, the average total assets includes long-term investments as well as the net operating assets.

To illustrate, the return on total assets by Mooney Company is computed as follows:

	20Y6	20Y5
Net income	$ 91,000	$ 76,500
Plus interest expense	6,000	12,000
Total	$ 97,000	$ 88,500
Total assets:		
Beginning of year	$1,230,500	$1,187,500
End of year	1,139,500	1,230,500
Total	$2,370,000	$2,418,000
Average total assets	$1,185,000 ($2,370,000 ÷ 2)	$1,209,000 ($2,418,000 ÷ 2)
Return on total assets	8.2% ($97,000 ÷ $1,185,000)	7.3% ($88,500 ÷ $1,209,000)

The return on total assets improved from 7.3% to 8.2% during 20Y6.

The *return on operating assets* is sometimes computed when there are large amounts of nonoperating income and expense. It is computed as follows:

$$\textbf{Return on Operating Assets} = \frac{\textbf{Operating Income}}{\textbf{Average Operating Assets}}$$

Since Mooney Company does not have a significant amount of nonoperating income and expense, the return on operating assets is not illustrated.

Return on Stockholders' Equity

The **return on stockholders' equity** measures the rate of income earned on the amount invested by the stockholders. It is computed as follows:

$$\textbf{Return on Stockholders' Equity} = \frac{\textbf{Net Income}}{\textbf{Average Total Stockholders' Equity}}$$

To illustrate, the return on stockholders' equity for Mooney Company is computed as follows:

	20Y6	20Y5
Net income	$ 91,000	$ 76,500
Stockholders' equity:		
Beginning of year	$ 787,500	$ 750,000
End of year	829,500	787,500
Total	$1,617,000	$1,537,500
Average stockholders' equity	$808,500 ($1,617,000 ÷ 2)	$768,750 ($1,537,500 ÷ 2)
Return on stockholders' equity	11.3% ($91,000 ÷ $808,500)	10.0% ($76,500 ÷ $768,750)

The return on stockholders' equity improved from 10.0% to 11.3% during 20Y6.

Leverage involves using debt to increase the return on an investment. The return on stockholders' equity is normally higher than the return on total assets. This is because of the effect of leverage.

For Mooney Company, the effect of leverage for 20Y6 is 3.1%, computed as follows:

Return on stockholders' equity	11.3 %
Less return on total assets	(8.2)
Effect of leverage	3.1 %

Exhibit 8 shows the 20Y6 and 20Y5 effects of leverage for Mooney Company.

Exhibit 8
Effects of Leverage

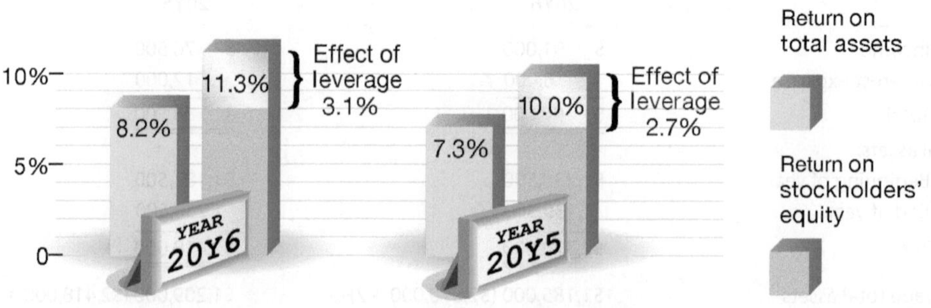

The Accounting Equation

Business Insight

Another term for leverage is "financial gearing." **Exxon Mobil Corporation (XOM)**, a worldwide-integrated energy company, is an example of a company that uses leverage for financial advantage. Exxon had a return on total assets of 4.0% for a recent year, while its return on stockholders' equity was 7.5%. Thus, Exxon is "geared" almost 2:1 by using debt on its balance sheet. Exxon is very profitable; thus, leverage is beneficial. In contrast, **Chesapeake Energy Corporation (CHK)**, an oil and gas exploration company, had return on assets of −2.0% for a recent 12-month period, and return on stockholders' equity of −10.7%. In this case, the approximate 5:1 leverage (−10.7% ÷ −2.0%) creates a financial disadvantage because the company is experiencing losses.

Return on Common Stockholders' Equity

The **return on common stockholders' equity** measures the rate of profits earned on the amount invested by the common stockholders. It is computed as follows:

$$\textbf{Return on Common Stockholders' Equity} = \frac{\textbf{Net Income} - \textbf{Preferred Dividends}}{\textbf{Average Common Stockholders' Equity}}$$

Because preferred stockholders rank ahead of the common stockholders in their claim on earnings, any preferred dividends are subtracted from net income in computing the return on common stockholders' equity.

Assuming $500,000 of common stock was outstanding in 20Y4, Mooney's common stockholders' equity is as follows:

	December 31		
	20Y6	20Y5	20Y4
Common stock, $10 par	$500,000	$500,000	$500,000
Retained earnings	179,500	137,500	100,000
Common stockholders' equity	$679,500	$637,500	$600,000

The retained earnings on December 31, 20Y4, of $100,000 is the same as the retained earnings on January 1, 20Y5, as shown in Mooney's comparative analysis of retained earnings shown in Exhibit 4.

Mooney Company had $150,000 of 6% preferred stock outstanding on December 31, 20Y6 and 20Y5. Thus, preferred dividends of $9,000 ($150,000 × 6%) are deducted from net income.

The return on common stockholders' equity for Mooney Company is computed as follows:

	20Y6	20Y5
Net income	$ 91,000	$ 76,500
Less preferred dividends	(9,000)	(9,000)
Total	$ 82,000	$ 67,500
Common stockholders' equity:		
Beginning of year	$ 637,500	$ 600,000
End of year	679,500	637,500
Total	$1,317,000	$1,237,500
Average common stockholders' equity	$658,500 ($1,317,000 ÷ 2)	$618,750 ($1,237,500 ÷ 2)
Return on common stockholders' equity	12.5% ($82,000 ÷ $658,500)	10.9% ($67,500 ÷ $618,750)

Mooney Company's return on common stockholders' equity improved from 10.9% to 12.5% in 20Y6. This rate differs from the returns earned by Mooney Company on total assets and stockholders' equity as shown as follows:

	20Y6	20Y5
Return on total assets	8.2%	7.3%
Return on stockholders' equity	11.3%	10.0%
Return on common stockholders' equity	12.5%	10.9%

These returns differ because of leverage, as discussed in the preceding section.

Nike Connection

In recent financial statements, Nike reported an asset turnover of 7.8, return on assets of 17.6%, and return on stockholders' equity of 42.7%. Nike has no preferred stock outstanding.

Earnings per Share on Common Stock

Earnings per share (EPS) on common stock measures the share of profits earned per share of common stock outstanding. Generally accepted accounting principles (GAAP) require the reporting of earnings per share on the income statement.[4] As a result, earnings per share (EPS) is often reported in the financial press. It is computed as follows:

$$\textbf{Earnings per Share (EPS) on Common Stock} = \frac{\textbf{Net Income} - \textbf{Preferred Dividends}}{\textbf{Shares of Common Stock Outstanding}}$$

When preferred and common stock are outstanding, preferred dividends are subtracted from net income to determine the income related to the common shares. Mooney Company had $150,000 of 6% preferred stock outstanding on December 31, 20Y6 and 20Y5. Thus, preferred dividends of $9,000 ($150,000 × 6%) are deducted from net income in computing earnings per share on common stock.

To illustrate, the earnings per share (EPS) of common stock for Mooney Company is computed as follows:

	20Y6	20Y5
Net income	$91,000	$76,500
Less preferred dividends	(9,000)	(9,000)
Total	$82,000	$67,500
Shares of common stock outstanding	50,000	50,000
Earnings per share on common stock	$1.64 ($82,000 ÷ 50,000)	$1.35 ($67,500 ÷ 50,000)

As shown above, Mooney's earnings per share (EPS) on common stock improved from $1.35 to $1.64 during 20Y6. Mooney did not issue any additional shares of common stock in 20Y6. If Mooney had issued additional shares in 20Y6, a weighted average of common shares outstanding during the year would have been used.

Mooney Company has a simple capital structure with only common stock and preferred stock outstanding. Many corporations, however, have complex capital structures with various types of equity securities outstanding, such as convertible preferred stock, stock options, and stock warrants. In such cases, the possible effects of such securities on the shares of common stock outstanding are considered in reporting earnings per share. These possible effects are reported separately as *earnings per common share assuming dilution* or *diluted earnings per share*.[5] This topic is described and illustrated in advanced accounting courses and textbooks.

4. FASB, *Accounting Standards Codification*, Section 260.10.
5. Ibid., Section 260.10.

Price-Earnings Ratio

The **price-earnings (P/E) ratio** on common stock measures a company's future earnings prospects. It is often quoted in the financial press and is computed as follows:

$$\text{Price-Earnings (P/E) Ratio} = \frac{\text{Market Price per Share of Common Stock}}{\text{Earnings per Share on Common Stock}}$$

To illustrate, the price-earnings (P/E) ratio for Mooney Company is computed as follows:

	20Y6	20Y5
Market price per share of common stock	$41.00	$27.00
Earnings per share on common stock	$ 1.64	$ 1.35
Price-earnings ratio on common stock	25 ($41 ÷ $1.64)	20 ($27 ÷ $1.35)

The price-earnings ratio improved from 20 to 25 during 20Y6. In other words, a share of common stock of Mooney Company was selling for 20 times earnings per share at the end of 20Y5. At the end of 20Y6, the common stock was selling for 25 times earnings per share. This indicates that the market expects Mooney to experience favorable earnings in the future.

In recent financial statements, Nike reported earnings per share of $2.55, which with a recent stock price of $77.14 yields a price-earnings ratio of 30.3. *Nike Connection*

Dividends per Share

Dividends per share measures the extent to which earnings are being distributed to common shareholders. It is computed as follows:

$$\text{Dividends per Share} = \frac{\text{Common Stock Dividends}}{\text{Shares of Common Stock Outstanding}}$$

To illustrate, the dividends per share for Mooney Company are computed as follows:

	20Y6	20Y5
Common stock dividends	$40,000	$30,000
Shares of common stock outstanding	50,000	50,000
Dividends per share of common stock	$0.80 ($40,000 ÷ 50,000)	$0.60 ($30,000 ÷ 50,000)

The dividends per share of common stock increased from $0.60 to $0.80 during 20Y6.

Dividends per share are often reported with earnings per share. Comparing the two per-share amounts indicates the extent to which earnings are being retained for use in operations. To illustrate, the dividends and earnings per share for Mooney Company are shown in Exhibit 9.

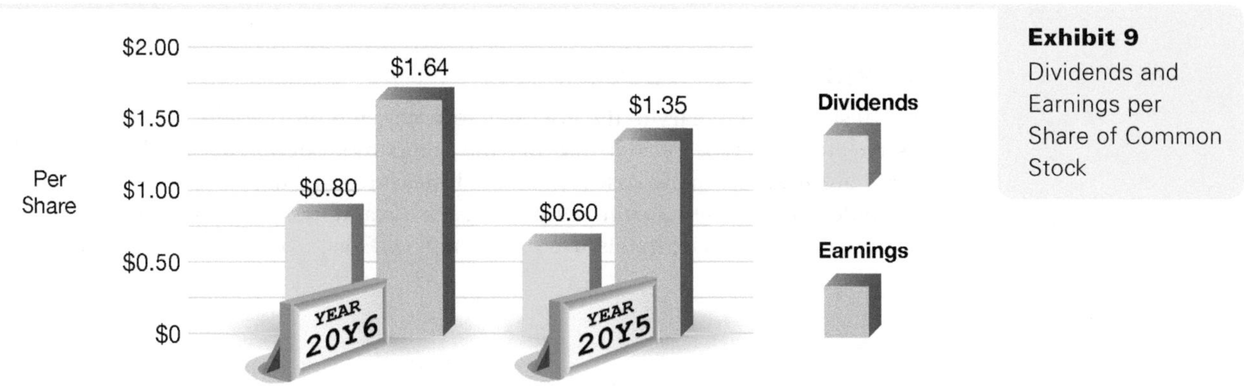

Exhibit 9 Dividends and Earnings per Share of Common Stock

Business Insight

Investing for Yield

Companies that provide attractive dividend yields are often mature companies found in stable industries. Examples of such industries are public utilities and food. Coca-Cola (KO), Procter & Gamble (PG), Kellogg's (K), Consolidated Edison (ED), Southern Company (SO), and General Mills (GIS) all have attractive dividend yields in excess of 3%. Procter & Gamble has had 63 consecutive years of dividend payouts, and Kellogg's has not reduced its dividend for 60 years. The stability of the food industry has allowed these companies to maintain dividends for many years. Growth companies, such as Alphabet (GOOG) or Facebook (FB), do not pay dividends, because they use their cash to grow the business. Investors in such growth companies expect to make their return from stock price appreciation, rather than dividends. Mark Cuban, billionaire, Shark Tank® investor, and owner of the Dallas Mavericks, stated, "I believe non-dividend stocks aren't much more than baseball cards. They are worth what you can convince someone to pay for it."

Quote source: Tim Parker, "The Top Ten Dividend Quotes," *Dividend.com*, August 29, 2012.

Dividend Yield

The **dividend yield** on common stock measures the rate of return to common stockholders from cash dividends. It is of special interest to investors, whose objective is to earn revenue (dividends) from their investment. It is computed as follows:

$$\textbf{Dividend Yield} = \frac{\textbf{Dividends per Share of Common Stock}}{\textbf{Market Price per Share of Common Stock}}$$

To illustrate, the dividend yield for Mooney Company is computed as follows:

	20Y6	20Y5
Dividends per share of common stock	$ 0.80	$ 0.60
Market price per share of common stock	$41.00	$27.00
Dividend yield on common stock	2.0% ($0.80 ÷ $41)	2.2% ($0.60 ÷ $27)

The dividend yield declined slightly from 2.2% to 2.0% in 20Y6. This decline was primarily due to the increase in the market price of Mooney's common stock.

In recent years, Nike paid dividends of $0.86 per share with a dividend yield of 1.1%.

Summary of Metrics

Exhibit 10 shows a summary of the liquidity, solvency, and profitability measures discussed in this chapter. The type of industry and the company's operations usually affect which measures are used. In many cases, additional measures are used for a specific industry. For example, airlines use *revenue per passenger mile* and *cost per available seat* as profitability measures. Likewise, hotels use *occupancy rates* as a profitability measure.

Exhibit 10 Summary of Metrics

	Method of Computation	
Liquidity and solvency measures:		
Working Capital	Current Assets − Current Liabilities	To indicate the ability to meet currently maturing obligations
Current Ratio	$\frac{\text{Current Assets}}{\text{Current Liabilities}}$	
Quick Ratio	$\frac{\text{Quick Assets}}{\text{Current Liabilities}}$	To indicate the ability to instantly pay debt
Accounts Receivable Turnover	$\frac{\text{Sales}}{\text{Average Accounts Receivable}}$	To assess the efficiency in collecting receivables and in the management of credit
Days' Sales in Receivables	$\frac{\text{Average Accounts Receivable}}{\text{Average Daily Sales}}$	
Inventory Turnover	$\frac{\text{Cost of Goods Sold}}{\text{Average Inventory}}$	To assess the efficiency in the management of inventory
Days' Sales in Inventory	$\frac{\text{Average Inventory}}{\text{Average Daily Cost of Goods Sold}}$	
Net Assets	Total Assets − Total Liabilities	To indicate the likelihood that creditors will be paid
Debt Ratio	$\frac{\text{Total Liabilities}}{\text{Total Assets}}$	
Ratio of Liabilities to Stockholders' Equity	$\frac{\text{Total Liabilities}}{\text{Total Stockholders' Equity}}$	
Ratio of Fixed Assets to Long-Term Liabilities	$\frac{\text{Fixed Assets (net)}}{\text{Long-Term Liabilities}}$	To indicate the likelihood that long-term creditors will be paid
Times Interest Earned	$\frac{\text{Income Before Income Tax + Interest Expense}}{\text{Interest Expense}}$	To assess the risk to creditors that interest will be paid if earnings decrease
Profitability measures:		
Asset Turnover	$\frac{\text{Sales}}{\text{Average Long-Term Operating Assets}}$	To assess the effectiveness in the use of operating assets
Return on Total Assets	$\frac{\text{Net Income + Interest Expense}}{\text{Average Total Assets}}$	To assess the profitability of the assets
Return on Stockholders' Equity	$\frac{\text{Net Income}}{\text{Average Total Stockholders' Equity}}$	To assess the profitability of the investment by stockholders
Return on Common Stockholders' Equity	$\frac{\text{Net Income − Preferred Dividends}}{\text{Average Common Stockholders' Equity}}$	To assess the profitability of the investment by common stockholders
Earnings per Share on Common Stock	$\frac{\text{Net Income − Preferred Dividends}}{\text{Shares of Common Stock Outstanding}}$	
Price-Earnings Ratio	$\frac{\text{Market Price per Share of Common Stock}}{\text{Earnings per Share on Common Stock}}$	To indicate future earnings prospects, based on the relationship between market value of common stock and earnings
Dividends per Share	$\frac{\text{Common Stock Dividends}}{\text{Shares of Common Stock Outstanding}}$	To indicate the extent to which earnings are being distributed to common stockholders
Dividend Yield	$\frac{\text{Dividends per Share of Common Stock}}{\text{Market Price per Share of Common Stock}}$	To indicate the rate of return to common stockholders in terms of dividends

Integrity, Objectivity, and Ethics in Business

Questionable Accounting?

A recent survey by *CFO* magazine reported that 47% of chief financial officers have been pressured by the chief executive officer to use questionable accounting. In addition, only 38% of those surveyed feel less pressure to use aggressive accounting today than in years past, while 20% believe there is more pressure. Perhaps more troublesome is the chief financial officers' confidence in the quality of financial information, with only 27% being "very confident" in the quality of financial information presented by public companies.

Source: D. Durfee, "It's Better (and Worse) Than You Think," *CFO*, May 3, 2004.

The analytical measures shown in Exhibit 10 are a useful starting point for analyzing a company's liquidity, solvency, and profitability. However, they are not a substitute for sound judgment. For example, the general economic and business environment should always be considered in analyzing a company's future prospects. In addition, any trends and interrelationships among the measures should be carefully studied.

Objective 6
Describe the corporate annual reports.

Corporate Annual Reports

Public corporations issue annual reports summarizing their operating activities for the past year and plans for the future. Such annual reports include the financial statements and the accompanying notes. In addition, annual reports normally include the following sections:

- Management's Discussion and Analysis
- Report on Internal Control
- Report on Fairness of the Financial Statements

Management's Discussion and Analysis

Management's Discussion and Analysis (MD&A) is required in annual reports filed with the Securities and Exchange Commission. It includes management's analysis of current operations and its plans for the future. Typical items included in the MD&A are as follows:

- Management's analysis and explanations of any significant changes between the current and prior years' financial statements.
- Important accounting principles or policies that could affect interpretation of the financial statements, including the effect of changes in accounting principles or the adoption of new accounting principles.
- Management's assessment of the company's liquidity and the availability of capital to the company.
- Significant risk exposures that might affect the company.
- Any "off-balance-sheet" arrangements such as leases not included directly in the financial statements. Such arrangements are discussed in advanced accounting courses and textbooks.

Investing Strategies

Business Insight

How do people make investment decisions? Investment decisions, like any major purchase, must meet the needs of the buyer. For example, if you have a family of five and are thinking about buying a new car, you probably wouldn't buy a two-seat sports car. It just wouldn't meet your objectives or fit your lifestyle. Alternatively, if you are a young single person, a minivan might not meet your immediate needs. Investors buy stocks in the same way, buying stocks that match their investment style and their financial needs. Two common approaches are value and growth investing.

Value Investing

Value investors search for undervalued stocks. That is, the investor tries to find companies whose value is not reflected in their stock price. These are typically quiet, "boring" companies with excellent financial performance that are temporarily out of favor in the stock market. This investment approach assumes that the stock's price will eventually rise to match the company's value. The most successful investor of all time, Warren Buffett, uses this approach almost exclusively. Naturally, the key to successful value investing is to accurately determine a stock's value. This will often include analyzing a company's financial ratios, as discussed in this chapter, compared to target ratios and industry norms. For example, the stock of Deckers Outdoor Corporation (DECK), the maker of TEVA™ sport sandals, was selling for $27.43 several years ago, a value relative to its earnings per share of $2.58. Over the next two years, the company's stock price increased more than 500%, reaching $166.50.

Tada Images/ShutterStock.com

Growth Investing

Growth investors identify companies that have the potential to grow sales and earnings through new products, markets, or opportunities. Growth companies are often newer companies that are still unproven but that possess unique technologies or capabilities. The strategy is to purchase these companies before their potential becomes obvious, hoping to profit from relatively large increases in the company's stock price. This approach, however, carries the risk that the growth may not occur. Growth investors use many of the ratios discussed in this chapter to identify high-potential growth companies. For example, lululemon athletica inc. (LULU), a leader in the athleisure industry, reported earnings per share of $0.83, when the company's stock price was trading near $15 per share. In the following decade, the company's sales increased by over 770%, earnings increased to $4.95 per share, and the company's stock price rose above $240 per share.

Report on Internal Control

The Sarbanes-Oxley Act requires management to prepare a report on internal control. The report states management's responsibility for establishing and maintaining internal control. In addition, management's assessment of the effectiveness of internal controls over financial reporting is included in the report.

Sarbanes-Oxley also requires a public accounting firm to verify management's conclusions on internal control. Thus, two reports on internal control, one by management and one by a public accounting firm, are included in the annual report. In some situations, these may be combined into a single report on internal control.

Audit Report

All publicly held corporations are required to have an independent audit (examination) of their financial statements. The Certified Public Accounting (CPA) firm that conducts the audit renders an opinion, called the *Report of Independent Registered Public Accounting Firm*, on the fairness of the statements.

An opinion stating that the financial statements present fairly the financial position, results of operations, and cash flows of the company is said to be an *unqualified opinion*, sometimes called a *clean opinion*. Any report other than an unqualified opinion raises a "red flag" for financial statement users and requires further investigation as to its cause.

Nike Connection

In recent financial statements, Nike received a clean audit opinion from its auditors, PricewaterhouseCoopers.

Key Points

1. Describe the usefulness of financial statements and methods of analysis.

General-purpose financial statements are useful in analyzing and interpreting a company's financial condition and performance, including its liquidity, solvency, and profitability. Methods of analysis include global and component analysis.

2. Describe basic financial statement analytical methods.

Global analysis computes changes in amounts, percentage of amounts, and percentage changes in amounts. The analysis of percentage increases and decreases in related items in comparative financial statements is called horizontal analysis. The analysis of percentages of component parts to the total in a single statement is called vertical analysis. Financial statements in which all amounts are expressed in percentages for purposes of analysis are called common-sized statements.

3. Describe and illustrate metrics used to analyze liquidity.

Liquidity is the ability to convert assets to cash. Liquidity metrics include working capital, current ratio, quick ratio, accounts receivable turnover, days' sales in receivables, inventory turnover, and days' sales in inventory.

4. Describe and illustrate metrics used to analyze solvency.

Solvency is the ability of a company to pay its debts as they become due over a long period of time. Solvency metrics include debt ratio, ratio of liabilities to stockholders' equity, ratio of fixed assets to long-term liabilities, and times interest earned.

5. Describe and illustrate metrics used to analyze profitability.

Profitability is the ability of a company to earn income (profits). Profitability metrics include asset turnover, return on total assets, return on stockholders' equity, earnings per share on common stock, price-earnings ratio, dividends per share, and dividend yield.

6. Describe the contents of corporate annual reports.

Corporate annual reports normally include financial statements and the accompanying notes, Management's Discussion and Analysis, the Report on Internal Control, and the Audit Report.

Key Terms

Accounts receivable turnover (469)
Asset turnover (475)
Common-sized statement (465)
Component analysis (461)
Current position analysis (467)
Current ratio (467)
Days' sales in inventory (471)
Days' sales in receivables (469)
Debt ratio (472)
Dividend yield (480)
Dividends per share (479)
Earnings per share (EPS) on common stock (478)
General-purpose financial statements (460)
Global analysis (461)
Horizontal analysis (461)
Inventory turnover (470)
Liquidity (460)
Management's Discussion and Analysis (MD&A) (482)
Net assets (472)
Price-earnings (P/E) ratio (479)
Profitability (461)
Quick assets (468)
Quick ratio (468)
Ratio of fixed assets to long-term liabilities (473)
Ratio of liabilities to stockholders' equity (472)
Return on common stockholders' equity (477)
Return on stockholders' equity (476)
Return on total assets (475)
Solvency (460)
Times interest earned (473)
Vertical analysis (464)
Working capital (467)

Illustrative Problem

Esmeralda Paint Co.'s comparative financial statements for the years ending December 31, 20Y4 and 20Y3, are as follows. The market price of Esmeralda Paint Co.'s common stock was $30 on December 31, 20Y3, and $25 on December 31, 20Y4.

ESMERALDA PAINT CO.
Comparative Income Statement
For the Years Ended December 31, 20Y4 and 20Y3

	20Y4	20Y3
Sales	$ 5,000,000	$3,200,000
Cost of goods sold	(3,400,000)	(2,080,000)
Gross profit	$ 1,600,000	$1,120,000
Selling expenses	$ (650,000)	$ (464,000)
Administrative expenses	(325,000)	(224,000)
Total operating expenses	$ (975,000)	$ (688,000)
Operating income	$ 625,000	$ 432,000
Other revenue and expense:		
Other revenue	25,000	19,200
Other expenses (interest)	(105,000)	(64,000)
Income before income tax	$ 545,000	$ 387,200
Income tax expense	(300,000)	(176,000)
Net income	$ 245,000	$ 211,200

ESMERALDA PAINT CO.
Comparative Statement of Stockholders' Equity
For the Years Ended December 31, 20Y4 and 20Y3

	20Y4			20Y3		
	Preferred Stock	**Common Stock**	**Retained Earnings**	**Preferred Stock**	**Common Stock**	**Retained Earnings**
Balances, Jan. 1	$500,000	$500,000	$723,000	$500,000	$500,000	$581,800
Net income			245,000			211,200
Dividends:						
Preferred stock			(40,000)			(40,000)
Common stock			(45,000)			(30,000)
Balances, Dec. 31	$500,000	$500,000	$883,000	$500,000	$500,000	$723,000

ESMERALDA PAINT CO.
Comparative Balance Sheet
December 31, 20Y4 and 20Y3

	Dec. 31, 20Y4	Dec. 31, 20Y3
Assets		
Current assets:		
Cash	$ 175,000	$ 125,000
Temporary investments	150,000	50,000
Accounts receivable (net)	425,000	325,000
Inventories	720,000	480,000
Prepaid expenses	30,000	20,000
Total current assets	$1,500,000	$1,000,000
Long-term investments	250,000	225,000
Property, plant, and equipment (net)	2,093,000	1,948,000
Total assets	$3,843,000	$3,173,000
Liabilities		
Current liabilities	$ 750,000	$ 650,000
Long-term liabilities:		
Mortgage note payable, 10%, due in eight years	$ 410,000	—
Bonds payable, 8%, due in 15 years	800,000	$ 800,000
Total long-term liabilities	$1,210,000	$ 800,000
Total liabilities	$1,960,000	$1,450,000
Stockholders' Equity		
Preferred 8% stock, $100 par	$ 500,000	$ 500,000
Common stock, $10 par	500,000	500,000
Retained earnings	883,000	723,000
Total stockholders' equity	$1,883,000	$1,723,000
Total liabilities and stockholders' equity	$3,843,000	$3,173,000

Instructions

Compute the following metrics for 20Y4:

1. Working capital
2. Current ratio
3. Quick ratio
4. Accounts receivable turnover
5. Days' sales in receivables
6. Inventory turnover
7. Days' sales in inventory
8. Debt ratio
9. Ratio of liabilities to stockholders' equity
10. Ratio of fixed assets to long-term liabilities
11. Times interest earned
12. Times preferred dividends earned
13. Asset turnover
14. Return on total assets
15. Return on stockholders' equity
16. Return on common stockholders' equity
17. Earnings per share on common stock
18. Price-earnings ratio
19. Dividends per share
20. Dividend yield

Solution

(Metrics are rounded to the nearest single digit after the decimal point.)

1. Working capital: $750,000
   $1,500,000 − $750,000
2. Current ratio: 2.0
   $1,500,000 ÷ $750,000
3. Quick ratio: 1.0
   $750,000 ÷ $750,000
4. Accounts receivable turnover: 13.3
   $5,000,000 ÷ [($425,000 + $325,000) ÷ 2]
5. Days' sales in receivables: 27.4 days
   $5,000,000 ÷ 365 days = $13,699
   $375,000 ÷ $13,699
6. Inventory turnover: 5.7
   $3,400,000 ÷ [($720,000 + $480,000) ÷ 2]
7. Days' sales in inventory: 64.4 days
   $3,400,000 ÷ 365 days = $9,315
   $600,000 ÷ $9,315
8. Debt ratio: 51.0%
   $1,960,000 ÷ $3,843,000
9. Ratio of liabilities to stockholders' equity: 1.0
   $1,960,000 ÷ $1,883,000
10. Ratio of fixed assets to long-term liabilities: 1.7
    $2,093,000 ÷ $1,210,000
11. Times interest earned: 6.2
    ($545,000 + $105,000) ÷ $105,000
12. Times preferred dividends earned: 6.1
    $245,000 ÷ $40,000
13. Asset turnover: 2.5
    ($2,093,000 + $1,948,000) ÷ 2 = $2,020,500
    $5,000,000 ÷ $2,020,500
14. Return on total assets: 10.0%
    ($245,000 + $105,000) ÷ [($3,843,000 + $3,173,000) ÷ 2]
15. Return on stockholders' equity: 13.6%
    $245,000 ÷ [($1,883,000 + $1,723,000) ÷ 2]
16. Return on common stockholders' equity: 15.7%
    ($245,000 − $40,000) ÷ [($1,383,000 + $1,223,000) ÷ 2]
17. Earnings per share on common stock: $4.10
    ($245,000 − $40,000) ÷ 50,000 shares
18. Price-earnings ratio: 6.1
    $25 ÷ $4.10
19. Dividends per share: $0.90
    $45,000 ÷ 50,000 shares
20. Dividend yield: 3.6%
    $0.90 ÷ $25

Self-Examination Questions

(Answers appear at the end of the chapter.)

1. What type of analysis is indicated by the following?

	Amount	Percent
Current assets	$100,000	20%
Property, plant, and equipment	400,000	80
Total assets	$500,000	100%

A. Vertical analysis
B. Horizontal analysis
C. Profitability analysis
D. Contribution margin analysis

2. Which of the following measures indicates the ability of a firm to pay its current liabilities?
A. Working capital
B. Current ratio
C. Quick ratio
D. All of the above

3. The ratio determined by dividing total current assets by total current liabilities is:
A. The current ratio
B. The working capital ratio
C. The bankers' ratio
D. All of the above

4. The ratio of the quick assets to current liabilities, which indicates the "instant" debt-paying ability of a firm, is the:
A. Current ratio
B. Working capital ratio
C. Quick ratio
D. Bankers' ratio

5. A measure useful in evaluating efficiency in the management of inventories is the:
A. Working capital ratio
B. Quick ratio
C. Days' sales in inventory
D. Ratio of fixed assets to long-term liabilities

Class Discussion Questions

1. What is the difference between horizontal and vertical analysis of financial statements?

2. What is the advantage of using comparative statements for financial analysis rather than statements for a single date or period?

3. The current year's amount of net income (after income tax) is 9% larger than that of the preceding year. Does this indicate an improved operating performance? Discuss.

4. How would you respond to a horizontal analysis that showed an expense increasing by over 70%?

5. How would the current and quick ratios of a service business compare?

6. For Belzer Corporation, the working capital at the end of the current year is $24,000 more than the working capital at the end of the preceding year, reported as follows:

	Current Year	Preceding Year
Current assets:		
Cash, temporary investments, and receivables	$ 81,000	$ 72,000
Inventories	171,000	126,000
Total current assets	$252,000	$198,000
Current liabilities	(90,000)	(60,000)
Working capital	$162,000	$138,000

Has the current position improved? Explain.

7. Why would the accounts receivable turnover ratio be different between Walmart (WMT) and Procter & Gamble (PG)?

8. A company that grants terms of n/30 on all sales has a yearly accounts receivable turnover, based on monthly averages, of 9. Is this a satisfactory turnover? Discuss.

9. a. Why is it advantageous to have a high inventory turnover?
   b. Is it possible for the inventory turnover to be too high? Discuss.
   c. Is it possible to have a high inventory turnover and a high days' sales in inventory? Discuss.

10. What do the following data taken from a comparative balance sheet indicate about the company's ability to borrow additional funds on a long-term basis in the current year as compared to the preceding year?

	Current Year	Preceding Year
Fixed assets (net)	$1,800,000	$1,260,000
Total long-term liabilities	450,000	350,000

11. a. How does the return on total assets differ from the return on stockholders' equity?
    b. Which return is normally higher? Explain.

12. a. Why is the return on stockholders' equity by a thriving business ordinarily higher than the return on total assets?
    b. Should the return on common stockholders' equity normally be higher or lower than the return on total stockholders' equity? Explain.

13. The net income (after income tax) of Fleming Inc. was $4.80 per common share in the latest year and $7.50 per common share for the preceding year. At the beginning of the latest year, the number of shares outstanding was doubled by a stock split. There were no other changes in the amount of stock outstanding. What were the earnings per share in the preceding year, adjusted for comparison with the latest year?

14. The price-earnings ratio for the common stock of In-Work Company was 15 at December 31, the end of the current fiscal year. What does the ratio indicate about the selling price of the common stock in relation to current earnings?

15. Why would the dividend yield differ significantly from the return on common stockholders' equity?

16. Favorable business conditions may bring about certain seemingly unfavorable ratios, and unfavorable business operations may result in apparently favorable ratios. For example, Shaddox Company increased its sales and net income substantially for the current year, yet the current ratio at the end of the year is lower than at the beginning of the year. Discuss some possible causes of the apparent weakening of the current position, while sales and net income have increased substantially.

17. Describe two reports provided by independent auditors in the annual report to shareholders.

Exercises

E12-1 Vertical analysis of income statement

Obj. 2

✔ a. 20Y8 net income: $42,750; 9.5% of sales

Revenue and expense data for Tribal Technologies Co. are as follows:

	20Y8	20Y7
Sales	$450,000	$362,500
Cost of goods sold	279,000	217,500
Selling expenses	58,500	58,000
Administrative expenses	31,500	32,625
Income tax expense	38,250	29,000

a. Prepare an income statement in comparative form, stating each item for both 20Y8 and 20Y7 as a percent of sales. Round to one decimal place.

b. Comment on the significant changes disclosed by the comparative income statement.

Obj. 2

SHOW ME HOW

✔ a. Year 2 income from continuing operations, 13.8% of revenues

E12-2 Vertical analysis of income statement

The following comparative income statement (in thousands of dollars) for two recent years was adapted from the annual report of International Speedway Corporation (ISCA), owner and operator of several major motor speedways, such as the Daytona International Speedway and the Talledega Superspeedway.

	Year 2	Year 1
Revenues:		
Admissions	$ 109,602	$ 121,505
Event-related revenue	508,505	491,664
Food, beverage, and merchandise	35,669	41,293
Other operating revenue	21,260	16,971
Total revenue	$ 675,036	$ 671,433
Expenses and other:		
Event-related expenses	$(145,093)	$(134,136)
NASCAR event management fees	(185,200)	(178,403)
Food, beverage, and merchandise	(27,278)	(29,593)
General and administrative	(224,303)	(233,145)
Total expenses	$(581,874)	$(575,277)
Income from continuing operations	$ 93,162	$ 96,156

a. Prepare a comparative income statement for Years 1 and 2 in vertical form, stating each item as a percent of revenues. Round to one decimal place.

b. Comment on the significant changes.

Obj. 2

SHOW ME HOW

EXCEL ONLINE

E12-3 Common-sized income statement

Revenue and expense data for the current calendar year for Dawg Electronics Company and for the electronics industry are as follows. Dawg Electronics Company data are expressed in dollars. The electronics industry averages are expressed in percentages.

	Dawg Electronics Company	Electronics Industry Average
Sales	$ 3,750,000	100.0%
Cost of goods sold	(2,062,500)	(61.0)
Gross profit	$ 1,687,500	39.0%
Selling expenses	$(1,125,000)	(23.0)%
Administrative expenses	(262,500)	(10.0)
Total operating expenses	$(1,387,500)	(33.0)%
Operating income	$ 300,000	6.0%
Other revenue and expense:		
Other revenue	15,000	3.0
Other expense	(3,750)	(1.0)
Income before income tax	$ 311,250	8.0%
Income tax expense	(93,750)	(2.5)
Net income	$ 217,500	5.5%

a. Prepare a common-sized income statement comparing the results of operations for Dawg Electronics Company with the industry average.

b. Comment on significant relationships revealed by the comparisons.

E12-4 Vertical analysis of balance sheet

Obj. 2

✔ Retained earnings, Dec. 31, 20Y2, 59.3%

Balance sheet data for a company for the years ended December 31, 20Y2 and 20Y1, are as follows:

	20Y2	20Y1
Current assets	752,000	602,000
Property, plant, and equipment	6,248,000	5,397,000
Intangible assets	1,000,000	1,001,000
Current liabilities	504,000	427,000
Long-term liabilities	1,504,000	1,197,000
Common stock	1,248,000	1,253,000
Retained earnings	4,744,000	4,123,000

Prepare a comparative balance sheet for 20Y2 and 20Y1, stating each asset as a percent of total assets and each liability and stockholders' equity item as a percent of the total liabilities and stockholders' equity. Round to one decimal place.

E12-5 Horizontal analysis of the income statement

Obj. 2

SHOW ME HOW

EXCEL ONLINE

✔ Net income increase, 36.4%

Income statement data for Cascade Images Inc. for the years ended December 31, 20Y5 and 20Y4, are as follows:

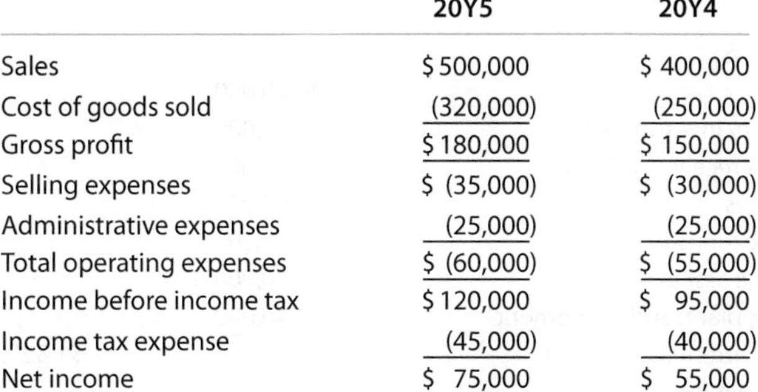

	20Y5	20Y4
Sales	$ 500,000	$ 400,000
Cost of goods sold	(320,000)	(250,000)
Gross profit	$ 180,000	$ 150,000
Selling expenses	$ (35,000)	$ (30,000)
Administrative expenses	(25,000)	(25,000)
Total operating expenses	$ (60,000)	$ (55,000)
Income before income tax	$ 120,000	$ 95,000
Income tax expense	(45,000)	(40,000)
Net income	$ 75,000	$ 55,000

a. Prepare a comparative income statement with horizontal analysis, indicating the increase (decrease) for 20Y5 when compared with 20Y4. Round to one decimal place.

b. What conclusions can be drawn from the horizontal analysis?

E12-6 Current position analysis

Obj. 3

SHOW ME HOW

EXCEL ONLINE

✔ 20Y9 working capital, $525,000

The following data were taken from the comparative balance sheet of Icon Living, Inc., for the years ended December 31, 20Y9 and December 31, 20Y8:

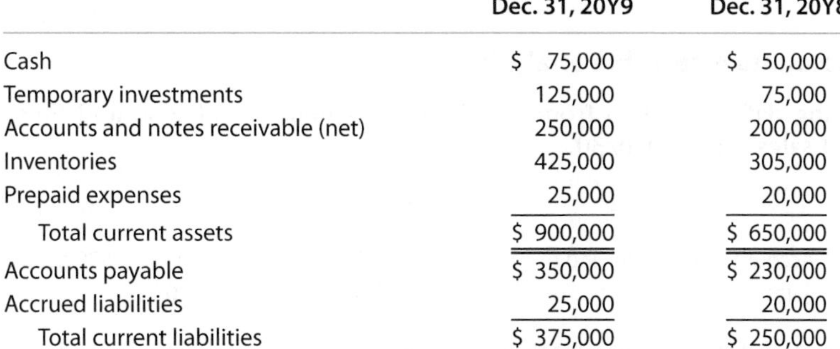

	Dec. 31, 20Y9	Dec. 31, 20Y8
Cash	$ 75,000	$ 50,000
Temporary investments	125,000	75,000
Accounts and notes receivable (net)	250,000	200,000
Inventories	425,000	305,000
Prepaid expenses	25,000	20,000
Total current assets	$ 900,000	$ 650,000
Accounts payable	$ 350,000	$ 230,000
Accrued liabilities	25,000	20,000
Total current liabilities	$ 375,000	$ 250,000

a. Determine for each year (1) the working capital, (2) the current ratio, and (3) the quick ratio.

b. What conclusions can be drawn from these data?

Obj. 3

✔ a. (1) Year 1 current ratio, 1.0

E12-7 Current position analysis

PepsiCo, Inc. (PEP), the parent company of Frito-Lay™ snack foods and Pepsi beverages, had the following current assets and current liabilities at the end of two recent years:

	Year 2 (in millions)	Year 1 (in millions)
Cash and cash equivalents	$5,509	$ 8,721
Short-term investments, at cost	229	2,269
Accounts and notes receivable, net	7,822	7,142
Inventories	3,338	3,128
Prepaid expenses and other current assets	747	633
Short-term obligations (liabilities)	2,920	4,026
Accounts payable and other current liabilities	17,541	18,112

a. Determine the (1) current ratio and (2) quick ratio for both years. Round to one decimal place.

b. What conclusions can you draw from these data?

Obj. 3

E12-8 Current position analysis

The bond indenture for the 10-year, 8% debenture bonds, dated January 2, 20Y8, required working capital of $200,000, a current ratio of 2.0, and a quick ratio of 1.0 at the end of each calendar year until the bonds mature. At December 31, 20Y9, the three measures were computed as follows:

1. Current assets:		
Cash	$120,000	
Temporary investments	150,000	
Accounts receivable (net)	240,000	
Inventories	190,000	
Prepaid expenses	50,000	
Intangible assets	30,000	
Property, plant, and equipment	540,000	
Total current assets (net)		$1,320,000
Current liabilities:		
Accounts and short-term notes payable	$440,000	
Accrued liabilities	160,000	
Total current liabilities		(600,000)
Working capital		$ 720,000
2. Current ratio	2.2	$1,320,000 ÷ $600,000
3. Quick ratio	1.5	$660,000 ÷ $440,000

a. List the errors in the determination of the three measures of current position analysis.

b. Is the company satisfying the terms of the bond indenture?

Obj. 3

✔ a. Accounts receivable turnover, Year 3, 6.4

E12-9 Accounts receivable analysis

The following data are taken from the financial statements of Rise and Shine Company. Terms of all sales are 2/10, n/30.

	Year 3	Year 2	Year 1
Accounts receivable, end of year	$ 450,000	$ 375,000	$300,000
Sales	2,640,000	1,957,500	

a. For Years 2 and 3, determine (1) the accounts receivable turnover and (2) the days' sales in receivables. Round to nearest dollar and one decimal place.

b. What conclusions can be drawn from these data concerning accounts receivable and credit policies?

E12-10 Accounts receivable analysis

Obj. 3

Bassett Stores Company and Fox Stores Inc. are large retail department stores. Both companies offer credit to their customers through their own credit card operations. Information from the financial statements for both companies for two recent years is as follows (all numbers are in millions):

	Bassett	Fox
Merchandise sales	$726,000	$2,470,000
Credit card receivables—beginning	75,000	350,000
Credit card receviables—ending	90,000	410,000

a. Determine (1) the accounts receivable turnover and (2) the days' sales in receivables for both companies. Round to nearest dollar and one decimal place.

b. Compare the two companies with regard to their credit card policies.

E12-11 Inventory analysis

Obj. 3

✔ a. Inventory turnover, current year, 12.0

The following data were extracted from the income statement of Brecca Systems Inc.:

	Current Year	Preceding Year
Sales	$9,700,000	$7,175,000
Beginning inventories	420,000	400,000
Cost of goods sold	5,820,000	4,305,000
Ending inventories	550,000	420,000

a. Determine for each year (1) the inventory turnover and (2) the days' sales in inventory. Round to nearest dollar and one decimal place.

b. What conclusions can be drawn from these data concerning the inventories?

E12-12 Inventory analysis

Obj. 3

✔ a. Costco inventory turnover, 11.8

Costco Wholesale Corporation (COST) and Walmart Stores Inc. (WMT) compete against each other in general merchandise retailing, gas stations, pharmacies, and optical centers. The following is selected financial information for both companies from a recent year's financial statements (in millions):

	Costco	Walmart
Sales	$152,703	$523,964
Cost of goods sold	132,886	394,605
Inventory, beginning of period	11,040	44,269
Inventory, end of period	11,395	44,435

a. Determine for both companies (1) the inventory turnover and (2) the days' sales in inventory. Round to one decimal place.

b. Compare and interpret the inventory metrics computed in (a).

Obj. 4

✔ a. Ratio of liabilities to stockholders' equity, Dec. 31, 20Y6, 0.6

E12-13 Ratio of liabilities to stockholders' equity and times interest earned

The following data were taken from the financial statements of Starr Construction Inc. for December 31, 20Y6 and 20Y5:

	Dec. 31, 20Y6	Dec. 31, 20Y5
Accounts payable and other liabilities	$ 1,700,000	$2,325,000
Current maturities of bonds payable	500,000	500,000
Serial bonds payable, 8%, issued 2008, due in five years	5,000,000	5,500,000
Common stock, $5 par value	250,000	250,000
Paid-in capital in excess of par	1,500,000	1,500,000
Retained earnings	10,250,000	7,500,000

The income before income tax was $2,816,000 and $2,640,000 for the years 20Y6 and 20Y5, respectively.

a. Determine the ratio of liabilities to stockholders' equity at the end of each year.

b. Determine the times (bond) interest earned during the year for both years.

c. What conclusions can be drawn from these data as to the company's ability to meet its currently maturing debts?

Obj. 4

✔ a. Hasbro, 66.4%

E12-14 Debt ratio, ratio of liabilities to stockholders' equity, and times interest earned

Hasbro (HAS) and Mattel, Inc. (MAT), are the two largest toy companies in North America. Liability and stockholders' equity data from recent balance sheets are shown for each company as follows (in millions):

	Hasbro	Mattel
Current liabilities	$ 1,257	$ 1,277
Long-term debt	4,663	3,557
Total liabilities	$ 5,920	$ 4,834
Total stockholders' equity	2,996	492
Total liabilities and stockholders' equity	$ 8,916	$ 5,326

The operating income and interest expense from the income statement for both companies were as follows (in millions):

	Hasbro	Mattel
Income (loss) from operations before tax	$594	$(158)
Interest expense	102	201

a. Determine the debt ratio for both companies. Round to one decimal place.

b. Determine the ratio of liabilities to stockholders' equity for both companies. Round to one decimal place.

c. Determine the times interest earned for both companies. Round to one decimal place.

d. Interpret the ratio differences between the two companies.

E12-15 Debt ratio, ratio of liabilities to stockholders' equity, and ratio of fixed assets to long-term liabilities

Obj. 4

✔ a. Hershey, 78.6%

Recent balance sheet information for two companies in the snack food industry, The Hershey Company (HSY) and Mondelez International, Inc. (MDLZ), is as follows (in millions of dollars):

	Hershey	Mondelez
Net property, plant, and equipment	$2,153	$ 8,733
Liabilities:		
Current liabilities	$2,009	$15,322
Long-term debt	3,531	14,207
Other long-term liabilities	856	7,669
Total liabilities	$6,396	$37,198
Stockholders' equity	1,745	27,351
Total liabilities and stockholders' equity	$8,141	$64,549

a. Determine the debt ratio for both companies. Round to one decimal place.

b. Determine the ratio of liabilities to stockholders' equity for both companies. Round to one decimal place.

c. Determine the ratio of fixed assets to long-term liabilities for both companies. Round to two decimal places.

d. Interpret the ratio differences between the two companies.

E12-16 Asset turnover

Obj. 5

✔ a. YRC Worldwide, 4.99

Three major transportation segments and a major company within each segment are as follows:

Segment	Company
Motor carriers	YRC Worldwide Inc. (YRCW)
Railroads	Union Pacific Corporation (UNP)
Transportation Arrangement	C.H. Robinson Worldwide Inc. (CHRW)

(amounts in millions)	YRC Worldwide	Union Pacific	C.H. Robinson Worldwide
Sales	$4,871	$21,708	$15,310
Average long-term operating assets	976	54,204	1,749

a. Determine the asset turnover for all three companies. Round to two decimal places.

b. Interpret the differences in the asset turnover in terms of the operating characteristics of each of the respective segments.

E12-17 Profitability metrics

Obj. 5

✔ a. Return on total assets, 20Y5, 21.5%

The following selected data were taken from the financial statements of The O'Malley Group Inc. for December 31, 20Y5, 20Y4, and 20Y3:

	December 31		
	20Y5	20Y4	20Y3
Total assets	$2,900,000	$2,400,000	$2,000,000
Notes payable (5% interest)	800,000	800,000	800,000
Common stock	250,000	250,000	250,000
Preferred $4 stock, $50 par (no change during year)	400,000	400,000	400,000
Retained earnings	1,450,000	950,000	550,000
Net income	530,000	430,000	330,000

No dividends on common stock were declared between 20Y3 and 20Y5.

a. Determine the return on total assets, the return on stockholders' equity, and the return on common stockholders' equity for the years 20Y4 and 20Y5. Round to one decimal place.

b. What conclusions can be drawn from these data as to the company's profitability?

Obj. 5

✔ a. Return on total assets, Year 3, 3.8%

E12-18 Profitability metrics

Macy's, Inc. (M), sells merchandise through company-owned retail stores and an Internet website. Recent financial information for Macy's is as follows (all numbers in millions).

	Year 3	Year 2
Net income	$564	$1,108
Interest expense	205	261

	Year 3	Year 2	Year 1
Total assets	$21,172	$19,194	$19,583
Total stockholders' equity	6,377	6,436	5,733

Assume the apparel industry's average return on total assets is 10.3%, and the average return on stockholders' equity is 15.2% for Year 3.

a. Determine the return on total assets for Macy's for Years 2 and 3. Round to one decimal place.

b. Determine the return on stockholders' equity for Macy's for Years 2 and 3. Round to one decimal place.

c. Evaluate the changes in the profitability ratios determined in (a) and (b).

Obj. 4, 5

✔ d. Asset turnover 1.32

E12-19 Seven metrics

The following data were taken from the financial statements of Woodwork Enterprises Inc. for the current fiscal year. Assuming that there are no intangible assets, determine the following: (a) debt ratio, (b) ratio of fixed assets to long-term liabilities, (c) ratio of liabilities to stockholders' equity, (d) asset turnover, (e) return on total assets, (f) return on stockholders' equity, and (g) return on common stockholders' equity. Round to two decimal places.

Property, plant, and equipment (net)			$ 5,000,000
Liabilities:			
Current liabilities		$ 400,000	
Mortgage note payable, 5%, ten-year note issued two years ago		3,600,000	
Total liabilities			$ 4,000,000
Stockholders' equity:			
Preferred $1 stock, $10 par (no change during year)			$ 1,000,000
Common stock, $5 par (no change during year)			2,000,000
Retained earnings:			
Balance, beginning of year	$8,000,000		
Net income	500,000	$8,500,000	
Preferred dividends	$ 100,000		
Common dividends	100,000	(200,000)	
Balance, end of year			8,300,000
Total stockholders' equity			$11,300,000
Sales			$ 6,250,000
Interest expense			$ 180,000
Beginning-of-the-year amounts:			
Property, plant, and equipment (net)			$ 4,500,000
Total assets			12,200,000
Retained earnings			8,000,000

E12-20 Six metrics

Obj. 4, 5

✔ d. Price-earnings ratio, 2.5

The balance sheet for Shryer Industries Inc. at the end of 20Y9 indicated the following:

Bonds payable, 5% (due in 30 years)	$ 8,000,000
Preferred $4 stock, $75 par	15,000,000
Common stock, $7 par	3,500,000

Income before income tax was $3,400,000, and income taxes were $1,000,000 for the current year. Cash dividends paid on common stock during the current year totaled $100,000. The common stock was selling for $8 per share at the end of the year. Determine each of the following: (a) times interest earned, (b) times preferred dividends earned, (c) earnings per share on common stock, (d) price-earnings ratio, (e) dividends per share of common stock, and (f) dividend yield. Round to one decimal place except earnings per share and dividends per share, which should be rounded to the nearest cent.

E12-21 Earnings per share, price-earnings ratio, dividend yield

Obj. 5

✔ b. Price-earnings ratio, 8.0

The following information was taken from the financial statements of Monarch Resources Inc. for December 31 of the current year:

Common stock, $125 par value (no change during the year)	$12,500,000
Preferred $6 stock, $90 par (no change during the year)	2,250,000

The net income was $1,300,000, and the declared dividends on the common stock were $460,000 for the current year. The market price of the common stock is $92 per share.

For the common stock, determine (a) the earnings per share, (b) the price-earnings ratio, (c) the dividends per share, and (d) the dividend yield.

E12-22 Price-earnings ratio, dividend yield

Obj. 5

The following table shows recent stock prices, earnings per share, and dividends per share for three companies:

	Price	Earnings per Share	Dividends per Share
Amazon.com (AMZN)	$1,847.84	$23.46	$0.00
McDonald's Corporation (MCD)	197.61	7.95	4.73
Microsoft (MSFT)	157.70	5.11	1.84

a. Determine the price-earnings ratio and dividend yield for the three companies. Round to one decimal place.

b. Discuss the differences in these ratios across the three companies.

Problems

Obj. 2

✔ 1. Sales 9.8% increase

P12-1 Horizontal analysis for income statement

For 20Y3, Greyhound Technology Company reported its most significant decline in net income in years. At the end of the year, Duane Vogel, the president, is presented with the following condensed comparative income statement:

GREYHOUND TECHNOLOGY COMPANY
Comparative Income Statement
For the Years Ended December 31, 20Y3 and 20Y2

	20Y3	20Y2
Sales	$ 862,000	$ 785,000
Cost of goods sold	(650,000)	(500,000)
Gross profit	$ 212,000	$ 285,000
Selling expenses	$ (44,000)	$ (40,000)
Administrative expenses	(27,000)	(25,000)
Total operating expenses	$ (71,000)	$ (65,000)
Operating income	$ 141,000	$ 220,000
Other revenue	2,300	2,000
Income before income tax	$ 143,300	$ 222,000
Income tax expense	(13,000)	(20,000)
Net income	$ 130,300	$ 202,000

Instructions

1. Prepare a comparative income statement with horizontal analysis for the two-year period, using 20Y2 as the base year. Round to one decimal place.
2. Comment on the significant relationships revealed by the horizontal analysis prepared in (1).

Obj. 2

✔ 1. Net income, 20Y6, 28.0%

P12-2 Vertical analysis for income statement

For 20Y6, Fishing Experiences Inc. initiated a sales promotion campaign that included the expenditure of an additional $45,000 for advertising. At the end of the year, Colt Schultz, the president, is presented with the following condensed comparative income statement:

FISHING EXPERIENCES INC.
Comparative Income Statement
For the Years Ended December 31, 20Y6 and 20Y5

	20Y6	20Y5
Sales	$1,200,000	$1,000,000
Cost of goods sold	(624,000)	(558,000)
Gross profit	$ 576,000	$ 442,000)
Selling expenses	(120,000)	(75,000)
Administrative expenses	(50,000)	(50,000)
Total operating expenses	$ (170,000)	$ (125,000)
Operating income	$ 406,000	$ 317,000
Other revenue	30,000	30,000
Income before income tax	$ 436,000	$ 347,000
Income tax expense	(100,000)	(90,000)
Net income	$ 336,000	$ 257,000

Instructions

1. Prepare a comparative income statement for the two-year period, presenting a vertical analysis of each item in relationship to sales for each of the years.
2. Comment on the significant relationships revealed by the vertical analysis prepared in (1).

P12-3 Effect of transactions on current position analysis

Obj. 3

✔ 2. c. Current ratio, 2.3

Data pertaining to the current position of Newlan Company are as follows:

Cash	$ 80,000
Temporary investments	160,000
Accounts and notes receivable (net)	235,000
Inventories	190,000
Prepaid expenses	10,000
Accounts payable	158,000
Notes payable (short-term)	80,000
Accrued expenses	12,000

Instructions

1. Compute (a) the working capital, (b) the current ratio, and (c) the quick ratio.
2. List the following captions on a sheet of paper:

Transaction	Working Capital	Current Ratio	Quick Ratio

Compute the working capital, the current ratio, and the quick ratio after each of the following transactions, and record the results in the appropriate columns. Consider each transaction separately and assume that only that transaction affects the data given above. Round to one decimal place.

a. Sold temporary investments for cash at no gain or loss, $50,000.
b. Paid accounts payable, $40,000.
c. Purchased goods on account, $75,000.
d. Paid notes payable, $30,000.
e. Declared a cash dividend, $15,000.
f. Declared a stock dividend on common stock, $24,000.
g. Borrowed cash from bank on a long-term note, $150,000.
h. Received cash on account, $72,000.
i. Issued additional shares of stock for cash, $300,000.
j. Paid cash for prepaid expenses, $10,000.

P12-4 Twenty metrics of liquidity, solvency, and profitability

Obj. 3, 4, 5

✔ 5. Days' sales in receivables, 22.8

The comparative financial statements of Automotive Solutions Inc. are as follows. The market price of Automotive Solutions Inc. common stock was $119.70 on December 31, 20Y8.

AUTOMOTIVE SOLUTIONS INC.
Comparative Income Statement
For the Years Ended December 31, 20Y8 and 20Y7

	20Y8	20Y7
Sales	$10,000,000	$ 9,400,000
Cost of goods sold	(5,350,000)	(4,950,000)
Gross profit	$ 4,650,000	$ 4,450,000
Selling expenses	$ (2,000,000)	$(1,880,000)
Administrative expenses	(1,500,000)	(1,410,000)
Total operating expenses	$ (3,500,000)	$(3,290,000)
Operating income	$ 1,150,000	$ 1,160,000
Other revenue and expense:		
Other revenue	150,000	140,000
Other expense (interest)	(170,000)	(150,000)
Income before income tax	$ 1,130,000	$ 1,150,000
Income tax expense	(230,000)	(225,000)
Net income	$ 900,000	$ 925,000

AUTOMOTIVE SOLUTIONS INC.
Comparative Statement of Stockholders' Equity
For the Years Ended December 31, 20Y8 and 20Y7

	20Y8			20Y7		
	Preferred Stock	**Common Stock**	**Retained Earnings**	**Preferred Stock**	**Common Stock**	**Retained Earnings**
Balances, Jan. 1	$500,000	$500,000	$5,375,000	$500,000	$500,000	$4,545,000
Net income			900,000			925,000
Dividends:						
Preferred stock			(45,000)			(45,000)
Common stock			(50,000)			(50,000)
Balances, Dec. 31	$500,000	$500,000	$6,180,000	$500,000	$500,000	$5,375,000

AUTOMOTIVE SOLUTIONS INC.
Comparative Balance Sheet
December 31, 20Y8 and 20Y7

	Dec. 31, 20Y8	**Dec. 31, 20Y7**
Assets		
Current assets:		
Cash	$ 500,000	$ 400,000
Marketable securities	1,010,000	1,000,000
Accounts receivable (net)	740,000	510,000
Inventories	1,190,000	950,000
Prepaid expenses	250,000	229,000
Total current assets	$3,690,000	$3,089,000
Long-term investments	2,350,000	2,300,000
Property, plant, and equipment (net)	3,740,000	3,366,000
Total assets	$9,780,000	$8,755,000
Liabilities		
Current liabilities	$ 900,000	$ 880,000
Long-term liabilities:		
Mortgage note payable, 10%	$ 200,000	$ 0
Bonds payable, 10%	1,500,000	1,500,000
Total long-term liabilities	$1,700,000	$1,500,000
Total liabilities	$2,600,000	$2,380,000
Stockholders' Equity		
Preferred $0.90 stock, $10 par	$ 500,000	$ 500,000
Common stock, $5 par	500,000	500,000
Retained earnings	6,180,000	5,375,500
Total stockholders' equity	$7,180,000	$6,375,000
Total liabilities and stockholders' equity	$9,780,000	$8,755,000

Instructions

Determine the following measures for 20Y8. Round all ratios to one decimal place. Round earnings per share and dividends per share to the nearest cent.

1. Working capital
2. Current ratio
3. Quick ratio
4. Accounts receivable turnover
5. Days' sales in receivables
6. Inventory turnover
7. Days' sales in inventory
8. Debt ratio
9. Ratio of liabilities to stockholders' equity
10. Ratio of fixed assets to long-term liabilities
11. Times interest earned
12. Times preferred dividends earned
13. Asset turnover
14. Return on total assets
15. Return on stockholders' equity
16. Return on common stockholders' equity
17. Earnings per share on common stock
18. Price-earnings ratio
19. Dividends per share of common stock
20. Dividend yield

P12-5 Trend analysis

Obj. 4, 5

Critelli Company has provided the following comparative information:

	Year 5	Year 4	Year 3	Year 2	Year 1
Net income	$1,785,000	$1,330,000	$ 990,000	$ 768,800	$ 664,000
Interest expense	400,000	350,000	300,000	240,000	200,000
Income tax expense	615,000	340,000	270,000	71,200	16,000
Average total assets	9,500,000	8,000,000	6,000,000	5,200,000	4,500,000
Average stockholders' equity	5,400,000	4,300,000	3,100,000	2,650,000	2,200,000

You have been asked to evaluate the historical performance of the company over the last five years.

Selected industry ratios have remained relatively steady at the following levels for the last five years:

	Industry Ratios
Return on total assets	15%
Return on stockholders' equity	18%
Times interest earned	3.5

Instructions

1. Prepare three line graphs, with the ratio on the vertical axis and the years on the horizontal axis for the following three ratios (rounded to one decimal place):

   a. Return on total assets

   b. Return on stockholders' equity

   c. Times interest earned

   Display both the company ratio and the industry benchmark on each graph. That is, each graph should have two lines.

2. Prepare an analysis of the graphs in (1).

Cases

Case 12-1 Analysis of financing corporate growth

Assume that the president of Elkhead Brewery made the following statement in the Annual Report to Shareholders:

"The founding family and majority shareholders of the company do not believe in using debt to finance future growth. The founding family learned from hard experience during Prohibition and the Great Depression that debt can cause loss of flexibility and eventual loss of corporate control. The company will not place itself at such risk. As such, all future growth will be financed either by stock sales to the public or by internally generated resources."

As a public shareholder of this company, how would you respond to this policy?

Case 12-2 Receivables and inventory turnover

Thornby Inc. completed its fiscal year on December 31. The auditor, Kim Holmes, has approached the CFO, Brad Potter, regarding the year-end receivables and inventory levels of Thornby Inc. The following conversation takes place:

Kim: We are beginning our audit of Thornby Inc. and have prepared ratio analyses to determine if there have been significant changes in operations or financial position. This helps us guide the audit process. This analysis indicates that the inventory turnover has decreased from 5.1 to 3.8, while the accounts receivable turnover has decreased from 12.5 to 9. I was wondering if you could explain this change in operations.

Brad: There is little need for concern. The inventory represents computers that we were unable to sell during the holiday buying season. We are confident, however, that we will be able to sell these computers as we move into the next fiscal year.

Kim: What gives you this confidence?

Brad: We will increase our advertising and provide some very attractive price concessions to move these machines. We have no choice. Newer technology is already out there, and we have to unload this inventory.

Kim: ... and the receivables?

Brad: As you may be aware, the company is under tremendous pressure to expand sales and profits. As a result, we lowered our credit standards to our commercial customers so that we would be able to sell products to a broader customer base. As a result of this policy change, we have been able to expand sales by 28%.

Kim: Your responses have not been reassuring to me.

Brad: I'm a little confused. Assets are good, right? Why don't you look at our current ratio? It has improved, hasn't it? I would think that you would view that very favorably.

Why is Kim concerned about the inventory and accounts receivable turnover ratios and Brad's responses to them? What action may Kim need to take? How would you respond to Brad's last comment?

Case 12-3 Vertical analysis

The condensed income statements through operating income for Apple Inc. (APPL) and Best Buy Co. Inc. (BBY) are reproduced for recent fiscal years as follows (numbers in millions of dollars).

	Apple	Best Buy
Sales	$ 260,174	$ 43,638
Cost of sales	(161,782)	(33,590)
Gross profit	$ 98,392	$ 10,048
Selling, general, and administrative expenses	(18,245)	(7,998)
Research and development expenses	(16,217)	(41)
Operating expenses	$ (34,462)	$ (8,039)
Operating income	$ 63,930	$ 2,009

Prepare comparative common-sized statements, rounding percents to one decimal place. Interpret the analyses.

Case 12-4 Profitability and stockholder ratios

Harley-Davidson, Inc. (HOG), is a leading motorcycle manufacturer in the United States. The company manufactures and sells a number of different types of motorcycles, a complete line of motorcycle parts, and brand-related accessories, clothing, and collectibles.The following information is available for three recent years (in millions except per-share amounts):

	Year 3	Year 2	Year 1
Net income (loss)	$ 424	$ 531	$ 522
Preferred dividends	None	None	None
Interest expense	$ 31	$ 31	$ 31
Shares outstanding for computing earnings per share	157	166	172
Cash dividend per share	$ 1.50	$ 1.48	$ 1.46
Average total assets	$10,597	$10,319	$9,931
Average stockholders' equity	$ 1,789	$ 1,809	$1,882
Average stock price per share	$ 36.38	$ 42.78	$54.99

1. Calculate the following ratios for each year. Round to one decimal place except dollar amounts, which should be rounded to the nearest cent.
   a. Return on total assets
   b. Return on stockholders' equity
   c. Earnings per share
   d. Dividend yield
   e. Price-earnings ratio using the average price per share of stock.

2. What is the average debt ratio and the ratio of liabilities to stockholders' equity for Years 1, 2, and 3?
3. Comment on the results in (1) and (2).

Case 12-5 Comprehensive profitability and solvency analysis

Hyatt Hotels Corporation (H) and **Marriott International Inc. (MAR)** are two major owners and managers of lodging and resort properties in the United States. Financial data (in millions) for a recent year for the two companies are as follows:

	Hyatt	Marriott
Income statement data:		
Interest expense	$ 75	$ 394
Income before income tax	1,006	1,599
Net income	766	1,273
Balance sheet data:		
Total assets	$8,417	$25,051
Total liabilities	4,450	24,348
Total stockholders' equity	3,967	703

The average liabilities, stockholders' equity, and total assets were as follows:

	Hyatt	Marriott
Average total assets	$8,030	$24,374
Average total liabilities	4,208	22,910
Average total stockholders' equity	3,822	1,464

1. Determine the following ratios for both companies (round to one decimal place after the whole percent):
   a. Return on total assets.
   b. Return on stockholders' equity.
   c. Times interest earned.
   d. Debt ratio for the most recent year.
   e. Ratio of liabilities to stockholders' equity for the most recent year.
2. Analyze and compare the two companies, using the information in (1).

Answers to Self-Examination Questions

1. **A** Percentage analysis indicating the relationship of the component parts to the total in a financial statement, such as the relationship of current assets to total assets (20% to 100%) in the question, is called vertical analysis (answer A). Percentage analysis of increases and decreases in corresponding items in comparative financial statements is called horizontal analysis (answer B). An example of horizontal analysis would be the presentation of the amount of current assets in the preceding balance sheet, along with the amount of current assets at the end of the current year, with the increase or decrease in current assets between the periods expressed as a percentage. Profitability analysis (answer C) is the analysis of a firm's ability to earn income. Contribution margin analysis (answer D) is discussed in a later managerial accounting chapter.

2. **D** Various liquidity and solvency measures, categorized as current position analysis, indicate a firm's ability to meet currently maturing obligations. Each measure contributes to the analysis of a firm's current position and is most useful when viewed with other measures and compared with similar measures for other periods and for other firms. Working capital (answer A) is the excess of current assets over current liabilities; the current ratio (answer B) is the ratio of current assets to current liabilities; and the quick ratio (answer C) is the ratio of the sum of cash, receivables, and temporary investments to current liabilities.

3. **D** The ratio of current assets to current liabilities is usually called the current ratio (answer A). It is sometimes called the working capital ratio (answer B) or bankers' ratio (answer C).

4. **C** The ratio of the sum of cash, receivables, and temporary investments (sometimes called quick assets) to current liabilities is called the quick ratio (answer C) or acid test ratio. The current ratio (answer A), working capital ratio (answer B), and bankers' ratio (answer D) are terms that describe the ratio of current assets to current liabilities.

5. **C** The days' sales in inventory (answer C), which is determined by dividing the average inventory by the average daily cost of goods sold, expresses the relationship between the cost of goods sold and inventory. It indicates the efficiency in the management of inventory. The working capital ratio (answer A) indicates the ability of the business to meet currently maturing obligations (debt). The quick ratio (answer B) indicates the "instant" debt-paying ability of the business. The ratio of fixed assets to long-term liabilities (answer D) indicates the margin of safety for long-term creditors.

Appendix A

Selected Topics

TOPIC 1: INVESTMENTS

TOPIC 2: FOREIGN CURRENCY TRANSACTIONS

TOPIC 3: CORPORATE TAXES

TOPIC 4: REPORTING UNUSUAL ITEMS AND COMPREHENSIVE INCOME

TOPIC 5: REVENUE RECOGNITION

TOPIC 6: INTERNATIONAL ACCOUNTING STANDARDS

Topic

1 Investments

What's Covered

Debt Investments
- Held-to-Maturity Securities (Obj. 1)
- Trading Securities (Obj. 1)
- Available-for-Sale Securities (Obj. 1)

Equity Investments
- Less Than 20% Ownership (Obj. 2)
- Between 20%–50% Ownership (Obj. 3)
- More Than 50% Ownership (Obj. 4)

Learning Objectives

Obj. 1 Describe and illustrate the accounting for debt investments classified as (a) held-to-maturity securities, (b) trading securities, and (c) available-for-sale securities.

Obj. 2 Describe and illustrate the accounting for equity investments of less than 20% ownership.

Obj. 3 Describe and illustrate the accounting for equity investments with 20%–50% ownership.

Obj. 4 Describe and illustrate the accounting for equity investments of more than 50% ownership.

Objective 1
Describe and illustrate the accounting for debt investments classified as (a) held-to-maturity securities, (b) trading securities, and (c) available-for-sale securities.

Debt Investments

Companies often invest in notes and bonds issued by corporations and governmental agencies. These **debt investments** may be purchased to earn interest or to earn profits from changes in their market price. Generally accepted accounting principles (GAAP) classify these investments as:

- Held-to-maturity securities
- Trading securities
- Available-for-sale securities

Held-to-Maturity Securities

Securities purchased with the primary objective of earning interest revenue and collecting the face value of the security at its maturity date are classified as **held-to-maturity securities**. Held-to-maturity securities are accounted for using the **cost method** of accounting.

Bonds are used to illustrate the accounting for held-to-maturity securities. The accounting for bonds involves the following three types of transactions:

- Purchase of bonds
- Receipt of interest revenue
- Sale of bonds

Purchase of Bonds The purchase of bonds is recorded by increasing an investments account for the cost of acquiring the bonds. If bonds are purchased between interest dates, the buyer must also pay the seller any accrued interest since the last interest payment date. Any accrued interest is recorded as an increase to an interest receivable account rather than to the investments account.

To illustrate, assume that Homer Company purchases $18,000 of bonds that were issued on January 31, 20Y3, at their face amount on March 17, 20Y3, plus accrued interest. The bonds have an interest rate of 6%, payable on July 31 and January 31.

Interest revenue is reported on the statement of cash flows as an operating activity. The effects of the bond purchase on the accounts and financial statements are as follows:

Financial Statement Effects

BALANCE SHEET

	Assets			= Liabilities	+ Stockholders' Equity
	Cash	+ Interest Receivable	+ Investments—Bonds		
20Y3 *Mar. 17*	(18,135)	135	18,000		

STATEMENT OF CASH FLOWS

Mar. 17 Investing	(18,000)
17 Operating	(135)

INCOME STATEMENT

Because Homer Company purchased the bonds on March 17, it is also purchasing the accrued interest for 45 days (January 31 to March 17), as shown in Exhibit 1.

Exhibit 1
Accrued Interest

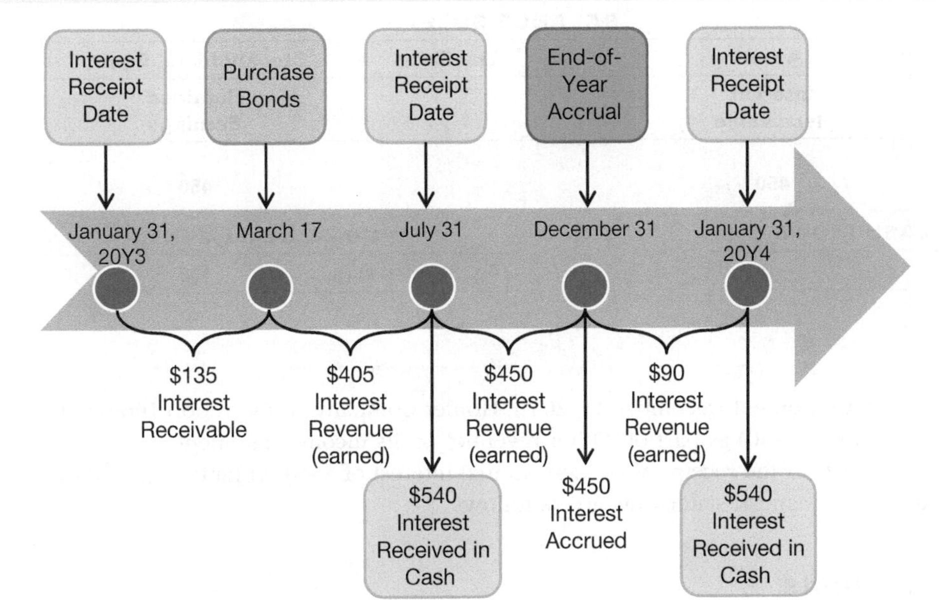

The accrued interest of $135 is computed as follows:[1]

$$\text{Accrued Interest} = \$18,000 \times 6\% \times (45 \div 360) = \$135$$

The accrued interest is recorded by increasing Interest Receivable for $135. Investments—Bonds is increased for the purchase price of the bonds of $18,000.

Receipt of Interest On July 31, Homer Company receives a semiannual interest payment of $540 ($18,000 × 6% × 6/12). The $540 interest includes the $135 accrued interest that Homer Company purchased with the bonds on March 17. Thus, Homer has earned $405 ($540 – $135) of interest revenue since purchasing the bonds, as shown in Exhibit 1.

[1] To simplify, a 360-day year is used to compute interest.

The effects of the receipt of the interest on July 31 on the accounts and financial statements are as follows:

Financial Statement Effects

BALANCE SHEET

	Assets		=	Liabilities	+	Stockholders' Equity
	Cash	+ Interest Receivable	=			Retained Earnings
20Y3 July 31.	540	(135)				405

STATEMENT OF CASH FLOWS

July 31. Operating	540

INCOME STATEMENT

July 31. Interest revenue	405

Homer Company's accounting period ends on December 31, 20Y3. Thus, an adjustment must be made to accrue interest for 5 months (August 1 to December 31) of $450 ($18,000 × 6% × 5/12), as shown in Exhibit 1. The effects of the adjustment for accrued interest on the accounts and financial statements are as follows:

Financial Statement Effects

BALANCE SHEET

	Assets	=	Liabilities	+	Stockholders' Equity
	Interest Receivable	=			Retained Earnings
20Y4 Dec. 31.	450				450

STATEMENT OF CASH FLOWS

INCOME STATEMENT

Dec. 31. Interest revenue	450

For the year ended December 31, 20Y3, Homer Company would report Interest Revenue of $855 ($405 + $450) as part of "Other revenue" on its income statement.

The effects of the receipt of the semiannual interest of $540 on January 31, 20Y4, on the accounts and financial statements are as follows:

Financial Statement Effects

BALANCE SHEET

	Assets		=	Liabilities	+	Stockholders' Equity
	Cash	+ Interest Receivable	=			Retained Earnings
20Y4 Jan. 31.	540	(450)				90

STATEMENT OF CASH FLOWS

Jan. 31. Operating	540

INCOME STATEMENT

Jan. 31. Interest revenue	90

Sale of Bonds Although the original intent of a company may have been to hold the bonds until maturity, it may have to sell bonds to raise cash for its operations. In such cases, the sale of bonds normally results in a gain or loss. If the proceeds from the sale exceed the balance of the bond investment account, then a gain is recorded. If the proceeds are less than the balance of the bond investment account, a loss is recorded.

To illustrate, on January 31, 20Y4, Homer Company sells the bonds at 98, which is a price equal to 98% of their face amount. The sale results in a loss of $360, computed as follows:

Proceeds from sale	$ 17,640*
Less book value (cost) of the bonds	(18,000)
Loss on sale of bonds	$ (360)

*$18,000 × 98%

The effects of the sale of the bonds on January 31, 20Y4, on the accounts and financial statements are as follows:

Financial Statement Effects

BALANCE SHEET

	Assets		=	Liabilities +	Stockholders' Equity
	Cash +	Investments—Bonds	=		Retained Earnings
20Y4 Jan. 31.	17,640	(18,000)			(360)

STATEMENT OF CASH FLOWS

Jan. 31. Investing	17,640

INCOME STATEMENT

Jan. 31. Loss on sale of investments	(360)

There is no accrued interest upon the sale because the interest payment date is also January 31. If the sale were between interest dates, interest accrued since the last interest payment date would be added to the sale proceeds and would be recorded as an increase to Interest Revenue. The loss on the sale of bond investments is reported as part of "Other revenue (loss)" on Homer Company's income statement.

If Homer Company had kept the bonds until their maturity instead of selling them, the entry to record the bonds' maturity would increase Cash and decrease Investments—Bonds for $18,000.

Reporting on Financial Statements If a held-to-maturity security will mature within a year, it is reported as a current asset on the balance sheet. Held-to-maturity securities maturing beyond a year are reported as noncurrent assets.

In the preceding illustration, Homer Company bonds were purchased at their face value. If the interest rate on bonds differs from the market rate of interest, the bonds may be purchased at a premium or discount. In such cases, the premium or discount is amortized over the life of the bonds and the bonds are reported on the balance sheet at their amortized cost. To simplify, we assume that all held-to-maturity securities are purchased at their face value.

Trading Securities

Debt securities that are purchased to earn profits from short-term changes in their market prices are classified as **trading securities**. Trading securities are reported as a current asset on the balance sheet. Trading securities are valued as a portfolio (group) of securities using the **fair value method**.[2] The **fair value** is the market price that the company would receive for a security if it were sold.

[2] The effect on the accounts and financial statements of the purchase, receipt of interest, and sale of trading securities are similar to those for held-to-maturity securities, which were illustrated earlier. For this reason, we focus on the end-of-period adjustments and reporting of trading securities.

To illustrate, assume that Maggie Company purchased a portfolio of debt securities issued by various companies during 20Y1.[3] Maggie Company expects to sell the securities within one year. On December 31, 20Y1, the cost and fair values of these trading securities were as follows:

Issuing Company	Cost (Face Value)	Fair Value
Armour Company	$ 5,000	$ 7,200
Maven, Inc.	11,000	7,500
Polaris Co.	8,000	10,600
Totals	$24,000	$25,300

The portfolio of trading securities is reported with a fair value of $25,300. An adjustment is necessary to record the increase in the fair value of $1,300 ($25,300 – $24,000). The effects of the adjustment for fair value of the portfolio of trading securities on December 31, 20Y1, on the accounts and financial statements are as follows:

Financial Statement Effects

BALANCE SHEET

	Assets	=	Liabilities +	Stockholders' Equity
	Valuation Allowance for Trading Investments	=		Retained Earnings
20Y1 *Dec. 31.*	1,300			1,300

STATEMENT OF CASH FLOWS

INCOME STATEMENT

Dec. 31. Unrealized gain on trading investments **1,300**

The **unrealized gain (loss) on trading investments** is reported on the income statement. Depending on its significance, it may be reported separately or as "Other revenue" on the income statement. The **valuation allowance for trading investments** is reported on the balance sheet as an addition or a deduction from the cost of the securities. The reporting of the preceding trading securities on Maggie Company's December 31, 20Y1, balance sheet is as follows:

Maggie Company
Balance Sheet (selected items)
December 31, 20Y1

Current assets:		
Cash		$120,000
Trading investments (at cost)	$24,000	
Valuation allowance for trading investments	1,300	
Trading investments (at fair value)		25,300

If the fair value of the portfolio of trading securities was less than the cost, then the adjustment would increase Unrealized Loss on Trading Investments and decrease Valuation Allowance for Trading Investments for the difference. Unrealized Loss on Trading Investments would be reported on the income statement as "Other expense." Valuation

[3] To simplify, we assume that all trading securities are purchased at their face value.

allowance for trading investments would be shown on the balance sheet as a *deduction* from trading investments (at cost).

Over time, the valuation allowance account is adjusted to reflect changes in the fair value of the portfolio. Thus, increases in the fair value of the portfolio from the beginning of the period will result in an adjustment to record an unrealized gain, similar to the preceding adjustment. Likewise, decreases in the fair value of the portfolio from the beginning of the period will result in an adjustment to record an unrealized loss.

To illustrate, assume that during 20Y2 no trading securities were purchased or sold and that the fair value of the portfolio of securities is $22,000 on December 31, 20Y2. In this case, the adjustment would increase Unrealized Loss on Trading Investments and decrease Valuation Allowance for Trading Investments for $3,300 ($25,300 – $22,000).

After the adjustment, Unrealized Loss on Trading Investments will have an adjusted balance of $3,300. Valuation Allowance for Trading Investments will have a balance of $(2,000), as follows:

Jan. 1, 20Y2 balance	$ 1,300
Dec. 31 Adjustment	(3,300)
Dec. 31, 20Y2 balance	$(2,000)

The unrealized loss of $3,300 would be reported on Maggie Company's 20Y2 income statement as "Other expense." The trading investments are reported on the December 31, 20Y2, balance sheet at their fair value of $22,000 (cost of $24,000 less valuation allowance of $2,000), as follows:

Maggie Company
Balance Sheet (selected items)
December 31, 20Y2

Current assets:		
Cash		$175,000
Trading investments (at cost)	$24,000	
Valuation allowance for trading investments	(2,000)	
Trading investments (at fair value)		22,000

Available-for-Sale Securities

Debt securities that a company intends to sell in the future, but not in the near term, are classified as **available-for-sale securities**. Available-for-sale securities are recorded at fair value using the fair value method similar to that used for trading securities. However, changes in the fair values are not reported on the income statement but are reported as part of stockholders' equity.

To illustrate, assume that Campbell Company purchased three debt securities during 20Y5 as available-for-sale securities.[4] On December 31, 20Y5, the cost and fair values of the securities were as follows:

Issuing Company	Cost (Face Value)	Fair Value
Bennett Company	$30,000	$32,200
MCT Industries Inc.	10,000	6,500
Randall Co.	50,000	55,000
Totals	$90,000	$93,700

[4] To simplify, we assume that all available-for-sale securities are purchased at their face value.

The portfolio of available-for-sale securities is reported at its fair value of $93,700. An adjustment is made to record the increase in fair value of $3,700 ($93,700 – $90,000). In order to maintain a record of the original cost of the securities, the increase in fair value of $3,700 is recorded as an increase to Valuation Allowance for Available-for-Sale Investments.

Unlike trading securities, the December 31, 20Y5, adjustment increases a stockholders' equity account instead of an income statement account. The $3,700 increase in fair value is recorded as an increase to Unrealized Gain on Available-for-Sale Investments.

The adjustment on December 31, 20Y5, to record the fair value of the portfolio of available-for-sale securities is as follows:

Financial Statement Effects

BALANCE SHEET

	Assets	=	Liabilities +	Stockholders' Equity
	Valuation Allowance for Available-for-Sale Investments	=		**Unrealized Gain (Loss) on Available-for-Sale Investments**
20Y5 Dec. 31.	3,700			3,700

STATEMENT OF CASH FLOWS

INCOME STATEMENT

The **unrealized gain (loss) on available-for-sale investments** is not reported on the income statement, but instead is reported as an addition to or deduction from stockholders' equity on the balance sheet. The **valuation allowance for available-for-sale investments** is reported on the balance sheet as an addition to or deduction from the cost of the securities. The reporting of the preceding trading securities on Campbell Company's December 31, 20Y5, balance sheet is as follows:

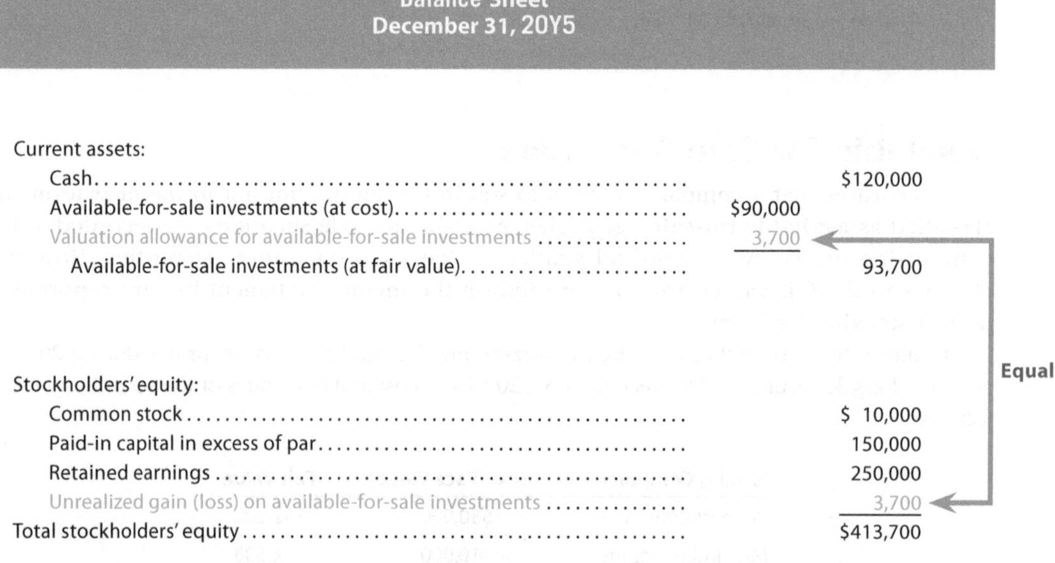

Campbell Company
Balance Sheet
December 31, 20Y5

Current assets:		
Cash		$120,000
Available-for-sale investments (at cost)	$90,000	
Valuation allowance for available-for-sale investments	3,700	
Available-for-sale investments (at fair value)		93,700
Stockholders' equity:		
Common stock		$ 10,000
Paid-in capital in excess of par		150,000
Retained earnings		250,000
Unrealized gain (loss) on available-for-sale investments		3,700
Total stockholders' equity		$413,700

As shown, Unrealized Gain on Available-for-Sale Investments is reported as an addition to stockholders' equity.[5] In future years, the cumulative effects of unrealized gains and losses are reported in this account.

[5] The effects of unrealized gains and losses on available-for-sale investments on stockholders' equity are also reported as part of comprehensive income, which is discussed in Appendix A, Topic 4: *Reporting Unusual Items and Comprehensive Income.*

If the fair value was less than the cost, then the adjustment would decrease (negative amount) the valuation account and decrease stockholders' equity as an unrealized loss. On the balance sheet, the Valuation Allowance for Available-for-Sale Investments would then be reported as a deduction from the cost of the investment and the Unrealized Loss on Available-for-Sale Investments would be reported in the "Stockholders' Equity" section as a deduction.

Over time, the valuation allowance account is adjusted to reflect the difference between the cost and the fair value of the portfolio. Thus, increases in the valuation allowance from the beginning of the period will result in an adjustment to record an increase in the valuation account and an increase in the unrealized gain (loss) account, similar to the adjustment illustrated earlier. Likewise, decreases in the valuation allowance from the beginning of the period will result in an adjustment to record a decrease in the valuation account and a decrease in the unrealized gain (loss) account.

To illustrate, assume that during 20Y6 no available-for-sale securities were purchased or sold and that the fair value of the portfolio of securities is $99,500 on December 31, 20Y6. In this case, the adjustment would increase Valuation Allowance for Available-for-Sale Investments and increase Unrealized Gain on Available-for-Sale Investments for $5,800 ($99,500 – $93,700).

After the adjustment, Valuation Allowance for Available-for-Sale Investments will have a balance of $9,500. Unrealized Gain on Available-for-Sale Investments will have a balance of $9,500. The adjusted accounts are as follows:

Valuation Allowance for Available-for-Sale Investments	
Jan. 1, 20Y6 Balance	$3,700
Dec. 31 Adjustment	5,800
Dec. 31, 20Y6 Adjusted balance	$9,500

Unrealized Gain (Loss) on Available-for-Sale Investments	
Jan. 1, 20Y6 Balance	$3,700
Dec. 31 Adjustment	5,800
Dec. 31, 20Y6 Adjusted balance	$9,500

The trading investments would then be reported on the December 31, 20Y6, balance sheet at their fair value of $99,500 ($90,000 + $9,500) as follows:

Campbell Company
Balance Sheet
December 31, 20Y6

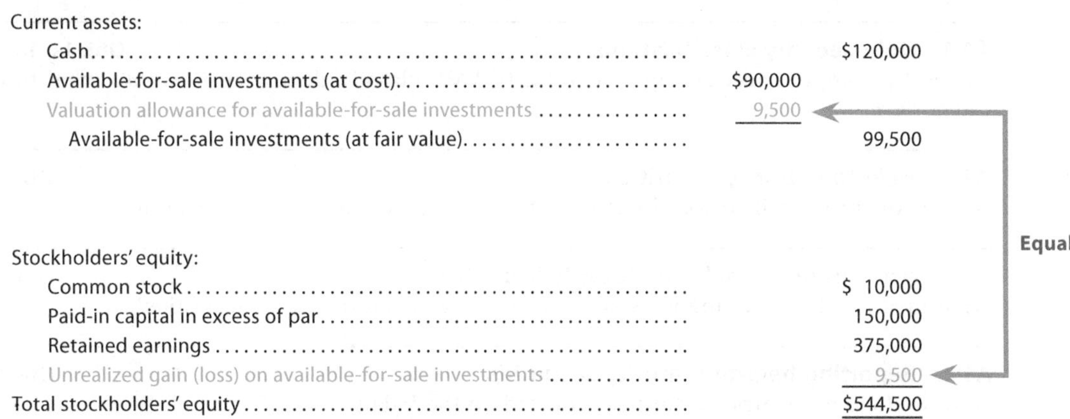

Current assets:		
Cash		$120,000
Available-for-sale investments (at cost)	$90,000	
Valuation allowance for available-for-sale investments	9,500	
Available-for-sale investments (at fair value)		99,500
Stockholders' equity:		
Common stock		$ 10,000
Paid-in capital in excess of par		150,000
Retained earnings		375,000
Unrealized gain (loss) on available-for-sale investments		9,500
Total stockholders' equity		$544,500

Let's Review

Debt Investments Summary

Investments in debt securities are classified as held-to-maturity, trading, or available-for-sale securities. Held-to-maturity securities are purchased with the primary objective of earning interest revenue and collecting the face value of the security at its maturity date. The purchase of, receipt of interest on, and sale of held-to-maturity securities are accounted for using the cost method of accounting.

Trading securities are debt securities that are purchased to earn profits from short-term changes in their market prices. The accounting for the purchase of, receipt of interest on, and sale of trading securities is similar to that for held-to-maturity securities. However, trading securities are valued at their fair value using a valuation allowance account. Increases and decreases in fair value are reported on the income statement as either an unrealized gain or a loss.

Available-for-sale securities are debt securities that a company intends to sell in the future, but not in the near term. The accounting for available-for-sale securities is similar to that for trading securities in that the securities are valued at their fair value using a valuation allowance account. However, increases and decreases in fair value are not reported on the income statement but are reported as part of stockholders' equity on the balance sheet as unrealized gains and losses.

Key Terms

available-for-sale securities (513)
cost method (508)
debt investments (508)
fair value (511)
fair value method (511)
held-to-maturity securities (508)
trading securities (511)
unrealized gain (loss) on available-for-sale investments (514)
unrealized gain (loss) on trading investments (512)
valuation allowance for available-for-sale investments (514)
valuation allowance for trading investments (512)

Assignments

A1-1 Debt security classifications **Obj. 1a, 1b, 1c**

Generally accepted accounting principles (GAAP) classify debt securities into what three categories?

A1-2 Held-to-maturity securities **Obj. 1a**

What is the primary investor objective of purchasing held-to-maturity securities?

A1-3 Accounting for held-to-maturity securities **Obj. 1a**

What method of accounting is used to account for held-to-maturity securities?

A1-4 Reporting held-to-maturity securities **Obj. 1a**

How are held-to-maturity securities reported on the balance sheet?

A1-5 Bond (held-to-maturity) investments **Obj. 1a**

✔ c. Loss on Sale of Investments, $2,100

Illustrate the effects on the accounts and financial statements of the following selected held-to-maturity investment transactions for Beacon Trust:

a. Purchased for cash $420,000 of Vasquez City 6% bonds at 100 plus accrued interest of $6,300.
b. Received first semiannual interest payment.
c. Sold $210,000 of the bonds at 99 plus accrued interest of $1,050.
d. Received face value of remaining bonds at their maturity.

A1-6 Bond (held-to-maturity) investments **Obj. 1a**

✔ c. Gain on Sale of Investments, $1,800

Illustrate the effects on the accounts and financial statements of the following selected held-to-maturity investment transactions for Marr Products:

a. Purchased for cash $180,000 of Hotline Inc. 5% bonds at 100 plus accrued interest of $1,500.
b. Received first semiannual interest payment.
c. Sold $90,000 of the bonds at 102 plus accrued interest of $750.
d. Received face value of remaining bonds at their maturity.

A1-7 Bond (held-to-maturity) investments **Obj. 1a**

✔ d. Accrued interest, $950

Demopoulos Company acquired $150,000 of Marimar Co. 6% bonds on May 1 at their face amount as a held-to-maturity investment. Interest is paid semiannually on May 1 and November 1. On November 1, Demopoulos Company sold $55,000 of the bonds for 98.

Illustrate the effects on the accounts and financial statements of the following:

a. The initial acquisition of the bonds on May 1.
b. The semiannual interest received on November 1.
c. The sale of the bonds on November 1.
d. The accrual of interest on December 31.

A1-8 Bond (held-to-maturity) investments **Obj. 1a**

✔ b. Interest Revenue, $4,800

Bula Investments purchased $240,000 of Effenstein Corp. 8% bonds at their face amount on October 1, 20Y1, as a held-to-maturity investment. The bonds pay interest on October 1 and April 1. On April 1, 20Y2, Bula sold $90,000 of Effenstein Corp. bonds at 102.

Illustrate the effects on the accounts and financial statements of the following selected transactions:

a. The initial purchase of the Effenstein Corp. bonds on October 1, 20Y1.
b. The adjustment for 3 months of accrued interest earned on the Effenstein Corp. bonds on December 31, 20Y1.
c. The receipt of semiannual interest on April 1, 20Y2.
d. The sale of $90,000 of Effenstein Corp. bonds on April 1, 20Y2, at 102.
e. The receipt of the face value of the remaining bonds at their maturity on October 1, 20Y8.

A1-9 Bond (held-to-maturity) investments **Obj. 1a**

✔ a. Interest Receivable, $2,400

Gillooly Co. purchased $360,000 of 6%, 20-year Lumpkin County bonds as a held-to-maturity investment on May 11, Year 1, directly from the county, at their face amount plus accrued interest. The bonds pay semiannual interest on April 1 and October 1. On October 31, Year 1, Gillooly Co. sold $90,000 of the Lumpkin County bonds at 98 plus $450 accrued interest.

Illustrate the effects on the accounts and financial statements of the following:

a. The purchase of the bonds on May 11 plus 40 days of accrued interest.
b. Semiannual interest on October 1.
c. Sale of the bonds on October 31.
d. Adjustment for accrued interest on December 31, Year 1. In computing the accrued interest, use the number of days divided by 360.
e. The receipt of the face value of the remaining bonds at their maturity on April 1, Year 20.

A1-10 Bond (held-to-maturity) investments **Obj. 1a**

✔ a. Jan. 31, Interest Receivable, $375

The following bond investment transactions were completed by Starks Company:

Jan. 31. Purchased $75,000 government bonds as a held-to-maturity investment at 100 plus accrued interest for 1 month. The bonds pay 6% annual interest on July 1 and January 1.

July 1. Received semiannual interest on bond investment.

Aug. 30. Sold $35,000 bonds at 98 plus accrued interest for 2 months.

a. Illustrate the effects on the accounts and financial statements of the preceding transactions.

b. Illustrate the effects on the accounts and financial statements of the December 31 adjustment for semiannual interest earned on the bonds.

c. Illustrate the effects on the accounts and financial statements of the receipt of $40,000 at the bonds' maturity on July 1.

A1-11 Trading securities **Obj. 1b**

What is the primary investor objective of purchasing trading securities?

A1-12 Accounting for trading securities **Obj. 1b**

What method of accounting is used to account for investments in trading securities?

A1-13 Reporting trading securities **Obj. 1b**

During its first year of operations, Coffman Inc. purchased trading securities with excess cash for $50,000. Coffman Inc. expects it will sell the securities within the next year. At the end of the year, these securities had a market value of $61,500.

a. Show how the securities would be reported on Coffman Inc.'s year-end balance sheet.

b. Explain how the increase in fair value of the securities would be reported on Coffman Inc.'s income statement for the year.

A1-14 Fair value adjustment for trading investments **Obj. 1b**

During the year ended December 31, 20Y3, trading securities were purchased for $346,000. On December 31, 20Y3, the securities had a fair value of $309,000.

Illustrate the effects on the accounts and financial statements of the December 31, 20Y3, adjustment to record the unrealized gain or loss on trading investments purchased in 20Y3.

A1-15 Fair value adjustment for trading investments **Obj. 1b**

During the year ended December 31, 20Y9, trading securities were purchased for $72,600. On December 31, 20Y9, the securities had a fair value of $79,100.

Illustrate the effects on the accounts and financial statements of the December 31, 20Y9, adjustment to record the unrealized gain or loss on trading investments purchased in 20Y9.

A1-16 Fair value adjustment for trading investments **Obj. 1b**

The investments of Charger Inc. include an investment of trading securities of Raiders Inc. purchased on February 24, 20Y7, for $551,000. The fair value of the securities on December 31, 20Y7, is $609,000.

a. Illustrate the effects on the accounts and financial statements of the February 24 purchase and the adjustment to fair value on December 31, 20Y7.

b. How is an unrealized gain or loss for trading investments reported on the financial statements?

A1-17 Fair value adjustment for trading investments **Obj. 1b**

✔ c. Unrealized Gain on Trading Investments, $24,550

Gruden Bancorp Inc. purchased a portfolio of trading securities during 20Y3, its first year of operations. The cost and fair value of this portfolio on December 31, 20Y3, are as follows:

Issuing Company	Cost	Fair Value
Griffin Inc.	$ 40,000	$ 44,800
Luck Company	37,500	33,750
Wilson Company	40,000	37,000
Totals	$117,500	$115,550

On May 10, 20Y4, Gruden Bancorp Inc. purchased trading securities of Carroll Inc. for $34,900.

a. Illustrate the effects on the accounts and financial statements of the adjustment for the portfolio of trading securities on December 31, 20Y3.

b. Journalize the May 10, 20Y4, purchase of Carroll Inc. securities.

c. Illustrate the effects on the accounts and financial statements of the adjustment for the portfolio of trading securities on December 31, 20Y4. Assume that except for the purchase of Carroll Inc. securities there were no other transactions involving trading securities in 20Y4. In addition, assume that the fair value of the portfolio of trading securities on December 31, 20Y4, is $175,000.

d. What amount should be reported for trading investments on the December 31, 20Y4, balance sheet?

A1-18 Accounting for available-for-sale securities **Obj. 1c**

What method of accounting is used to account for investments in available-for-sale securities?

A1-19 Reporting available-for-sale securities **Obj. 1c**

During its first year of operations, Giovani Foods purchased available-for-sale securities for $37,500. Giovani Foods expects it will sell the securities within the next year. At the end of the year, these securities had a market value of $33,900.

Explain how the decrease in fair value of the securities would be reported on Giovani Foods' financial statements for the year?

A1-20 Available-for-sale securities; adjustment to fair value **Obj. 1c**

✔ a. $6,100

Using the data from Assignment A1-19, assume that Giovani Foods did not purchase or sell any available-for-sale securities during its second year of operations. At the end of the second year, the market value of the available-for-sale securities is $40,000.

a. What would be the amount of the adjustment to fair value for the available-for-sale securities?

b. After the adjustment is posted to the accounts, what is the balance of the valuation allowance for available-for-sale securities account?

c. How would the increase in the fair value of the securities in the second year be reported on Giovani Foods' financial statements?

A1-21 Fair value adjustment for available-for-sale investments **Obj. 1c**

On January 1, 20Y5, Valuation Allowance for Available-for-Sale Investments had a zero balance. On December 31, 20Y5, the cost of the available-for-sale securities was $43,290, and the fair value was $39,120.

Illustrate the effects on the accounts and financial statements of the adjustment to record the unrealized gain or loss on available-for-sale investments on December 31, 20Y5.

A1-22 Fair value adjustment for available-for-sale investments **Obj. 1c**

On January 1, 20Y7, Valuation Allowance for Available-for-Sale Investments had a zero balance. On December 31, 20Y7, the cost of the available-for-sale securities was $19,040, and the fair value was $22,870.

Illustrate the effects on the accounts and financial statements of the adjustment to record the unrealized gain or loss on available-for-sale investments on December 31, 20Y7.

A1-23 Fair value adjustment for available-for-sale investments **Obj. 1c**

✔ c. Unrealized Gain on Available-for-Sale Investments, $2,500

M. Jones Inc. purchased the following available-for-sale securities during 20Y5, its first year of operations:

Issuing Company	Cost
Arden Enterprises Inc.	$150,000
French Broad Industries Inc.	66,000
Pisgah Construction Inc.	104,000
	$320,000

The fair value of the various available-for-sale securities on December 31, 20Y5, was as follows:

Issuing Company	Fair Value, Dec. 31, 20Y5
Arden Enterprises Inc.	$170,000
French Broad Industries Inc.	71,500
Pisgah Construction Inc.	96,000
	$337,500

a. Illustrate the effects on the accounts and financial statements of the adjustment for the fair value of the portfolio of securities on December 31, 20Y5.

b. If the fair value of the portfolio of securities were the same on December 31, 20Y6, illustrate the effects on the accounts and financial statements to adjust the portfolio to fair value?

c. If the fair value of the portfolio of securities was $340,000 on December 31, 20Y6, illustrate the effects on the accounts and financial statements to adjust the portfolio to fair value?

d. If the fair value of the portfolio of securities was $330,000 on December 31, 20Y6, illustrate the effects on the accounts and financial statements to adjust the portfolio to fair value?

A1-24 Fair value adjustment for available-for-sale investments **Obj. 1c**

Wheeler Inc. owned the following available-for-sale investments as of December 31, 20Y4:

Issuing Company	Cost	Fair Value
Bernard Co.	$ 38,250	$ 37,500
Chadwick Co.	65,520	63,770
Totals	$103,770	$101,270

During 20Y5, Wheeler Inc. did not purchase or sell any available-for-sale securities. The fair value of the Bernard Co. and Chadwick Co. securities as of December 31, 20Y5, were as follows:

Issuing Company	Fair Value
Bernard Co.	$ 40,000
Chadwick Co.	66,000
	$106,000

a. What was the balance of Valuation Allowance for Available-for-Sale Investments as of January 1, 20Y5?

b. Illustrate the effects on the accounts and financial statements of the adjustment to fair value for the available-for-sale investments as of December 31, 20Y5.

c. After the adjustment in (b), what is the balance of Valuation Allowance for Available-for-Sale Investments?

d. Do changes in fair value of available-for-sale securities affect Wheeler Inc.'s net income?

e. If the portfolio of securities held by Wheeler Inc. had been classified as trading securities, how would the investment be reported on the income statement for the year ending December 31, 20Y5, and the December 31, 20Y5, balance sheet?

Equity Investments: Less Than 20% Ownership

Objective 2
Describe and illustrate the accounting for equity investments of less than 20% ownership.

A company may invest in the preferred or common stock of another company as an equity investment. An **equity investment** is an investment in preferred stock or common stock of another company. The company investing in another company's stock is the **investor**. The company whose stock is purchased is the **investee**.

The percent of the investee's outstanding stock purchased by the investor determines the degree of control that the investor has over the investee. This, in turn, determines the accounting method used to record the equity investment.

If the investor purchases less than 20% of the outstanding stock of the investee, the investor is considered to have *no control* over the investee. In this case, it is assumed that the investor purchased the stock primarily to earn dividends or to realize gains on price increases of the stock.

All equity investments of less than 20% of the investee's outstanding stock are accounted for using the fair value method.[6] Under the **fair value method**, the following transactions are recorded:

- Purchase of stock
- Receipt of dividends
- Sale of stock
- Change in fair value

Purchase of Stock

The purchase of stock is recorded at its cost. To illustrate, assume that on May 1, 20Y7, Tindell Company purchases 2,000 shares of Lisa Company common stock at $50 per share. The effects of the purchase of the stock on the accounts and financial statements are as follows:

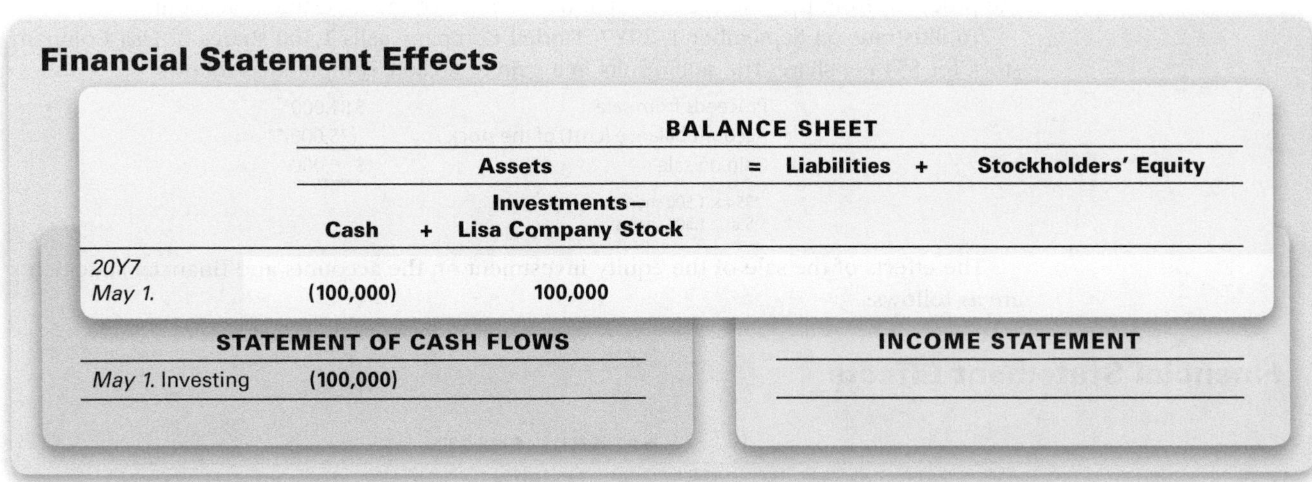

Financial Statement Effects

BALANCE SHEET

	Assets		=	Liabilities	+	Stockholders' Equity
	Cash	+ Investments—Lisa Company Stock				
20Y7 *May 1.*	(100,000)	100,000				

STATEMENT OF CASH FLOWS

May 1. Investing	(100,000)

INCOME STATEMENT

[6] This discussion is consistent with *Financial Instruments, Subtopic 825-10, FASB Accounting Standards Update*, Financial Accounting Standards Board, Norwalk, CT, January 2016.

Receipt of Dividends

On July 31, 20Y7, Tindell Company receives a dividend of $0.40 per share from Lisa Company. The effects of the receipt of the dividend on the accounts and financial statements are as follows:

Financial Statement Effects

BALANCE SHEET

	Assets	=	Liabilities	+	Stockholders' Equity
	Cash	=			**Retained Earnings**
20Y7 July 31.	800				800

STATEMENT OF CASH FLOWS

July 31. Operating	800

INCOME STATEMENT

July 31. Dividend revenue	800

Dividend Revenue is reported as part of "Other revenue" on Tindell Company's income statement. Cash dividends received are reported as an operating cash inflow on Tindell Company's statement of cash flows.

Sale of Stock

The sale of an equity investment normally results in a gain or loss. A gain is recorded if the proceeds from the sale exceed the balance of the investment account. A loss is recorded if the proceeds from the sale are less than the balance of the investment account.

To illustrate, on September 1, 20Y7, Tindell Company sells 1,500 shares of Lisa Company stock for $54 per share. The sale results in a gain of $6,000, computed as follows:

Proceeds from sale	$ 81,000*
Account balance (cost) of the stock	(75,000)**
Gain on sale	$ 6,000

*$54 × 1,500 shares
**$50 × 1,500 shares

The effects of the sale of the equity investment on the accounts and financial statements are as follows:

Financial Statement Effects

BALANCE SHEET

	Assets			=	Liabilities	+	Stockholders' Equity
	Cash	+	**Investments—Lisa Company Stock**	=			**Retained Earnings**
20Y7 Sept. 1.	81,000		(75,000)				6,000

STATEMENT OF CASH FLOWS

Sept. 1. Investing	81,000

INCOME STATEMENT

Sept. 1. Gain on sale of investments—Lisa Company stock	6,000

The gain on the sale of investments is reported as part of "Other revenue" on Tindell Company's income statement.

Change in Fair Value

At the end of the accounting period, an adjustment is made to record the change in the fair value of the investment. **Fair value** is the market price that would be received if the security were sold. A change in fair value of an equity investment is recognized in net income as an **unrealized gain or loss on equity investments** for the period.[7]

To illustrate, assume that Tindell Company's year-end is December 31, 20Y7, and that the remaining 500 shares of Lisa Company stock have a fair value of $55 per share. The increase in fair value results in an unrealized gain of $2,500, computed as follows:

Fair value of investment	$ 27,500*
Less balance of the investment account	(25,000)**
Change in fair value	$ 2,500

*500 shares × $55
**$100,000 – $75,000

In order to maintain a record of the original cost of the equity securities, a valuation account, called Valuation Allowance for Equity Investments, is increased for $2,500, and Unrealized Gain on Equity Investments is increased for $2,500. The adjustment to record the increase in fair value of the equity investment is as follows:

Financial Statement Effects

BALANCE SHEET

	Assets	=	Liabilities	+	Stockholders' Equity
	Valuation Allowance for Equity Investments	=			Retained Earnings
20Y7 Dec. 31.	2,500				2,500

STATEMENT OF CASH FLOWS

INCOME STATEMENT

Dec. 31. Unrealized gain on equity investments	2,500

On the income statement, Tindell Company would report an unrealized gain on equity investments of $2,500. On its December 31, 20Y7, balance sheet, the Lisa Company stock is reported as "Equity investment at cost" under "Current assets." The **valuation allowance for equity investments** is reported as an addition to the cost of the investment, as follows:

Tindell Company
Balance Sheet
December 31, 20Y7

Current assets:		
Cash		$ 75,000
Accounts receivable		190,000
Equity investment at cost	$25,000	
Valuation allowance	2,500	
Equity investment at fair value		27,500

When a company owns more than one equity security, the securities are valued and reported as a group (portfolio) using the securities' fair values. The unrealized gain on equity investments would be reported as part of "Other revenue" on Tindell Company's income statement.

[7] *Financial Instruments, Subtopic 825-10, FASB Accounting Standards Update.*

Over time, the valuation allowance account is adjusted to reflect changes in the fair value of the portfolio. Thus, increases in fair value from the beginning of the period will result in an adjustment to record an unrealized gain, similar to the preceding journal entry. Likewise, decreases in fair value from the beginning of the period will result in an adjustment to record an unrealized loss.

To illustrate, assume that on December 31, 20Y8, the fair value of the 500 shares of Lisa Company stock is $64 per share or $32,000 (500 shares × $64). The adjustment for increase in fair value of $4,500 ($32,000 – $27,500) increases Valuation Allowance for Equity Investments and increases Unrealized Gain on Equity Investments for $4,500. After the adjustment, Valuation Allowance for Equity Investments would have a balance of $7,000, as follows:

Valuation Allowance for Equity Investments	
Jan. 1, 20Y8 Balance	$2,500
Dec. 31 Adjustment	4,500
Dec. 31, 20Y8 Adjusted balance	$7,000

The unrealized gain of $4,500 would be reported on Tindell Company's 20Y8 income statement. The equity investment in Lisa Company stock is reported on the December 31, 20Y8, balance sheet at its fair value of $32,000, as follows:

Tindell Company
Balance Sheet
December 31, 20Y8

Current assets:		
Cash		$ 75,000
Accounts receivable		190,000
Equity investment at cost	$25,000	
Valuation allowance	7,000	
Equity investment at fair value		32,000

Let's Review

Equity Investments: Less Than 20% Ownership Summary

If an investor purchases less than 20% of the outstanding stock of an investee, the investor is considered to have *no control* over the investee. In this case, the equity investment is accounted for using the fair value method.

Under the fair value method, entries are recorded for the purchase of, receipt of any dividends on, and sale of the stock. In addition, at the end of the accounting period, an adjustment is made to record the change in the fair value of the investment. Any change in fair value of the investment is recorded using a valuation account, which is reported on the balance sheet as an addition or deduction from the investment's original cost. Any related unrealized gain or loss for the period is reported on the income statement under "Other revenue and expense."

Key Terms

equity investment (521)
fair value (523)
fair value method (521)
investee (521)
investor (521)
unrealized gain or loss on equity investments (523)
valuation allowance for equity investments (523)

Assignments

A1-25 Accounting for equity investments — Obj. 2

Williamson Inc. owns 15% of the outstanding common stock of Olson Corporation.

For purposes of determining the proper accounting for Williamson Inc.'s investment in Olson Corporation, is it proper to assume that Williamson Inc. controls Olson Corporation? Explain.

A1-26 Accounting for equity investments — Obj. 2

What method of accounting is used to account for equity investments of less than 20% ownership?

A1-27 Accounting for equity investments; less than 20% ownership — Obj. 2

✔ c. Gain on sale, $6,000

Bellows Inc. purchased 10,000 shares of Nesbitt Inc.'s common stock for $7.50 per share. Nesbitt Inc. has 100,000 shares of common stock outstanding.

a. What account and amount is used by Bellows Inc. to record the investment in Nesbitt Inc.?

b. Assuming that Nesbitt Inc. paid a dividend of $0.40 per share, what account and amount is used by Bellows Inc. to record the receipt of the dividend?

c. If Bellows Inc. sold 4,000 shares of Nesbitt Inc.'s common stock for $9.00 per share, how much gain on the investment would Bellows Inc. recognize?

A1-28 Determining fair value — Obj. 2

In recording the change in fair value of an equity investment with less than 20% ownership, what is used to determine fair value?

A1-29 Reporting change in fair value — Obj. 2

Explain how a change in fair value of an equity investment with less than 20% ownership is reported on the investor's (a) income statement and (b) balance sheet.

A1-30 Equity investment transactions; less than 20% ownership — Obj. 2

✔ c. Gain on Sale of Investments, $36,000

On January 23, 15,000 shares of Aurora Company's common stock are acquired at a price of $25 per share. On April 12, a $0.50-per-share dividend was received on the Aurora Company stock. On June 10, 6,000 shares of the Aurora Company stock were sold for $31 per share. At the end of the accounting period (December 31), the fair value of the remaining 9,000 shares of Aurora Company's stock was $30 per share. Aurora Company has 200,000 shares of common stock outstanding.

Illustrate the effects on the accounts and financial statements of (a) the purchase of the stock, (b) the receipt of the dividends, (c) the sale of 6,000 shares, and (d) the change in fair value.

A1-31 Equity investment transactions; less than 20% ownership — Obj. 2

✔ c. Loss on Sale of Investments, $4,800

On September 12, 3,000 shares of Denver Company's common stock are acquired at a price of $40 per share. On October 15, an $0.80-per-share dividend was received on the Denver Company stock. On November 10, 1,600 shares of the Denver Company stock were sold for $37 per share. At the end of the accounting period (December 31), the fair value of the remaining 1,400 shares of Denver Company's stock was $35 per share. Denver Company has 400,000 shares of common stock outstanding.

Illustrate the effects on the accounts and financial statements of (a) the purchase of the stock, (b) the receipt of the dividends, (c) the sale of 6,000 shares, and (d) the change in fair value.

A1-32 Equity investment transactions; less than 20% ownership — Obj. 2

✔ Sept. 10, Loss on Sale of Investments, $18,000

The following equity investment transactions were completed by Vintage Company during a recent year:

Apr. 10. Purchased 11,000 shares of Delew Company's common stock for a price of $60 per share. Delew Company has 250,000 shares of common stock outstanding.

July 8. Received a quarterly dividend of $0.85 per share on the Delew Company investment.

Sept. 10. Sold 3,000 shares for a price of $54 per share.

Dec. 31. At the end of the accounting period, the fair value of the remaining 8,000 shares of Delew Company's stock was $58 per share.

Illustrate the effects on the accounts and financial statements of the preceding transactions.

A1-33 Equity investment transactions; fair value method — Obj. 2

✔ July 26, Gain on Sale of Investments, $22,500

Quan Corp. manufactures construction equipment. Illustrate the effects on the accounts and financial statements of the following selected equity investment transactions completed by Quan during a recent year using the fair value method:

Feb. 2. Purchased for cash 3,100 shares of Celeste Inc.'s common stock for $32 per share. Celeste Inc. has 80,000 shares of common stock outstanding.

Mar. 6. Received dividends of $0.45 per share on Celeste Inc. stock.

June 7. Purchased an additional 1,400 shares of Celeste Inc. stock for $38.

July 26. Sold 2,500 shares purchased on February 2 for $41 per share.

Sept. 25. Received dividends of $0.62 per share on Celeste Inc. stock.

Dec. 31. At the end of the accounting period, the fair value of the remaining 2,000 shares of Celeste Inc. stock was $40 per share.

A1-34 Equity investment transactions; fair value method — Obj. 2

✔ Aug. 12, Loss on Sale of Investments, $2,250

Seamus Industries Inc. buys and sells investments as part of its ongoing cash management. The following investment transactions were completed during the year:

Feb. 24. Purchased 1,000 shares of Tett Co.'s common stock for $85 per share.

May 16. Purchased 2,500 shares of Isaacson Co.'s common stock for $36.

July 14. Sold 400 shares of Tett Co. stock for $100 per share.

Aug. 12. Sold 750 shares of Isaacson Co. stock for $33 per share.

Oct. 31. Received dividends of $0.40 per share on Tett Co. stock.

Dec. 31. At the end of the accounting period, the fair value of the remaining 600 shares of Tett Co.'s stock was $110 per share. The fair value of the remaining 1,750 shares of Isaacson Co.'s stock was $30 per share.

Illustrate the effects on the accounts and financial statements of the preceding transactions.

A1-35 Fair value adjustment for equity investments; less than 20% ownership — Obj. 2

✔ a. $8,500 balance

Malia Industries owned the following equity investments as of December 31, 20Y3:

Issuing Company	Cost	Fair Value
Jolliff Co.	$ 75,000	$ 82,500
Polich Inc.	50,000	48,300
Shaklee Corporation	25,000	27,700
	$150,000	$158,500

Each of the preceding equity investments was purchased in 20Y3 and is less than 20% ownership of the issuing company. During 20Y4, Malia Industries did not purchase or sell any of the equity securities. The fair value of the equity securities as of December 31, 20Y4, was as follows:

Issuing Company	Cost
Jolliff Co.	$ 80,000
Polich Inc.	45,000
Shaklee Corporation	24,500
	$149,500

a. What was the balance of Valuation Allowance for Equity Investments as of December 31, 20Y3?

b. Illustrate the effects on the accounts and financial statements of the adjustment to fair value for the equity investments as of December 31, 20Y4.

c. After the adjustment in (b), what is the balance of Valuation Allowance for Equity Investments?

d. Does the change in fair value of the equity securities in 20Y4 affect Malia Industries' net income?

Equity Investments: 20%–50% Ownership

Objective 3
Describe and illustrate the accounting for equity investments with 20%–50% ownership.

If a company (investor) purchases between 20% and 50% of the outstanding stock of another company (investee), the investor is considered to have a *significant influence* over the investee. Investments of between 20% and 50% of the investee's outstanding stock are accounted for using the **equity method**.

Under the equity method, a stock investment is recorded at its initial cost. However, the investor's share of the investee's operating results and dividends are also recorded in the investment account as follows:

- *Net Income:* The investor records its share (percent) of the net income of the investee as an increase to the investment account. Its share (percent) of any net loss is recorded as a decrease to the investment account.
- *Dividends:* The investor's share (percent) of cash dividends received from the investee decreases the investment account.

Purchase of Stock

To illustrate, assume that Simpson Inc. purchased a 40% interest in Flanders Corporation's common stock on January 2, 20Y6, for $350,000. The effects of the stock purchase on the accounts and financial statements are as follows:

Financial Statement Effects

BALANCE SHEET

	Assets		=	Liabilities	+	Stockholders' Equity
	Cash	+ Investment in Flanders Corp. Stock				
20Y6 *Jan. 2.*	(350,000)	350,000				

STATEMENT OF CASH FLOWS

Jan. 2. Investing	(350,000)

INCOME STATEMENT

Recording Investee Net Income

For the year ended December 31, 20Y6, Flanders Corporation reported net income of $105,000. Under the equity method, Simpson Inc. (investor) records its share (percent) of Flanders net income. The effects of recording Simpson Inc.'s share of Flanders net income on the accounts and financial statements are as follows:

Financial Statement Effects

BALANCE SHEET

	Assets	=	Liabilities	+	Stockholders' Equity
	Investment in Flanders Corp. Stock	=			Retained Earnings
20Y6 *Dec. 31.*	42,000*				42,000

STATEMENT OF CASH FLOWS

INCOME STATEMENT

Dec. 31. Income of Flanders Corp.	42,000

*$105,000 x 40%

Income of Flanders Corporation is reported on Simpson Inc.'s income statement separately or as part of "Other revenue." If Flanders Corporation had a net loss during the period, the loss would be recorded as an increase to Loss from Flanders Corporation and a decrease to Investment in Flanders Corporation Stock.

Recording Investee Dividends

During the year ended December 31, 20Y6, Flanders Corporation declared and paid cash dividends of $45,000. Under the equity method, Simpson Inc. (investor) records its share (percent) of Flanders dividends. The effects of receiving the Flanders' Corporation dividend on the accounts and financial statements are as follows:

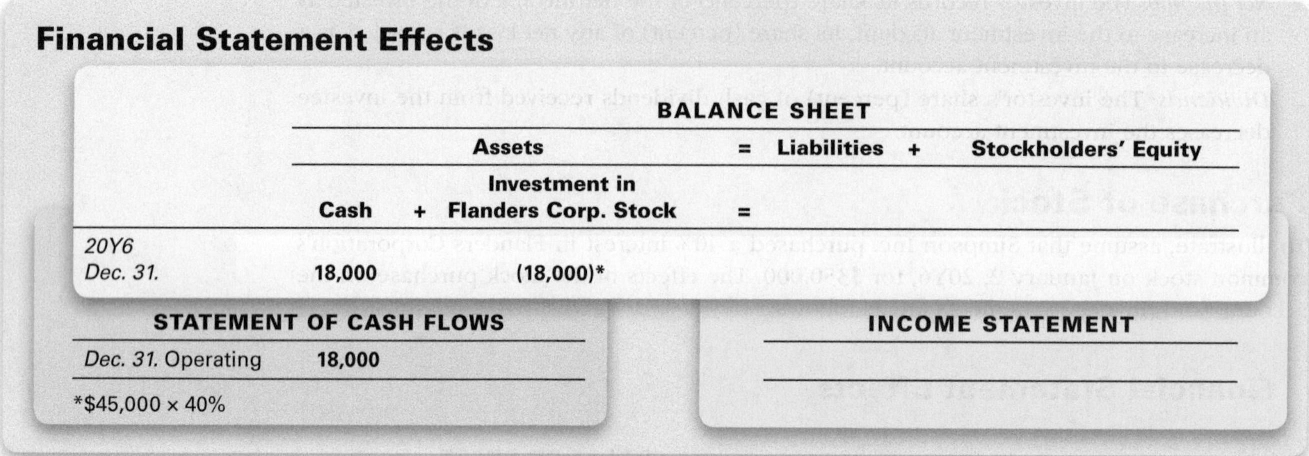

Financial Statement Effects

BALANCE SHEET

	Assets		= Liabilities +	Stockholders' Equity
	Cash	+ Investment in Flanders Corp. Stock	=	
20Y6 *Dec. 31.*	18,000	(18,000)*		

STATEMENT OF CASH FLOWS

Dec. 31. Operating	18,000

*$45,000 × 40%

INCOME STATEMENT

The effect of recording 40% of Flanders Corporation's net income and dividends is to increase the investment account by $24,000 ($42,000 − $18,000). Thus, Investment in Flanders Corporation Stock increases from $350,000 to $374,000, as shown in Exhibit 2.

Exhibit 2
Investment and Dividends

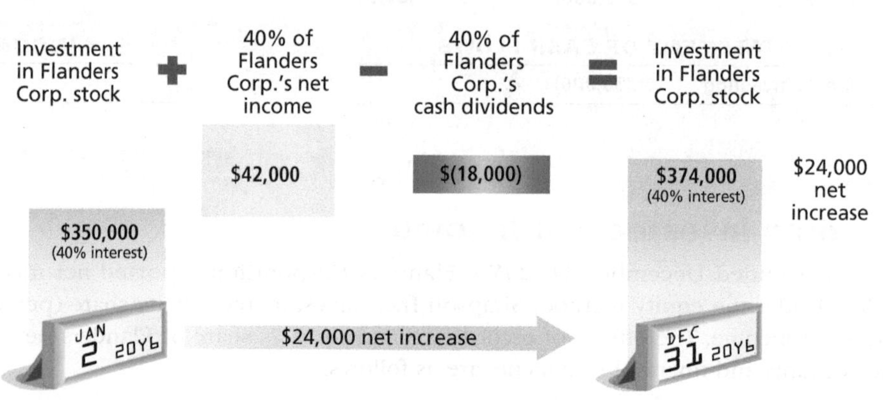

Investments accounted for under the equity method are reported on the balance sheet as noncurrent assets and are not adjusted to fair value. Any dividends received are reported as a cash inflow from operating activities on the statement of cash flows.

Recording Sale of Stock

Under the equity method, a gain or loss is normally recorded from the sale of an investment. A gain is recorded if the proceeds exceed the balance of the investment account. A loss is recorded if the proceeds are less than the balance of the investment account.

To illustrate, if Simpson Inc. sold Flanders Corporation's stock on January 1, 20Y7, for $400,000, a gain of $26,000 would be reported, computed as follows:

Proceeds from sale	$ 400,000
Balance in the stock investment account	(374,000)
Gain on sale	$ 26,000

The effects of selling the Flanders Corporation stock on the accounts and financial statements are as follows:

Financial Statement Effects

BALANCE SHEET

	Assets		=	Liabilities +	Stockholders' Equity
	Cash	+ Investment in Flanders Corp. Stock	=		Retained Earnings
20Y7 *Jan. 1.*	400,000	(374,000)			26,000

STATEMENT OF CASH FLOWS

Jan. 1. Investing	400,000

INCOME STATEMENT

Jan. 1. Gain on sale of Flanders Corporation stock	26,000

Let's Review

Equity Investments: 20%–50% Ownership

Summary

If a company (investor) purchases between 20% and 50% of the outstanding stock of another company (investee), the investor is considered to have a *significant influence* over the investee. Investments of between 20% and 50% of the investee's outstanding stock are accounted for using the equity method.

Under the equity method, a stock investment is recorded at its initial cost. However, the investor records its share (percent) of the net income of the investee as an increase to the investment account and an increase to the investor's income. The investor's share (percent) of any investee's net loss is recorded as a decrease to the investment account and a decrease to the investor's income. The investor's share (percent) of cash dividends received from the investee increases cash and decreases the investment account.

Under the equity method, a gain or loss is normally recorded from the sale of an investment. A gain is recorded if the proceeds exceed the balance of the investment account. A loss is recorded if the proceeds are less than the balance of the investment account.

Investments accounted for under the equity method are reported on the balance sheet as noncurrent assets and are not adjusted to fair value.

Key Term

equity method (527)

Assignments

A1-36 Equity investments; significant influence **Obj. 3**

What percentage of an investee's outstanding common stock must an investor acquire in order to be considered to have significant influence over the investee?

A1-37 Accounting for equity investments **Obj. 3**

What method of accounting is used for investments between 20% and 50% of the investee's outstanding common stock?

A1-38 Accounting for equity investments; 20%–50% ownership **Obj. 3**

Lynch Corporation owns 35% of the outstanding common stock of Katherine Interiors Inc.

a. Explain how Lynch Corporation would account for its share of Katherine Interiors' net income of $500,000.

b. Explain how Lynch Corporation would account for the receipt of $30,000 of dividends from Katherine Interiors Inc.

A1-39 Reporting equity investments; 20%–50% ownership **Obj. 3**

Pascal Inc. acquired 40% of the outstanding common stock of Andres Corporation for $1,200,000. During the year, Andres Corporation reported net income of $220,000 and paid dividends of $45,000.

Explain how Pascal Inc. would report its investment in Andres Corporation on its year-end balance sheet (classification and amount).

A1-40 Equity investment transactions; 20%–50% ownership **Obj. 3**

On January 2, 20Y7, Mikedes Company acquired 30% of the outstanding stock of Violet Company for $720,000. For the year ended December 31, 20Y7, Violet Company earned income of $190,000 and paid dividends of $40,000. On January 31, 20Y8, Mikedes Company sold all of its investment in Violet Company stock for $770,000.

Illustrate the effects on the accounts and financial statements of Mikedes Company of (a) the purchase of the stock, (b) the share of Violet Company income, (c) the dividends received from Violet Company, and (d) the sale of the Violet Company stock.

A1-41 Equity investment transactions; 20%–50% ownership **Obj. 3**

On January 2, 20Y4, Whitworth Company acquired 40% of the outstanding stock of Aloof Company for $340,000. For the year ended December 31, 20Y4, Aloof Company earned income of $180,000 and paid dividends of $10,000. On January 31, 20Y5, Whitworth Company sold all of its investment in Aloof Company stock for $405,000.

Illustrate the effects on the accounts and financial statements of Whitworth Company of (a) the purchase of the stock, (b) the share of Aloof income, (c) the dividends received from Aloof Company, and (d) the sale of the Aloof Company stock.

A1-42 Equity investment transactions; 20%–50% ownership **Obj. 3**

At a total cost of $5,600,000, Herrera Corporation acquired 280,000 shares of Tran Corp. common stock as a long-term investment. Tran Corp. has 800,000 shares of common stock outstanding, including the shares acquired by Herrera Corporation.

a. Illustrate the effects on the accounts and financial statements of Herrera Corporation of the following information:

   1. Tran Corp. reports net income of $600,000 for the current period.
   2. A cash dividend of $0.50 per common share is paid by Tran Corp. during the current period.

b. Why is the equity method appropriate for the Tran Corp. investment?

A1-43 Equity investment transactions; 20%–50% ownership **Obj. 3**

✔ b. $14,900,000

On January 4, 20Y4, Ferguson Company purchased 480,000 shares of Silva Company's common stock directly from one of the founders for a price of $30 per share. Silva has 1,200,000 shares outstanding, including the Ferguson shares. On July 2, 20Y4, Silva paid $750,000 in total dividends to its shareholders. On December 31, 20Y4, Silva reported a net income of $2,000,000 for the year.

a. Illustrate the effects on the accounts and financial statements of Ferguson Company of the preceding transactions involving the investment in Silva Company during 20Y4.

b. Determine the December 31, 20Y4, balance of the investment in Silva Company stock account.

A1-44 Equity investment transactions; 20%–50% ownership **Obj. 3**

✔ b. $184,800

On January 6, 20Y8, Bulldog Co. purchased 34% of the outstanding common stock of Gator Co. for $212,000. Gator Co. paid total dividends of $24,000 to all shareholders on June 30, 20Y8. Gator had a net loss of $56,000 for 20Y8.

a. Illustrate the effects on the accounts and financial statements of Bulldog's purchase of the stock, receipt of the dividends, and the equity loss in Gator Co. stock.

b. Compute the balance of Investment in Gator Co. Stock on December 31, 20Y8.

c. How does valuing an investment under the equity method differ from valuing an investment at fair value?

A1-45 Equity method **Obj. 3**

Hawkeye Company's balance sheet reported, under the equity method, its long-term investment in Raven Company for comparative years as follows:

	Dec. 31, 20Y6	Dec. 31, 20Y5
Investment in Raven Company stock (in millions)	$281	$264

In addition, the 20Y6 Hawkeye Company income statement disclosed equity earnings in the Raven Company investment as $25 million. Hawkeye Company neither purchased nor sold Raven Company stock during 20Y6. The fair value of the Raven Company stock investment on December 31, 20Y6, was $310 million.

Explain the change in Investment in Raven Company Stock from December 31, 20Y5, to December 31, 20Y6.

Equity Investments: More Than 50% Ownership

Objective 4

Describe and illustrate the accounting for equity investments with more than 50% ownership.

If an investor purchases more than 50% of the outstanding common stock of an investee, the investor is considered to have *control* over the investee. The purchase of more than 50% ownership of the investee's stock is termed a **business combination**. The corporation owning all or a majority of the voting stock of another corporation is called the **parent company**. The corporation that is controlled is called the **subsidiary company**.

A company may acquire more than 50% of the outstanding common stock of an investee for a variety of strategic reasons. For example, by obtaining control over the subsidiary, the parent may be able to rapidly expand its operations into new markets or diversify its operations. In other cases, a company may be able to guarantee and streamline its supply chain by acquiring a supplier.

Although the corporations that make up a parent and subsidiary relationship may operate as a single economic unit, they normally maintain separate accounting records and prepare separate financial statements for internal reporting purposes. For external reporting, however, results of operations and the financial position of a parent and subsidiary are combined and reported as a single economic unit. Such financial statements are more relevant and useful to external stakeholders because the parent company, in substance, controls the subsidiary.

The separate financial statements of the parent and subsidiary are combined and reported as a consolidated entity. These combined financial statements are called **consolidated financial statements**. Such statements are normally identified by adding *and Subsidiary(ies)* to the name of the parent corporation or by adding *Consolidated* to the statement title.

Preparing Consolidated Financial Statements

Consolidated financial statements are prepared by combining the separate financial statements of the parent and subsidiary into a single set of financial statements. In doing so, the accounts for the parent and subsidiary are added together (consolidated) using the following two principles:

1. The effects of any intercompany, parent-subsidiary transactions must be eliminated.
2. The parent's investment account is offset (eliminated) against the subsidiary's equity accounts.

When the separate parent and subsidiary financial statements are combined into consolidated statements, special attention should be given to intercompany transactions. **Intercompany transactions** by their very nature affect accounts of both the parent and subsidiary. For example, assume that the parent issued a $100,000 note payable to its subsidiary for cash. In this case, the parent's general ledger would include Notes Payable with a $100,000 balance. Likewise, the subsidiary's general ledger would include Notes Receivable with a $100,000 balance. These corresponding accounts in the parent and subsidiary's ledgers are called **reciprocal accounts**. Examples of other accounts often affected by intercompany transactions include Accounts Receivable, Interest Expense, Interest Revenue, Sales, Cost of Goods Sold, and Inventory.

The effects of intercompany transactions must be eliminated when the financial statements of the parent and subsidiary are consolidated. For example, the preceding reciprocal accounts, the $100,000 Notes Payable and Notes Receivable, must be eliminated (offset). This is because consolidated financial statements are prepared as if the parent and subsidiary were one economic entity (company). In other words, in the preceding example the consolidated company cannot owe itself a $100,000 note.

The parent's investment in subsidiary account is also reciprocal to the subsidiary's stockholder equity accounts. For example, assume that Schofield Inc. has stockholders' equity consisting of $75,000, no par common stock, and retained earnings of $645,000. Parkdale Corp. purchases all of Schofield Inc.'s common stock for $720,000. In this case, Parkdale Corp.'s investment account, Investment in Schofield Inc., is reciprocal to Schofield's accounts, Common Stock ($75,000) and Retained Earnings ($645,000). Since the consolidated entity cannot own itself, Investment in Schofield Inc. of $720,000 is eliminated (offset) against Schofield Inc.'s Common Stock of $75,000 and Retained Earnings of $645,000.

The elimination of reciprocal accounts is not actually recorded by the parent and subsidiary. The effects are only eliminated in preparing the consolidated financial statements. This is normally done using a spreadsheet (work sheet), which is illustrated next.

Illustration of Consolidated Financial Statements

To illustrate the preparation of consolidated financial statements, assume that Pierson Inc. owns 100% of the common stock of Smith Corporation.[8] Pierson Inc. and Smith Corporation maintain separate accounting records, prepare separate financial statements, and use a common fiscal year ending on December 31. Balance sheets for Pierson Inc. and Smith Corporation for the year ending December 31, 20Y5, are shown in Exhibit 3.

Exhibit 3

Balance Sheets for Pierson Inc. and Smith Corporation

	A	F	G
1	**Pierson Inc. and Subsidiary**		
2	**Balance Sheets**		
3	**December 31, 20Y5**		
4		**Pierson Inc.**	**Smith Corporation**
5	**Assets**		
6	Cash	275,000	100,000
7	Accounts Receivable	750,000	400,000
8	Inventory	1,200,000	800,000
9	Investment in Smith Corporation	500,000	—
10	Other assets	3,275,000	700,000
11	Total assets	6,000,000	2,000,000
12			
13	**Liabilities**		
14	Accounts Payable	850,000	280,000
15	Other liabilities	1,500,000	1,220,000
16	Total liabilities	2,350,000	1,500,000
17			
18	**Stockholders' Equity**		
19	Common Stock	100,000	50,000
20	Retained Earnings	3,550,000	450,000
21	Total stockholders' equity	3,650,000	500,000
22	Total liabilities and stockholders' equity	6,000,000	2,000,000

Assume that except for Pierson's ownership of Smith Corporation, the companies have no intercompany transactions or other reciprocal accounts.

[8] To simplify, we assume that the parent company owns 100% of the common stock of the subsidiary. Ownership of less than 100% is discussed in advanced accounting courses.

The consolidated balance sheet is prepared by eliminating the balance of Pierson Inc.'s Investment in Smith Corporation of $500,000 against Smith Corporation's Common Stock of $50,000 and Retained Earnings of $450,000. This elimination is shown in color in Exhibit 4. The remaining accounts are added together in the Consolidated Balance Sheet column of Exhibit 4.

Exhibit 4
Consolidated Work Sheet (Spreadsheet)

	A	C	D	E	F
1	**Pierson Inc. and Subsidiary**				
2	**Consolidated Balance Sheet Work Sheet**				
3	**December 31, 20Y5**				
4		**Pierson Inc.**	**Smith Corporation**	**Eliminations**	**Consolidated Balance Sheet**
5	**Assets**				
6	Cash	275,000	100,000		375,000
7	Accounts Receivable	750,000	400,000		1,150,000
8	Inventory	1,200,000	800,000		2,000,000
9	Investment in Smith Corporation	500,000	—	**(500,000)**	—
10	Other assets	3,275,000	700,000		3,975,000
11	Total assets	6,000,000	2,000,000		7,500,000
12					
13	**Liabilities**				
14	Accounts Payable	850,000	280,000		1,130,000
15	Other liabilities	1,500,000	1,220,000		2,720,000
16	Total liabilities	2,350,000	1,500,000		3,850,000
17					
18	**Stockholders' Equity**				
19	Common Stock	100,000	50,000	**(50,000)**	100,000
20	Retained Earnings	3,550,000	450,000	**(450,000)**	3,550,000
21	Total stockholders' equity	3,650,000	500,000		3,650,000
22	Total liabilities and stockholders' equity	6,000,000	2,000,000		7,500,000
23					

The consolidated balance sheet would be prepared from the right-hand column of Exhibit 4. Since there were no other reciprocal accounts (intercompany transactions), the consolidated income statement would be prepared by adding the separate income statements of Pierson Inc. and Smith Corporation together.

If any intercompany transactions did occur during the year or if there were other reciprocal accounts, their effects would also be eliminated in preparing the consolidated financial statements. To illustrate, assume that during 20Y5 Smith Corporation sold and received payment of $300,000 for merchandise purchased by Pierson Inc. The merchandise sold to Pierson Inc. cost Smith Corporation $180,000. In turn, Pierson Inc. sold the merchandise to another (nonaffiliated) company for $450,000.

Since the consolidated entity cannot sell merchandise to itself, Smith Corporation's sale of $300,000 to Pierson Inc. must be eliminated. When Pierson Inc. sold the merchandise to another company for $450,000, it recorded cost of goods sold of $300,000. However, the merchandise only cost the consolidated entity $180,000, which was recorded by Smith Corporation when it sold the merchandise to Pierson Inc. As result, the elimination must be made that decreases Sales for $300,000 and decreases Cost of Goods Sold for $300,000. The consolidated entity would then report a sale of $450,000 and related cost of goods sold of $180,000.

Let's Review

Equity Investments: More Than 50% Ownership

Summary

The corporation owning all or a majority of the voting stock of another corporation is called the parent company. The corporation that is controlled is called the subsidiary company. Since the parent company has control over the subsidiary company, consolidated financial statements are reported to external stakeholders as one economic entity. In preparing consolidated financial statements, (1) the effects of any intercompany, parent-subsidiary transactions are eliminated and (2) the parent's investment account is offset (eliminated) against the subsidiary's equity accounts.

Key Terms

business combination (531)
consolidated financial statements (531)
intercompany transactions (531)
parent company (531)
reciprocal accounts (531)
subsidiary company (531)

Assignments

A1-46 Reporting equity investments; more than 50% ownership **Obj. 4**
Why are consolidated financial statements reported to external stakeholders?

A1-47 Preparing consolidated statements **Obj. 4**
What are two principles used in preparing consolidated financial statements?

A1-48 Preparing consolidated statements **Obj. 4**
Why are the effects of intercompany transactions eliminated in preparing consolidated financial statements?

A1-49 Preparing consolidated statements **Obj. 4**
The parent company's account, "Investment in Subsidiary," is eliminated against what subsidiary accounts in preparing consolidated financial statements?

A1-50 Preparing consolidated statements **Obj. 4**
Are the elimination entries used in preparing consolidated financial statements recorded in the accounts (ledgers) of the parent and subsidiary companies?

A1-51 Preparing a consolidated balance sheet — Obj. 4

Pryor Corp. owns 100% of the common stock of Stark Inc. Pryor Corp.'s investment in Stark Inc. is recorded in its ledger as "Investment in Stark Inc." with a balance of $11,150,000. The stockholders' equity of Pryor Corp. and Stark Inc. for the year ending December 31, 20Y6, is as follows:

	Pryor Corp.	Stark Inc.
Common stock	$ 12,000,000	$2,500,000
Retained earnings	125,000,000	8,650,000

a. What elimination entry would be made in the spreadsheet for preparing the consolidated balance sheet?

b. Show how the stockholders' equity of Pryor Corp. and Subsidiary would be reported on the consolidated balance sheet.

A1-52 Preparing a consolidated balance sheet — Obj. 4

Phelps Corporation owns all of the common stock of Stern Company. Each company maintains its own accounting records and prepares separate financial statements. Balance sheets for each company as of December 31, 20Y8, are as follows:

	A	F	G
1	**Phelps Corporation and Subsidiary**		
2	**Balance Sheets**		
3	**December 31, 20Y8**		
4		**Phelps Corporation**	**Stern Company**
5	**Assets**		
6	Cash	30,500	20,500
7	Accounts Receivable	29,100	22,500
8	Inventory	75,750	35,250
9	Investment in Stern Company	92,500	—
10	Other assets	300,000	44,250
11	Total assets	527,850	122,500
12			
13	**Liabilities and Stockholders' Equity**		
14	Accounts Payable	75,000	30,000
15	Common Stock	300,000	50,000
16	Retained Earnings	152,850	42,500
17	Total liabilities and stockholders' equity	527,850	122,500

a. Prepare a spreadsheet for consolidating the balance sheets of Phelps Corporation and Stern Company.

b. Prepare a December 31, 20Y8, consolidated balance for Phelps Corporation and Subsidiary.

c. Assume that the accounts receivable of Phelps Corporation include $3,000 that is due from Stern Company. What would the consolidated balance sheet report for accounts receivable and accounts payable?

A1-53 Preparing a consolidated income statement **Obj. 4**

For the year ended December 31, 20Y2, the operating results of Paley Corporation and its wholly owned subsidiary, Sims Enterprises, are as follows:

	A	F	G
1		**Paley Corporation**	**Sims Enterprises**
2	Sales	3,200,000	900,000
3	Cost of goods sold	(1,900,000)	(550,000)
4	Gross profit	1,300,000	350,000
5	Operating expenses	(750,000)	(125,000)
6	Operating income	550,000	225,000
7	Interest revenue	20,000	
8	Interest expense		(15,000)
9	Net income	570,000	210,000

During 20Y2, Sims Enterprises sold and received payment of $80,000 for merchandise that was purchased by Paley Corporation. The merchandise sold to Paley cost Sims Enterprises $45,000. Paley Corporation sold the merchandise to another (nonaffiliated) company for $110,000.

a. Prepare a consolidated income statement for Paley Corporation and Subsidiary. *Hint:* Eliminate the effect of the intercompany sale.

b. Assume that as of December 31, 20Y2, Paley Corporation had not sold the merchandise purchased from Sims Enterprises. How would this affect the preparation of the consolidated financial statements?

c. Assume that $15,000 of the interest revenue that Paley Corporation reported on its income statement was from a note payable from Sims Enterprises. Sims paid the note payable at its maturity in 20Y2. How would the loan affect the preparation of the consolidated financial statements?

Topic

2 Foreign Currency Transactions

What's Covered

Foreign Currency Transactions
- Cash Transactions (Obj. 1)
- Credit Transactions (Obj. 2)

Learning Objectives

Obj. 1 Describe and illustrate the accounting for cash foreign currency transactions.

Obj. 2 Describe and illustrate the accounting for foreign currency transactions on account.

Many United States (U.S.) companies enter into transactions with foreign companies as either sellers or buyers of products or services. When the transactions require receipt or payment in U.S. dollars, the transactions are recorded like those illustrated earlier in this text.

A foreign company may, however, require the receipt or payment in a foreign currency. When funds are received in a foreign currency, the amount of the foreign currency received must be converted into its equivalent U.S. dollars for recording in the accounts. When a payment is to be made in a foreign currency, U.S. dollars must be exchanged for the foreign currency for payment.

A transaction with a foreign company may also occur "on account" with credit terms such as n/30 (due in 30 days). If the transaction involves receipt or payment in a foreign currency, the value of the foreign currency may change between when the initial transaction is recorded and when the receipt or payment in the foreign currency is due. In this case, a foreign exchange gain or loss must be recorded.

Foreign Currency: Cash Transactions

Objective 1
Describe and illustrate the accounting for cash foreign currency transactions.

The simplest foreign currency transactions are cash transactions that do not involve credit. These transactions require payment or receipt in a foreign currency when the product or service is purchased or when the product or service is rendered.

Cash Purchases

To illustrate a cash purchase from a foreign company, assume that on June 30, 20Y6, Beacon Inc., a U.S. company, purchased merchandise from Le Sueur Company, located in Toulouse, France, for €16,500 euros. Le Sueur Company requires Beacon Inc. to submit its payment in euros.

Since Le Sueur Company requires payment in euros, Beacon Inc. must exchange U.S. dollars for euros. The conversion of one country's currency for another involves the use of an exchange rate. An **exchange rate** is the rate at which a country's currency can be converted into another country's currency. Exhibit 1 shows the exchange rate for converting euros (EUR) to U.S. dollars (USD).[1]

[1] Each country's currency has a standard abbreviation. For example, the abbreviation for the U.S. dollar is USD, while the abbreviation for euros is EUR. Throughout this discussion, we use the standard abbreviation for each country's currency.

Exhibit 1
Exchanging Euros for U.S. Dollars

Euros to U.S. Dollars

Exchange Rate: $0.90 USD per EUR

1 EUR ⟶ **$0.90 USD**

The exchange rate of $0.90 USD per EUR means that U.S. dollars are worth more than euros. As a result, in the preceding illustration, Beacon Inc. will need to exchange only $14,850 USD to obtain €16,500 EUR (€16,500 EUR × $0.90 USD).

Since Beacon Inc.'s records are in USDs, it would record the purchase of merchandise from Le Sueur Company on June 30, 20Y6, in USD. The effects of the purchase on the accounts and financial statements are as follows:

Financial Statement Effects

BALANCE SHEET

	Assets			=	Liabilities	+	Stockholders' Equity
	Cash	+	**Inventory**				
20Y6 *June 30.*	(14,850)*		14,850				

STATEMENT OF CASH FLOWS

June 30. Operating	(14,850)

INCOME STATEMENT

*€16,500 EUR x $0.90 USD

Cash Sales

Sales to a foreign company that pays in a foreign currency rather than USDs are recorded in a similar manner. The foreign currency that is received is first exchanged for USDs. The transaction is then recorded in a normal manner.

To illustrate, assume that Smith Industries, a U.S. company, sold merchandise that cost $25,000 to Jose' Rafael Co., a Mexican company, on July 7, 20Y1, receiving $210,000 pesos (MXN). Assuming an exchange rate of $0.20 USD per MXN, the effects of the sale on the accounts and financial statements of Smith Industries are as follows:

Financial Statement Effects

BALANCE SHEET

	Assets			=	Liabilities	+	Stockholders' Equity
	Cash	+	**Inventory**	=			**Retained Earnings**
20Y1 *July 7.*	42,000*		(25,000)				17,000

STATEMENT OF CASH FLOWS

July 7. Operating	42,000

INCOME STATEMENT

July 7. Sales	42,000
Cost of goods sold	(25,000)
Gross profit	17,000

*$210,000 MXN × $0.20 USD

As shown in the preceding illustrations, cash foreign currency transactions are recorded in the same manner as cash transactions in earlier chapters. The only difference is that a foreign currency must be converted to U.S. dollars (USD).

Foreign Currency: Credit Transactions

Objective 2
Describe and illustrate the accounting for foreign currency transactions on account.

The purchase or sale to a foreign company may be "on account" and, thus, involve a credit period. In this case, if the exchange rate changes between the time of purchase or sale and the payment or receipt of the foreign currency, a foreign exchange gain or loss must be recorded.

Purchases on Account

A U.S. company may purchase from a foreign company on credit that requires payment in a foreign currency. The initial purchase is recorded in USD using the exchange rate on the date of purchase. If at the time of payment, the value of USD increases relative to the foreign currency, a **foreign currency exchange gain** is recorded. If at the time of payment, the value of USD decreases relative to the foreign currency, a **foreign currency exchange loss** is recorded.

Exhibit 2 summarizes the recording of foreign currency exchange gains and losses for purchases on account.

Exhibit 2
Foreign Currency Exchange Gains and Losses: Purchases on Account by a U.S. Company

USD Relative to Foreign Currency	Foreign Exchange Gain or Loss
Increases in value	Gain
Decreases in value	Loss

To illustrate, assume that on November 4, 20Y3, Bishop Industries, a U.S. company, purchased merchandise on account from TC Chang Inc., located in Beijing, China, for ¥1,200,000 Chinese yuan (CNY). The payment is due November 23, 20Y3, in CNY.

Assume an exchange rate of $0.15 USD per CNY on November 4, 20Y3. The effects of the purchase on the accounts and financial statements of Bishop Industries are as follows:

Financial Statement Effects

BALANCE SHEET

	Assets	=	Liabilities	+	Stockholders' Equity
	Inventory	=	Accounts Payable		
20Y3					
Nov. 4.	180,000*		180,000		

STATEMENT OF CASH FLOWS

INCOME STATEMENT

*¥1,200,000 CNY × $0.15 USD

Assume that on November 23, 20Y3, the exchange rate is $0.16 USD per CNY. In other words, the USD has decreased in value relative to the CNY. As a result, on November 23, Bishop Industries will need to exchange $192,000 USD (¥1,200,000 × $0.16 USD) to receive ¥1,200,000 CNY to pay the TC Chang Inc. account payable. In this case, Bishop Industries has incurred a foreign currency exchange loss of $12,000 ($192,000 – $180,000).

The effects of the payment to TC Chang Inc. on November 23 on the accounts and financial statements of Bishop Industries are as follows:

Financial Statement Effects

BALANCE SHEET

	Assets	=	Liabilities	+	Stockholders' Equity
	Cash	=	Accounts Payable	+	Retained Earnings
20Y3					
Nov. 23.	(192,000)*		(180,000)		(12,000)

STATEMENT OF CASH FLOWS

Nov. 23.	Operating	(180,000)
	Financing	(12,000)

INCOME STATEMENT

Nov. 23.	Foreign currency exchange loss	(12,000)

* ¥1,200,000 CNY × $0.16 USD

The exchange loss of $12,000 is a result of the exchange rate changing from $0.15 USD per CNY on November 4 to $0.16 USD per CNY on November 23. The exchange loss can be computed as follows:

Exchange Loss: $12,000 = ¥1,200,000 CNY × ($0.16 USD per CNY – $0.15 USD per CNY)

If the exchange rate had been $0.13 USD per CNY on November 23, Bishop Industries would have only needed $156,000 (¥1,200,000 CNY × $0.13 USD) to pay TC Chang Inc. In other words, the USD has increased in value relative to the CNY. In this case, Bishop Industries would have recorded an exchange gain of $24,000 ($180,000 – $156,000), which can also be computed as follows:

Exchange Gain: $24,000 = ¥1,200,000 CNY × ($0.15 USD per CNY – $0.13 USD per CNY)

The cash effects of foreign currency exchange gains and losses are normally reported as a separate item on the statement of cash flows. To simplify, we classify foreign exchange gains and losses as a financing activity.

Sales on Account

Sales on account to a foreign company that pays in a foreign currency rather than USDs are recorded in a similar manner. The initial sale is recorded in USD using the exchange rate on the date of sale. If at the time of the receipt of the foreign currency the value of the USD has increased, a foreign currency exchange loss is recorded. If at the time of receipt of the foreign currency the value of the USD has decreased, a foreign currency exchange gain is recorded.

Exhibit 3 summarizes the recording of foreign currency exchange gains and losses for sales on account.

Exhibit 3
Foreign Currency Exchange Gains and Losses: Sales on Account by U.S. Company

USD Relative to Foreign Currency	Foreign Exchange Gain or Loss
Increases in value	Loss
Decreases in value	Gain

To illustrate, assume that SuperMart Inc., a U.S. company, sold merchandise that cost $200,000 to Bjorn Markets, a Swedish company located in Stockholm, on March 19, 20Y8, for kr3,750,000 Swedish krona (SEK). Bjorn Markets pays kr3,750,000 SEK to SuperMart Inc. on April 18, 20Y8.

Assume an exchange rate of $0.100 USD per SEK on March 19, 20Y8. The effects of the sale to Bjorn Markets on March 19 on the accounts and financial statements of SuperMart Inc. are as follows:

Financial Statement Effects

BALANCE SHEET

	Assets			=	Liabilities +	Stockholders' Equity
	Accounts Receivable	+	Inventory	=		Retained Earnings
20Y8 *Mar. 19.*	375,000*		(200,000)			175,000

STATEMENT OF CASH FLOWS

INCOME STATEMENT

Mar. 19. Sales	375,000
Cost of goods sold	(200,000)
Gross profit	175,000

*kr3,750,000 SEK x $0.100 USD

Assume that on April 18, 20Y8, the exchange rate is $0.104 USD per SEK. In other words, the USD has decreased in value relative to the SEK. As a result, on April 18 SuperMart will receive kr3,750,000 SEK that is worth $390,000 USD (kr3,750,000 × $0.104). In this case, SuperMart has a foreign currency exchange gain of $15,000 ($390,000 – $375,000).

The effects of the receipt of the 3,750,000 SEK on April 18 by SuperMart on its accounts and financial statements are as follows:

Financial Statement Effects

BALANCE SHEET

	Assets			=	Liabilities	+	Stockholders' Equity
	Cash	+	Accounts Receivable	=			Retained Earnings
20Y8 Apr. 18.	390,000*		(375,000)				15,000

STATEMENT OF CASH FLOWS

Apr. 18. Operating	375,000
Financing	15,000

INCOME STATEMENT

Apr. 18. Foreign currency exchange gain	15,000

*kr3,750,000 SEK x $0.104 USD

The exchange gain of $15,000 is a result of the exchange rate changing from $0.100 USD per SEK on March 19 to $0.104 USD per SEK on April 18. In contrast, if the exchange rate on April 18 had been $0.097, SuperMart would have received kr3,750,000 SEK worth only $363,750 USD (kr3,750,000 × $0.097), and SuperMart would have recorded a foreign currency exchange loss of $11,250 ($375,000 – $363,750).

Exhibit 4 summarizes the accounting for transactions with foreign companies.[2]

Exhibit 4 Accounting for Transactions with Foreign Companies

Type of Transaction	Foreign Currency Exchange Gain or Loss
Cash purchase or sale with payment or receipt in foreign currency.	
Convert foreign currency into USD and record as normal purchase or sale	**No Gain or Loss**
Cash purchase or sale with foreign company with payment or receipt in USD.	
Record as normal purchase or sale	**No Gain or Loss**
Credit purchase with payment in foreign currency.	
Date of purchase:	
Convert amount due in foreign currency into USD and record as normal purchase.	**No Gain or Loss**
Date of payment:	
Convert USD into foreign currency:	
If USD *increases* in value from date of purchase, record payment with:	Gain
If USD *decreases* in value from date of purchase, record payment with:	Loss
Credit sale with receipt in foreign currency.	
Date of sale:	
Convert amount due in foreign currency into USD and record as normal sale.	**No Gain or Loss**
Date of receipt:	
Convert foreign currency into USD:	
If USD *increases* in value from date of sale, record receipt with:	Loss
If USD *decreases* in value from date of sale, record receipt with:	Gain

[2] Foreign currency exchange gains and losses may also be recorded as an adjustment when there are outstanding accounts receivables or payables requiring receipt or payment in a foreign currency at the end of the accounting period.

Let's Review

Summary

1. When transactions require receipt or payment in U.S. dollars, the transactions with foreign companies are recorded in the normal manner. When funds are received in a foreign currency, the amount of the foreign currency received must be converted into its equivalent U.S. dollars for recording in the accounts. When a payment is to be made in a foreign currency, U.S. dollars must be exchanged for the foreign currency for payment.

2. When a transaction with a foreign company occurs with credit terms and involves receipt or payment in a foreign currency, a foreign currency exchange gain or loss may arise. A foreign currency exchange gain or loss is recorded if the value of the foreign currency changes relative to the U.S. dollar between the date of the initial transaction and the receipt or payment in the foreign currency. Exhibit 4 summarizes the accounting for transactions with foreign companies.

Key Terms

exchange rate (537)
foreign currency exchange gain (539)
foreign currency exchange loss (539)

Assignments

A2-1 Accounting for cash transaction with foreign company **Obj. 1**

How does the accounting for a cash transaction with a foreign company differ from a transaction with a U.S. company if (a) the payment or receipt is in USD and (b) the payment or receipt is in a foreign currency?

A2-2 Foreign currency conversion **Obj. 1**

King Manufacturing Inc. received ₹1,500,000 Indian rupees (INR) from a cash sale of merchandise to Krishna LLC, located in New Delhi, India. Assuming an exchange rate of $0.014 USD per INR, how much will King Manufacturing record in USD?

A2-3 Foreign currency conversion **Obj. 1**

Mays Inc. purchased merchandise from Takaoka Industries located in Osaki, Japan, for ¥21,800,000 Japanese yen (JPY). Takaoka Industries requires payment in JPY at the time of sale. Assuming an exchange rate of $0.009 USD per JPY, how much will Mays Inc. record for the purchase of the merchandise in USD?

A2-4 Cash purchase from foreign company **Obj. 1**

On August 7, 20Y1, Boise Co., a U.S. company, purchased merchandise from Red Deer Inc., located in Edmonton, Canada, for $67,500 Canadian dollars (CAD). Red Deer Inc. requires payment in CAD at the time of purchase. On August 7, 20Y1, the exchange rate was $0.74 USD per CAD. Illustrate the effects of the purchase on the accounts and financial statements of Boise Co.

A2-5 Cash purchase from foreign company **Obj. 1**

On November 15, 20Y4, Butler Wholesale, a U.S. company, purchased merchandise from Shetland Wool, located in Wellington, New Zealand, for $331,100 New Zealand dollars (NZD). Shetland Wool requires payment in NZD at the time of purchase. On November 15, 20Y4, the exchange rate was $0.65 USD per NZD. Illustrate the effects of the purchase on the accounts and financial statements of Butler Wholesale.

A2-6 Cash sale to foreign company **Obj. 1**

On February 3, 20Y8, Sullivan Manufacturing, a U.S. company, sold merchandise that cost $42,000 to Cikan Stores, located in Prague, Czech Republic, receiving kč1,600,000 Czech koruna (CZK) at the time of sale. The exchange rate on February 3, 20Y8, was $0.044 USD per CZK. Illustrate the effects of the sale on the accounts and financial statements of Sullivan Manufacturing.

A2-7 Cash sale to foreign company **Obj. 1**

On May 17, 20Y3, Summerfield LLC, a U.S. company, sold merchandise that cost $500,000 to Harman Stores, located in Riyadh, Saudi Arabia, receiving ﷼3,000,000 Saudi riyal (SAR) at the time of sale. The exchange rate on May 17, 20Y3, was $0.27 USD per SAR. Illustrate the effects of the sale on the accounts and financial statements of Summerfield LLC.

A2-8 Foreign currency exchange gain or loss **Obj. 2**

When would a U.S. company record a foreign currency exchange gain or loss?

A2-9 Foreign currency exchange gain or loss **Obj. 2**

A U.S. company purchases merchandise on account (on credit) from a foreign company that requires payment in a foreign currency. (a) When would the U.S. company record a foreign currency exchange loss? (b) When would the U.S. company record a foreign currency exchange gain? (c) Is a foreign currency exchange loss or gain recorded at the initial date of the transaction or at the date of payment?

A2-10 Foreign currency exchange gain or loss **Obj. 2**

A U.S. company sells merchandise on account (on credit) to a foreign company that pays in a foreign currency. (a) When would the U.S. company record a foreign currency exchange gain? (b) When would the U.S. company record a foreign currency exchange loss? (c) Is a foreign currency exchange loss or gain recorded at the initial date of the transaction?

A2-11 Purchase on account with foreign company **Obj. 2**

✔ b. Foreign Currency Exchange Loss, $30,000

On April 22, 20Y5, Beyer Inc., a U.S. company, purchased merchandise from Kindersley Co., located in Saskatchewan, Canada, for $1,000,000 Canadian dollars (CAD). Kindersley Co. requires payment in CAD on May 15, 20Y5.

a. Assume an exchange rate of $0.75 USD per CAD on April 22. Illustrate the effects of the purchase on April 22 on the accounts and financial statements of Beyer Inc.
b. Assume an exchange rate of $0.78 USD per CAD on May 15. Illustrate the effects of the payment on May 15 on the accounts and financial statements of Beyer Inc.
c. Assume an exchange rate of $0.73 USD per CAD on May 15. Illustrate the effects of the payment on May 15 on the accounts and financial statements of Beyer Inc.

A2-12 Sale on account with foreign company **Obj. 2**

✔ b. Foreign Currency Exchange Gain, $32,500

On January 18, 20Y4, Sentinel Inc., a U.S. company, sold merchandise costing $180,000 to Outback Expeditions, located in Perth, Australia, for $650,000 Australian dollars (AUD). Outback Expeditions pays on February 9, 20Y4, in AUD.

a. Assume an exchange rate of $0.70 USD per AUD on January 18. Illustrate the effects of the sale on January 18 on the accounts and financial statements of Sentinel Inc.
b. Assume an exchange rate of $0.75 USD per AUD on February 9. Illustrate the effects of the receipt of the $650,000 AUD on February 9 on the accounts and financial statements of Sentinel Inc.
c. Assume an exchange rate of $0.69 USD per AUD on February 9. Illustrate the effects of the receipt of the $650,000 AUD on February 9 on the accounts and financial statements of Sentinel Inc.

Topic

3 Corporate Taxes

What's Covered

Corporate Income Taxes
- Payment of Taxes (Obj. 1)
- Allocation of Taxes (Obj. 2)

Learning Objectives

Obj. 1 Journalize the quarterly estimated tax liability and its related payment.
Obj. 2 Explain and account for differences between income before income taxes on the income statement and taxable income on the tax return.

Corporations are taxable entities that normally pay income taxes. Some corporations pay not only federal income taxes, but also state and local income taxes. Although the following discussion is limited to federal income taxes, the basic concepts also apply to state and local income taxes.[1]

Objective 1
Journalize the quarterly estimated tax liability and its related payment.

Payment of Income Taxes

Most corporations are required to pay federal income taxes in four quarterly installments throughout the year.[2] For example, assume that a corporation with an accounting period ending December 31 estimates its income tax expense for the year to be $600,000. The effects on the accounts and financial statements on April 15 of the first quarter estimated tax liability and its related payment of $150,000 ($600,000 ÷ 4) are as follows:

Financial Statement Effects

BALANCE SHEET

	Assets	= Liabilities	+ Stockholders' Equity
		Income Tax Payable	Retained Earnings
Apr. 15. Estimated taxes		150,000	(150,000)
15. Tax payment	(150,000)	(150,000)	

STATEMENT OF CASH FLOWS

Apr. 15. Operating	(150,000)

INCOME STATEMENT

Apr. 15. Income tax expense	(150,000)

After the end of the year, the actual taxable income and related income tax are determined. If additonal taxes are owed, an income tax liability is recorded. If the total estimated tax payments are greater than the actual tax, the overpayment is an increase to a prepaid tax asset and a decrease to Income Tax Expense.

[1] Because state tax laws vary, this section focuses on federal income taxes.
[2] Estimated taxes are due for a corporation on the 15th day of the 4th, 6th, 9th, and 12th months of its tax year.

Since income tax is often a significant amount, it is normally reported separately on the income statement. To illustrate, an excerpt from a recent **Apple Inc. (AAPL)** income statement follows:

Operating income	$ 63,930
Other income (expense)	1,807
Income before income taxes	$ 65,737
Income taxes	(10,481)
Net income	$ 55,256

Allocation of Income Taxes

Objective 2
Explain and account for differences between income before income taxes on the income statement and taxable income on the tax return.

The **taxable income** of a corporation is determined using tax laws and regulations. As shown in Exhibit 1, taxable income is different than **income before income taxes** that is reported on the income statement using generally accepted accounting principles. As a result, the income tax based upon taxable income on a corporation's tax return differs from income tax expense on the corporation's income statement. These differences may need to be allocated among various financial statement periods depending upon the nature of the item causing the difference.

Exhibit 1
Tax Return and Income Statement

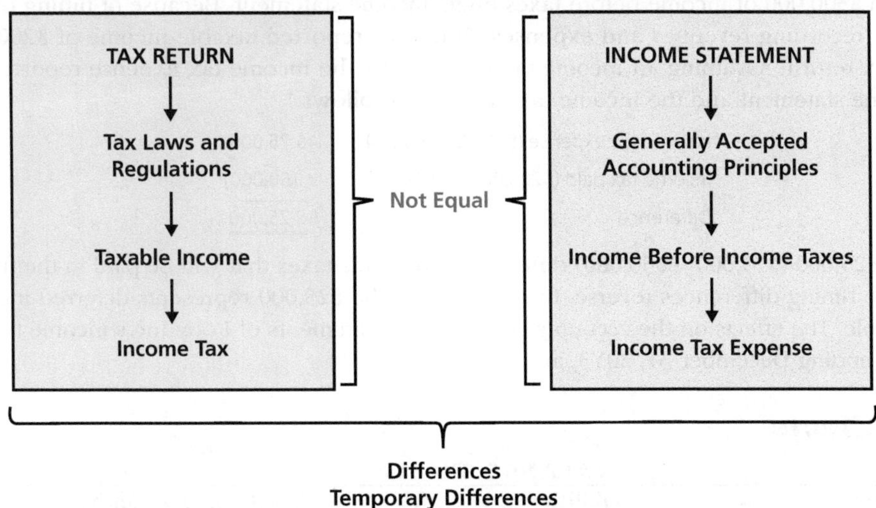

Some differences between taxable income and income before income taxes are created, because items are recognized in one period for tax purposes and in another period for income statement purposes. Such differences, called **temporary tax differences**, reverse or turn around in later years. Some examples of items that create temporary differences are as follows:

1. Some revenues or gains are taxed *after* they are reported on the income statement. An example is the use of the point-of-sale method of recognizing revenue on the income statement and the installment method of recognizing revenue for tax purposes.
2. Other revenues or gains are taxed *before* they are reported on the income statement. For example, cash received in advance for magazine subscriptions is included in taxable income but reported as income when earned on the income statement.
3. Some expenses or losses are deducted in determining taxable income *after* they are reported on the income statement. An example is estimating product warranty expense on the income statement when a product is sold while recognizing warranty expense when it is paid for tax purposes.
4. Other expenses or losses are deducted in determining taxable income *before* they are reported on the income statement. An example is MACRS depreciation used for tax purposes and the straight-line method used for financial statement purposes.

Over the life of a corporation, temporary differences do not change the *total* amount of tax paid. Temporary differences affect only the *timing* of when the taxes are paid. Corporations normally use tax-planning methods so that temporary differences defer (delay) the payment of taxes to later years. As a result, the income tax expense reported on the income statement is normally related to two liabilities that are reported on the balance sheet. Income taxes related to current income are reported as a current liability. Income taxes resulting from temporary tax differences are reported as a long-term liability, called **deferred income tax payable.**[3]

Exhibit 2 shows the relationship between the income tax expense and the related current and long-term liabilities.

Exhibit 2
Current and Deferred Income Tax Liabilities

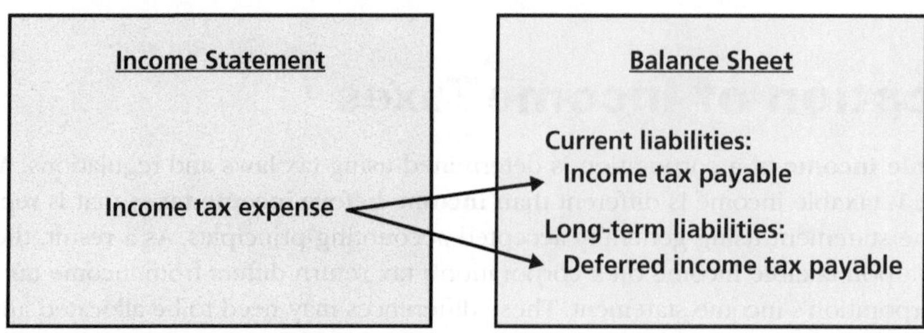

To illustrate, assume for its first year of operations ending December 31, 20Y3, Roby Inc. reported $300,000 of income before taxes on its income statement. Because of timing differences in recording revenues and expenses, Roby Inc. reported taxable income of $200,000 on its tax return. Assuming an income tax rate of 25%, the income tax expense reported on its income statement and the income tax paid are as follows:[4]

Income tax expense ($300,000 × 25%)	$ 75,000
Income tax paid ($200,000 × 25%)	(50,000)
Difference	$ 25,000

The $25,000 ($75,000 – $50,000) difference represents taxes that will be paid in the future when the timing differences reverse. In other words, the $25,000 represents deferred income tax payable. The effects on the accounts and financial statements of Roby Inc.'s income tax for the year ending December 31, 20Y3, are as follows:[5]

Financial Statement Effects

BALANCE SHEET

	Assets	=	Liabilities			+	Stockholders' Equity
			Income Tax Payable	+	Deferred Income Tax Payable		Retained Earnings
20Y3 Dec. 31.			50,000		25,000		(75,000)

STATEMENT OF CASH FLOWS

INCOME STATEMENT

Dec. 31. Income tax expense	(75,000)

The income tax expense of $75,000 is matched against the income before taxes of $300,000 on Roby Inc.'s income statement. The income tax payable of $50,000 is reported as a current liability and the deferred income tax payable is reported as a long-term liability on the balance sheet.

Differences between taxable income and income before taxes on the income statement may also arise because some revenues are exempt from taxes and some expenses are not deductible for tax purposes. For example, interest revenue from municipal bonds is exempt from federal taxes. Such differences, referred to as **permanent tax differences,** create no special financial statement reporting issues. This is because the income tax determined under the tax laws is the same as the amount that would be reported as tax in the financial statements.

[3] In some cases, a deferred tax asset may arise from tax benefits a corporation is expected to receive in the future. Such assets are reported as a long-term asset. Deferred tax assets are discussed in advanced accounting courses.

[4] For purposes of illustration, the 25% tax rate is assumed to include all federal, state, and local income taxes.

[5] To simplify, we assume no estimated tax payments.

Let's Review

Summary

1. Corporations are taxable entities that normally pay income taxes in four quarterly installments. The tax liability is initially recorded by increasing Income Tax Expense and Income Tax Payable. Income Tax Payable and Cash are decreased when the taxes are paid.
2. The taxable income is determined using tax laws and regulations, while income before income taxes on the income statement is determined using generally accepted accounting principles. As a result, the income tax based upon taxable income on a corporation's tax return differs from income tax expense on the corporation's income statement. When these differences are caused by temporary timing differences, GAAP requires tax effects to be allocated among financial statement periods. These allocations are made using a deferred income tax payable account.

Key Terms

deferred income tax payable (546)
income before income taxes (545)
permanent tax differences (546)
taxable income (545)
temporary tax differences (545)

Assignments

A3-1 Quarterly tax payments **Obj. 1**

A corporation with an accounting period ending December 31 estimates that its taxable income for the year will be $1,200,000.

a. When will the corporation's first quarterly estimated tax payment be due?

b. Assuming an income tax rate of 20%, how much will each quarterly estimated tax payments be?

A3-2 Tax return and income statement **Obj. 2**

Does the *taxable income* reported on a corporation's tax return normally equal *income before income taxes* that is reported on the income statement? If not, why?

A3-3 Tax return and income statement **Obj. 2**

Differences between taxable income and income before income taxes may be created because an item is recognized in one period for tax purposes and in another period for income statement purposes. (a) What are these differences called? (b) Give an example of a revenue item that creates such differences. (c) Give an example of an expense item that creates such differences.

A3-4 Tax return and income statement **Obj. 2**

Over the life of a corporation, will the total tax expense reported on the income statement differ from the total tax paid on the tax return? Explain.

A3-5 Deferred income tax **Obj. 2**

When recording a corporation's income taxes for the year, (a) why would Deferred Income Tax Payable be increased? (b) How is Deferred Income Tax Payable reported in the financial statements?

A3-6 Estimated and deferred income taxes **Obj. 1, 2**

For its first year of operations ended December 31, 20Y6, Hunter-Jones Inc. reported income before income taxes of $2,800,000. By using temporary revenue and expense timing differences, Hunter-Jones Inc. reduced its taxable income to $2,300,000. Hunter-Jones Inc.'s income tax rate is 25%.

a. What is the amount of income tax expense reported on the income statement?

b. What is the amount of income tax due on the tax return?

c. Illustrate the effects on the accounts and financial statements of Hunter-Jones Inc.'s income tax for the year ended December 31, 20Y6. Assume no estimated tax payments were made during the year.

A3-7 Estimated and deferred income taxes **Obj. 1, 2**

Using the data from Assignment A3-6, illustrate the effects on the accounts and financial statements of the following selected transactions for Hunter-Jones Inc. for the year ended December 31, 20Y7:

a. The first quarter estimated tax liability and payment on April 15 of $200,000.

b. The second quarter estimated tax liability and payment on June 15 of $200,000.

c. Assume that the third and fourth estimated tax liabilities and payments of $200,000 were made during the year. Illustrate the effects on the accounts and financial statements on January 15, 20Y8, of an additional income tax liability and payment for the year ending December 31, 20Y7, assuming that $100,000 of timing differences from 20Y6 reversed in 20Y7.

A3-8 Estimated and deferred income taxes **Obj. 1, 2**

Illustrate the effects on the accounts and financial statements of the following income-tax-related transactions for Resnick & Sons Inc. for the year ending June 30, 20Y6:

20Y5

Oct. 15. Recorded the first quarter estimated tax liability and payment of $100,000.

Dec. 15. Recorded the second quarter estimated tax liability and payment of $100,000.

20Y6

June 30. Recorded the additional income tax and deferred income tax liabilities for the year ending June 30, 20Y6, based upon the preceding estimated tax payments and the following data:

Income tax rate	28%
Income before income taxes*	$1,750,000
Taxable income*	1,500,000
Third quarter estimated taxes paid	100,000
Fourth quarter estimated taxes paid	100,000

*Difference due to temporary timing differences.

A3-9 Estimated and deferred income taxes **Obj. 1, 2**

Illustrate the effects on the accounts and financial statments of the following income-tax-related transactions for Yang & Daughters Inc. for the year ending December 31, 20Y7:

20Y7

Apr. 15. Recorded the first quarter estimated tax liability and payment of $75,000.

June 15. Recorded the second quarter estimated tax liability and payment of $75,000.

Dec. 31. Recorded the additional income tax and deferred income tax liabilities for the year based upon the preceding estimated tax payments and the following data:

Income tax rate	25%
Income before income taxes*	$1,400,000
Taxable income*	1,280,000
Third quarter estimated taxes paid	75,000
Fourth quarter estimated taxes paid	75,000

*Difference due to temporary timing differences.

A3-10 Deferred income taxes **Obj. 1, 2**

Temporary revenue and expense timing differences between income before income taxes and taxable income for Broadway Suites Inc.'s first four years of operations ended December 31 are as follows:

	20Y1	20Y2	20Y3	20Y4
Income before taxes	$5,000,000	$6,500,000	$7,200,000	$8,300,000
Taxable income	4,500,000	5,100,000	8,300,000	9,100,000

Assume that the income tax rate for each year is 25% and that all tax payments are made when due.

a. Fill in the amounts in the following table for each year:

			Deferred Income Tax Payable	
Year	Tax Expense on Income Statement	Tax Paid on Tax Return	Year's Addition (Deduction)	December 31 Balance
20Y1				
20Y2				
20Y3				
20Y4				
Totals				

b. Over the life of a corporation, will the *total* tax expense on the income statements equal the total tax paid on the tax returns? Explain.

c. At any point in the life of a corporation, will there normally be a balance in Deferred Income Tax Payable? Explain.

A3-11 Deferred income taxes **Obj. 1, 2**

Temporary revenue and expense timing differences between income before income taxes and taxable income for four years of Jaffe Corporation's operations are as follows:

	20Y4	20Y5	20Y6	20Y7
Income before taxes	$12,000,000	$14,100,000	$15,800,000	$20,500,000
Taxable income	10,500,000	12,400,000	14,200,000	18,700,000

Assume that Jaffe Corporation's income tax rate for each year is 20% and that all tax payments are made when due.

a. Assume that Deferred Tax Payable has a balance of $275,000 on December 31, 20Y3. Complete the following table:

			Deferred Income Tax Payable	
Year	Tax Expense on Income Statement	Tax Paid on Tax Return	Year's Addition (Deduction)	December 31 Balance
20Y3				$275,000
20Y4				
20Y5				
20Y6				
20Y7				
Totals				

b. Over the life of a corporation, will the *total* tax expense on the income statements equal the total tax paid on the tax returns? Explain.

c. On December 31, 20Y3, Jaffe Corporation had a balance of $275,000 in Deferred Income Tax Payable. Using your answer to part (a), did this balance increase or decrease from January 1, 20Y4, to December 31, 20Y7? If so, why?

A3-12 Permanent tax differences **Obj. 2**

What is an example of a permanent difference between taxable income and income before income taxes?

Topic

4 Reporting Unusual Items and Comprehensive Income

What's Covered

Unusual Items on the Financial Statements
- Discontinued Operations (Obj. 1)
- Prior Period Adjustments (Obj. 1)

Comprehensive Income
- Income Statement (Obj. 2)
- Statement of Comprehensive Income (Obj. 2)
- Balance Sheet (Obj. 2)

Learning Objectives

Obj. 1 Describe and illustrate the reporting of unusual items in the financial statements.
Obj. 2 Define and illustrate the reporting of comprehensive income.

Objective 1
Describe and illustrate the reporting of unusual items in the financial statements.

Unusual Items in the Financial Statements

Generally accepted accounting principles (GAAP) require special accounting and financial statement reporting for unusual items. This is because such items do not occur frequently and are normally unrelated to a company's current operations. As a result, unusual items may impact a user's interpretation of a company's operating results and financial condition.

GAAP identifies the following two types of unusual items:

- Discontinued operations
- Prior period adjustments

Discontinued Operations

A **discontinued operation** occurs when a company sells or disposes of an operating segment or component of its business. A discontinued operation may result from a company selling a subsidiary or from a strategic shift in business operations.[1] For example, a retailer might decide to discontinue selling its merchandise in retail stores and instead sell only online.

A gain or loss normally results when a company discontinues an operation. This gain or loss is reported on the income statement as a *"Gain (or loss) from discontinued operations"* following *"Income from continuing operations."* Companies with discontinued operations should also report earnings per share separately for income from continuing operations, discontinued operations, and net income.[2]

To illustrate, assume that Dillon Corporation produces and sells electrical products, hardware supplies, and lawn equipment. In 20Y2, Dillon Corporation decided to discontinue selling electrical products and sold its electrical product assets at a loss of $150,000, which resulted in a tax savings of $30,000. Assuming the company has 200,000 shares of common stock outstanding, Dillon Corporation would report the loss on discontinued operations as shown in Exhibit 1.

[1] A strategic shift includes items such as the disposal of a major geographic area or major line of business.
[2] Generally accepted accounting principles require that earnings per share for income from continuing operations and net income be reported on the income statement. Other per-share amounts are normally reported in the notes to the financial statements.

Exhibit 1
Reporting of Discontinued Operations

Dillon Corporation
Income Statement
For the Year Ended December 31, 20Y2

Sales	$12,350,000
Cost of goods sold	(5,800,000)
Gross profit	$ 6,550,000
Selling and administrative expenses	(5,240,000)
Income from continuing operations before income tax expense	$ 1,310,000
Income tax expense	(320,000)
Income from continuing operations	$ 990,000
Loss from discontinued operations	
(net of $30,000 income tax savings)	(120,000)
Net income	$ 870,000
Earnings per common share:	
Income from continuing operations	$ 4.95
Loss from discontinued operations	(0.60)
Net income	$ 4.35

A note to the financial statements should also describe why the operations were sold, when the operations were discontinued, and the assets, liabilities, income, and expenses of the discontinued operations.

Prior Period Adjustments

An unusual item that affects a prior period's financial statements is called a **prior period adjustment**. The two most common types of prior period adjustments are as follows:

- Adjustments for accounting errors
- Adjustments for a change in accounting principle

An **accounting error** results from making mathematical mistakes or incorrectly applying generally accepted accounting principles. For example, if a company incorrectly counts its ending inventory, its income statement and balance sheet will be in error.

A **change in accounting principle** occurs when a company changes from one generally accepted accounting principle to another. For example, a change from the first-in, first-out (FIFO) cost method to the weighted average cost method is a change in accounting principle.

Although errors and changes in accounting principles are called prior period adjustments, their effects on the financial statements are applied to prior as well as current financial statements. For example, a prior period adjustment for an error requires a restatement of the beginning balance of retained earnings as well as prior period financial statements. A change in accounting principle requires that the prior periods' financial statements be reported as if the new accounting principle had always been used.[3]

A prior period adjustment does not affect current-period earnings. Only the earnings in the prior periods are restated. However, because the prior earnings are restated, the beginning balance of Retained Earnings is restated. This may also cause the restatement of other balance sheet accounts.

To illustrate, assume that Bynum Company computed depreciation expense in 20Y4 as $86,000. In 20Y5, Bynum Company discovered that the correct amount of depreciation expense for 20Y4 should have been $100,000. Thus, depreciation expense for 20Y4 is understated by $14,000 ($100,000 – $86,000) and net income was overstated by $14,000.[4]

[3] Changes from one generally accepted depreciation method to another generally accepted depreciation method are an exception to this general rule and are treated prospectively as a change in estimate, as discussed in Chapter 9.

[4] The correction of the error would also require a correction of income tax owed through the filing of an amended tax return for the years affected. To simplify, we ignore the tax effects of corrections of errors.

Since the 20Y4 net income was closed to Retained Earnings, the effects on the accounts and financial statements of the prior period adjustment is as follows:

Financial Statement Effects

BALANCE SHEET

	Assets	=	Liabilities +	Stockholders' Equity
	Accumulated Depreciation	=		Retained Earnings
20Y5				
Jan. 1.	(14,000)			(14,000)

STATEMENT OF CASH FLOWS

INCOME STATEMENT

On Bynum Company's statement of stockholders' equity, retained earnings would be reported as shown in Exhibit 2.

Exhibit 2
Reporting Prior Period Adjustments

Bynum Company
Statement of Stockholders' Equity
For the Year Ended December 31, 20Y5

	Common Stock	Retained Earnings	Total
Balances, January 1, 20Y5	$200,000	$320,000	$520,000
Less: Prior period adjustment—correction of error		**(14,000)**	**(14,000)**
Balances, January 1, 20Y5 (adjusted)	$200,000	$306,000	$506,000
Issued common stock	50,000		50,000
Net income		105,000	105,000
Dividends		(25,000)	(25,000)
Balances, December 31, 20Y5	$250,000	$386,000	$636,000

Objective 2
Define and illustrate the reporting of comprehensive income.

Comprehensive Income

A company's income consists of revenues, expenses, gains, and losses. However, GAAP allows certain nonowner transactions to bypass the income statement and be recorded directly in stockholders' equity. These items, along with net income, are reported as part of other comprehensive income.

Generally accepted accounting principles define **comprehensive income** as all changes in stockholders' equity during a period, except those changes resulting from investments by owners and dividends.[5] The items that are not reported on the income statement are classified as **other comprehensive income.**[6]

Other comprehensive income is added to net income to determine comprehensive income, as follows:

Net income	$ xxx
Other comprehensive income	xxx
Comprehensive income	$ xxx

An other comprehensive loss would be subtracted from net income.

[5] *FASB Accounting Standards Codification*, Glossary.

[6] Other comprehensive income includes changes in the fair value of certain investment securities, foreign currency exposures, changes in the fair value of derivative financial instruments, and certain gains/losses from pension plans. These four items are discussed in detail in advanced accounting texts.

Reporting Comprehensive Income

Generally accepted accounting principles (GAAP) allow companies to report comprehensive income in the following ways:

- On the income statement, directly below net income
- On a separate statement of comprehensive income

To illustrate, assume that Bart Company held available-for-sale securities that increased in fair value by $2,600 during the year. GAAP requires this increase in fair value of $2,600 to be reported as other comprehensive income.[7]

Assuming that Bart Company elects to report other comprehensive income on the income statement, it would be reported as shown in Exhibit 3.

Exhibit 3
Comprehensive Income Reported on the Income Statement

Bart Company Income Statement For the Year Ended December 31, 20Y2	
Sales	$1,200,000
Cost of goods sold	(960,000)
Gross profit	$ 240,000
Operating expenses	(144,500)
Operating income	$ 95,500
Income tax expense	(25,000)
Net income	$ 70,500
Other comprehensive income	2,600
Comprehensive income	$ 73,100

Assume that Bart Company elects to report comprehensive income on a separate **statement of comprehensive income**. This statement is shown in Exhibit 4 for Bart Company and would follow the income statement.

Exhibit 4
Income Statement and Statement of Comprehensive Income

Bart Company Income Statement For the Year Ended December 31, 20Y2	
Sales	$1,200,000
Cost of goods sold	(960,000)
Gross profit	$ 240,000
Operating expenses	(144,500)
Operating income	$ 95,500
Income tax expense	(25,000)
Net income	$ 70,500

Bart Company Statement of Comprehensive Income For the Year Ended December 31, 20Y2	
Net income	$70,500
Other comprehensive income	2,600
Comprehensive income	$73,100

[7] A more in-depth discussion of the accounting for available-for-sale securities can be found in Appendix B, Topic 1: *Investments*.

The cumulative effects of other comprehensive income items are reported as **accumulated other comprehensive income.** These cumulative effects are reported on the statement of stockholders' equity and the balance sheet as shown in Exhibit 5 for Bart Company.

Exhibit 5
Reporting Accumulated Other Comprehensive Income

Bart Company
Statement of Stockholders' Equity
For the Year Ended December 31, 20Y2

	Common Stock	Paid-in Capital in Excess of Par	Retained Earnings	Accumulated Other Comprehensive Income	Total
Balances, January 1, 20Y2	$18,000	$292,000	$184,500	$ 0	$494,500
Issued common stock	2,000	8,000			10,000
Net income			70,500		70,500
Dividends			(5,000)		(5,000)
Increase in fair value of available-for-sale securities				2,600	2,600
Balances, December 31, 20Y2	$20,000	$300,000	$250,000	$2,600	$572,600

Bart Company
Balance Sheet
December 31, 20Y2

Stockholders' Equity

Common stock	$ 20,000
Paid-in capital in excess of par	300,000
Retained earnings	250,000
Accumulated other comprehensive income	2,600
Total stockholders' equity	$572,600

Let's Review

Summary

1. GAAP requires special accounting for discontinued operations and prior period adjustments. When a company sells or disposes of an operating segment or component of its business, it reports a gain or loss from discontinued operations on the income statement following "Income from continuing operations."

   Prior period adjustments are required due to accounting errors and changes in accounting principle. An error requires a restatement of the beginning balance of retained earnings as well as prior period financial statements. A change in accounting principle requires that the prior periods' financial statements be reported as if the new accounting principle had always been used.

2. Comprehensive income is defined as all changes in stockholders' equity during a period except those changes resulting from investments by owners and dividends. Comprehensive income consists of net income plus other comprehensive income and is reported either on the income statement, directly below net income, or on a separate statement of comprehensive income.

Key Terms

accounting error (551)
accumulated other comprehensive income (554)
change in accounting principle (551)
comprehensive income (552)
discontinued operation (550)
other comprehensive income (552)
prior period adjustment (551)
statement of comprehensive income (553)

Assignments

A4-1 Earnings per share, discontinued operations **Obj. 1**

The income from continuing operations before income tax expense of Cutler Co. was $3,600,000. During the year, Cutler Co. reported discontinued operations that resulted in a gain of $500,000 before taxes. There were 500,000 shares of $10 par common stock and 100,000 shares of $2 preferred stock outstanding throughout the current year. The applicable income tax rate was 20%.

Determine the per-share figures for common stock for (a) income from continuing operations, (b) gain on discontinued operations, and (c) net income.

A4-2 Income statement and earnings per share for discontinued operations **Obj. 1**

Apex Inc. reports the following for a recent year:

Income from continuing operations before income taxes	$1,000,000
Loss from discontinued operations (before taxes)	$(300,000)
Applicable tax rate	20%
Weighted average number of shares outstanding	20,000

a. Prepare a partial income statement for Apex Inc. beginning with net income from continuing operations before income tax expense.
b. Determine the earnings per share for Apex Inc. including per-share amounts for unusual items.

A4-3 Errors and prior period adjustments **Obj. 1**

Explain whether Colston Company correctly reported the following items in the financial statements:

a. In a recent year, the company discovered a clerical error in the prior year's accounting records. As a result, the reported net income for the previous year was overstated by $45,000. The company corrected this error by adjusting the beginning balance of retained earnings for the effect of the error and restating the prior year financial statements.
b. In a recent year, the company voluntarily changed its method of accounting from point-in-time recognition of revenue to recognition of revenue over time. Both methods are acceptable under generally accepted accounting principles. The cumulative effect of this change was reported as a separate component of income on the current period income statement.

A4-4 Depreciation error — Obj. 1

Everdeen Inc. had common stock of $2,300,000 and retained earnings of $865,000 at January 1, 20Y7. During 20Y7, Everdeen reported the following:

Net income	$430,000
Cash dividends declared and paid	24,000
Common stock issued	35,000

The company discovered that net income for 20Y6 was overstated by $28,000 due to an error in computing depreciation expense.

a. Illustrate the effects on the accounts and financial statements of correcting the error.

b. Prepare a statement of stockholders' equity for Everdeen Inc. for the year ended December 31, 20Y7.

A4-5 Depreciation error — Obj. 1

Huldquist Company had common stock of $1,000,000 and retained earnings of $475,000 at January 1, 20Y2. During 20Y2, Huldquist Company reported the following:

Net income	$380,000
Cash dividends declared and paid	30,000
Common stock issued	40,000

The company discovered that the 20Y1 depreciation expense of $300,000 should have been $225,000.

a. Illustrate the effects on the accounts and financial statements of correcting the error.

b. Prepare a statement of stockholders' equity for Huldquist Company for the year ended December 31, 20Y2.

A4-6 Change in accounting principle — Obj. 1

On January 1, 20Y5, Gaius Company changed from the weighted average cost method to the first-in, first-out (FIFO) cost method of valuing inventory. This change caused prior year earnings to be overstated by $15,000.

a. Explain how Gaius Company would report this accounting change.

b. Illustrate the effects on the accounts and financial statements of the prior period adjustment.

A4-7 Comprehensive income — Obj. 2

Anson Industries, Inc., reported the following information on its 20Y1 income statement:

Sales	$4,000,000
Cost of goods sold	2,300,000
Operating expenses	1,000,000
Income tax expense	280,000
Other comprehensive income	450,000

a. Prepare an income statement that includes comprehensive income.

b. Prepare an income statement and a separate statement of comprehensive income.

A4-8 Comprehensive income — Obj. 2

Sprouts Farmers Market, Inc. (SFM) is a supermarket chain that offers a wide selection of fresh, natural, and organic foods. At the beginning of Year 1, the company reported no accumulated other comprehensive income. The company recently reported the following information:

Sprouts Farmers Market, Inc.
Consolidated Statements of Comprehensive Income
(in thousands)

	Year 3	Year 2	Year 1
Net income	$149,629	$158,536	$158,440
Other comprehensive income (loss)	(5,816)	1,918	(784)
Comprehensive income	$143,813	$160,454	$157,656

Determine the amount reported on the balance sheet as accumulated other comprehensive income (loss) at the end of Year 3.

Topic

5 Revenue Recognition

Companies recognize revenue when services have been performed or products have been delivered to customers. For example, when **McDonald's (MCD)** sells a hamburger, the revenue is earned when the hamburger is delivered to the customer. In this example, revenue recognition is simple because the hamburger is delivered and cash is received at a single point in time.

Complex Revenue Transactions

Revenue recognition is more complex, however, when a transaction includes several items that are sold together, items that are delivered over time, or items whose prices depend upon future events. To address these more complex transactions, the Financial Accounting Standards Board (FASB) issued a new accounting standard in May 2014.[1] The new Standard uses a five-step method for determining when revenue should be recognized. The five steps are as follows:

- Step 1. *Identify the contract with the customer.* The new Standard treats every revenue transaction as a contract. A contract is an agreement by the seller to provide a good or service in exchange for payment from the buyer. A contract may be verbal and implicit, such as the purchase of a **McDonald's** hamburger, or written and explicit, such as a cell phone contract.
- Step 2. *Identify the separate performance obligations in the contract.* Every contract requires the seller and buyer to perform. For example, when you purchase a McDonald's hamburger, you (the buyer) perform by paying and McDonald's (the seller) performs by delivering a hamburger. When you purchase a cell phone from **Verizon (VZ)**, the transaction is more complex. You perform by paying cash or charging your credit card and signing a written contract. Verizon performs by delivering you the phone and promising to provide you cellular service in the future. In this case, Verizon has two performance obligations: (1) to provide the phone and (2) to provide cellular service in the future.
- Step 3. *Determine the transaction price.* The transaction price is the amount the seller is entitled to receive in exchange for the goods and services it has provided. In the case of the McDonald's hamburger, the transaction price is the amount paid for the hamburger. In the case of Verizon, the transaction price is the total price to be paid for the phone (the first performance obligation) and cellular service (the second performance obligation).
- Step 4. *Allocate the transaction price to the separate performance obligations.* Since the sale of a McDonald's hamburger involves the sale of a single item that is immediately delivered, the entire transaction price is allocated to the hamburger. In more complex transactions, such as a Verizon cellular service contract, the revenue received from the customer must be allocated among the performance obligations. This allocation is based on the stand-alone (separate) price of each good or service. For example, Verizon should allocate the revenue from the customer between the phone (first performance obligation) and the commitment to provide cellular service (second performance obligation).
- Step 5. *Recognize revenue when each separate performance obligation is satisfied.* The seller should recognize (record) revenue as each performance obligation is satisfied. The performance obligation could be satisfied either at a point in time or over time. In the case of McDonald's, the performance obligation is satisfied when the clerk delivers the hamburger to the customer. At this point, the control of the hamburger has passed to the customer. In the case of Verizon,

[1] Accounting Standards Update, *Revenue from Contracts with Customers (Topic 606),* Financial Accounting Standards Board, May 2014, Norwalk, CT.

it satisfies its first performance obligation when it delivers you the phone. Verizon satisfies its second performance obligation over time by providing you cellular service. Thus, Verizon should record a portion of the total revenue at the time you sign the contract and receive your phone and the remaining revenue over the period cellular service is provided.

To illustrate, assume that on March 1, Chandler Evans upgrades (replaces) his cell phone with Star Cellular at no cost by signing a two-year agreement. The new agreement cannot be canceled and requires a payment of $90 per month. The cell phone selected by Evans cost Star Cellular $250.

The five-step method for recognizing revenue from this transaction would be applied as follows:

- Step 1. *Identify the contract with the customer.* The contract with Chandler Evans is the two-year cellular service agreement that includes delivery of a new cell phone.
- Step 2. *Identify the separate performance obligations in the contract.* Star Cellular has two separate performance obligations under this contract. First, Star Cellular must deliver a new cell phone at the time that Evans signs the service agreement. Second, Star Cellular must provide Evans with cell service for two years.
- Step 3. *Determine the transaction price.* The transaction price is the total amount Star Cellular will receive over the contract period. In this case, Star Cellular will receive $2,160 ($90 × 24 months) over the contract period.[2]
- Step 4. *Allocate the transaction price to the separate performance obligations.* If Star Cellular sold the cell phone and cell service separately, the individual prices would be as follows:

Cell phone (sold separately)	$ 600
Cell service for two years	3,000
Total price if sold separately	$3,600

The transaction price is allocated to each performance obligation based upon what each obligation would sell for separately as a stand-alone product. To illustrate, the cell phone is allocated $360 of the transaction price of $2,160, computed as follows:

$$\text{Cell Phone} = \text{Transaction Price} \times \frac{\text{Price of Cell Phone Sold Separately}}{\text{Total Price of Cell Phone and Cell Service Sold Separately}}$$

$$= \$2{,}160 \times \frac{\$600}{\$3{,}600} = \$360$$

The cell service is allocated $1,800 of the transaction price of $2,160, computed as follows:

$$\text{Cell Service} = \text{Transaction Price} \times \frac{\text{Price of Cell Service Sold Separately}}{\text{Total Price of Cell Phone and Cell Service Sold Separately}}$$

$$= \$2{,}160 \times \frac{\$3{,}000}{\$3{,}600} = \$1{,}800$$

- Step 5. *Recognize revenue when each separate performance obligation is satisfied.* The $360 of revenue assigned to the cell phone is recognized when the customer signs the service agreement and receives the phone. At this point, the first performance obligation has been satisfied by Star Cellular and the control of the phone has passed to the customer. The $1,800 of cell service revenue will be recognized in increments as the performance obligation is satisfied over the two-year term of the contract.

[2] An interest component may need to be considered in long-term contracts. To simplify, we ignore interest.

Recording Contract Revenue

The effects on the accounts and financial statements of the sale of the cell phone on March 1 are as follows:

Financial Statement Effects

BALANCE SHEET

	Assets		= Liabilities +	Stockholders' Equity
	Accounts Receivable	+ Inventory	=	Retained Earnings
Mar. 1.	360	(250)		110

STATEMENT OF CASH FLOWS

INCOME STATEMENT

Mar. 1. Sales	360
Cost of goods sold	(250)
Gross profit	110

The $1,800 of cell service revenue is recognized as the performance obligation is satisfied over the two-year term of the contract. For example, $75 ($1,800 ÷ 24 months) of service revenue would be recorded each month. The effects on the accounts and financial statements of receiving the service revenue for March are as follows:

Financial Statement Effects

BALANCE SHEET

	Assets		= Liabilities +	Stockholders' Equity
	Cash	+ Accounts Receivable	=	Retained Earnings
Mar. 31.	90	(15)[1]		75[2]

STATEMENT OF CASH FLOWS

Mar. 31. Operating	90

INCOME STATEMENT

Mar. 31. Cell service revenue	75

[1]$360 ÷ 24 months
[2]$1,800 ÷ 24 months

The preceding journal entries illustrate how over the life of the two-year contract the total revenue from the contract of $2,160 is divided between the sale of the cell phone ($360 of revenue) and providing of cell service ($1,800 of revenue). In addition, the journal entries illustrate when revenue from the phone and service is recorded.

Exhibit 1 summarizes the division of revenue and its recording over the two-year contract.

Exhibit 1
Recording Revenue over Two-Year Contract

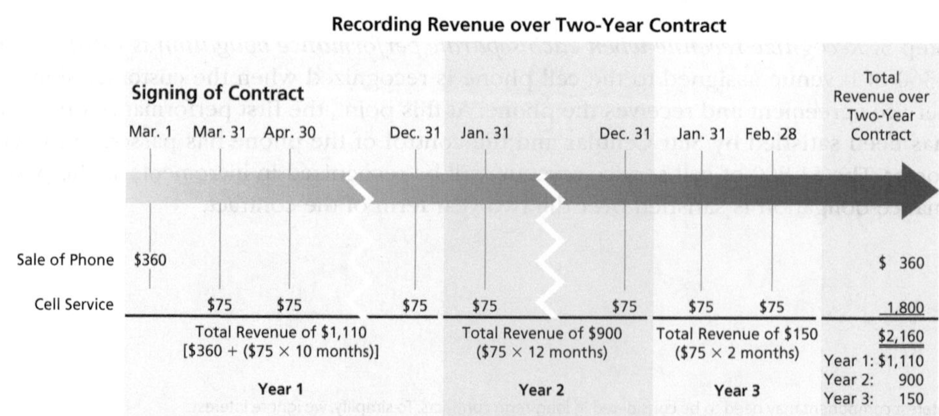

6 International Accounting Standards

The Need for Global Accounting Standards

As discussed in Chapter 1, the Financial Accounting Standards Board (FASB) establishes generally accepted accounting principles (GAAP) for public companies in the United States. Of course, there is a world beyond the borders of the United States. In recent years, the removal of trade barriers and the growth in cross-border equity and debt issuances have led to a dramatic increase in international commerce. As a result, often companies are reporting financial results to users outside of the United States.

Historically, accounting standards have varied considerably across countries. These variances have been driven by cultural, legal, and political differences and resulted in financial statements that were not easily comparable and difficult to interpret. A common set of International Financial Reporting Standards (IFRS) has begun to emerge to reduce cross-country differences in accounting standards. While much of the world has migrated to IFRS, the United States has not. Because of the size of the United States and its significant role in world commerce, U.S. GAAP still has a global impact. As a result, there are currently two major accounting standard-setting efforts in the world, U.S. GAAP and IFRS. These two sets of accounting standards add cost and complexity for companies operating internationally.

Overview of IFRS

International Financial Reporting Standards are designed to meet the financial reporting needs of an increasingly global business environment.

What Is IFRS? International Financial Reporting Standards are a set of global accounting standards developed by an international standard-setting body called the International Accounting Standards Board (IASB). Like the Financial Accounting Standards Board, the IASB is an independent entity that establishes accounting rules. Unlike the FASB, the IASB does not establish accounting rules for any specific country. Rather, it develops accounting rules that can be used by a variety of countries, with the goal of developing a single set of global accounting standards.

Who Uses IFRS? IFRS applies to companies that issue publicly traded debt or equity securities, called public companies, in countries that have adopted IFRS as their accounting standards. For example, public companies in the European Union (EU) are required to prepare financial statements using IFRS. Exhibit 1 shows the approximately 140 countries and jurisdictions that have adopted or permit the use of IFRS for financial reporting.

Exhibit 1 IFRS Adopters

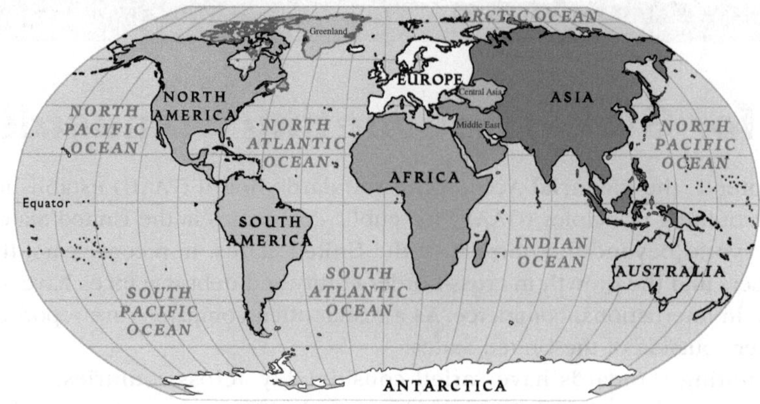

Afghanistan
Albania
Angola
Anguilla
Antigua and Barbuda
Argentina
Armenia
Australia
Austria
Azerbaijan
Bahamas
Bahrain
Bangladesh
Barbados
Belarus
Belgium
Belize
Bermuda
Bhutan
Bolivia
Bosnia and Herzegovina
Botswana
Brazil
Brunei
Bulgaria
Cambodia
Canada
Cayman Islands
Chile
China
Colombia
Costa Rica
Croatia
Cyprus
Czech Republic
Denmark
Dominica
Dominican Republic
Ecuador
Egypt
El Salvador
Estonia
European Union
Fiji
Finland
France
Georgia
Germany
Ghana
Greece
Grenada
Guatemala
Guinea-Bissau
Guyana
Honduras
Hong Kong
Hungary
Iceland
India
Indonesia
Iraq
Ireland
Israel
Italy
Jamaica
Japan
Jordan
Kenya
Korea (South)
Kosovo
Latvia
Lesotho
Liechtenstein
Lithuania
Luxembourg
Macao
Macedonia
Madagascar
Malaysia
Maldives
Malta
Mauritius
Mexico
Moldova
Mongolia
Montserrat
Myanmar
Nepal
Netherlands
New Zealand
Nicaragua
Niger
Nigeria
Norway
Oman
Pakistan
Palestine
Panama
Paraguay
Peru
Philippines
Poland
Portugal
Romania
Russia
Rwanda
Saint Lucia
Saudi Arabia
Serbia
Sierra Leone
Singapore
Slovakia
Slovenia
South Africa
Spain
Sri Lanka
St Kitts and Nevis
St Vincent and the Grenadines
Suriname
Swaziland
Sweden
Switzerland
Syria
Taiwan
Tanzania
Thailand
Trinidad and Tobago
Turkey
Uganda
Ukraine
United Arab Emirates
United Kingdom
United States
Uruguay
Uzbekistan
Venezuela
Vietnam
Yemen
Zambia
Zimbabwe

Source: *Financial Reporting Standards for the World Economy*, IFRS, June 2015.

U.S. GAAP and IFRS: The Road Forward

The United States has not formally adopted IFRS for U.S. companies. The wide acceptance being gained by IFRS around the world, however, has placed considerable pressure on the United States to align U.S. GAAP with IFRS. There are two possible paths that the United States could take to achieve this: (1) adoption of IFRS by the U.S. Securities and Exchange Commission (SEC) or (2) convergence of U.S. GAAP and IFRS. These two options are briefly discussed in this section.

Adoption of IFRS by the SEC The U.S. Securities and Exchange Commission is the governmental agency that has authority over the accounting and financial disclosures for U.S. public companies. Only the SEC has the authority to adopt IFRS for U.S. public companies. After considerable deliberation over a period of nearly five years, the SEC published a Final

Report on the issues surrounding IFRS adoption.[1] Notably, this report did not include a final policy decision or recommendation in favor of U.S. public companies adopting IFRS. Indeed, since this report, the SEC has distanced itself from the adoption position, and it is now acknowledged as unsupported.

Convergence of U.S. GAAP and IFRS Convergence involves aligning IFRS and U.S. GAAP one topic at a time, by slowly merging IFRS and U.S. GAAP into two broadly uniform sets of accounting standards. To this end, the FASB and IASB have agreed to work together on a select number of difficult and high-profile accounting issues. These issues frame a large portion of the disagreement between the two sets of standards and, if accomplished, will significantly reduce the differences between U.S. GAAP and IFRS. The projects selected for the convergence effort represent some of the more technical topics in accounting and are covered in intermediate and advanced accounting courses.

One of the major limitations of convergence is that both the FASB and IASB continue to operate as the accounting standard-setting bodies for their respective jurisdictions. As such, convergence would not result in a single set of global accounting standards. Only those standards that go through the joint FASB–IASB standard-setting process would be released as uniform. Standards that do not go through a joint standard-setting process may create inconsistencies between U.S. GAAP and IFRS.

Differences Between U.S. GAAP and IFRS

U.S. GAAP and IFRS differ both in their approach to standard setting, as well as their financial statement presentation and recording of transactions.

Rules-Based Versus Principles Approach to Standard Setting

U.S. GAAP is considered to be a "rules-based" approach to accounting standard setting. The accounting standards provide detailed and specific rules on the accounting for business transactions. There are few exceptions or varying interpretations of the accounting for a business event. This structure is consistent with the U.S. legal and regulatory system, reflecting the social and economic values of the United States.

In contrast, IFRS is designed to meet the needs of many countries. Differences in legal, political, and economic systems create different needs for and uses of financial information in different countries. For example, Germany needs a financial reporting system that reflects the central role of banks in its financial system, while the Netherlands needs a financial reporting system that reflects the significant role of outside equity in its financial system.

To accommodate economic, legal, and social diversity, IFRS must be broad enough to capture these differences while still presenting comparable financial statements. Under IFRS, there is greater opportunity for different interpretations of the accounting treatment of a business event across different business entities. To support this, IFRS often has more extensive disclosures that support alternative assumptions. Thus, IFRS provides more latitude for professional judgment than typically found in comparable U.S. GAAP. Many countries find this feature attractive in reducing regulatory costs associated with using and auditing financial reports. This "principles-based" approach presents one of the most significant challenges to adopting IFRS in the United States.

Technical Differences Between IFRS and U.S. GAAP

Although U.S. GAAP is similar to IFRS, differences arise in the presentation format, balance sheet valuations, and technical accounting procedures. A comprehensive summary of the key differences between U.S. GAAP and IFRS that are relevant to an introductory accounting course is provided in Exhibit 2.

[1] Work Plan for the Consideration of Incorporating International Financial Accounting Standards into the Financial Reporting System for U.S. Issuers: Final Staff Report, U.S. Securities Exchange Commission, July 13, 2012.

Exhibit 2 Comparison of Accounting for Selected Items Under U.S. GAAP and IFRS

	U.S. GAAP	IFRS	Text Reference
General:			
Financial statement titles	Balance Sheet Statement of Stockholders' Equity Statement of Cash Flows	Statement of Financial Position Statement of Changes in Equity Statement of Cash Flows	General
Financial periods presented	Public companies must present two years of comparative information for income statement, statement of stockholders' equity, and statement of cash flows	One year of comparative information must be presented	General
Conceptual basis for standard setting	"Rules-based" approach	"Principles-based" approach	General
Internal control requirements	Sarbanes-Oxley Act (SOX) Section 404		Chs 5, 12
Balance Sheet:	***Balance Sheet***	***Statement of Financial Position***	
Terminology differences	"Payable" "Stockholders' Equity" "Net Income (Loss)"	"Provision" "Capital and Reserves" "Profit or (Loss)"	Ch 9 Ch 10 General
Inventory—LIFO	LIFO allowed	LIFO prohibited	Ch 7
Inventory—valuation	Reversal of lower-of-cost-or-market write-downs not allowed	Reversal of lower-of-cost-or-market write-downs allowed	Ch 7
Long-lived assets	May NOT be revalued to fair value	May be revalued to fair value on a regular basis	Ch 8

(Continued)

Exhibit 2 Comparison of Accounting for Selected Items Under U.S. GAAP and IFRS (*Concluded*)

	U.S. GAAP	IFRS	Text Reference
Land held for investment	Treated as held for use or sale, and recorded at historical cost	May be accounted for on a historical cost basis or on a fair value basis with changes in fair value recognized through profit and loss	Ch 8
Property, plant, and equipment—valuation	Historical cost If impaired, impairment loss may NOT be reversed in future periods	May select between historical cost or revalued amount (a form of fair value) If impaired, impairment loss may be reversed in future periods	Ch 8
Cost of major overhaul (Capital and revenue expenditures)	Different treatment for ordinary repairs and maintenance, asset improvement, extraordinary repairs	Typically included as part of the cost of the asset or asset component if future economic benefit is probable and can be reliably measured	Ch 8
Intangible assets—valuation	Acquisition cost, unless impaired	Fair value permitted if the intangible asset trades in an active market	Ch 8
Intangible assets—impairment loss reversal	Prohibited	Prohibited for goodwill but allowed for other intangible assets	Ch 8
Income Statement:	***Income Statement***	***Statement of Comprehensive Income***	
Classification of expenses on income statement	Public companies must present expenses on the income statement by function (e.g., cost of goods sold, selling, administrative)	Expenses may be presented based either by function (e.g., cost of goods sold, selling) or by the nature of expense (e.g., wages expense, interest expense)	Chs 1, 2, 3, 4
Statement of Cash Flows:	***Statement of Cash Flows***	***Statement of Cash Flows***	
Classification of interest paid or received	Treated as an operating activity	Interest paid may be treated as either an operating or a financing activity; interest received may be treated as an operating or investing activity	Ch 11
Classification of dividend paid or received	Dividend paid treated as a financing activity, dividend received treated as an operating activity	Dividend paid may be treated as either an operating or a financing activity; dividend received may be treated as an operating or investing activity	Ch 11

Appendix B

Nike Inc., Form 10-K for the Fiscal Year Ended May 31, 2020 Selected Excerpts*

NIKE, Inc.

(Exact name of Registrant as specified in its charter)

Management's Annual Report on Internal Control over Financial Reporting

Management is responsible for establishing and maintaining adequate internal control over financial reporting, as such term is defined in Rule 13(a) - 15(f) and Rule 15(d) - 15(f) of the Securities Exchange Act of 1934, as amended. Internal control over financial reporting is a process designed to provide reasonable assurance regarding the reliability of financial reporting and the preparation of the financial statements for external purposes in accordance with generally accepted accounting principles in the United States of America. Internal control over financial reporting includes those policies and procedures that: (i) pertain to the maintenance of records that, in reasonable detail, accurately and fairly reflect the transactions and dispositions of assets of the Company; (ii) provide reasonable assurance that transactions are recorded as necessary to permit preparation of financial statements in accordance with generally accepted accounting principles, and that receipts and expenditures of the Company are being made only in accordance with authorizations of our management and directors; and (iii) provide reasonable assurance regarding prevention or timely detection of unauthorized acquisition, use or disposition of assets of the Company that could have a material effect on the financial statements.

Because of its inherent limitations, internal control over financial reporting may not prevent or detect misstatements. Also, projections of any evaluation of effectiveness to future periods are subject to the risk that controls may become inadequate because of changes in conditions, or that the degree of compliance with the policies or procedures may deteriorate.

Under the supervision and with the participation of our Chief Executive Officer and Chief Financial Officer, our management conducted an evaluation of the effectiveness of our internal control over financial reporting based upon the framework in *Internal Control — Integrated Framework (2013)* issued by the Committee of Sponsoring Organizations of the Treadway Commission (COSO). Based on the results of our evaluation, our management concluded that our internal control over financial reporting was effective as of May 31, 2020.

PricewaterhouseCoopers LLP, an independent registered public accounting firm, has audited (1) the Consolidated Financial Statements and (2) the effectiveness of our internal control over financial reporting as of May 31, 2020, as stated in their report herein.

John J. Donahoe II
President and Chief Executive Officer

Matthew Friend
Executive Vice President and Chief Financial Officer

* The entire NIke Inc., Form 10-K is available on the companion website at cengage.com

Report of Independent Registered Public Accounting Firm

To the Board of Directors and Shareholders of NIKE, Inc.

Opinions on the Financial Statements and Internal Control over Financial Reporting

We have audited the accompanying consolidated balance sheets of NIKE, Inc. and its subsidiaries (the "Company") as of May 31, 2020 and 2019, and the related consolidated statements of income, of comprehensive income, of shareholders' equity and of cash flows for each of the three years in the period ended May 31, 2020, including the related notes and financial statement schedule listed in the index appearing under Item 15(a)(2) (collectively referred to as the "consolidated financial statements"). We also have audited the Company's internal control over financial reporting as of May 31, 2020, based on criteria established in *Internal Control - Integrated Framework* (2013) issued by the Committee of Sponsoring Organizations of the Treadway Commission (COSO).

In our opinion, the consolidated financial statements referred to above present fairly, in all material respects, the financial position of the Company as of May 31, 2020 and 2019, and the results of its operations and its cash flows for each of the three years in the period ended May 31, 2020 in conformity with accounting principles generally accepted in the United States of America. Also in our opinion, the Company maintained, in all material respects, effective internal control over financial reporting as of May 31, 2020, based on criteria established in *Internal Control - Integrated Framework* (2013) issued by the COSO.

Changes in Accounting Principles

As discussed in Note 1 to the consolidated financial statements, the Company changed the manner in which it accounts for leases as of June 1, 2019 and the manner in which it accounts for revenue from contracts with customers and the manner in which it accounts for income taxes related to intra-entity transfers other than inventory as of June 1, 2018.

Basis for Opinions

The Company's management is responsible for these consolidated financial statements, for maintaining effective internal control over financial reporting, and for its assessment of the effectiveness of internal control over financial reporting, included in the accompanying Management's Annual Report on Internal Control over Financial Reporting. Our responsibility is to express opinions on the Company's consolidated financial statements and on the Company's internal control over financial reporting based on our audits. We are a public accounting firm registered with the Public Company Accounting Oversight Board (United States) (PCAOB) and are required to be independent with respect to the Company in accordance with the U.S. federal securities laws and the applicable rules and regulations of the Securities and Exchange Commission and the PCAOB.

We conducted our audits in accordance with the standards of the PCAOB. Those standards require that we plan and perform the audits to obtain reasonable assurance about whether the consolidated financial statements are free of material misstatement, whether due to error or fraud, and whether effective internal control over financial reporting was maintained in all material respects.

Our audits of the consolidated financial statements included performing procedures to assess the risks of material misstatement of the consolidated financial statements, whether due to error or fraud, and performing procedures that respond to those risks. Such procedures included examining, on a test basis, evidence regarding the amounts and disclosures in the consolidated financial statements. Our audits also included evaluating the accounting principles used and significant estimates made by management, as well as evaluating the overall presentation of the consolidated financial statements. Our audit of internal control over financial reporting included obtaining an understanding of internal control over financial reporting, assessing the risk that a material weakness exists, and testing and evaluating the design and operating effectiveness of internal control based on the assessed risk. Our audits also included performing such other procedures as we considered necessary in the circumstances. We believe that our audits provide a reasonable basis for our opinions.

Definition and Limitations of Internal Control over Financial Reporting

A company's internal control over financial reporting is a process designed to provide reasonable assurance regarding the reliability of financial reporting and the preparation of financial statements for external purposes in accordance with generally accepted accounting principles. A company's internal control over financial reporting includes those policies and procedures that (i) pertain to the maintenance of records that, in reasonable detail, accurately and fairly reflect the transactions and dispositions of the assets of the company; (ii) provide reasonable assurance that transactions are recorded as necessary to permit preparation of financial statements in accordance with generally accepted accounting principles, and that receipts and expenditures of the company are being made only in accordance with authorizations of management and directors of the company; and (iii) provide reasonable assurance regarding prevention or timely detection of unauthorized acquisition, use, or disposition of the company's assets that could have a material effect on the financial statements.

Because of its inherent limitations, internal control over financial reporting may not prevent or detect misstatements. Also, projections of any evaluation of effectiveness to future periods are subject to the risk that controls may become inadequate because of changes in conditions, or that the degree of compliance with the policies or procedures may deteriorate.

Critical Audit Matters

The critical audit matter communicated below is a matter arising from the current period audit of the consolidated financial statements that was communicated or required to be communicated to the audit committee and that (i) relates to accounts or disclosures that are material to the consolidated financial statements and (ii) involved our especially challenging, subjective, or complex judgments. The communication of critical audit matters does not alter in any way our opinion on the consolidated financial statements, taken as a whole, and we are not, by communicating the critical audit matter below, providing a separate opinion on the critical audit matter or on the accounts or disclosures to which it relates.

Accounting for Income Taxes

As described in Note 9 to the consolidated financial statements, the Company recorded income tax expense of $348 million for the year ended May 31, 2020, and has net deferred tax assets of $732 million, including a valuation allowance of $26 million, and total gross unrecognized tax benefits, excluding related interest and penalties, of $771 million as of May 31, 2020, $536 million of which would affect the Company's effective tax rate if recognized in future periods. The Company is subject to taxation in the United States, as well as various state and foreign jurisdictions. As disclosed by management, the use of significant judgment and estimates, as well as the interpretation and application of complex tax laws is required by management to determine its provision for income taxes.

The principal considerations for our determination that performing procedures relating to the accounting for income taxes is a critical audit matter are the significant judgment by management when assessing complex tax laws and regulations, including new temporary regulations and recent court rulings, as it relates to determining the provision for income taxes and other tax positions. This in turn led to a high degree of auditor judgment, subjectivity and effort in performing procedures and evaluating audit evidence relating to the provision for income taxes and other tax positions. In addition, the audit effort involved the use of professionals with specialized skill and knowledge to assist in performing procedures and evaluating the audit evidence obtained.

Addressing the matter involved performing procedures and evaluating audit evidence in connection with forming our overall opinion on the consolidated financial statements. These procedures included testing the effectiveness of controls relating to the provision for income taxes and other tax positions. These procedures also included, among others, evaluating the effect on the Company's tax provision of changes in its legal entity structure and tax laws, testing management's tax calculations and considering the Company's compliance with tax laws. We also used professionals with specialized skill and knowledge to assist in evaluating the application of relevant tax laws, the provision for income taxes and the reasonableness of management's assessments of whether certain tax positions are more-likely-than-not of being sustained.

/s/ PricewaterhouseCoopers LLP
Portland, Oregon
July 24, 2020

We have served as the Company's auditor since 1974.

NIKE, Inc. Consolidated Statements of Income

	YEAR ENDED MAY 31,		
(In millions, except per share data)	**2020**	**2019**	**2018**
Revenues	$ 37,403	$ 39,117	$ 36,397
Cost of sales	21,162	21,643	20,441
Gross profit	16,241	17,474	15,956
Demand creation expense	3,592	3,753	3,577
Operating overhead expense	9,534	8,949	7,934
Total selling and administrative expense	13,126	12,702	11,511
Interest expense (income), net	89	49	54
Other (income) expense, net	139	(78)	66
Income before income taxes	2,887	4,801	4,325
Income tax expense	348	772	2,392
NET INCOME	**$ 2,539**	**$ 4,029**	**$ 1,933**
Earnings per common share:			
Basic	$ 1.63	$ 2.55	$ 1.19
Diluted	$ 1.60	$ 2.49	$ 1.17
Weighted average common shares outstanding:			
Basic	1,558.8	1,579.7	1,623.8
Diluted	1,591.6	1,618.4	1,659.1

The accompanying Notes to the Consolidated Financial Statements are an integral part of this statement.

NIKE, Inc. Consolidated Statements of Comprehensive Income

(Dollars in millions)	YEAR ENDED MAY 31, 2020	2019	2018
Net income	$ 2,539	$ 4,029	$ 1,933
Other comprehensive income (loss), net of tax:			
Change in net foreign currency translation adjustment	(148)	(173)	(6)
Change in net gains (losses) on cash flow hedges	(130)	503	76
Change in net gains (losses) on other	(9)	(7)	34
Total other comprehensive income (loss), net of tax	(287)	323	104
TOTAL COMPREHENSIVE INCOME	**$ 2,252**	**$ 4,352**	**$ 2,037**

The accompanying Notes to the Consolidated Financial Statements are an integral part of this statement.

NIKE, Inc. Consolidated Balance Sheets

(In millions)	MAY 31, 2020	2019
ASSETS		
Current assets:		
Cash and equivalents	$ 8,348	$ 4,466
Short-term investments	439	197
Accounts receivable, net	2,749	4,272
Inventories	7,367	5,622
Prepaid expenses and other current assets	1,653	1,968
Total current assets	20,556	16,525
Property, plant and equipment, net	4,866	4,744
Operating lease right-of-use assets, net	3,097	—
Identifiable intangible assets, net	274	283
Goodwill	223	154
Deferred income taxes and other assets	2,326	2,011
TOTAL ASSETS	**$ 31,342**	**$ 23,717**
LIABILITIES AND SHAREHOLDERS' EQUITY		
Current liabilities:		
Current portion of long-term debt	$ 3	$ 6
Notes payable	248	9
Accounts payable	2,248	2,612
Current portion of operating lease liabilities	445	—
Accrued liabilities	5,184	5,010
Income taxes payable	156	229
Total current liabilities	8,284	7,866
Long-term debt	9,406	3,464
Operating lease liabilities	2,913	—
Deferred income taxes and other liabilities	2,684	3,347
Commitments and contingencies (Note 18)		
Redeemable preferred stock	—	—
Shareholders' equity:		
Common stock at stated value:		
Class A convertible — 315 and 315 shares outstanding	—	—
Class B — 1,243 and 1,253 shares outstanding	3	3
Capital in excess of stated value	8,299	7,163
Accumulated other comprehensive income (loss)	(56)	231
Retained earnings (deficit)	(191)	1,643
Total shareholders' equity	8,055	9,040
TOTAL LIABILITIES AND SHAREHOLDERS' EQUITY	**$ 31,342**	**$ 23,717**

The accompanying Notes to the Consolidated Financial Statements are an integral part of this statement.

NIKE, Inc. Consolidated Statements of Cash Flows

	YEAR ENDED MAY 31,		
(Dollars in millions)	**2020**	**2019**	**2018**
Cash provided (used) by operations:			
Net income	$ 2,539	$ 4,029	$ 1,933
Adjustments to reconcile net income to net cash provided (used) by operations:			
Depreciation	721	705	747
Deferred income taxes	(380)	34	647
Stock-based compensation	429	325	218
Amortization, impairment and other	398	15	27
Net foreign currency adjustments	23	233	(99)
Changes in certain working capital components and other assets and liabilities:			
(Increase) decrease in accounts receivable	1,239	(270)	187
(Increase) decrease in inventories	(1,854)	(490)	(255)
(Increase) decrease in prepaid expenses, operating lease right-of-use assets and other current and non-current assets	(654)	(203)	35
Increase (decrease) in accounts payable, accrued liabilities, operating lease liabilities and other current and non-current liabilities	24	1,525	1,515
Cash provided (used) by operations	2,485	5,903	4,955
Cash provided (used) by investing activities:			
Purchases of short-term investments	(2,426)	(2,937)	(4,783)
Maturities of short-term investments	74	1,715	3,613
Sales of short-term investments	2,379	2,072	2,496
Additions to property, plant and equipment	(1,086)	(1,119)	(1,028)
Other investing activities	31	5	(22)
Cash provided (used) by investing activities	(1,028)	(264)	276
Cash provided (used) by financing activities:			
Proceeds from borrowings, net of debt issuance costs	6,134	—	—
Increase (decrease) in notes payable, net	49	(325)	13
Proceeds from exercise of stock options and other stock issuances	885	700	733
Repurchase of common stock	(3,067)	(4,286)	(4,254)
Dividends — common and preferred	(1,452)	(1,332)	(1,243)
Other financing activities	(58)	(50)	(84)
Cash provided (used) by financing activities	2,491	(5,293)	(4,835)
Effect of exchange rate changes on cash and equivalents	(66)	(129)	45
Net increase (decrease) in cash and equivalents	3,882	217	441
Cash and equivalents, beginning of year	4,466	4,249	3,808
CASH AND EQUIVALENTS, END OF YEAR	**$ 8,348**	**$ 4,466**	**$ 4,249**
Supplemental disclosure of cash flow information:			
Cash paid during the year for:			
Interest, net of capitalized interest	$ 140	$ 153	$ 125
Income taxes	1,028	757	529
Non-cash additions to property, plant and equipment	121	160	294
Dividends declared and not paid	385	347	320

The accompanying Notes to the Consolidated Financial Statements are an integral part of this statement.

NIKE, Inc. Consolidated Statements of Shareholders' Equity

	COMMON STOCK				CAPITAL IN EXCESS OF STATED VALUE	ACCUMULATED OTHER COMPREHENSIVE INCOME (LOSS)	RETAINED EARNINGS (DEFICIT)	TOTAL
	CLASS A		CLASS B					
(In millions, except per share data)	SHARES	AMOUNT	SHARES	AMOUNT				
Balance at May 31, 2017	**329**	**$ –**	**1,314**	**$ 3**	**$ 5,710**	**$ (213)**	**$ 6,907**	**$ 12,407**
Stock options exercised			24		600			600
Repurchase of Class B Common Stock			(70)		(254)		(4,013)	(4,267)
Dividends on common stock ($0.78 per share) and preferred stock ($0.10 per share)							(1,265)	(1,265)
Issuance of shares to employees, net of shares withheld for employee taxes				4	110		(28)	82
Stock-based compensation					218			218
Net income							1,933	1,933
Other comprehensive income (loss)						104		104
Reclassifications to retained earnings in accordance with ASU 2018-02						17	(17)	–
Balance at May 31, 2018	**329**	**$ –**	**1,272**	**$ 3**	**$ 6,384**	**$ (92)**	**$ 3,517**	**$ 9,812**
Stock options exercised			18		539			539
Conversion to Class B Common Stock	(14)	14						–
Repurchase of Class B Common Stock		(54)			(227)		(4,056)	(4,283)
Dividends on common stock ($0.86 per share) and preferred stock ($0.10 per share)							(1,360)	(1,360)
Issuance of shares to employees, net of shares withheld for employee taxes		3			142		(3)	139
Stock-based compensation					325			325
Net income							4,029	4,029
Other comprehensive income (loss)						323		323
Adoption of ASU 2016-16 (Note 1)							(507)	(507)
Adoption of ASC Topic 606 (Note 1)							23	23
Balance at May 31, 2019	**315**	**$ –**	**1,253**	**$ 3**	**$ 7,163**	**$ 231**	**$ 1,643**	**$ 9,040**
Stock options exercised			20		703			703
Repurchase of Class B Common Stock			(34)		(161)		(2,872)	(3,033)
Dividends on common stock ($0.955 per share) and preferred stock ($0.10 per share)							(1,491)	(1,491)
Issuance of shares to employees, net of shares withheld for employee taxes			4		165		(9)	156
Stock-based compensation					429			429
Net income							2,539	2,539
Other comprehensive income (loss)						(287)		(287)
Adoption of ASC Topic 842 (Note 1)							(1)	(1)
Balance at May 31, 2020	**315**	**$ –**	**1,243**	**$ 3**	**$ 8,299**	**$ (56)**	**$ (191)**	**$ 8,055**

The accompanying Notes to the Consolidated Financial Statements are an integral part of this statement.

NOTE 1 — Summary of Significant Accounting Policies

Description of Business

NIKE, Inc. is a worldwide leader in the design, development and worldwide marketing and selling of athletic footwear, apparel, equipment, accessories and services. NIKE, Inc. portfolio brands include the NIKE Brand, Jordan Brand, Hurley and Converse. The NIKE Brand is focused on performance athletic footwear, apparel, equipment, accessories and services across a wide range of sport categories, amplified with sport-inspired lifestyle products carrying the Swoosh trademark, as well as other NIKE Brand trademarks. The Jordan Brand is focused on athletic and casual footwear, apparel and accessories using the Jumpman trademark. Sales and operating results of Jordan Brand products are reported within the respective NIKE Brand geographic operating segments. The Hurley brand is focused on action sports and youth lifestyle apparel and accessories under the Hurley trademark. Sales and operating results of Hurley brand products, prior to its divestiture, are reported within the NIKE Brand's North America geographic operating segment. Refer to Note 20 — Acquisitions and Divestitures for information regarding the divestiture of the Company's wholly-owned subsidiary, Hurley. Converse designs, distributes, licenses and sells casual sneakers, apparel and accessories under the Converse, Chuck Taylor, All Star, One Star, Star Chevron and Jack Purcell trademarks. In some markets outside the U.S., these trademarks are licensed to third parties who design, distribute, market and sell similar products. Operating results of the Converse brand are reported on a stand-alone basis.

Basis of Consolidation

The Consolidated Financial Statements include the accounts of NIKE, Inc. and its subsidiaries (the "Company" or "NIKE"). All significant inter-company transactions and balances have been eliminated.

Revenue Recognition

Beginning in fiscal 2019, the Company adopted Accounting Standards Update (ASU) No. 2014-09, *Revenue from Contracts with Customers* (Topic 606). Prior to fiscal 2019, amounts have not been restated and continue to be reported in accordance with the Company's historical accounting policies. The Company's revenue recognition policies under Topic 606 are described in the following paragraphs and references to prior period policies under Accounting Standard Codification Topic 605 — *Revenue Recognition* (Topic 605), are included below in the event they are substantially different.

Revenue transactions associated with the sale of NIKE Brand footwear, apparel and equipment, as well as Converse products, comprise a single performance obligation, which consists of the sale of products to customers either through wholesale or direct to consumer channels. The Company satisfies the performance obligation and records revenues when transfer of control has passed to the customer, based on the terms of sale. A customer is considered to have control once they are able to direct the use and receive substantially all of the benefits of the product.

Transfer of control passes to wholesale customers upon shipment or upon receipt depending on the country of the sale and the agreement with the customer. Control passes to retail store customers at the time of sale and to substantially all digital commerce customers upon shipment. Prior to fiscal 2019, the requirements for recognizing revenue were met upon delivery to the customer. The transaction price is determined based upon the invoiced sales price, less anticipated sales returns, discounts and miscellaneous claims from customers. Payment terms for wholesale transactions depend on the country of sale or agreement with the customer and payment is generally required within 90 days or less of shipment to or receipt by the wholesale customer. Payment is due at the time of sale for retail store and digital commerce transactions.

Consideration for trademark licensing contracts is earned through sales-based or usage-based royalty arrangements and the associated revenues are recognized over the license period.

Taxes assessed by governmental authorities that are both imposed on and concurrent with a specific revenue-producing transaction, and are collected by the Company from a customer, are excluded from *Revenues* and *Cost of sales* in the Consolidated Statements of Income. Shipping and handling costs associated with outbound freight after control over a product has transferred to a customer are accounted for as a fulfillment cost and are included in *Cost of sales* when the related revenues are recognized.

Sales-Related Reserves

Consideration promised in the Company's contracts with customers is variable due to anticipated reductions such as sales returns, discounts and miscellaneous claims from customers. The Company estimates the most likely amount it will be entitled to receive and records an anticipated reduction against *Revenues*, with an offsetting increase to *Accrued liabilities* at the time revenues are recognized. The estimated cost of inventory for product returns is recorded in *Prepaid expenses and other current assets* on the Consolidated Balance Sheets. Prior to fiscal 2019, the Company's reserve balances were reported net of the estimated cost of inventory for product returns and recognized within *Accounts receivable, net* for wholesale transactions and *Accrued liabilities* for the Company's direct to consumer business, on the Consolidated Balance Sheets.

The provision for anticipated sales returns consists of both contractual return rights and discretionary authorized returns. Provisions for post-invoice sales discounts consist of both contractual programs and discretionary discounts that are expected to be granted at a later date.

Estimates of discretionary authorized returns, discounts and claims are based on (1) historical rates, (2) specific identification of outstanding returns not yet received from customers and outstanding discounts and claims and (3) estimated returns, discounts and claims expected, but not yet finalized with customers. Actual returns, discounts and claims in any future period are inherently uncertain and thus may differ from estimates recorded. If actual or expected future returns, discounts or claims were significantly greater or lower than the reserves established, a reduction or increase to net revenues would be recorded in the period in which such determination was made.

Cost of Sales

Cost of sales consists primarily of inventory costs, as well as warehousing costs (including the cost of warehouse labor), third-party royalties, certain foreign currency hedge gains and losses and product design costs. Shipping and handling costs are expensed as incurred and included in *Cost of sales*.

Demand Creation Expense

Demand creation expense consists of advertising and promotion costs, including costs of endorsement contracts, complimentary product, television, digital and print advertising and media costs, brand events and retail brand presentation. Advertising production costs are expensed the first time an advertisement is run. Advertising media costs are expensed when the advertisement appears. Costs related to brand events are expensed when the event occurs. Costs related to retail brand presentation are expensed when the presentation is complete and delivered.

A significant amount of the Company's promotional expenses result from payments under endorsement contracts. In general, endorsement payments are expensed on a straight-line basis over the term of the contract. However, certain contract elements may be accounted for differently based upon the facts and circumstances of each individual contract. Prepayments made under contracts are included in *Prepaid expenses and other current assets* or *Deferred income taxes and other assets* depending on the period to which the prepayment applies.

Certain contracts provide for contingent payments to endorsers based upon specific achievements in their sport (e.g., winning a championship). The Company records *Demand creation expense* for these amounts when the endorser achieves the specific goal.

Certain contracts provide for variable payments based upon endorsers maintaining a level of performance in their sport over an extended period of time (e.g., maintaining a specified ranking in a sport for a year). When the Company determines payments are probable, the amounts are reported in *Demand creation expense* ratably over the contract period based on the Company's best estimate of the endorser's performance. In these instances, to the extent actual payments to the endorser differ from the Company's estimate due to changes in the endorser's performance, adjustments to *Demand creation expense* may be recorded in a future period.

Certain contracts provide for royalty payments to endorsers based upon a predetermined percent of sales of particular products, which the Company records in *Cost of sales* as the related sales occur. For contracts containing minimum guaranteed royalty payments, the Company records the amount of any guaranteed payment in excess of that earned through sales of product within *Demand creation expense*.

Through cooperative advertising programs, the Company reimburses its wholesale customers for certain costs of advertising the Company's products. The Company records these costs in *Demand creation expense* at the point in time it is obligated to its customers for the costs. This obligation may arise prior to the related advertisement being run.

Total advertising and promotion expenses, which the Company refers to as *Demand creation expense*, were $3,592 million, $3,753 million and $3,577 million for the years ended May 31, 2020, 2019 and 2018, respectively. Prepaid advertising and promotion expenses totaled $686 million and $773 million at May 31, 2020 and 2019, respectively, of which $326 million and $333 million, respectively, was recorded in *Prepaid expenses and other current assets*, and $360 million and $440 million, respectively, was recorded in *Deferred income taxes and other assets*, depending on the period to which the prepayment applied.

Operating Overhead Expense

Operating overhead expense consists primarily of wage and benefit-related expenses, research and development costs, bad debt expense, as well as other administrative expenses, such as rent, depreciation and amortization, professional services, meetings and travel.

Cash and Equivalents

Cash and equivalents represent cash and short-term, highly liquid investments, that are both readily convertible to known amounts of cash, and so near their maturity they present insignificant risk of changes in value because of changes in interest rates, including commercial paper, U.S. Treasury, U.S. Agency, money market funds, time deposits and corporate debt securities with maturities of 90 days or less at the date of purchase.

Short-Term Investments

Short-term investments consist of highly liquid investments, including commercial paper, U.S. Treasury, U.S. Agency, time deposits and corporate debt securities, with maturities over 90 days at the date of purchase. Debt securities the Company has the ability and positive intent to hold to maturity are carried at amortized cost. At May 31, 2020 and 2019, the Company did not hold any short-term investments classified as trading or held-to-maturity.

At May 31, 2020 and 2019, *Short-term investments consisted* of available-for-sale debt securities, which are recorded at fair value with unrealized gains and losses reported, net of tax, in *Accumulated other comprehensive income (loss)*, unless unrealized losses are determined to be other than temporary. Realized gains and losses on the sale of securities are determined by specific identification. The Company considers all available-for-sale debt securities, including those with maturity dates beyond 12 months, as available to support current operational liquidity needs and, therefore, classifies all securities with maturity dates beyond 90 days at the date of purchase as current assets within *Short-term investments* on the Consolidated Balance Sheets.

Refer to Note 6 — Fair Value Measurements for more information on the Company's short-term investments.

Allowance for Uncollectible Accounts Receivable

Accounts receivable, net consist primarily of amounts receivable from customers. The Company makes ongoing estimates relating to the collectability of its accounts receivable and maintains an allowance for estimated losses resulting from the inability of its customers to make required payments. In addition to judgments about the creditworthiness of significant customers based on ongoing credit evaluations, the Company considers historical levels of credit losses, as well as macroeconomic and industry trends, such as the impacts of COVID–19, to determine the amount of the allowance. Accounts receivable with anticipated collection dates greater than 12 months from the balance sheet date and related allowances are considered non-current and recorded in *Deferred income taxes and other assets*. The allowance for uncollectible accounts receivable was $214 million and $30 million as of May 31, 2020 and 2019, respectively.

Inventory Valuation

Inventories are stated at lower of cost and net realizable value, and valued on either an average or a specific identification cost basis. In some instances, the Company ships product directly from its suppliers to the customer, with the related inventory and cost of sales recognized on a specific identification basis. Inventory costs primarily consist of product cost from the Company's suppliers, as well as inbound freight, import duties, taxes, insurance and logistics and other handling fees.

Property, Plant and Equipment and Depreciation

Property, plant and equipment are recorded at cost. Depreciation is determined on a straight-line basis for land improvements, buildings and leasehold improvements over 2 to 40 years and for machinery and equipment over 2 to 15 years.

Depreciation and amortization of assets used in manufacturing, warehousing and product distribution are recorded in *Cost of sales*. Depreciation and amortization of all other assets are recorded in *Operating overhead expense*.

Software Development Costs

Internal Use Software: Expenditures for major software purchases and software developed for internal use are capitalized and amortized over a 2 to 12-year period on a straight-line basis. The Company's policy provides for the capitalization of external direct costs associated with developing or obtaining internal use computer software. In addition, the Company also capitalizes certain payroll and payroll-related costs for employees who are directly associated with internal use computer software projects.

The amount of capitalizable payroll costs with respect to these employees is limited to the time directly spent on such projects. Costs associated with preliminary project stage activities, training, maintenance and all other post-implementation stage activities are expensed as incurred.

Computer Software to be Sold, Leased or Otherwise Marketed: Development costs of computer software to be sold, leased or otherwise marketed as an integral part of a product are subject to capitalization beginning when a product's technological feasibility has been established and ending when a product is available for general release to customers. In most instances, the Company's products are released soon after technological feasibility has been established. Therefore, software development costs incurred subsequent to achievement of technological feasibility are usually not significant, and generally most software development costs have been expensed as incurred.

Impairment of Long-Lived Assets

The Company reviews the carrying value of long-lived assets or asset groups to be used in operations whenever events or changes in circumstances indicate the carrying amount of the assets might not be recoverable. Factors that would necessitate an impairment assessment include a significant adverse change in the extent or manner in which an asset is used, a significant adverse change in legal factors or the business climate that could affect the value of the asset or a significant decline in the observable market value of an asset, among others. If such facts indicate a potential impairment, the Company would assess the recoverability of an asset group by determining if the carrying value of the asset group exceeds the sum of the projected undiscounted cash flows expected to result from the use and eventual disposition of the assets over the remaining economic life of the primary asset in the asset group. If the recoverability test indicates that the carrying value of the asset group is not recoverable, the Company will estimate the fair value of the asset group using appropriate valuation methodologies, which would typically include an estimate of discounted cash flows. Any impairment would be measured as the difference between the asset group's carrying amount and its estimated fair value.

Goodwill and Indefinite-Lived Intangible Assets

The Company performs annual impairment tests on goodwill and intangible assets with indefinite lives in the fourth quarter of each fiscal year or when events occur or circumstances change that would, more likely than not, reduce the fair value of a reporting unit or an intangible asset with an indefinite life below its carrying value. Events or changes in circumstances that may trigger interim impairment reviews include significant changes in business climate, operating results, planned investments in the reporting unit, planned divestitures or an expectation that the carrying amount may not be recoverable, among other factors.

For purposes of testing goodwill for impairment, the Company allocates goodwill across its reporting units, which are considered the Company's operating segments. The Company may first assess qualitative factors to determine whether it is more likely than not that the fair value of a reporting unit is less than its carrying amount. If, after assessing the totality of events and circumstances, the Company determines it is more likely than not that the fair value of the reporting unit is greater than its carrying amount, an impairment test is unnecessary. If an impairment test is necessary, the Company will estimate the fair value of its related reporting units. If the carrying value of a reporting unit exceeds its fair value, the goodwill of that reporting unit is determined to be impaired and the Company will proceed with recording an impairment charge equal to the excess of the carrying value over the related fair value.

Indefinite-lived intangible assets primarily consist of acquired trade names and trademarks. The Company may first perform a qualitative assessment to determine whether it is more likely than not that an indefinite-lived intangible asset is impaired. If, after assessing the totality of events and circumstances, the Company determines it is more likely than not that the indefinite-lived intangible asset is not impaired, no quantitative fair value measurement is necessary. If a quantitative fair value measurement calculation is required for these intangible assets, the Company primarily utilizes the relief-from-royalty method. This method assumes trade names and trademarks have value to the extent their owner is relieved of the obligation to pay royalties for the benefits received from them. This method requires the Company to estimate the future revenues for the related brands, the appropriate royalty rate and the weighted average cost of capital. If the carrying value of the indefinite-lived intangible exceeds its fair value, the asset is determined to be impaired and the Company will proceed with recording an impairment charge equal to the excess of the carrying value over the related fair value.

Operating Leases

Beginning in fiscal 2020, the Company adopted Accounting Standards Update (ASU) No. 2016-02, *Leases (Topic 842)*. Prior period amounts have not been restated and continue to be reported in accordance with the Company's historical accounting policies. The Company's lease recognition policies under Topic 842 are described in the following paragraphs.

The Company primarily leases retail store space, certain distribution and warehouse facilities, office space, equipment and other non-real estate assets. The Company determines if an arrangement is a lease at inception and begins recording lease activity at the commencement date, which is generally the date in which the Company takes possession of or controls the physical use of the asset. Right-of-use (ROU) assets and lease liabilities are recognized based on the present value of lease payments over the lease term with lease expense recognized on a straight-line basis. The Company's incremental borrowing rate is used to determine the present value of future lease payments unless the implicit rate is readily determinable.

Lease agreements may contain rent escalation clauses, renewal or termination options, rent holidays or certain landlord incentives, including tenant improvement allowances. ROU assets include amounts for scheduled rent increases and are reduced by the amount of lease incentives. The lease term includes the non-cancelable period of the lease and options to extend or terminate the lease when it is reasonably certain the Company will exercise those options. Certain lease agreements include variable lease payments, which are based on a percent of retail sales over specified levels or adjust periodically for inflation as a result of changes in a published index, primarily the Consumer Price Index.

Fair Value Measurements

The Company measures certain financial assets and liabilities at fair value on a recurring basis, including derivatives, equity securities and available-for-sale debt securities. Fair value is the price the Company would receive to sell an asset or pay to transfer a liability in an orderly transaction with a market participant at the measurement date. The Company uses a three-level hierarchy established by the Financial Accounting Standards

Board (FASB) that prioritizes fair value measurements based on the types of inputs used for the various valuation techniques (market approach, income approach and cost approach).

The levels of the fair value hierarchy are described below:

- Level 1: Quoted prices in active markets for identical assets or liabilities.
- Level 2: Inputs other than quoted prices that are observable for the asset or liability, either directly or indirectly; these include quoted prices for similar assets or liabilities in active markets and quoted prices for identical or similar assets or liabilities in markets that are not active.
- Level 3: Unobservable inputs with little or no market data available, which require the reporting entity to develop its own assumptions.

The Company's assessment of the significance of a particular input to the fair value measurement in its entirety requires judgment and considers factors specific to the asset or liability. Financial assets and liabilities are classified in their entirety based on the most conservative level of input that is significant to the fair value measurement.

Pricing vendors are utilized for a majority of Level 1 and Level 2 investments. These vendors either provide a quoted market price in an active market or use observable inputs without applying significant adjustments in their pricing. Observable inputs include broker quotes, interest rates and yield curves observable at commonly quoted intervals, volatilities and credit risks. The fair value of derivative contracts is determined using observable market inputs such as the daily market foreign currency rates, forward pricing curves, currency volatilities, currency correlations and interest rates and considers nonperformance risk of the Company and its counterparties.

The Company's fair value measurement process includes comparing fair values to another independent pricing vendor to ensure appropriate fair values are recorded.

Refer to Note 6 — Fair Value Measurements for additional information.

Foreign Currency Translation and Foreign Currency Transactions

Adjustments resulting from translating foreign functional currency financial statements into U.S. Dollars are included in the foreign currency translation adjustment, a component of *Accumulated other comprehensive income (loss)* in *Total shareholders' equity*.

The Company's global subsidiaries have various assets and liabilities, primarily receivables and payables, which are denominated in currencies other than their functional currency. These balance sheet items are subject to re-measurement, the impact of which is recorded in *Other (income) expense, net*, within the Consolidated Statements of Income.

Accounting for Derivatives and Hedging Activities

The Company uses derivative financial instruments to reduce its exposure to changes in foreign currency exchange rates and interest rates. All derivatives are recorded at fair value on the Consolidated Balance Sheets and changes in the fair value of derivative financial instruments are either recognized in *Accumulated other comprehensive income (loss)* (a component of *Total shareholders' equity*), *Long-term debt* or *Net income* depending on the nature of the underlying exposure, whether the derivative is formally designated as a hedge and, if designated, the extent to which the hedge is effective. The Company classifies the cash flows at settlement from derivatives in the same category as the cash flows from the related hedged items. For undesignated hedges and designated cash flow hedges, this is primarily within the *Cash provided by operations* component of the Consolidated Statements of Cash Flows. For designated net investment hedges, this is within the *Cash used by investing activities* component of the Consolidated Statements of Cash Flows. For the Company's fair value hedges, which are interest rate swaps used to mitigate the change in fair value of its fixed-rate debt attributable to changes in interest rates, the related cash flows from periodic interest payments are reflected within the *Cash provided by operations* component of the Consolidated Statements of Cash Flows. Refer to Note 14 — Risk Management and Derivatives for additional information on the Company's risk management program and derivatives.

Stock-Based Compensation

The Company accounts for stock-based compensation by estimating the fair value, net of estimated forfeitures, of equity awards and recognizing the related expense as *Cost of sales* or *Operating overhead expense*, as applicable, in the Consolidated Statements of Income on a straight-line basis over the vesting period. Substantially all awards vest ratably over four years of continued employment, with stock options expiring ten years from the date of grant. The fair value of options, stock appreciation rights, and employees' purchase rights under the employee stock purchase plans (ESPPs) is determined using the Black-Scholes option pricing model. The fair value of restricted stock and restricted stock units is established by the market price on the date of grant.

Refer to Note 11 — Common Stock and Stock-Based Compensation for additional information on the Company's stock-based compensation programs.

Income Taxes

The Company accounts for income taxes using the asset and liability method. This approach requires the recognition of deferred tax assets and liabilities for the expected future tax consequences of temporary differences between the carrying amounts and the tax basis of assets and liabilities. The Company records a valuation allowance to reduce deferred tax assets to the amount management believes is more likely than not to be realized.

The Company recognizes a tax benefit from uncertain tax positions in the financial statements only when it is more likely than not the position will be sustained upon examination by relevant tax authorities. The Company recognizes interest and penalties related to income tax matters in *Income tax expense*.

Refer to Note 9 — Income Taxes for further discussion.

Earnings per Share

Basic earnings per common share is calculated by dividing *Net income* by the weighted average number of common shares outstanding during the year. Diluted earnings per common share is calculated by adjusting weighted average outstanding shares, assuming conversion of all potentially dilutive stock options and awards.

Refer to Note 12 — Earnings per Share for further discussion.

Management Estimates

The preparation of financial statements in conformity with generally accepted accounting principles requires management to make estimates, including estimates relating to assumptions that affect the reported amounts of assets and liabilities and disclosure of contingent assets and liabilities at the date of financial statements and the reported amounts of revenues and expenses during the reporting period. Actual results could differ from these estimates. Additionally, the extent to which the evolving COVID-19 pandemic impacts the Company's financial statements will depend on a number of factors, including the magnitude and duration of the pandemic. The Company expects it may have a material, adverse impact on future revenue growth as well as overall profitability and may continue to lead to higher than normal inventory levels, revised payment terms with certain wholesale customers, higher sales-related reserves, factory cancellation costs and a volatile effective tax rate driven by changes in the mix of earnings across the Company's jurisdictions.

Recently Adopted Accounting Standards

In February 2016, the Financial Accounting Standards Board (FASB) issued Accounting Standards Update (ASU) No. 2016-02, *Leases (Topic 842)*, which replaced existing lease accounting guidance. The new standard is intended to provide enhanced transparency and comparability by requiring lessees to record ROU assets and corresponding lease liabilities on the balance sheet. ROU assets represent the Company's right to use an underlying asset for the lease term and lease liabilities represent the Company's obligation to make lease payments arising from the lease. The new guidance requires the Company to continue to classify leases as either an operating or finance lease, with classification affecting the pattern of expense recognition in the income statement. In addition, the new standard requires enhanced disclosure surrounding the amount, timing and uncertainty of cash flows arising from leasing agreements.

In July 2018, the FASB issued ASU No. 2018-11, which provided entities with an additional transition method. Under the new transition method, an entity initially applies the new standard at the adoption date, versus at the beginning of the earliest period presented, and recognizes a cumulative-effect adjustment to the opening balance of retained earnings in the period of adoption. The Company elected this transition method and adopted Topic 842 using a modified retrospective approach in the first quarter of fiscal 2020 with the cumulative effect of initially applying the new standard recognized in *Retained earnings* at June 1, 2019. Comparative prior period information has not been adjusted and continues to be reported in accordance with previous lease accounting guidance in Accounting Standards Codification (ASC) Topic 840 - *Leases*.

Upon adoption, the Company elected the package of transition practical expedients which allowed the Company to carry forward prior conclusions related to: (i) whether any expired or existing contracts are or contain leases, (ii) the lease classification for any expired or existing leases and (iii) initial direct costs for existing leases. Additionally, the Company elected the practical expedient to not separate lease components from nonlease components for all real estate leases within the portfolio. The Company made an accounting policy election to not record leases with an initial term of 12 months or less on the Consolidated Balance Sheets and will recognize related lease payments in the Consolidated Statements of Income on a straight-line basis over the lease term.

In preparation for implementation, the Company executed changes to business processes, including implementing a software solution to assist with the new reporting requirements. The adoption of Topic 842 resulted in a $2.7 billion increase to total assets and total liabilities as of June 1, 2019. Upon adoption, the Company recognized $3.2 billion of total operating lease liabilities and $2.9 billion of operating lease ROU assets, as well as removed $348 million of existing deferred rent liabilities, which was recorded as an offset against the ROU assets. In addition, the Company removed $184 million of existing assets and liabilities related to build-to-suit lease arrangements. Several other asset and liability line items in the Company's Consolidated Balance Sheets were also impacted by immaterial amounts. The adoption of the standard did not have a material impact on the Consolidated Statements of Income or Consolidated Statements of Cash Flows. For more information on the Company's lease arrangements refer to Note 19 — Leases.

In October 2016, the FASB issued ASU No. 2016-16, *Income Taxes (Topic 740): Intra-Entity Transfers of Assets Other Than Inventory*. The updated guidance requires companies to recognize the income tax consequences of an intra-entity transfer of an asset other than inventory when the transfer occurs. Income tax effects of intra-entity transfers of inventory will continue to be deferred until the inventory has been sold to a third party. The Company adopted the standard on June 1, 2018, using a modified retrospective approach, with the cumulative effect of applying the new standard recognized in *Retained earnings* at the date of adoption. The adoption resulted in reductions to *Retained earnings, Deferred income taxes and other assets,* and *Prepaid expenses and other current assets* of $507 million, $422 million and $45 million, respectively, and an increase in *Deferred income taxes and other liabilities* of $40 million on the Consolidated Balance Sheets.

Nike Annual Report: Analysis and Interpretation

Using the Nike Annual Report (Form 10-K) provided in this Appendix, perform the following analyses and interpret your results.

Exercises

Chapter 1 Return on assets — Obj. 6

1. Assume that total assets at the beginning of 2019 is $22,536 million. Compute the return on assets for 2020 and 2019 presented. Round to one decimal place.
2. Interpret the change in return on assets from 2019 to 2020.

Chapter 2 Common-sized income statements — Obj. 6

1. Prepare common-sized income statements for 2020 and 2019. Round to one decimal place.
2. Using your analysis in part (1), analyze and comment on the performance of Nike.

Chapter 3 Quick ratio — Obj. 6

1. Compute the quick assets for 2020 and 2019.
2. Compute the quick ratio for 2020 and 2019. Round to two decimal places.
3. Analyze and assess any change in liquidity for 2020 and 2019.

Chapter 4 Gross profit percent and markup percent — Obj. 8

1. Compute the gross profit percent for 2020 and 2019. Round to one decimal place.
2. Compute the average markup percent for 2020 and 2019. Round to one decimal place.
3. Compare the results in parts (1) and (2) for 2020 and 2019. Comment on your comparison.

Chapter 5 Internal control and cash — Obj.8

1. Based on the information in Nike's most recent annual report, answer the following questions:
   a. How much cash does Nike have at the end of 2020? Round to the nearest million.
   b. What percentage of total assets is cash for 2019 and 2020? Has this percentage increased, decreased, or remained the same during this period? Round to one decimal place.
2. Review Management's Annual Report on Internal Control over Financial Reporting. Based on this information, answer the following questions:
   a. Who has responsibility for establishing and maintaining adequate internal controls over a company's financial reporting?
   b. How is "internal control over financial reporting" defined in this report?

Chapter 6 Accounts receivable turnover and days' sales in receivables — Obj. 7

Assume that accounts receivable at the begining of 2019 is $3,498 million.

1. Compute the accounts receivable turnover for 2019 and 2020. Round all computations to two decimal places.
2. Compute the days' sales in receivables for 2019 and 2020. Use 365 days and round your results to the nearest whole day.
3. What conclusions can be drawn from these analyses regarding Nike's efficiency in collecting receivables?

Chapter 7 Inventory turnover and days' sales in inventory — Obj. 6

Assume that inventory at the beginning of 2019 was $5,261 million.

1. Compute the inventory turnover for 2019 and 2020. Round to two decimal places.
2. Compute the days' sales in inventory for 2019 and 2020. Use 365 days and round your results to the nearest whole day.
3. Interpret the change in inventory efficiency during 2020.

Chapter 8 Asset turnover ratio **Obj. 7**

Assume that total assets at the beginning of 2019 is $22,536 million.

1. Compute the asset turnover rate for 2020 and 2019. Round to two decimal places.
2. Interpret the change in the asset turnover ratio from 2019 to 2020.

Chapter 9 Debt ratio **Obj. 6**

1. Compute the debt ratio for 2019 and 2020. Round all computations to one decimal place.
2. Are Nike's operations financed primarily with debt or equity?

Chapter 10 Price-earnings ratio **Obj. 7**

Assume that the market price of Nike's stock at the end of its fiscal year was $77.14 in 2019 and $98.58 in 2020.

1. Compute the price-earnings ratio for 2019 and 2020. Round to two decimal places.
2. Analyze and comment on your results from part (1).

Chapter 11 Free cash flow and cash flow adequacy **Obj. 6**

Assume that the average amount of debt maturing over the next 5 years is $300.6 million, $101.8 million, and $103.0 million for 2020, 2019, and 2018, respectively.

1. Compute the free cash flow for 2018, 2019, and 2020.
2. Compute the cash flow adequacy ratio. Round to one decimal place.
3. Interpret Nike's free cash flow and cash flow adequacy ratio.

Appendix C

Double-Entry Accounting Systems

Throughout this text, transactions are recorded and summarized by using the accounting equation and the integrated financial statement framework. Transactions were recorded as pluses or minuses for each item affected by a transaction. At the same time, the effects of the transaction on the financial statements were shown. The equality of the accounting equation aided in preventing and detecting errors. That is, total assets must always equal total liabilities plus stockholders' equity.

Double-entry accounting also uses the accounting equation. However, double-entry accounting uses debit and credit rules as an additional control on the accuracy of recording transactions. This appendix describes and illustrates the basic elements of double-entry accounting.

In a double-entry accounting system, transactions are recorded in accounts. An **account**, in its simplest form, has three parts:

1. A title, which identifies the accounting equation element recorded in the account
2. A space for recording increases in the amount of the element
3. A space for recording decreases in the amount of the element

The account form presented next is called a **T account** because it resembles the letter T. The left side of the account is called the debit side, and the right side is called the credit side.[1]

Title	
Left side	Right side
debit	*credit*

Amounts entered on the left side of an account, regardless of the account title, are called debits to the account. When debits are entered in an account, the account is said to be *debited*. Amounts entered on the right side of an account are called credits, and the account is said to be *credited*. Debits and credits are sometimes abbreviated as *Dr.* and *Cr.*

To illustrate, a T account for Cash is shown next.

	Cash				
Debit side of account	(a)	25,000	(b)	20,000	Credit side of account
	(d)	7,500	(e)	3,650	
			(f)	950	
			(h)	2,000	
	Balance	5,900			

Balance of account → 5,900

Recording transactions in accounts using double-entry accounting follows certain rules. For example, increases in assets are recorded on the debit (left) side of the account. Likewise, decreases in assets are recorded on the credit (right) side of the account. With an asset account, the excess of debits over its credits is the balance of the account.

To illustrate, the preceding cash account is used. The receipt of cash (increase in Cash) of $25,000 in transaction (a) is entered on the debit (left) side of the cash account. A reference notation (letter or date of the transaction) is also entered into the account. The reference notation provides a means of backtracking to the underlying transaction data, should any questions arise.

1. The terms *debit* and *credit* are derived from the Latin *debere* and *credere*.

The payment of cash (decrease in Cash) of $20,000 in transaction (b) is entered on the credit (right) side of the account. The balance of the cash account of $5,900 is the excess of debits over credits, as shown here:

Debits ($25,000 + $7,500)	$ 32,500
Less credits ($20,000 + $3,650 + $950 + $2,000)	(26,600)
Balance of Cash	$ 5,900

The balance of the cash account is inserted in the Debit column. In this way, the balance is identified as a debit balance.

Rules of Debit and Credit

A standard method of recording debits and credits in accounts is essential to ensure that businesses record transactions in a similar manner. The rules of debit and credit are shown in Exhibit 1.

Exhibit 1 Rules of Debit and Credit; Normal Balances of Accounts

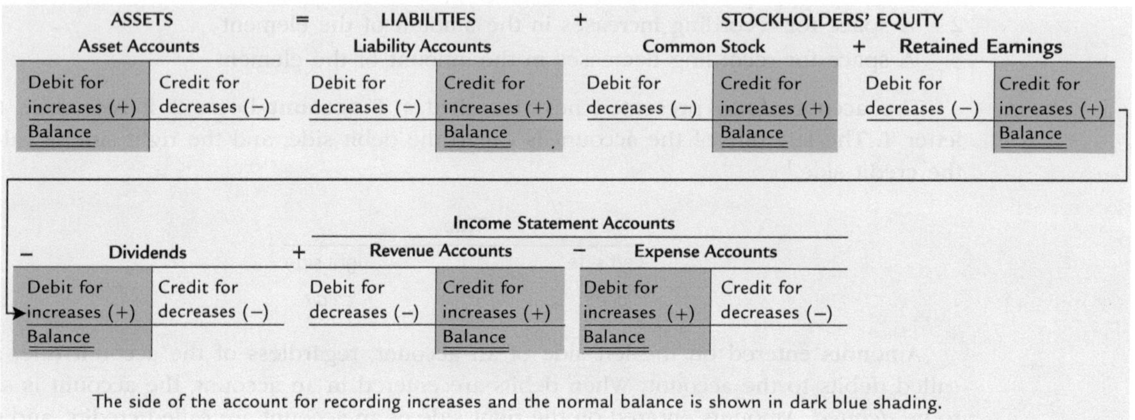

The side of the account for recording increases and the normal balance is shown in dark blue shading.

Exhibit 1 illustrates the following characteristics of the rules of debit and credit:

1. The normal balance of an account is the side of the account used to record increases. Thus, the normal balance of an asset account is a debit balance; the normal balance of a liability account is a credit balance. This characteristic is often useful in detecting errors in the recording process. That is, when an account normally having a debit balance actually has a credit balance, or vice versa, an error has occurred or an unusual situation exists.
2. Asset accounts (on the left side of the accounting equation) are increased by debits and have a normal debit balance. The only exception is that some asset accounts, called *contra asset accounts,* are increased by credits and have normal credit balances. As the words *contra asset* imply, these accounts offset the normal debit balances of asset accounts. For example, accumulated depreciation, an offset to plant assets, is increased by credits and has a normal credit balance. Thus, accumulated depreciation is a contra asset account.
3. Liability and stockholders' equity accounts (on the right side of the accounting equation) are increased by credits and have normal credit balances.
4. Dividend accounts appear on the right side of the accounting equation and decrease stockholders' equity (retained earnings). Thus, dividends accounts are increased by debits and have a normal debit balance. In this sense, the dividends accounts can be thought of as a type of contra account to retained earnings.

5. Revenue accounts appear on the right side of the accounting equation and increase stockholders' equity (retained earnings). Thus, revenue accounts are increased by credits and have normal credit balances.
6. Expense accounts appear on the right side of the accounting equation and decrease stockholders' equity (retained earnings). Thus, expense accounts are increased by debits and have a normal debit balance. Expense accounts can be thought of as a type of contra account. In this case, expense accounts can be thought of as contra accounts to revenues.

The rules of debit and credit require that for each transaction, the total debits equal the total credits. That is, each transaction must be recorded so the total debits for the transaction equal the total credits.

To illustrate, assume a company pays cash of $500 for supplies. The asset account Supplies is debited (increased) by $500 and Cash is credited (decreased) by $500. Likewise, if the company provides services and receives $2,000 from customers, Cash is debited (increased) and Fees Earned is credited (increased) by $2,000. This equality of debits and credits for each transaction provides a control over the recording of transactions.

To summarize, under double-entry accounting each transaction is recorded using the rules shown in Exhibit 1. In doing so, the total debits equal the total credits for each transaction.

The Journal

Under double-entry accounting, each transaction is initially entered in chronological order in a record called a **journal**. In this way, the journal documents the history of the company. The process of recording transactions in the journal is called **journalizing**. The specific transaction record entered in the journal is called a **journal entry**.

In practice, companies use a variety of formats for recording journal entries. A small company may use one all-purpose journal, sometimes called a **general journal**. Alternatively, another company may use **special journals** for recording different types of transactions. To simplify, a basic two-column general journal is used in this appendix.

Illustration of Double-Entry Accounting

Assume that on November 1, 20Y7, Lee Dunbar organizes a corporation that will be known as Web Solutions. The first phase of Lee's business plan is to operate Web Solutions as a service business providing assistance to individuals and small businesses by developing Web pages and configuring and installing application software. Lee expects this initial phase of the business to last one to two years. During this period, Web Solutions will gather information on the software and hardware needs of customers. During the second phase of the business plan, Web Solutions will expand into an Internet-based retailer of software and hardware to individuals and small business markets.

To start the business, Lee deposits $25,000 in a bank account in the name of Web Solutions in return for shares of stock in the corporation. This first transaction increases Cash and Common Stock by $25,000. This transaction is recorded in the journal using the following three steps:

Step 1. The date of the transaction is entered in the Date column.

Step 2. The title of the account to be debited is recorded at the left-hand margin under the Description column, and the amount to be debited is entered in the Debit column.

Step 3. The title of the account to be credited is listed below and to the right of the debited account title, and the amount to be credited is entered in the Credit column.

Using the preceding steps, the transaction is recorded in the journal as follows:

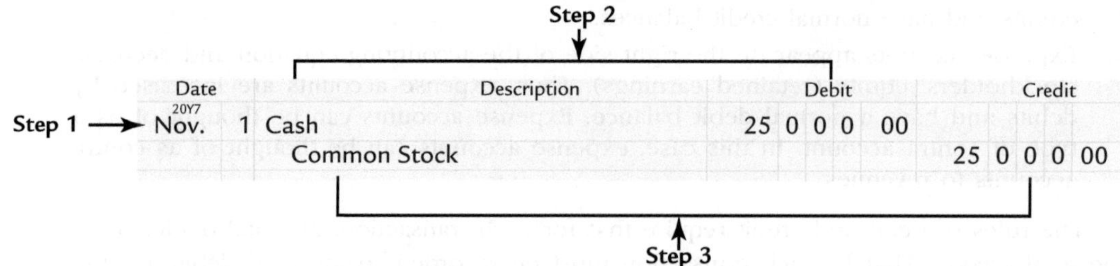

The increase in the asset is debited to the cash account. The increase in stockholders' equity (capital stock) is credited to the common stock account. As other assets are acquired, the increases are also recorded as debits to asset accounts. Likewise, other increases in stockholders' equity will be recorded as credits to stockholders' equity accounts.

Web Solutions entered into the following additional transactions during the remainder of November:

Nov. 5 Purchased land for $20,000, paying cash. The land is located in a new business park with convenient access to transportation facilities. Web Solutions plans to rent office space and equipment during the first phase of its business plan. During the second phase, the company plans to build an office and a warehouse on the land.

10 Purchased supplies on account for $1,350.

18 Received $7,500 for services provided to customers for cash.

30 Paid expenses as follows: wages, $2,125; rent, $800; utilities, $450; and miscellaneous, $275.

30 Paid creditors on account, $950.

30 Paid stockholder (Lee Dunbar) dividends of $2,000.

The journal entries to record these transactions follow.

Date		Description	Debit	Credit
Nov.	5	Land	20 0 0 0 00	
		Cash		20 0 0 0 00
	10	Supplies	1 3 5 0 00	
		Accounts Payable		1 3 5 0 00
	18	Cash	7 5 0 0 00	
		Fees Earned		7 5 0 0 00
	30	Wages Expense	2 1 2 5 00	
		Rent Expense	8 0 0 00	
		Utilities Expense	4 5 0 00	
		Miscellaneous Expense	2 7 5 00	
		Cash		3 6 5 0 00
	30	Accounts Payable	9 5 0 00	
		Cash		9 5 0 00
	30	Dividends	2 0 0 0 00	
		Cash		2 0 0 0 00

Posting to the Ledger

The journal lists the chronological history of businesses' transactions. Periodically, the journal entries must be transferred to the accounts. The group of accounts for a business is called its **general ledger**. The list of accounts in the general ledger is called the **chart of accounts**. The accounts are normally listed in the order in which they appear in the financial statements, beginning with the balance sheet and concluding with the income statement.

The chart of accounts for Web Solutions is shown in Exhibit 2.

Exhibit 2
Chart of Accounts for Web Solutions

Balance Sheet Accounts	Income Statement Accounts
Assets	**Revenue**
Cash	Fees Earned
Accounts Receivable	Rent Revenue
Supplies	**Expenses**
Prepaid Insurance	Wages Expense
Office Equipment	Rent Expense
Accumulated Depreciation	Depreciation Expense
Land	Utilities Expense
Liabilities	Supplies Expense
Accounts Payable	Insurance Expense
Wages Payable	Miscellaneous Expense
Unearned Rent	
Stockholders' Equity	
Common Stock	
Retained Earnings	
Dividends	

The process of transferring the journal entry debits and credits to the accounts in the ledger is called **posting**. To illustrate the posting process, Web Solutions' November 1 transaction, along with its posting to the cash and common stock accounts, is shown in Exhibit 3.

Exhibit 3
Posting a Journal Entry

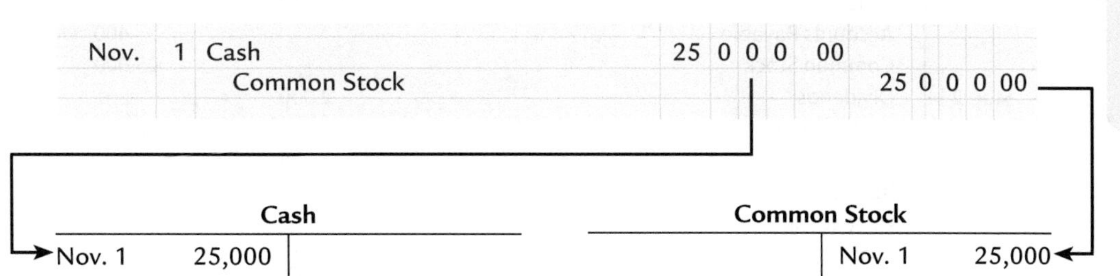

The debits and credits for each journal entry are posted to the accounts in the order in which they occur in the journal. In posting to the accounts, the date is entered followed by the amount of the entry. After the journal entries have been posted, the ledger becomes a chronological history of transactions by account.

Trial Balance and Financial Statements

Errors may occur in posting debits and credits from the journal to the ledger. One way to detect such errors is by preparing a **trial balance**. Double-entry accounting requires that debits must always equal credits. The trial balance verifies this equality. The four steps in preparing a trial balance are as follows:

Step 1. List the name of the company, the title of the trial balance, and the date the trial balance is prepared.

Step 2. List the accounts from the ledger and enter their debit or credit balance in the Debit or Credit column of the trial balance.

Step 3. Total the Debit and Credit columns of the trial balance.

Step 4. Verify that the total of the Debit column equals the total of the Credit column.

The trial balance for Web Solutions as of November 30, 20Y7, is shown in Exhibit 4. The account balances in Exhibit 4 are taken from the November 30 balances, which are shown in a darker green screen in the ledger shown in Exhibit 6.

The trial balance does not provide complete proof of the accuracy of the ledger. It indicates only that the debits and the credits are equal. However, this proof is still of value as errors often affect the equality of debits and credits.

If the two totals of a trial balance are not equal, an error has occurred. In such a case, the error must be located and corrected before financial statements are prepared. This ability to detect errors in recording when the trial balance totals are not equal is a primary control feature of the double-entry accounting system.

The trial balance can be used as the source of data for preparing financial statements. The financial statements prepared in a double-entry accounting system are similar to those described and illustrated in the text. For this reason, the financial statements are not illustrated in this appendix.

Exhibit 4 Trial Balance

Step 1 → **Web Solutions**
Trial Balance
November 30, 20Y7

Step 2	Account	Debit Balances	Credit Balances
	Cash	5,900	
	Supplies	1,350	
	Land	20,000	
	Accounts Payable		400
	Common Stock		25,000
	Dividends	2,000	
	Fees Earned		7,500
	Wages Expense	2,125	
	Rent Expense	800	
	Utilities Expense	450	
	Miscellaneous Expense	275	
		32,900	32,900

Steps 3–4

Review of Double-Entry Accounting

As a review of the double-entry accounting financial reporting system, Web Solutions' transactions for December are used. The journal entries for the following December transactions are shown in Exhibit 5.

Dec. 1 Paid a premium of $2,400 for a comprehensive insurance policy covering liability, theft, and fire. The policy covers a two-year period.

1 Paid rent for December, $800. The company from which Web Solutions is renting its store space now requires the payment of rent on the first day of each month rather than at the end of the month.

1 Received an offer from a local retailer to rent the land purchased on November 5. The retailer plans to use the land as a parking lot for its employees and customers. Web Solutions agreed to rent the land to the retailer for three months with the rent payable in advance. Web Solutions received $360 for three months' rent beginning December 1.

4 Purchased office equipment on account from Executive Supply Co. for $1,800.

6 Paid $180 for a newspaper advertisement.

11 Paid creditors $400.

13 Paid a receptionist and a part-time assistant $950 for two weeks' wages.

16 Received $3,100 from fees earned for the first half of December.

16 Earned fees on account totaling $1,750 for the first half of December.

20 Paid $1,800 to Executive Supply Co. on the debt owed from the December 4 transaction.

21 Received $650 from customers in payment of their accounts.

23 Purchased $1,450 of supplies by paying $550 cash and charging the remainder on account.

27 Paid the receptionist and the part-time assistant $1,200 for two weeks' wages.

31 Paid $310 telephone bill for the month.

31 Paid $225 electric bill for the month.

31 Received $2,870 from fees earned for the second half of December.

31 Earned fees on account totaling $1,120 for the second half of December.

31 Paid dividends of $2,000 to stockholder.

Exhibit 5
Journal Entries: December Transactions for Web Solutions

Date		Account	Debit	Credit
Dec.	1	Prepaid Insurance	2,400.00	
		Cash		2,400.00
	1	Rent Expense	800.00	
		Cash		800.00
	1	Cash	360.00	
		Unearned Rent		360.00
	4	Office Equipment	1,800.00	
		Accounts Payable		1,800.00
	6	Miscellaneous Expense	180.00	
		Cash		180.00
	11	Accounts Payable	400.00	
		Cash		400.00
	13	Wages Expense	950.00	
		Cash		950.00

Exhibit 5
Continued

Date		Description	Debit	Credit
Dec.	16	Cash	3 1 0 0 00	
		Fees Earned		3 1 0 0 00
	16	Accounts Receivable	1 7 5 0 00	
		Fees Earned		1 7 5 0 00
	20	Accounts Payable	1 8 0 0 00	
		Cash		1 8 0 0 00
	21	Cash	6 5 0 00	
		Accounts Receivable		6 5 0 00
	23	Supplies	1 4 5 0 00	
		Cash		5 5 0 00
		Accounts Payable		9 0 0 00
	27	Wages Expense	1 2 0 0 00	
		Cash		1 2 0 0 00
	31	Utilities Expense	3 1 0 00	
		Cash		3 1 0 00
	31	Utilities Expense	2 2 5 00	
		Cash		2 2 5 00
	31	Cash	2 8 7 0 00	
		Fees Earned		2 8 7 0 00
	31	Accounts Receivable	1 1 2 0 00	
		Fees Earned		1 1 2 0 00
	31	Dividends	2 0 0 0 00	
		Cash		2 0 0 0 00

The posting of the journal entries to the ledger accounts is shown in Exhibit 6.

Exhibit 6
Ledger for Web Solutions

Cash			
Nov. 1	25,000	Nov. 5	20,000
18	7,500	30	3,650
		30	950
		30	2,000
	32,500		26,600
Nov. 30 Bal.	5,900	Dec. 1	2,400
Dec. 1	360	1	800
16	3,100	6	180
21	650	11	400
31	2,870	13	950
		20	1,800
		23	550
		27	1,200
		31	310
		31	225
		31	2,000
	12,880		10,815
Dec. 31 Bal.	2,065		

Accounts Receivable			
Dec. 16	1,750	Dec. 21	650
31	1,120		
Dec. 31 Bal.	2,220		

Supplies			
Nov. 10	1,350		
Dec. 23	1,450		
Dec. 31 Bal.	2,800		

Prepaid Insurance			
Dec. 1	2,400		

Office Equipment			
Dec. 4	1,800		

Land			
Nov. 5	20,000		

Accounts Payable			
Nov. 30	950	Nov. 10	1,350
		Nov. 30 Bal.	400
Dec. 11	400	Dec. 4	1,800
20	1,800	23	900
	2,200		3,100
		Dec. 31 Bal.	900

Exhibit 6 Continued

Unearned Rent

		Dec. 1		360

Common Stock

		Nov. 1		25,000

Dividends

Nov. 30	2,000		
Dec. 31	2,000		
Dec. 31 Bal.	4,000		

Fees Earned

		Nov. 18	7,500
		Dec. 16	3,100
		16	1,750
		31	2,870
		31	1,120
		Dec. 31 Bal.	16,340

Wages Expense

Nov. 30	2,125		
Dec. 13	950		
27	1,200		
Dec. 31 Bal.	4,275		

Rent Expense

Nov. 30	800		
Dec. 1	800		
Dec. 31 Bal.	1,600		

Utilities Expense

Nov. 30	450		
Dec. 31	310		
31	225		
Dec. 31 Bal.	985		

Miscellaneous Expense

Nov. 30	275		
Dec. 6	180		
Dec. 31 Bal.	455		

The trial balance shown in Exhibit 7 indicates that after posting December transactions to the general ledger, the total of the debit balances of accounts equals the total of the credit balances.

Exhibit 7 Trial Balance for Web Solutions

Web Solutions
Trial Balance
December 31, 20Y7

	Debit Balances	Credit Balances
Cash	2,065	
Accounts Receivable	2,220	
Supplies	2,800	
Prepaid Insurance	2,400	
Office Equipment	1,800	
Land	20,000	
Accounts Payable		900
Unearned Rent		360
Common Stock		25,000
Dividends	4,000	
Fees Earned		16,340
Wages Expense	4,275	
Rent Expense	1,600	
Utilities Expense	985	
Miscellaneous Expense	455	
	42,600	42,600

Exercises

E-1 Rules of debit and credit

The following table summarizes the rules of debit and credit. For each of the items (a) through (l), indicate whether the proper answer is a debit or a credit.

	Increase	Decrease	Normal Balance
Balance sheet accounts:			
Asset	Debit	(a)	(b)
Liability	Credit	(c)	(d)
Stockholders' equity:			
Common stock	(e)	Debit	(f)
Retained earnings	(g)	Debit	Credit
Dividends	Debit	(h)	Debit
Income statement accounts:			
Revenue	(i)	(j)	(k)
Expense	(l)	Credit	Debit

E-2 Identifying transactions

Pack Your Bags Inc. is a travel agency. The nine transactions recorded by Pack Your Bags during May 20Y5, its first month of operations, are indicated in the following T accounts:

Cash

(1)	12,500	(2)	875
(7)	5,000	(3)	1,800
		(4)	1,350
		(6)	3,750
		(9)	1,250

Equipment

(3)	9,000		

Dividends

(9)	1,250		

Accounts Receivable

(5)	6,750	(7)	5,000

Accounts Payable

(6)	3,750	(3)	7,200

Service Revenue

		(5)	6,750

Supplies

(2)	875	(8)	525

Common Stock

		(1)	12,500

Operating Expenses

(4)	1,350		
(8)	525		

Indicate the following for each debit and each credit: (a) whether an asset, liability, capital stock, dividend, revenue, or expense account was affected and (b) whether the account was increased (+) or decreased (−). Present your answers in the following form, with transaction (1) given as an example:

	Account Debited		Account Credited	
Transaction	Type	Effect	Type	Effect
(1)	asset	+	capital stock	+

E-3 Journal entries

Based upon the T accounts in Exercise 2, prepare the nine journal entries from which the postings were made.

E-4 Trial balance

Based upon the data presented in Exercise 2, prepare a trial balance, listing the accounts in their proper order.

✔ Total Debit column: $22,700

E-5 Normal entries for accounts

During the month, Be You Co. has a substantial number of transactions affecting each of the following accounts. State for each account whether it is likely to have (a) debit entries only, (b) credit entries only, or (c) both debit and credit entries.

1. Accounts Payable
2. Accounts Receivable
3. Cash
4. Fees Earned
5. Insurance Expense
6. Dividends
7. Supplies Expense

E-6 Normal balances of accounts

Identify each of the following accounts of Shakti Yoga Co. as an asset, liability, stockholders' equity, revenue, or expense, and state in each case whether the normal balance is a debit or a credit.

a. Accounts Payable
b. Accounts Receivable
c. Common Stock
d. Cash
e. Dividends
f. Fees Earned
g. Office Equipment
h. Rent Expense
i. Supplies
j. Wages Expense

E-7 Cash account balance

During the month, Shogun Co. received $515,000 in cash and paid out $331,000 in cash.

a. Do the data indicate that Shogun Co. had net income of $184,000 during the month? Explain.
b. If the balance of the cash account is $222,350 at the end of the month, what was the cash balance at the beginning of the month?

E-8 Account balances

✔ c. $283,600

a. During October, $100,000 was paid to creditors on account, and purchases on account were $115,150. Assuming the October 31 balance of Accounts Payable was $39,000, determine the account balance on October 1.
b. On May 1, the accounts receivable account balance was $36,200. During May, $315,000 was collected from customers on account. Assuming the May 31 balance was $41,600, determine the fees billed to customers on account during May.
c. On June 1, the cash account balance was $20,000. During June, cash receipts totaled $279,100 and the June 30 balance was $15,500. Determine the cash payments made during June.

E-9 Transactions

Winter Solstice Co. has the following accounts in its ledger: Cash, Accounts Receivable, Supplies, Office Equipment, Accounts Payable, Common Stock, Retained Earnings, Dividends, Fees Earned, Rent Expense, Advertising Expense, Utilities Expense, and Miscellaneous Expense.

Journalize the following selected transactions for July 20Y9 in a two-column journal.

July 1 Paid rent for the month, $900.
2 Paid advertising expense, $360.

July 5 Paid cash for supplies, $180.
6 Purchased office equipment on account, $2,460.
10 Received cash from customers on account, $820.
15 Paid creditor on account, $240.
27 Paid cash for repairs to office equipment, $100.
30 Paid telephone bill for the month, $36.
31 Fees earned and billed to customers for the month, $5,360.
31 Paid electricity bill for the month, $63.
31 Paid dividends, $400.

E-10 Journalizing and posting

On November 2, 20Y3, Fibrosis Co. purchased $1,800 of supplies on account.

a. Journalize the November 2, 20Y3, transaction.
b. Prepare a T account for Supplies. Enter a debit balance of $1,050 as of November 1, 20Y3.
c. Prepare a T account for Accounts Payable. Enter a credit balance of $15,600 as of November 1, 20Y3.
d. Post the November 2, 20Y3, transaction to the accounts and determine November 30 balances.

E-11 Transactions and T accounts

The following selected transactions were completed during January of the current year:

1. Billed customers for fees earned, $8,346.
2. Purchased supplies on account, $360.
3. Received cash from customers on account, $7,830.
4. Paid creditors on account, $220.

a. Journalize the preceding transactions in a two-column journal, using the appropriate number to identify the transactions.
b. Post the entries prepared in (a) to the following T accounts: Cash, Supplies, Accounts Receivable, Accounts Payable, and Fees Earned. To the left of each amount posted in the accounts, place the appropriate number to identify the transactions.

E-12 Trial balance

✔ Total of Credit column: $350,000

The accounts in the ledger of Angel Co. as of December 31, 20Y7, are listed in alphabetical order as follows. All accounts have normal balances. The balance of the cash account has been intentionally omitted.

Accounts Payable	$ 14,000	Notes Payable	$ 30,000
Accounts Receivable	29,950	Prepaid Insurance	2,250
Common Stock	25,000	Rent Expense	45,000
Cash	?	Retained Earnings	41,750
Dividends	15,000	Supplies	1,575
Fees Earned	232,500	Supplies Expense	5,925
Insurance Expense	4,500	Unearned Rent	6,750
Land	63,750	Utilities Expense	31,125
Miscellaneous Expense	6,675	Wages Expense	131,250

Prepare a trial balance, listing the accounts in their proper order and inserting the missing figure for cash.

Problems

P-1 Journal entries and trial balance

✔ Total of credit column: $16,325

On March 1, 20Y1, Sadie May established Pampered Pet, which completed the following transactions during the month:

a. Sadie May transferred cash from a personal bank account to an account to be used for the business in exchange for common stock, $10,000.

b. Purchased supplies on account, $500.

c. Earned sales commissions, receiving cash, $6,125.

d. Paid rent on office and equipment for the month, $1,900.

e. Paid creditor on account, $300.

f. Paid dividends, $1,500.

g. Paid automobile expenses (including rental charge) for month, $750 and miscellaneous expenses, $200.

h. Paid office salaries, $1,550.

i. Determined that the cost of supplies used was $363.

Instructions

1. Journalize entries for transactions (a) through (i), using the following account titles: Cash, Supplies, Accounts Payable, Common Stock, Dividends, Sales Commissions, Rent Expense, Office Salaries Expense, Automobile Expense, Supplies Expense, and Miscellaneous Expense.
2. Prepare T accounts, using the account titles in part (1). Post the journal entries to these accounts, placing the appropriate letter to the left of each amount to identify the transaction. Determine the account balances, after all posting is complete. Accounts containing only a single entry do not need a balance.
3. Prepare a trial balance as of March 31, 20Y1.

P-2 Journal entries and trial balance

✔ 4. Total of Debit column: $286,675

Orange Realty acts as an agent in buying, selling, renting, and managing real estate. The trial balance on October 31, 20Y4, is shown next.

ORANGE REALTY
Trial Balance
October 31, 20Y4

	Debit Balances	Credit Balances
Cash	16,960	
Accounts Receivable	34,900	
Prepaid Insurance	3,600	
Office Supplies	800	
Land	—	
Accounts Payable		4,960
Unearned Rent		—
Notes Payable		—
Common Stock		5,000
Retained Earnings		26,540
Dividends	12,800	
Fees Earned		176,000
Salary and Commission Expense	112,000	
Rent Expense	14,000	
Advertising Expense	11,440	
Automobile Expense	5,120	
Miscellaneous Expense	880	
	212,500	212,500

The following business transactions were completed by Orange Realty during November 20Y4:

Nov. 1 Purchased office supplies on account, $1,050.
2 Paid rent on office for month, $2,000.
3 Received cash from clients on account, $22,300.
5 Paid annual insurance premiums, $2,850.
9 Returned a portion of the office supplies purchased on November 1, receiving full credit for their cost, $200.
17 Paid advertising expense, $2,750.
23 Paid creditors on account, $2,475.
29 Paid miscellaneous expenses, $250.
30 Paid automobile expense (including rental charges for an automobile), $750.
30 Discovered an error in computing a commission; received cash from the salesperson for the overpayment, $500.
30 Paid salaries and commissions for the month, $13,900.
30 Recorded revenue earned and billed to clients during the month, $41,500.
30 Purchased land for a future building site for $37,500, paying $5,000 in cash and giving a note payable for the remainder.
30 Paid dividends, $2,500.
30 Rented land purchased on November 30 to a local university for use as a parking lot for athletic events; received advance payment of $1,800.

Instructions

1. Record the November 1, 20Y4, balance of each account in the appropriate balance column of a T account, and write Balance to identify the opening amounts.
2. Journalize the transactions for November in a two-column journal.
3. Post the journal entries to the T accounts, placing the date to the left of each amount to identify the transaction. Determine the balances for all accounts.
4. Prepare a trial balance of the ledger as of November 30, 20Y4.

Glossary

A

Accelerated depreciation method A depreciation method that provides for a higher depreciation amount in the first year of the asset's use, followed by a gradually declining amount of depreciation.

Account A record in which increases and decreases in a financial statement element are recorded.

Accounting An information system that provides reports to stakeholders about the economic activities and condition of a business.

Accounting cycle The process that begins with analyzing transactions and ends with preparing the financial statements.

Accounting equation Assets = Liabilities + Stockholders' Equity

Accounting error A mathematical mistake entered in the accounting records or the incorrect application of a generally accepted accounting principle.

Accounting period concept An accounting concept in which accounting data are recorded and summarized in a period process.

Accounts payable Liabilities for amounts incurred from purchases of products or services in the normal operations of a business.

Accrual basis of accounting A system of accounting in which revenue is recorded as it is earned and expenses are recorded and matched against the revenue they generate.

Accruals Recognition of revenue when earned or expenses when incurred regardless of when cash is received or disbursed.

Accrued assets Revenues that have been earned at the end of an accounting period but have not been recorded in the accounts; sometimes called *accrued revenues*.

Accrued expenses Expenses that have been incurred at the end of an accounting period but have not been recorded in the accounts; sometimes called *accrued liabilities*.

Accrued liabilities Expenses that have been incurred at the end of an accounting period but have not been recorded in the accounts; sometimes called *accrued expenses*.

Accrued revenues Revenues that have been earned at the end of an accounting period but have not been recorded in the accounts; sometimes called *accrued assets*.

Accumulated depreciation An offsetting or contra asset account used to record depreciation on a fixed asset.

Accumulated other comprehensive income The cumulative effect of other comprehensive income items, which is reported separately in the "Stockholders' Equity" section of the balance sheet.

Activity base A measure of activity that is related to changes in cost and is used in the denominator in calculating the predetermined factory overhead rate to assign factory overhead costs to cost objects; also called an *allocation base* or *activity driver*.

Activity-based costing (ABC) An accounting framework based on determining the cost of activities and allocating these costs to products using activity rates.

Activity cost pools Cost accumulations that are associated with a given activity, such as machine usage, inspections, moving, and production setups.

Adequate disclosure concept An accounting concept that requires financial statements to include all relevant data a reader needs to understand the financial condition and performance of a business.

Adjustment process A process required by the accrual basis of accounting in which the accounts are updated prior to preparing financial statements.

Administrative expenses Expenses incurred in the administration or general operations of the business; costs not directly related to selling, such as officer salaries.

Amortization The periodic transfer of the cost of an intangible asset to expense.

Annuity A series of equal cash flows at fixed intervals.

Assets The resources owned by a business.

Asset turnover A profitability metric used to assess how efficiently a company is using its operating assets to generate sales, computed as sales divided by average long-term operating assets.

Available-for-sale securities Debt securities that a company intends to sell in the future (before maturity), but not in the near term.

Average rate of return A method of evaluating capital investment proposals that focuses on the expected profitability of the investment.

B

Balanced scorecard A performance evaluation approach that incorporates multiple performance dimensions by combining financial and nonfinancial measures.

Balance sheet A list of the assets, liabilities, and owner's equity as of a specific date, usually at the close of the last day of a month or a year.

Bank reconciliation The analysis that details the items responsible for the difference between the cash balance reported in the bank statement and the cash balance in the ledger.

Bank statement A summary of all transactions mailed to the depositor by the bank each month.

Bonds payable A type of long-term debt financing with a face amount that is in the future with interest that is normally paid semiannually.

Book value The cost of a fixed asset minus accumulated depreciation on the asset.

Book value of a fixed asset The value of an asset as indicated by the company's records of historical cost less accumulated depreciation.

Break-even point The level of business operations at which revenues and expired costs are equal.

Budget An accounting device used to plan and control resources of operational departments and divisions.

Budgetary slack Excess resources set within a budget to provide for uncertain events.

Budgeted variable factory overhead The standard variable overhead for the actual units produced.

Budget performance report A report comparing actual results with budget figures.

Business An organization in which basic resources (inputs), such as materials and labor, are assembled and processed to provide goods and services (outputs) to customers.

Business combination The purchase of more than 50% ownership of the investee's stock.

Business entity concept An accounting concept that limits the economic data in the accounting system of a specific business or entity to data related directly to the activities of that business or entity.

Business stakeholder A person or entity that has an interest in the economic performance of a business.

Business-to-business (B2B) Transactions between suppliers and retailers.

Business-to-consumer (B2C) Transactions between retailers and consumers.

C

Capital expenditures The costs of acquiring fixed assets, adding a component, or replacing a component of a fixed asset.

Capital expenditures budget The budget summarizing future plans for acquiring plant facilities and equipment.

Capital investment analysis The process by which management plans, evaluates, and controls long-term capital investments involving fixed assets.

Capital rationing The process by which management allocates available investment funds among competing capital investment proposals.

Cash Coins, currency (paper money), checks, money orders, and money on deposit available for unrestricted withdrawal from banks and other financial institutions.

Cash basis of accounting A system of accounting in which only transactions involving increases or decreases of the entity's cash are recorded.

Cash budget A budget of estimated cash receipts and payments.

Cash equivalents Highly liquid investments that are usually reported with cash on the balance sheet.

Cash flow adequacy ratio An indicator of the company's credit quality. It is calculated by dividing free cash flow by the average amount of debt maturing over the next five years.

Cash flows from (used for) financing activities The cash flows from transactions that affect the debt and equity of the company.

Cash flows from (used for) investing activities The cash flows from transactions that affect the investments in the noncurrent assets of the company.

Cash flows from (used for) operating activities The cash flows from transactions that affect the net income of the company.

Cash payback period The expected period of time that will elapse between the date of a capital expenditure and the complete recovery in cash (or equivalent) of the amount invested.

Cash refund An amount paid by the seller to the buyer for merchandise that is defective, is damaged during shipment, or does not meet the buyer's expectations.

Cash short and over The account used to record the difference between the amount of cash in a cash register and the amount of cash that should be on hand according to the records.

Change in accounting principal When a company changes from one generally accepted accounting principle to another, such as a change from FIFO to the weighted average cost method of valuing inventory.

Chief financial officer The head of the accounting department in a company; also called the *comptroller*.

Classified balance sheet A balance sheet prepared with various sections, subsections, and captions that aid in its interpretation and analysis.

Common-sized balance sheet A balance sheet where each amount is expressed as a percent of total assets or total liabilities plus stockholders' equity.

Common-sized financial statements Financial statements that express each amount as a percent of a base amount.

Common-sized income statement An income statement where each amount is expressed as a percent of sales.

Common-sized statement A financial statement in which all items are expressed only in relative terms.

Compensating balance A requirement by some banks that depositors maintain minimum cash balances in their bank accounts.

Component analysis A method of analysis that computes metrics for liquidity, solvency, and profitability for components of financial statements.

Comprehensive income All changes in stockholders' equity during a period, except those resulting from dividends and investments by owners.

Comptroller The head of the accounting department in a company; also called the *chief financial officer*.

Consigned inventory Merchandise that is shipped by manufacturers to retailers who act as the manufacturer's selling agent.

Consignee The retailer in a consigned inventory arrangement.

Consignor The manufacturer in a consigned inventory arrangement.

Consolidated financial statements The financial statements resulting from combining parent and subsidiary statements.

Constraint (or bottleneck) A point in the manufacturing process where the demand for the company's products exceeds its ability to produce the products.

Continuous budgeting A method of budgeting that provides for maintaining a 12-month projection into the future.

Contribution margin Sales less variable cost of goods sold and variable selling and administrative expenses.

Contribution margin ratio The percentage of each sales dollar that is available to cover the fixed costs and provide income from operations.

Controllable expenses Costs that can be influenced by the decisions of a manager of a cost, profit, or investment center.

Controllable revenues Revenues that can be influenced by the decisions of a manager of a profit or investment center.

Controllable variance The difference between the actual amount of variable factory overhead cost incurred and the amount of variable factory overhead budgeted for the standard product.

Controlling account The account in the general ledger that summarizes the balances of the accounts in the subsidiary ledger.

Conversion costs The combination of direct labor and factory overhead costs.

Copyright An exclusive right to publish and sell a literary, artistic, or musical composition.

Corporation A business organized under state or federal statutes as a separate legal entity.

Cost A payment of cash (or a commitment to pay cash in the future) for the purpose of generating revenues.

Cost accounting system A system used to accumulate manufacturing costs for decision-making and financial reporting purposes.

Cost allocation The process of assigning indirect costs to a cost object, such as a job.

Cost behavior The manner in which a cost changes in relation to its activity base (driver).

Cost center A decentralized unit in which the department or division manager has responsibility for the control of costs incurred and the authority to make decisions that affect these costs.

Cost concept An accounting concept that determines the amount initially entered into the accounting records for purchases.

Cost method A method of accounting for bond investments in which the purchase is recorded at original cost, including any fees charged by a broker in acquiring the bonds, and any accrued interest is recorded separately.

Cost object A product, a sales territory, a department, or an activity by which costs are classified and assigned.

Cost of goods sold The cost of products sold; also may be referred to as *cost of merchandise sold* or *cost of sales*.

Cost of goods sold budget A budget of the estimated direct materials, direct labor, and factory overhead consumed by sold products.

Cost of merchandise sold The cost of products sold; also may be referred to as *cost of sales* or *cost of goods sold*.

Cost of sales The cost of products sold; also may be referred to as *cost of merchandise sold* or *cost of goods sold*.

Cost price approach An approach to transfer pricing that uses cost as the basis for setting the transfer price.

Cost variance The difference between the actual cost and the standard cost at actual volumes.

Cost-volume-profit analysis The systematic examination of the relationships among costs, expenses, sales, and operating profit or loss.

Cost-volume-profit graph A chart that graphically shows the sales, costs, and related profit or loss for various levels of units sold; also called a *break-even graph*.

Coupon A sales incentive or promotion that provides the customer a discount when purchasing a product.

Credit memorandum A form used by a seller to inform the buyer of the amount the seller proposes to decrease the account receivable due from the buyer.

Credit period The amount of time the buyer is allowed in which to pay the seller.

Credit terms Terms for payment on account by the buyer to the seller.

Cumulative preferred stock Stock that has a right to receive regular dividends that were not declared (paid) in prior years.

Currency exchange rates The rates at which currency in another country can be exchanged for U.S. dollars.

Current assets Cash and other assets that are expected to be converted to cash or sold or used up through the normal operations of the business within 1 year or less.

Currently attainable standards Standards that represent levels of operation that can be attained with reasonable effort.

Current position analysis Analysis of a company's ability to pay its current liabilities.

Current ratio A financial ratio that is computed by dividing current assets by current liabilities.

Customer refunds payable A liability recording the amount of refunds and allowances expected to be granted in the future, which is estimated at the end of the period as part of the adjusting process.

D

Data analytics The science of analyzing raw data to discover patterns, identify anomalies, or gain other useful insights.

Debit (bank) cards A card used for electronic payment by which the money required by the purchase is deducted instantly from the customer's bank account.

Debit memorandum A form used by a buyer to inform the seller of the amount the buyer proposes to decrease the account payable due the seller.

Debt investments Notes and bonds issued by corporations and governmental agencies, purchased to earn interest or to earn profits from changes in their market price.

Deferrals Delayed recordings of expenses or revenues.

Deferred expenses Items that are initially recorded as assets but are expected to become expenses over time or through the normal operations of the business; sometimes called *prepaid expenses*.

Deferred income tax payable Taxes payable beyond a year.

Deferred revenues Items that are initially recorded as liabilities but are expected to become revenues over time or through the normal operations of the business; sometimes called *unearned revenues*.

Defined benefit plan pension plan that promises employees a fixed annual pension benefit at retirement, based on years of service and compensation levels.

Defined contribution plan A pension plan in which the contributions into the plan are defined but the employee's pension may vary depending on investment performance.

Depletion expense The portion of the cost of a natural resource that has been harvested or mined.

Depreciable cost The amount of an asset's cost that is allocated over its useful life as depreciation expense; calculated as initial cost less residual value.

Depreciation The systematic periodic transfer of the cost of a fixed asset to an expense account during its expected useful life.

Differential analysis The area of accounting concerned with the effect of alternative courses of action on revenues and costs.

Differential cost The amount of increase or decrease in cost expected from a particular course of action compared with an alternative.

Differential income (or loss) The difference between differential revenue and differential cost.

Differential revenue The amount of increase or decrease in revenue expected from a particular course of action as compared with an alternative.

Direct labor Consists of wages of factory workers directly involved in manufacturing the product.

Direct labor cost Wages of factory workers who are directly involved in converting materials into a finished product.

Direct labor cost budget A budget that estimates the direct labor hours and related costs needed to support budgeted production.

Direct labor rate variance The cost associated with the difference between the standard rate and the actual rate paid for direct labor used in producing a commodity.

Direct labor time variance The cost associated with the difference between the standard hours and the actual hours of direct labor spent producing a commodity.

Direct materials Consists of the costs of acquiring a product's component materials.

Direct materials cost The cost of materials that are an integral part of the finished product.

Direct materials price variance The difference between the actual price and standard price times the actual quantity.

Direct materials purchases budget A budget that uses the production budget as a starting point.

Direct materials quantity variance The cost associated with the difference between the standard quantity and the actual quantity of direct materials used in producing a commodity.

Direct method A method of reporting the cash flows from operating activities as the difference between the operating cash receipts and the operating cash payments.

Discontinued operation An operating segment of a business that has been sold or disposed of.

Dividends Distributions of the earnings of a corporation to its stockholders.

Dividends per share Measures the extent to which earnings are being distributed to common shareholders.

Dividend yield A ratio, computed by dividing the annual dividends paid per share of common stock by the market price per share at a specific date, which indicates the rate of return to stockholders in terms of cash dividend distributions.

Double-declining balance method A method of depreciation that provides periodic depreciation expense based on the declining book value of a fixed asset over its estimated life.

DuPont formula An expanded expression of return on investment determined by multiplying the profit margin by the investment turnover.

E

Earnings per share (EPS) A measure of profitability computed by dividing net income, reduced by preferred dividends, by the number of shares outstanding.

Earnings per share (EPS) on common stock Net income per share of common stock outstanding during a period.

Electronic funds transfer (EFT) A system in which computers rather than paper (money, checks, etc.) are used to effect cash transactions.

Elements of internal control The control environment, risk assessment, control activities, information and communication, and monitoring.

Employee fraud The intentional act of deceiving an employer for personal gain.

Equity investment An investment in the preferred or common stock of another company.

Equity method A method of accounting for equity securities in which the investment is initially recorded at cost with subsequent adjustments made for the investor's share of the net income of the investee company and dividends received from the investee company.

Estimated Coupons Payable A current liability account for the estimated amount of coupons printed out with sales receipts that will be redeemed by customers.

Estimated Returns Inventory An asset representing inventory expected to be returned in the future, which is estimated at the end of the period as part of the adjusting process.

Exchange rate The rate at which a country's currency can be converted into another country's currency.

Expected useful life An estimate of the duration that an asset will be in service or provide benefit to the company.

Expense recognition principle An accounting principle that states that the expenses incurred in generating revenue should be reported in the same period as the related revenue; by matching revenues and expenses, net income or loss for the period can properly be determined and reported.

Expenses Costs used to earn (generate) revenues.

F

Factory overhead Consists of all factory costs other than direct materials and direct labor, such as equipment depreciation, supervisory salaries, and utility costs.

Factory overhead cost All of the costs of operating the factory except for direct materials and direct labor.

Factory overhead cost budget A budget that estimates the cost for each item of factory overhead needed to support budgeted production.

Factory overhead cost variance report Reports budgeted and actual costs for variable and fixed factory overhead for each cost element along with the related controllable and volume variances.

Fair value The price that would be received for a security if it were sold today.

Fair value method A method of accounting for securities in which the book value of the portfolio is adjusted for changes in fair value.

Favorable cost variance Actual cost is less than standard cost.

Fees earned Revenues received from providing services.

Financial accounting The area of accounting that focuses on recording transactions and events so that general-purpose financial statements can be prepared.

Financial Accounting Standards Board (FASB) The authoritative body that has the primary responsibility for developing accounting principles.

Financial accounting system A system that includes (1) a set of rules for determining what, when, and the amount that should be recorded for an economic event; (2) a framework for facilitating preparing financial statements; and (3) one or more controls to determine whether errors could have occurred in the recording process.

Financial statements Financial reports that summarize the effects of events on a business.

Financing activities Business activities that involve obtaining funds to begin and operate a business.

Finished goods inventory The cost of finished products on hand that have not been sold.

Finished goods ledger The subsidiary ledger that contains the individual accounts for each kind of commodity or product produced.

Fiscal year The annual accounting period adopted by a business.

Fixed assets Long-lived or relatively permanent tangible assets that are used in the normal business operations; sometimes called *plant assets*.

Flexible budget A budget that adjusts for varying rates of activity.

Fixed costs Costs that tend to remain the same in amount, regardless of variations in the level of activity.

FOB (free on board) destination Freight terms in which the seller pays the transportation costs from the shipping point to the final destination.

FOB (free on board) shipping point Freight terms in which the buyer pays the transportation costs from the shipping point to the final destination.

Foreign currency exchange gain The gain realized if the value of the U.S. dollar increases relative to a foreign currency between the purchase transaction date and payment date when the payment must be made in the foreign currency.

Foreign currency exchange loss The loss realized if the value of the U.S. dollar decreases relative to a foreign currency between the purchase transaction date and payment date when the payment must be made in the foreign currency.

Free cash flow A liquidity metric that represents the cash available after maintaining and expanding current operating capacity; computed as operating cash flows less investing cash flows.

Freight The cost of transportation when shipping or receiving goods.

G

General expenses Expenses incurred in the administration or general operations of the business; sometimes called administrative expenses.

General-purpose financial statements Basic financial statements, such as the balance sheet and income statement, which are made available to a wide range of potential users so that the company's financial condition and performance may be assessed.

Generally accepted accounting principles (GAAP) Rules for the way financial statements should be prepared.

Global analysis A method of analysis that computes changes in amounts, percentages of amounts, and percentage changes in amounts for each financial statement.

Goal conflict Situation when individual self-interest differs from business objectives.

Going concern concept An accounting concept that assumes that a company will continue in business indefinitely.

Goodwill An intangible asset of a business that is created from favorable factors such as location, product quality, reputation, and managerial skill, as verified from a merger transaction.

Gross profit Sales minus the cost of merchandise sold.

Gross profit percent Gross profit divided by net sales.

H

Held-to-maturity securities Securities purchased with the primary objective of earning interest revenue and collecting the face value of the security at its maturity date.

High-low method A technique that uses the highest and lowest total cost as a basis for estimating the variable cost per unit and the fixed cost component of a mixed cost.

Horizontal analysis Financial analysis that compares an item in a current statement with the same item in prior statements.

I

Ideal standards Standards that can be achieved only under perfect operating conditions, such as no idle time, no machine breakdowns, and no materials spoilage; also called *theoretical standards*.

In arrears In a state of being behind; cumulative preferred stock dividends that have not been paid in prior years are said to be in arrears.

Income before income taxes The income reported on the income statement before income tax expense is deducted.

Income statement A summary of the revenue and expenses for a specific period of time, such as a month or a year.

Indirect method A method of preparing the statement of cash flows that reconciles net income with net cash flows from operating activities.

Inflation A period when prices in general are rising and the purchasing power of money is declining.

Initial cost of a fixed asset The purchase price of a fixed asset plus all the costs incurred to obtain and ready it for use.

Intangible assets Long-lived assets that are useful in the operations of a business, are not held for sale, and are without physical qualities.

Intercompany transactions Business transactions between a parent and subsidiary company.

Interest payable A liability to pay interest on a due date.

Internal control The policies and procedures used to safeguard assets, ensure accurate business information, and ensure compliance with laws and regulations.

Internal rate of return (IRR) method A method of analyzing proposed capital investments that focuses on using present value concepts to compute the rate of return from the net cash flows expected from the investment.

International Accounting Standards Board (IASB) An authoritative body that establishes accounting principles and practices for companies in many countries outside of the United States.

Inventory shortage The amount by which the merchandise for sale, as indicated by the balance of the merchandise inventory account, is larger than the total amount of merchandise counted during the physical inventory; sometimes called *inventory shrinkage*.

Inventory shrinkage The amount by which the merchandise for sale, as indicated by the balance of the merchandise inventory account, is larger than the total amount of merchandise counted during the physical inventory; sometimes called *inventory shortage*.

Investee The company whose stock is purchased by an investor.

Investing activities Business activities that involve obtaining the necessary resources to start and operate the business.

Investment center A decentralized unit in which the manager has the responsibility and authority to make decisions that affect not only costs and revenues but also the fixed assets available to the center.

Investment turnover A component of the rate of return on investment computed as the ratio of sales to invested assets.

Investor The company investing in another company's stock.

Invoice The bill that the seller sends to the buyer.

J

Job cost sheet An account in the work-in-process subsidiary ledger in which the costs charged to a particular job order are recorded.

Job order cost system A type of cost accounting system that provides for a separate record of the cost of each particular quantity of product that passes through the factory.

Just-in-time (JIT) processing A business philosophy that focuses on eliminating time, cost, and poor quality within manufacturing processes.

K

Kanban A Japanese term for cards; the cards used to signal the need to move materials within a just-in-time (JIT) manufacturing system.

L

Lease A contract for the use of an asset for a period of time.

Liabilities The rights of creditors that represent a legal obligation to repay an amount borrowed according to terms of the borrowing agreement.

Limited liability company (LLC) A form of corporation that combines attributes of a partnership and a corporation.

Liquidity Refers to the ability to convert an asset to cash.

Low-cost strategy A strategy where a company designs and produces products or services at a lower cost than its competitors.

M

Management's Discussion and Analysis (MD&A) An annual report disclosure that provides management's analysis of the results of operations and financial condition.

Managerial accounting The branch of accounting that aids management in making financing, investing, and operating decisions for the company.

Manufacturing business A type of business that changes basic inputs into products that are sold to customers.

Manufacturing cells Work centers in a just-in-time (JIT) manufacturing system.

Margin of safety The difference between current sales revenue and the sales at the break-even point.

Market price approach An approach to transfer pricing that uses the price at which the product or service transferred could be sold to outside buyers as the transfer price.

Markup An amount that is added to a "cost" amount to determine product price.

Markup percent The amount expressed as a percentage that is added to the cost of a product to determine its selling price.

Merchandise inventory Merchandise on hand (not sold) at the end of an accounting period.

Master budget The comprehensive budget plan linking the individual budgets related to sales, cost of goods sold, operating expenses, capital expenditures, and cash.

Matching concept An accounting concept that requires expenses of a period to be matched with the revenue generated during that period.

Materials inventory The cost of materials that have not yet entered into the manufacturing process.

Materials ledger The subsidiary ledger containing the individual accounts for each type of material.

Materials requisition The form or electronic transmission used by a manufacturing department to authorize the issuance of materials from the storeroom.

Merchandising business A type of business that purchases finished products from other businesses to sell to its customers.

Metric A quantitative measure.

Metric-based analysis The use of metrics to assess a business's financial condition, performance, and decisions.

Mixed costs Costs with both variable and fixed characteristics.

Monthly cash burn The net cash outflow used for expenses, also called *monthly cash expenses*.

Monthly cash expenses Computed for companies with negative cash flows from operations as net cash flows from operations divided by 12.

Multiple-step income statement A form of income statement that contains several sections, subsections, and subtotals.

N

Natural business year A fiscal year that ends when business activities have reached the lowest point in an annual operating cycle.

Negotiated price approach An approach to transfer pricing that allows managers of decentralized units to agree (negotiate) among themselves as to the transfer price.

Net assets A company's stockholders' equity, computed as total assets less total liabilities.

Net income The excess of revenues over expenses.

Net Income—Accrual Basis A profitability metric determined as the excess of revenues over expenses in an accounting system in which revenue is recorded as it is earned and expenses are recorded and matched against the revenue they generate.

Net loss The excess of expenses over revenues.

Net present value method A method of analyzing proposed capital investments that focuses on the present value of the cash flows expected from the investments.

Note payable A type of short- or long-term financing that requires payment of the amount borrowed plus interest.

O

Objectivity concept An accounting concept that requires accounting records and data reported in financial statements be based on objective evidence.

Occupancy rate An output metric for assessing the performance and the efficient use of assets for the hotel industry, computed as rooms occupied by the available room nights; also known as the *utilization rate*.

Operating activities Business activities that involve using the business's resources to implement its business strategy.

Operating cycle The business process of spending cash to acquire assets used to generate revenue, earning revenues, and receiving cash from customers.

Operating income The excess of gross profit over total operating expenses.

Operating leverage A measure of the relative mix of a business's variable costs and fixed costs, computed as contribution margin divided by income from operations.

Opportunity cost The amount of income forgone from an alternative to a proposed use of cash or its equivalent.

Other comprehensive income Specified items that are reported separately from net income, including foreign currency items, pension liability adjustments, and unrealized gains and losses on investments.

Other expense Expenses that cannot be traced directly to operations.

Other revenue Revenue from sources other than the primary operating activities of a business.

Overapplied factory overhead The amount of factory overhead applied in excess of the actual factory overhead costs incurred for production during a period.

Owner's equity The financial rights of the owner.

P

Paid-in capital in excess of par The excess of the amount received over par value of Common Stock or Preferred Stock that has been issued.

Par value The monetary amount printed on a stock certificate.

Parent company The corporation owning all or a majority of the voting stock of another corporation.

Partnership A business owned by two or more individuals.

Patents Exclusive rights to produce and sell goods with one or more unique features.

Pension A cash payment to retired employees.

Period costs Those costs that are used up in generating revenue during the current period and that are not involved in the manufacturing process.

Periodic inventory system The inventory method in which the inventory records do not show the amount available for sale or sold during the period.

Permanent tax differences Differences between taxable income and income before taxes on the income statement that arise because some revenues are exempt from taxes and some expenses are not deductible for tax purposes.

Perpetual inventory system The inventory system in which each purchase and sale of merchandise is recorded in an inventory account.

Petty cash fund A special-purpose cash fund to pay relatively small amounts.

Physical inventory A physical count and listing of goods on hand used to determine the balance of the inventory account at the end of an accounting period.

Predetermined factory overhead rate The rate used to apply factory overhead costs to the goods manufactured. The rate is determined from budgeted overhead cost and estimated activity usage data at the beginning of the fiscal period.

Premium-price strategy A strategy where a company tries to design and produce products or services that serve unique market needs, allowing it to charge premium prices.

Prepaid expenses Assets resulting from the prepayment of future expenses such as insurance or rent that are expected to become expenses over time or through the normal operations of the business; often called *deferred expenses.*

Present value concept Cash today is not the equivalent of the same amount of money to be received in the future.

Present value index An index computed by dividing the total present value of the next cash flow to be received from a proposed capital investment by the amount to be invested.

Present value of an annuity The sum of the present values of a series of equal cash flows to be received at fixed intervals.

Prime costs The combination of direct materials and direct labor costs.

Prior period adjustment An unusual item that affects a prior period's financial statements, usually as a result of an accounting error or a change in accounting principal.

Process cost system A type of cost accounting system in which costs are accumulated by department or process within a factory.

Process yield An output metric that indicates the efficiency of a process, computed as units passing inspection divided by units entering the process.

Product cost concept A concept used in applying the cost-plus approach to product pricing in which only the costs of manufacturing the product, termed the *product costs*, are included in the cost amount to which the markup is added.

Product costs The three components of manufacturing costs: direct materials, direct labor, and factory overhead costs.

Production budget A budget of estimated unit production.

Profitability The ability of a company to generate net income related to its invested assets.

Profit The excess of the amounts received from customers for goods or services and the amounts paid for the inputs used to provide the goods or services.

Profit center A decentralized unit in which the manager has the responsibility and the authority to make decisions that affect both costs and revenues (and thus profits).

Profit margin The ratio of operating income to sales.

Profit-volume graph A chart that graphically shows only the difference between total sales and total costs (or profits) and allows managers to determine the operating profit (or loss) for various levels of units sold.

Proprietorship A business owned by one individual.

Purchase returns and allowances From the buyer's perspective, returned merchandise or an adjustment for defective merchandise.

Pull manufacturing A just-in-time method wherein customer orders trigger the release of finished goods, which triggers production, which triggers release of materials from suppliers.

Q

Quick assets Cash and other current assets that can be quickly converted to cash, such as marketable securities and receivables.

Quick ratio A financial ratio that measures the ability to pay current liabilities with quick assets (cash, marketable securities, accounts receivable).

R

Rate of return on investment (ROI) A measure of managerial efficiency in the use of investments in assets computed as income from operations divided by invested assets.

Ratio The expression of a financial statement item or set of items as a percentage of another financial statement item in order to measure an important economic relationship as a single number.

Ratio of cash to monthly cash expenses A ratio that is useful in assessing how a company with negative cash flows from operations can continue to operate. Computed as cash and cash equivalents divided by monthly cash expenses.

Ratio of fixed assets to long-term liabilities A leverage ratio that measures the margin of safety of long-term creditors, calculated as the net fixed assets divided by the long-term liabilities.

Ratio of liabilities to stockholders' equity A comprehensive leverage ratio that measures the relationship of the claims of creditors to stockholders' equity.

Rebate A sales incentive or promotion that provides the customer a refund after the product is purchased.

Receiving report The form or electronic transmission used by the receiving personnel to indicate that materials have been received and inspected.

Reciprocal accounts Corresponding accounts in the parent and subsidiary's ledgers that are affected by intercompany transactions and must be offset against each other when preparing consolidated financial statements.

Relevant range The range of activity over which changes in cost are of interest to management.

Residual income The excess of divisional income from operations over a "minimum" acceptable income from operations.

Residual value The estimated value of a fixed asset at the end of its useful life.

Responsibility accounting The process of measuring and reporting operating data by areas of responsibility.

Responsibility center A budgetary unit within a company for which a manager is assigned responsibility over costs, revenues, or assets.

Retained earnings Net income retained in a corporation.

Return on assets A profitability metric often used to compare a company's performance over time and with competitors, computed by dividing net income by average total assets.

Return on common stockholders' equity A profitability metric that indicates the rate of profits earned on the amount invested by the common stockholders; computed by dividing net income less preferred dividends by average common stockholders' equity.

Return on sales A profitability metric computed by dividing net income by total sales.

Return on stockholders' equity A profitability metric that indicates the rate of profits earned on the amount invested by stockholders; computed by dividing net income by average total stockholders' equity.

Return on investment (ROI) A measure of managerial efficiency in the use of investments in assets, computed as operating income divided by invested assets.

Return on total assets A profitability metric that indicates the rate of profits earned on total assets without considering how the assets are financed; computed as the sum of net income plus interest expense divided by average total assets.

Revenue The increase in assets from selling products or services to customers.

Revenue expenditures Costs that benefit only the current period or costs incurred for normal maintenance and repairs of fixed assets.

Revenue recognition principle An accounting principle that states that revenues should be recorded at the time a product is sold or a service is rendered.

S

Sales Revenues received from selling products; the total amount charged to customers for merchandise sold, including cash sales and sales on account.

Sales budget A budget that indicates for each product (1) the quantity of estimated sales, and (2) the expected unit selling price.

Sales mix The relative distribution of sales among the various products available for sale.

Sarbanes-Oxley Act An act passed by Congress in 2002 designed to reduce the likelihood and mitigate the impact of financial fraud so as to restore public confidence and trust in the financial statements of companies.

Securities and Exchange Commission (SEC) An agency of the U.S. government that has authority over the accounting and financial disclosures for corporations whose stock is traded and sold to the public.

Selling expenses Costs directly related to the selling of a product or service such as sales salaries and advertising expenses.

Service business A type of business that provides services rather than products to customers.

Service department charges The costs of services provided by an internal service department and transferred to a responsibility center.

Single-step income statement A form of income statement that deducts the total of all expenses in one step from the total of all revenues.

Solvency The ability of a company to pay its debts as they become due over the long term.

Special-purpose cash funds Cash funds designated for special needs, such as payroll or travel expenses.

Standard cost A detailed estimate of what a product should cost.

Standard cost systems Accounting systems that use standards for each manufacturing cost entering into the finished product.

Standards Performance goals.

Stated value A value, similar to par value, approved by the board of directors of a corporation for no-par stock.

Statement of cash flows A financial statement that provides a summary of the cash receipts and cash payments and reports the change in financial condition due to the change in cash during a specific period of time.

Statement of comprehensive income A separate statement from the income statement showing the effects of other comprehensive income on net income.

Statement of financial condition Reports the financial condition as of a point in time; often referred to as the *balance sheet.*

Statement of stockholders' equity A financial statement that reports the change in financial condition due to the changes in stockholders' equity items for a specific period of time.

Static budget A budget that does not adjust to changes in activity levels.

Stock Shares of ownership of a corporation.

Stockholders Investors who purchase stock in a corporation.

Stockholders' equity The stockholders' rights to the assets of a business.

Straight-line method A method of depreciation that provides for equal periodic depreciation expense over the estimated life of a fixed asset.

Subsidiary company A corporation that is controlled by another company through the ownership of all or a majority of its voting stock.

Subsidiary ledger A ledger containing individual accounts with a common characteristic.

Sunk cost A cost that is not affected by subsequent decisions.

T

Tangible assets Assets such as machinery, buildings, computers, office furnishings, trucks, and automobiles that have physical characteristics.

Target costing A concept used to design and manufacture a product at a cost that will deliver a target profit for a given market-determined price.

Taxable income The income of a corporation subject to income taxes as determined using tax laws and regulations and reported on the corporation's tax return.

Temporary tax differences Differences between taxable income and income before taxes on the income statement that arise because items are recognized in one period for tax purposes and another period for income statement purposes and that reverse in later years.

Theoretical standards Standards that can be achieved only under perfect operating conditions, such as no idle time, no machine breakdowns, and no materials spoilage; also called *ideal standards*.

Theory of constraints (TOC) A manufacturing strategy that attempts to remove the influence of bottlenecks (constraints) on a process.

Times interest earned A solvency metric that determines the degree of risk that interest payments will not be made if earnings decrease, computed as income before interest and taxes divided by interest expense; also known as the *fixed charge coverage ratio*.

Time tickets The form on which the amount of time spent by each employee and the labor costs incurred for each individual job, or for factory overhead, are recorded.

Time value of money concept The concept that an amount of money invested today will earn interest.

Total cost concept A concept used in applying the cost-plus approach to product pricing in which all the costs of manufacturing the product plus the selling and administrative expenses are included in the cost amount to which the markup is added.

Total manufacturing cost variance The difference between the total actual cost and the total standard cost for the units produced.

Trademark A name, term, or symbol used to identify a business and its products.

Trade discounts Discounts from the list prices in published catalogs or special discounts offered to certain classes of buyers.

Trade receivables Notes and accounts receivables that result from sales transactions.

Trading securities Equity and debt securities that are purchased to earn profits from short-term changes in their market prices.

Transaction An economic event that, under generally accepted accounting principles (GAAP), affects an element of the accounting equation and must be recorded.

Transfer price The price charged one decentralized unit by another for the goods or services provided.

U

Underapplied factory overhead The actual factory overhead costs incurred in excess of the amount of factory overhead applied for production during a period.

Unearned revenues Items that are initially recorded as liabilities but are expected to become revenues over time or through the normal operations of the business.

Unfavorable cost variance Actual cost exceeds standard cost.

Unit contribution margin The dollars available from each unit of sales to cover fixed costs and provide income from operations.

Unit of measure concept An accounting concept requiring that all economic data be recorded in dollars.

Unrealized gain (loss) on available-for-sale investments An increase (decrease) in the fair value of available-for-sale securities that have not been sold.

Unrealized gain (loss) on equity investments An increase (decrease) in the fair value of equity securities that have not been sold.

Unrealized gain (loss) on trading investments An increase (decrease) in the fair value of trading securities that have not been sold.

Utilization rate An output metric for assessing the performance and the efficient use of assets, computed as service units used divided by available service units.

V

Valuation allowance for available-for-sale investments An addition to or deduction from the cost of available-for-sale securities to reflect their fair value.

Valuation allowance for equity investments An addition to or deduction from the cost of equity securities to reflect their fair value.

Valuation allowance for trading investments An addition to or deduction from the cost of trading securities to reflect their fair value.

Variable cost concept Often referred to as *variable costing*, a method of reporting variable and fixed costs that includes only the variable manufacturing costs in the cost of the product.

Variable costing A method of reporting variable and fixed costs that includes only the variable manufacturing costs in the cost of the product.

Variable costs Costs that vary in total dollar amount as the level of activity changes.

Vertical analysis An analysis that compares each item in a current statement with a total amount within the same statement.

Volume variance The difference between the budgeted fixed overhead at 100% of normal capacity and the standard fixed overhead for the actual units produced.

Voucher Any document that serves as proof of authority to pay cash.

Voucher system A set of procedures for authorizing and recording liabilities and cash payments.

W

Working capital The excess of the current assets of a business over its current liabilities.

Work-in-process (WIP) inventory The direct materials costs, the direct labor costs, and the factory overhead costs that have entered into the manufacturing process but are associated with products that have not been finished.

Z

Zero-based budgeting A concept of budgeting that requires all levels of management to start from zero and estimate budget data as if there had been no previous activities in their units.

Subject Index

A

D

E

F

G

T

U

V

W

Company Index

The Basics

Types of Business

Service
Merchandising
Manufacturing

Forms of Business

Proprietorship
Partnership
Corporation
Limited liability company

Business Stakeholders

Capital market
Product or service market
Government
Internal

Business Activities

Operating
Investing
Financing

Financial Statements

Income statement
Statement of stockholders' equity
Balance sheet
Statement of cash flows

Integration of Financial Statements

Net income → income statement and statement of stockholders' equity
Cash → balance sheet and statement of cash flows
Common stock and retained earnings → balance sheet and statement of stockholders' equity

Accounting Concepts

Business entity
Cost
Going concern
Matching
Objectivity
Unit of measure
Adequate disclosure
Accounting period

Type of Metrics

Liquidity (amounts/ratios)
Profitability (amounts/ratios)

Accounting Equation

Assets = Liabilities + Stockholders' Equity

Types of Adjustments

Deferrals
Accruals

Elements of Internal Control

Control environment
Risk assessment
Control procedures
Monitoring
Information and communication

Bank Reconciliation

Cash balance according to bank		$XXX
Add: Increases to cash not on bank statement (deposits in transit, etc.)	$XXX	
Deduct: Decreases to cash not on bank statement (outstanding checks, etc.)	(XXX)	XXX
Adjusted balance		$XXX

Cash balance according to company		$XXX
Add: Unrecorded bank increases to cash (credit memos) (notes collected by bank)	$XXX	
Deduct: Unrecorded decreases to cash (debit memos) (NSF checks, service charges, etc.)	(XXX)	XXX
Adjusted balance		$XXX

Must be equal

Shipping Terms:

	FOB Shipping Point	FOB Destination
Ownership (title) passes to buyer when merchandise is............	delivered to freight carrier	delivered to buyer
Freight costs are paid by...................	buyer	seller

Interest Computation

Interest = Face Amount × Rate × Time

Inventory Cost Flows

First-in, First-out (FIFO)
Last-in, First-out (LIFO)
Weighted average

Depreciation Methods

Straight-line

$$\text{Annual Depreciation} = \frac{\text{Cost} - \text{Residual Value}}{\text{Useful Life}}$$

Double-declining-balance

Annual Depreciation = Rate* × Book Value at Beginning of Period

* Rate = 2 × Straight-line Rate;
Straight-line Rate = 1 ÷ Useful Life

Depletion

$$\text{Depletion Rate} = \frac{\text{Cost of Resource}}{\text{Estimated Total Units of Resource}}$$

Depletion Expense = Depletion Rate × Quantity Removed

Adjustments to Net Income (Loss) Using the Indirect Method:

Net income (loss)	$ XXX	
Adjustments to reconcile net income to net cash flow from operating activities:		
Depreciation of fixed assets	XXX	
Amortization of intangible assets	XXX	
Losses on disposal of assets	XXX	
Gains on disposal of assets	(XXX)	
Changes in current operating assets and liabilities:		
Increases in noncash current operating assets	(XXX)	
Decreases in noncash current operating assets	XXX	
Increases in current operating liabilities	XXX	
Decreases in current operating liabilities	(XXX)	
Net cash flow from operating activities		$XXX

Subtract	Add
Increases in accounts receivable	Decreases in accounts receivable
Increases in inventory	Decreases in inventory
Increases in prepaid expenses	Decreases in prepaid expenses
Decreases in accounts payable	Increases in accounts payable
Decreases in accrued expenses payable	Increases in accrued expenses payable
Decreases in income taxes payable	Increases in income taxes payable

Summary of Metrics

Liquidity and Solvency Metrics

Working Capital	Current Assets − Current Liabilities
Current Ratio	$\frac{\text{Current Assets}}{\text{Current Liabilities}}$
Quick Ratio	$\frac{\text{Quick Assets}}{\text{Current Liabilities}}$
Accounts Receivable Turnover	$\frac{\text{Sales}}{\text{Average Accounts Receivable}}$
Days' Sales in Receivables	$\frac{\text{Average Accounts Receivable}}{\text{Average Daily Sales}}$
Inventory Turnover	$\frac{\text{Cost of Goods Sold}}{\text{Average Inventory}}$
Days' Sales in Inventory	$\frac{\text{Average Inventory}}{\text{Average Daily Cost of Goods Sold}}$
Net Assets	Total Assets − Total Liabilities
Debt Ratio	$\frac{\text{Total Liabilities}}{\text{Total Assets}}$
Ratio of Liabilities to Stockholders' Equity	$\frac{\text{Total Liabilities}}{\text{Total Stockholders' Equity}}$
Ratio of Fixed Assets to Long-Term Liabilities	$\frac{\text{Fixed Assets (net)}}{\text{Long-Term Liabilities}}$
Times Interest Earned	$\frac{\text{Income Before Income Tax} + \text{Interest Expense}}{\text{Interest Expense}}$

Profitability Metrics

Asset Turnover	$\frac{\text{Sales}}{\text{Average Long-Term Operating Assets}}$
Return on Total Assets	$\frac{\text{Net Income} + \text{Interest Expense}}{\text{Average Total Assets}}$
Return on Stockholders' Equity	$\frac{\text{Net Income}}{\text{Average Total Stockholders' Equity}}$
Return on Common Stockholders' Equity	$\frac{\text{Net Income} - \text{Preferred Dividends}}{\text{Average Common Stockholders' Equity}}$
Earnings per Share on Common Stock	$\frac{\text{Net Income} - \text{Preferred Dividends}}{\text{Shares of Common Stock Outstanding}}$
Price-Earnings Ratio	$\frac{\text{Market Price per Share of Common Stock}}{\text{Earnings per Share on Common Stock}}$
Dividends per Share	$\frac{\text{Common Stock Dividends}}{\text{Shares of Common Stock Outstanding}}$
Dividend Yield	$\frac{\text{Dividends per Share of Common Stock}}{\text{Market Price per Share of Common Stock}}$